PERSONNEL MANAGEMENT

THE IRWIN SERIES IN MANAGEMENT
AND THE BEHAVIORAL SCIENCES

Consulting Editors
L. L. CUMMINGS and E. KIRBY WARREN

Advisory Editor
JOHN F. MEE

Personnel Management

MICHAEL J. JUCIUS, Ph.D.

Professor of Management
University of Arizona

 Eighth Edition • 1975

RICHARD D. IRWIN, INC.   Homewood, Illinois   60430

Irwin-Dorsey International   Arundel, Sussex   BN18 9AB
Irwin-Dorsey Limited   Georgetown, Ontario   L7G 4B3

Eighth Edition

First Printing, March 1975
Second Printing, November 1975
Third Printing, February 1976
Fourth Printing, July 1976

ISBN 0-256-01644-5
Library of Congress Catalog Card No. 74–24447

Printed in the United States of America

To
MY DAUGHTERS
Barbie, Cathy, and Lisa

PREFACE

The basic aim of earlier editions of *Personnel Management* was to supply college students with a realistic survey of this area. It was thought that others in various positions in business also might find it useful.

But the college student was of uppermost concern. A balance of descriptive, interpretive, and case materials was sought to provide students with an insight into the operations and problems of personnel management. This would serve as a basis for fruitful interactions with their instructors and peers in the classroom and ultimately for useful induction into the actual world of affairs.

There has been no reason to drop these views as guides of the current revision. The basic structure and subject matter has been retained. But a variety of materials has been inserted throughout which serve to bring in refinements and new developments and emphasis. As a consequence the blend of the old and the new provides a more credible and viable picture of current working in this field.

Moreover, various users including students have suggested changes in presentation and content that have been adopted with gratitude. And a large number of additions and revisions have been made in the questions and case problems presented at the end of each chapter.

The text is organized around the basic functions that management must perform in order to build and work with an effective and satisfied group of people. At the outset, attention is directed to the scope, guiding principles, and background of personnel management. Then consideration is given to the managerial functions of planning and organizing that are universally significant in dealing with all personnel activities.

After consideration of these basic matters, attention is turned to the major operative tasks of procuring, developing, maintaining, and utilizing a working force. Taken up are such topics as specifying job and manpower requirements; attracting, screening, interviewing, and testing people;

training and developing employees, including executives; establishing merit evaluation, compensation, and service programs; dealing with collective bargaining, grievances, and disciplinary cases; and carrying on research and auditing programs.

These materials have been developed and organized to be a useful resource of help to the good instructor. In working through them, some instructors may desire to follow sequences differing from those in the outline. Some, for example, may prefer to take up the materials on cooperation and conflict earlier than they are presented in the text. Or the materials on job evaluation may be taken up in conjunction with those on job specifications. Such rearrangements are readily pursuable within the framework of the text.

To acknowledge the numerous fellow-workers, executives, associates, and, above all, students whose aid and ideas are incorporated in this text is impossible. I am particularly indebted to Bernard A. Deitzer of the University of Akron for his reading of the manuscript and for his preparation of teaching materials which accompany the text. To all I am appreciative beyond words but not beyond grateful remembrance and indebtedness.

February 1975   MICHAEL J. JUCIUS

CONTENTS

part I
Basic Aspects of Personnel Management   1

1. **The Field of Personnel Management**   3

The Human Factor in Business. The Concept of Personnel Management. Definition of Personnel Management. Responsibility for Personnel Management. Basic Guides in Personnel Management. Personnel Executives. OUTLINE OF SUBSEQUENT CHAPTERS.

2. **A Perspective of Personnel Management**   17

Importance and Scope of Perspective. HISTORICAL CHANGES: Technological Conditions. Cultural and Social Background. Governmental Relations. Trends in Employee Roles. Management Attitudes. The Force of Education. PRESENT STATUS: General Nature of Problems. Management's Role. Approaches to Personnel Problems. Obstacles to Problem Solving. Future Prospects.

3. **Human Aspects of Personnel Management**   34

The Human Factor. Dealing with the Human Factor. Dimensions of the Human Factor. Human Aspects of Motivation. Human Aspects of Executive Behaviour.

4. **Personnel Programming**   50

Scope and Importance. OBJECTIVES: The Importance of Objectives. Classes of Personnel Objectives. FUNCTIONS: Nature of Functions. Assignment of Responsibility for Functions. PERSONNEL POLICIES: Nature and Purposes. Coverage. Responsibility for Establishing Policies. Policy Control. BUDGETARY ASPECTS OF PROGRAMS. INFORMATIONAL NEEDS OF PROGRAMMING.

5. **Organization of Personnel Management**   68

Scope of Organization. SYSTEMS OF PERSONNEL MANAGEMENT: Nature of Systems. Systems in Personnel Management. ORGANIZATION STRUCTURE:

xi

Formal Structures. Informal Authority. Relations between Executives. Responsibility in Organization Structure. FACTORS IN SPECIFIC STRUCTURAL DESIGNS: Attitude of Management. Interaction of Personnel and Structure. Physical Factors. Effect of Legislation and Unions upon Structure. Problems Faced. TESTS OF GOOD STRUCTURE. INTEGRATION OF PERSONNEL FUNCTIONS AND FACTORS.

part II
The Procurement Phase of Personnel Management   87

6. Job and Personnel Requirements   89

The Hiring Function. JOB AND EMPLOYEE SPECIFICATIONS: Definitions. Job Specification Information. Employee Specification Information. Responsibility for Collecting Information. Methods of Gathering Data. Writing Specifications. QUANTITATIVE REQUIREMENTS: Methods of Estimation. Personnel Requirements and Production Estimates. Labor Turnover. Technical and Managerial Employee Requirements.

7. Sources of Personnel Supply   109

Variability of Sources of Supply. Types of Personnel Sources. The Internal Source. The External Source. Evaluation of Alternative Sources. Layout and Location of Employment Office.

8. The Selection Procedure   122

Scope of the Selection Procedure. Design of Procedural and Structural Relations. Initiation of Selection Procedure. Gathering Information about Candidates. Reports and Records. Induction of New Employee.

9. Interviewing and Counseling   144

The Role of Interviewing and Counseling. Purposes. Types of Interviewing. Technical Factors. Procedures of Interviewing. Rules of Interviewing.

10. Tests   161

Popularity of Tests. Basic Fundamentals. Areas of Usage. Types of Tests. Operating a Testing Program. Rules of Testing.

11. Transfers and Promotions   180

Scope of Transfers and Promotions. Purposes. Operational Aspects. Limitations. Seniority. Summary.

12. Merit Evaluation   198

Evaluation Programs. Objectives of Evaluation. Fundamental Issues of Evaluation. Designs of Evaluation Forms. Accuracy of Evaluations. Rules of Evaluating.

part III
The Development Phase of Personnel Management   223

13. **Training Operative Employees**   225

Training and Education. JUSTIFICATION AND SCOPE. COURSES OF TRAINING:
On-the-Job Training. Vestibule Training. Apprenticeship Training. Intern-
ship Training. Outside Courses. Programmed Learning. Retraining and
Upgrading. FACTORS IN A TRAINING PROGRAM: Planning the Program.
Organizational Aspects. Selection of Trainees and Instructors. Evaluation
of Training Program. Rules and Principles of Learning.

14. **Executive Development**   243

Significance of Executive Development. PLANNING EXECUTIVE DEVELOP-
MENT: Executive Capacities. Candidates for Development. Conditions of
Executive Development. TYPES OF DEVELOPMENT PROGRAMS: On-the-Job
Development. Understudy Plans. Short-Term Courses. Position Rotation
Plan. Other Supervisory Programs. Decision-Making Training. Business
Games. Role Playing. Sensitivity Training. CONTENT OF DEVELOPMENT
PROGRAMS. FOLLOW-UP AND EVALUATION: Evaluation of Trainees.

15. **Education**   261

Importance and Scope of Education. UPWARD EDUCATION: Subject Matter.
Learning Methods. DOWNWARD EDUCATION: Subject Matter. Learning
Methods. ROLE OF COMMUNICATION: Basic Concepts of Communication.
Rules of Communication.

part IV
The Maintenance Phase of Personnel Management   275

16. **Remuneration Policies**   277

Significance of Remuneration. The Problems of Remuneration. Scope of
Present Discussion. Economic Explanations. Noneconomic Aspects. Com-
pensation Levels. Influence of Unions and Collective Bargaining. Govern-
mental Regulations. The Walsh-Healey Public Contracts Act. The Bacon-
Davis (Public Construction) Act. Equal Pay Act. Safeguards in Wage
Programming.

17. **Job Evaluation and Wage Classification**   294

Introduction. Organizational Aspects. Selection of Jobs to Be Evaluated.
Making the Job Analysis. Job Evaluation Plans. Summary.

18. **Plans of Remuneration**   310

Introduction. Basic Kinds of Plans. Tests of Wage Plans. Types of Wage
Payment Plans. Remuneration of Salesmen. Executive Compensation
Plans. Records.

19. **Fringe Benefits**   **328**

Scope of Discussion. Fringe Benefits. Insurance Programs. Pension Plans. Unemployment Compensation Plans.

20. **Related Compensation Problems**   **342**

Introduction. TIME PROBLEMS: Variables. Daily Time Problems. Portal-to-Portal Issues. Weekly Time Problems. Yearly Time Problems. STABILIZA-TION PROGRAMS: Job Stabilization. Individual Plans. Intercompany Co-operation. Governmental Influences. WAGE STABILIZATION: Scope of Plans. Employee Coverage. Guarantee Periods and Amounts. Examples of Voluntary Plans. Conditions of Feasible Use.

21. **Service and Participation Programs**   **360**

Scope of Plans. RECREATIONAL, SOCIAL, AND ATHLETIC PROGRAMS: Purposes of Programs. Recreational and Social Programs. Athletic Programs. Music in the Plant and Office. PARTICIPATION PROGRAMS: Company Periodicals. Suggestion Systems. CONVENIENCE SERVICES: Restaurant Facilities. Company Stores. Credit Unions. Home Purchasing. Medical Services. Consultative Services. Retirement Consultation. ORGANIZATION FOR SERVICE PLANS: Example of Service Organization. Organizational Plan under Decentralized Operations. Company Experts. RULES OF OPERATION.

22. **Physical Security**   **382**

Introduction. Objectives. WORKING CONDITIONS: General Considerations. Phases of Working Conditions. HEALTH: Pertinent Factors. Medical Examinations. Health Services. Organization for Medical Services. SAFETY: Importance and Scope. Measures of Accidents. Human Phases of Safety. Safety Organization.

23. **Areas of Special Personnel Interest**   **406**

Scope. Minority and Disadvantaged Groups. Handicapped Workers. The Older Employee. Women Employees. Technological Innovations. International Personnel Programs.

part V
The Utilization Phase of Personnel Management   **423**

24. **Cooperation and Conflict**   **425**

Scope. ORGANIZATIONAL BEHAVIOUR: Nature and Characteristics of an Organization. Interactions of People and Organizations. The Role of Personnel Management in an Organization. EMPLOYEE MORALE: Meaning of Morale. Theory of Morale Development. Factors of Morale Development. CONFLICT: Nature and Impact. Handling Conflicts.

25. **Union-Management Relations**   **439**

Scope of Discussion. GENERAL BACKGROUND OF UNIONIZATION: The Role of Unions. Historical Aspects of Union Growth. Legal Changes and

Status. Types of Unions. THE LABOR MANAGEMENT RELATIONS ACT: Scope of Act. Rights of Parties. Coverage of the Act. Operations under the Act. RELATIONS WITH THE UNION: Preparing for Negotiation. Negotiating. Subject Matter of Agreements. Living with the Contract.

26. Handling Grievances   458

Employee Dissatisfactions. BASIC CONSIDERATIONS: Meaning of Grievances. Implications of the Definition. Channels for Handling Grievances. STEPS IN HANDLING GRIEVANCES: Describing Grievances. Gathering Facts. Establishing Tentative Solutions. Checking Tentative Solutions. Applying Solutions. Follow-Up of the Grievance. PRINCIPLES OF HANDLING GRIEVANCES: Principles of Interviewing. Management's Attitudes toward Employees. Management's Responsibilities. Long-Run Principles. MACHINERY FOR HANDLING GRIEVANCES: Organizational Responsibility. Grievance-Handling Procedures.

27. Disciplinary Action   475

INTRODUCTION: Definition of Terms. Procedures of Disciplinary Action. Statement of Problem. Gathering Facts. Establishing Tentative Penalties. Choosing the Penalty. Applying Penalties. Follow-Up of Disciplinary Action. PRINCIPLES OF DISCIPLINARY ACTION: Desirability of Disciplinary Action. Attitude toward Employees. Implications of Disciplinary Action. Union-Management Relations.

28. Personnel Research and Evaluation   488

Introduction. PERSONNEL RESEARCH: Nature and Scope. Basic Considerations. EXAMPLES OF RESEARCH: Absenteeism. Contributors to Personnel Research. EVALUATION: Nature and Scope. Basic Considerations. Subjects and Methods of Evaluation. SUMMARY.

Appendix: Example of a Job Analysis Schedule   513

Instructions for Filling Out the Job Analysis Schedule   520

Selected Bibliography   530

Index   535

part I
Basic Aspects of Personnel Management

This Part of the text is devoted to laying a foundation upon which succeeding parts can be built more firmly. It has been imperative at the outset to describe the field and major elements of personnel management. With such an overall view in mind, it is then useful to consider the factors which have influenced the evolution of personnel management, which affect its present status, and which are likely to have an impact upon future trends.

With these basic dimensions covered, this Part is then at an appropriate juncture to be concerned with the central core of personnel management—the human factor, its composition, its motivational characteristics, and its executive manifestations. After drawing this picture of the human factor it is then useful and desirable to look at the managerial functions of planning and organizing which are essential to the performance of other functions of personnel management included in subsequent Parts of this text.

CHAPTER 1

THE FIELD OF
PERSONNEL MANAGEMENT

The Human Factor in Business

From many sides, we are constantly being reminded of the importance of the human factor in business. News media give prominence to various incidents in labor-management relations. Politicians, governmental agencies, educators, and various community groups express their interest in the aims and problems of employees. Business and labor leaders voice their deep concern with people. And ever widening research in the behavioral sciences is casting new light on interpersonal relations in the working environment.

But perhaps more impressive than the foregoing to most individuals are their own personal experiences. From childhood to old age, a large segment of their lives is encompassed by business affairs. Their standard of living and earning power are dependent upon their jobs and general economic conditions. Much of what and how they think is determined by job factors. Their aspirations and fears, as well as those of their families, are bound up in the business environment.

Thus, in numerous ways, all employees, from top administrators to unskilled, from professional to manual, are made aware of their dependence on business affairs. All consequently are concerned with their stake, roles, and involvement in business.

The Concept of Personnel Management

At the outset of this study, it is well to make clear what is meant by the terms labor and personnel. Some restrict labor to mean operative workers, and some use personnel either to mean higher level employees or as a more euphonious term for labor. But here, it is proposed to use each interchangeably as the human factor in the business enterprise.

Thus, everyone from the president of an enterprise to the salesperson, mechanic, or clerk is labor or personnel. To be sure, operative levels of employees have received much attention in personnel managment, but interest here is also directed to professional, scientific, technical, staff, and managerial groups of labor. Thus, a vice president may be concerned with subordinate levels of labor, but nonetheless is also encompassed in the term labor or personnel.

A number of terms have been used to designate various aspects of the subject of people in business. *Industrial relations,* for example, has been used to refer to multilateral relations between employees, employers, and government. To others, it means the relations between employees and management within the confines of a given enterprise. *Labor relations,* in the language of one user, many refer to collective bargaining and, in that of another, to grievance handling. And still others have tagged some of these subjects with such terms as *human engineering, labor management, human relations, personnel services, personnel administration,* and *employee management.*

Such a variety of terms has evolved because the subject of people in business can be studied from a number of viewpoints. To begin with, emphasis may be placed upon the needs and roles of people themselves as individuals. For example, interest may be in such questions as why do people work, what are their reactions to work, or how should they be treated as human beings. Or emphasis may be upon the overall scheme of people in the total industrial and national picture. For example, interest may be in such problems as unemployment, social security, living conditions, education, and political relations. Or emphasis may be upon how people fit into the operations of a given business enterprise. For example, of interest here are such matters as hiring, training, and motivation of people as a resource of a particular company.

Each of these approaches—the individual, the national, and the enterprise—are very important. But in this text, study is directed to the latter—people in the business enterprise—and is entitled personnel management. The other approaches will be brought in when particularly relevant to business operations.

What then is the relation of personnel management to the factor of people in business. To answer this question, attention is directed in this chapter to the following aspects of the meaning and scope of personnel management:

1. Definition and description of the field of personnel management
2. Groups of managers concerned with personnel management
3. Basic guides in personnel management
4. Qualifications and training of personnel executives

Definition of Personnel Management

No definition can be expected to describe fully any concept or subject. It can, however, serve as a springboard for fruitful analysis and amplification. With these thoughts in mind, personnel management is defined here as follows:

The field of management which has to do with planning, organizing, directing, and controlling the functions of procuring, developing, maintaining, and utilizing a labor force, such that the—

a.   Objectives for which the company is established are attained economically and effectively.
b.   Objectives of all levels of personnel are served to the highest possible degree.
c.   Objectives of society are duly considered and served.

1. Dimensions of Labor.   Labor is the basic term of this definition. But what are its dimensions? Certainly, labor's physical and mental attributes are pertinent to business productivity. And it is also true that emotional and group aspects, ethical and cultural qualities, perceptions and aspirations, and various needs and drives of people impinge on the affairs of a business enterprise. Thus, the human being in business is a multi-dimensional creature.

But are all dimensions equally significant? The brains and brawn required to do given jobs were once—and still are very often—all the business manager wanted from or would be concerned about labor. As time has gone on, however, the impacts of the other dimensions have made themselves felt, although as yet their roles in business are often accorded a lower order.

How to deal with this complex of dimensions is surely perplexing. But not to deal with all of them can lead to varying degrees of trouble. Hence, all of them are viewed here as falling in the concerns of personnel management.

2. Managerial Phases.   Next, this definition makes the point that personnel management is a part of management. This does not preclude others from participating in consideration of matters important to them. It does mean, however, that constructive leadership in personnel work is a basic obligation of management. Such leadership encompasses four broad managerial functions: planning, organizing, directing, and controlling.

The planning functions pertain to the steps taken in developing a personnel program and in specifying what operative personnel functions are to be performed, and how. Such plans are sometimes unwritten, but it is usually preferable to set them down in printed form. More is said on this subject in Chapter 4.

After plans have been developed, organizing is next in order. This calls for procuring the resources necessary to carry out the plan, designing appropriate systems for carrying out the plans, and establishing lines of authority and communication between the various people working with or receiving benefit from the personnel plans. In Chapter 5, various schemes of organizing personnel work will be described.

Directing refers to the function of actively running the organization units responsible for executing specific personnel plans. Thus, it is particularly relevant to the work of leadership both at the operative and higher managerial levels. In this activity, attention must be given to such tasks as motivating and supervising people. Specific examples of direction will be noted throughout various parts of the text.

By means of the function of control, management evaluates results of personnel work in comparison with desired objectives. Controls, first of all, measure the progress of the personnel ship along the lines laid out in the program. When the ship docks (at the end of the program year, let us say), controls then are exercised to determine how effectively desired personnel objectives were attained. Thus, through direct observation and supervision, as well as reports, records, and audits, management assures itself that its organization is carrying out planned programs. Reference to controls will be made throughout subsequent chapters.

3. Technical Phases of Personnel Work.   The foregoing definition also places emphasis upon four broad and fundamental phases of personnel work. These arise out of the fact that a working force must be procured, developed, maintained, and utilized. These phases, briefly defined here, will be surveyed more fully in later chapters.

Procurement calls for performing such functions as locating sources of supply, interviewing, giving tests, and inducting selected applicants. *Development* calls for training and education, morale building, good communications, promotion and transfer plans, suggestions systems, and similar plans. *Maintenance* encompasses activities which serve to support the skills and favorable attitudes of employees, such as adequate wages and working conditions, supervision, grievance machinery, recreational and social programs, and health service plans. Of course, all of the foregoing impinge upon the *utilization* of labor, which is concerned with the working effectiveness of the employee.

To perform these tasks, management must employ a variety of tools, devices, forms, records, and procedures. As a consequence, these sometimes seem to be the substance of personnel work. They are a means to an end, however, and should be viewed as such. To allow forms to become the keystone of a personnel program is to convert personnel management into a clerkship. Appropriate references to these tools will be made in subsequent chapters.

4. Objectives.   The description of personnel management, in the fourth place, stresses the point that personnel work is intended to attain a number of important objectives. High place must at once be given here to success in producing a service or commodity which earns a reasonable profit. This is patently dependent upon the effectiveness with which the various members of the business team work together. Personnel management must seek, therefore, to make employees effective contributors to the success of the enterprise. Unless a particular enterprise is successful, it can neither continue to exist nor have use for labor or management.

The foregoing definition recognizes clearly and unequivocally that the performance of personnel duties must also keep in view the objectives of people. Nonfinancial as well as financial needs of people must be fairly and sincerely considered in the plans of management. If not, others will be more than eager, in ways which may run counter to those considered good by the employer, to help people attain desired goals.

And finally, the definition recognizes that personnel management must make appropriate contributions to social needs and norms. This encompasses three levels of obligations. A company must:

a. Be a good neighbor in its immediate locale.
b. Live according to the best interests of its regional and national location.
c. Where applicable, give consideration to its international obligations.

Briefly, this means that a business, though an economic institution, is also an inseparable part of the social complex.

The foregoing picture of personnel management may seem somewhat idealistic. After all, not all companies perform all of the personnel functions cited here, nor do all take the views proposed here. Nevertheless, the practices and viewpoints of companies which have had the best results from their personnel programs are closely in line with the foregoing suggestions.

Responsibility for Personnel Management

The responsibility for performing functions to achieve desired objectives has in the foregoing been placed upon management. As noted earlier, this does not mean to exclude others, such as unions, governmental agencies, and employees themselves from roles in managerial decision-making. Some of their roles will be noted in this text at appropriate points. How are personnel responsibilities divided among various levels of managers, and between line and staff executives? Answers to this question will be proposed in greater detail in Chapter 5, but a few comments are in order here.

The primary responsibility for personnel management must be assumed by the top management of a company. To the president, subject to the approval of the board of directors, must be assigned the task of setting the tone of human relations; of establishing the broad objectives, plans, and policies of personnel management; of assigning to various subordinate executives the duties they are to carry out; of coordinating personnel efforts, and checking to see that personnel plans are executed. Evaluation of the effectiveness with which desired objectives have been attained shows where (1) future personnel plans can be improved and (2) responsible executives can be appropriately rewarded or penalized.

Of course, the chief executive cannot—except in the smallest companies—perform the functions of personnel management throughout all levels of the organization. Executives at each level must carry out personnel duties appropriate to their respective organizational units. These are the ones who actually put personnel practices into effect. How well they manage personnel depends upon their skills, the guidance they get from above, and the help they may get from a personnel department, if there is one.

The personnel department provides a third segment of personnel management. It has attained a formal stature in most companies having about 100 employees. It serves by helping to hire employees, train them, operate a variety of personnel programs, and carry on relations with labor unions. But its services must be approved by those it serves or by some higher authority. Since it does so much personnel work, it is often assumed to be personnel management. While the contributions of this department may be great, its role in the personnel area must be that of a companion to the line executives.

These three groups of executives are the personnel managers in business. No one should be ignored nor anyone given exclusive jurisdiction; hence all are the concern of this text.

Basic Guides in Personnel Management

The field of personnel management cannot be adequately described, however, by defining its functions, listing its objectives, and denoting its responsible leaders. Stopping here establishes the form of personnel management. But to what degree should various objectives be sought? How balance the interests of various groups? To what extent should the several functions be performed? What ideals and ethics should guide management?

Answers to these questions add substance to form; they determine what personnel management really is in any given company. And how such answers are derived depends in turn upon the philosophy and principles adopted by a given company.

1. A Philosophy of Personnel Management.   The most basic guide to personnel action in any company derives from its philosophy toward people. The mere fact that a business philosophy is not written down does not mean that none exists. Informally or subconsciously, if not openly, a philosophy exists in every company.

Broadly speaking, a personnel philosophy may tend toward either of two directions. First, labor may be viewed as a technical factor which more or less passively or actively resists managerial leadership. People must therefore be molded, controlled, and closely supervised by management to achieve company goals. Such views have prevailed in many business quarters.

Second, more recently, labor has been viewed as a human factor with inherently constructive potentials. Various research as well as the experiences of a small but increasing number of practitioners support the thesis that constructive forces in people are better realized when a participative attitude underlies management's programs. And there is a growing acceptance of the idea that helping people to grow is as important as business growth.

2. *Principles of Personnel Management.* The broad terms of a philosophy to be practically useful should serve to derive specific guidelines for personnel programs and practices. Such guidelines and bench marks—or principles—are not immutable or inflexible laws. They should be amended as conditions change and as more is learned about the behavioral patterns of the human factor, individually and in groups.

Without implying that the list is complete, the following discussion is intended to illustrate the lines along which a set of principles could be built.

a. Deal with people as complete individuals. Employees may be hired for their technical capabilities and economic usefulness. But their cooperation and interactions with management are largely influenced by their personal feelings, cultural and social attitudes, and ethical norms. So these as well as technical factors must be programmed into the organizational operations. Managerial action should be sensitive to how employees feel about these matters, such as, contemplated work assignments, personnel policies, and decisions which affect employee interests. And such sensitivity should be in line with group as well as individual relations.

b. Make employees feel worthwhile and related. "People do not live by bread alone" applies to workers too. Of course all of us are pleased to get a good pay check. But what makes for personal significance between paydays? Then, personal feelings of accomplishment, pride in one's craft or profession, and an harmonious kinship with fellow workers as well as with one's company are day-to-day needs if technical productivity is to be of the highest order.

c. Add to fairness the appearance of fairness. Be fair, but also appear to be fair. It is not argued here that appearance of fairness is coequal with being fair (although some seem to give it equal or superior status).

The maxim as stated here recognizes merely the simple truth that all of us are influenced by how things are presented to us, as well as by what is presented.

d. Rewards should be earned, not given. Gift giving is not the province of business, is not wanted by mature employees, and is rarely appreciated. Yet, one often hears that employees were given a 30-cent-an-hour raise, were given a vacation with pay, or were given a paid-up insurance policy. Such gifts invariably induce no extra efforts. Indeed, employees soon assume that the gifts must be continued as a deserved reward.

If these rewards are earned, they should not be termed gifts. The relationship between effort and reward should be clearly stated as earnings. Then the worker is not put in the position of having to be grateful. It is unwise to subject a person to the feeling of subservience when the situation reflects accomplishment and satisfaction with a job well done.

e. Supply employees with relevant information. Communication on matters of mutual interest is imperative. There is little reason for believing that important information can be kept from employees. Sooner or later, the hidden information turns up, often in a form which tends to weaken the confidence of employees in their company.

Moreover, it is unwise to withhold information on the ground that employees cannot understand or are likely to misinterpret complicated information. Whether they can or cannot understand an accounting statement, for example, is irrelevant. To employees, the availability of such a statement (and particularly one drawn in a form designed for their benefit) is assurance that the company has nothing to hide.

f. Do not underestimate the intelligence or strength of people. It is courting trouble to assume that employees (organized or not) are neither strong nor generally intelligent. Sometimes management so assumes because people are slow to action. Once aroused, however, employees have shown that they know not only what they want but also how to get it, both in the national area and in the individual company.

An interesting point can be made here regarding the charge that employees are not wise enough to participate in decisions affecting their interests. But the point is irrelevant. Employees exert an influence upon every decision management reaches. When employees have no direct voice in bargaining, for example, they may malinger, seek employment elsewhere, or have recourse to the ballot box. In short, they act indirectly when not invited to do so directly. Hence the real issue is how and by what means employees should be brought into the decision-making processes.

g. "Sell" the personnel program. This follows because employees will learn by themselves or from others, if management does not teach them.

Time must be taken and effort exerted through understandable language to sell management's beliefs. On the one hand, it should be clear that policies and programs that have taken executives perhaps months to develop cannot be assimilated in the time it takes to read a notice on the bulletin board or in the company magazine. On the other hand, the selling should be done in terms—whether oral or printed—that can be clearly understood.

In the last analysis, the real significance of one's principles will be found in whether or not they are a part of daily routines and executive acts. All the talk in the world is ineffective unless it is backed with action. In short, the "good" life must be lived by management in order that labor can be sure that what is said is really meant.

Personnel Executives

Some comments are now in order regarding the qualifications, breadth of knowledge, and education expected of those whose jobs entail personnel management. Obviously, what is said here must be somewhat general. Conditions are certainly not the same in all kinds and sizes of businesses. And the kind and degree of personnel responsibilities within the same company will not be the same for top, middle, first-line, and staff executives. Hence a standard specification for everyone is out of the question. Nevertheless, there are points which have some application to all.

1. Qualifications. As to qualifications, one frequently hears from those seeking to prepare themselves for personnel work that they made the choice because they "like to work with people." This is highly commendable but should scarcely be the deciding factor. After all, one must like to work with people in almost all fields of professional and technical endeavor. Moreover, the words "working with people" are too indefinite —they may mean such things as helping others out of trouble (of which there are many kinds, and not all are of interest to the business enterprise); simply liking to work side by side with others (no more than ordinary gregariousness); and telling people what they should or should not do (often a mere desire for power).

Success in personnel management depends upon skill and ability in three areas: managerial, technical, and behavioral. By its very emphasis in the title, it should be patent that managerial talents are involved. In the case of top, middle, bottom, and staff managers, a premium is placed on ability to plan, organize, direct, and control the work of others. The emphasis is upon managing the work of others, not upon doing the work oneself. Therefore, any executive concerned with personnel activities must be proficient in leading others and in coordinating the organizational unit with the systems and organizations of other executives.

Managers must, by definition, manage somebody regarding something, and must therefore possess competence in the technical field being managed. In the personnel area, they must be skilled in the tools, techniques, and practices of procuring, developing, maintaining, and utilizing a labor force. If the executives in question happen to be personnel managers, the depth of their technical skill should be much more detailed and comprehensive than that of line executives. The latter should concern themselves with policy determination and programming technical matters the higher they are in the organization, and with application of technical matters the lower they are.

And since managers must manage somebody, they must possess skill in working personally with subordinates. The way a leader reacts to or behaves toward subordinates determines in part how effective will be the execution of managerial and technical functions. The top executive, for example, may be autocratic or democratic in relationships with subordinate executives. The personnel manager may be patronizing, cooperative, officious, or contemptuous toward other workers. And the supervisor may be "work-centered" or "person-centered" in dealing with employees. The behavioral pattern—friendly, stern, standoffish, pleasant, gruff, or understanding, to cite but a few examples—has a significant effect upon the reactions an executive will get from colleagues and associates.

2. Breadth of Knowledge.   Another useful view of executives concerned with personnel may be taken by (a) viewing the fields of knowledge that can contribute to their work and (b) discussing the extent of specialization in the various fields.

a. Fields of Knowledge.   The following listing illustrates the major fields of knowledge which have a contribution to make in the personnel area:

1. Philosophy, which seeks for the underlying explanations of human nature and conduct
2. Ethics, which is concerned with moral and value judgments
3. Logic, which is concerned with rules and principles of reasoning
4. Mathematics, which treats of exact relations between quantities, magnitudes, and systems
5. Psychology, which deals with the phenomena of individual consciousness and behavior
6. Sociology, which deals with the forms and functions of human groups
7. Anthropology, which is concerned with physical and environmental relations to people's social and cultural patterns
8. Medicine, which in all its branches is concerned with our well-being
9. History, which seeks to record and explain past events
10. Economics, whose interests are in optimizing choices among competing uses of limited resources

11. Management, which is concerned with skillful leadership of organized groups
12. Political science, which in the best sense is concerned with how people are governed and govern themselves

b. Extent of Specialization. For how many of the foregoing fields should an executive be responsible? Some interesting trends may be noted. Going back only a little more than a century or two, a person was not considered educated unless a master of many fields. In our own country, such men as Washington, Jefferson, and Franklin were not only governmental figures of renown, but were also proficient in military, agricultural, business, philosophical, and cultural affairs. And in other countries, too, business leaders could claim the same cosmopolitan skill and knowledge.

Then, gradually, came the era of specialization. The outpouring of knowledge in each field seemed to require the full attention and time of anyone who pretended to be an expert. The philosopher had time only for philosophy, the doctor only for medicine, the psychologist only for psychology, the manager only for business, etc. To each, vocation monopolized time to such an extent that other endeavors rated at best only amateur standing.

But in recent years, there has been a swing back. And of particular interest in the study of human problems in business is the growth of the behavioral sciences. This trend proceeds on the lines that to specialized effort must be added collaboration. The psychologist, the sociologist, the economist, the mathematician, etc., must join forces to solve human problems.

Such joining of forces involves a number of things. It is desirable, for example, to improve communication between fields, to compare theories of human behavior, to study approaches and skills used by each other, to note similarities and differences of findings about human beings, to discuss systems of measurement and empirical research, and to seek generalizations about human behavior.

This trend undoubtedly will accelerate. People in the business environment cannot be effectively studied like the elephant which was examined by the blind men. Each in his specialized "view" was partly right and partly wrong. And difficult though it is, the studies of specialists must be brought together. Fortunately, the developments in mathematics, decision making, electronic computers, interdisciplinary research, and mixing of professional groups and societies are providing major breakthroughs. In this text, it is deemed axiomatic that the interrelations of employee and management are best approached through combined viewpoints.

3. Education. It is undoubtedly true that many executives engaged in personnel work gained managerial and technical competence on the job and through self-education. The school of experience was once the only one available. It is exacting and thorough. But it is also somewhat haphazard, costly, and time-consuming. Indeed, by the time one "graduated," it was time to receive a pension.

It is not surprising, therefore, that graduates of this school themselves advocate formal education whenever possible. And more and more companies prefer such training. As a consequence, formal offerings at the collegiate level have in the past several decades been increasing steadily.

Formal education need not, nor should it, stop with a college degree. For example, special short courses and executive development programs in many of the foregoing areas are also made available by such groups as professional management associations, private companies, consulting organizations, trade associations, and colleges and universities.

Thus, through appropriate combinations of formal education and working experience, competence in personnel work will be better achieved. Indeed, this may well raise personnel management to a professional status. But such a level cannot be attained so long as personnel work is viewed as a routine set of procedures. Professional status of personnel work calls for (a) technical study and training beyond the borders of mere trade knowledge, (b) large responsibilities toward those served, and (c) a high level of ethics in dealing with labor, management, and the community. When appropriate standards in these areas are promulgated and accepted generally, the field of personnel management will deserve inclusion in the family of professions.

OUTLINE OF SUBSEQUENT CHAPTERS

It is the task of the following chapters to fill out the outline of personnel management sketched in this chapter. The next four chapters of Part I, *Basic Aspects of Personnel Management* provide materials that are pertinent to all aspects of personnel management. Perspective, human relations, programming, and organization cut across all areas and specific tasks of personnel work.

Part II, covered by Chapters 6–12, is concerned with the procurement function of personnel management. Subjects taken up here include job and personnel requirements, sources of labor supply, the selection procedure, interviewing, testing, and transfers and promotions. Some of these are also important to topics taken up in later parts, in particular the development and utilization phases.

Part III (Chapters 13–15) has to do with the development phase of personnel management. Emphasis here is upon training, education, and communication both for operative and executive levels of the organization.

Part IV (Chapters 16–23) has to do with the maintenance phase of personnel management. Various aspects of compensation, service, participation, safety, and health programs are specific subjects considered here.

Finally, Part V (Chapters 24–28) has to do with some aspects of the utilization phase of personnel management. Union-management relations, grievance and disciplinary handling, and research and audits provide the headings of interest in this phase.

QUESTIONS

1. Check the definition of personnel management given in the text against personnel practices in a company in your community or in a company with which you are acquainted. Are there any differences?
2. What is the difference between managerial and operative functions of personnel management?
3. Does business have social obligations? If so, what are they? Do they change over time?
4. Where is personnel management performed in a business organization?
5. Why is a philosophy important in personnel management? What is the relation of principles to a philosophy of personnel management?
6. How far would you go in supplying employees with confidential company information? Would your answer be the same for all levels of employees? During a strike as well as during a period of relative peace?
7. Why is it important for a company to "sell" its personnel programs and policies to its employees?
8. What qualifications should executives possess in relation to their obligations in personnel management?
9. How much weight would you give to "liking to work with people" as a critical factor in selecting a personnel manager?
10. Why has formal training tended to supplant the "school of hard knocks" as preparation for personnel management?

CASE 1–1. EXTRACOMPANY BEHAVIOR OF EMPLOYEES

In a given company, two somewhat related incidents have brought on some soul-searching sessions on policy by the management of a given company. The first case arose when the company restaurant unexpectedly could not operate one day. Employees therefore had to go out into the neighborhood for their lunches. One of the employees, Bill Calm, a supervisor, happened to take a few alcoholic drinks with his lunch. In his happy condition, he made some bright (as he thought) but ungentlemanly remarks to one of the secretaries who was eating lunch at the same restaurant. When she returned to work, she indignantly reported Bill's conduct and remarks to the personnel manager.

The second case arose in connection with Art Swift, a valued engineer, who, after working hours, used to follow the primrose path to various taverns in the town. This part of his life did not affect his work. But stories started to drift back to management that Swift's actions reflected unfavorably on the company. Some of the comments implied that one couldn't put much confidence in the company's products if they were made by employees such as Swift.

Questions

1. What action, if any, should management take in each case?
2. What policy would you advocate, if any, governing the personal lives of one's employees?

CASE 1-2.   WORKING CONDITIONS

Bill had been raised in ranch country. Until he finished college he spent his vacations and free time working on various ranches. Two in particular impressed him, but for different reasons.

In the first of these, as well as the second, hours were long, pay was relatively low, and working conditions were rough and hard. But being away from city life, expenses were low so it was not hard to save a few dollars. But if the existence of a ranch hand didn't interest one, he didn't stay around very long.

In the first ranch, the manager of the ranch had a standoffish attitude, lacked interest in the ranch hands as individuals, and gave his help no more technical information than was absolutely necessary. On this ranch turnover was high, employee morale nonexistent, and workmanship of minimum quality or output.

Results in the second ranch were reversed though working conditions, living conditions, and wages were about the same. But the manager in this case took an interest in the hands as individuals; he willingly gave time, assistance, and advice on personal matters; he talked to the hands about their long-range plans; and he had the hands in his home for friendly and social visits. And he requested and got help and advice from his men on how to improve operations and conditions.

As Bill reviewed his experiences in the light of a job which he was taking in a city-located, industrial company, he wondered if what he had seen in his two ranch experiences had applicability in his new life. He wondered if the city would require an impersonal approach or whether the human being was the same in a big plant as on a ranch.

Question

1. How do you view his experiences and his possible conclusions based on his experiences?

A PERSPECTIVE OF 2
PERSONNEL MANAGEMENT

Importance and Scope of Perspective

Personnel management must deal with the present and be concerned with the future. It must build programs that solve problems in the framework of today and tomorrow. But if it is to perform its tasks as effectively as possible, it must also be aware of the past. Forces and factors and experiences in the past have their impact upon the present and future.

Study in this text of personnel matters can proceed on firmer grounds, therefore, by directing attention at the outset to (1) a review of some pertinent trends of the past, (2) a survey of current conditions, and (3) an estimate of future prospects.

HISTORICAL CHANGES

Many impressive changes have taken place in the status and positions of employees in the United States. And a variety of forces and conditions have brought on these changes. Space here is insufficient to examine fully all of these matters. But a useful appreciation of historical changes can be gained by reviewing the following areas of changes:

1. Technological conditions
2. Cultural and social background
3. Governmental relations
4. Trends in employee roles
5. Management attitudes
6. The force of education

Technological Conditions

Technological changes have had a profound effect upon the working population. Work was once performed manually with the aid of simple tools. Now thousands of workers have been brought into modern factories, offices, and distributing units. And now increasingly, operations are being carried on by complex, integrated, power-driven, automatic, and electronically controlled equipment.

As might be expected, such technological changes have left their impact upon employees. Where once there were large numbers of artisans, the working population is now made up largely of machine tenders, desk workers, and service employees. Where once there were opportunities for personal expression, the average job, in and of itself, is now repetitive and restrictive.

Of course, the technological revolution has provided some offsetting gains. For one, there are increased goods and services. And such trends as automation, electronic data processing, and computerization presage new and improved job opportunities. Hence, as technology advances, the

FIGURE 2-1

Employment Trends among Major Occupational Categories, 1960 and 1972 (actual) and 1980 and 1985 (projected)

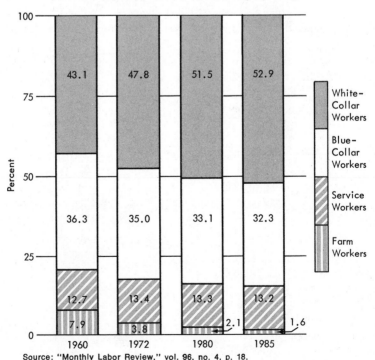

Source: "Monthly Labor Review," vol. 96, no. 4, p. 18.

FIGURE 2–2

Employment in Major Occupational Groups, 1960 and 1972 (actual) and 1980 and 1985 (projected)

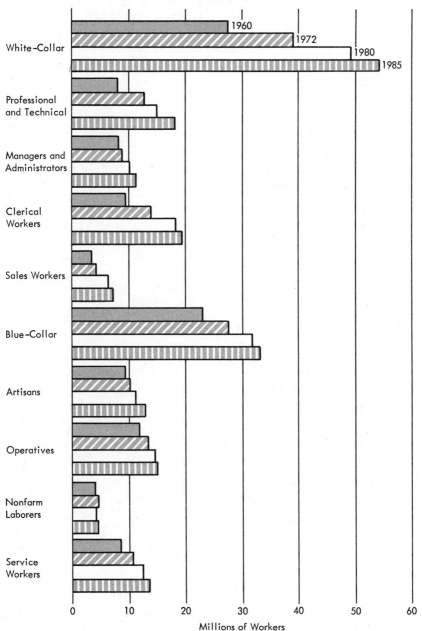

Millions of Workers

Source: "Monthly Labor Review," vol. 96, no. 4, p. 19.

highest skills of people are increasingly required. The trends are in the direction of a challenging, not a dismal, prospect for the employment of human energies.

The call for higher levels of skills increases in urgency. Since 1960, about 80 percent of the increase in total employment in the United States has been in the white-collar occupations (professional, technical, managerial, clerical, and sales). Looking ahead to 1985, it is estimated that industrial jobs percentagewise will show some increase, whereas the demand for professional and technical workers will be up about 50 percent, for clerical workers about 40 percent, and for service workers about 25 percent as shown in Figures 2–1 and 2–2. In some industries, such as aerospace, white-collar workers now exceed production workers.

Cultural and Social Background

Cultural and social changes have a striking impact upon attitudes and actions of employees. In these respects some significant changes have taken place in education, rural and urban conditions, age groups and some sociological patterns of business.

1. Educational Background. In regard to education, a much larger percentage of the population is now exposed to formal education. For example, in the age group of 25 and over the median level of education is now more than 12 years of schooling—yet just prior to World War II, the average was 9 years.

But it must be noted that some groups in the population are proportionately not as well educated as others. Such disadvantaged groups often find it difficult to find jobs in more advanced fields.

The consequences of both increasing education and of educational shortages are serious. As the base of education broadens, management must plan to deal with employees on a higher plane of logical interactions. Employees want a voice in affairs affecting their interests and want to have provision made for advancement in business. And for the disadvantaged, provision must be made to upgrade their employability capacities. Upgrading is becoming a direct challenge to business management as well as to community agencies.

2. Urban Conditions. Sources of labor supply have also changed strikingly in terms of a move from a rural to an urban orientation. Whereas about 15 percent of the population lived in urban areas in the middle 1800s, about 80 percent now do in the 1970s, and about 90 percent are expected to be living in urban areas by the year 2000.

As greater numbers congregate in cities, their viewpoints tend to change. First, people become far more dependent. They no longer can fall back on a plot of ground to sustain themselves when depressions hit. They are increasingly concerned with attaining economic security. Second, people have been confronted with the problems of city living—congestions, slums, tensions, and crimes. So people have increasingly moved to the position that business has a large responsibility to provide economic security, to provide training and jobs for school dropouts, and to assist in making our cities a better place to live and to earn a living. In short, the social responsibilities placed upon business are being expanded to include far more than mere contributions to welfare units but rather active participation in solving community problems.

3. Age Groups. The dispersion of workers according to age groups also has interesting implications. As seen in Figure 2–3, estimates indicate that the younger age groups constitute the larger share of the population in moving from 1970 to 1980. This implies that more attention will have to be directed to provide programs of training for younger workers, programs to hold experienced middle-aged workers, and programs effectively to utilize older workers.

Moreover, age dispersion has made it necessary to make adjustments for the "generation gap." Business has been confronted with an influx of youths impatient with either the views of their elders or with opportunities for advancement. It therefore has had to give attention to the demands of youth, yet to do so without upsetting too much the status, roles, and rewards expected by the elders.

4. Sociological Patterns. Another significant trend is that pertaining to the social status of people in the community and in their place of

FIGURE 2–3

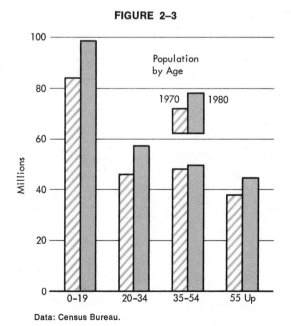

Data: Census Bureau.

work. Earlier, the job a person held represented a definite station in the eyes of colleagues and neighbors. The scale of prestige values was informal, yet generally known and respected. If a person's current occupation was low in the scale of values, there was a ladder of jobs of greater prestige to climb, aided by ability and luck.

But this stable structure has been undermined in a number of ways. First, drastic and accelerating changes in mobility of workers, transportation, communication, and new occupations have reduced the stability of social relations. Second, bringing together large numbers of people (often from a variety of areas and backgrounds) under the single roof of a factory, store, or office added new frameworks of social relationships and abolished older ones. Third, status tended to be aligned to other factors than jobs; operative employees derived prestige, if they had any at all, from their company's reputation whereas technical employees tended to be more concerned with their professional organizations. And fourth, minority groups refused to stand still for continued relegation to the lowest scale of jobs and opportunities.

Governmental Relations

Momentous changes have also taken place in the relation of government to labor and business. This may be seen by reviewing trends in governmental attitudes toward labor and management, and its own role in the business community.

1. Earlier Governmental Attitudes. From an earlier attitude of general disinterest and passiveness in labor-management matters, government has in some cases taken giant steps in the direction of positive intervention. And from a role in which it tended invariably to side with property owners, government has turned more and more in the direction of becoming a protagonist and guardian of the interests of employees.

About the time of the Civil War and for some time afterward, employees possessed few powerful friends in governmental circles. The concept of interstate commerce had not been extended to include manufacturing so that the legislative and executive branches of the federal government had no interest in labor's problems. State legislative bodies were preoccupied with agricultural, pioneering, and maritime affairs so that they too had neither time nor interest to spare on the problems arising in industry. And the judicial branch based its views on the preeminence of property rights so that it invariably ruled for capital interests whenever labor issues were placed before it. Indeed, court injunctions were a favored and easily obtained weapon of employers to combat picketing and boycotts, to stop strikes, and to limit union activities.

2. *Changing Conditions.* But a number of forces acted to change the role of government. Several costly strikes at the turn of the century focused attention upon the injury being done to the public welfare as well as to the parties involved. In addition, the public was aroused about sweatshops and poor working conditions as exposed by concerned reformers and organized labor. And workers grew in numbers so that their voting power made politicians more alert to their problems.

Hence, from the beginning of the 20th Century onward, significant changes evolved. Some protective legislation, primarily at the state level, could be found pertaining to child labor and industrial safety. State after state began to provide for worker's compensation in the event of industrial accidents. And the federal government passed important labor laws pertaining to accidents to railroad employees, the eight-hour day on the railroads, and the issuance of labor injunctions in the federal courts. During the Thirties, particularly significant were federal legislation and executive action on such subjects as collective bargaining, minimum and overtime wages, and social security.

And in recent years the federal government has asserted itself on a wide range of labor matters. It has proposed, for example, that wage increases sought through collective bargaining be restricted to noninflationary wage-price levels. It has experimented with direct wage controls. It has funded plans for upgrading skills of various unemployed and underprivileged groups. It has set safe working rules. And it has enacted laws for equalizing employment opportunities irrespective of race, color, sex, age, or creed.

Trends in Employee Roles

No perspective of personnel management would be complete without a view of the changing role of employees in business. For a long time it was the opinion of management—and one accepted by employees—that management was the boss and employees were to follow obediently management's decisions. If they did not like the boss, they were free to seek employment elsewhere. But gradually there ensued dissatisfaction with this relationship. Employees wanted to have some share in decisions which affected their interests.

Three methods have been used to gain this change by employees. First, employees have individually or in informal groups asked management to adjust grievances or to consider suggested improvements. This method continues to the present though it has not been very effective in getting management to share its powers with employees. Second, employees have sought to share decision-making powers through legal compulsion. For example, in Western Germany, labor has by law been given minority representation on the boards of directors and equal representation on work councils of specified types of business concerns under a plan called "co-determination." Although such a movement has not been introduced here, nevertheless it represents a concept which cannot be discounted. Third, employees have organized into unions through whose combined strength they have been able to gain a substantial voice in managerial decision making.

Although unions have existed for a long time in this country, their influence became significant from the 1930s onward, as illustrated in

FIGURE 2–4

Union Membership (1940–1980)

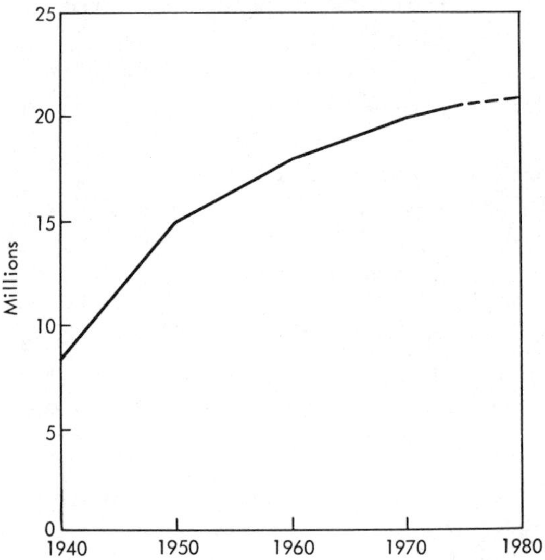

Figure 2–4. Now, out of a total working force of over 85 million, about one of every four workers is a union member.

As labor, through unions, has pursued its role in business, there has come a significant readjustment in employee-employer relations. The authority of the employer is no longer unquestioned. Employees not only have strong views regarding what they want but also have shown that they know how to achieve their goals. And it might well be argued that equality of strength is a prerequisite to mutual understanding of each other's problems and for equitable balancing of interests.

Management Attitudes

Another perspective of this field may be had by examining the attitudes employers have taken toward employees. There is much overlapping in conceptual trends, but a number of views stand out.

Until the turn of the century, labor was most widely viewed strictly as a factor of production. As such, it was to be handled like any other technical or economic resource of production. The main considerations were costs and returns. This view overlooks the influence which emotional and social characteristics have upon the working situation. Hence, this view has proved untenable, although some employers occasionally cast longing glances on the factor-of-production concept.

The first departures from the factor-of-production concept took place around 1900. Some employers became concerned with employees as human beings. Believing that they knew what was best for employees, they installed recreational, pension, and insurance programs at their own expense. Many such employer-initiated programs have been termed paternalism.

With the passage of time, paternalism encountered serious opposition. On the one hand, employees began to resist being treated like children. They wanted a voice in programs which affected their interests. On the other hand, some employers themselves saw that as employees matured, the limitations of paternalism should be removed. As a result, business has either been forced to or has voluntarily tended to accept employees as joint collaborators in defining its economic and social responsibilities.

In recent years concern with the human aspect has been expanded to include sociological factors and human values. There is growing recognition that employees must be dealt with in terms not only of their group perceptions and needs, but also their own value as meaningful human beings.

Another concept which has pushed itself into the foreground is derived from the political power of labor. The AFL-CIO Committee on Political Education and the Alliance for Labor Action of the U.A.W. are examples of this movement. This trend of labor in politics is likely to accelerate rather than slow down. As a consequence, some companies have undertaken various political programs either to counter labor's programs or to bring more education into the political arena.

In summary, management may approach its dealings with employees from any one of several viewpoints: the economic or factor-of-production point of view, various shades of human and social aspects, and various degrees of the political and partnership variety. It does seem that the trend is strong toward giving greater weight to the human, social, and democratic dimensions of management's relations with employees.

The Force of Education

And finally, this perspective of personnel management must give a prominent place to educational forces, informal and formal, conducted by individuals or by the professions. Certainly, much progress in labor-management relations is due to the long campaigns of various writers who cried out against sweatshops, child labor, unsafe and unsanitary working conditions, willful disregard for elementary needs of people, the underprivileged in ghettos, and unethical dealings with labor. Those who in novels, in various liberal periodicals, or in muckraking attacks dwelt on the shortcomings of business had much to do with awakening the conscious of the public—and eventually of management—to the need for more humane and ethical practices in business.

To formal educational institutions also a debt is owed for essential improvements in personnel management. Once our institutions of higher learning were involved, as far as business was concerned, with providing professional scientists—engineers, physicists, and chemists. Later, education was directed to such areas as psychology, sociology, and law, but only insofar as these contributed to a better technical employment of people. And finally, higher education in the humanities and the social sciences have been directed toward human problems in business. And specialized schools of business at the graduate level as well as the undergraduate level have allocated some of their resources to the field of personnel management.

PRESENT STATUS

It is now appropriate to outline the present status of the role and task of personnel management. To do this, it is desirable (1) to draw an overall picture of personnel problems, (2) to examine management's role in their solutions, (3) to note possible approaches to the solutions of these problems, and (4) to note obstacles to solutions.

General Nature of Problems

Management must allocate some of its time, skill, and resources to personnel because of various problems that call for solution. At this juncture, therefore, it is desirable to note the range of problems that arise in connection with employees. These include the following categories:

1. Measurement of Quantities. How much, for example, is a fair wage, a fair day's pay, or a fair pension payment? Or what is the right number of hours to be worked, the right length of a vacation, or the right number of holidays with pay?

2. Dimensions of the Human Factor. To what extent should consideration be given to the technical, economic, psychological, sociological, political, and ethical aspects of the human factor in business?

3. External Relationships. In what ways and in regard to what topics should management work with governmental agencies, labor groups, community agencies, and educational institutions in the matter of personnel problems?

4. Internal Relationships. Through what systems and structures should management and employees work out solutions to common problems?

Management's Role

Such problems are the province, though not the exclusive domain, of management. Either directly or indirectly, however, management is involved in all of them. But the same can also be said of other groups. How and to what degree each should participate in their solution is debatable. As noted in earlier discussions of trends, the roles of the several groups have been in a state of flux. And there is no reason to assume that the situation will be otherwise in the future.

There are areas, however, wherein the prerogatives of management are sharper than in others. Its rights of decision are more clearly defined over internal business operations. At least, it is invariably accorded the primary role of leadership in the internal framework. Others—such as unions and governmental agencies—have inserted themselves into the internal picture in varying degrees and ways, usually in the form of controls, agreements, and limitations over unrestricted freedom of managerial decision making.

Approaches to Personnel Problems

A number of approaches may be taken by management in tackling the problems with which it is confronted. These may be grouped into three large classes according to (1) the extent to which the problems are anticipated, (2) the nature of facts brought to bear upon problems, and (3) the kinds of knowledge required in dealing with these problems.

1. Cure and Prevention. Looking first at the extent to which problems are anticipated, personnel management can tackle problems after or before they develop. For example, after an employee expresses a grievance or after a work stoppage occurs, steps are taken to correct the situation. Unfortunately, personnel management has often tended to use such tardy, curative steps.

Opposed to this, there is a trend toward the use of preventive measures. Management is attempting more frequently to anticipate possible sources of trouble by establishing constructive personnel programs. Job evaluation, attitude surveys, and merit-rating plans, to be discussed later in this text, are cases in point.

The preventive approach can be strengthened by studying companies which have experienced long years of relatively satisfactory personnel relations. This is analogous to studying healthy individuals to learn how better to maintain physical well-being.

2. Factual Basis of Personnel Problems. Another way of looking at the approach to personnel problems which management employs is to note the basis used to solve problems. Such solutions may be founded in one's own experiences, in the experiences of others, or in scientific analysis of problems.

Under the first-mentioned plan, the personnel executive reaches decisions in terms of personal experience, which are therefore subject to the wisdom a limited experience can provide. It is very simple and quick in execution but results are unpredictable and often beyond explanation. Nevertheless, it is undoubtedly a widely used plan in personnel as well as in other areas of management.

Next, the executive may add the experience of others before reaching a decision. By means of attendance at conventions, discussions with other experts, visits to the plants of others, and study of business literature, the executive broadens the horizons of limited self experience. This approach is relatively simple, not too expensive to use, and hence frequently applied. But finding plans of others that will fit one's own problems is sometimes equivalent to looking for the proverbial needle in the haystack.

Finally, some executives attempt to solve their problems by scientific methods. Here solutions are sought by gathering, analyzing, and interpreting pertinent data. Obviously, this approach to problems is time consuming, usually costly, and invariably calls for close attention to details. Hence, this approach, though the best in theory, is the hardest to apply and thus the least frequently used. Yet, it represents the line along which attempts must increasingly be made, since it is the only one that has a logical basis for continued success. And it is the only one in which both employees and management can join forces without fear that a solution prejudicial to the other is being sought.

3. Knowledge Requirements. What areas of knowledge are pertinent to the solution of personnel problems? Specific areas were noted in the preceding chapter in the section devoted to the education of executives concerned with personal matters. It will suffice here to comment upon the basic human aspects for which knowledge is indispensable. The business executive must learn as much as possible about three aspects of people: what they do, why they do what they do, and by what means they seek to attain their goals.

What do people do? They think, feel, act. So such fields of knowledge as logic, psychology, medicine, etc., are helpful in learning how people, for example, think, feel, and act in regard to various subjects of interest.

Why do they do what they do? They have certain values, needs, goals, and interests. So ethics, for example, seeks to throw light on grades of values in human life. Sociology is interested in group needs and satisfactions. And history has given us clues on how various goals have shaped human events.

What means do they use to accomplish their goals? They have striven to attain desired ends through either individual or group effort. So psychology, sociology, and political science are contributors to our knowledge of such efforts. And economics and management have contributed to the wisdom and organizing skills needed for such decisions.

The foregoing listing does not imply that enough is now known in all areas to provide quick and simple solutions. The listing merely recites basic subject matter which cannot safely be left unstudied.

Obstacles to Problem Solving

It is well to recognize also that the problems that confront personnel management are by no means simple. It is not child's play to tussle with such issues as fair wages, the way in which employees should exercise their voice in matters of interest to them, reactions to political activities, and how far one has a right to go into matters pertaining to private lives and community affairs.

Complex though these problems are, their solutions are made even more difficult by the following obstructions:

1. Precise methods of measuring labor's interests or contributions are lacking.
2. The human factor is hard to interpret, and its probable future actions are difficult to forecast.
3. The common human shortcomings of ignorance, selfishness, and prejudice interfere with the application of logical methods.

If these obstructions could be removed, a long stride would be taken in reducing labor problems. For example, how much room for argument could there be if a measuring device were available that could determine precisely what an employee in a given case was worth? Imagine how quickly wage disputes could be settled with a thermometer of wage rates. But such a device is nonexistent, and it is improbable that one will be developed in the foreseeable future. Of course, methods of giving approximate answers are available, but they all leave something to be desired. Is it any wonder, therefore, that disputants over wage matters so often have recourse to tests of power in order to reach decisions in their quarrels?

The human factor also is a source of perplexing problems. It acts in ways that are often difficult to understand, let alone forecast. Even the fairest of us are not above some selfishness or ignorance—sometimes reasonably so and sometimes not. Although it may be argued that the human race is improving in these matters, we still have a long way to go in learning how to live together peacefully and equitably.

These difficulties are cited as a warning to the student to be realistic about personnel matters. It would be much better if logic could always be used. Unfortunately, the perversity of human nature must be considered. When trial-and-error methods must sometimes be used, this should not give rise to cynicism; rather, it is only realistic to recognize the complete nature of things as they are. Under such conditions, measurable improvement rather than artificial perfection should be the test of results achieved.

Future Prospects

From the foregoing, it is clear that labor in business has traveled many roads and has involved many groups. Changes in relationships have been numerous and continuous. It is not unreasonable, therefore, to expect that present patterns will be reconstructed with the passage of time. What are the future prospects?

What the future may bring is of course conjectural. But several possibilities are worth mentioning. In the first place, it is almost certain that employees will exert more influence on decisions which affect their interests. Whether this influence will emphasize voluntary cooperation with management, intervention through union representatives, legislative controls, or some combination of these is uncertain. Undoubtedly employees, through their unions, will push for increased rights to decide work rules and policies.

In the second place, it is almost certain that the government will take an increasing role in labor-management affairs. It will be forced to do so by the growing voting power of labor. Those aspiring to political office will be careful to avoid being tagged as an enemy of labor. Conversely, they will seek to aid in the enactment of laws which are favorable to labor. But government as an agency of all the people must seek ways and means of balancing the interests and protecting the rights of all who are involved in and affected by labor relations.

In the third place, technological changes can be expected to be more striking in their impact upon personnel relations. Merely to list the following is enough to illustrate the problems that must be solved as automation gains momentum: how to provide for employees displaced by machines, how to share in the productive powers of mechanization, how to develop the needed engineers and technicians, and how to design supervisory and organizational techniques to meet these new challenges.

Technological changes will also affect the factor of mobility of workers. This will involve changes in jobs, employers, occupations, industry, and geographic area, as well as movements in and out of the labor force itself. The increasing rate at which technology and business have been changing will see increased movements in the dimensions just mentioned. And such changes will call for (1) greater flexibility on the part of people, (2) more attention by management to personnel problems of a more dynamic society, and (3) better solutions to the needs of those displaced or adversely affected.

In the fourth place, it is certain that new insights and broader attitudes are needed if employees and management are to work together more harmoniously and effectively. New insights must come from the behavioral sciences. Business applications of psychology, sociology, and anthropology are particularly needed. And new attitudes must recognize that people are more than technical and economic factors but also total human beings. In all its operations, business must consider and allow for the feelings, perceptions, and values of people as people.

Varied research has pointed up the fruitful possibilities of improvement that lie in the areas of industrial sociology, group dynamics, and interpersonal relations. Perhaps most gratifying is the realization that human problems in business should be approached from an interdisciplinary rather than a specialized point of view.

And last, one can expect business to take a broader view of its responsibilities than it has in the past. Once, it was rather universally accepted that business should be judged primarily by the profit test. Management was appraised according to how well it protected the interests of the financial investor. But signs are abundant that management also must be judged on its concerns for human values and on its development of a social conscience. This trend will be accelerated as the productivity of our business system moves beyond meeting subsistence levels and supports an increasingly affluent society.

QUESTIONS

1. How have technological changes affected the types of skills required of employees?
2. What have been the effects of cultural and social changes in the United States since the late 1800s upon the problems of employee-employer relations?
3. What has the age distribution of the population to do with management problems?
4. How has the role of government in employee-employer relations changed?
5. Do you expect the concept that business should accept responsibility for labor's economic security will receive greater or lesser acceptance in the next five or ten years?
6. What are the various attitudes which management has taken toward employees and relations with employees since 1900?
7. What are the major problems that arise in connection with dealing with employees?
8. What approaches to problem solving are available to management? Which do you prefer?

9. What obstacles stand in the way to solutions to personnel problems? Which do you prefer?

10. What do you think will be the status of personnel by the year 2000? You might find it of interest to keep a record of your forecast and check it with what does happen.

CASE 2–1. EMPLOYMENT TESTS AND MINORITIES

For more than a decade, the Over-the-Road Trucking Co. had, among other selection devices, given some simple psychological tests to candidates for employment. These were paper-pencil tests which gave some clue to abilities to interpret, to judge, and make choices. The company felt that they contributed to weeding out the poorer candidates.

The company has recently been charged with unfair discrimination by the hiring practices it follows, particularly the use of the tests. The charges arose when Jane Direct, a candidate, "failed" the tests and was, therefore, not hired. Jane claimed that she had driven trucks for five years and had an excellent work record—which proved to be true. The company argued that it used tests because they helped to select the best available drivers from those who were applying at any given time.

The local representative of the federal Equal Employment Opportunity Commission (EEOC) that heard the case asked a number of questions about the company's hiring practices, but two stood out: first, what evidence do you have in validation of the tests, and, second, how many members of the minority group of which Jane Direct is a member have you hired?

The company representative answered by saying that, first, it felt that tests helped screen out the poorer candidates and to pick out the better ones, and, second, out of 25 candidates of this group in the past two years none had been hired because none could meet the tests.

Questions

1. What do you think should be the decision in this case?
2. What must the company do to make the use of tests acceptable to the EEOC?

CASE 2–2. NEED SATISFACTION

Jim Tackus had in a few years worked himself up from a relief truck driver to a division supervisor of road operations over 40 drivers. He knew all the ropes and technicalities of the driver's job. But to help him acquire and to improve his managerial and people skills, he was sent to supervisory training sessions operated by the industry's trade association.

In one of the sessions, the common problem of unsafe driving practices was under discussion. The men in the group were asked if they had any particular cases of their own they would like to have discussed and Jim volunteered one of his pet problems. Jim cited the case of Daring Joe who had a good record except for a tendency to take unnecessary chances in passing slower drivers in the face of oncoming traffic. Jim stated that he had tried to motivate Daring Joe by pointing out the dangers to Joe, the possible losses to the company, and the effect upon public relations —all without effect upon Joe.

The group leader after some talk by various group members asked, "Why not use the behavioral approach to the problem?" Jim and the others wanted to know what he meant. The group leader responded by saying that Daring Joe was evidently satisfying a need such as excitement, danger, and challenge, recognition, and power by his reckless driving. He went on to say that by closer examination it would then be possible to ascertain which need Joe was satisfying and thereby arrive at a decision as to how to handle the satisfaction of the particular need. Then Joe would be advised to adopt the plan to satisfy the need—such as mountain climbing—or he would be forced to resign.

Jim threw up his hands on hearing this saying that his company expected him to motivate truck drivers not to play motivational games with adolescents.

Question

1. Is Jim right or wrong? Why?

CHAPTER 3

HUMAN ASPECTS OF PERSONNEL MANAGEMENT

The Human Factor

Personnel management seeks, as already noted, to help build an effective and satisfied working team. All executives, in their personnel responsibilities, must therefore give due consideration to the technical skills required of people. This is the factor-of-production aspect of people.

But people possess other attributes. They bring to the work place, whether management likes it or not, various personal feelings, desires, perceptions, motives, values, and drives. Thus, people—at operative, technical, professional, and managerial levels—may be concerned about such matters as security, relations with fellow workers, status, roles, and personal and family needs. When a person is unsettled about these, efficiency will be impeded and cooperation difficult to obtain. An individual whose various dimensions are harmoniously attuned will be more effective in the working situation.

Dealing with the Human Factor

An employee must, therefore, be dealt with as a human being as well as a technical factor. Human beings manifest themselves through group interactions as well as individual actions. Human aspects are subjective and changeable, qualitative and dynamic, varying with cultural and personal backgrounds, economic events, and with the passage of time: indeed a complex of perplexing forces.

Is management's task here then mystical, and dependent upon some nebulous, occult touch? An answer in the affirmative seems supported

34

by the paucity of scientific knowledge regarding human behavior. Yet there are some grounds for arguing that management can make constructive progress in this area. By careful attention to what is known about people, management can accomplish much good.

It is important at the outset of this text, therefore, to note aspects of the human factor which are practically pertinent to all personnel activities. These materials are taken up in this chapter under the following headings:

1. Dimensions of the human factor
2. Human aspects of motivation
3. Human aspects of executive behavior

Dimensions of the Human Factor

In dealing with people in business, it is essential to encompass all dimensions of the human factor. These dimensions, first, must be defined, second, their dynamic character must be considered, and, third, they must be incorporated into the programs of building an effective and satisfied working force.

1. Defining the Human Factor. Close observation of employees serves to reveal that they are complex creatures. On the surface, and in the exterior phases of their work, they are obviously physiological creatures. They are technical machines in physical, muscular, manipulative, and energy-exerting operations. And to sustain these technical machines, they require various inputs of food, rest, and environmental conditions. Thus, they both act physiologically and have physiological needs.

Sustaining the physiological dimensions also requires that protection be provided against harmful or destructive forces. Hazards which might lead to physical disabilities or death concern them. They want to avoid physical pain and also loss of income that result from an inability to continue work. They therefore need physiological security.

Such concerns naturally suggest that an employee has a feeling dimension: likes and dislikes of a very personal nature. Some things cause happiness and others bring on sadness. Some things cause excitement and enthusiasm; others cause apathy and depression. He is, in short, an emotional creature. People possess a psychological dimension. In this area, as in the case of the physiological, they act psychologically and also have psychological needs.

In observing employees, it will soon be apparent that they like to interact with people—they have a social dimension. This propensity has implications of interaction and needs. Employees need the approval, protection, and feeling of belonging which only the acts of commingling can provide. They want status, prestige, compliments—all things which, in part, can only come if they interact appropriately in various group situations. Here too they both act socially and have social needs.

And, finally, one is impressed with the fact that they have an ethical dimension. They have ideas of what is right and wrong. This does not mean that an individual alone is correct in personal standards of fairness or of the means of attaining fairness. But it does mean that ethics are an important part of individuals' actions and needs. Again, they both act ethically and have ethical needs.

In brief, it is contended that employees must be viewed as physiological, psychological, sociological, and ethical creatures. They both act and have needs in these major areas. There may be differences of opinions regarding the proportions of or intensities of these dimensions but not that they are basic parts of the human factor.

2. Dynamics of the Human Dimension. It is important, moreover, that one be aware of the dynamic nature of these dimensions. Life consists of a continuous series of inputs and outputs of these complex facets. This fact is basic to a useful understanding of what motivates humans, what their defense mechanisms are, and what is meant by a mature or normal person.

Although more will be said about motivation later in this chapter, it is well to note here that time is an important ingredient of this subject. Attempts to stimulate employees will not necessarily bring forth immediate responses or satisfactions. Such practices usually must have time to work themselves out. Moreover, no one stimulus will serve for all time. Rather the efforts of management must consist of a series of unending, interacting motivational sequences.

The defense mechanisms of people are also dynamic in character. In various ways, most individuals prepare and carry out plans either to enhance or to defend their psychological, physiological, sociological, and ethical needs and standards. Threats or imagined threats to these bring forth individual and group reactions of varying degrees and kinds. Management must be alert to react correctly to defensive behavior and defense-causing behavior.

But how is the balance struck on these on-going positive and negative forces and effects? Only by working with people as maturing, not static, individuals. People are unlike inert metal; they are in a continuous process of change and of maturing. In maturing they are characterized by increasing self determination in place of a passive activity; increasing varieties of behavior in place of limited ways of behavior; increasing ability to concentrate in place of short interest span; increasing time span of planning in place of short-range perspective; increasing movement to equality with others in place of subordinate positions; and increasing awareness of others in place of self-concern and just self-awareness. If, for example, a maturing employee is kept on an unchanging job, motivation is difficult.

In sum, human dimensions must be viewed dynamically if management expects to build realistic personnel programs. Dealing with people is a continuing challenge. And it is a challenge related to a growth factor, a maturing individual.

3. Building the Human Work Force. But how are these dimensions of people handled by management? The answer lies in how programs are designed to procure, develop, maintain, and utilize people. Extended treatment of these functions is accorded in later chapters, but some brief comments are in order now.

Human relations can be no better than the kind of people who are hired. And if procurement is to do its job, attention must be directed to specifying the kinds of human characteristics that are needed on various jobs. Then applicants should be screened in terms of such human factors as personality patterns, social awareness, emotional stability, interests, and growth potentials.

Having hired people with good human relations features, the next step is to develop them as fully as needed. Training should be directed to technical skills, but as important is increasing the understanding of people about their personal relations with fellow workers, to supervisors, and to various company associates.

But trained employees must be properly maintained. First, procedures should be established to reduce dissatisfactions of aggrieved employees. Second, management must proceed with firmness and sensitivity in dealing with disciplinary cases. And third, management should concern itself with positive morale building, motivation, and conditions of gaining the willingness of people to cooperate.

The payoff in dealing with the human factor comes in how it is utilized on the job. Two points are important here. First, supervisory practices are significant here and will be discussed in later chapters. Second, job design affects worker satisfaction and productivity. And it is enough to say now that management's efforts here are often repaid when it institutes careful job studies, job enrichment, job enlargement, and employee suggestion plans.

Human Aspects of Motivation

Perhaps the most unique aspect of the human factor is that relating to motivation. People, undoubtedly more than any other living creature, are captains of their destiny. They can vary the intensity of their efforts over a wide range; how they apply technical skills depends upon their motivation—partly a financial matter but also a human matter. To examine the latter phase, attention is here directed to basic aspects, classes, steps, and rules of motivating.

1. Basic Aspects. Motivation, simply defined, is the act of stimulating someone or oneself to take a desired course of action. This may be illustrated as follows:

For example, such stimuli as wage incentives or better job opportunities are expected to yield such responses as higher output. But this relationship is easy to question because such responses are not always achieved. Obviously, something else intrudes upon the simple S-R Theory and can be illustrated as follows:

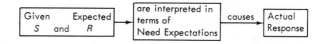

For example, an employee working on piece work knows that it is an incentive for increased production and higher earnings. But if the worker concludes that higher output will lead to rate cutting or running out of work which would adversely affect personal needs of future income or job security, production will fall below potential. Such other needs as respect of fellow workers or for one's own standards of fairness would weigh heavily in interpreting responses to various stimuli. Moreover as one evaluates the affect of actual responses upon one's interests (or those of others), this will affect future interpretations and responses. Thus, the diagram may be expanded as follows:

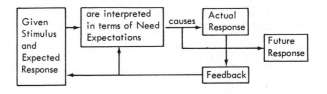

There also are a number of perplexities of which one must be aware if one's chances of success in motivation are to be increased. To begin with, there are stimuli, or buttons, without number which may be pushed in seeking a given response. Which should be pushed—a compliment, a preferred job location, a promotion, a new title, or more authority?

Moreover, a particular button may stimulate one individual but fail with another. Or, how hard should the respective buttons be pushed? Sometimes a light touch is enough, and sometimes one must be heavy-handed. Then too, a given button works at one time with a particular person and then fails at another time. And finally, there is the problem of conflicting buttons being pushed at the same time. Thus, management may be pushing one set of buttons, the union another, and the employee a third set.

Care must be taken, also, to be aware of the particular circumstances and environment in which stimuli are being applied. Thus, one must be a close student of individual differences among people. Motivating plans must be adjusted to given conditions of race, color, sex, creed, nationality, and customs in a particular area and community. And what might work in a company with a long history of union relations, for example, would undoubtedly be questionable in one with a long history of no unions. The general attitudes of people and management toward each other are pertinent in motivational planning. And to cite but one more example, economic conditions of prosperity or depression have a large impact upon motivational possibilities.

2. Classes of Motivators. The range and conditions of application of motivators is as wide as human experience. Yet progress in motivation can be made if management makes use of available motivators. These may be classified as financial, discussed in later chapters, and non-financial, discussed here as individual, group, and company motivators.

Turning first to individual motivators, it is obvious that as human beings, people have certain basic needs. Unless these are satisfied, life may either be lost or lose its significance. So in various ways and in varying degrees, people strive to satisfy these needs. Food, sex, clothing, and shelter come immediately to mind. Physiological safety and economic security are common needs. Who would deny the needs of gregariousness and social interaction. And as quickly there come to mind such needs as those of creativity, self-esteem, human dignity, and self-fulfillment.[1]

Also significant are motivators which arise out of social interactions. There is need to associate with others, to be gregarious, to help and be helped by others, and to interact with others. And we are very strongly affected by what others think of us and our actions. Even the basic areas of wants—food, sex, shelter, and religion—are invariably influenced by group opinion. Our families, neighbors, and working associates have some influence on where we live, what kinds of clothing we wear, and the kinds of jobs we prefer.

---

[1] A. H. Maslow, *Motivation and Personality.* New York: Harper & Bros., 1954. Maslow has had considerable influence in devising this hierarchy of human needs.

In terms of the company itself, motivators may be indirect or direct. Indirectly, many of the individual and group motivators just cited are often based upon the work situation. The degree to which we satisfy personal and social needs is determined in part by how well we earn economic support for them in our company. Moreover, business need not be inimical to human needs. In few types of human activity is the relation between working hours and leisure hours so favorable.

Turning now to direct company motivators, a number may be mentioned. To begin with, work itself can be the source of many satisfactions. This does not imply that work, like play, will be pleasurable in all ways. But it is suggested that work has potentialities for satisfactions such as feelings of accomplishment, of significance, of craftsmanship, of creativity, of pride, of self-respect, and of respect of others. Just to go through a modern business enterprise is to be struck by the complex tasks which can challenge the skill, imagination, and ambitions of anyone.

But some justifiably retort that many jobs are neither challenging nor satisfying but boring and dull. Here, however, business can point to two favorable trends. First, it is turning more and more of such work over to machines; boring work is being reduced thereby. Second, business is seeking ways to make jobs more interesting. Some companies have found that programs of job enlargement and enrichment can reduce boredom as well as increase interest. And some companies have encouraged employee participation in the design of more effective and satisfying job arrangements. In both instances, needs such as significance, pride of accomplishment, and creativity are served.

But it is argued by some students of motivation in business that one must be aware of what factors are motivators and which are not.[2] Some factors do lead to superior job satisfaction and performance. Thus possibility for growth, responsibility, achievement, advancement, and recognition are motivators. But there are other factors—termed hygiene, maintenance, or dissatisfiers—whose absence lead to dissatisfaction but whose presence do not motivate but merely prevent dissatisfaction. Thus, management should not expect good working conditions to be a motivator; they can only reduce dissatisfaction. For positive motivation one must turn to the motivators such as growth and achievement possibilities.

3. Steps of Motivation. It is now appropriate to see how management may actually proceed to motivate employees. This activity divides itself into two parts: (a) what is to be done, and (b) how and why what is done is done. The former are steps in motivation, and the latter are rules governing the steps. Both are performed simultaneously, of course. But

---

[2] F. Herzberg. *Work and the Nature of Man.* Cleveland: World Publishing Company, 1966.

for purposes of discussion, it is preferable to take them up separately. This section is devoted, therefore, to steps and the next to rules of motivation. The major steps include the following:

a. Sizing up situations requiring motivation
b. Preparing a set of motivating tools
c. Selecting and applying the appropriate motivator
d. Following up the results of the application

  a. *The Size-up.* The first stage of motivation is to ascertain motivational needs. Which employees need motivation? All, of course, but of varying kinds of degrees. Thus, one person will work to get champagne and caviar; another wants only beer and pretzels. Some worry about a college education for the children; others are more than satisfied if their children learn how to read and write. Or one takes pride in producing quality work, while another is simply interested in quantity. Stress in the size-up stage must therefore be laid upon individual differences.

  b. *Preparing a Set of Motivating Tools.* Having determined the motivational needs of a particular person or group, an executive must then be ready to select and apply specific tools of motivation. But this means that a list must be available from which choices may be made. An executive, from personal experience, from the experiences of others, and with the help of the personnel division, can distill a list of what devices seem to work, with what types of people, and under what conditions.

  c. *Selecting and Applying Motivational Plans.* The critical stage in motivation is, of course, application. This involves selection of the appropriate plan, the method of application, and the timing and location of applications.

  The choice of a plan depends on answers to a number of pertinent questions. Who is involved? What has worked or not worked in the past? Are there any precedents or other employees involved? What does the selected motivational device require in terms of executive time, skill, and resources?

  Having decided, for example, that an employee is to be complimented on craftsmanship, thought must be given to application. One must think through the words to use, the tone of voice, and gestures when paying the compliment; rehearse the contemplated act. In this connection, role playing and sensitivity training have proved effective as advance preparation.

  And finally, consideration should be given to where and when motivation is to be applied. Using the compliment as an example, some employees like to be told in public of their good deeds; others prefer to avoid the spotlight. Timing, too, is important. How soon after a good deed has been done should an employee be told of management's appreciation? Too late may be worse than useless. So it is imperative that the time factor be watched in the application of a motivational plan.

d. Feedback. Feedback is needed to determine if an individual has been motivated. If not, some other device must be applied. This is necessary because the desired objective—whether higher output, lower costs, greater loyalty, or whatnot—has not been attained. A secondary purpose of follow-up is to evaluate motivational devices for future reference. It provides information regarding how devices should be classified as to their possible future use.

4. Rules of Motivating.   In the performance of the steps of motivation, management should be guided by some fundamental rules or bench marks. These are not laws; we do not as yet know enough about motivation to be that certain. But past experience has taught some useful lessons which provide a basis for building one's own list of guides.

a. Variability.   Of utmost significance in motivation is its unending and changeable nature. Management must not act on the premise that its motivational program is set if a given set of stimuli bring forth favorable responses. One will soon learn otherwise for a number of reasons. First, given motivators continuously repeated lose some of their power. Thus, a first time compliment may make an employee feel good; repeated compliments become old stuff and less effective. Second, restricting motivation to a particular type—such as a given wage incentive plan—suffers from sameness. People fundamentally like some change in practically all phases of their lives, motivation included. Third, no one set of motivators will retain the same degree of forcefulness for all people or for the same person over a period of time. To be sure, employees are people, in that sense they are all alike. But individual differences exist between people and even the same person is different from time to time. One may be discouraged by these warnings but they nevertheless are motivational facts of life.

b. Self-Interest and Motivation.   Without doubt, motivation is largely built on selfishness. This may seem to be an undesirable foundation. To the extent that selfishness tends toward greediness, undesirability is not denied. But selfishness may be intelligent. This is so when a person realizes that personal purposes are best served by helping others, too, to attain their goals. For example, employees ambitious to climb the executive ladder may try to accomplish this by climbing over others and letting the devil take the hindmost. Or they can try to climb by helping others become more effective team members. Both methods are selfish, but one is intelligent.

c. Attainability.   It may seem too obvious to say so, but motivation must establish attainable goals. What we hold out for a particular person must be attainable by that person. This does not mean easily or at once.

Such a goal as a better job or a supervisory position may take years to attain. But it must be within reach.

Attainability should be related to a sense of personal effort. Interest in work is enhanced when employees can see that each of their efforts served to attain a given goal. There is a kind of reciprocity here. Reaching a goal is satisfying but working to reach the goal is also satisfying; and so both can be mutually reinforcing. For example, some companies have found that productivity has been increased when employees were allowed to establish both the goals to be attained and the means to attain them.

d. Participation. Along these lines, the desirability of participation of those to be motivated in the plans of motivation is increasingly being recognized. Such co-operation serves to reduce suspicion of management's motivational aims. And participation serves to make the employees feel worthwhile.

e. Proportioning Rewards. Good motivation is dependent also upon proportioning rewards between people and for the same person at different times. But how much of a stimulus is to be applied to attain a given response? For example, how much commission is to be paid to salespeople to gain how much in the way of sales effort? Scientifically accurate answers are as yet unavailable. Yet careful attention to this aspect of all motivational devices can bring improvement and can serve to avoid under- or over-motivation.

f. The Human Element. It is well to refer again to the idea that the actions of people are caused by their feelings as well as by their thinking. One needs to work with employees for only a short time to learn how quickly their actions can turn into undesirable channels if their feelings are hurt, their egos or personalities insulted, or their pet ideas slighted. An executive may have been absolutely right in facts, logic, and decisions. But by giving a wrong impression, or by rubbing a person's fur the wrong way, the executive's actions do not bring off the desired results.

g. Individual-Group Relationships. Motivation must be based upon group- as well as individual-centered stimuli. For a long time, management acted as though employees were solely and simply ego-centered creatures. If action was desired, attention had only to be paid to the individual drives and needs of people. To an extent, this is true. Each of us is to a large degree an island.

But at times, individuals are group-influenced. For example, office workers tend to act and feel somewhat differently than shop workers, and artisans take a different view of their work than unskilled labor. Or a person may like the job but nevertheless go out on a strike because of peer loyalty. Hence, an executive must determine what group-inspired differences exist in individuals as well as what egocentric drives motivate them.

h. Situational. And finally, business must be aware of the fact that motivation is affected by the work situation. Wages, for example, cannot be viewed as something alone. But how is a given wage plan affected by how a job is designed, by physical conditions, by supervisory relationships, by attitudes of fellow workers, by contemplated job changes, by relationships with other jobs and processes, by communication channels, etc.? A given motivational device can neither make up for shortcomings in other influential factors nor be fully effective without proper attention to the inter-affects of other factors upon it. This calls, as some have rightfully argued, for a system—not a piece-meal approach to the design of motivational programs.

Human Aspects of Executive Behavior

In dealing with individuals and groups, an executive affects people not only by the functions performed but also by acts, demeanor, and appearance. Hence, managers should concern themselves with how their behavior and attitudes influence human relations.

Behavior Patterns. It is not surprising to hear such comments from employees as the following. "Keep away from the boss today; she just passed me without seeing me." "The boss smiled this morning; I wonder who is going to get the ax today?" "The boss is wearing his brown suit today; don't ask him for any favors."

By reading such signs, people learn when to avoid the boss and when the individual can be favorably approached. Subordinates become aware that such overt manifestations are indicative of the way an executive is likely to act on a given day. The way an executive talks, and about which subjects, posture, dress, and bodily mannerisms also provide clues to moods. Or an executive's office decor often notifies people what relations with others are likely to be expected.

Executive Attitudes. Of great significance in affecting individual and group reactions is the set of attitudes an executive holds toward how the organization should be operated. Differences may be found in attitudes toward (a) group control, (b) factors of success, and (c) latitude of action.

a. Type of Group Action. How an executive directs the organization can fall into a variety of categories. For a long time in this country— and it is still true in many other countries—the theory of the autocrat prevailed. The executive was supreme and expected orders to be obeyed loyally, completely, and without question. There were no human relations problems. The "problems" kept to themselves or were discharged. As long as everyone thought that management had the right to act autocratically, the system operated with relative efficiency and satisfaction.

All autocratic executives have not been heartless. Many have felt a strong responsibility for providing for the personal needs and welfare of their employees. So it was not uncommon to find managers who provided various recreational, health, and benefit services. It was not unlike good parents who take care of their children; hence the term *paternalism* has been applied to this type of management behavior.

But children grow up and want to do things and decide things for themselves. As a consequence, the autocrat and the paternalist in business, by force or by choice, have tended to move toward participative actions. Participation may take such limited forms as suggestion systems, grievance plans, and joint conferences. The final plans and decisions remain in the hands of management.

A more advanced stage of human relations is attained when management shares decision-making powers with employees. This stage has been reached already in the subjects covered by collective bargaining. Labor and management work out the basis upon which wages, hours, and working conditions will be established in return for the skills and effort of the working force.

There is no doubt that each of these types of leadership will be found to exist in the United States today. Indeed, each executive uses some of these forms and is seldom, if ever, always a pure autocrat, paternalist, or participative-oriented. Sometimes, it pays to be decisive; sometimes, it is better to be a complete humanitarian; and, sometimes, it is well to be an equal partner. An executive should adjust so that the person with whom cooperation is sought will react most favorably for the total good, under various conditions.

b. Factors of Success. Executives differ, too, regarding the factors they consider important in measuring success and progress. Since most people are interested in getting ahead—or at least likes to think they are so motivated—it is important to know how one's superior measures success.

Of particular relevance in this connection is the attention which has been directed to the "work-centered" versus the "person-centered" boss, as shown in Figure 3–1. Studies of these types indicate that more work is accomplished under the latter type of supervisor than the former. Thus the work-oriented executive deals with subordinates in terms of meeting schedules, getting out production, keeping down costs and spoilage, and being careful with machines and tools. The more successful person-oriented executive, on the other hand, shows concern for the problems subordinates have and with the difficulties they encounter on the job.

An executive need not tend to be work-centered or person-centered, but may take both aspects into consideration, as indicated in Figure

FIGURE 3–1

Supervisory Effectiveness

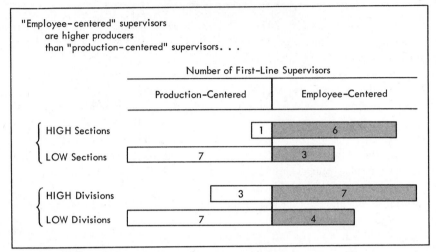

"Employee–centered" supervisors
    are higher producers
    than "production–centered" supervisors. . .

	Number of First–Line Supervisors	
	Production–Centered	Employee–Centered
HIGH Sections	1	6
LOW Sections	7	3
HIGH Divisions	3	7
LOW Divisions	7	4

Source: Rensis Likert, *Motivation: The Core of Management*, Personnel Series, no. 155 (New York: American Management Association), p. 6.

3–2. The use of a "managerial grid" is an excellent device for obtaining a graphical view of an executive's tendencies in both directions at the same time.

Other examples may be cited of executive attitudes toward success factors. Some executives rate a subordinate high for a neatly ordered desk. Another is impressed by on-time performance. Some like a particular style of report writing and dislike others. Some rate terseness as a sign of ability, and others consider it as a sign of emptiness. Some are impressed by quantity and others by quality. Is it any wonder that subordinates are on the alert as to how a particular superior evaluates things?

These likes and dislikes also run along lines of personal qualities. An executive may show partiality toward sorority sisters or fraternity brothers, those of a given nationality or religion, members of a particular club, those from a particular part of a town or a social stratum, those who dress well or have polished manners, or those of a particular coloration or physiognomy. Sooner or later, these bases of evaluation become known. The smarter employees shy clear of those whose standards they cannot meet and attach themselves to those with whom their success is more apt to be assured. So again, it is human rather than technical factors which are affecting the success (or lack of it) in management.

c. *Latitude of Action.* Another aspect of executive behavior is the degree of freedom accorded subordinates. This has, first of all, a positive

FIGURE 3–2

Where Five Executive Types Fit on the Managerial Grid

9,1: The production man. He doesn't let human factors interfere with efficiency. Output outweighs everything else.

1,9: The morale builder. He figures that a comfortable work tempo will let production take care of itself.

1,1: The cynic. He believes workers are naturally lazy and sets production standards low so they can meet them.

9,9: The rarest of all. He expects results will be best when managers and workers have a common stake in company goals.

5,5: The compromiser. He wants to keep employees happy, production adequate—and doesn't want to rock the boat.

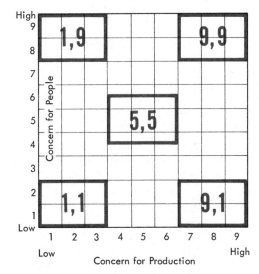

Source: "Grid Puts Executives on the Griddle," *Business Week,* Oct. 18, 1969, p. 159.

phase in terms of how free employees feel in taking action. Some executives go to the extreme of holding subordinates only for results; they may use whatever means they desire. In such instances of "management by objectives," management is then unconcerned with methods or excuses; it either gets results from present managers or hires new ones. This may give subordinates freedom of action, which is desired by many people; however, it also provides for swifter penalties but, by the same token, greater rewards, when one is successful.

There is also a negative phase in regard to the mistakes subordinates may make. Some executives look with such contempt upon errors that subordinates are immobilized for fear of penalties. They avoid mistakes by slowing down action until they can be assured of the desires of their superiors. Their mistake records are low but so also is their production.

Some executives believe, however, that subordinates should be freed of this fear, that they have a right to make mistakes. And this finds foundation in the theory of learning which states that we learn from our mistakes as well as from our successes. Of course, the proponents of this idea do not contend that success will be in proportion to mistakes. Rather, the idea is that removal of fear opens powers of constructive action which hitherto have been walled up by fear of executive displeasure. Moreover, review of mistakes is a good way to clear the road for better future planning and action.

QUESTIONS

1. With what dimensions of the human factor must management be concerned?

2. Why is it desirable to view the human factor in a dynamic sense?

3. In what ways can the procurement of an effective working force be performed so as to take into account the human aspects of people?

4. What is the theory of motivation? What makes its application difficult?

5. Into what classes may motivators be grouped?

6. What steps should be taken and what principles followed when motivating?

7. Why are group forces seemingly of equal if not greater importance in affecting individual behavior?

8. What is your opinion of the importance of executive behavior in influencing individual actions? Should subordinates allow such personal factors to affect their attitudes and performance?

9. Which type of executive attitude toward the organization do you think is most effective and desirable. How do you take into account the influence of time and situation upon the attitude an executive might assume?

10. In what ways may executives differ regarding the factors they consider important in measuring the success of their subordinates? How would you rate these factors in terms of their usefulness and fairness?

CASE 3–1.   Participation in Decision Making

In American business, it has been traditional for management (or the owner or entrepreneur) to assume the right to make decisions regarding the operations of the business. Because of the risks owners were taking with personal finances, it was argued that they should have control over how the risks of their investments were to be handled. And the rights of decision-making included personal as well as property-involved subjects.

But over the past 100 years, there has been a gradual whittling of this tradition. Employees in particular have raised some interesting points and questioning arguments. They claim more and more that they too take risks, investing the time of their working lives which involve risks to them which are just as important and critical as the financial risks of management. Hence they argue that they should participate in decisions which affect their risks and their interests such as working conditions, earnings, the kinds of working associates, opportunities for growth, and personal security.

And to gain support for their contentions, they are turning for help to the government and unions as well as to the public and their own individual efforts.

Having seen many of these developments, M. A. Wright, President and chief stockholder of the Wright Corp., is seeking to determine how decision-making over what subjects should be shared between management and the employees and by what means.

Question

1. What suggestions would you make to Wright?

CASE 3–2.   Ethnic and Cultural Considerations

The Foreign-Make Company decided to establish a manufacturing operation in a fairly remote area of the southwest. The locale was chosen because of available material resources, proximity to a transportation terminal, and an abundant labor supply.

The workers would come from surrounding small Indian villages, the Mexican-American residents of the area, and a few transplanted employees from the home site of the company. Two religions were predominant: Mormon and Catholic. Ethnic loyalties were very evident. Spanish and Indian dialects were openly spoken, with some English.

The company reasoned that it could take advantage of the cheap labor supply yet at the same time make a contribution to the area's standard of living with the jobs it would provide. It was realized that the workers were relatively uneducated but no difficulties were expected on that score because the machinery and manual operations were very simple.

Mary Sullit was chosen to head up this unit because she was successful in the home operation, having an excellent record of getting things done. Sullit was provided with a few key people to manage the new plant, included among which was a personnel manager who spoke Spanish as well as English. Recruiting workers was easy because the company was almost the only source of employment.

Within a year, it was evident that things were not going right. Productivity was lower than expected. Turnover and absenteeism were excessive. Orders were casually disobeyed. Some workers lost interest in working. Once all the Indian workers stayed away for two weeks during a tribal festival. The cultural differences of the workers surfaced. The Indians and Mexican-Americans were suspicious of the whites. The workers had little feeling for an achievement-oriented society, and though fascinated by tedious, intricate tasks, disliked plain manual labor. And the Mormons and Catholics were often at odds.

Question

1. As the company does not deem it advisable to close down the operation and take the attendant losses, what would you suggest?

CHAPTER 4

PERSONNEL PROGRAMMING

Scope and Importance

The manner in which the human factor is fitted into the pattern of a company's operations may be like a patchwork or like a map of well-defined dimensions. In the former case, personnel management will be characterized by gaps and duplications of functions, contradictions between policies, and poorly budgeted operations. In the latter case, the various phases of personnel work will have been arranged into a well-designed system. The difference between the two lies in managerial planning—the degree of predetermining the objectives to be sought in a forthcoming period and how they are to be attained.

By establishing a plan, management recognizes that all parts of personnel work must be interacting and complementary if they are to be most effective. Good selection procedures, for example, reduce excessive training. Again, such work as collective bargaining is not left to chance but is based upon careful research regarding wages, hours, and working conditions. Or auditing of personnel work is not an afterthought but is planned for at the same time as the activities to be evaluated. This illustrates the point that controls must be planned.

Planning a program requires the integration of several factors. Assuming that a basic foundation of philosophy and principles (as outlined in Chapter 1) has been devised, attention must be directed to the following aspects of programming.

1. Objectives to be sought through the program
2. Functions to be performed in seeking desired objectives
3. Policies guiding those responsible for programs
4. Budgetary aspects of programs
5. Informational needs of programming

OBJECTIVES

The Importance of Objectives

Perhaps the most fundamental factor in a personnel program, next to a basic philosophy, is that of objectives. It is impossible, on the one hand, to establish effective personnel plans until one has definite ideas of what results one hopes to accomplish. For example, a motivational program cannot be designed just to motivate; it must be based upon some estimate of the degree by which it is hoped to increase productivity. Or a pension plan, to be successful, must serve specific needs of employee as well as company goals.

On the other hand, it is difficult to prescribe remedies for (i.e., a plan to correct) personnel shortcomings if one does not know what the specific results should have been. If a hiring procedure is to be improved, for example, it is necessary to know how far it has fallen short of producing desired results. Only then can one decide whether the procedure should be completely replaced or merely changed in some parts. Moreover, when objectives are established only after troubles are encountered with particular programs, employees suspect that executives are making a case to suit themselves.

Classes of Personnel Objectives

Personnel objectives should include all personnel goals of interest to the company and to the participants therein. In general, and in varying degrees, personnel functions are expected to help attain the following goals:

1. Produce and distribute an acceptable product or service
2. Continuously yield satisfactory profits to investors and satisfactory wages, salaries, and other personal values to employees at all levels
3. Meet community and social obligations
4. Attain the foregoing objectives economically and effectively

1. Service Objectives. At the outset, it is imperative to recognize the fundamental importance of the objective of service. Business is an institution by means of which society seeks to satisfy its needs for goods and services. Various resources, among them people, are needed to produce such goods and services. To those who help to attain the service objectives, personal rewards are forthcoming, such as profits to the owners and wages, salaries, and other personal satisfactions to employees at various organizational levels.

The design of a personal program thus starts with a clear picture of the service objectives of a company. On this basis, efforts of personnel management can then be directed to designing plans of dealing with people so that planned services are effectively derived.

2. Personal Objectives. Of course, the objectives of service, efficiency, and profits do not take precedence over the personal goals employees seek, nor vice versa. Obviously, the goals of employees also must be attainable, or trouble will ensue. Hence, personnel management must give due consideration to the aims of employees. But what are the personal goals which must be satisfied?

It is not difficult to list the kinds of goals that are generally in the minds of employees, but the question of how much of each kind is desired is another matter. Quantitative answers have to be hammered out on the anvil of actual experience, but qualitative wants of employees may be classified as follows:

a. Fair wages, hours, and working conditions
b. Participation and involvement in decisions
c. Economic security
d. Opportunity for advancement and self-improvement
e. Worthwhile accomplishment and individual significance
f. Positive group feeling

a. Fair Wages, Hours, and Working Conditions.   The keystone of any personnel program is an acceptable wage structure. Unless employees are reasonably satisfied that their wages are fair, it is invariably futile to expect much good from other parts of a personnel program, such as recreational plans, company periodicals, suggestion systems, training plans, and insurance plans. Hence, it is imperative (1) to establish as fair a wage policy as possible and (2) to seek to convince the employees of the intrinsic fairness of the plan.

In the matter of hours of work, there is less probability of trouble as long as rules governing working periods, rest periods, holidays, vacations, and shift rotations are definitely stated, are uniformly applied, and conform to general community practice.

Working conditions also merit attention in a personnel program. Physical aspects of working conditions, such as heating, lighting, safety devices, and clean work places, can usually be established without too much difficulty. In this regard, job content, or what tasks should be assigned to better balance technical and human needs, is of growing concern. Supervision—the human aspect of managerial working conditions—is also important and not easy to perform. And what constitutes correct work loads and reasonable rights of employees to participate in determining job assignments can cause deep-seated controversies.

b. Participation.   Participation and involvement in decisions which affect their interests are increasingly desired by all levels of employees. Fair wages, for example, seem fairer when employees have something to say about their establishment. Even on such matters as deciding on the adoption of new work assignments or equipment, ultimate efficiency depends upon the manner in which employees are involved in the decision-making process. Although this seems to run counter to the prerogatives of management, what good are such prerogatives if they are nullified by the noncooperation of labor? If an end is desirable, the appropriate question is what means are most effective in their attainment.

c. *Economic Security.* Another group of personal objectives in which employees are interested is that of economic security. Such events as accidents, seasonal or cyclical depressions, or technological changes hold a constant threat to an employee's earning power. To be sure, federal and state legislation has been enacted that serves to alleviate some of these losses. And unions have obtained concessions along the lines of supplementary unemployment benefits and are working toward the guaranteed annual wage. But these efforts do not relieve private industry from a responsibility to add to employee security.

d. *Opportunity for Employees.* Less tangible than the foregoing, and for that reason perhaps less frequently considered, is the desire of employees for the opportunity for self-improvement and self-fulfillment. There is a subtle distinction here that must be grasped. All employees do not want promotions; to many, the responsibilities of new jobs are too great, and the feeling of security in their present positions is too satisfying to give up. But there are very few employees who do not like to think that if they wanted to get ahead, the opportunity for such development would be open to them. Providing opportunities for personal and job growth is a desirable aspect of personnel planning.

e. *Individual Feeling of Significance.* Perhaps the most deep-seated need of employees is that of self-fulfillment. People need to feel that their working hours are significant and worthwhile. Herein is one of the most serious challenges to management. How can all work, from manual to creative, and from routine to varied, instill in employees a sense of a meaningful life? How convince, for example, many college students that they should not turn away from careers in business; that business is a constructive life work? Good wages and salaries, though important are not enough, nor are mere words unsupported by substantiating evidence. One answer lies in opportunities to contribute to a company's efforts of providing a useful service to its customers and to society. Another lies in assuring employees that their brains as well as their brawn are important. There must be evidence that business is a place where all of the human dimensions can be satisfactorily utilized.

f. *Group Feeling of Significance.* There is growing recognition, too, that personnel management must consider the feelings generated by interpersonal relations within groups. If a group feels, for example, that a job or company is inferior, that the status of various positions is of a low order, or that cooperation with management is undesirable, individuals will feel likewise. Hence, it is wise for management to build its personnel programs with a view to favorable development of group perceptions, feelings, and values.

3. Community and Social Objectives. Many forces have been at work for many years to bring about the realization that what happens within the walls and during the working hours of a business organization has an effect upon the community and, in turn, upon the efficiency of the company. For example, failure to provide safe working conditions, taking advantage of lower wages for women, child labor or sweatshop wage rates have in their time adversely affected the community. Or to business has been assigned part of the blame for failure to provide helpful programs for such groups as those in ghettos, the underprivileged, and various minority groups. Eventually, there has been a reaction against all business as well as the offending companies.

It is not implied that all business has been callously indifferent. Indeed, increasing numbers of companies are voluntarily undertaking programs to alleviate such community shortcomings by locating branches

FIGURE 4–1

Relation of Management, Personnel Program, and Objectives

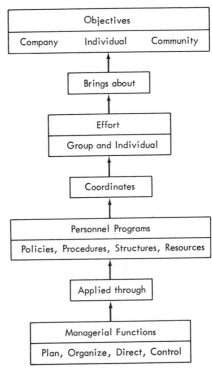

in ghettos and also special training for underprivileged groups. Nevertheless, the failure of enough employers to take constructive action has led to the enactment of various restrictive laws by the states as well as by the federal government. In recent years the passage of compensatory and welfare legislation concerning such matters as unemployment insurance, old-age pensions, and medical care is additional evidence of what happens when business itself has not (and, some argue, for good reason) accepted such social obligations itself.

4. Economy and Effectiveness. All the foregoing objectives must invariably be attained economically and effectively. This follows for the simple reason that a company's resources are not unlimited. If its resources, and that includes personnel, are not utilized effectively, a company will eventually lose out in the competitive race. The need for economy and effectiveness must be understood by employees since their personal goals can best be attained only by successfully operated companies.

In summary, the various objectives the employer and employees seek must be incorporated in a well-designed personnel program. This relation between objectives and the program is aptly summarized in Figure 4–1.

FUNCTIONS

Nature of Functions

Having established the objectives of personnel management, the next important question to be settled is that of how desired goals are to be attained. The answer, basically, is through the performance of functions (activities).

The kind and quality of functions chosen in any given case are affected by the company's objectives. For example, a company that recognizes the psychological needs of employees will have to undertake a variety of activities that would be unnecessary if these objectives were not considered. Or in a company that is conscious of the need for economy and effectiveness in its personnel programs, control and audit functions will be installed which others would ignore. And a company that proposes, for example, to set wages upon community levels must undertake surveys which are of no interest to those that follow a traditional or hit-or-miss system of setting wage differentials.

Although details of actual practice vary considerably, the general outline of personnel functions is much the same among progressive companies. These functions fall into two major classes: operative and managerial. Since they have been described in the first chapter and will be taken up in detail in succeeding chapters, only a brief comment on each is needed now. The operative functions of personnel management include the activities specifically concerned with procuring, developing, utilizing, and maintaining an efficient working force. The managerial functions pertain to the activities concerned with planning, organizing, directing, and controlling the work of those performing operative personnel functions.

It is essential to grasp the significance of this dual division of personnel functions. Otherwise, preoccupation with detailed problems leads to the neglect of managerial duties. It is easy, as many executives have learned to their regret, to become so busy with such tasks as hiring, transferring, counseling, and training that they fail to foresee shifting conditions which call for changes in operative functions, fail to organize the work of subordinates satisfactorily, and fail to keep a good check upon the work of subordinates.

Assignment of Responsibility for Functions

The personnel program must not only spell out needed functions but must also establish them into organized responsibility patterns. This requires the design of (1) procedural or systems structures and (2) organization structures.

1. Procedural Responsibility. Procedural or systems responsibility refers to the manner in which functions are arranged in complementary and sequential relationships for the accomplishment of desired objectives. The relation between functions, projects, and information flows in a selected area of personnel work is aptly illustrated in Figure 4–2. References to other procedures will be made throughout the text, hence only a few comments are in order here.

A personnel procedure is the basic tool for getting work done, i.e., accomplishing objectives. The broad function of hiring, for example, to be effective, must consist of an orderly sequence of a number of detailed functions. Each subfunction must feed into the next, so that good candidates are retained and poor ones rejected. Such details as application forms, interviews, tests, and references should be arranged so that evaluation of candidates can proceed effectively in arriving at correct decisions. Or on a larger scale, various broad personnel procedures—training, motivation, counseling, wage administration, collective bargaining—should be orderly not only within themselves but also in relation to each other and to the major functions of the business, such as production, sales, finance, research, and engineering.

The management of personnel systems has taken on an increasing importance as companies have grown in size. Information data and flows have increased to such an extent that decision making in personnel matters would be obstructed without carefully designed and integrated procedures. The economical and full use of computers, data-processing equipment, and communication devices is impossible unless their incorpo-

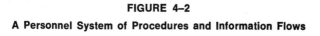

FIGURE 4–2

A Personnel System of Procedures and Information Flows

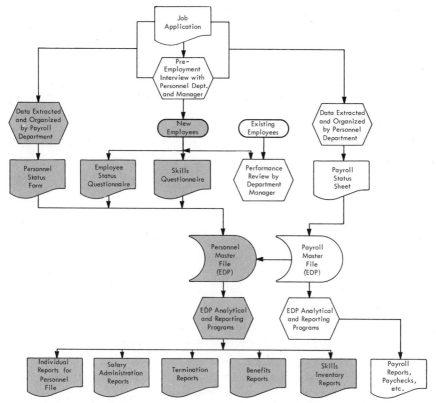

Source: James G. Howard, "A Low-Cost Approach to Computerized Personnel Data Systems," *Personnel Journal*, vol. 48, no. 9., p. 704.

ration into personnel systems is carefully planned to the smallest detail. The demands of coordinating the personnel activities of a large and often geographically decentralized organization have underlined indelibly the need of refined systems in a personnel program.

2. Organizational Responsibility. Organizational responsibility refers to the manner in which functions and procedures are grouped under particular executives and to the relationships between these executives. This aspect is the concern of the next chapter, so only a few comments are in order now.

The organization structure must specify three areas of responsibility for the preparation, execution, and control of personnel functions. First, the personnel duties and responsibilities of each member of the management team must be specified. Second, the role of staff personnel units must be established, designating over what functions they have authority and which of their services are subject to approval by line executives. And third, the relationship between line and staff executives needs to be clearly indicated as to their specific areas of authority, responsibility, and conditions of cooperation and consultation.

PERSONNEL POLICIES

Many personnel functions are repeated frequently. Hiring, for example, takes place every time a new person is added to the payroll. Or, disciplining is an oft-repeated function. And so on through the whole gamut of personnel work. Handling each repetition as an independent incident would be very wasteful of executive time. So most companies establish guidelines—called policies—to govern repeated cases of personnel activities.

Nature and Purposes

Policies are basic rules established to govern functions so that they are performed in line with desired objectives.[1] A few comments will serve to clarify this definition. First, while policies are guides to action they

FIGURE 4–3

Relation of Policies, Procedures, and Objectives

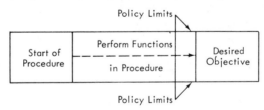

are not the action. Functions and procedures constitute the action. For example, a selection policy might state: "Hire only high-school graduates or the equivalent." The hiring would be done through the selection process; the policy restricts those going through the process. Second, while policies guide action toward objectives, they are not the objectives, as illustrated in Figure 4–3. Thus, in the selection policy just cited, policies help achieve effectiveness in hiring by removing some candidates from the selection process who presumably are undesirable. And third,

---

[1] To some, the term *policies* has reference to the basic principles or philosophy upon which an organization is built or operated. While such principles or philosophy are basic to policy making. it is preferred here to follow the more restricted connotation of *policy*.

while personnel policies are a tool of management, they cannot think for or replace management. Management must design appropriate policies and see that they are properly applied.

Policies serve two major purposes. On the one hand, they restrain subordinates from performing undesirable functions or from mishandling specified functions. As an example of the former, a policy which states that unauthorized collections among employees shall not be permitted on company premises upon penalty of discharge serves to prevent such activities from being performed. Or as an example of the latter, a policy which states that candidates for employment shall be selected only from those who possess a high school education or its equivalent serves to screen out those who would, in the opinion of the company in question, fail to succeed if employed.

On the other hand, policies are positive in nature by providing standard decisions when action has to be taken. Hence, they make it unnecessary for subordinates to ask their superiors how a given problem or case should be handled. Consider, as an example, the policy that all employees will be evaluated every four months to determine which ones deserve raises. This policy is restrictive, to be sure, in that the subject of raises is to be taken up only at specified time periods; but it states definitely when each employee can expect to have a record review, which certainly is not true in the absence of such a policy. As a consequence of this policy, an executive asked about raises is in a position to give a prompt answer.

Coverage

In general terms, policies should cover situations which tend to repeat themselves. A useful classification can be derived by grouping policies according to the organizational areas to which they pertain and the kinds of functions they are intended to guide. Study of all of these is beyond the scope of this book. From time to time in subsequent chapters, however, the subject of policies will be discussed in connection with various subjects. Some insight can be gained at this juncture from the following listing and the brief examples in each:

1. Organizational grouping of policies:
    a. General company policies which must be followed by all units of a company; e.g., it may be a company policy to subsidize educational programs of study carried on by any executive or employee in various schools.
    b. External policies which guide an organization in relation to outside groups and agencies; e.g., it may be the policy to approve the participation of executives in part-time assistance to community, charity, and welfare agencies.

    c. Internal policies which guide the internal relations between organization units; they may be vertical or horizontal.

        (1) A vertical policy is intended to guide a lower level in an organization; e.g., the sales manager may rule that all district managers are to evaluate salespeople every quarter.

        (2) A horizontal policy is intended to guide relationships between departments on the same level, e.g., a policy may be set to the effect that the personnel department must consult with and get approval of departments it serves before establishing, let us say, training procedures.

    d. Centralized policies which have pertinence for companies with several locations and have reference to the degree of autonomy local units will have in setting policies and procedures which fit their respective conditions.

2. Functional grouping of policies:

    a. Policies which guide managerial functions of personnel planning, organizing, directing, and controlling; e.g., it may be the policy that every manager must submit a plan of action for personnel activities in his/her unit by December 1 for the next operating year.

    b. Policies which guide technical functions of procuring, developing, maintaining, and utilizing labor; e.g., it may be the policy that any employees having a grievance have the unqualified right to go to their superior or the personnel division, as they may choose.

Responsibility for Establishing Policies

Many personnel policies undoubtedly have, like Topsy, just grown. In such instances, everyone seems to know, without being told and without knowing where it originated, that a certain type of decision will be made in certain situations. Such policies are informal, and their establishment is beyond analysis. But useful comments can be made about formal methods of establishing policies.

Most personnel policies are best established at the higher levels of management with the advice and assistance of staff personnel. To see the desirability of this, take the matter of severity of penalties. Every executive must at one time or another take disciplinary action. It would be unwise, however, to allow each executive to set personal policies on penalties. The result would be inconsistent and nonuniform penalties. Hence, such policies should be set at a high level to cover all parts of the organization in which discipline is a recurring problem.

Middle and supervisory levels will be more concerned with transmission and application of policies. Middle management will be responsible for communicating the policy formulations to operating levels. Such communications would involve interpreting policies, clarifying areas of uncertainty and misunderstanding, and training lower levels in policy application. And the first-line supervision and, in some instances, the personnel department would be responsible for applying personnel policies in their respective areas of duties.

There is an important question of the form in which policies should be communicated. As already noted, many are informal or stated in oral form. It is not uncommon, for example, to hear an executive say: "Our policy is to pay wages equal to or above the community rate." But nowhere is this written down, and the amount of the premium seems to vary with the passage of time and business conditions. Written policies are an obvious improvement. They require more time to prepare and issue. They have advantages of permanence and ease of transmission, can be used as training manuals, and can be quickly arranged for auditing and evaluation. Hence, many companies find it desirable to prepare carefully worded printed statements of their policies.

Policy Control

Personnel policies will be most effective if they are established in accordance with good standards and are carefully reviewed from time to time. A set of standards is very useful in checking to see if a proposed personnel policy will be a good policy. Without seeking the answers, note how the following questions immediately give clues regarding such a policy as "Hire only high-school graduates or the equivalent."

1. Is the policy based upon a careful analysis of the objectives and ideals of the company?
2. Is it definite, unambiguous, complete, and accurately stated?
3. Is it reasonably stable and not subject to change because of temporary changes in existing conditions?
4. Does it have sufficient flexibility to handle normal variations in conditions?
5. Is it related to policies of other sections of the company so that a proper balance of complementary policies is established?
6. Is it known and understood by all who must work with it or are affected by it?

Periodic review of personnel policies is also needed to determine which should be changed or dropped and where additional policies are needed. A variety of appraisal methods is available, as follows:

1. All policies should be subject to some, if not extended, evaluation annually.
2. Some policies should come up for review at specific times, such as when collective bargaining agreements must be renegotiated.

3. Policies of each department or division may be reviewed when budgetary requests are made.
4. Spot or overall appraisal of policies may be made by outside consultants. This could be done after trouble develops; but preferably, it should be a constructive preventive measure.
5. Policies should be subject to review when the desirability is indicated by employee suggestions, employee grievances, or unsatisfactory reports on employee performance or behavior.
6. Policies should be subject to review whenever a company plans a major expansion or contraction, a change to a new location, or a change of methods.

BUDGETARY ASPECTS OF PROGRAMS

The budget is a particularly useful device in personnel programming. It shows, in financial terms for a coming period of time, the amounts which may be spent for various personnel activities. It is, therefore, a quantitatively expressed plan of action. During the period covered by the budget, it is useful in guiding the actions of those performing personnel functions. But in addition, at the end of the budget period, it can be used as a basis of comparison with actual expenditures. Hence a personnel budget assists management in performing not only its functions of planning and organizing but also that of controlling.

The possible contributions of budgeting to programming may be seen by describing the steps of budgetary preparation and usage. To begin with, establishing budgets involves a forecast of the specific goals which are to be sought and the tasks which must be undertaken in a forthcoming period. Such questions as the following must be answered:

1. How many people are to be hired, trained, counseled, transferred, and pensioned?
2. ˙ What types of recreational, social, and athletic activities shall be scheduled, and how often?
3. How many grievance or collective bargaining sessions are likely to be held?
4. How many workers are likely to have accidents, become sick or disabled, or require hospitalization?
5. How much of a staff—administrative, technical, and clerical—will be needed to carry out personnel functions?
6. What equipment, space, and other resources will be needed to carry out personnel functions?

Obviously, answers to these questions depend in part on the basic attitude of a company toward human relations. For example, a company which believes, as some do, that it is desirable to provide facilities for religious contemplation on company premises will entail expenditures that would not be incurred by those that feel otherwise. Thus the budget aids in giving concrete expression to basic personnel philosophy and principles.

In setting forth estimates of personnel expenditures, it is invariably necessary, in the second place, to communicate extensively between organization levels. Thus, it is usually customary to ask lower levels of an organization to submit their estimates of what personnel duties must be performed by them and how much money will be required for these purposes. These are reviewed as they ascend the organization structure. The top management then combines all estimates, checks to see if they conform with total business prospects, and then returns the budgets in amended or original form. At times, it may be desirable to go up and down the channels more than once before all parties are satisfied. In any

TABLE 4–1

The Standard Manufacturing Co. Operating Budget (personnel division, 1975)

Administrative expenses:
Administrative salaries	$60,000	
Clerical salaries	12,000	
Office supplies	2,000	
Traveling expenses	8,000	
Telephone and telegraph	1,600	
Total		$ 95,600

Employment division:
Manager's salary	$19,000	
Interviewers' salaries	30,000	
Technical salaries	20,000	
Clerical salaries	24,000	
Advertising	6,000	
Office supplies	8,000	
Traveling expenses	12,000	
Telephone and telegraph	5,000	
Total		124,000

Training division:
Manager's salary	$17,000	
Trainers' salaries	28,000	
Technical salaries	19,000	
Clerical salaries	12,000	
Training supplies	9,000	
Traveling expenses	4,200	
Telephone and telegraph	1,200	
Total	90,400	
Medical division*		65,400
Safety division*		43,600
Employee relations division*		123,600
Benefits and service division*		146,600
Auditing and research division*		39,000
Grand total		$738,200

* Breakdown of detail not shown.

TABLE 4–2

**The Standard Manufacturing Co. Labor Budget
(department #1)**

Supervisory salaries		$ 34,000
Clerical salaries		32,000
Training costs		8,400
Safety engineer		16,800
Drill press operators:		
Grade 1	$98,600	
Grade 2	63,000	
Grade 3	24,500	
Total		186,100
Bench hands:		
Grade 1	$42,000	
Grade 2	9,800	
Total		51,800
Truckers		12,000
Grand total		$341,100

event, this up-and-down process of communication provides an excellent means of educating all levels on personnel matters and of integrating the various elements of an organization into a more effective team as regards personnel goals.

In the third place, working up a budget can serve to minimize gaps, imbalance, or duplications in programming. This can be illustrated in Tables 4–1 and 4–2. By reviewing the subdivisions in Table 4–1, management can be sure that all phases of personnel have been covered. Dividing the budget according to organizational divisions, as evidently has been done in this case, is a particularly useful plan. And by comparing elements of expense in various budgets, duplication of effort can be uncovered. Thus, in Table 4–2, Department #1 has a budgeted amount for training and safety salaries. If these have been approved, it is only because they are valid supplements to the amounts requested for training and safety work in the budget of the staff personnel division.

Finally, such budgets can be useful in comparing what happened with original expectations. Thus, at the end of the budget period, actual expenditures can be entered in a column adjacent to budgeted amounts. Differences can then be entered either as absolute or as percentage values. Reasons and explanations for deviations can then be sought. Search for causes of variations can serve two purposes: (1) to determine who deserves censure or praise and (2) to adjust future plans to take advantage of past successes and avoid past mistakes.

Through the use of budgets, comparisons may also be made with other companies or with industry-wide data. In the past decade, more and more information has been forthcoming on such relationships as personnel expenditures per employee and the number of personnel staff members per 100 employees on the payroll. It would be most helpful to a company if its records were kept so that it could make comparisons with others similar to it.

INFORMATIONAL NEEDS OF PROGRAMMING

It should be apparent by this time that much information will be required in programming personnel work. How well this job of collecting information is done will determine how successfully responsible executives can reach decisions on personnel objectives, functions, policies, and principles. Reliance in such matters is often placed upon personal experience or the experience of others. Yet, it is contended here that much more emphasis will have to be placed upon, first, logical, scientific research for needed information, and, second, informational systems which funnel data quickly and in usable form to executives.

As to the research side, a number of tools are already available for these purposes and will be touched upon in later chapters. It is worth noting here, however, a few examples of information gathering through research. Such techniques as job analysis and employee specifications, merit rating and job evaluation analysis, procedural analysis, turnover and absenteeism studies, morale and attitude surveys, wage and salary surveys, and policy audits and evaluations can provide indispensable information basic to program development. Such investigations need not be perfect analyses of these subjects. Of course, the more thorough, the better. But for all practical purposes, much data can be gathered with a minimum of fanfare and expenditure. There is needed only the sincere desire to seek facts for decisions in the place of personal hunches and limited experience.

In the matter of informational systems, this phase has in recent years for the first time received the attention it deserves. Business in many respects is so complex and the personnel problems with which it is faced are so involved that decision making is passing out of the intuitional stage. An executive must have built-in systems of informational flows that will serve personnel planning and controlling needs. Fortunately with computers, electronic data processing, and systems designs, tools exist to gather, compile, store, and retrieve the data needed for quantitative personnel programming.

The purpose of this chapter has been to call attention to certain basic factors to which consideration must be given early in the study or development of any personnel program. Decisions must be reached on such matters as objectives, functions, assignment of responsibilities, policies, and principles in building an effective personnel plan. Some believe that such matters may be resolved by cut-and-dried methods. But there is no shortcut solution to the complex problems of human relations. The only hope in the long run for fair and equitable solutions is along the path of facts and information. Hence the subject of research has been given special emphasis in this chapter on programming. Research is without doubt the key to effective planning of personnel activities.

QUESTIONS

1. What are the purposes of a personnel program? Are these purposes solely for the interests of the company?
2. Of all personnel objectives, which do you think would be the most difficult to attain?
3. How would you prove in a given case that investment in a personnel program was justified?
4. How would you classify the needs of employees? To what extent are these selfish?
5. To what extent is it feasible to include in a personnel program all of the personnel functions listed in this chapter?
6. What is the difference between procedural responsibility and organizational responsibility?
7. Why should a company have personnel policies? Should employees have a voice in their determination?
8. How does one check the effectiveness of personnel policies?
9. What contributions do budgets make to personnel programming? Is it reasonable to put a dollar sign on personnel work and human relations?
10. Why is information a basic need of personnel programming and personnel control?

CASE 4–1. THE SLEEPING EMPLOYEE

In conference were the Personnel Director, the Production Manager, and the President of the company. The subject was policy regarding the oft-repeated question, "shall we give him another chance?" The subject arose in this instance because of the "case of the sleeping employee."

The previous day, Charles Fox had been found asleep on the job by his supervisor. This was the third such incident in the past four months. In the other incidents, the supervisor had warned Fox, and did so again this time. Such warnings had to be entered on the employee's personnel record. After reading about this last incident, the Personnel Director asked for the present meeting so that a policy could be established as to how many "last chances" were desirable and useful.

The Production Manager was for "one more chance" when workers were scarce, when the employee in question was a valued one, or when production quotas had to be met. The Personnel Director claimed that such an indefinite posture failed to discourage rule breaking and also partook of partiality. And the President added no thoughts but did say, "Let me know what you decide and I'll likely go along with your recommendation."

Question

1. What would you add to this conference had you been there?

CASE 4–2. A NARCOTICS PROBLEM

Approximately a year ago, a situation arose that was not covered by any of the policies of the company. An employee, Bob by name, began coming to work obviously under the influence of some type of narcotic. His supervisor noticed a definite change in his work. His output declined, he made more mistakes in both his records and reports, his inventory of parts was carelessly handled, and he spent time in apparent daydreaming.

Knowing Bob needed the job, his supervisor approached him about his working deficiencies and warned him that if he did not improve, disciplinary action would have to be taken. Bob denied that he was on drugs of any sort but did agree that his work had slipped and needed to be improved.

Bob's work and attitude improved slowly for about two weeks but then began to slip again. The supervisor decided to report the case to the personnel manager. Together they confronted Bob with the facts about his poor performance and their suspicions as to the cause. They asked Bob what he believed would be the best thing to do. Bob begged them to allow him to keep his job and give him another chance, again without admitting that he was on narcotics. He promised them he would straighten up and improve on all aspects of his job. They agreed to allow Bob to remain on his job but he would have to report to his supervisor directly each day upon coming to work. For a while all went well but again Bob's performance began to revert to that of one who was evidently on drugs.

Questions

1. What help can the company give if it does not have the skills to deal with an employee with this problem?
2. If discharge is an answer here, how and when should it be handled?

ORGANIZATION OF 5
PERSONNEL MANAGEMENT

Scope of Organization

To attain the various objectives of personnel management, the efforts of numerous people in a company must be effectively coordinated. An appropriate operational organization must, therefore, be designed and maintained. Such an organization would include (1) the systems and procedures which incorporate the various functions to be performed, and (2) the organizational structures of authority-responsibility relationships of the people who perform the functions. These two subjects comprise the major divisions of this chapter.

SYSTEMS OF PERSONNEL MANAGEMENT

It has been noted that personnel management must procure, develop, maintain, and utilize people. Even the briefest consideration of any of these four functions is sufficient to disclose that each consists of more than one step. Procurement, for example, invariably involves a number of subfunctions. How these subfunctions are arranged in orderly sequences determines the system of procurement used in a particular case. It is important, therefore, that systems be carefully established if each of the basic four functions is to attain desired goals. To understand the role of systems in personnel management, the discussion here is concerned with (1) the nature of systems and (2) systems in personnel management.

It is important to recognize this dual aspect of organization. An organization structure establishes authority-responsibility relationships.

But these do not get any work done. Work gets done through organized systems.

Nature of Systems

A system, as already noted, is a sequential and interrelated arrangement of functions leading to the attainment of desired objectives. Such an arrangement consists of the following parts:

1. The objectives of the system
2. The functions and subfunctions to be performed
3. The information flows needed to operate and control functions
4. The resources (technical and human) to operate and manage the various parts
5. The relationships between the foregoing

The relationships in a system can be seen more clearly by reference to the simple hiring system illustrated in Figure 5–1. The objective of filling a vacancy is the justification for the existence of the system. The six steps that deal with candidates must be performed with that end in mind. Each step is dependent upon previous flows of information, derives information for its own needs, and serves to advance subsequent steps. For example, the interviewer in the personnel department derives information useful (1) in deciding whether or not to reject a given candi-

FIGURE 5–1

A Hiring System

Step #1	Step #2	Step #3	Step #4	Step #5	Step #6	OBJECTIVE
FUNCTIONS						
Hiring Requisition Authorized	Applicant Fills out Application Blank	Interviewer Talks to Applicant	Candidate Takes Psychological Tests	Supervisor Talks to Candidate	Personnel and Payroll Records Are Completed	Vacancy Filled by Candidate
INFORMATION FLOWS						
Job and Employee Specifications	Various Information on Application Blank	Interviewer's Evaluation	Test Scores	Supervisor's Evaluation	Final Decision	
RESOURCES						
Executive Authority	Office– Space Analyst	Office– Space Interviewer	Test Forms Norms Analyst	Working Situation	Records and Record Section	

Feedback

Result Feedback

date and (2) to others later in the procedure. But the interviewer would not be as effective without the information supplied from the application blank, job specifications, and employee specifications. And each step requires technical, physical, and human resources as specified. After the vacancy has been filled, subsequent records of the degree of success of the candidate can be fed back to various steps in the system so that improvements can be incorporated into future hirings.

Hiring can be used to illustrate decision-making aspects of systems in personnel work. As noted, hiring invariably involves rejections as well as selections. Each stage of the hiring process provides a basis for deciding whether or not a given candidate is to be retained as a candidate. The decision presumably is based upon the information generated by the various stages of the process. Quantity and quality of information are therefore critical to decision making. As a consequence, systems design in personnel requires that attention be directed to the input and channeling of information to and through the various stages of every personnel procedure.

Building such a system consists of four steps. First, it is necessary to determine the components of the system. Second, the components must be arranged into an orderly sequence. Third, the amount of time needed for the performance of each component must be calculated. And finally, space and equipment must be provided for the performance of each component. Obviously these steps involve much detail which are beyond the scope of this text but whose importance should be apparent.

Systems in Personnel Management

Inasmuch as discussion of systems is best related to particular tasks of personnel management, various references to this subject are made throughout the text. It is appropriate here, however, to note the growing awareness to a systems approach to personnel management as business enterprises become more complex. As long as business units were relatively small and stable in their operations, it was feasible to let systems just grow and, in a sense, take care of themselves.

But as a company grows and is subject to various changes in operations, the traditional approach to systems building leads to informational strangulation and excessive costs. Growth generates tremendous amounts of personnel information that can be handled only by expensive technical and human resources. But the use of well-designed electronic data-processing equipment makes possible the efficient and rapid flow of information to both line and staff departments. Moreover, a well-designed system of such equipment can be flexible enough to handle various new informational needs that develop after the original installation.

Another phase of system design that merits attention is how the personnel management system ties in with the total company and divisional systems. Personnel management cannot be considered as something that is off somewhere by itself in a personnel department. It must be fitted into an ongoing, developing, changing operation incorporated throughout all units of a company. Thus a supervisory training program for project leaders in the engineering division is not a self-contained, isolated undertaking. It must be related to such matters as overall company long-range planning, current production plans, budgetary requirements, promotional plans, and appraisal plans covering the ambitions of particular staff members. So this training plan, like all subsystems, must be blended into other subsystems and into the total company operating system. Such an approach makes for a total procedural and informational system for personnel management.

ORGANIZATION STRUCTURE

If personnel procedures and systems could be made self-coordinating, our general survey of organizations could have ended with the preceding section. But the people who are an essential part of working procedures must be made accountable to and given direction by superiors. This is accomplished by an organization structure. The present section is concerned with the place of personnel management in various schemes and patterns of organization structure. The discussion is taken up under the following headings:

1. Formal organization structures
2. Informal authority
3. Relations between executives
4. Determinants of structural design
5. Tests of good structure
6. An integrated view of structural factors

Formal Structures

A formal structure is one which has been expressly established in an enterprise to spell out who has authority and responsibility over whom and for what. There are three major types of formal structures: the line, the functional, and the line and staff.

1. Line Form of Structure.   The line form is simplicity itself, as shown in Figure 5–2. Executives are given complete charge of the work assigned to them, subject only to the superior to whom they report. In the line form, each executive is his/her own personnel manager. One handles all personnel duties which are helpful in the performance of one's primary task whether that be production, sales, or finance.

FIGURE 5–2

The Line Form of Organization Structure

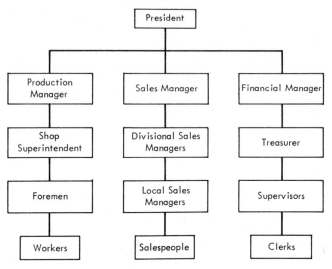

There are good and bad sides to this form. The line form is simple, it permits quick decision making, and responsibility for personnel matters is easy to determine. But it is asking much of an executive to be a good personnel manager and a good technical manager at the same time.

The advantages of the line form tend to outweigh the disadvantages when (a) a company is relatively small, (b) the executives at all levels and in all parts of the company are well seasoned, and (c) the problems of the company are neither complex nor changing rapidly. Obviously, its sphere of usefulness is limited.

2. Functional Form of Structure. The pure functional form of struc-

FIGURE 5–3

The Functional Form of Organization Structure

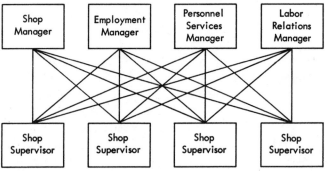

ture is illustrated in Figure 5–3, with only part of an organization shown for the sake of simplicity. Here, each shop supervisor receives specialized services from a number of specialized personnel managers whose authority in their respective special fields must be obeyed.

The advantage of the functional form lies in the specialized leadership for personnel work. This advantage is heavily offset by the fact that the areas of authority of the specialists cannot be separated in practice as easily as they can be drawn on a chart. The result is divided lines of authority that encourage squabbling between experts which frustrates subordinates.

Wherever the functional form has been tried on a broad scale, it has eventually failed. Yet, its use on a restricted or temporary basis is an efficient way of handling complex or emergency personnel problems or duties imposed by governmental regulations or union relations. And its advantage of specialized leadership can be adapted, without disadvantage, in the line and staff form.

3. Line and Staff Form of Structure. The most widely used form in personnel work is the line and staff, a simple diagram of which is shown in Figure 5–4. The most striking feature of the line and staff form is that in it each person reports to one and only one superior, yet receives specialized service and help from various experts. To illustrate, let us look at the hiring procedure, which is operated by the employment section of the personnel division, as shown in Figure 5–4. This unit

FIGURE 5–4

The Line and Staff Form of Organization Structure

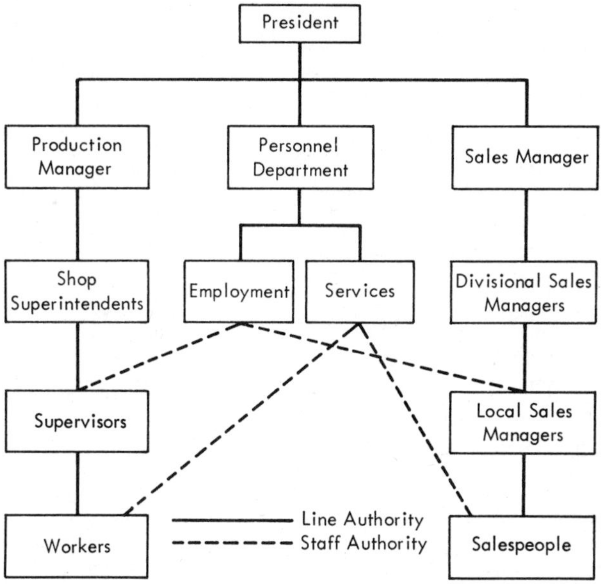

Line Authority
Staff Authority

screens applicants for jobs and then directs those selected as desirable employees to the supervisors for their acceptance or rejection. Since the employment unit cannot compel supervisors to follow its recommendations, the line of authority between the supervisor and the superintendent remains undivided and the allegiance of the former to the latter is not placed in question.

The advantages of the line and staff form are readily apparent. Experts are available for service, but their services need not be accepted by the line. Obviously, it would ordinarily be unwise to refuse to avail oneself of such services, since the staff frees line executives so that they may concentrate upon their primary responsibilities.

The major disadvantage of the line and staff form is that staff specialists sometimes attempt to force their suggestions and services upon others. In such a situation, subordinate executives do not know whether to obey their immediate superiors or the staff. This leads to the divided-line weakness of the functional form, which can be avoided if staff experts are expressly warned against exceeding their assigned scope of activity.

But the line and staff form has evolved as the most widely used in personnel management, particularly as companies have grown in size

FIGURE 5–5

Project Line and Staff Personnel Relations

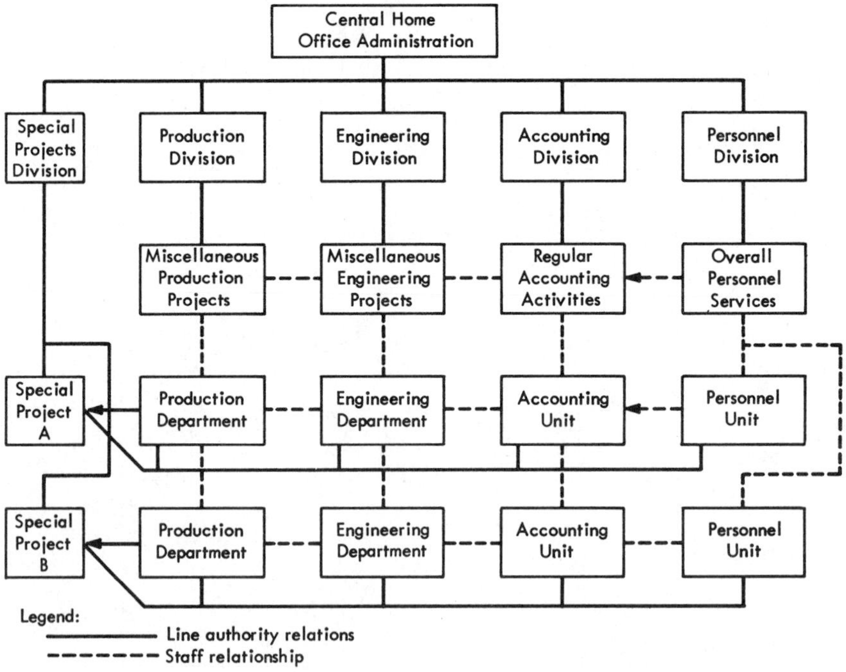

Legend:
———————— Line authority relations
– – – – – – Staff relationship

and complexity. Of interest in this connection is the aerospace industry in which companies have grown to a point that specific projects such as contracts for new types of missiles, space vehicles, or planes tend to become businesses within a business. As a consequence, it is desirable to establish personnel staff units for each project. And the project personnel staff units can receive staff advice and monitoring from a central personnel staff unit. Thus as illustrated in Figure 5–5, Project Personnel Units A and B which service Projects A and B, respectively, are in turn served by the Home Office Personnel Department. Such a type of line and staff organization is sometimes called a matrix or grid structure.

Informal Authority

Even casual observation is usually sufficient to show that there are differences between the formal authority an executive is assigned and that which he actually possessed. Some executives have high titles but wield little power, whereas others of lower status in the organization chart exercise authority beyond their assigned station.

More careful studies disclose such differences even more strikingly. Of particular interest here are sociometric studies that seek to show graphically various types of working relationships between members of an organization. An example of this is shown in Figure 5–6. The solid lines depict the formal lines of relationship between levels of the organization structure. The arrowed lines show the relationships between those with whom most time is spent in getting work done. It is clear from the

FIGURE 5–6

Sociometric Analysis of an Organization Structure

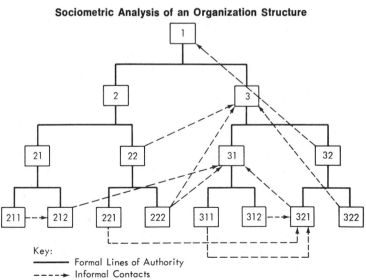

Key:
——— Formal Lines of Authority
----➤ Informal Contacts

heavy lines running to the positions marked, 3, 31 and 321 that because of their respective levels in the structure, their significance is greater than that of the other positions.[1]

Such informal relations develop for a number of reasons. First, it may be time-consuming to go through channels; a friendly visit to the personnel department may get a transfer arranged, for example, quickly and quietly. Second, an accounting supervisor, for example, having little confidence in or respect for the accounting manager, tries a short-cut when seeking a raise. Third, it may give a person a greater feeling of prestige in contacting executives other than one's own supervisor. Fourth, some executives attract followers because of personal qualities of sympathetic understanding and wisdom. And finally, and perhaps foremost, informal relations develop because the formal structures fail to provide for the full needs of the organization and the people. Thus a structure which is based on the technical procedures soon will be interlaced with channels which provide for the personal, psychological, and sociological needs of people.

Relations between Executives

It is now pertinent to inquire into the particular roles of line executives and of staff executives in personnel matters. This may perhaps best be done by commenting upon the concepts of authority and responsibility and how these are related to personnel activities.

Authority in Organization Structure. Authority, in its broadest sense, means the right to command the performance of others. It implies the right to give orders to others and to expect obedience from those to whom the orders are given.

But what is the source of authority, and how far does authority extend? In a formal sense, any executive obtains authority by delegation from a superior. Thus a personnel director may be empowered by the vice president (1) to organize and operate a personnel department and (2) to render personnel services to various other groups in the organization. The first part of this delegation gives the director authority over the staff and the workings of the organization unit. The second part of the delegation indicates that the direct line of authority stops at the borders of the personnel department. Beyond these limits the director's authority is advisory, which, in the final analysis, means that there is no authority.

In an informal sense, the authority derived by delegation may be strengthened and the borders of authority may be extended by earning

---

[1] It is to be noted that such sociometric measurements may be superimposing procedural analysis upon structural elements, in which case they may be depicting procedural relationships as well as structural importance.

the right to lead. In the case of line executives, this means incorporating some degree of participation and consultation in dealing with subordinates. In the case of staff executives, such as the personnel director, this means serving the interests of others with proficiency and sensitivity.

Responsibility in Organization Structure

An executive who has authority, also has responsibilities. By responsibility is meant the obligation (1) to do an assigned task and (2) to look to someone for the assignment. Obligation implies a willingness to accept, for whatever rewards one may see in the situation, the burden of a given task and the risks which attend in the event of failure. Usually, more than one person or organization unit incurs obligations in a personnel procedure. For example, in selecting a salesclerk, the employment section suggests hiring a given candidate, but the departmental sales manager approves or disapproves the recommendation. Then, who is responsible if the salesclerk eventually proves unsatisfactory?

An answer to this question could be provided if the areas of responsibility had been defined before the hiring took place. In that event, assignment would have been made for each step of hiring. Such assignments could have specified the procedural responsibilities of both the staff and the line units. It would have been a relatively simple matter to determine which one failed to eliminate the salesclerk in the screening process.

To sum up, it should be apparent that authority over and responsibility for each phase of personnel work should be clearly assigned to a given individual or organization unit. Take training as an example. Planning of program development, teaching methods, and training aids may well be assigned to a training section in the personnel division. Actual training may be assigned to each supervisor who will use these services and aids. Here, there is a clear division of authority and responsibility for particular phases of training. Such an analysis of training also serves to emphasize the need of line and staff cooperation. Delineation of obligations for all other personnel functions should be made in the same manner.

FACTORS IN SPECIFIC STRUCTURAL DESIGNS

It is now appropriate to note the formal place given to personnel in the organization in actual practice. Practice varies, depending upon a number of factors, the more important of which are the following:

1. The degree to which top management considers personnel subjects important

2. Interaction of people and organizations
3. The size of the company and the location of its units
4. Influence of such outside factors as legislation and labor unions
5. Types of labor or company problems calling for solution

Of course, these are more or less interrelated; but for the sake of simplicity, the foregoing will be used as an outline of exposition.

Attitude of Management

The opinion of top management of the importance of personnel is undoubtedly the most compelling factor in determining its place in the organization structure. In some companies, there is no personnel department worthy of the name, nor are line executives expected to spend much time on personnel duties. Opposed to the foregoing are other companies that have elaborate and highly placed personnel divisions as well as personnel-minded line executives.

FIGURE 5–7

Composite Personnel Relations Functional Chart

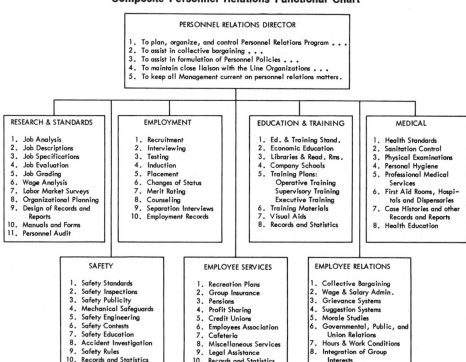

PERSONNEL RELATIONS DIRECTOR
1. To plan, organize, and control Personnel Relations Program . . .
2. To assist in collective bargaining . . .
3. To assist in formulation of Personnel Policies . . .
4. To maintain close liaison with the Line Organizations . . .
5. To keep all Management current on personnel relations matters.

RESEARCH & STANDARDS
1. Job Analysis
2. Job Descriptions
3. Job Specifications
4. Job Evaluation
5. Job Grading
6. Wage Analysis
7. Labor Market Surveys
8. Organizational Planning
9. Design of Records and Reports
10. Manuals and Forms
11. Personnel Audit

EMPLOYMENT
1. Recruitment
2. Interviewing
3. Testing
4. Induction
5. Placement
6. Changes of Status
7. Merit Rating
8. Counseling
9. Separation Interviews
10. Employment Records

EDUCATION & TRAINING
1. Ed. & Training Stand.
2. Economic Education
3. Libraries & Read. Rms.
4. Company Schools
5. Training Plans:
    Operative Training
    Supervisory Training
    Executive Training
6. Training Materials
7. Visual Aids
8. Records and Statistics

MEDICAL
1. Health Standards
2. Sanitation Control
3. Physical Examinations
4. Personal Hygiene
5. Professional Medical Services
6. First Aid Rooms, Hospitals and Dispensaries
7. Case Histories and other Records and Reports
8. Health Education

SAFETY
1. Safety Standards
2. Safety Inspections
3. Safety Publicity
4. Mechanical Safeguards
5. Safety Engineering
6. Safety Contests
7. Safety Education
8. Accident Investigation
9. Safety Rules
10. Records and Statistics

EMPLOYEE SERVICES
1. Recreation Plans
2. Group Insurance
3. Pensions
4. Profit Sharing
5. Credit Unions
6. Employees Association
7. Cafeteria
8. Miscellaneous Services
9. Legal Assistance
10. Records and Statistics

EMPLOYEE RELATIONS
1. Collective Bargaining
2. Wage & Salary Admin.
3. Grievance Systems
4. Suggestion Systems
5. Morale Studies
6. Governmental, Public, and Union Relations
7. Hours & Work Conditions
8. Integration of Group Interests
9. Records and Statistics

In instances in which top management takes a comprehensive and understanding view of the subject, a personnel division approximately along the lines of that shown in Figure 5–7 would be the result. It should be noted that this chart is a composite developed from actual practice, and not just a theoretical conception.

Interaction of Personnel and Structure

Although only in the threshold stage, the introductory work of the behavioral sciences gives evidence of the need of adjusting structure to personnel as well as accommodating personnel to structure. Thus, different types of organization structure have varying influences on employee attitudes, reactions, and needs. And employees can influence, for good or bad, the structure employed in a given company. Because of such interaction, the design of structure must be one of reciprocal accommodation with personnel, and not a unilateral decision.

To see this in its practical aspect, a subordinate in a line and staff organization must relate to (and is, in turn, affected by) not only an immediate superior but also such staff units as the personnel department. A subordinate feeling adversely controlled by an autocratic line superior and more at ease with the permissive role of the staff department, can readily tend to undermine the former. Particularly is this probable as rights of employees gain more legal and union support, which tends to reduce the autocratic powers of management. But the reverse is possible, in that structures may be weak in dealing with personnel. At times and with particular kinds of employees, strong executive action may be called for.

This restrictive impact of organization structure has been particularly evident in large enterprises. As a consequence, developments in decentralization and the splitting-off of product units as self-contained organizations have been favored by some. These seem to raise employee efficiency and satisfaction. Personnel as well as other problems can be handled more effectively in relation to the particular situational conditions of the decentralized units. And the personnel have a greater feeling of association with such units than with the total organization of which they are a part.

Physical Factors

As suggested earlier, size of company, location of offices and plants, and the importance of labor problems affect the specific place such a division would be given in a particular organization. For example, a medium-sized company with one plant and no unusual labor problems

FIGURE 5–8

Personnel Functions in a Small Company

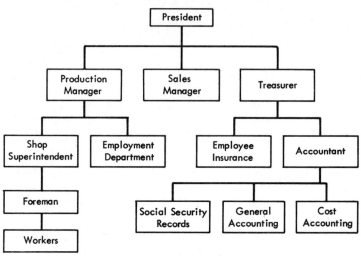

might get along very well with the setup shown in Figure 5–8. As illustrated there, an employment section has been installed in the production division to serve its needs, whereas employment functions apparently are performed by the sales manager. (A larger company might establish a setup such as that shown in Figure 5–7.) In the case of personnel matters affecting all employees, central units have been established in the accounting department to handle social security records and in the treasurer's department to handle pension and insurance programs. Most of the relations with employees are handled directly by shop superintendents and line supervisors.

But as an organization grows, the volume of personnel work increases to a point where it becomes a burden on all line executives. It is therefore as desirable for the sales manager, let us say, to give up some personnel duties as it was in earlier decades for the production manager. As a consequence, as illustrated earlier in Figure 5–4, the employment section "hires" for all line executives. Thus, in larger companies (employees running into the thousands), a centralized personnel department performs many service and advisory duties, thereby freeing line executives to concentrate on (a) important decisions in personnel matters and (b) face-to-face human relations.

When growth of an enterprise takes place by establishing additional locations, the question arises as to where and by whom personnel functions should be performed. One answer is illustrated in Figure 5–9. A personnel department, subject to the plant manager, is established at

FIGURE 5–9

Decentralization of Personnel Functions

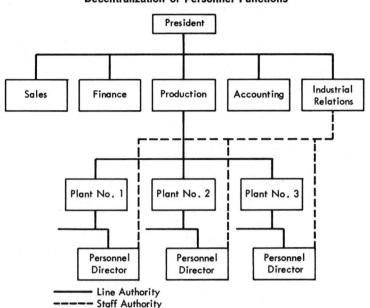

each location. In addition, there is a central personnel unit to which each may turn for expert advice and from which uniform plans and policies are derived. By this arrangement, local autonomy, with its advantages, is secured; yet, uniform practices are assured for the company. In some instances the foregoing arrangement is changed by making the local personnel units responsible to the central personnel unit instead of to the respective plant managers. This relationship is used because of the more specialized direction which is given to the local personnel units. This advantage is attained only at the cost of lowered cooperation between the local personnel units and the plants they serve.

Effect of Legislation and Unions upon Structure

Such factors as legislation and labor unions have also influenced the design of organization structures. For example, the installation of such units as equal employment opportunity, safety, and unemployment compensation can be ascribed almost entirely to legislative regulations or requirements. Also, the right of employees to organize and bargain collectively has resulted in the addition of organization relationships, as illustrated in Figure 5–10.

FIGURE 5–10

Structure of Union-Company Relationships

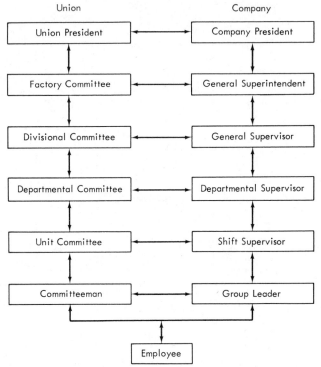

Problems Faced

In the last analysis, the type of personnel functions performed depends largely upon the problems to be solved. This explains why personnel management usually developed first in the production divisions of most companies. Here, labor problems among large aggregations of workers were encountered.

But as other areas of problems developed, personnel units were established to deal with them. For example, it is not uncommon to find personnel units concerned primarily with such groups as research and development personnel, engineering staffs, women workers, and night-shift employees.

TESTS OF GOOD STRUCTURE

The foregoing discussion of the theory and practice of organization structure has been undertaken with a view to providing the student with a background of material essential to, and an understanding of the place of personnel management in, an enterprise. In conclusion, it is worth pointing some remarks toward the matter of tests by which it may be possible to determine whether or not a given personnel department is well organized. In general, a good personnel department should possess the following characteristics.

1. Stability, or the ability to replace key personnel executives or employees with a minimal loss of effectiveness
2. Flexibility, or the capacity to handle effectively short-run changes in the volume of personnel work or in the personnel problems encountered
3. Growth, or the feature of being prepared with advance plans to handle permanent changes in personnel problems or in underlying labor conditions
4. Balance, or the feature of having authority and resources adequate in amount to handle the functions and problems for which the personnel department is made responsible
5. Simplicity, or the feature of keeping personnel lines of relationship to other departments clear and simple
6. Objectivity, or the feature of having definite objectives for each unit in the personnel department

INTEGRATION OF PERSONNEL FUNCTIONS AND FACTORS

From what has been said in this and earlier chapters, it is apparent that a number of executives, functions, factors, and dimensions are involved in personnel management. The relationships between them can be summarized and visualized in the integrated illustration of personnel management in Figure 5–11. This shows that the:

1. managerial functions of planning, organizing, directing, and controlling are related to
2. the technical functions of procuring, developing, maintaining, and utilizing
3. the physiological, mental, psychological, sociological, political, and ethical characteristics of human beings which pertain to
4. the objectives, policies, and functions of the
5. various divisions of the company and
6. are subject to environmental factors, available resources, and philosophical constraints.

This diagram may also serve to illustrate the check list principle. It depicts the functions, factors, departments, and human resources related to personnel. A user of this as a check list can go through all departments shown therein to determine what each is doing or not doing about the

FIGURE 5–11

The Integrated Nature of Personnel Factors

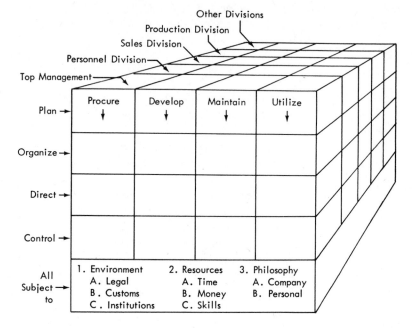

Each of the human characteristics is to be placed in each of the cubes

Physiological
Mental
Psychological
Sociological
Political
Ethical

Each of the factors must be considered in each of the cubes

Objectives
Policies
Functions

various personnel factors. From such a review, gaps, duplications, or errors in personnel matters will be revealed and appropriate remedial action taken.

QUESTIONS

1. What is meant by and included in a personnel system?
2. What must be done in order to design a personnel system?
3. Of what use is the functional form of organization structure in personnel management?
4. What are the advantages and disadvantages of the line and staff form of organization structure?
5. What is the matrix (or grid) form of structure and where would it be used?

6. What is the purpose of a sociometric analysis of an organization?
7. For what reasons do informal relations develop among executives?
8. What should be the relation between authority and responsibility of personnel work?
9. Upon what factors does the place accorded the personnel department in a company organizational structure usually depend?
10. Under what conditions can centralization and decentralization of personnel functions exist at the same time?

CASE 5–1. PERSONNEL ORGANIZATION

The Surface Grinder Company has expanded from a one-location operation to a point that now there are six branches in addition to the home site. This growth, while very profitable, has also raised a number of organizational problems, one of them related to personnel management.

When the company operated out of one location, any questions about such matters as hiring decisions or wage policies could be and were quickly handled. Now the situation is more complicated because each branch has its own personnel functions and problems. Consistency of personnel matters among the branches is lacking yet the conditions or problems are similar. But to assume that each should go on its own raises questions of inter-branch policies and equity.

The problem has received little formal attention. The company has grown rather informally in its personnel relations. The home office has its own operating practices and takes up local labor problems as they come up. Every branch has personnel supervisors who report to the branch manager. They handle routine hiring, training, wage matters and grievances as they think best in line with the individual manager's ideas and what they consider to be home-office thinking.

Now it is felt by the home office that the organization of the personnel function needs more formal determinations. In particular three basic questions seem to need resolution: (1) what technical personnel functions should be decentralized into each branch and which centralized in the home office, (2) to what company policies should each location conform, and (3) how should lines of communication be established so that flows of personnel information between all units may be accomplished expeditiously?

Question

1. What suggestions do you have to give this company on these questions?

CASE 5–2.   ORGANIZING PERSONNEL RELATIONS

In a large branch drug store, as happened to be the case in the Medicinal Drug Company, personnel management as well as over-all management can be a confusing and confused situation to its employees. In the branch in question, there seemed to be two types of management and four types of employees. The two types of management were the senior pharmacists, who were the store managers also; and long-term employees who were the departmental supervisors. The four types of employees were the temporary or short-hour employees; the long-term, full-time employees; the apprentice pharmacists; and the full-time pharmacists. Authority relationships were not spelled out but one became acquainted with some of them in day-to-day experiences. But there was much uncertainty particularly as shifts overlapped and day assignments during the week often brought people together who didn't know one another too well.

As to personnel management, that—what there was of it—was the task of the managing pharmacist plus what help came from the area offices. Turnover was high and was a continuing problem to the manager who was neither trained nor interested in this aspect of the work. The temporary help was generally irresponsible and lacking in motivation. Most employees considered their wages inadequate. The long-term employees resented the pharmacists, first, because only they could become store managers, and, second, because the apprentice pharmacists tended to exhibit an air of superiority over the non-professionals.

Question

1. What is the fundamental question that calls for solution in the matter of personnel management here, and what two alternative solutions could be made to work?

part II
The Procurement
Phase of Personnel
Management

The kind of people with which an organization is staffed is of utmost importance. People significantly affect the success of an organization. People will bring many or few problems to management. People make their own as well as organizational life relatively pleasant or unpleasant.

This Part is devoted to the tasks and methods of building a team— effective for the organization and satisfactory to its own personal needs. Concern here is therefore with such matters as determination of personnel needs, sources of employee supply, selection procedures and tools, and induction and placement of people. These matters receive so much space because if procurement is well done, other personnel tasks are made much easier and the people affected thereby are better served in all respects.

JOB AND PERSONNEL 6 REQUIREMENTS

The Hiring Function

The foregoing chapters have served to provide a description of and insight into the meaning, background, scope, and basic factors of personnel management. It is now time to turn specific attention to the operative functions of personnel management. These, as will be recalled, include procuring, developing, maintaining, and utilizing an employee force. Each of these involves detailed activities, specific methods, and underlying principles. As a consequence, it will be necessary to devote the next several chapters to a discussion of procurement; the other functions will be studied in subsequent chapters.

Personnel procurement may be defined as the task of hiring people to fill current or future job vacancies. If hiring practices are to be most effective, answers must be sought to a number of important questions, among which are the following.

1. What are the requirements of the jobs to be filled?
2. What kinds of and how much personnel must be procured?
3. From what sources may the required personnel be procured?
4. What procedures should be used to screen candidates for employment?
5. What is the use of such tools as interviewing and testing in the selection procedure?
6. What is the place of transfers and promotions in the procurement function?

The present chapter is devoted to the first two of these questions; the other questions are considered in the next several chapters.

JOB AND EMPLOYEE SPECIFICATIONS

Since employees are hired to carry out specific tasks, it would seem desirable to know, first, what are the facts about the jobs to be filled, and, second, what kinds of people are needed to fill such jobs. Such knowledge is often kept only in the minds of line executives. But the best practice, certainly in companies of any size, calls for the preparation of job and employee specifications. And when hiring is done by a personnel department, such specifications are indispensable.

The task of developing such information may be conveniently discussed under the following headings:

1. Definitions.
2. Job specification information.
3. Employee specification information.
4. Responsibility for collecting information.
5. Methods of gathering information.
6. Writing up specifications.

Definitions

Unfortunately, definitions for terms used in this field are not standardized. For present purposes, definitions have been selected which have currency among technicians, although they do not conform with the loose usage of the non-professional. In this section, definitions are given for the concepts of jobs, specifications, and job studies.

1. Job Terms. A number of terms are used in connection with the work people perform. By a *job* is meant an assignment of work calling for a set of duties, responsibilities, and conditions that are different from those of other work assignments. A job refers to the contents of a particular task, not its location. For example, two salesclerks who are performing similar duties and who require similar training, experience, and personal characteristics would, according to the foregoing definition, be said to hold the same kind of job. Yet, these two clerks may be working in widely separated parts of the store. On the other hand, two other salesclerks who do not have the same range of duties would be said to be working on different jobs, even though they happened to be located side by side.

The term *job* may be clarified by comparing it with "position" and "occupation." The term *position* is sometimes used as a synonym for "job," although in technical usage a distinction is made between the two. Thus, when several persons are doing similar work, each one is said to have the same job. But "position" refers to the number of people at work, not to the nature of their work assignments. The term *stations* is similar in meaning to that of "positions." There invariably are more positions or stations in a company than jobs.

The term *occupation* refers to a group of jobs with common characteristics. Although selling, for example, may be divisible into a number of jobs, depending on the complexity of the selling work, a group of closely related selling jobs may be considered as an occupation. *Job families* is another term used to cover the idea of groupings of similar jobs.

Within a particular job, two or more *grades* may also be recognized. For example, a wide range of work may be performed in the case of a single-spindle drill press operation. Some of the work might involve intricate drilling, and other batches might be more or less simple. Hence, it would be desirable to distinguish between operators on this machine according to whether they were, let us say, Class I, Class II, or Class III operators.

2. Specifications. *Specifications* are statements which describe something about the jobs of a company. They may describe the job itself (strictly speaking, a job specification). They may describe the kind of a person who should fill a given job (strictly speaking, an employee specification). The difference between the two may be seen in connection with a middle management position which, as a job, is illustrated in Figure 6–1, and which, as a person, is illustrated in Figure 6–2. Or they may describe both job and employee characteristics (strictly speaking, a job and employee specification). In practice, the term *job specification* is often used to include varying amounts of both job and employee information.

Practice is not uniform regarding how much detail is included in a specification. About all that can be said in this connection is that detail should be sufficient for the purposes of a particular company. In some cases, it might be sufficient to specify that a stenographer, for example, takes dictation, transcribes shorthand notes, types, and keeps various files. In other cases, it might be very desirable to specify in some detail, as is illustrated in Figure 6–3, how much work is expected from a stenographer on various duties. And in many cases, it might be wise to translate job requirements into statements of human characteristics such as finger dexterity, physical strength, hand-eye coordination, and emotional poise needed on the job.

3. Job Studies. Terms used in connection with the derivation of job and employee specifications also merit definition at this juncture. *Job analysis* refers to the process of gathering information about the operations, duties, and organizational aspects of jobs in order to write up specifications or, as they are called by some, *job descriptions*. Another term of interest is *job classification*, which refers to a system of relating jobs with similar or family characteristics into a logical grouping of classes. The term *job evaluation*, which subject is studied in a later chapter, has reference to monetary measurement of jobs. And *employee evaluation*, also studied later, has reference to process by which the relative value of employees is measured.

FIGURE 6–1

Job Description Form

Position Title: __Middle Management__   Under Supervision of:_____

Definition of Job Purpose:

To be a link between management and production, responsible for seeing that company policies are executed to the company's benefit.

Definition of Job Duties:

1. Informing management on price and trend forecasts.
2. Informing management on profit and loss in each department.
3. Knowing specific duties of each department under his supervision.
4. Supervising job training.
5. Giving authority on job assignments.

Additional Responsibility Requirements:

1. Representing company at conventions, service clubs, etc.
2. Maintaining good employer-employee relations.

Extent and Limits of Decision-Making Authority Granted:

1. These are specified by top management and Board of Directors.
2. Primarily sees that top management's decisions are carried out, but also initiates some action in so doing (extent depends on size of company)
3. Direct supervision depends on size of company.

Working Conditions:

As many hours as are needed to fulfill job duties without neglecting family and community activities.

FIGURE 6–2

Employee Specifications Form

Position Title: <u>Middle Management</u>

<u>Age:</u>   Minimum: <u>25-30</u>

Education: Number of years of formal schooling: <u>College not required</u>
              Type of education: <u>General, with emphasis on business</u>
              Special subjects required: <u>Some background in accounting,</u>
                                         <u>selling, floriculture; record of</u>
                                         <u>school leadership and extra-</u>
                                         <u>curricular activity is an asset</u>

<u>Physical and Health:</u> Good health; emotional stability

<u>Energy Level and Tempo:</u> High--ability to adjust to increasing or changing tempo

<u>Appearance, Dress and Bearing:</u> Neat; should wear generally accepted clothing

<u>Mental Abilities:</u> Alertness; ability to listen with an open mind

<u>Special Abilities:</u> Flexibility; ability to lead

<u>Previous Work Experience:</u> Work experience in most phases of flower industry, with a record of job stability

<u>Special Knowledge or Skills:</u> Must have knowledge and appreciation of flowers; a keen appreciation of finance

<u>Skill in Operating Special Equipment or Machinery:</u> None

<u>Degree of Personal Traits:</u> (Stability, Dependability) High degree of both

<u>Maturity:</u> Must be capable of accepting responsibility in company and community affairs

<u>Self-Reliance:</u> Must be a self-starter, a strong person who sticks with own decisions

<u>Dominance:</u> Must be able to give orders in a personable way, with appreciation of strengths and weaknesses of subordinates

<u>Creativeness:</u> Desirable

<u>Other:</u>

FIGURE 6–3

Performance Standards—Stenographer-Typist and File Clerk

	Hours	Minutes	%
1. Total Hours Paid for: (Daily)	8	480	100
Total Hours Allowance: (Daily)	1	60	12.5
Total Net Productive Hours: (Daily)	7	420	87.5

LINES

2. 30 Lines per Letter: Dictated and Transcribed
   30 Lines per Letter: Straight Copy

LETTERS

3. Production (net production time) – in Seven (7) Hours, or 420 Minutes:
   Dictated and Transcribed Letters (30 lines each) = 10-1/2 letters, or Straight Copy Work
   (30 lines each) = 21 letters

TIME STUDY ANALYSIS

4. Fifteen (15) Minutes Average Dictation Time for 30-Line Letter
   Twenty-Five (25) Minutes Average Transcription Time for 30-Line Letter
   Twenty (20) Minutes Average Copy Time for 30-Line Letter

AVERAGE DAILY TIME

5. Net Production Time: Seven (7) Hours, or 420 Minutes:
   Minutes per Dictated Letter (40) = 10-1/2 – 30-Line Letters in Seven (7) Hours
   Minutes per Copied Letter (20) = 21 – 30-Line Letters in Seven (7) Hours

FILING

6. (a) Fifty (50) Units of Mail per Hour using a numerical file system is the average and
   includes General File upkeep.
   (b) One hundred fifty (150) Units of Mail per Hour, filing alphabetically, is the average
   and includes General File upkeep.

Production standards are based on surveys of stenographic work and represent actual production
of stenographers having average ability.

It is well to note here that although interest in these tools at present is in relation to hiring, they are also of use in connection with other personnel tasks. For example, training, counseling, safety work, job evaluation, promotion plans, and personnel research are scarcely possible without a good plan of job analysis, specifications, and classifications. These uses are discussed in later chapters.

Job Specification Information

The first step in a well-rounded program of job specifications is to prepare a list of all jobs in the company and where they are located.

Information on job titles may be derived by checking payroll records, organization chart titles, supervisors, and employees. The *Dictionary of Occupational Titles*, a publication of the federal government, may be used as a basis of industry-wide comparison.

The second step is to gather and write up information about each of the jobs in a company. In general, such information usually includes the following:

1. Job titles, including trade nicknames
2. Number of employees on the job and their organizational location
3. Names of immediate supervisors
4. Materials, tools, and equipment used or worked with
5. Work or instructions received from whom and to whom delivered
6. Salary or wage levels and hours of work
7. Conditions of work
8. Complete listing of duties, separated according to daily, weekly, monthly, and casual, and estimated according to time spent on each
9. Educational and experience requirements
10. Skills, aptitudes, and abilities required
11. Promotional and transfer lines from and to the job
12. Miscellaneous information and comments

Figure 6–4 illustrates how such information was gathered by means of a questionnaire in the retail field. Such job information should be based on well-designed jobs. Those jobs which are not well-designed must first be restructured. Methods of restructuring are beyond the scope of this text, but what basically constitutes good design is not.

FIGURE 6–4

Questionnaire for Job Analysis

Your Name　　　*Jane White*　　　　　　Date　　*2-9-*
_____

Title or Designation of Your Job　　　　*Inspector-wrapper*
_____

Regular or Extra　　　　*Regular*
_____

Your Department　　　*Coat and Gown Room*
_____

To Whom Do You Report Directly (Name and Title):　*Miss Nancy Brown*

floor supervisor.
_____

The purpose of this questionnaire is to ask each person here to write down exactly what his or her job is and also to write down the duties and the responsibilities of that job. This information will be of great assistance in carrying out the store's employment, training, and promotion program.

In the space below, please write a brief description of your work under the

FIGURE 6–4 (*continued*)

eight main headings indicated. To do this successfully, reflect for a few minutes on your activities, making a few notes of the things you do daily, periodically, and occasionally; any supervision of others which you may do; your contacts with other individuals and departments; any business contacts outside the Company, and whether personally, by telephone, or by correspondence; finally a notation of the equipment and material you use. Endeavor to put the essential things first and in order of their performance, then the lesser items.

Next, write four or five sentences covering that portion of your work falling under each of the headings. Do any revising necessary to make the statements more concise. Whenever possible, begin each statement with word denoting action. For example: "open mail, type forms," etc. (Omit "I"). Finally, copy this below in legible print or longhand (on typewriter if convenient).

Use additional paper if necessary and attach securely.

1. **Description of Work**

   A—DAILY DUTIES: Describe in detail the work you perform regularly each day. In case of selling, include the lines of merchandise sold and the price range. Where there are several steps involved in your job, show each separately and in order of performance.

   1. *Check and put away supplies received from supply department.*
   2. *Straighten and clean wrapping desk including washing paste jar, filling tape machine with water and tape.*
   3. *Complete wrapping of after-four merchandise.*
   4. *Receive sales check and merchandise from salesperson to be wrapped for takewith or delivery giving precedence to takewiths.*
   5. *Open tube carriers for authorized saleschecks and check same against merchandise, noting quantity, price and condition of merchandise.*
   6. *If salescheck is unauthorized, notify section manager. If there is change to be returned to customer, count and call salesperson.*
   7. *Select correct size box, line with tissue, fold merchandise and prepare box for takewith or delivery, according to routines learned in training period.*
   8. *Paste customer's address docket on packages and pin triplicate of sales-check on packages to be delivered in town or out of town and make record of shipments.*
   9. *Bag layaways, fold sales check and place in slot of layaway tag and place on hook of the hanger.*
   10. *Keep stubs for stock record purposes.*
   11. *Answer phone calls for section managers and salespeople.*
   12. *Check supplies and make requisition for needed items.*
   13. *Count dockets of merchandise wrapped the previous day.*
   14. *Make out desk report if there is more than one person in the desk.*

   B—PERIODICAL DUTIES: Describe in detail the work you perform regularly at stated periods, as, for instance, each week, each month, etc. If none, so state.

   None.

   C—OCCASIONAL DUTIES: Describe those duties you are called upon to perform at irregular intervals, that is, duties which are special or fill-in work.

   None.

FIGURE 6–4 *(concluded)*

2. **Job Knowledge Requirements**
   A—STORE PROCEDURE AND METHODS:
   1. *Handling of sales transactions and authorizations according to store procedure.*
   2. *Handling of wrapping according to store procedure.*
   3. *Handling of inspector-wrapper reports according to store procedure.*
   4. *Handling of delivery record of coat department.*
   5. *Type and quantity of supplies needed.*

   B—MERCHANDISE:
   1. *Check merchandise for defects.*

3. **What Equipment Do You Use?**
   Inspector stamp, tape machine, paste bottle, scissors.

4. **What Materials Do You Work with or Sell?**
   Wrapping paper, tissue paper, boxes, tape, twine and miscellaneous forms.

5. **If You Supervise the Work of Others, State How Many and What Their Jobs Are (for example: Two file clerks).**
   None.

6. **What Persons in Other Jobs Do You Contact Regularly in Your Work?**
   A—WITHIN THE COMPANY

Section manager	*Assistant buyer*
Salesperson	*Floor supervisor*
Buyer	*Head supervisor*

   B—OUTSIDE OF THE COMPANY
   Answer customers' phone calls to salespeople and questions of customers at desk.

7. **To What Job Would You Normally Expect to Be Promoted?**
   Stock record clerk, Credit Department clerk, Adjustment office clerk, Shopping Service, Salesperson.

8. **From What Job Were You Transferred to Your Present Job?**
   Hired for job—no previous retail experience.

Source: M. J. Jucius, H. H. Maynard, and C. L. Shartle, *Job Analysis for Retail Stores* (Columbus, Ohio: Bureau of Business Research, Ohio State University, 1945), pp. 15–17.

A job should be of such design that a person on it is most productive. Theoretically, this is most likely to occur when jobs are highly specialized. Thus each worker would then be a technical expert doing an assigned task, such as, clerk, machinist, shipper, typist, assembler, etc. Somebody else (various managers and staff specialists) plan, organize, direct, and control the *doer*. But such specialization is more or less boring, demanding, without personal satisfaction, and non-challenging to the worker who consequently is less productive.

To overcome these negative aspects, the contention is—enlarge and enrich the job. How? Turn over to the workers some of the planning of their work; let them exercise self-supervision and self-control of what they do; permit them to evaluate their own work; and give them some added technical tasks beyond a numbing specialized repetition. In these ways workers gain the satisfaction of being meaningful contributors, of seeing a wholeness in their work, of being challenged to develop their work and to face up to their responsibilities—of having a sense of growth rather than of stagnation.

Such views of building individual job content do theoretically reduce the advantages of specialization. But they also reduce the disadvantages of over-specialization and increase the advantages due to utilizing the total capacities of an employee. That this is true has been shown in a number of instances in which job enlargement and enrichment have been adopted.

Employee Specification Information

A job specification, in and of itself, does not describe what kind of person is needed to fill a job. Hence, for hiring purposes, job information must be converted into required employee characteristics. An employee specification is called for which describes needed physical, mental, emotional, social, and behavioral requirements.

1. Physical Specifications. An easy approach to the task of writing employee specifications is to list the physical qualifications which are called for on given jobs. This has reference to the obvious fact that various kinds and degrees of physical capacities are required on different jobs. Thus a stock chaser has to do a lot of walking, whereas a drill press operator works primarily sitting or standing. And an assembler of parts in the tail section of an airplane should be small in stature, whereas a warehouseman should possess a large and strong physique. A specification of physical demands for the position of an electric motor repairperson is illustrated in Figure 6–5.

2. Mental Specifications. In regard to mental specifications, this has reference to the various mental processes called for on particular jobs, such as an ability to perform arithmetical calculations, to interpret blue prints, to read electrical circuits, etc. A general approach to mental processes has been to specify for a given job the required schooling or experience. In this way a given educational level, let us say four years of high school in the case of a stenographer, may be used as an indirect measure of the level of mental processes required on a particular job. The intelligent quotient (IQ) measured by the psychologist is also a generally accepted measure in this area.

More detailed are attempts to specify particular types and degrees of

FIGURE 6–5

Physical Demands Record

TITLE OF JOB: ELECTRIC MOTOR REPAIRMAN | **SURVEYED BY:** | **DATE:** 10/14 | **ACCEPTED BY:** | **APPROVED BY:** | **OCC. CODE:** | **PLANT:** | **DEPT.:** | **JOB CODE:**

Supersedes Physical Demands Record of 12-21-

PHYSICAL DEMANDS RECORD

HEALTH & SAFETY SECTION OF THE PERSONNEL DEPARTMENT

EXPLANATION OF ENTRIES
A NUMBER OR FRACTION — ACTUAL NUMBER OF HOURS THE ACTIVITY IS REQUIRED IN 8 HRS.
E — EITHER RIGHT OR LEFT ALONE WILL DO THE JOB.

EXPLANATION OF ENTRIES
BLANK NO ENTRY — PARTICULAR FACTOR NOT REQUIRED.
X — PARTICULAR FACTOR IS REQUIRED.

PHYSICAL FACTORS

No./Fraction	#	Factor
6	1	TOTAL HOURS ON FEET
6	2	STANDING
2	3	WALKING – Level surfaces
1/4	4	CLIMBING – Stairs, ramps
1/4	5	11-20 lbs. — FLOOR TO FOUR FEET (TOTAL EFFORT IN LIFTING)
1/4	6	21-35 lbs.
1/4	7	36-50 lbs.
1/4	8	51-65 lbs.
	9	66-80 lbs.
1/4	10	11-20 lbs. — FOUR FEET TO SEVEN FEET
	11	21-35 lbs.
1/4	12	36-50 lbs.
1/4	13	51-65 lbs.
1/4	14	21-35 lbs. — BENCH TO BENCH (CARRYING)
1/2	15	36-50 lbs.
	16	51-65 lbs.
	17	66-80 lbs. (PUSHING / PULLING)
	18	See Remarks For Weights
1	19	BACK & HIP BENDING (30°–90°)
	20	CRAWLING, LYING
1/2	21	CROUCHING, SQUATTING
6	22	SITTING
6	23	Right — FINGERING (Pinching or Manual Dexterity)
3	24	Left
5	25	Right — HANDLING (Grasping or Coarse Hand Motion)
5	26	Left
6	27	Right — ELBOW BENDING 30°–90° from straight
6	28	Left
1/4	29	Right — 91°–120° from straight
1/4	30	Left
1/4	31	Right — REACHING, Above shoulders
1/4	32	Left
6	33	Right — Below shoulders
6	34	Left
1/4	35	Right — KNEE BENDING 30°–90° from straight
1/4	36	Left
1/2	37	Right — 91°–120° from straight
1/2	38	Left

REMARKS

(1) Locate trouble and repair or overhaul a variety of defective AC and DC electric motors and electrical apparatus such as heaters, switches, electric hand grinders and drills, fans and miscellaneous electric hand equipment. Visually checks parts for imperfections. Checks dials and gages on testing equipment.

(8) Uses a variety of hand tools and hand power tools. Operates various machines, etc. Performs some operations from a sitting position at bench. Moves material manually with help, by hand truck, tricycle, and chain hoist. Lifts alone 10 to 50 lbs. parts, tools, motors, fixtures, etc. Items 5-8, 10, 14, 15, all or any combination required for single work day.

(17) Pulling and pushing effort equal to 15 to 35 lbs. Total effort does not exceed 1/2 hour.

(4) Climbs stairs.

(40) Equipment dials and gages.

(44) Fine wiring, etc. (48) Wire color coding.

(49-50) Discuss problem, receive instructions. Hearing to detect foreign noises in equipment.

(52) Electric hoist. (53) Drill press, bench. grinders, coil wiring machine, etc.

(54) Airgun, Dunore Grinders (55) Rides tricycles to pick up and deliver motors.

(56) Icy ground. (58) Material stacked on floor, etc. (59) Stepladder in crib. (61) Soldering acid, fluxes. (63) Paints, varnish, lacquer, thinner, 9004, 9054, 9001, 9101, 9006, (65) 9831, 9805, 9636, 9054, Residual oils and greases (66) Indoor and outdoor conditions. (73) Soldering fumes, abrasive dusts. (74) 9004, 9001, 9006 Thinner, paints, etc.

Gen. Foreman H. Flagg Reviewed and Accepted

PERSONAL PROTECTIVE EQUIPMENT
Eye, hand protection. Protective cream.

SENSORY AND EXPOSURE FACTORS

Factor	#	Entry
EYESIGHT — FAR RATING A	39	
B	40	X
C	41	
D	42	
NEAR RATING A	43	
B	44	X
C	45	
D	46	
THREE DIMENSION VISION	47	
COLOR VISION	48	X
TALKING	49	X
HEARING	50	X
POWER VEHICLES (OPERATING EXPOSURES)	51	X
POWER HOISTS	52	X
EXPOSED MACHINES	53	X
POWER HAND TOOLS	54	X
TRICYCLES	55	X
SLIPPERY SURFACES (WALKING EXPOSURES)	56	X
HOLES AND PITS	57	
OBSTRUCTIONS	58	X
LADDERS (ELEVATIONS)	59	X
UNGUARDED (over 5 ft.)	60	
PRIMARY IRRITANTS (acids, alkalis, etc.)	61	X
SENSITIZERS (synthetic resins, etc.)	62	
DEFATTERS (solvents, strippers, etc.)	63	X
SOAPS (soluble cutting oils, soaps, etc.)	64	
FOLLIC. IRR. (insol. oils, greases, etc.)	65	X
HIGH (10° above shop) (TEMPERATURE)	66	X
LOW (10° below shop)	67	
RAPID CH'NG'S (30° ±)	68	
COLD WATER	69	
40-50 DECIBELS (NOISE)	70	X
51-60 DECIBELS	71	
61-70 DECIBELS	72	
Dusts, Fumes (AIR CONTAMINANTS)	73	X
Mists, Gases, Vapors	74	X
X-Ray, Gamma Rays, etc. (RADIATION)	75	
Ultra-Violet, Infra Red, etc.	76	

Source: Adapted from "Job Redesign for Older Workers," Bulletin No. 1523, U.S. Dept. of Labor, p. 18.

mental characteristics. The following list is illustrative of characteristics that might be considered under this heading:

General intelligence	Ability to plan
Memory for names and places	Arithmetical abilities
Memory for abstract ideas	Reading abilities
Memory for oral directions	Scientific abilities
Memory for written directions	Judgment
Memory for spatial relations	Ability to concentrate
Ability to estimate quantities	Ability to handle variable factors
Ability to estimate qualities	

3. Emotional and Social Specifications. Although the trend is by no means widespread, nevertheless there is a growing realization that perhaps the most important aspects of personnel requirements are those pertaining to emotional and social characteristics. Various studies have shown that for most factory and sales jobs, human rather than technical requirements are more difficult to meet. Moreover, other studies have shown that most personnel problems stem from poor emotional and social adjustments of employees.

Specifying required emotional and social characteristics is, however, a very difficult task. Yet, as illustrated in the following excerpt from the job analysis form of a large retail establishment, some companies appraise the social factors in all jobs.

Social Characteristics of the Job (Contacts)

A. Requirements for social adaptability in human relationships:
   1. Limited social relationships in situations of minor importance.
   2. Limited simple social relationships of major importance.
   3. Frequent social relationships; must deal repeatedly with unpleasant attitudes and situations of minor importance with immediate adjustment.
   4. Constant delicate social emergencies of major importance.
B. Relationship that exists between this job and store reputation:
   1. None to very little; little opportunity for work results to affect opinion.
   2. Close relationship between manner of doing job and outside opinion of store efficiency, etc.
   3. Constant major effect of work results on public and/or employee opinion of store.
   4. Major responsibility is to mold and influence the reputation of the store in the minds of public and/or employees.
C. Personal appearance, including dress, posture, poise, features, and voice required by the job:
   1. Social relationships and type of work require only average personal appearance.
   2. Social relationships require above-average personal appearance.
   3. Outstanding personal appearance required as part of the job.

In most instances, however, about the best that can be done along these lines is to rely upon the interpretative judgment of executives who are aware of the significance of personality and social factors. For example, in one company the supervisors have been given short courses in elementary and applied psychology. They have been advised to note the personal problems employees encounter in their respective departments. By this means, at least a rough form of personal and social specifications has been developed in the minds of the supervisors. Such specifications are far from precise, but they are much better than nothing at all.

4. Behavioral Specifications.   At higher levels, behavioral descriptions are increasingly being included in specifications. This approach seeks to describe the overt acts of people rather than the traits that cause or underlie the acts. For example, it is generally agreed that an executive should have, among other traits, judgment; or a research engineer, creativity; or a sales manager, teaching ability. But at present, descriptions of the amounts of such traits, let alone their definitions, reveal very little agreement either among practical people or among theorists.

Hence, attention is being directed in some quarters to how people should act on a given job and toward others. For example, as noted in Chapter 1, executives have an effect upon subordinates in terms of such observable features as their physical behavior and dress, their use of various forms of authority, the use of various measures of success, and the degree of freedom allowed their staffs. Consequently, some companies are examining candidates for promotion in these as well as the traditional trait terms. Or in the case of creativity of research engineers, some companies are checking on the degree of nonconformity, "free wheeling," and innovations candidates have shown in past and present positions, whether or not directly in research. And in the case of teaching ability, evidence is sought in terms of such factors as interest in learning, concern for the problems of others, and sensitivity to the feelings of others.

Responsibility for Collecting Information

Most companies assign the task of preparing specifications to the personnel department. Its work is subject, of course, to approval of line executives. This is a logical assignment because the personnel unit is commonly responsible for selection, training, and salary administration, all of which are served by job specifications. In some instances, job analysis is assigned to the time-study or engineering departments because of the interest of these units in the operational aspects of jobs.

Two alternatives are available for staffing the unit which prepares specifications. Either trained help may be brought in from the outside, or members currently on the staff who seem to have abilities along these lines may be given special training in job analysis methods. The advantage of the former alternative is that competent specialists are secured at once, but its disadvantage is that outsiders must learn the personality of the company and its special problems. The latter alternative reverses the merits and demerits. Most companies select analysts from their own ranks because it is easier to train such specialists than to find them in the labor market.

Methods of Gathering Data

Information for job studies is obtained in either of two ways—questionnaires or personal interviews.

In the questionnaire method a standard form is prepared by the job analysts and sent either to each worker or to the supervisors. Some companies prefer to gather job data from the workers, believing that they obtain more detailed information thereby, whereas others feel that the supervisor is a better judge of what should be included for each job. After the completed questionnaires are returned, the job analysts in the personnel department group them by jobs and then examine the findings, job by job. As may be expected, it is possible to survey all the jobs and positions in a company much more quickly by this method than by the interviewing method.

Under the interview method the job analyst obtains information by personal conference with the workers or supervisors, and generally both. If well trained for the work, the job analyst can gather more relevant information by interviewing than is possible with questionnaires. Moreover, a personal appraisal of the job contributes greatly to the accuracy of the studies. Usually, personal interviews are more costly and time-consuming than questionnaires. Which should be used depends upon the value received and required as compared to the costs and time involved.

Writing Specifications[1]

In writing specifications, a number of requirements must be carefully handled. Language problems are always present. It must be remembered that the written word, unless carefully chosen, may not convey to the reader what the writer intended. Trade terms are particularly elusive and often colloquial; hence, when used, they should be defined in non-technical language, if possible.

It is also essential to avoid overestimating the requirements of jobs.

---

[1] The appendix of this text contains a detailed example of a job specification and serves to illustrate the care that must go into its preparation. To those who examine such materials for the first time, they may appear to be unduly complex. But with practice they become less formidable and their usefulness is fully appreciated.

The specifications should define the minimum acceptable standards for employment and performance on the job. Exceptional functions, only occasionally performed, should not be permitted to influence the overall description. Nor should specifications be colored by the personalities of or special skills exhibited by particular employees from whom job information may have been obtained.

In writing job descriptions, particularly when they are to be used in making work assignments, care must be exercised to minimize the chances of their becoming straitjackets. Thus, it is not uncommon for workers (1) to get into jurisdictional disputes over who is to do particular parts of jobs or (2) to claim that certain tasks need not be done because they were not included in the job description. Jurisdictional disputes may be reduced by seeing to it that two or more jobs are not assigned the same tasks. And avoidance of responsibility may be suppressed by including a catchall clause stating that management reserves the right to add or remove duties from particular jobs when circumstances (such as emergencies, changes in work load, rush jobs, or technological developments) dictate.

QUANTITATIVE REQUIREMENTS

Methods of Estimation

Job and personnel requirements must be quantified as well as described. In many companies, steps are taken to find replacements only after vacancies occur or are likely to occur. Although this method of estimating quantitative needs is simple, it possesses little else to commend it. On the contrary, its use aggravates interruptions to production and tends to result in hurried and hence poorly evaluated selection of replacements. Therefore, its continued use can probably be condoned only when replacements are few and far between.

The effectiveness of hiring can be raised by forecasting operative, technical, and executive requirements. Such forecasts may be based upon (1) production estimates, (2) past turnover records, and (3) expected technical and managerial needs.

Personnel Requirements and Production Estimates

Personnel requirements in some cases vary closely with fluctuations in production. Hence, forecasts of the latter are basic to estimates of the former. And production forecasts depend upon sales forecasts; hence, sales forecasts are the basis upon which the estimates of personnel requirements are built. Thus, how much personnel is needed in a given department of a company depends upon factory schedules which, in turn, are worked out from sales forecasts and storage policies.

Inasmuch as sales ordinarily fluctuate more than is desired for purposes of production, most companies do not produce strictly to the sales curve. Instead, a production schedule is derived which levels out somewhat the peaks and valleys of sales estimates. The degree is largely dependent upon the storability of the products in question and their nonsusceptibility to the style factor. After factory schedules are computed, departmental work loads can be established. The departmental schedules provide the basis for determining labor needs in each department.

After employee requirements are determined, it is then necessary to ascertain how much personnel of various kinds is available to produce the output scheduled for the period of time in question. These two classes of information can be compared to compute the employees to be added to or removed from the payroll. In equation form, this computation resolves itself as follows:

> Total personnel requirements *less* Available personnel
> *equals* Personnel to be added
> (*or* removed from) the payroll

The computation of available personnel begins with a listing of the present employees. From this is subtracted the estimated number who will leave for various reasons. This figure is then the net available figure which is introduced into the foregoing formula.

Labor Turnover

One of the oldest devices of estimating labor requirements is through labor turnover calculations. Inasmuch as vacancies are created by employees leaving the company, it is only wise to estimate statistically how many are likely to leave. Thus, it may be possible to learn about the number of job vacancies, even though who specifically is to leave cannot be ascertained. Such estimates are best made in terms of past turnover. Knowing trends of turnover is an excellent means of appraising how many vacancies are likely to occur in the future.

Labor turnover may be measured simply by relating accessions or separations during a given period to the average payroll for that period. For purposes of consistency and comparability, the month is the period commonly used. For example, if a company had an average payroll during a given month of 600 (585 at the beginning, plus 615 at the end, divided by 2), took on 50 employees, and 20 were separated from the payroll, then:

1. Based upon accession figures, turnover is calculated as follows:

$$\frac{50}{600} \times 100 = 8.33 \text{ percent}$$

2. Based upon separation figures, turnover is calculated as follows:

$$\frac{20}{600} \times 100 = 3.33 \text{ percent}$$

Depending upon whether a company expects a stable or a growing trend in the same month in the future, it can quickly determine what provisions must be made to fill personnel requirements.

Technical and Managerial Employee Requirements

Increasingly, interest is turning to predetermining technical and managerial employee needs. Waiting for vacancies to occur before seeking replacements of higher level employees is too risky in this highly competitive and complex age. So both small and large companies have turned their attention to filling future needs for executives and technicians. What may be done in this connection is described here in terms of positions covered and methods of expressing needs.

This area of needs covers a wide range of tasks. First is the managerial category, which includes top executives, middle management groups, and supervisory levels. Second is the professional group, which includes such areas as engineers, chemists, accountants, economists, and lawyers. And third in the specialist group which includes such personnel as technical maintenance people, research assistants, computer programmers, and commercial artists.

Calculating needs in all of these areas is difficult. Their numbers do not vary directly with production, as in the case with production workers. And estimating when incumbents are likely to leave is seldom subject to statistical averages in most companies. Nonetheless, useful attempts in these directions have been made. For example, Table 6–1

TABLE 6–1

Five-Year Executive Replacement Plan*

Position	No. of Positions	Quits	Normal Retire- ment	Death and Early Retire- ment	Total	Cumu- lative Pro- motions
President	1	—	1	—	1	1
Executive staff	13	—	4	—	4	5
General staff	39	—	11	5	16	21
Fourth level	115	6	40	14	60	81
Fifth level	162	2	36	19	57	138
	330	8	92	38	138	246

* Briefly, we must be prepared (1) to produce at least one new top executive, (2) to produce two department managers per year, (3) to upgrade 22 people per year at the middle management level, and (4) to hire and retain annually 14 young people with good management potential.

FIGURE 6–6

An Example of Personnel Audit

| Roy D. Roeber |
| Supervisor – Test Instrumentation |

| 26 yrs.   James, T.B. |
| Instrumentation Engineer   BSEE |
| Insufficient evidence but very bright; has leadership. Looks like a very good instrument designer. Needs to improve technical knowledge and supervisory skills. Little evidence of his personal characteristics. |

| 31 yrs.   Williams, O.S. |
| Instrumentation Engineer   HS Gd. |
| Really only a technician. Lacks formal engineering training. Personality not so good. Paper work poor. A poor risk. Willing and conscientious worker. |

| 37 yrs.   Frank, A.P.   BS |
| Instrumentation Engineer   Physics |
| Very weak basic abilities, especially in technical areas. Poorly qualified for this job. Best suited where he can use numerical ability, e.g. test data evaluation. Overall growth and potential limited. |

| 39 yrs.   Fred, X. |
| Measurements Specialist |
| Solid background of experience for this job. Interest, initiative, perseverance. Lacks technical training or understanding for other engineering work. Limited to present job but is happy on it. |

| 32 yrs.   Ann, A.C. |
| Instrumentation Engineer   BSAE |
| Bright, sharp, aggressive. Good leadership skills. Record of technical accomplishment. A bit too blunt and direct. Has lots of drive and anxious to learn. Demanding of self and others. Needs to improve supervisory skills. |

| 44 yrs.   Louise, M.R. |
| Instrumentation Engineer   BSME |
| Adequate abilities. Varied engineering background. Appears to lack aggressiveness and initiative. Probably better placed in project or equipment design. |

CODE

Promotable   Satisfactory   Misplaced   Unsatisfactory

Source: Adapted from D. R. Lester and M. L. Owen, "How to Conduct a Manpower Audit," *Personnel*, vol 36, no. 3, p. 49.

shows the replacements that are estimated to be necessary at all executive levels in a given company over a five-year period. And Figure 6–6 shows how a company estimates which engineers are promotable, thus obtaining a picture of those capable of filling advanced positions as well as those for whom replacements will have to be found.

QUESTIONS

1. What is the difference between the terms job, position, grade, and occupation?
2. Why are both job specifications and employee specifications useful in hiring?

3. What kinds of information are usually included in a job specification?

4. What are emotional and social traits perhaps more important than technical characteristics on many jobs?

5. What is the difference between behavioral descriptions and trait descriptions?

6. Select a job on which you can get first-hand information and write a job and employee specification following the illustration outlined in this chapter and in the Appendix. (Typist, bus driver, meter reader, housewife, fraternity cook, stenographer, or salesclerk are a few examples that come to mind in addition to actual factory or office experiences one might have had.)

7. In studying jobs, what are the relative advantages of the interview and questionnaire methods?

8. By what methods may estimates of quantitative requirements for personnel be estimated?

9. How may the labor turnover method be used to estimate employee requirements?

10. What suggestions do you have for estimating future management position requirements?

CASE 6-1.   JOB SPECIFICATIONS

This case is concerned with a grievance that arose out of an interpretation of job specifications. A machine operator spilled a large quantity of liquid on the floor around his machine. The supervisor told the operator to clean up the spill. The operator refused stating that the specification for his job did not include clean up. Not having time to check the exact wording of the specification, the supervisor called a service man—a general helper-type of worker assigned to the department—to do the cleaning. The service man was called at 2:55 P.M., which happened to be just before the scheduled afternoon general ten-minute rest period shut down. But he refused to do the clean-up because he claimed that his job specification did not include such chores.

The supervisor threatened to discharge the service man who then complied but immediately afterward filed a grievance.

In preparing for the grievance hearing, the company executives reviewed the three job specifications. It was found that the job specification of the machine operator stated that the operator was responsible for keeping his machine in clean, operating order but nothing about floor cleaning. The job specification for the service man stated that he was responsible in assisting operators in various ways such as getting materials and tools and when called on for assistance, but nothing was said about clean up. Although not present at the time, the janitor's job specification was also checked; it did include all forms of cleaning, but his specification stated that his hours of work commenced after the shift ended.

Question

1. What suggestions do you have to settle this case and also to prevent a recurrence of such conflicts of opinion?

CASE 6–2. AN OPPORTUNITY IN PERSONNEL

Ms. Fiber had been a pioneer in the synthetic filament field. She was an engineering genius, developing unique operations. She restricted her interests to technical matters; she let others handle routine production matters and was not concerned with how others used her output. Her mind was technically oriented and her creativity gave her company one big profitable result after another.

She was the chief operating officer of the company in addition to being its technical genius. Since she gave all of her attention to new inventions, other matters, such as personnel, were left to subordinates. As the company grew and prospered there seemed to be no personnel problems because there always were opportunities for growth and earnings for all.

As time went on, competition from others in the industry grew and the expansion of the company was reduced. And it seemed that personnel problems grew as opportunities decreased. Ms. Fiber sensed that she had given no attention to people-oriented problems, that she had little interest for people problems, and that she had surrounded herself with a like-minded group of chemical and engineering professionals.

She turned to a consulting search organization to find her a qualified personnel executive at a vice presidential level to build up this phase of her business. Her present personnel manager had been kept in a subordinate position and did not have the qualifications or experience for the top level job.

Question

1. Assume you were recommended for the job and it was offered to you, what would you want in your job contract before you would be willing to undertake this responsibility and challenge?

CHAPTER 7

SOURCES OF PERSONNEL SUPPLY

Variability of Sources of Supply

Suitable candidates must be attracted before actual hiring can take place. A knowledge of sources of supply and how they may be tapped are prerequisites to a program of attracting candidates. These matters are the concern of this chapter.

Ordinarily, all of the sources of supply to be discussed here do not remain at a constant degree of usefulness but are affected by the general state of the labor market. For example, during war emergencies, sources such as older workers are utilized, contrary to normal practice, and sources such as casual applicants that had previously been satisfactory dry up.

Or looking into the future, as illustrated in Figure 7–1, by forecasts of national trends in employment, demands in higher level positions will place much greater strain upon personnel sources than will manual occupations. Hence a particular company must give consideration to local, statewide, and national conditions in studying sources of supply. Such surveys should concern themselves with the advantages, disadvantages, and conditions of most favorable usage of various sources of supply.

Types of Personnel Sources

Sources of employee supply are commonly divided into internal and external sources. Internal sources refer to the present working force of a company. In the event of a vacancy, someone already on the payroll is upgraded, transferred, promoted, or sometimes demoted. Usually, the

FIGURE 7–1

Employment by Occupations, 1950–80

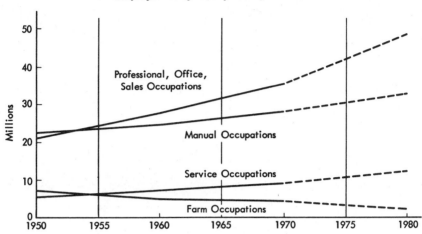

Source: U.S. Department of Labor, *Manpower—Challenge of the 1960's* (Washington, D.C.: U.S. Government Printing Office, 1960), p. 10, and *Monthly Labor Review*, April 1970, p. 19.

definition is expanded (and for understandable reasons) to include the following:

1. Those not on the payroll of a particular company but in the employment of affiliated or subsidiary companies
2. Those who were once on the payroll of a particular company but who plan to return or whom the company would like to rehire—for example, those on leave of absence, those who quit voluntarily, or those on production layoffs

External sources refer to employment agencies, schools, floating labor, and persons recommended by present employees.

The Internal Source

1. Advantages. The internal source is often credited with being better than the external. This contention is based, in the first place, upon the argument that the morale of employees is raised by cultivating the internal source. Employees are thereby given concrete evidence that they are preferred over outsiders when good vacancies occur. This policy is commendable if it induces present employees to prepare themselves for transfers or promotions, thereby making themselves better than those who might have been hired from the outside.

Another and cogent argument in favor of the internal source is that the employer is in a better position to evaluate those presently employed than outside candidates. This argument is valid if the company maintains a satisfactory record of the progress, experience, and service of its employees, and if transfers and promotions are based upon measured merit. Otherwise, the internal source will degenerate into an undeserved monopoly for those on the payroll.

2. Disadvantages. The chief weaknesses of the internal source are twofold: danger of "inbreeding" and possible inadequacy of supply. The first of these weaknesses arises out of the fact that the learner seldom has ideas or notions that differ widely from those of the teacher. As a consequence, startling innovations or suggestions are seldom contributed, which are so important in our competitive economy. The company, therefore, is not likely to be known for its progressiveness and, indeed, may be left behind in the parade. Consequently, on jobs in which originality counts heavily, such as advertising, style designing, and basic research, the practice of always filling vacancies from within is seldom followed.

The policy of using internal sources also breaks down when there are numerous vacancies. During periods of rapid expansion, for example, the internal source is inadequate.

3. Conditions of Favorable Use. For most favorable use of the internal source of supply, then, conditions must be right. The vacancies to be filled must be within the capacities of present employees, adequate employee records must be maintained, and opportunities should be provided in advance for employees to prepare themselves for promotion.

The External Source

Ultimately, of course, all vacancies must be filled from the outside. Even the company that prides itself upon its policy of filling vacancies exclusively from within must go to the outside to fill vacancies at the bottom of the promotional ladder. Hence, every company must be acquainted in some degree with the kinds of external sources. Among the external sources are public employment agencies, private employment agencies, advertising, casual labor, recommended labor, minority groups, recruiting, and labor unions.

1. Public Employment Agencies. The public employment agencies have achieved a significant role in the field of employment. These agencies are represented by the several state employment services and the U.S. Employment Service, commonly known as USES. The USES came into existence when it was established as a unit of the U.S. Department of Labor. During World War I it acted as the sole recruiting agency for civilian workers in war industries. Since then its main role has been to set national policies and to oversee the operations of the state employment services.

The state services are now the main agency of public employment.

They began their growth in the depression years of the Thirties. Then the Social Security Act provided that laid-off workers, to be eligible for unemployment benefits, had to register with the state agencies. This gave these agencies a roster of the unemployed—in a sense, of the available worker supply.

These agencies experienced further growth in World War II. Then they were given wide powers over hiring, classification of essential jobs (draft deferment status), and job changes between companies by employees.

And in the past few years, the public agencies have expanded their importance by moving from a simple employment agency to a comprehensive personnel service agency, as illustrated in Figure 7–2. Overall, the public agencies have assumed a leading role in the labor market in a variety of ways.

FIGURE 7–2

Public Employment Personnel Services

APPLICANT CHARACTERISTICS	**JOB INFORMATION**		Applicant Flow Service

LEVEL I — Job-Ready, Competitive, Motivated — Jobs — Self-Help Referral, Current Job Listing, Job Inventory, Wage Information, Occupational Information, Ed. & Training Library — Reception, Screening, Routing, Group Information Service

LEVEL II — Marginal Skills, Undermotivated, Minor Employment Barriers, Poor Occupational Attachment, Veteran, Minority, Claimant, Handicapped, Older Worker, Youth — EMPLOYABILITY EXPLORATION: Outreach, Specific Information Service (group or individual), Occupational Guidance, Referral to Job Openings and Training, Job Search Assistance – Job Development, Counseling (voc. choice), Stop-Gap Employment, Initial Assessment, Referral to Support Services, Personal Promotional Support — Jobs

LEVEL III — Noncompetitive, Significant Employment Barriers, Low Skill Level, Educational Deficiencies, Minority – Veteran – Handicapped, Claimant — EMPLOYABILITY DEVELOPMENT: Outreach, Assessment – Testing, Team Services – Counseling – Coaching, Training, Education, Personal Support (medical, legal, etc.), Job Development, On-Job Training, Work Experience, Follow-through Support — Jobs

SUPPORT – INPUTS

Personnel Research, NAB-JOBS, Chamber of Commerce, Apprenticeship Information, Economic Research, Automated Job Matching, Interarea Clearance

Counseling, Vocational Guidance, Job Development, Employer Services, Automated Job Matching, Orientation

Counseling, Coaching, Training – MDTA, OJT, JOBS 70, Personal Supportive Services, Education, Job Development, Follow – through after Placement, CEP – WIN – SUN, Vocational Rehabilitation, Vocational Education

The state agencies provide a wide range of services, the cost of which is paid for by employer contributions to the unemployment compensation funds. Basically, they provide a clearinghouse for jobs and job information. Employers send them requests for employees. And candidates for employment can learn from them what jobs are available and be referred thereby to employers.

This basic service is refined and implemented in numerous ways, as follows:

1. Applicants are counseled about their own capabilities in relation to job requirements and labor market conditions.

2. A variety of psychological, trade, and aptitude tests are available to applicants for better guidance and counseling.

3. A selective placement service for handicapped workers is provided to match their capacities to demands of various jobs.

4. Help is available to military veterans in seeking to match skills with civilian jobs.

5. Effort is directed toward helping minority groups and the underprivileged to find jobs and to be trained for employability.

6. Special service is also provided for college, technical, and professional applicants.

7. A nationwide network of the state agencies utilizes job bank computers to provide job information throughout the country as well as locally.

8. The services have special duties when critical labor shortages occur either in peace or war time.

9. Their information on labor supply, wage rates, hirings, and layoffs is useful to companies contemplating plant relocations or decentralization.

2. Private Employment Agencies. Private employment agencies also are significant in the labor market. These have tended to serve either in the technical and professional areas or in the relatively unskilled fields. In the former case, private services usually specialize according to such groups as office and clerical help, accountants and computer staffs, engineers, salespeople, and executives. Such specialization enhances their capacity to interpret the needs of their clients, to seek out particular types of people, and to develop proficiency in recognizing the talents of specialized personnel. These agencies have increased the value of their services by associating local agencies into national organizations through which information of interregional information can be exchanged.

Some private employment agencies have, as noted above, restricted their clientele to the lower levels of worker skills. In such instances, they serve to attract applicants in numbers that the employer personally could not. This is particularly true of companies that have seasonal problems or are located away from the larger labor markets. Thus a company that has a seasonal logging operation, for example, may need quickly, but temporarily, a large but miscellaneous crew, including such workers as cooks and carpenters as well as lumberjacks. By turning to the employment agencies in larger cities, the employer can gather and ship out a group of floating workers that could scarcely be recruited in any other way.

In essence, then, the private agencies are brokers, bringing employers and employees together. For this service, they are compensated by fees charged against either the employee or the employer. The fee is usually computed as a percentage of a week's, two weeks', or a month's pay.

Charging for this service is of course legitimate, but the practice has led to abuses which, for a time, cast suspicion upon almost all private employment agencies. Such abuses led to state and local control being exercised over private agencies. Many of the employment agencies themselves, through their trade association, led in the fight to remove unscrupulous operators.

For a time after the USES had strengthened its position in the labor market, some felt that the day of the private agency had ended. Perhaps some of the weaker units were forced out, but the remaining ones certainly seem far from finished. Indeed, the competition has served as a tonic because the services of the private agencies have improved over those of earlier years. Some private agencies are no longer content merely to bring employer and employee together but are computerizing lists of available talent, are utilizing testing devices to classify and evaluate applicants, are adopting scientific counseling services to interpret the abilities of their clientele, and are employing advanced techniques of vocational guidance to increase the probabilities of correct placements. These advances have made private agencies even more attractive to employees who prefer their more personal and selective characteristics.

3. Advertising for Labor.   Advertising in various media is also a widely used method of attracting labor. How much advertising is done usually depends upon the urgency of the demand for labor. Sometimes the classified sections of metropolitan newspapers have been well filled with such advertisements. But this source is scarcely used when other channels supply sufficient candidates. The main shortcomings of this source are its uncertainty and the range of candidates that are attracted. Perhaps some of this is due to poor copy work, because many ads are uninspired, uninteresting, and not clear. Even when an advertisement is properly written and timed, the employer cannot be sure that it will pull the desired number of applicants. Moreover, the candidates must be culled very carefully, since a good proportion of those who do present themselves are unqualified.

Such advertisements should not be expected to do more than any advertisement can do—that is, attract attention and create a desire, which must be followed up by other appeals and selective devices. Nevertheless when the medium of advertising is chosen carefully, the attention of desirable applicants can be attracted with a high degree of selectivity. For example, advertisements placed in trade journals or professional magazines can be directed so that only specific groups will be reached.

4. Casual Labor Sources. Most companies rely to some extent upon the casual labor which daily applies at the employment office or gate. Here again, the source is uncertain, and the candidates cover a wide range of abilities. Although it cannot be relied upon and does call for very careful screening, few companies care to shut off this source. In the first place, it is an inexpensive source; the applicant comes to the door of the employer. Second, there always is an occasional good find that makes up for the expense of culling. And third, some companies believe it is good public relations—those in consumer goods industries particularly (bakeries, food products, public utilities, etc.)—to receive cordially all who come to the company premises, whether or not jobs are or will be available.

5. Recommended Labor. Recommended labor refers to all applicants who come to the employer on the direct suggestion of a present employee or other employers. Some employers cultivate this source, feeling that it provide a preselected class of applicants. When employees recommend friends for jobs, it is likely that they do this with some degree of care. They know that to recommend someone who is unsatisfactory will reflect upon their own good judgment; and they recognize that a friend will not appreciate a lead that does not materialize in a good job.

6. Minority Groups. More and more, companies are seeking candidates among women and also from minority groups. The approaches include specific search programs as well as involvement in the ghettos.

A variety of programs have been instituted to attract employees from minority groups. Of course, many companies rely upon the public employment agencies for help. Recourse is also had to private employment agencies. Much intensive search is conducted among colleges and universities, particularly for technical and professional positions. Some companies rely upon their own employees of minority groups to suggest ways and means of finding candidates. Of noteworthy significance is the developing attitude that special attention must be given to the feelings and viewpoints of minority members in attracting, interviewing, and communicating with them.

Business is beginning also to get more involved with the ghettos as a source of labor supply. A few have gone to the extent of establishing branch plants and units in the ghettos to utilize minorities right at the source. Most have tried to attract candidates to their regular units. In part this step is taken voluntarily as a social responsibility. And in part, there is a recognition that these areas contain very valuable employee potential. Disadvantaged persons who previously were shunned as being inadequately equipped for entry into business are now being invited into employment. The inadequacies are being overcome by various training and educational programs. Some of the improvement programs are being supported by business alone and some under the various training programs of the federal government. And the results attained from these sources and programs are proof that tapping the ghettos is very good business as well as a contribution to community and social improvements.

7. Recruitment Sources.   During periods of general labor scarcity, or in connection with scarcity of applicants for specific occupations, positive steps of seeking employees must be taken. What may be done is discussed in terms of usual factory and office jobs, highly skilled jobs, and technical and professional positions.

a. General-Run Jobs.   Industry must take a particularly active role in seeking employees during periods of a tight labor market. For example, in one company during a critical shortage of employees, a concentrated house-to-house canvass by its own women employees brought in a large number of housewives willing to work temporarily during the pinch.

Another company struck on the idea of recruiting blind workers for such jobs as sorting rough pieces of mica. The blind by touch alone were able to do as well or better than those with normal vision who used a micrometer.

In some areas, intercompany and community exchanges of labor supply were carried out. By pooling information regarding projected hiring and discharges, it was found in some communities that employees could be exchanged in a mutually satisfactory manner.

b. Highly Skilled Workers.   The foregoing cases also serve to illustrate methods of recruiting highly skilled workers. Also noteworthy is the plan of dividing complicated jobs into relatively simple operations. When, for example, the shortage of skilled toolmakers became dangerously acute, many companies found it desirable to divide this work into its components. Then, trainees were assigned to the simple aspects of the toolmaker's job, while the craftsman retained the complicated operations. Thus, specialized talents were utilized to the highest possible degree and spread over the largest number of jobs possible.

c. Technical and Professional Positions.   Many companies have turned to the schools to look for desirable applicants for such positions. They send representatives to college campuses to seek the cream of the graduating classes. In a few cases the practice has been to offer summer employment to outstanding juniors and even sophomores with a view to permanent employment later. This practice enables the employer to try out the students and thus be in a better position to evaluate their potentialities. And the students not only gain useful work experience but also can better judge the desirability of making a permanent connection. Some college recruitment programs have been extended to the point that companies are willing to pay for postgraduate training of students in particularly scarce, specialized job areas. In all cases of college recruitment, it is highly desirable to be very careful in screening candidates.

In recent years, the high demand for professional and managerial talent has seen the emergence of "search specialists." These look for technicians and high-level executives who, though employed, could be induced to move to more challenging and remunerative positions. Such searchers may be a unit within a consulting firm or an independent employment agency.

8. Unions. Unions have played, and are likely to play, an increasing role in the matter of sources of labor supply. In some industries, such as the building trades, unions have carried the responsibility of supplying employers with needed skilled employees. This not only has been of real service to employers but has also removed from their shoulders the obligation of how to allocate limited amounts of work during slack periods. The union has determined the order in which available workers are assigned to employers.

When unions have completely taken over the hiring function, as in the case of the hiring halls of the maritime industry, this practice has been restricted by the Taft-Hartley Act. Such halls must not discriminate against nonunion members.

Where unions do not actively engage in providing employment information or service to their members, they invariably take an interest in seeing that members laid off are given preference in rehiring. Most union contracts contain some reference to the responsibility of the employer to rehire former employees, and usually in some order of seniority.

Evaluation of Alternative Sources

A knowledge of available sources of supply should be augmented by an evaluation of their relative merits. Some plan should be devised by which it is possible to measure how good or how poor various sources have proved to be. Some reference has been made in the foregoing discussion regarding the advantages and disadvantages of various sources, but such generalized conclusions should in particular cases be checked by objective measurements.

Perhaps the most accurate way of evaluating the effectiveness of sources of employee supply is to run statistical correlations. In this manner, it is possible to relate the factor of success on the job with particular sources of supply. A simple illustration of how this is done is shown by the study made in one company which, among other things, wanted to know how well people from various parts of the city in which it was located succeeded on the job. The map of the community in question was divided into parts that had somewhat common characteristics—for example, purchasing power, nationalities, and schools. The records of employees selected from these areas were then correlated with the degree of job success as measured by the plan of employee rating operated by the company. It was found that the employees who came from certain areas rated higher than those who came from other areas. As a consequence, it was decided to restrict hirings to those candidates who came from the areas from which the better employees had come in the past. It was

TABLE 7–1

Source of Hiring

	Gate Hiring		Referred by Present Employees		Rehiring of Layoffs		Total	
	No.	%	No.	%	No.	%	No.	%
January	27	71	5	13	6	16	38	100
February	15	60	4	16	6	24	25	100
March	12	70	2	12	3	18	17	100

recognized that as a result of this policy, a few good employees from the restricted areas would be passed up, but it was felt that this loss would be less than that which would be incurred by hiring from the low-rated areas.

A simpler plan of evaluating alternative sources of supply is to use such measures as turnover, grievances, and disciplinary action. For example, by classifying turnover data according to the original sources from which employees came, it is possible to contrast the relative merits of sources of supply. The same result may be obtained by tabulating grievances and disciplinary action according to classes of hiring sources. Table 7–1 provides an illustration of such a tabulation. Such studies are not conclusive, but they do throw light upon a subject that otherwise is beclouded by personal opinions and even prejudices.

Layout and Location of Employment Office

The physical layout and location of the employment office has an indirect, though nonetheless important, effect upon the attraction of suitable candidates. An office with comfortable furnishings and a pleasing

FIGURE 7–3
Employment Office of a Small Plant

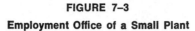

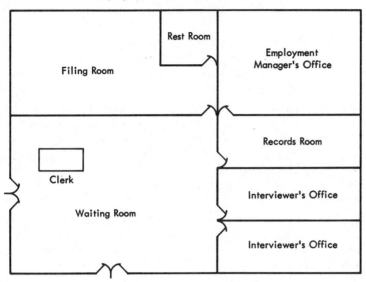

appearance leaves a favorable impression upon applicants and adds to the efficiency of the employing staff. Also, one that is conveniently located is more likely to attract candidates than one that is not so easily reached. Indeed, this matter of location has become so important at times that some unique experiments have been conducted to make employment offices more accessible. For example, one company established branch employment offices in downtown locations, from which applicants found suitable were taken to the plant by station wagon. Other organi-

FIGURE 7–4
Personnel Layout of a Medium-Sized Company

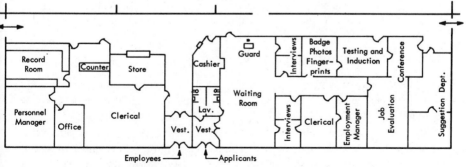

Source: Cyril T. Tucker, "Three Ways to Lay Out a Personnel Department," *Factory Management and Maintenance,* vol. 101, no. 9, pp. 154–55.

zations have also employed auto trailers as added means of reaching and attracting labor. When the labor market is exceedingly tight, recourse to such methods is justifiable, though it might prove too expensive to use as a regular practice.

The layout and appointments of the employment office require careful consideration. The main problem here is that the volume of hirings varies so widely that it is difficult to arrive at a satisfactory compromise as to size. Usually, the employment office is too large or too small. Some examples of office layouts are shown in Figures 7–3 and 7–4. It will be noted that all of the plans are designed to facilitate an efficient flow of applicants through the hiring process. Care must be exercised that the layout does not imply or lead to ethnic, color, or sex discrimination.

QUESTIONS

1. For what kinds of position or occupations will there tend to be more of a demand as the years go by?
2. What conditions must be met for favorable use of the internal source of labor supply?
3. What kinds of services are performed by the public employment agencies?
4. How might the trend of growth of prestige of private employment agencies in recent years be explained?
5. Examine the classified advertising section of a newspaper carrying ads for employees. What would be examples of good and poor advertisements?
6. What are the particular advantages of the recommended source of labor supply?
7. What are the advantages of college recruitment programs as sources of labor supply?
8. What roles may the unions play in regard to the subject of sources of labor supply?
9. How can the relative merits of alternative sources of labor supply be measured objectively?
10. What can a good physical location and layout of an employment office contribute in the matter of sources of labor supply?

CASE 7–1.   CONDITIONS OF WORK

Among the jobs in a "drug store" at a large airport is that of combination cashier and stock clerk. The pay scale of all cashiers—men or women—is $2.10 an hour to start plus a commission of $2.50 a day minimum. A larger commission can be earned on selected merchandise which is sold. After three months the rate per hour is increased to $2.25. The hours are 7:30 to 4:00 P.M.; 3:30 to 12:00 Midnight; and 11:30 to 7:00 A.M. There are no pay differentials between the various shifts although the early shift offers a better chance of earning a higher commission because it is the busiest. A 15 percent discount is available to all employees.

The schedule of hour assignments is made up on Friday for the following week although one's shift does not change except for vacations or openings because of leaving by an employee. There is no extra pay for holidays or weekends. There is a high rate of turnover, tardiness, and absenteeism. The company is not concerned about this because it argues "there's always someone looking for a job."

There is a high rate of stealing, evidently by employees (as well as customers), and periodic lie-detector tests must be taken by all employees.

Question

1. What support can you give for improving conditions of work in the light of the company's views on the availability of candidates for employment?

CASE 7–2. HIRING WOMEN EMPLOYEES

For a long time, and up to the present, the Double Strength Structural Steel Corporation has hired only male employees except in the office departments. In its advertisements for help, however, it has recently included the statement, "An Equal Opportunity Employer" with the intent of clarifying its policy on hiring members from minority groups.

It was surprised recently when two young women applied for jobs in the shop in reply to an ad specifying openings in the warehouse and in the cutting and shaping departments. The employment manager turned down the applicants on the grounds that the work involved moving heavy materials, required strength to manipulate machine controls, required association with men whose shop talk was none too gentle, consisted of dusty, grimy, and greasy conditions, and was in an environment that had no facilities for women.

The women replied that they were aware of these conditions, had experience in shop work, and knew their rights under the law against discrimination on the grounds of sex.

The employment manager backed off, stating an unwillingness to hire them but offering to check with higher authority. They were asked to come back the next day.

Question

1. What answer would you give the women when they returned?

CHAPTER 8

THE SELECTION PROCEDURE

Scope of the Selection Procedure

The selection procedure is the system of functions and devices adopted in a given company for the purpose of ascertaining whether or not candidates possess the qualifications called for by a specific job or for progression through a series of jobs. The procedure cannot be effectively placed in operation until, as noted in earlier chapters, three major steps have been taken:

1. Requirements of the job to be filled have been specified
2. Qualifications people must possess have been specified
3. Candidates for screening have been attracted

With these steps completed, it is then the task of selection to match the qualifications of candidates with the requirements of the job. Undesirable candidates are screened out and the qualified retained.

Selection processes of companies differ widely. Some companies are content with a cursory personal interview and a simple physical examination. At the other extreme, elaborate series of tests, examinations, interviews, and reference checks are employed.

Although there are differences in detail, almost all selection procedures, formally or informally, include the following broad steps:

1. Designing procedural and structural relations
2. Initiating the selection process
3. Gathering information about candidates
4. Interpreting findings
5. Making decisions and recording results
6. Inducting successful candidates

Design of Procedural and Structural Relations

The selection procedure is like a sequence of hurdles. Successful candidates leap over them and arrive at the finish line; the unsuccessful do not. This is well illustrated in Figure 8–1. Three important questions must be answered in connection with these hurdles. First, what should be the design of these hurdles? Second, who is responsible for checking the candidates as they try to go over each hurdle? And third, what are the characteristics of a good set of selection hurdles?

1. Procedural Arrangements.   Procedural design should consider a number of subjects. Attention must be directed first to the number and kinds of hurdles to be included. Specifically, a decision must be made as to how many of such hurdles as the following are to be used: application blanks, reference letters, psychological tests, interviews, personal observations, and physical examinations. Second, the height of each hurdle must be set. Shall application blanks, for example, be comprehensive, and shall interviews be in depth and conducted by several executives? And third, in what sequence shall investigations be made? For example, should psychological tests be given before or after personal interviews?

How thoroughly these questions are answered depends in part upon the significance placed upon procurement as a phase of personnel management. Those who feel that good selection is at the heart of employee productivity and good human relations will spend much time and money on it. They believe that when good employees are hired, subsequent functions of personnel work and of supervision are easier to perform. But casual hiring leads to higher costs of training, dealing with, motivating, and supervising subordinates.

How these questions are answered depends, too, upon other factors. For example, business conditions are important. When labor is scarce, a company which sets high standards of selection will be unable to hire as many people as it needs. Conversely, in a depression, standards can be raised. Cost is another factor affecting the design of hurdles, particularly in relation to the sequence of arrangement. Thus, it is usually desirable to give extended psychological tests only after some less expensive, preliminary steps have weeded those that are obviously unqualified. Nor would it be desirable to have higher executives interview candidates before lower levels have performed some screening operations. And finally, tradition is a factor affecting procedural design. For example, physical examinations were once conducted by the town doctor and so had to be given last. Nowadays, the physical examination is given on the premises of most companies and could therefore be moved up in the procedure. Yet, for tradition's sake, it is often kept at the end.

2. Organizational Relationships.   Very important in the design of a selection procedure is the matter of how line and staff executives should share the tasks and responsibilities for accepting or rejecting candidates.

FIGURE 8–1

Summary of a Selection Procedure

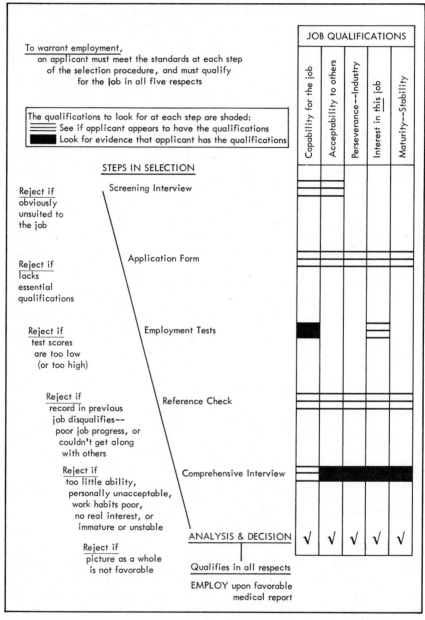

Source: Adapted from Milton M. Mandell, *The Employment Interview*, Research Study no. 47 (New York: American Management Association).

To begin with, to the personnel department is usually assigned responsibility for operating the selection procedure. In this capacity the personnel department, as a staff unit, assists the line departments; it does not dictate to them. First, unsuccessful candidates should be eliminated by the staff so that the time of the line executives is not spent needlessly on such people. Second, candidates who can meet line requirements should be made available promptly as required.

Such assistance does not relieve the line executive of responsibility or authority. The line executive should supply the personnel department with information needed for good hiring. For example, the sales manager should help to establish good job and employee specifications for each of the positions under that jurisdiction, and should be ready to participate in particular phases of the selection process—such as technical interviewing—when that is required. And the ultimate authority of the sales manager, let us say, to accept or reject a candidate must not be contravened by the personnel department. The latter has the right to offer what it considers good candidates, but the sales manager must have the right to accept or reject (subject, of course, to review by higher authority, but not subject to the dictates of the personnel department, which has the right to petition for such a review). Thus, each executive complements the other in this vital task.

3. Characteristics of a Good Procedure. A number of characteristics must be built into a procedure if it is to be rated as a good selection plan. Of course, the essential feature of a selection procedure is that it produces results effectively and economically. To do this, each step in the selection sequence must be assigned a place so that it may contribute its fullest share to the final result. Moreover, each step or phase of the selection procedure must be equipped and performed to a degree commensurate with its importance. For each step, too, it is necessary to establish (a) standards of performance and (b) means of allocating and determining responsibility for results. In designing the procedure, care should be taken to make it reasonably flexible so that it can manage effectively temporary changes in volume, yet be sufficiently stable so that it is not subject to whimsical changes. The selection process should have definitely established starting and finishing points, so that unauthorized or dangling procedures will not be in operation. Each step should give due consideration to cost, time taken, and local customs. And finally, the procedure should not transgress laws relating to discrimination on grounds of race, color, creed, age, sex, or nationality.

Initiation of Selection Procedure

The selection process is placed in operation by means of a release of authority to fill an existing or expected vacancy. How such authority is

FIGURE 8–2

An Employment Requisition

EMPLOYMENT REQUISITION				
Number Required			Date of Request	
Department		Position		
Duties and Responsibilities				
Addition to Present Force	Permanent	Temporary	If Temporary, How Long?	
Reasons for Addition				
Replacement	Permanent	Temporary	If Temporary, How Long?	
If Replacement, Give Names of Employees Replaced				
Rate of Pay	Per Hour	Per Week	Is Application for Bond Required?	Yes No

EDUCATION REQUIRED		
Elementary School	High School	College or University
Special Training		
Other Requirements		

EXPERIENCE			
Kind	Years Desired	Kind	Years Desired
Technical		Clerical	
Typing		Mechanical	
Stenographic		Special	

Report to (Supervisor)	Location	Date	Time	A.M. P.M.
Requested by		Department		
Approved by		Department		
Remarks				

(NOTE Type in Duplicate Original to Personnel Dept. Duplicate for your File)
PLEASE ANTICIPATE YOUR WANTS AS FAR IN ADVANCE AS IS POSSIBLE AND GIVE SUFFICIENT DETAILS SO THAT THE PERSONNEL DEPARTMENT CAN MAKE AN INTELLIGENT SELECTION OF APPLICANTS.

TELEPHONE REQUESTS MUST BE COVERED BY A WRITTEN REQUISITION WITHOUT DELAY.

released, by whom, and to whom differs from company to company. In its simplest form, where the company is small and the line form of organization structure is in use, each executive decides when vacancies should be filled.

As an organization grows, release of authority is clothed in formalized records and systems. Very common in such instances is the use of a form called the hiring requisition as illustrated in Figure 8–2, issued to the employment office. Some companies permit first-line supervisors and superintendents to issue hiring requisitions for any vacancies that occur. Other companies grant this right to supervisors in regard to direct help, such as machine operators, but require higher approval in the case of indirect or so-called nonproduction help, such as truckers, messengers, and clerks. Still other companies require all requisitions made out by supervisors and superintendents to carry the signatures of higher executives. The purpose of such requirements is to control more closely the number of hirings and thus reduce the possibility of needless employment.

As requisitions are received, they may be recorded in a labor journal or register, so that the status of unfilled requisitions may readily be ascertained and controlled. Employment requisitions are then assigned to employment assistants, who acquaint themselves with job and employee specifications and thus prepare themselves to check on available candidates.

Gathering Information about Candidates

The task of gathering information about candidates may be viewed in terms of (1) what information is sought, and how, and (2) how the information is interpreted after it is collected.

1. Information Sought. A variety of information may be gathered from and about candidates for vacancies. The efforts exerted in gathering such information may be studied in terms of (*a*) the information which is sought and (*b*) the means of deriving desired information. In the first of these divisions, the general classes of information include the following:

a. Training, experience, and general background
b. Mental ability and level of intelligence
c. Physical condition, aptitudes, and skills
d. Moral and emotional characteristics and skills
e. Psychological and sociological aspects

Under the second of these divisions, the general groups of means of gathering information include the following:

a. Interviews
b. Tests and examinations
c. Personal observation
d. Application blanks, references, and similar reports
e. Union sources

In the present section the discussion will be restricted to application blanks, references, personal observation, and union sources, inasmuch as the use of tests, examinations, and interviews for collecting desired information is treated more thoroughly in the next few chapters.

a. *The Application.* The application blank is undoubtedly one of the most common tools of selection. It invariably occupies a leading role because information gathered in this manner provides a clue to the need of and a basis for other selective processes. Its design differs widely from company to company, but commonly sought are the following classes of information:

1. Identifying information, such as name, address, telephone number, and social security number.
2. Personal information, such as marital status and dependents.
3. Physical characteristics, such as height, weight, health, defects.
4. Education.
5. Experience, usually through the last three or four employers only.
6. References, personal and business.
7. Miscellaneous remarks and comments.

Details included under the foregoing headings may be noted by a study of the form illustrated in Figure 8–7.

In determining what information is to be asked for on an application blank, it is invariably necessary to reach a compromise between what is wanted and needful and what can be obtained effectively on such a form.

The application blank is seldom used as the sole basis of hiring decisions. Its main usefulness is to provide information for reference checking, good interviewing, and correlation with testing data. Of course, when an applicant discloses a lack of needed training or experience, the application blank may serve to reject him or her.

The design and form of the application blank also deserves mention. On the one hand, it must be designed from the viewpoint of the applicant. In this connection the use of such devices as the following have been found helpful: grouping similar questions in adjacent blocks of space; using "yes" and "no" questions, as well as questions that can be checked off, whenever possible; and using legible print. On the other hand, it must be designed with the company's purpose in mind. It should be relatively easy to handle in the employment office. This calls for consideration of such matters as ease of filing, durability throughout frequent handling, and prominence of the most pertinent information. In addition, it may be desirable to adopt two or more types of blanks so that they will fit the various classes of personnel to be selected—for example, general factory employees, general office employees, and executive and technical employees.

b. Use of References. The use of references is also common to most selection procedures. This practice places reliance upon the evaluation of

FIGURE 8–3
A Sample Reference Form

_____, Social Security No._____,
has applied to us for a position as _____. Applicant claims to
have been in your employ from _____ to_____ . Having
had an opportunity to observe above applicant as an employee, your frank answers
to the questions on the reverse side of this card will be valuable to us, and would
be greatly appreciated. We assure you that your replies will not be revealed to
the applicant, or anyone else, under any circumstances.

(Reverse)

1. When was applicant in your employ? From _____ to _____.
2. Position held: _____
3. Attendance regular? Yes _____ No _____. If not, what was the cause
   of absences?_____
4. Liked by his co-workers (well-liked, acceptable, sometimes criticized)?
   _____
5. Rate of progress slow, average, above average? _____
6. Asked to resign, or resigned voluntarily?_____
7. Would you re-employ for a similar position? Yes _____ No _____
   If not, why?_____
8. In view of your knowledge of applicant's character, ability, and
   dependability, how would you rate him/her as an employee?
   Below average _____ Above average _____ Average _____
9. If you prefer, we will call you on telephone No. _____.

Source: Adapted from C. W. Brooks, "Checking Applicants' References," *Management Review*, vol. XXXVII no. 9, p. 465.

former employers, friends, and professional acquaintances. Inasmuch as most people are reluctant to make reports that may hinder the chances of others, their opinions are not likely to result in accurate appraisals unless carefully controlled. For example, the probability of receiving an accurate appraisal is increased when a personnel officer seeking information knows and has the confidence of the personnel officer whose company has been given as a reference. Such close acquaintances are found in localities in which associations of personnel executives have been formed. Or if a reference form, such as that shown in Figure 8–3, is used which requires specific answers, the chances of getting unbiased references are increased.

The usefulness of references is also dependent upon the speed with which they can be checked. During times when the need for people is great, decisions may have to be made about candidates very quickly. In urgent cases the telephone and the telegraph are employed.

c. Personal Observation. Despite the increased use of various types of formal tests, and despite the high probabilities of error due to personal prejudice or ineffectiveness, personal observation is undoubtedly widely used and weighs heavily in reaching decisions in the selection process. Certainly, interviewing, which essentially is a form of personal observation, has been accorded a higher role in selection since its techniques have been studied more scientifically in recent years.

Indeed, interviewing is such a useful tool that a fuller discussion of it is undertaken in the following chapter. In any event, much useful information can be obtained by talking to and sizing up candidates. It would be unwise to forgo its inclusion in the selection process simply because it can be easily misused. After all, any tool can be mishandled; the moral is that users should be properly trained to use such tools.

d. Union Sources. Information may also be obtained from local union offices regarding the preference to be given candidates. Indeed, in some instances, as noted earlier, the union hall would be the first and perhaps the only source of supply of labor. In such cases the union would sift out the candidates for employment. And it seems probable that as time goes on, the union office is likely to take a greater interest in who among their members is hired, in their competency to hold jobs, and in the company's tests of selection.

2. Interpreting Findings. The next major step in the selection process is to interpret findings and make decisions. Of course, this is a phase of selection that takes place at all stages of the process. Inasmuch as the selection process is also a rejection process, some candidates will fall by the wayside after each step. Some candidates may be rejected before they are even permitted to fill out an application blank, others will be rejected because of information received on the application blank, and still others will not fail until a final survey of all evidence is made.

This task of separating acceptable from nonacceptable candidates is very difficult, particularly in borderline cases and in cases where the candidates succeed in passing the preliminary hurdles. Let us assume that on a test used in connection with a particular job, the minimum passing grade is 75, and that a candidate gets 74. What should be done if personal qualities, as well as training, experience, and references, are satisfactory? The tendency is to accept the candidate in such instances in spite of the test score. But what if the test score is 73 or 72 or 71 or

70? When does the weight of the test outbalance the other factors? Most companies leave this to the personal judgment of the employment officer, or to a higher executive in important cases.

Reports and Records

1. Rejections. As decisions are reached regarding applicants, it is necessary to make out reports and records. These records may be classified according to whether the candidates are rejected, are not hired but

FIGURE 8–4
Acceptance or Rejection Form

```
        NOTICE OF ACCEPTANCE or REJECTION OF APPLICATION FOR EMPLOYMENT


                              Dept.
To SAMUEL MARKUM              Head    PAUL SMITH              Date  10-1        19   7

                  THIS IS TO ADVISE YOU THAT THE APPLICATION OF:

Name  JOHN DOE              Address  1754 South Sixth St.          Phone  297-2046


          Accepted        XXXXXXXXX
Has been          for            Employment.   (If accepted , date starts to work)  10-5-7
          Rejected        Permanent

If Rejected , Give Reasons for Rejection_____


THIS GOES TO FOREMAN AT TIME OF INTERVIEW AND MUST BE COMPLETED AND RETURNED TO
SUPERINTENDENT'S DESK FOR REVIEW.
(This form to be signed and returned
DIRECT to superintendent's desk)
                                        _____Foreman
```

would be desirable employees if vacancies were available, or are hired.

Keeping records of candidates not hired may seem a useless gesture, but it is not necessarily so. In the first place, if considerable study has been made of a candidate who is found unsuitable, records of the case will prevent a restudy if the applicant should later reapply, as sometimes happens. Since microfilming has come into use, such records can be kept in a minimum of space. Figure 8–4 illustrates a record that could be used for rejected candidates. In the second place, a record of reasons for rejection is highly desirable in cases in which a company might be accused of discriminatory or unfair labor practices. This factor grows in importance as rules governing fair employment practices become formalized in state laws and for companies seeking federal contracts.

Practically all companies maintain a file of information on candidates who would make desirable employees if vacancies existed. The usefulness of such a file depends on the economic position of the industrial and business community. In a tight labor market, applications filed by candidates are usually found to be useless as a source of supply unless followed up within a day or two. On the other hand, during recession periods, applications may be a useful source even weeks after being filed.

2. Records of Hired Employees.   As to candidates who are hired, the systems of recording fall into three major groups. First, some companies place all hiring information for each employee in a folder. As time goes on, additional data, such as merit ratings, job and rate changes, educational accomplishments, and disciplinary cases are also placed in the folder.

Second, some companies compile, in addition to the folder, a card

FIGURE 8–5

**Kardex Equipment Makes Personnel Records
Available Quickly at Point of Use**

FIGURE 8–5 (continued)

**Supporting Papers Are Kept in Insulated Files
for Reference when Needed**

Courtesy of Sperry Univac-Remington. (Reproduced by permission)

recapitulating important information in the folder. The card is filed separately from the folder and becomes the working source of information about the employee. Figure 8–5 illustrates such a card system. References to the card can be quickly made without disturbing the detailed materials in the folder.

And third, some companies have turned to data-processing equipment to keep personnel records. In some cases, records are stored in computers into which information is fed as it becomes available and from which it is retrieved as needed. This system is adopted when the number of employees results in voluminous records. Sometimes, tabulating cards, as illustrated in Figure 8–6, are used for this purpose.

Careful planning of personnel records will make it possible to maintain them at minimum expense. It is reported, for example, that in one case the personnel records of 900 employees are kept by one clerk.[1] An-

[1] R. D. McMillen, "Personnel Records," *Factory Management and Maintenance,* vol. CV, no. 6, p. 109.

FIGURE 8–6

A Personnel Tabulating Card

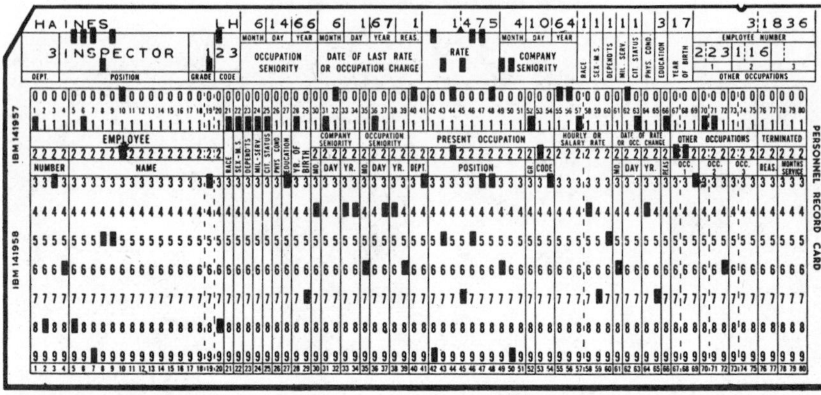

Source: International Business Machines Corporation, *I.B.M. Accounting.*

other interesting example of a personnel record for a smaller company is the multipurpose form illustrated in Figure 8–7. It may be used in the following ways:

a. Application blank (pp. 1 and 2).

b. Interview rating, test record, and reference checkup (p. 3).

c. Basic payroll record (pp. 3 and 4).

d. Medical examination form (p. 4).

e. Record of other personnel data, such as attendance, salary or job changes, and efficiency rating (p. 4).

Induction of New Employee

The final step in the selection process is that of inducting new employees into their new surroundings and placing them on their new jobs. In many companies, this stage of an employee's tenure is handled very superficially. But there is a strong movement in the direction of handling this stage with great care because turnover among new employees is higher than among workers with greater seniority.

The stage of induction should take into account two major aspects: (1) acquainting the new employee with the new surroundings and company rules and regulations, and (2) indoctrination in the "philosophy" of the company and its reasons for existence. More companies build their programs around the first of these aspects than the second.

1. Getting Acquainted.   In acquainting the new employee with the new surroundings and company regulations, practice tends toward giving introductory materials and instructions away from the working center. Either a classroom lecture, a movie, or a group conference is used by a

FIGURE 8-7

A Multipurpose Personnel Form

(Page 1)

FILL IN BOTH SIDES COMPLETELY

EMPLOYMENT APPLICATION

DATE:

NAME: (Last) (First) (Initial.)

SOCIAL SECURITY NO.:

SEX:　　HEIGHT　　WEIGHT

ADDRESS:

TELEPHONE NO.

DATE OF BIRTH:

U. S. CITIZEN: YES ( ) NO ( )　MARRIED ( ) SINGLE ( )　SEPARATED ( ) DIVORCED ( )　WIDOW(ER) ( )

NO OF DEPENDENTS CLAIMED FOR INCOME TAX EXEMPTIONS:

CHILDREN ( )　OTHERS (,　PARENTS ( )

AGES OF CHILDREN:

IF FEMALE AND MARRIED STATE MAIDEN NAME

IF YOU HAVE NO TELEPHONE, THROUGH (Give name WHOM CAN YOU BE LOCATED?　& Tel. No.)

DO YOU OWN YOUR OWN HOME?　YES ( )　NO ( )

DESCRIBE PHYSICAL DEFECTS, IF ANY:

DO YOU HAVE ANY INCOME OTHER THAN WHAT YOU GET FROM WORKING?　YES ( ) NO ( ) IF YES, WHAT?

MILITARY EXPERIENCE: FROM _____ TO _____

BRANCH OF SERVICE

HIGHEST RANK OBTAINED

HONORABLE YES ( ) DISCHARGE: NO ( )

IF IN ACTIVE ( ) RESERVES: INACTIVE ( )

ARE YOU A FORMER EMPLOYEE?　WHEN?

WHY DID YOU LEAVE?

NAMES AND RELATIONSHIP OF RELATIVES WORKING HERE:

MACHINES YOU CAN OPERATE:

POSITION DESIRED:　　SHIFT DESIRED:　　WAGES EXPECTED:

WHEN CAN YOU BEGIN WORK?

RECORD OF EDUCATION

	NAME OF SCHOOL	No. of Years	DID YOU GRADUATE?	DATE YOU LEFT	COURSE	AVERAGE GRADE	DESCRIBE COLLEGE OR OTHER TRAINING:—
GRAMMAR							
HIGH							
TRADE							

RECORD OF PREVIOUS EMPLOYMENT — SHOW PRESENT OR LAST POSITION FIRST

STARTING DATE	NAME AND ADDRESS OF COMPANY:	NAME OF SUPERVISOR	WAGES RECEIVED
LEAVING DATE	TYPE OF WORK DONE:	REASON FOR LEAVING:	
STARTING DATE	NAME AND ADDRESS OF COMPANY:	NAME OF SUPERVISOR	WAGES RECEIVED
LEAVING DATE	TYPE OF WORK DONE:	REASON FOR LEAVING:	
STARTING DATE	NAME AND ADDRESS OF COMPANY:	NAME OF SUPERVISOR	WAGES RECEIVED
LEAVING DATE	TYPE OF WORK DONE:	REASON FOR LEAVING:	

Source: J. S. Kornreich, "Personnel Records for a Small Company," *Personnel*, vol. 29, no. 5, pp. 431–36.

FIGURE 8-7 *(continued)*

(Page 2)

FAMILY INFORMATION (HUSBAND, WIFE, FATHER, MOTHER, BROTHERS AND SISTERS)

RELATIONSHIP TO YOU	PRESENT OR LAST OCCUPATION	CITY WHERE NOW LIVING	RELATIONSHIP TO YOU	PRESENT OR LAST OCCUPATION	CITY WHERE NOW LIVING

HOW LONG HAVE YOU LIVED AT YOUR PRESENT ADDRESS?

IF LESS THAN ONE YEAR, GIVE PREVIOUS ADDRESS:

WHAT TRANSPORTATION WILL YOU USE TO GET TO WORK?

☐ DO
☐ DO NOT OWN AN AUTO

IF YOU OWN AUTO, STATE MAKE AND YEAR:

REFERENCES GIVE THREE REFERENCES WHO KNOW YOU WELL. DO NOT GIVE RELATIVES OR FORMER EMPLOYERS.

1. _____ _____ _____
   (NAME)   (OCCUPATION)   (ADDRESS)

2. _____ _____ _____
   (NAME)   (OCCUPATION)   (ADDRESS)

3. _____ _____ _____
   (NAME)   (OCCUPATION)   (ADDRESS)

GIVE NAMES OF PEOPLE WORKING HERE WHO KNOW YOU VERY WELL:

Additional Remarks and Information
(DESCRIBE OTHER EXPERIENCE, RELATED HOBBIES OR SPECIAL QUALIFICATIONS)

_____

_____

_____

READ CAREFULLY ➤

I UNDERSTAND THAT IF EMPLOYED, FALSE STATEMENTS ON THIS APPLICATION SHALL BE CONSIDERED SUFFICIENT CAUSE FOR DISMISSAL.

_____
(Applicant's Signature)

SIGN HERE ➤

APPLICANT — DO NOT WRITE BELOW THIS LINE

FIGURE 8-7 (continued)

(Page 3)

INVESTIGATION

DATES		DATES	
ATTENDANCE		ATTENDANCE	
WORK RECORD		WORK RECORD	
REASON FOR LEAVING		REASON FOR LEAVING	
REHIRE		REHIRE	

DATES		DATES	
ATTENDANCE		ATTENDANCE	
WORK RECORD		WORK RECORD	
REASON FOR LEAVING		REASON FOR LEAVING	
REHIRE		REHIRE	

TEST SCORES AND INTERPRETATION

PHYSICAL EXAMINATION	DATE
BY DR.	

RESULTS—

INTERVIEWED BY	DATE	GENERAL COMMENT	WORK ATT.:	ALERTNESS:	APPEARANCE:
1.					
2.					
3.					

STARTING DATE:	STARTING POSITION:	DEPT.:	SHIFT OR WORK HOURS:
STARTING WAGE:	AUTOMATIC INCREASE: YES ( ) NO ( ) AMOUNT?	DATE?	APPROVED BY

FIGURE 8-7 (concluded)

(Page 4)

MEDICAL EXAMINATION

DATE

HT.   WT.

GENERAL APPEARANCE:

EYES: (R.

  (L.

EARS: HEARS WATCH   (R.

  (L.

NOSE

THROAT

TONGUE

TEETH

NECK

CHEST CONTOUR

HEART

PULSE

BLOOD PRESSURE

LUNGS

ABDOMEN

EXTREM. (U.

  (L.

ING. REG.

PAST MEDICAL HISTORY

G. U.

URINE

SPINE

SKIN

NOTES:

SIGNED: DR.

PERSONNEL RECORD (Attendance, Salary or Job Changes, Efficiency Rating, Awards, etc.)

DATE	ACTION	EXPLANATION	DATE	ACTION	EXPLANATION

member of the personnel department. In any event, such subjects as the following are covered:

a. Company history, products, and major operations.
b. General company policies and regulations.
c. Relation of supervisors and personnel department.
d. Rules and regulations regarding:
   (1) Wages and wage payment.
   (2) Hours of work and overtime.
   (3) Safety and accidents.
   (4) Holidays and vacations.
   (5) Methods of reporting tardiness and absences.
   (6) Discipline and grievances.
   (7) Uniforms and clothing.
   (8) Parking.
   (9) Badges and parcels.
e. Economic and recreational services available:
   (1) Insurance plans.
   (2) Pensions.
   (3) Athletic and social activities.
f. Opportunities:
   (1) Promotion and transfer.
   (2) Job stabilization.
   (3) Suggestion systems.

It is ordinarily not expected that much of the foregoing will be remembered, but this preliminary step does serve to prove that the company is taking a sincere interest in getting the inductee off to a good start. Moreover, booklets and pamphlets may be supplied which provide a permanent record of the materials that have been seen and heard.

After preliminary sessions in the personnel department, new employees are conducted to their working center. At one time employees were given oral instructions and left to find their own way, and some companies still use this system. Better practice, however, is to have either a representative of the personnel department act as a guide or someone from the operating department come over and take the new employee in hand.

Upon arriving at the assigned department, the inductee is introduced to the supervisor and fellow workers. The supervisor or a key employee then instructs the employee on such matters as to how to ring in and out, where the lockers are, departmental rules, and how the job is to be done. It is better practice to have the supervisor handle this phase of induction to personally prove at a critical time management's desire to build a friendly and helpful relationship.

After an employee has been placed on the job, good induction practice also involves periodic follow-up. Either by reports or, better, by personal visits from the supervisor or a representative of the personnel department, the status of the new employee is ascertained after a couple of periods of 30 or 60 days. This serves to check whether the employee has been properly placed, whether the promises the company made have been kept, and whether any problems have arisen that require attention.

2. Indoctrination. The induction stage provides an excellent opportunity to develop favorable attitudes of new employees toward their new employment and surroundings. Hence, more and more companies are taking advantage of this opportunity to sell their philosophies, the whys and wherefores of private enterprise, the advantages of the capitalistic system, the need for productivity, and the reasons why the firm operates as it does. This approach to induction should be taken by both the personnel department and the line supervisors.

Perhaps the essence of indoctrination is to convince the employee that what is good for the company is also good for the employee. If the company honestly practices this philosophy, indoctrination is not to be criticized. If the approach is concerned, however, only with the best interests of the employer, the indoctrination is built on sand. Indoctrination based on mutual self-interest, moreover, must be a continuous process, beginning when a person is hired and persisting throughout the relationship.

QUESTIONS

1. What is the relation of a selection procedure to selection functions?
2. In what order should a company place the various hurdles (functions) included in its selection procedure and how high (difficult) should they be?
3. Who should have authority for performing the various parts of a selection procedure?
4. How does one go about determining if one's selection procedure is a good one?
5. By what methods are the various classes of information sought from candidates obtained?
6. In what ways is the application blank most useful in screening candidates?
7. How can the level of confidence in reference letters be increased?
8. Why is it desirable to retain records of candidates not hired?
9. Why is the induction of new employees a matter of significant importance?
10. Upon what grounds can indoctrination of new employees be justified?

CASE 8-1.   EMPLOYEE MOBILITY

Among the questions on the application blank of the MultiCountry Company is, *Are you free to move?* Bill Jones, just out of college and anxious for some action, answered, *"Yes, exclamation mark, period."* Later when he was invited to company headquarters for additional conversations, he began to note some curious reactions from some of the people who interviewed him.

One of those who interviewed him, asked, "Is your wife enthusiastic about foreign assignments? And what about your children?" Bill replied, "I haven't any of either yet." The interviewer smiled quietly and went on to another subject.

Another interviewer asked Bill what cities abroad he liked and which ones he disliked. But Bill could not say because he hadn't been abroad. And he mentioned that travel pictures he saw had not indicated enough about them to give him a good clue.

A third interviewer asked about the particular features of travel in American cities that impressed him. All Bill could think of was the common-place comment that one meets interesting people.

As he later reviewed these examples of his answers to the particular questions, he realized that although he might be free and desirous to travel, he didn't know (1) if a future family would, (2) why he might like or be willing to put up with some of the rigors of travel, and (3) why the company and its executives asked the questions and what they hoped to get out of the answers.

Question

1. Of what use might the questions really be to the company and to the interviewee?

CASE 8–2. INDUCTION PROCEDURES

This is a report on the induction procedures used in a job-order foundry employing from 150 to 200 people.

Originally, new employees were inducted as follows: Upon completion of the hiring process the employee was escorted from the employment office to the foundry by an office messenger. Entering the foundry, the new worker was taken directly to the superintendent's office, whereupon the messenger presented the superintendent or superintendent's assistant with a slip of paper bearing the employee's name, age, home address, telephone number, and previous foundry experience, if any. There was no other introduction.

The superintendent or assistant would then briefly explain that the policy was to have new employees work their first week in the grinding and inspection department, where the products of the foundry were given the finishing touches and inspected. The new employee was then escorted to grinding and inspection; on the way the superintendent would make some such comment as this, "You will find your time card in that rack over there," and point in the general direction of the foundry time clock.

In the grinding room the new employee was put to work with other people loading and unloading rough castings into large drums which rotated, in order to grind off sharp edges and to detect any flaws in the castings.

The second week the inductee was returned to the superintendent's office and assigned to the supervisor in charge of the type of work for which he or she was hired, or wherever there was a need. The supervisor usually assigned a new person as an assistant to one of the older workers for the purpose of learning the job. This was particularly true in the case of molders and sandcutters.

The above is a complete and accurate account of the induction procedure used by this company for several years.

A new personnel director, fresh out of college and inexperienced, arrived on the scene and took immediate steps to correct the method of inducting new employees. A brief resumé of the number of grievances, and the fact that 50 percent of all employees leaving did so during the first three months of their employment, indicated something was wrong with the original breaking-in process.

The personnel director installed the following induction procedure:

1. Each new employee is presented with a small handbook containing the rules and regulations of the company. Sufficient time is taken to elaborate on some of the more important rules, thus eliminating the possibility of some of the misunderstandings which frequently result in grievances.
2. A 15-minute film is shown on the production process as well as how the product is used and distributed. The counselor is careful to emphasize certain key points of the film and at the same time attempts to instill a certain feeling of confidence in the company product. Generally speaking, most workers want to be a part of a good production team.
3. The pay scale and promotional possibilities are discussed in detail. New employees are assured that promotion is possible, providing of course, that they produce satisfactorily in accordance with established standards. This gives new workers something to look forward to and constitutes somewhat of a challenge to them.
4. Sufficient time is taken to show and explain the following facilities:

    a. Location of time clocks and how to ring in and out properly
    b. Location of rest rooms, showers and lockers
    c. Location of facilities for eating lunch (most of the employees carry their lunch)
    d. Location and use of the employee parking lot
    e. Location of the first-aid room

f. Recreational activities, which include company-sponsored softball and basketball teams, and a picnic each year

5. At the conclusion of the orientation, each employee is invited to come back to the personnel office to discuss and talk over any problems pertaining to work or personal matters relative to housing, transportation, medical problems, and so on. The personnel director feels that this procedure is essential to good morale, since it instills a feeling of security in the new worker.

6. The personnel director or an assistant personally escorts each new person to the foundry superintendent's office and makes a proper introduction. This is a prime prerequisite for getting the work relationship off on the right foot.

Questions

1. Under what conditions might the casual induction procedure as originally employed have been effective?
2. Do you think the new procedure is more effective? Why?
3. In what ways might the new procedure of induction be made more effective?

CHAPTER 9

INTERVIEWING AND COUNSELING

The Role of Interviewing and Counseling

The interview is one of the most commonly used methods of seeking information from job applicants. It is a face-to-face, oral, observational, and personal appraisal method. Usually, it is more than a means of getting information. It also involves giving (1) information that will help the applicant decide about the company and (2) advice that may serve to change the mental or emotional attitude of the interviewee.

Interviewing and counseling are taken up at this point because they are useful in hiring. These techniques are also important in connection with grievances, disciplinary action, vocational guidance, employees being separated from the payroll, employees with personal problems, transfers and promotions, and training sessions.

Good interviewing is not easily achieved. It must be based upon sound rules and applied by skilled personnel. How this may be done can be seen by examining the following aspects of the subject:

1. Purposes.
2. Types.
3. Technical factors.
4. Procedures
5. Rules.

Purposes

As already noted, interviewing has uses in a variety of personnel areas. It is desirable, therefore, to note what purposes interviewing is

144

intended to serve in the important areas of employment, training, human relations, and labor relations.

1. Employment. Viewing employment in the broadest sense, interviewing has a contribution to make in selecting, testing, inducting, placing, transferring, and terminating employees.

Interviewing has been a widely used tool in selection. The employer, by means of talk and observation, seeks to determine the degree to which the applicant possesses desired qualities and to appraise the applicant's mental, physical, emotional, and social qualities—potential or developed. Thus, the primary purpose is to select the candidate who will best advance the business' objectives.

But the interview is not all one-sided. The applicant usually hopes for more than a job—but for a good job. So the employer in the interview must also serve the purposes of the applicant by giving information and conveying an attitude that will help the applicant decide whether or not to accept a job if it is offered. The selection process is therefore a rejection process by the candidate as well as the employer. And it is far better for an applicant to turn down an offer that would result in an unsatisfactory situation in the long run even though there may be short-run advantages.

A particularly critical area of interviewing is that concerned with counseling those who have taken psychological tests. Candidates tend to be tense yet curious about tests and testing results. When a battery of tests has been given, it is best to discuss interests of candidates first; discussion of this aspect seldom implies any threat to the candidate. Then it is wise to move to ability and aptitude scores. Here care must be taken to point out the relevance of these scores to particular jobs without implying that the candidate has scored too high or too low. Lastly, personality scores should be taken up; the candidate can be led to use these scores as a basis for self evaluation of the testing process.

Turning now to induction, the interview both in the personnel department and by the supervisor is a desirable way to give the new employee information on company objectives, policies, procedures, and details pertinent to the position. But perhaps more important is the opportunity to communicate an attitude of friendliness toward and interest in the inductee. For this purpose, the interview is a particularly effective tool.

Similarly, interviewing has a real contribution to make when employees are placed on a job, transferred, or promoted. Well-planned interviews can serve to impress employees with the opportunities of the job, to compliment them on the reasons why they were selected, to indicate dangers to be avoided, and to suggest avenues of advancement. Placement is a particularly favorable occasion for talk and discussion. A person is at a stage of achievement and also in a mood to receive a message.

But employees also leave their jobs. An exit interview can serve to determine why the separation is taking place. Discussions may point to some shortcomings on the part of the company or sources of irritation to employees. Such interviews are helpful to the company in indicating what it needs to do to increase its effectiveness in dealing with the labor factor. They are helpful to the employees who remain because of the improvements which follow. And they may be helpful to the departing employee who (a) may stay on after a constructive interview and (b) may clarify his own thinking and improve his behavior on future jobs.

2. Training. The interview is a very useful tool in training. In such instances, it sometimes goes under the name of "coaching." The interviewer or coach seeks to transmit "know-how" and "know-why" by talk, example, and demonstration. Coaching has very desirable features. It can put a person at ease, reduce tensions, and thereby release the powers within to perform at optimum level. Mistakes can be readily corrected, answers quickly provided, and assurances of good progress immediately given.

The interview is obviously a good training tool. But far more than that, it can serve to develop loyalty toward management. The employee who has been coached toward success will unconsciously if not openly cooperate with the person who gave needed help. Hence, if an executive is serious about gaining the confidence and respect of subordinates, there are few ways that will pay higher dividends than training, and few tools of training that are better than personal coaching.

An interesting example of interviewing as a training device (and also for selection) is the "stress-type" interview. Here, candidates are exposed to a variety of difficulties, obstacles, embarrassments, rudeness, and accusations. Then they are evaluated on how well they handled themselves under these circumstances or how long it took before they broke under them. Obviously, such interviewing would be justifiable only where the job specification called for qualities to meet highly unusual and severe stresses and strains.

3. Human Relations. Using the term *human relations* in the more restricted sense of encompassing personal problems and difficulties, interviewing has a particularly useful sphere of application. In this connection, interviewing often goes by the name of counseling. The intent is to help employees help themselves in solving problems with which they are perplexed, or simply to provide an environment in which unsolvable problems can be borne with some grace and courage.

The problem areas may be company- or noncompany-caused, as illustrated by such cases as the following: An employee is having marital difficulties; has lost a loved one; is not making satisfactory job progress; is drinking excessively; cannot seem to get along with the superior; or is frustrated or bored. No matter what the source, the problems obviously will affect the employee on the job. For that reason, some companies try to be helpful no matter what the source. Other companies restrict their attention to company business.

In either event, counseling may be helpful in a number of ways. For example, an appraisal interview can be useful to subordinates who wonder why they are not making satisfactory job progress. They can thereby be shown strong and weak points and what must be done to gain favorable consideration for promotions. Or counseling may help a person find the sources of personal difficulties. Suggesting a person to quit excessive drinking, for example, is seldom effective. But counseling may be helpful in uncovering the reason for drinking; then the employee can make a logical attack upon the problem and not feel like a hopeless case.

4. Labor Relations. Interviewing is an invaluable tool of disciplinary action, grievance handling, and relations with unions. These phases will be examined more fully in later chapters. Worthy of note in passing, however, is the point that labor relations sometimes involve deviations from desired practice or differences of opinion. In disciplinary action, for example, an employee has departed from a desired course; in grievances the company has not confirmed the expectations of employees; and in collective bargaining, there are differences regarding standards of wages, hours, or working conditions which should be maintained.

The contributions of interviewing in such instances may be fourfold. First, good interviewing can help to determine the truth: i.e., to what extent the employee or the company was in error and what fair wages, hours, and working conditions are. Second, interviewing can serve as a platform from which to convey the good and honorable intentions of management and, for that matter, of the other parties concerned. Third, interviewing can help management to learn directly the attitudes, reactions, and viewpoints of its employees and of the representatives of its employees. And finally, interviewing can disclose the areas of personnel management regarding which the skills of executives need improvement and increased attention.

Types of Interviewing

The attainment of the foregoing purposes may be sought by any of a number of types of interviewing. In actual practice, there are undoubtedly as many types of interviewing as there are interviewers. By and large, much interviewing has been unplanned and unskilled. In such cases the interviewer may have some notion of the information desired or the purpose meant to be accomplished. Beyond that, reliance upon spur-of-the-moment questions or insight may guide the actual interview. Such practices are not very successful, nor do they serve to contribute to a student's understanding of good principles and practices of interviewing. Much more can be learned from study of the following methods:

1. Planned interview.
2. Nondirective interview.
3. Depth interview.
4. Group interview.

   1. Planned Interviews. Many interviewers have improved themselves by following definite plans of action. Before entering into the actual interview, they work out in their minds, if not on paper, what they hope to accomplish, what kinds of information they are to seek or give, how they will conduct the interview, and how much time they will allot to it. During the interview, deviations from the plan may be made; but when the interviewers deviate, they do so with knowledge of what they are doing and how far off they are from the intended track. Although there is some formality about such a plan, flexibility is one of its major advantages.

   A more formalized type of planning is that illustrated by the patterned interview. It is based on the assumption that to be most effective, every pertinent detail must be worked out in advance. And equally important, the interviewer must be skilled—not necessarily a trained psychologist, but able to cultivate the uncommon faculties of common sense and interpretative ability.

   A set of specific questions is used in patterned interviewing. These are prepared from three sources. First, job and employee specifications provide a guide to important questions. Second, information that may be derived from application forms and references provides a clue to what should be asked. And third, experience with past interviews will indicate useful types of questions. The result is a formal list, such as the excerpt illustrated in Figure 9–1.

   Thus the formal list of questions is but a device to aid the memory of the interviewer. He or she follows through a check list and devises additional questions to amplify knowledge of the candidate wherever needed. This is the point at which the psychological skill of the interviewer comes into play. As information is gathered from the candidate, it must be interpreted in the light of the interviewer's understanding of normal standards of human behavior and attainments. Finding from questions on recreation habits, for example, that a given candidate seems immature for the job in question, the interviewer will be more vigilant when other classes of questions are asked, in order to ascertain whether or not the clue to immaturity is substantiated.

   2. The Nondirective Interview. In recent years, some interest has been shown in the nondirective interview. As its name implies, applicants in

FIGURE 9–1

Excerpt from Patterned Interview Form

DOMESTIC AND SOCIAL SITUATION

Married	Single	Widowed	Divorced	Separated	Date of marriage		Is couple compatible?

Living with spouse? Yes No (If no) Specify _____ Dependents: Number _____

Ages _____ What plans do you have for your children?
Do dependents provide adequate motivation?

What difficulties or serious arguments have you had with your spouse?
Financial? Social? Personal?

Have you been married previously? Yes No (If yes) How many times?

When and what was the reason for end of marriage or marriages? Death Divorce

Separation _____ (Unless death) What were the reasons?

Do domestic difficulties indicate immaturity?

What do you do for recreation? _____ What hobbies do you have?
Does recreation show maturity? Will hobbies help work?

To what extent do you and your spouse entertain?
Does applicant seem socially well-adjusted?

When did you last drink intoxicating liquor? _____ To what extent? _____ (Doesn't drink)
Is this sensible drinking?

What types of people do you actively dislike?
Is applicant biased?

Source: Adapted from Robert N. McMurray, "Validating the Patterned Interview," *Personnel*, vol. XXIV, no. 6, p. 266.

such an interview are not directed by questions or comments as to what they should talk about. While the interviewer may intersperse brief phrases, these should be noncommittal, so that a candidate determines the trend of conversation.

The theory of such interviews is that a candidate is thus more likely to reveal his true self than when answering set questions. With set questions, the candidate tends to respond as the interviewer seems to want, or with favorable answers, whether they are true or not. But in the nondirective approach the candidate obviously does not know how to slant replies or commentary. Unstructured talking will reveal much about goals, interests, and competency by what is revealed as well as what is excluded.

As in the case of the patterned interview, a major step of the nondirective technique is to study the requirements of the job to be filled and then learn as much as possible about the candidate from such sources as the application blank, reference letters, and tests. From such studies the interviewer ascertains what to listen for while the candidate is talking.

Such interviews are started by putting candidates at ease by the usual introductions, courtesies, and idle talk. Then candidates are requested by an appropriate statement or opening question to talk about their personal history. After a candidate starts talking, the interviewer must, without leading, keep the candidate talking. Particularly effective in this connection is the use of questions which merely repeat what the candidate says. For example, a candidate might say, "I like to work on challenging jobs." For the interviewer to ask "why?" would tend to be a leading question, so the query might be, "So you like challenging jobs?" Then the candidate must go on without a guiding hint.

The task of the nondirective interview is to determine what kind of person the candidate really is. The interviewer must be skilled in measuring the story the candidate tells against the normal standards of human behavior, attitudes, and attainments. In terms of how the candidate conducts himself, from his disclosures of training and experience, and from his statements on recreational and social activities, the interviewer must appraise the candidate's qualifications to fill the job in question.

3. The Depth Interview.   Although not strictly a distinct type, the depth interview is worthy of special note. It is used to go into considerable detail on particular subjects of an important nature, the idea being that intensive examination of a candidate's background and thinking is indispensable for correct evaluations and decisions.

As a case in point, assume that one candidate for employment has noted that one of his hobbies is sailing. In the common types of interviewing, this subject will not be pursued much further, if at all; the interviewer will undoubtedly reach a conclusion based on his stereotype of amateur sailors. In a depth interview, however, the subject might be chosen for exhaustive analysis. The interviewee would be asked when he got into sailing, and why; where he sails, and why; with whom he sails, and why; how often he sails, and why; how much time and money he invests in his hobby, and why; what types of equipment he owns and prefers, and why; in what kinds of weather he prefers to sail, and why; and what kinds of friends he selects for his crew, and why. The emphasis is upon the "why," and, if possible, the why of the why. Of course, the questions are not asked crudely and belligerently. Finesse is called for. Only through such exhaustive analysis and questioning can one get a truer picture of the interviewee.

4. The Group Interview. An interesting departure is to interview groups rather than individuals. This may be done either by having one or more executives question a group of candidates or by having a group of executives observe a number of candidates talking over some assigned questions or problems. Such an approach has two major advantages. First, the time of busy executives is conserved because all candidates are interviewed at one time. And second, it is possible to get a better picture of candidates when they have to react to and against each other.

Technical Factors

The effectiveness of any type of interviewing is basically dependent upon the skill with which certain factors common to all interviewing are utilized. These factors are language, the senses, and mechanical aids.

1. Language. Interviewing takes place largely through the use of words. Words are representatives of ideas, thoughts, and feelings; they are not the actual ideas, thoughts, and feelings. Unfortunately, words are not precise and universally accepted representatives. Hence a given word such as *union* does not mean, signify, or denote the same thing to every user. Indeed, to a top executive, it might denote a dastardly conspiracy; while to a worker, it might connote a bond of security and friendship.

Good interviewers do not, therefore, take it for granted that their ideas will be conveyed to another simply because they choose words which have a given meaning to them. They become instead a student of the meaning of words. They know that words not only have sounds— phonetics—but also, as noted in an earlier chapter, shades of meaning —semantics. They thereby learn to avoid words which are likely to arouse needless antagonism and doubt, and to select words which are likely to convey thoughts precisely and with a favorable reaction.

Appropriate selection of words thus helps to clarify exchanges between interviewer and interviewee, and serves to minimize undesirable reactions. But going further, appropriate usage of language can avoid embarrassment and mistakes, and can lead conversations along desired channels. On the one hand, words whose meanings are not known to the listener should be avoided. If polysyllabic verbiage which the interviewee does not understand is used, seldom, if ever, will the candidate reveal ignorance; so the exchange of information is not achieved as desired by both parties. And on the other hand, the interviewer who can ask suggestive questions, use descriptive terms, and draw clear word pictures will get fuller answers. This will reduce the number of "yes-no" answers, and particularly answers which the interviewee thinks the interviewer wants to hear.

2. The Senses.   The interviewer must use human senses to good advantage, especially those of sight and hearing. By careful practice, the interviewer can improve observational skills and can note the behavioral patterns of the interviewee. What mannerisms or expressive movements are exhibited, such as excessive hand movements, ear pulling, and nervous jerking? How is physical posture controlled during the interview? Do face and eyes show unusual changes as questions become more intensive or border on the personal or embarrassing? Are there evidences on the clothing or hands of poor personal habits or lack of cleanliness? Observation of such items will provide some clues as to how a person acts.

Hearing, too, is deserving of special attention. Most people believe they are good listeners, but that is far from the truth. Only through conscious practice can one become a good listener. In the first place, there is a psychological barrier that must be circumvented. People can generally receive (listen) about four to five times as fast as they can send (talk). It is hard, therefore, to concentrate attention under such circumstances. In the second place, good listeners must listen, must avoid talk until the time is ripe for it. They should restrain the desire to talk that almost everyone has. They do not argue, interrupt, or disapprove without due cause. In the third place, good listeners listen with sincerity, interest, and apparent attention. They get involved in the problem, exercises their minds in grasping the ideas being expressed, and apply their logical faculties to the case at hand. And in the fourth place, good listeners, through behavior and expressions, convey to interviewees undivided concern for what is being said.

3. Mechanical Aids.   The efficacy of interviewing is also being raised by the use of mechanical aids. Recorders of various types are being used to obtain transcriptions of interviews. The record can be replayed as often as needed to verify and evaluate the information so obtained. In a few instances, movies have been taken, so that a visual record is also obtained. Of interest as an observational aid is the use of window glass which is unidirectional. A number of people can observe an interview without themselves being seen. If a hidden microphone is used, the observers can also hear the conversations.

It would not be amiss to note the contribution of surroundings to good interviewing. An appropriately equipped room which is private is very desirable. This may seem to contradict what was said in the foregoing paragraph about recordings and hidden observers. In some instances, it may be defensible and useful to refrain from telling interviewees about hidden observers. But in most cases, they should be informed of the reasons for their use, and permission for their use should be obtained.

Procedures of Interviewing

From what has been said thus far, it can be seen that interviewing involves (1) establishment of the purposes of interviewing; (2) design of a plan to gather, record, and analyze information and reach conclusions thereupon; and (3) development of skillful interviewers. Enough has been said on the first of these points. Attention is now directed to the second and third points.

1. Gathering and Interpreting Information. Interviewing, to be well done, must be viewed as more than a simple incident of talk and listen. It should consist of a sequence of events, thought processes, and awareness. This is well-illustrated in Figure 9–2. Here it is seen that a sequence of stages is followed in a well-designed procedure. At each stage, the interviewer listens to and observes the interviewee; is cognizant of making tentative decisions; is aware of the actions to be taken at various stages depending upon how the interviewee is revealed; and is careful to keep appropriate notes and good records. Through such a total-concept of interviewing, this task can be undertaken most effectively.

Since interviewing is such a complex technique, information may be easily forgotten or distorted with the passage of time unless recorded. Some companies use sound recordings for this purpose but the far greater number employ the written word to preserve pertinent data and findings. In addition to what the interviewee reveals, such records should show specific interpretations, evaluations, and recommendations.

The final test of interviewing and counseling is, of course, whether or not they achieve established goals satisfactorily. It may be noted that interviewing was once considered to be an unreliable tool of selection; and to this day it remains so when performed in an unplanned manner by unskilled executives. But skillful practitioners are in general agreement that rating of prospective employees by interviewing correlates very closely with ultimate success on the job. This suggests interviewing procedures and the judgments derived therefrom must be tested against the ultimate performance of candidates on the job.

2. Developing Skillful Interviewers. It has already been noted that an important element in interviewing is the skill of the interviewer. This suggests the need for careful selection and training of interviewers.

FIGURE 9–2
Recruiting Interviewing Procedure

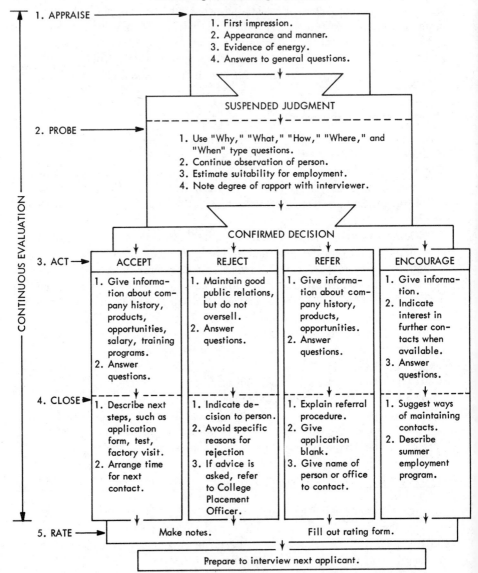

CONTINUOUS EVALUATION

1. APPRAISE
1. First impression.
2. Appearance and manner.
3. Evidence of energy.
4. Answers to general questions.

SUSPENDED JUDGMENT

2. PROBE
1. Use "Why," "What," "How," "Where," and "When" type questions.
2. Continue observation of person.
3. Estimate suitability for employment.
4. Note degree of rapport with interviewer.

CONFIRMED DECISION

3. ACT

ACCEPT	REJECT	REFER	ENCOURAGE
1. Give information about company history, products, opportunities, salary, training programs. 2. Answer questions.	1. Maintain good public relations, but do not oversell. 2. Answer questions.	1. Give information about company history, products, opportunities. 2. Answer questions.	1. Give information. 2. Indicate interest in further contacts when available. 3. Answer questions.

4. CLOSE

1. Describe next steps, such as application form, test, factory visit. 2. Arrange time for next contact.	1. Indicate decision to person. 2. Avoid specific reasons for rejection 3. If advice is asked, refer to College Placement Officer.	1. Explain referral procedure. 2. Give application blank. 3. Give name of person or office to contact.	1. Suggest ways of maintaining contacts. 2. Describe summer employment program.

5. RATE   Make notes.   Fill out rating form.

Prepare to interview next applicant.

Courtesy Richard S. Uhrbrock, Procter & Gamble Co. (Adapted)

In selecting interviewers, practice varies considerably. Some companies select for such work only those who are college trained in psychology and psychiatry. Others place emphasis upon mature experience in the type of work for which people are going to be interviewed. But allowing for variations, a list of qualifications would include the following:

a. A suitable background of experience similar to that of those who are to be interviewed

b. Maturity of action and viewpoint, so that the others unconsciously tend to assume an attitude of confidence and cooperation

c. Experience and training in sizing up people from their behavior and actions (as opposed to mere physical build or appearance)

d. A combination of an objective viewpoint and an appreciation of human feelings and attitude

e. Good judgment, so that the "chaff may be separated from the wheat" during the interview, and so that the proper weight is assigned to information obtained from the interview in relation to other sources of information

f. An ability to work through organizational channels with supervisors and other executives

g. An ability to plan the work of interviewing and to see the total as well as individual implications

Individuals with such capacities or potentials for their development are not too difficult to find in most companies. Usually, the main thing to be done is to train available talent properly. A review of such training programs is therefore in order.

The practices of training interviewers and counselors are varied. Some companies use the conference method to conduct training sessions. Others give trainees the opportunity to attend evening courses at local colleges. Some prepare instruction manuals which cover such points as factors common to all interviews, subjects to be covered during interviews, how to conduct follow-up interviews, and how to counsel employees. Interviewers have also been helped by giving them first-hand experience in various shop and office departments.

In one company the training given interviewers consists of ten lessons which cover such materials as the following:

1. Preparation for conducting practice interviews.
2. Conducting practice interviews.
3. Recording, interpreting, and evaluating one's findings.
4. Closing the interview with a candidate.

In addition, trainees study plant operating departments and write job specifications. Later, follow-up training is given interviewers as specific cases and needs require. Another good training device is a check list, which may be used by the interviewer to review personal methods.

Rules of Interviewing

This discussion can best be closed by summarizing a number of rules of good interviewing. They have been developed largely by trial and error, although it is encouraging to note that research is beginning to make contributions. Adoption of these rules does not provide an unfailing high road to successful interviewing but serves to increase the probability of a useful exchange of information or views. Nor does a mere listing provide automatic success; they must be practiced in order to assure proficiency.

1. Perhaps the basic rule of interviewing is to respect the interests and individuality of the interviewee. Unless one conveys a sympathetic understanding of the other person's point of view and desires, it is difficult to develop feelings of confidence and empathy, which are essential to getting or giving information. On the one hand, one should be sensitive to the ideas and feelings of others. And on the other hand, one should not underestimate the intelligence of employees, display an attitude of superiority, or use trick questions.

2. It is also of high importance in interviewing to preestablish clearly the objectives to be gained or purposes to be served by interviews. Until this is done, it is impossible either to plan an interview effectively or to act convincingly during one. A practical difficulty, however, is that many interviews must be conducted on the spur of the moment. The pressure of other jobs may make it impossible to schedule interviews so that allowances may be made for preplanning time. This excuse should seldom be used in employment interviewing, but lack of time often affects the interviewing that takes place between executives at various levels and their subordinates.

3. There is no principle of interviewing that has been more frequently stated—and deservedly so—than that of making the interviewee feel at ease. To this end, the interviewer must act and be relaxed and at ease too. Any failure in this respect, particularly where grievances or disciplinary action are concerned, results in an atmosphere of tension and belligerence unconducive to a free exchange of ideas. In the employment interview, too, the feeling of newness that obstructs the interview must be reduced by placing the interviewee at ease. As good a way as any to attain a relaxed discussion is to start slowly with some topic known to both parties. No matter how busy the interviewer is, the impression at the outset should be that sufficient time for an unhurried discussion is available. When time is short, it is preferable to postpone the interview.

4. Another principle of good interviewing is to allow—indeed, to encourage—the interviewee to talk copiously. In the case of grievances, for example, this practice serves not only to draw out the whole complaint but also to cool off the aggrieved party. Only by encouraging a full discussion is it possible to lead the interviewee to unburden to the point that nothing important or relevant is left unsaid. Fifteen- or twenty-minute interviews, for example, scarcely allow ample opportunity for full expression. Indeed, hours are to be preferred.

5. An important suggestion to the interviewer is to be a close student

of the meaning of words, i.e., of the field of semantics: Know what meaning an applicant gives to such words as *capitalism, profits, rights,* and *merit:* guard against using words that might arouse unnecessary antagonism or reservations, such as *low intelligence, boss, governmental interference,* or *psychoneurosis:* and although it is very difficult to do, try to ascertain how words used by a particular individual may be colored by past working experiences or charged with the emotionalism of personal experiences.

6. The interviewer should avoid personal views and opinions unless they are of significance to the interviewee or until the latter has had sufficient opportunity to talk. Even though keeping quiet is difficult, developing this virtue is a must. Moreover, after deciding what is to be done, the interview should not end abruptly but should be closed diplomatically, so that the interviewee feels satisfied that a full hearing has been accorded. In the case of a job refusal, for example, the applicant may otherwise feel that the decision was hasty or based on an incomplete picture of the facts. Or in the case of a grievance, the interviewee may gain the impression that the company was prejudiced from the start.

7. In concluding an interview, the interviewer should know how to draw it to a close and should be prepared to state views or decisions clearly and concisely and, if possible, conclusively. A final and positive answer need not be made; but if such an answer is possible, so much the better. If an answer cannot be given with finality, it is a good rule to indicate what other steps are to be taken, and why. In addition, a definite time schedule for a decision or another meeting should be set. In this way the interviewee is more likely to feel that the interviewer is capably and reasonably seeking a fair solution.

8. Physical conditions and layout should be selected that are suitable to the purposes of the interview. Insofar as practicable, quiet and secluded (out-of-hearing, if not out-of-sight) surroundings should be available. Few interviewees, whether looking for a job, airing a grievance, or being rebuked, want to be overheard by others. Most of us like to have others hold the opinion that we are accepted members of the group; an open interview may give evidence to the contrary. An unobtrusive location also makes it possible for the interview to proceed without interruption and with a minimum of distracting influences.

9. It is well to note that the use of interviews should be considered part of an effective and economical plan of exchanging information. For example, where or how should the following type of question be posed: "What financial obligations do you have?" The matter raised is of such a personal nature, however, that it is likely to prove less embarrassing to a candidate if it is asked during an interview when the reason for asking it can be given.

Some go so far as to say that interviews should be used to gather personal and qualitative information, whereas other devices, such as application blanks and tests, should be used to secure objective or quantitative information. This suggestion has some merit, although it is often difficult to draw a clear boundary line between qualitative and quantitative information. Perhaps a more practical rule to follow is to gather as much factual and biographical data as possible on the application blank and then follow up in the interview with detailed questions on those subjects which appear, in a particular case, to have potentialities for adding useful clues. Thus, in nine cases out of ten, there may be no reason for following up the answers that applicants give regarding hobbies, let us say; but occasionally, the listing may provide a basis for further personal questioning.

QUESTIONS

1. For what purposes may interviews be used?
2. In the case of an interview given in connection with a battery of psychological tests, in what order is it preferable to discuss the test results?
3. In what ways may interviewing prove useful in connection with various aspects of labor relations?
4. How much use would you make in business of the nondirective and the depth types of interviewing?
5. Why must the interviewer be a student of semantics?
6. How can the effectiveness of interviewing be measured?
7. What qualities should an interviewer possess?
8. How can the average executive find time to give employees unhurried interviews?
9. By what ways may an interviewer draw an interview to a close gracefully, yet conclusively?
10. What types of questions is it better to ask in an interview than on an application blank?

CASE 9–1.   STATUS OF EMPLOYEES

The Elite Airline has recently placed in service a new large-type plane that is to be its "blue ribbon" plane. To handle the maintenance, repair, and servicing of these planes, a select group of service mechanics have had to be trained. As it turned out these selectees soon acquired an informal higher status. Those who worked on the older types of aircraft felt a lowering in prestige. The publicity with which the airline advertised the superiority of its new service also rubbed off favorably on the select mechanics.

Were this all, there might have been little to worry about. But a check of records showed that absenteeism, tardiness, and petty grievances had increased among the old-plane mechanics. And supervisors comments showed that cooperation and friendliness among the two groups of mechanics had decreased. Although all mechanics were on the same wage scale system, an informal feeling existed among the non-select group that the select group of mechanics seemed to gain available advantages and privileges faster.

Management felt that the problem was minor yet something ought to be done about it. It was concluded that the basic cause of these problems was the status which accrued to the select mechanics and the subsequent decrease in prestige of the other group. Moreover, management felt that motivation was the best possible cure.

Questions

1. Assume that management is right about motivation, what motivational plan would you suggest?
2. Do you believe some other plan would work better?

CASE 9–2. AN INEFFECTIVE EMPLOYEE

Ed Smith had been employed in four different departments in seven months. In none of them did he get a rating of better than "fair." Yet, according to his tests and interviews during hiring, the personnel director thought Ed should have done much better.

Now, Mr. O. L. Wade, Smith's present and fifth supervisor, reports that Smith is loafing on the job, stepping out for frequent smokes, and occasionally interfering with other operators by his gossiping.

Wade called Smith into his office for a talk, his intention being to find out why Smith didn't work more effectively. The conversation in its essential parts was as follows:

WADE: How do you like the job you're on?

SMITH: Oh, it's all right.

WADE: Well, I've noticed you seem to have a lot of spare time on your hands. Seems like you might put out a little more effort.

SMITH: I think I do as much as anyone else on this job.

WADE: But Ed, you don't keep yourself busy.

SMITH: There's nothing else to do; if you look at the charts, you'll see I do as much as the guy on the shift before me.

WADE: Well, let's see if we can't keep a little busier in the future.

SMITH: O.K. (*He leaves.*)

A review of Smith's personnel and work records revealed the following information:

Age: *20*	Days lost: None
Experience: *None previously in a factory*	Days late: None
	Accidents: None

Education: *1 year college;*
    studied art, quit, no funds
Military Status: Deferred,
    perforated eardrums

Productivity: Average
Characteristics: Quiet,
    slow-moving, defensive
    when talking with superiors,
    lacks initiative

A review of job reports showed the following:

First job: Carbon cutting; broke in with Old Harvey. Didn't exert himself on this job. Supervisor asked to transfer him out.

Second job: Carting saggers; temporary during vacation period for regular man. Did the job passably.

Third job: Piecework in forcing department, traying carbons. Earned above-average per hour at regular rate. This was a vacation fill-in.

Fourth job: Helper in mixing room; worked slowly.

Fifth job: Transferred to new CWS plant as helper in calcining room, where he is presently employed.

Questions

1. What would your decision be now as to what to do with Smith?
2. Could anything have been done to prevent this situation from developing?

TESTS 10

Popularity of Tests

Since World War I, when psychological tests were adopted by the United States Army as an aid in the placement of army personnel, much has been written about tests, their development, application, and usefulness. But usage has not come up to the volume of writings.

The limited usage is due to a number of reasons. Some companies became discouraged because tests did not solve their hiring problems, a conclusion they should have reached before seeking a cure-all. Others think that their selection problems are susceptible to more understandable solutions. And many companies do not care to invest the time and money needed to build a successful testing program.

Tests have made and can make effective contributions to a personnel program. But their use calls for much study and skill. The subject is so complex that no more than a general discussion is possible in this chapter, which is divided under the following headings:

1. Basic concepts and assumptions of testing.
2. Areas of usage.
3. Types of tests.
4. Operating a testing program.
5. Rules in testing.

Basic Fundamentals

It is desirable to understand at the outset that a test—any test—is a process of measurement. By such measurement, it is hoped to determine how well a person has done something or may do something in the future. The measurement may be in either intangible or quantitative terms. Thus, upon being introduced to someone, we decide immediately or soon after that our new acquaintance is "okay" or perhaps someone who should not be trusted. Our judgment is qualitative, since we do not specify how right or how untrustworthy. Nevertheless, in our own fashion, we have given a test and reached a conclusion regarding the other's future performance.

Our conclusions may also be expressed quantitatively. As a result of a formal intelligence test, a definite score would be obtained for each person—e.g., an intelligence quotient of 102. A quantitative score is better, in the sense that it can be communicated to others more readily, than qualitative scores or verbal descriptions.

Tests, moreover, are based upon samples. This need not destroy one's confidence in them. So long as steps are taken to see that given samples are representative of the areas of which they presumably are samples, their usefulness is not questionable on that basis.

Test results provide measures of past aspects and future events and must therefore be used with care. The score of a test, which is intended to reveal how much experience, training, or ability one has acquired, does not disclose unerringly what may happen in the future. This is so because it is difficult to estimate with how much enthusiasm the skills may be applied as time goes on.

But tests which are intended to provide predictions about the future are as yet more accurate in their negative implications than in their positive significance. For example, if candidate A receives a high score on a battery of tests and candidate B receives a low score, the reasonable deduction is that B is not likely to succeed if hired and hence should not, other things considered, be hired. As for A, it is plausible to expect success, but not that that success will be in proportion as the grade is high.

Even the most enthusiastic supporters of tests do not insist, however, that decisions regarding applicants or employees be reached solely on the basis of test scores. Tests should be added to the sum of information gathered from such sources as application blanks, references and interviews. Indeed, it is arguable that selection of candidates can be much more effective with the addition of tests than without them.

Areas of Usage

Tests have been used in a variety of areas. To illustrate this, examples will be cited in the areas of selection, guidance and placement, and training.

1. Selection. Testing has had its widest application in the area of selection. Its success there has been highest in connection with shop and clerical jobs and less so—but still on the promising side—with professional and executive positions.

Looking first at operative jobs, examples of successful testing are numerous. Good results have been derived in terms of reductions in the percentage of subsequent failures on the job. Through testing training costs have been reduced by eliminating poor learners. And on inspection and routine production jobs, simple eye tests have served to reject unfit candidates.

Turning to the executive area, much study is being devoted to testing, although the surface has been little more than scratched. One conclusion that stands out is the necessity of combining ratings and interviews with selected batteries of tests, to be able to screen potentially good from inferior executives. Thus, to results of tests on such factors as interests, emotional stability, general intelligence, and personality must be added opinions on such factors as training, experience, social responsibilities and relationships, production record, and hobbies.

As a case in point, a selection procedure was heavily weighted with psychological testing, interviewing, and performance studies. Before using these, one out of every two supervisors failed, on the average. After using them, success in promotions to the supervisory level reached ninety per cent.

The right combination of selection factors is even more significant at higher executive levels. This is so because no one combination of factors and personal characteristics has been found to describe all successful executives. Hence the establishment of an employee specification of the "ideal" executive is as yet impossible. Nevertheless, careful studies over a number of years have shown that tests have useful predictive value. In one instance, a battery of tests has been helpful in predicting progress from operative levels to first-line supervision and upwards to higher executive positions. The test battery measured such characteristics as problem solving ability, linguistic ability, sociability, optimism, social leadership, dominance, self-confidence, objectiveness, and tolerance.

Turning now to the technical area, testing of sales engineers is noteworthy. In one instance, tests of vocational interest, mental maturity, personality, and mechanical aptitude were used in addition to other selection devices. Selection and placement of sales engineers was improved up to twenty percent by these methods. This success points to an important moral: a selection device should not be judged by whether or not it provides perfect results but rather by its capacity to make a reasonably significant improvement in results.

2. Guidance and Placement. A significant use of tests is found in connection with guidance and placement. When it is realized that most young people do not know for what field of endeavor they are best suited, it can be seen what a vast field of service for testing is available. All that can be done here is to note some contributions of testing to guidance in the business field.

One study has some interesting comments on vocational predictability. Recognizing the limitations of the samples studied and the importance of "other things not being equal," a number of tests have been found useful (by no means perfect) in predicting occupational success. In the case of accounting, for example, tests of arithmetic reasoning, reading comprehension, and reaction speed tended to discriminate between above-average and below-average accountants. A spatial relations test was useful in discriminating among engineers and a reading comprehension test was useful in the case of managers.

An interesting example of test usage in placement is found in the case of a company that compared success of apprentices selected with and without tests. Results on the job showed that half of the tested apprentices outranked all of the nontested apprentices. This shows rather strikingly that job placements without tests were not only expensive for the company but also unfair to those who were placed on jobs in which they were not apt to achieve a satisfactory degree of success.[1]

In another case it was found that applicants for advanced technical training had a 100 percent chance of success if they scored 70 or better on an aptitude test but only a 37 percent chance if their score was between 40–49. Of course, the test did not measure motivation to succeed, which factor could well offset aptitude.[2]

3. Training.   Tests have also been useful in strengthening training programs. An interesting example of this is reported in using tests to determine who should be trained, where training should begin, and whether training has been adequate. It was found that the learning cost of employees who had scored lowest on a finger dexterity test, as measured by a simple pegboard, was close to twice as much as of those who had scored highest as shown in Figure 10–1. Obviously, savings in training costs would more than offset the cost of such selection tests.

Tests can also save training costs by determining where training should begin. On a simple measurement question asked about an illustration showing some blocks adjacent to a scale, it was found that most applicants were unable to read to $\frac{1}{32}$ of an inch. Obviously, training would be wasted in these cases unless the training were started at a level low enough to teach measuring fundamentals.

The question of whether training has been adequate is also of significance. Figure 10–2 illustrates the relation between scores on an electrical information test and hours of instruction. By preestablishing a measure to indicate when a person has sufficient knowledge to handle a particular job, it is possible to determine how many hours of training are ordinarily

---

[1] C. A. Drake, "Aptitude Tests Help You Hire," *Factory Management and Maintenance,* vol. 95, no. 6, p. 57.

[2] P. J. Chartrand, "Research and Entry Criteria," *Personnel Journal,* vol. 46, no. 11, p. 713.

FIGURE 10–1

Relationship between scores on a finger-dexterity test and average learning cost to the plant in minimum makeup pay

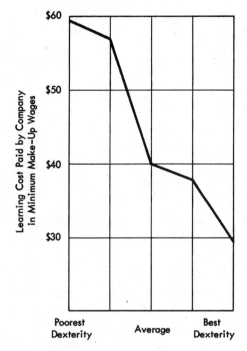

Source: C. H. Lawshe and Joseph Tiffin, "How Tests Can Strengthen the Training Program," *Factory Management and Maintenance*, vol. 102, no. 3, pp. 119–21.

required to attain the desired score. Thus, if it is decided that anyone who has a grade of 80 may be turned loose on a job, then, by the use of such a chart as that in Figure 10–2, it may be noted that training would be needed for about 200 hours. Obviously, any figure above or below this would be wasteful either by overtraining or by poor production due to undertraining.

Even in such technical tasks as computer programming, tests can play a role in selecting trainees. This may be seen in one instance in which test scores were compared to grades received after training. As displayed in Table 10–1, those with high test scores on a Revised Programmer Aptitude Test tended to be more successful in subsequent training. The reverse was true of those with low test scores. It is not hard to conclude that it would generally be undesirable to train low test scorers.

FIGURE 10–2

Relationship between length of training period and scores on an electrical information test

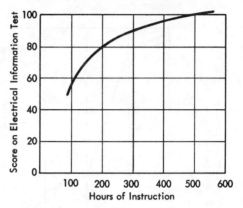

Source: C. H. Lawshe and Joseph Tiffin, "How Tests Can Strengthen the Training Program," *Factory Management and Maintenance*, vol. 102, no. 3, pp. 119–21.

TABLE 10–1

Results of an Aptitude Test

Test Letter Grades	Number	Class Standing on Final Grades	
		Percent in Lowest Third	Percent in Highest Third
A	53	13	57
B	50	24	42
C	38	42	13
D	34	68	6

Source: W. J. McNamara and J. L. Hughes, "A Review of Research in the Selection of Computer Programmers," *Personnel Psychology*, vol. 14, no. 1, p. 42.

Types of Tests

Having seen the uses to which tests have been put, it would now be desirable to examine various kinds of tests. Time and space preclude this because estimates show that thousands of tests have been developed. Some good can be derived, however, by describing and illustrating tests under the following headings: (1) characteristics tested and (2) individual tests and batteries of tests.

1. Characteristics Tested. The characteristics measured by tests fall into four major categories: physical, abilities and skills, interests, and personality. As suggested in Figure 10–3, each of these is divisible into more specific characteristics. Almost everyone has some acquaintance with physical tests such as those of height, weight, strength, eyesight, and hearing. Hence, this group need detain us no longer.

The nature of abilities and skills calls for some amplification. This has reference to competence in getting things done. But competence can be viewed in two ways: (*a*) one may already be proficient in getting things done, or (*b*) one may merely possess the potential. The first is referred

FIGURE 10–3

Measures of Human Characteristics

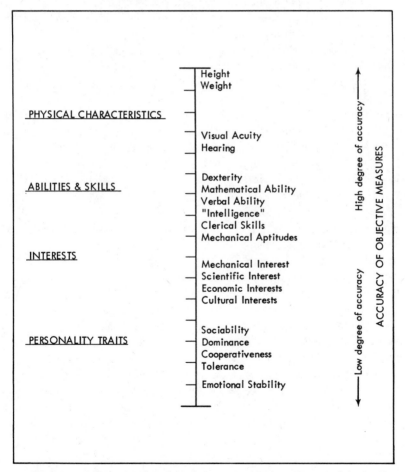

Source: H. H. Meyer and H. M. Bertotti, "Uses and Misuses of Tests in Selecting Key Personnel," *Personnel*, vol. 33, no. 3, p. 280.

to as proficiency or achievement; and the second, aptitude. Tests that fall in this grouping are illustrated by the following:

a. Tweezer dexterity tests are used to determine whether a candidate possesses sufficient finger performance and control to handle small parts efficiently and without undue fatigue.
b. A test of mechanical ability may be obtained by checking the speed with which a candidate can assemble oddly shaped jigsaw blocks.
c. Another test used to determine mechanical ability is the spatial relations test. This serves as a measure of a candidate's ability to visualize the shape of physical objects.
d. Tests of machine skill have been designed in which the operator is checked (1) for speed and accuracy in controlling two cranks turned at different speeds and in different directions, and (2) for hand-eye coordination in turning a crank while following with the eyes a line drawn on a revolving drum.
e. A test used to screen candidates for fine assembly work has been based upon dexterity in handling small parts.
f. Inspection tests are usually made up of sample jobs which check visual acuity and finger dexterity.
g. Technical intelligence has been measured by the use of pictorial multiple-choice questions, as has mechanical comprehension to understand various types of physical relationships.
h. A classification and placement test designed to measure individual performance in 12 basic skills of seeing is incorporated in a testing instrument called the "Ortho-rate."

These skills are not as pure as their names might indicate. Intelligence is a case in point; it is perhaps irrevocably mixed up with other phases of human characteristics, such as learning, experience, background, personality, mechanical ability, executive talent, sales ability, and interests. Moreover, intelligence can be further divided into such elements as numerical memory, verbal memory, reasoning, imagination, and spatial memory. Hence, in the design of tests, it is necessary first to specify what particular aspects of a trait such as intelligence are to be measured. Otherwise, a general measure, such as the IQ, must be interpreted not as a pure score but as one covering a variety of similar characteristics.

Testing of abilities and skills alone is invariably insufficient in predicting job success because interest and motivation are also important. Tests have been devised to measure interest but not much has been done as yet with the motivational factor. In checking interests of people, following are some samples from tests:

a. Below are names and accomplishments of persons who have attained fame. If the life and work of a man interest you, circle the L before

his name; if you are indifferent to his accomplishments, encircle the
I; if you dislike the type of activity he stands for, encircle the D.

L   I   D   1.   Johann Gutenberg—movable type for printing presses
L   I   D   2.   Hervey Allen—author of *Anthony Adverse*
L   I   D   3.   George Corliss—valve gear for steam engines
L   I   D   4.   Thomas Edison—incandescent lamp

b. Below are listed several paired occupations. Suppose that each occupation pays the same salary, carries the same social standing, and
offers the same future advancement. Place a check (√) in front of
the one occupation of each pair which you would prefer as a life
work. *Be sure to mark one of each pair.*

__Research chemist   __Sales manager
__Factory superintendent   __Advertising manager

__Budget director   __Research chemist
__Sales manager   __Personnel director

__Office manager   __Factory superintendent
__Construction engineer   __Office manager

__Research chemist   __Design engineer
__Sales manager   __Traffic manager

__Personnel director   __Budget director
__Office manager   __Design engineer

Personality also conditions the application of abilities and skills. Tests
in this category have been perhaps least successful in measuring what
can be expected of a person. This is due to the fact that:

a. The degree to which personality is important in various occupations
has not been established with certainty.
b. The components of personality have not been defined to the satisfaction of all concerned.
c. Personality is more nebulous than other human characteristics and
therefore harder to measure.

The truth of this can be seen by even a casual glance at the following
listing of categories of traits used to describe and measure personality:

a. General level of activity—e.g., active, vigorous, calm, alert, elated,
jumpy, jittery, and compulsive behavior
b. Attitudes toward life, individuals, and society—e.g., contented, be-
wildered, immature, cautious, tolerant, submissive, belligerent, prejudiced, and realistic
c. Control and intensity of feelings—e.g., extroverted, stable, self-
sufficient, worried, depressed, alienated, masculine, paranoic, and
schizophrenic

2. Individual Tests and Batteries of Tests. Tests may be part of a

FIGURE 10–4

General Aptitude Test Battery

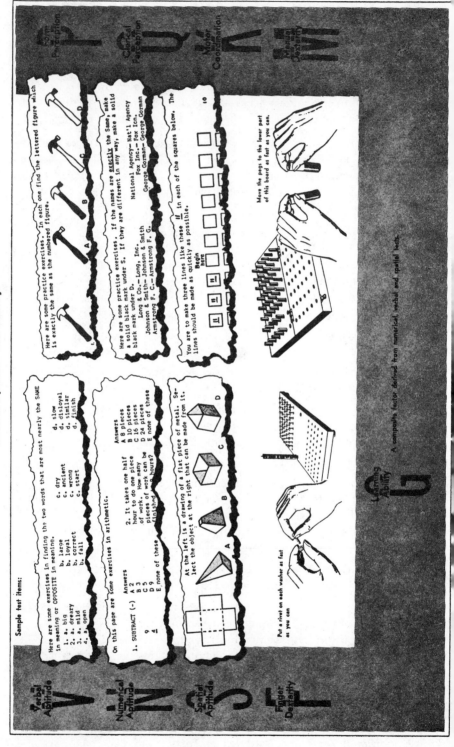

group or battery (as illustrated in Figure 10–4), or may be given singly. A battery of tests is considered to give much better results. This does not mean that a candidate must receive high grades on all the tests given. On the contrary, some of the tests included in a battery may be given with a view to finding what things a candidate is neither equipped to do nor interested in doing. This tends to strengthen conclusions reached on the positive tests included in the battery.

Operating a Testing Program

Since it has been impractical to analyze even a part of all tests in use, some useful suggestions regarding any tests may be provided by commenting upon (1) staffing and organizing a testing program, (2) recording and interpreting test results, and (3) measuring the accuracy of tests.

1. Staffing and Organizing. Undoubtedly, a most important requirement of a good testing program is that of assigning it to competent personnel. Immediately, there comes to mind the psychologist, trained in the theory of tests, their construction, their uses, and their meaning. When possible, such a person should be given responsibility for operating the testing program. However, it is not always possible to utilize full time the services of a professional psychologist. A part-time consultant may be employed in such cases, or it is possible to find some individual with the required potential to assign to and train in this field. Some executives have become proficient in operating a testing program after study of and experimentation with tests.

From an organizational point of view, a number of suggestions are in order. To begin with, the top executives must be convinced of the desirability of testing. Until and unless they are "sold," the battle with the lower levels of an organization will be eventually lost or hard-won. Next, top management should be kept abreast of the developmental stages of the program. And it should be kept informed of progress by means of reports illustrating the success of the testing program.

Those on lower levels of an organization will also have to be convinced of the usefulness of testing. Unless one wants a forced acceptance—and consequently, an unstable position—it is best in these levels to go slowly. Usually, only a department or two should be selected as the area of installation. Results here should then be so self-apparent that the program will expand of its own accord.

2. Recording Test Results. Another operational aspect worthy of consideration is that of recording test results. Such records can be expressed simply in arithmetic or verbal terms, or they may be displayed graphically. Arithmetic or verbal terms have simplicity and ease of recording in their favor, but they lack the desirable characteristic of visualization. For example, Figure 10–5 illustrates the graphical method

FIGURE 10–5

Visual Performance Profile

Visual patterns desirable for electric soldering operations, and the actual score made by one of the employees in the highest hourly rating group. Scores in the darkened area are undesirable.

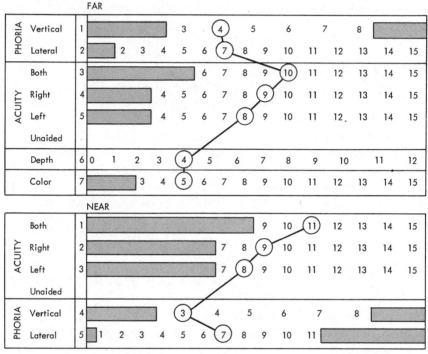

Source: N. Frank Stump, "Vision Tests Predict Worker Capacity," *Factory Management and Maintenance*, vol. 104, no. 2, pp. 121–22.

of displaying test results in regard to visual measurements. The "profile," or line connecting various test scores, quickly and clearly reveals to the reader the coordination of given operators as compared to desirable limits.

On a broader scale, the value of profile recording may be seen in Figure 10–6. Here, test scores on nine tests are recorded. The tests were as follows: (*a*) pinboard, (*b*) right-right turning, (*c*) special inspection, (*d*) case sorting, (*e*) visual perception, (*f*) controlled turning, (*g*) right-left turning, (*h*) hand-foot coordination, and (*i*) rhythm. The profiles of the four candidates shown in Figure 10–6 make it possible to draw conclusions much more quickly than if the scores had merely been expressed arithmetically.

FIGURE 10–6

Inspection Test Profile

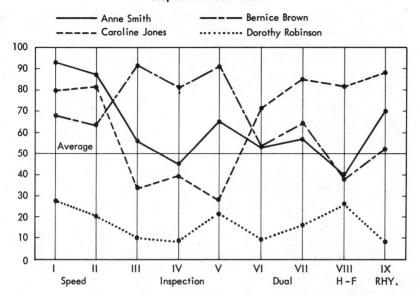

Source: C. A. Drake and H. D. Oleen, "The Technique of Testing," *Factory Management and Maintenance*, vol. 96, no. 3, pp. 77–78.

3. Measures of Accuracy of Tests. Tests are usually measured in terms of their validity and reliability. Tests are obviously developed and designed to test something—e.g., intelligence, temperament, finger dexterity, or reading ability. The degree to which a given test does this is a measure of its validity and is commonly expressed by means of the statistical device of coefficient of correlation as shown in Table 10–2. Simply, this refers to a measure of the degree to which those who have high, average, and low scores also have high, average, and low production records, as illustrated in Table 10–3.

TABLE 10–2

How Tests Take the Gamble out of Personnel Selection

Validity Coefficient of Test	Percent Improvement over Chance
.20	2
.30	5
.40	8
.50	13
.60	20
.70	29

An example of a simple determination of validity is provided by the following case of selection of office employees:

After administering five different tests we found two which predicted success to a fairly high degree. The critical score on each test is such that, of the 20 best operators, 15 made good scores; and of the 20 poorest, only 5 made good scores; or, in other words, if we had discharged all the operators with scores below the critical point of either test, we would have lost 25 percent of our best operators, but no less than 75 percent of our poorest.

This is not as high a degree of correlation between test scores and performance as is often obtained; we believe we can improve it by further experimentation with other tests.

TABLE 10–3
Illustrations of Test Validity

Job Performance	Test Scores		
	Low	Middle	High
Diagrammatic illustration of perfect validity:			
High	0	0	100
Middle	0	100	0
Low	100	0	0
Diagrammatic illustration of zero validity:			
High	33	34	33
Middle	33	34	33
Low	33	34	33
A more "realistic" illustration of validity:			
High	5	30	65
Middle	20	50	30
Low	65	25	10

Source: "Basics of Testing," *Personnel*, vol. 32, no. 6, pp. 550–51. Adapted from a manual prepared for the Navy Department by the U.S. Civil Service Commission, Washington, D.C.

The correlation indicates, however, the probability of a very substantial degree of success in selecting operators who will subsequently prove satisfactory. As a matter of fact, of 5 operators employed in the last three years as beginners, that is, without experience, 4 are now among the 20 best girls [women] and only 1 is in the lower group. That one is well up in the lower 20 and, we think, will move higher after a little more experience.[3]

In other words, the higher the validity of a test, the more accurately can a prediction be made about those tested. This is shown in Table 10–2 in terms of chances of improvement increasing as validity increases.[4]

---

[3] Edward N. Hay, *Inaugurating a Test Program, Personnel Series,* no. 43 (New York: American Management Association), p. 32.

[4] Bernard Hanes, "How Psychological Tests *Can* and *Can't* Help," *Factory Management and Maintenance,* vol. 115, no. 11, pp. 152–53.

A test which is supposed to measure something should yield approximately the same answer for the same person at different times (allowing for the memory factor and improvement on the job because of experience). The degree to which a given test does yield consistently the same scores is a measure of its reliability and is also commonly expressed as a coefficient of correlation.

An example of a simple determination of reliability is provided by the following case in which pupils who had been given a test in blueprint reading were later retested:

Months later, people were retested at random, the same test being used. There was an improvement in the scores, but not more than 7 points. Seven points out of 100 is a negligible figure which could be charged to remembrance or practice. Theoretically, we could say that each person hit his own level again on a retest, and that the test was reliable. Or, in other words, that each time it was used one could depend on getting accurate results. The reliability of a test can be bettered by lengthening it. This should not be done to extremes because the element of writing fatigue may void any good results. Employment tests should not run more than 30 minutes to be practical.[5]

Rules of Testing

This discussion can perhaps best be summarized by noting some rules of good testing practice. Such rules may be grouped under the headings of (1) human relations aspects, (2) operational suggestions, and (3) uses of test scores.

1. Human Relations Aspects.   The user of tests must be extremely sensitive to the feelings of people about tests. Most people are relatively concerned about whether tests will disclose fairly their real capacities or will be used fairly in appraising them. It is well known by test administrators that people will often try either to give the "right" answers or slant their reactions. As a consequence, insofar as possible, tests must be constructed and administered so as to minimize the probabilities of getting distorted results.

Steps must be taken to reduce the reasonable fears and suspicions of people. Careful explanation of the purposes and uses of tests are helpful. Pointing out that tests alone are not the sole criterion in making decisions is desirable. Explaining that high scores on all factors are not required is useful. Stressing the fact that tests are not intended merely to seek out weaknesses is reassuring. And above all, proving through actions subsequent to testing that one takes cognizance of the whole person—both strengths and weaknesses—serves to bring out favorable reactions to tests.

Of particular significance in human relations is the Civil Rights Act

[5] R. W. Gillette, "Tests Help You Hire Right," *Factory Management and Maintenance,* vol. 99, no. 10, p. 80.

of 1964 (Title VII) which makes illegal using tests to discriminate against candidates because of race, color, creed, or sex. Moreover, under this Act, charges have been brought questioning the fairness of using tests for those who have been disadvantaged in getting an education. In such cases, charges of discrimination have been upheld to a degree that indicates that tests must be "race-free" and nondiscriminatory for the underprivileged if their inclusion in the selection program is to be legally permissible.

The EEOC (Equal Employment Opportunity Commission) is particularly concerned about the use of tests (or interviews) which might discriminate against members of minority groups. It is unwilling to accept an employer's use of tests unless the test has been validated against job performance and unless no alternative method of selection is available. For example, a test which measures general verbal skills but is not directly related to job-related performance would be considered unacceptable. Nor would a test be acceptable (except temporarily until more representative validation studies were made) if the original validating group of employees did not contain a representative proportion of minority members.

2. Operational Suggestions.   Several operational suggestions are in order. It is highly desirable to make careful job and position studies as a basis for building tests. Job analysis is essential in order to determine the skills, aptitudes, or other characteristics for which tests must be designed. Until this information is obtained, the selection or development of tests can only be based on guesswork.

Moreover, it is generally agreed that tests should be selected or developed with a view to particular jobs in a particular company. Although there are tests which may have general reliability, such as the general intelligence test, specific adaptations are invariably called for. Local conditions, variations in jobs (even with the same title), and differences in company policies and operation methods are sufficient reason for making individual adaptations.

Another operational rule is that reliance should not be placed solely upon tests in reaching decisions. Tests are most useful when they are given a part in the task of selection, placement, or training of employees. Other devices such as application forms, interviews, and rating scores should be given a prominent role. There is a danger that one's initial enthusiasm for tests may tend unwarrantedly to relegate these other instruments to a small role. When this first flush has passed, there is equal danger that tests may be discarded for failing to provide all the answers.

There also are operational rules related to testing. Adequate time and resources must be provided to design, validate, and check tests. Any attempt to hurry is an almost inevitable invitation to ineffectual results. The effect of time upon people must also be considered. Most people change with time. Hence a test used to select for initial employment should be used only to judge a candidate for that job. If it is desired to test for promotability or potential, interest and aptitude tests are in order. The latter, it must be remembered, are less accurate than trade tests. The accuracy of tests of both aptitude and proficiency is not such a high order that they can be applied indiscriminately.

3. Uses of Test Scores.   Some comments on the use of test scores are also in order. Care must be exercised in determining the critical score of a test. This is the point at which unsuccessful candidates are to be cut off, and is illustrated in Table 10–4. But it is well to establish upper as

TABLE 10–4

How a Critical Score Separates Good and Poor Workers

Test Score	Poor Employees	Good Employees
100.....................		1
90.....................		4
80.....................		6
70.....................	2	5
60.......Critical Score..	0	4
50.....................	7	2
40.....................	8	
30.....................	6	
20.....................	4	
10.....................	2	
0.....................	1	

Source: Bernard Hanes, "How Psychological Tests *Can* and *Can't* Help," *Factory Management and Maintenance*, vol. 115, no. 11, pp. 152–53.

well as lower cutoff points. A person who is too good for the job in question may eventually prove unsatisfactory.

Care must also be exercised to interpret and use correlation figures correctly. A high validity rating does not mean that the given test can be used with impunity. For example, an individual may score low on a test of high validity, yet, through high personal motivation, may more than make up for, let us say, a minimum of technical skill. But a test with a low validity rating may nevertheless give a valuable clue to a particular applicant's strength or weakness.

Organizationally speaking, some rules on test usage are worth noting. Only the expert—the psychologist, consultant, or staff specialist—should be allowed to design, select, and interpret tests. This person should be the keeper of the tests, scores, and related information. Others have an interest in them and have a right to the benefit of testing. So the line and staff executives and supervisors should cooperate in the use of tests, but it should be a relation of doctor and patient. The expert should be and will be recognized as the authority, if, like the doctor, expertise proves worth in supplying needed help.

In the final analysis, tests must be judged in terms of their contribution to the solution of problems of selection, placement, training, productivity, and employee satisfaction. Such judgments might not be too difficult to arrive at were it always possible to try out various tests by comparing test scores with the production records of employees. But unlimited resources are seldom provided for such research. As a consequence, most tests must be devised and evaluated within time limits and budget expenditures that do not allow all the latitude that might be desired.

QUESTIONS

1. Why can confidence be placed in testing even though tests are based on samples?
2. What usefulness is there in tests in connection with the selection of executives?
3. What do the terms diagnostic and prognostic have to do with the use of tests?
4. What would your decision be in the case of an applicant who receives a score of 69 on a battery of tests for which the passing grade has been set at 70?
5. Why is a test of abilities and skills insufficient to predict a candidate's degree of success on a job requiring the tested abilities and skills?
6. What line and staff organizational relationships must be worked out in setting up a testing program?
7. Of what use are "profiles" in depicting test scores?
8. What is meant by validity and reliability of tests? How are measures of each obtainable?
9. Why is the EEOC particularly concerned about the use of tests in hiring?
10. Upon what basic information should the development and selection of tests be based?

CASE 10–1. TAKING A TEST

Jane Steel, just graduated from college, was applying for a job of management trainee with the Sedate Appliances Company. Jane was in the process of answering a test which sought to get a line on a candidate's goals, viewpoints, attitudes, interests, moral standards, and ways of thinking about business, politics, community affairs, and family relations.

In answering the questions, Jane was in a dilemma. Personally, she knew she was very liberal in her views, quite radical at times, critical of some accepted business practices, and out of sympathy with old-line executives. She also knew the reputation of the Sedate Company and its executives as being quite old-fashioned and being out of patience with the idiocies—as they put it—of the younger generation.

If Jane answered as she really felt, she knew the job would not be hers. If Jane answered as she knew the executives would like to hear—and she was smart enough to put herself in their shoes—she knew the job in all likelihood would be hers.

Question

1. How would you answer if you were Jane?

CASE 10–2.   TESTS AND HIRING POLICIES

Being dissatisfied with its practice of selecting apprentices for tool-making on the basis of education and recommendations of present tool-makers, a company decided to try out a program of psychological testing. It procured the services of a private consulting concern which recommended a battery of tests covering various aptitude, interest, manipulative, and mental areas. The tests were given over a period of two years with hirings continuing on the old basis irrespective of the test scores. In this way success or lack of success on the job could be correlated with test scores.

Having compiled a record of the relative degree of job success, test scores and job rating scores were reported as follows:

Battery Score	No. Receiving Job Scores of				
	Superior	Very Good	Good	Passable	Failure
90–95	7	4	2	0	0
85–89	2	6	4	1	0
80–84	1	3	8	2	0
75–79	0	1	4	4	1
70–74	0	1	2	4	1
65–69	0	1	1	4	2
60–64	0	1	1	2	3

After examining this report, there was considerable discussion by a committee of executives as to how this battery of tests should be used, if at all.

Question

1. What is your opinion in this matter?

TRANSFERS AND 11
PROMOTIONS

Scope of Transfers and Promotions

Many vacancies are filled by internal movements of present employees. These movements are termed transfers and promotions. The former term refers to changes in which the pay, status, and job conditions of the new position are approximately the same as of the old. In the case of promotions, the new position has higher pay, status, and job conditions as compared with the old.

Handling a program of transfers and promotions requires attention to a number of details, which are discussed here under the following headings:

1. Purposes of transfer and promotion programs.
2. Operational aspects.
3. Practical limitations.
4. Seniority aspects.

Purposes

The primary purpose of a transfer or promotion is to increase the effectiveness of the organization in attaining its service and profit objectives. When employees are placed in positions in which they can be most productive, chances for successful results of the organization for which they work are consequently increased. It should be the aim, therefore, of any company to change positions of employees as soon as their capacities increase and opportunities warrant.

Another significant purpose of transfers and promotions is of a personal nature. Job changes provide an opportunity for present employees to move into jobs that provide greater compensation, personal satisfaction, and prestige. Being transferred to a new job may open up new avenues of advancement or add the spice of variety to daily routines. Often, too, prestige is a factor, in that the person transferred is publicly recognized for accomplishments. Of course, not all employees want to be transferred or promoted. Many like the assurance of a settled security; yet, most like to feel that opportunities for transfer or promotion are available.

Operational Aspects

Transfer and promotion systems are either informal or formal. Under the informal plan, decisions as to who should be transferred or promoted usually await the occurrence of a vacancy. Moreover, the bases upon which decisions are made vary from vacancy to vacancy and from time to time. As a consequence, no employees know what their status is or is likely to be under this system. But its use is often justified because of its simplicity or because of the infrequency of job changes.

The informal plan gives way, as a company grows or as the losses in morale flowing from it become evident, to some formal program. The plan may be based upon a system of pertinent job and personnel information or upon the seniority of employees. In this section, attention is directed first to the informational systems and then to seniority plans.

A systematic plan of transfers and promotions which pretends to be complete must contain the following:

1. A plan of job relationships.
2. A plan and policy for selecting appropriate employees.
3. A plan of records and reports.

1. Plan of Job Relationships. The basic step in building a plan of transfer and promotion is that of determining the horizontal and vertical relations between jobs. Thus, for each job a schedule must be provided of the jobs (a) to which transfers may be made and (b) to which promotions may be made.

Job analysis is an indispensable tool for making such determinations. It provides information on the skill, experience, training, responsibility, and environmental factors involved in each job. Comparing such information for various jobs serves to disclose which jobs are related because of similar job requirements. Then, on each job specification, as illustrated in Figure 11–1, the jobs from and to which changes can logically be made are listed. Here, it is shown that a molding machine operator may be promoted to a divider man, promoted from a pan greaser or a molding machine helper, or transferred to a cake-baker helper or wrapping machine helper.

Establishing such job relationships does not imply that lines of trans-

FIGURE 11–1

Job Specification

Job Title: <u>MOLDING MACHINE OPERATOR</u>   Department: <u>MAKE-UP</u>

EMPLOYEE QUALIFICATIONS

ENGLISH S: <u>X</u> R: <u>X</u>

EDUCATION: Public _____ High ___X___ or Baker's _____

EXPERIENCE: 2 months Pan Greaser and Molding Machine Helper.

PHYSICAL REQUIREMENTS: No contagious or venereal disease, pass physical examination of food handler; normal eyesight.

MISCELLANEOUS: Worker must be careful, honest, cooperative, dependable, and alert. Must have fine sense of touch and good memory. Must have ability to move hands rapidly and skillfully to twist pieces of dough.

CONDITION OF WORK

Machine ___X___ Hand _____ Heavy _____ Light _____ Medium ___X___

Stand ___X___ Sitting _____ Stooping _____ Hazard ___X___

Rough ___X___ Accurate _____ Inside ___X___ Outside _____

Dusty ___X___ Hot ___X___ Cold _____ Dirty _____ Greasy _____

Quick ___X___ Slow _____ Humid _____ Sticky ___X___

Miscellaneous:

EMPLOYEE INFORMATION

RATE OF PAY: $4.40 hr.; time and $\frac{1}{2}$ for overtime.
HOURS OF WORK: 8-hr. day, 48-hr. week, Sunday to Friday; longer hours overtime.
WORK SHIFT: 1 P.M. to 9 P.M.
VACATION: One year, one week; five years, two weeks.
PROMOTIONS: May be promoted to Divider Man.
    May be promoted from Pan Greaser and Molding Machine Helper.
    May be transferred to Cake Baker apprentice or Wrapping Machine Helper.
PERSONAL EFFECTS REQUIRED: White uniform, hat, and apron.

DUTIES

1. Under general supervision of Divider Man to properly mold all bread into cylindrical form.
2. To uniformly twist pieces of dough together.
3. To put into pans twisted pieces of dough.
4. Supervise Pan Greaser and Molding Machine Helper to see that proper types and amount of pans are greased prior to beginning of run and to see that panned bread is properly racked.

fer and promotion are unbending. If it happens that a particular person filling a job has the qualifications to jump into another line of progression, this should be permitted. However, this is a matter of personal qualifications and does not destroy the validity of natural job relationships.

FIGURE 11–2

A Progression Chart

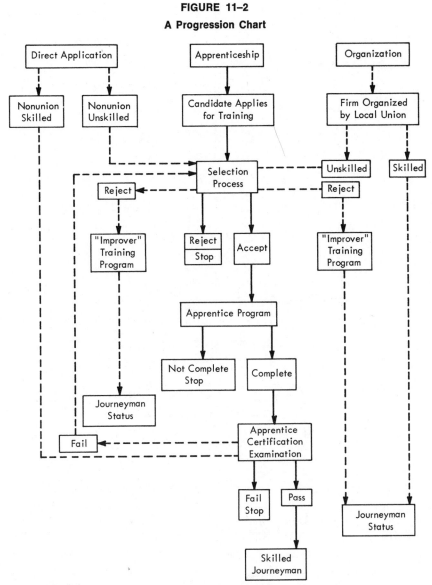

FIGURE 11–3

Upgrading and Transfer Chart for Machine Shop and Tool Department

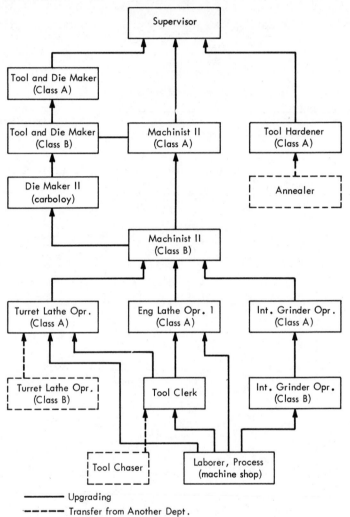

When job relationships have been fully explored in this manner, it is desirable to construct promotion and transfer charts, samples of which are shown in Figures 11–2 and 11–3. Such diagrams may appear to be complicated, but study of them quickly provides an answer regarding the jobs to which changes can be made. Moreover, such diagrams are superior to the images of job relationships that exist merely in the minds of executives and employees. And such images are seldom identical.

2. Selecting Candidates for Promotion. The next important part of a transfer and promotion plan is that by which employees are selected for available job vacancies. The significance of this to employees cannot be overestimated. In their eyes, this is the crucial test of the fairness of a company's plan. Hence, care should be exercised to select employees objectively, according to agreed-upon standards and not upon personal whim. Where a union is involved, such agreement will usually include a balancing of seniority (discussed later in this chapter) and merit.

The merit factor requires a good procedure for evaluating employees. The quantity and quality of performance should be measured periodically. This evaluation should cover such factors as output, cooperation, willingness to accept responsibility, degree of iniative, and ability to get along with others. An excellent illustration of how this may be done is shown in Figure 11–4 in connection with the supervisory position. The summary comparing a given candidate's rating with job requirements is supported by detailed statements evaluating such matters as the following:

a. Character of group to be supervised.
b. Administrative responsibilities.
c. General nature of operation to be supervised.
d. Potential abilities in the areas of human relations, administration, and job knowledge.
e. Recommendations of training needs.
f. Estimate of future growth.

The general subject of evaluation and ratings is discussed more fully in the next chapter.

The plan of employee evaluation should include an arrangement for consultation and perhaps vocational guidance. By discussing a person's strong and weak points before vacancies occur, a two-edged weapon is employed. Those who are ambitious can get suggestions on how to improve themselves. And a record of such discussions can be cited to those who did not get a desired job because they failed to follow suggestions. When discussions with employees take place only after transfers or promotions are not received, it is difficult to convince disgruntled employees that they were fairly treated. This is an example of the principle that, to be acceptable, standards should be discussed before as well as after application.

In promoting to managerial levels, particularly supervisory, an interesting plan is the assessment center technique. In one case, twelve prospective supervisors are brought together for five days in special surroundings. For three days they work on a variety of cases, situational materials, and samples of managerial roles. A group of managers observe the group in action, interview them, and carry on discussions with them. Then the observers spend two days making evaluations and recommendations. Experience with this plan indicates that subsequent success

FIGURE 11–4

Supervisory Selection Summary Sheet

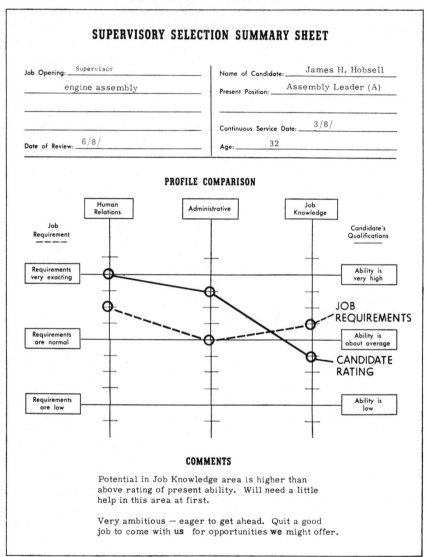

SUPERVISORY SELECTION SUMMARY SHEET

Job Opening: _Supervisor_

engine assembly

Date of Review: _6/8/_

Name of Candidate: _James H. Hobsell_

Present Position: _Assembly Leader (A)_

Continuous Service Date: _3/8/_

Age: _32_

PROFILE COMPARISON

| Human Relations | Administrative | Job Knowledge |

Job Requirement
– – – –

Candidate's Qualifications

Requirements very exacting — Ability is very high

JOB REQUIREMENTS

Requirements are normal — Ability is about average

CANDIDATE RATING

Requirements are low — Ability is low

COMMENTS

Potential in Job Knowledge area is higher than above rating of present ability. Will need a little help in this area at first.

Very ambitious -- eager to get ahead. Quit a good job to come with **us** for opportunities **we** might offer.

on the supervisory jobs correlates to a high degree with the evaluations.

3. Records and Reports. A third important part of a transfer and promotion plan is that of designing adequate records and reports. The system should include the following:

a. Forecasts of job vacancies
b. Central reporting of vacancies
c. Locating qualified employees
d. Notification of all parties concerned
e. Follow-up of transferred and promoted personnel

a. Forecasting Vacancies. Efforts should be made to determine how many vacancies are likely to occur during coming periods on various jobs. Advance preparations can then be made to locate qualified employees. As a consequence, the stability of the organization can be maintained. Moreover, the danger of overselling present employees on the probabilities of advancement will be minimized. It is indeed destructive of morale when employees are led to expect job changes that do not materialize.

Such forecasts are not overly difficult to make, provided that information on future sales volume and personnel turnover is available. As noted in Chapter 6, "Job and Personnel Requirements," it is then possible to estimate with a practical degree of accuracy how many vacancies will have to be filled. For example, in a company that has 40 supervisors at present, turnover of supervisors has been 10 percent annually, and increases in volume of business are expected to increase the supervisory force by about 5 percent annually; hence, six vacancies will have to be filled in the supervisory ranks during the coming year.

Another effective way of forecasting vacancies is to show the ages of executives on the organization chart. This can be done graphically by using different colors for different age groups—e.g., red for ages 50 and over, orange for 40—49, blue for 30—39, green for 20—29, and brown for 19 and under. Such an organization chart will immediately show the general areas which may be out of balance in terms of age groups and in which steps should be taken to provide for transfers or promotions. In what areas training of executives for transfer and promotion should be undertaken may also be disclosed.

b. Reporting Vacancies. Central reporting of vacancies is an essential of a good transfer and promotion plan. Otherwise, some vacancies will be filled from the outside rather than from within. As a consequence, employees will tend to lose confidence in the company's interest in them. The procedure which suggests itself here is (1) to have all hiring done on a requisition basis and (2) to have all requisitions pass through the hands of a transfer and promotion section in the personnel department. In this way, requisitions can be reviewed with an eye to filling vacancies from within before outside sources are explored. This may result in some delay during rush periods, but it is offset by increased employee confidence in management's consideration of employee interests.

c. Locating Candidates. Locating qualified (whether by merit or seniority) employees requires a search of personnel records. This is a formidable task when files of written records must be examined personally. But the use of tabulating equipment or electronic computers to store and search for information speeds up the process immeasurably. Reference to such records was made in Chapter 9. See also Figure 11–5.

FIGURE 11–5
Employee Information Card

Employee No. ________

Name ________ Address ________ Town ________

Dept. ________ Code ____ Position ________ Code ____ Emp. Date ________

Emp. Status = Reg. 1 ☐ Temp. 2 ☐ Part Time 3 ☐ Co-op 4 ☐ | Shift 1 ☐ 2 ☐ 3 ☐

Marital Status = Married 1 ☐ Single 2 ☐ Divorced 3 ☐ Separated 4 ☐ Widowed 5 ☐

No. Dep. Children 1 ☐ 2 ☐ 3 ☐ 4 ☐ 5 ☐ | Relatives in Co. = Yes 1 ☐ No 2 ☐ | Who ________

Union = AFL - CIO 1 ☐ Other 1 ☐ | Emp. Clubs = Gasco 1 ☐ Three Star 1 ☐ Other 1 ☐ Veterans 1 ☐

Experiences of Skills = Clerical 1 ☐ Mechanical 1 ☐ Sales 1 ☐ Supervisory 1 ☐ Other 1 ☐

Special Training = Departmental 1 ☐ J.R.T. 1 ☐ J.I.T. 1 ☐ J.M.T. 1 ☐ Other 1 ☐

Accidents = Lost Time 1 ☐ 2 ☐ 3 ☐ 4 ☐ 5 ☐ | Auto 1 ☐ 2 ☐ 3 ☐ 4 ☐ 5 ☐ | Other 1 ☐ 2 ☐ 3 ☐ 4 ☐ 5 ☐ 6 ☐ 7 ☐ 8 ☐

Company Insurance = Yes 1 ☐ No 2 ☐ | Hospitalization = Yes 1 ☐ No 2 ☐ | Credit Union Member = Yes 1 ☐ No 2 ☐

Absenteeism = Days = 001 ☐ 002 ☐ 003 ☐ 004 ☐ 005 ☐ 006 ☐ 007 ☐ 008 ☐ 009 ☐ 010 ☐ 011 ☐ 012 ☐ Any No. ________

Punch Card Operations Completed Date ________ Operator ________

Separation Information

RESIGNED

Disliked Outside Work	0	____
Disliked Inside Work	1	____
Disliked Supervisor	2	____
Disliked Coworker	3	____
Disliked Rate of Pay	4	____
Disliked Working Conditions	5	____
Disliked Type of Work	6	____
Disliked Promotional Opportunities	7	____
Because of Lack of Proper Tools	8	
Other Reasons What? ________	9	____

RELEASED

Lack of Work	00	____
Dishonest	01	____
Intoxication	02	____
Loaf or Sleep on Job	03	____
Inadaptability	04	____
Destruction to Company Property	05	____
Disloyal to Company	06	____
Lost Interest in Job	07	____
Unsafe Practices	08	____
Would Not Follow Instructions	09	____
Would Not Accept Responsibilities	10	____
Outside Distractions	11	____
Other Reason = Explain ________	12	____

IN GENERAL

		1 Yes	2 Doubtful	3 No
Was Work Satisfactory?	68			
Would You Rehire?	69			
Did Worker Work Out Two Weeks' Notice?	70			
Does Worker Agree with the Reasons Reported as to Separation?	71			
Could this Separation Have Been Avoided?	72			
Did Worker Leave Our Company for Another Job?	73			
Was Attitude toward the Company Good When Worker Left?	74			
Would You Recommend Worker to Another Company?	75			

If Not, Why? ________

General Comments ________

Of course, a record should also be maintained of employees who specifically request or are recommended by their superiors for transfer or promotion.

Another method of locating candidates is that of job posting. Under this method, notice of vacancies (as illustrated in Figure 11–6) is posted on bulletin boards and on the time clock or is announced through the company newspaper or some other form of communication. Such posting may be limited to the department or division in which the vacancy occurs, or it may be posted on a company-wide basis. The notice may be posted for some limited time—e.g., a week or 10 days—or it may remain posted until the job is filled, no matter how much time is needed. This practice of posting has grown out of union desires that present employees be allowed an opportunity to bid on good jobs before outsiders are given a chance at them.

d. *Authorizations and Notifications.* Another important aspect of a procedure of transfers and promotions is that of proper authorizations and notifications. On the one hand, the central unit responsible for locating qualified workers should not be permitted to initiate transfers of its own accord. It should request superiors of qualified employees to authorize a job change. It may have to "sell" its requests, but this is better than staff interference with line authority. Then, too, the personnel department should be ready to suggest replacements to the superior who is losing a good worker.

On the other hand, the system should provide for proper notification of all concerned. It is usually best for the supervisor to inform the person being changed. In that way, line authority is not divided. In addition, subordinates are impressed favorably by executives who show signs of looking after the interests of employees. The approval of the new superior under whom the employee is to work must also be obtained by the personnel department. In this way the staff position of the personnel department does not intrude upon the authority of the line department served. And finally, notices of the change should go to the payroll department, personnel history section of the personnel department, and any other sections that keep records of employees.

e. *Follow-up.* The final step of a good transfer and promotional plan is that of follow-up. After an interval of a month or two, a brief interview would suffice to determine whether all is going well or whether some form of corrective action is in order. This form of feedback is similar to that recommended for new employees. After all, the changed employee is a new employee in a new job, even though an old employee in the company.

Some companies allow the feedback to come from the employee in the form of a grievance or complaint. This assumes that all employees will air their dissatisfactions, which is not true. Moreover, it places upon the employee the responsibility for a function that is largely managerial.

FIGURE 11–6

Job Postings

JOB CODE NO.	JOB DESCRIPTION	WORKING SCHEDULE	JOB RATE
283	LUBRICATION MECHANIC (Req 567) Checks for lubrication and lubricates, according to schedule, the moving parts or wearing surfaces of mechanical equipment. Cleans machines and equipment. Reports defective parts of equipment such as worn belts, worn bearings, loose flywheel, etc. Makes recommendations for safety measures concerning equipment on which he works. Makes simple bearing replacements. Checks motor bearing spacing, works to fit into production schedule. Makes recommendations for change in frequency or type of lubrication. Supv: J. Lunt, Preventative Maintenance. Should have good mechanical sense. Knowledge of lubricating procedure essential.	6:00 a.m. 2:30 p.m.	Group 17
252	ESTIMATOR (Req 622) Estimates cost on all jobs in Machine Shop. Sets up and maintains records on all estimates. Checks prints with Engineers for cost saving methods. Procures and evaluates estimates for work to be done on breakdown orders by other departments. Sets up and maintains records on drawing changes. Sets up and maintains method for checking actual costs against estimated costs. Supv: R. Wilkins, Machine Shop. High School or equivalent – 2 years in practical machine shop experience or mechanical estimating experience. (Must be good at figures and have neat hand writing.) Ability to learn and maintain good office procedures.		Group 15
253	Q.C. TESTER (Req 457) To conduct special tests, evaluate data and write reports. Supv: G. Thibeault, Quality Control. Q.C. experience helpful – should be able to write reports clearly and easily. This is a summer job.	8:00 – 4:45	Group 18

It is our general policy to fill job openings from within the company when there are qualified candidates among our own people. If you are interested in any of the above jobs, please tell your supervisor or contact Personnel immediately. Jobs will be posted for three days before being filled. Occasional exceptions may be made when particular speed is necessary in filling the vacancy, and recent postings of similar jobs have brought no response. The details of how the Job Posting System operates are contained in Personnel Instructions 52-12 which your Supervisor can show you.

POSTING DATE: 7/10/--

Source: H. G. Pearson, "Pros and Cons of Job Posting," *Personnel*, vol. XXXIII, no. 3, p. 274.

Limitations

Whether or not, and to what extent, a transfer and promotion plan can be put into operation depends upon a number of factors. Obviously, there must be sufficient vacancies to warrant investment in an involved plan. That is why a small company or one in which turnover is very low would be foolish to waste time and resources on a formal plan. The objectives to be gained would not be worth the effort.

In organizations where new ideas, initiative, and originality are important, outside hirings are to be preferred. Otherwise, replacements are bound to be made with employees who are not likely to know more than those whom they replaced. The results are bound to be unsatisfactory in a highly competitive situation.

Again, a plan of transfers and promotions may reveal that for some jobs satisfactory horizontal or vertical job progressions cannot be readily established. For example, some jobs are commonly known as "blind alley" jobs. In such cases a plan of training should be established so that those who desire or deserve transfers or promotions can be prepared to get into a job with progressive possibilities.

Perhaps the most serious problem of transfer and promotion plans arises out of the difficulty of measuring the overall qualifications of employees. It is a formidable task to measure and weigh together such factors as quantity and quality of output, cooperation, acceptance of responsibility, and aptitude for progress. Nor is it easy to explain the results to those who are affected by such measurements. To face up to the development of a good measuring plan or to accept the simpler but less logical plan of seniority is a perplexing choice.

Seniority

Length of service—or seniority—is the governing factor in transfers and promotions below the supervisory level in many companies. It is also of significance in collective bargaining, which is discussed in Chapter 25. Attention to it is directed here under the following headings:

1. Calculating length of service.
2. Balancing merit and seniority.
3. Privileges affected by seniority.
4. Areas of application.
5. Summary of arguments.

1. Calculating Seniority. The method of calculating length of service is an important part of a seniority plan. It should provide for the following factors: (a) when seniority starts to accumulate, (b) effect of various interruptions to employment, and (c) the effect of transfers and promotions upon seniority calculation.

a. Accumulating Seniority. When there are no outside factors involved, seniority begins to accumulate as soon as an employee is hired. This should be specifically stated, particularly when a company undertakes collective bargaining. Otherwise, there is a possibility that the seniority of employees hired before a contract goes into effect may be dated from the date of the contract. Also, in the case of union contracts, it is important to note whether or not new employees have seniority rights during their period of probation and whether or not the probationary period will be included in the calculation of seniority. Again, where large numbers of employees are hired on the same date, a question of seniority may arise unless a basis for priority is established. In such instances, priority may be established upon such an arbitrary basis as order of clock numbers assigned or alphabetical listing.

b. Interruptions to Service. After seniority begins to accumulate, there are a number of interruptions to service for which provisions should be made. Ordinarily, interruptions that are due to the company's actions or are relatively short are customarily not deducted in calculating seniority. Examples would be time off for short personal absences, layoffs, and sick leave included in seniority accumulations. However, extended leaves of absence, layoffs beyond designated periods of time, and extended sick leaves are sometimes deducted in computing seniority. These aspects of calculating seniority will not cause difficulty so long as they are provided for and understood in advance.

c. Job Changes and Seniority. More difficult to handle is the effect of transfers and promotions upon seniority calculations. For example, workers may be unwilling to accept or may even refuse transfers if the change means a loss of seniority. Or workers who have been promoted to a supervisory position and later demoted have sometimes found themselves at the bottom of a seniority list. Except in a few industries, such as the building trades, where the seniority of supervisors is protected, the seniority status of supervisors and transferees is not protected traditionally unless specifically stated by company policy or union agreement.[1] Hence, it is desirable, when questions of this type are likely to arise, to specify what the seniority privileges will be. Perhaps the fairest provision is to allow demoted supervisors the seniority they had before the promotion took place. In the case of transferees, it would seem fair to allow them to retain their seniority if they return to their old jobs and to have some measure of adjusted seniority if they remain on their new jobs. Otherwise, only the most adventuresome will be willing to transfer.

Exemptions from seniority rules may also be desirable for technical and professional employees and for trainees. In order to avoid discrimi-

---

[1] Giving a person such as a supervisor, shop steward, or committeeman preference in layoffs or rehirings without regard to service is also termed superseniority or preferential seniority.

natory practices in connection with such groups, unions sometimes require that the number of exempted employees must be limited to some percentage of nonexempted groups. In any event, to prove its fairness to all employees, it is well for management to define specifically exempt jobs and positions, and to restrict the conditions under which the exemptions shall apply.

2. Merit versus Seniority. A second important part of any seniority plan is the matter of balancing seniority in relation to merit. This will occasion much debate unless carefully defined. It might seem that a statement such as the following would be clear and fair: "As between two employees with equal ability, the one with the greater seniority will be given preference." Does ability refer to the minimum required for the job or to relative abilities of candidates? Employees usually argue for the former, while management argues for the latter. Moreover, there is the usual conflict about the accuracy of management in measuring ability.

Whatever hope a company may have to work out a plan balancing merit and seniority will depend, therefore, upon a number of factors. First, a set of job and employee specifications should be carefully prepared, so that claimants for jobs can be shown that requirements are objective and not capricious. Second, a complete and thoroughly understood transfer and promotion plan should be promulgated. Third, a good system of employee merit rating should be installed. Merit must be measurable, or its proponents have built their house of arguments upon sand. This system must consider the views of the union, and ratings under it should be subject to some set plan of review. Fourth, performance standards should be set as objectively as possible, so that measurements of employee productivity and cooperation may be more readily acceptable by all. And lastly, a well-thought-out grievance procedure should be established which is acceptable to employees and to the union, if employees are so represented. These requirements are not easily met; until they are, there is little use in arguing for merit in place of seniority.

3. Employment Privileges Affected. The relative weight that seniority will have upon various classes of employment privileges also should be carefully defined. For example, it may be completely controlling in such matters as length of vacations and choice of vacation periods; or it may be controlling in choice of work periods, shifts, or runs in the case of transportation services, and it may be only partly controlling in such matters as transfers and promotions. Similarly, in the matter of discharges and layoffs, seniority may be given part or total weight.

Moreover, how seniority shall apply in each class must also be determined. For example, limitations must be placed on senior employees who replace or "bump" junior employees. Senior employees may be required within a given period of time to demonstrate that they can competently perform the jobs of employees they bump, or junior employees may be protected if they hold special types of jobs or if they have been with the company for a specified number of years.

On recall of employees after a production layoff, seniority rules vary. In some companies, no new employees may be hired until all available laid-off employees are recalled. In other cases the company may have some discretion in hiring new employees as compared to those laid off. In addition, the sequence of recalling senior employees should be carefully indicated in terms of area of work to which their seniority applies and in terms of its importance relative to merit.

4. Area of Application. Finally, the application of the seniority principle should give consideration to the area to which it applies. For example, it is unwise to give seniority company-wide application in such matters as transfers. Otherwise, the result will be that workers unqualified for vacancies will nevertheless apply for them if they have company-wide seniority.

The usual areas of application are the department, the occupation (the "family" classification), or the company. No one of these of itself is without disadvantages. As noted above, the company-wide plan unduly favors the senior employee who wants to bump more qualified employees in departments outside the immediate experience of the senior employee. In the case of departmental plans, very capable and key employees may be lost because they cannot replace less qualified employees with less service in other departments. And the occupational plan may be affected by the disadvantages of the departmental or company-wide plan, depending upon how narrow or wide the job family in a given occupation happens to be.

To minimize disadvantages arising out of seniority areas, it may be desirable to establish restrictive rules. For example, company-wide seniority may be applied to all unskilled and semiskilled jobs, departmental seniority may be applied to skilled jobs, and occupational seniority may be applied to certain highly specialized classifications. Another restrictive rule, of course, is that of adding merit qualification to pure seniority measures.

Summary

In summary, the seniority plan of determining employment changes has the advantage of apparent simplicity in its favor. However, as may be deduced from the foregoing discussion, extreme care must be exercised in writing the seniority clauses; otherwise, troubles will arise that may be more bothersome than those it had been hoped to avoid. The major disadvantage of the seniority plan is that merit and ability tend to receive a minor place in reaching employment decisions.

Yet the position taken by some unions in favor of seniority is readily understandable. For one thing, one can scarcely argue about such a definite matter as the date on which an employee started to work with the company. But ratings of the relative abilities of employees for promotion are subject to some debate even when the best of systems is employed. So a union cannot be overly blamed for preferring not to embroil itself in such arguments. For another thing, some unions hold to the thesis that all employees in a given occupation or unit of work are to be treated alike. To recognize individual differences would lead to intra-union arguments. Such disagreements tend to weaken union solidarity in dealing with the company. Hence, it is more sensible for the union to forego theoretical accuracy to enhance membership unity.

It is imperative, however, that seniority rules avoid illegal discriminatory results. Too often in the past, blacks, women, and some ethnic groups—despite their skills and abilities—have been precluded from moving to better jobs and supervisory positions because of some seniority rules. Recent court decisions have looked with disfavor upon seniority rules which have served to maintain such discriminatory results.

In sum, until more acceptable methods of calculating and balancing ability and merit are devised, seniority may be expected to remain a useful method of determining employment practices.

QUESTIONS

1. What purposes are served by transfers and promotions?
2. How are plans of job relationships established for use in programs of transfers and promotions?
3. How does the assessment center technique work?
4. What methods may be used to estimate future job vacancies?
5. What are the advantages of job posting?
6. What arguments may be employed to convince supervisors to approve of releasing their best employees to other departments and to better jobs?
7. Under what conditions would you advise against filling job vacancies by transfers or promotions?
8. What situations must be considered in determining length of seniority?
9. If both merit and seniority are to be used in matters of transfers and promotions, what factors must be considered in such a plan?
10. For what reasons is the seniority plan looked upon with favor in the event of transfers or promotions?

CASE 11–1. THE OUTCOME OF A PROMOTIONAL POLICY

A few years ago Bill Changer, the set-up man in his department, and the highest paid nonsupervisor in the department, was offered a promotion to supervisor. He took the supervisor's job because it paid more money and because, under the union contract, he could reclaim his old job if it became necessary to return to his bargaining unit.

Not long after his appointment to supervisor, the set-up job classification was abolished because of changed methods but Bill gave this little thought because he had proved satisfactory to the company and to himself in the supervisory job. Several months later, due to declining business, Bill was not needed as a supervisor and had to return to the operative ranks. The company returned Bill to the highest paid job in the department which now was multiple tool operator. To do this one of the multiple tool operators had to be bumped.

But as soon as this happened, the union objected claiming that the deposed supervisor could, according to the contract, claim his job if it existed. But since it didn't, he would have to take a lower classification job and work his way back into a seniority claiming status.

The company argued that since Bill had the top-paying job in the bargaining unit that equity demanded that he be returned to the same level even though it meant a difference in responsibility as long as he was qualified to do the work, which all agreed he was.

Question

1. On what grounds would you decide this case were you called in to do so?

CASE 11–2.   EXECUTIVE PROMOTION

Airway Tools is a manufacturer of a variety of home and industrial tools. A situation involving promotion has arisen on the production side of the company. Under the president is a vice president of production under whom are the engineering manager, the maintenance manager, the quality control manager, the production manager, and the factory superintendent.

A year ago, the vice president died unexpectedly. Of the five executives just mentioned, each felt in line for the promotion. Three weeks later the quality control manager was promoted to the vice presidency. This particularly irked Don Donald, the production manager, who felt that he deserved the promotion. He talked to the president about the decision pointing to his own length of service, experience in production matters, and high merit evaluation ratings. The president was sympathetic but said that Donald was needed more urgently on the line as production manager than as the vice president.

Six months later, the work of the newly appointed vice president was judged to be unsatisfactory and his resignation was requested. Search for a new vice president was undertaken. The other four executives were again evaluated by the president and his advisors. This time the engineering manager was promoted.

This action enraged Donald, who felt betrayed and misused. The engineering manager had been with the company only five years whereas Donald had fifteen years of service with the company. Donald asked the president to explain why he was passed over again. The president replied, "Our decision is based on several criteria. First, we look at leadership and executive growth potential. Then we look at the executive's qualifications and contributions in the present and to the future. We promote the person whom we feel has the ability to lead effectively at the top side. Anyway our decision has been made and I can't see the use of any further discussion on this subject."

Question

1. Are or are you not satisfied with the criteria and process of selection stated by the president? Why or why not?

MERIT EVALUATION 12

Evaluation Programs

As noted in the preceding chapter, employment privileges may be earned by superior performance. In such cases, some plan of evaluating performance must be used. The plans go by such names as merit rating, service appraisal, progress rating, performance evaluation, and merit evaluation. And they have other uses such as in counseling, training, compensation, and handling grievances and disciplinary cases.

Evaluation of employees is one of the most universal practices of management. It is applied formally or informally to all employees—operative, technical, professional, and executive. Many companies use formal plans primarily in connection with operative employees. However, a good rating program should encompass all employees. Hence, concern in this chapter will be for rating suggestions which are useful for all levels and categories of employees.

Some managements have given up—or have been forced to give up—formal plans in favor of the seniority plan for determining rewards and privileges. They were discarded because of some defect in the design or use of the plans. The moral is that formal evaluation plans will not, in and of themselves, operate effectively or be accepted unquestioningly.

The success of formal plans of evaluation depends upon the care with which they are planned, operated, and controlled. How this may be accomplished is discussed here under the following headings:

1. Objectives.
2. Fundamental issues of evaluation.
3. Design of evaluation forms.
4. Accuracy of evaluations.
5. Rules of evaluation.

Objectives of Evaluation

Any number of objectives may be sought by means of rating programs. First and foremost is the objective of determining more accurately which employees should receive pay increases, which should be given transfers or promotions, and which should be given preferred status and privileges. Second, evaluations are very useful in counseling, that is, in suggesting what a person should do to improve performance and chances for advancement. Third, when disputes arise over pay, promotions, etc., the availability of a series of ratings provides management with information when conferring with the aggrieved. Fourth, from the viewpoint of management, supervisors and executives who know that they will be expected periodically to fill out rating forms (and be prepared to justify their estimates) will tend to be more observant of their subordinates and hence to become better day-to-day supervisors. In the fourth place, when supervisors follow uniform rules of rating, the treatment received by all employees will be more consistent throughout the organization.

An evaluation plan need not encompass all these objectives. Indeed, by union agreement, it may be decided that merit shall have little or nothing to do with choosing candidates for transfer or promotion, let us say. Yet, merit rating could serve as a basis for counseling employees about their strengths and weaknesses or for improving supervisory-employee relations.

This discussion of objectives would be incomplete without the admonition that rating plans must not be used for purposes beyond their capacities. To be specific, some plans have been wrecked by using them to grant general or individual compensation increases that really stemmed from labor market conditions and not from individual merit. When the news gets around that a supervisor has granted someone an increase to avoid a resignation, others soon demand the same treatment. Such misuse of merit rating makes everyone a participant in a crooked game that leads to mistrust not only of merit rating but also of other personnel practices of management.

Fundamental Issues of Evaluation

Perhaps the best place to begin a description of merit evaluation is with the fundamental issues raised by evaluation. These include (1) the basic theory of evaluation, (2) the bases of comparison involved in evaluation, and (3) the question of how evaluations should be discussed with employees.

1. Basic Theory of Evaluation. Evaluation, as noted, is the act of estimating the worth of employees in order to, first, determine rewards and penalties, and, second, provide a basis for counseling. In regard to

FIGURE 12–1

Engineer Appraisal Form

BELL & HOWELL COMPANY

NAME _____ CLOCK NO. _____ POSITION _____ DATE _____

APPRAISED BY _____ DATE INTERVIEWED _____

	UNSATISFACTORY			FAIR (Somewhat below average)		GOOD		EXCELLENT (Somewhat above average)		OUTSTANDING (Well above average)		
	1	2	3	4	5	6	7	8 9 10	11	12 13	14	5
1. INITIATIVE Enterprises; drive; capacity for independent action; degree to which he assumes responsibility when orders are lacking; degree to which he follows through on a job despite obstacles.												
2. COOPERATIVENESS The trait of working wholeheartedly both with and for others in an open-minded objective fashion; possession of the qualities of tact, courtesy, friendliness and tolerance.												
3. EXPRESSION Facility in expressing ideas both orally and in writing. This implies the ability to communicate ideas in a logical, coherent fashion and the ability to summarize.												
4. QUANTITY OF WORK Amount of useful output in the light of the opportunities afforded by the job. The output may be written or otherwise.												

5.	QUALITY OF WORK											
	The general excellence of all kinds of output, including written material, with consideration given to the difficulty of the job. Accuracy, thoroughness and dependability of output should be considered, but not quantity. In the case of supervisors, this trait includes skill in directing and guiding others.											
6.	CREATIVENESS											
	Originality, including imagination and inventiveness.											
7.	ENGINEERING OR TECHNICAL JUDGEMENT											
	Skill in analyzing situations and arriving at sound conclusions from available facts even though the available data may be incomplete or seemingly contradictory.											
8.	VERSATILITY & ADAPTABILITY											
	Willing and capable of doing successfully several lines of work, as need arises.											
9.	GENERAL COMPANY INFORMATION											
	The degree of understanding of procedures of major and minor company policies and conformance to them. (See Inst. 3 B)											
10.	BUDGET AND/OR SCHEDULES											
	Ability to perform within budget limitations and/or according to schedules and commitments.											
11.	PROFESSIONAL INTEGRITY											
	Degree of willingness to face facts and follow course of action indicated.											

the former, one measure of worth is the contribution made by each employee. In simple form, this may be diagrammed as follows:

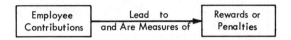

However, it is not always possible to measure employee contributions. Or when it can be done, it nevertheless may be desirable to advise employees how their contributions may be increased. In such instances, it is necessary to ask: What is there about the individual that caused the contribution? For example, individual characteristics, instead of contributions, may be used as the basis of rewards and penalties, as shown in the following diagram:

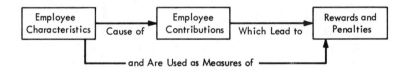

Let us assume that employees *A* and *B* receive $4 an hour on a given job and are being considered for raises. Their respective contributions to service objectives should be weighed because the contributions that anyone makes to the ultimate customers of a company are the justification for compensation. But if, in the first place, it is impossible to measure such contributions because an individual's work is intermixed with that of others, ratings may be made of the characteristics that caused the contributions. Or second, if it is desired to tell employees individually why their contributions are as they are, a rating should be made of employee characteristics and behavior as the basis for counseling. This aspect of evaluation may be diagrammed as follows:

2. Basis of Comparison. Another fundamental issue of rating concerns the bases of comparing personal characteristics or contributions. When it is said, for example, that employee *A* is better than employee *B*, the comparison may be based upon any of the following:

a. The two employees relative to each other.
b. *A* and *B* as compared to other workers.

c. *A* and *B* as compared to an ideal worker.

d. Arbitrary yardsticks of various factors.

Perhaps there is no more common method than that of comparing two or more people in a given situation. To be sure, this practice suffers from the lack of a common and unvarying standard, but it is simple. Hence, some of the earliest attempts to rate employees were based upon a simple ranking of workers. The names of all employees were placed on cards, and the cards were sorted in order, from highest to lowest.

A more modern version is the paired-comparison method. Cards are prepared with two names on each, every employee being paired with every other one in a given unit. The supervisor (or two or more raters) checks on each card the name of the employee the supervisor considers to be the better one. A tabulation can then be made showing which employee has received the most checks down to the one who has received the least. These methods do not indicate the relative differences in employees, and the ratings depend upon who is on the payroll at a given time. At least, the rater has been put on record and is therefore likely to be more careful in making estimates.

Accuracy of ratings may be advanced by comparing all employees with selected employees who are considered to be representative of the best, above average, average, below average, and the poorest. In this way, an employee who rated "above average," for example, could be given a better impression of relative worth than when informed of a rating of 12th, let us say, in a list of 40 employees. This form of worker-to-worker rating may be improved in two ways. First, several factors may be used in rating worker-to-worker. For example, an employee may be compared to a five-person standard in terms of such factors as initiative, cooperation, and dependability. These factor ratings are then arranged to establish an overall grade. Second, instead of using actual employees as standards for best, above average, and so forth, ideal descriptions may be developed. This avoids changes in standards that occur when employees who have been used as models leave the department or company.

While some companies use refined systems of worker-to-worker rating plans, the trend has been toward plans in which measuring sticks of factors common to all employees are used. For example, Figure 12–2 illustrates a form in which raters evaluate subordinates by checking along lines divided into various lengths to indicate degrees of contribution or personal characteristics. Such graphical methods have gained in favor because qualitative differences are easier to visualize.

3. Consultations with Employees. Another important question is how results of evaluations should be discussed with employees. The decision not to do so may be reached for two reasons. First, some companies feel

FIGURE 12–2

Employee Progress Rating

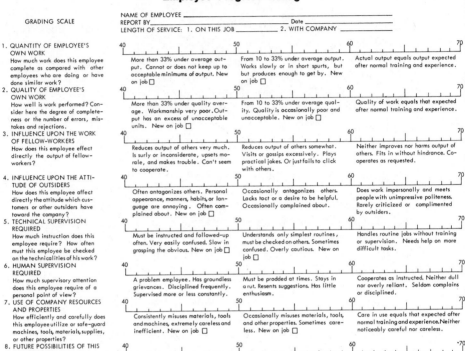

that rating discussions lead to needless controversy and recrimination. And second, in connection with the forced-choice plan of rating, to be described later, it is necessary that the method of scoring the rater's opinions be kept secret.

Although there may be occasions when ratings should be withheld from employees, it seems better to work toward a relationship of frank discussion between employer and employee. If grievances exist, or if employees have shortcomings, they cannot be reduced or removed simply by waiting. Sooner or later, the matters must be discussed. The question is one of timing: when is it most appropriate to open discussions? Of course, after a rating program has been installed, the first ratings will raise what appears to be a hornet's nest of controversy. Once these are cleared up, subsequent ratings will result in fewer controversies.

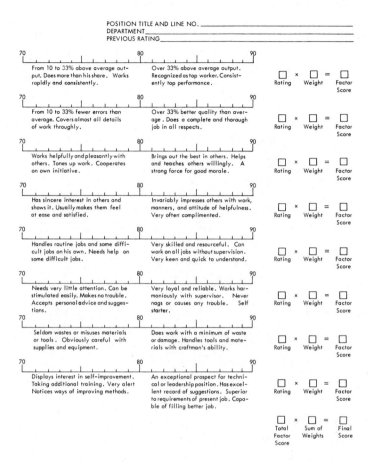

The most cogent reason for discussing evaluations is that they are helpful in counseling employees. If workers want to improve, they must know, first, their strong and weak points, and, second, what they must do to improve. Such knowledge can be helpfully obtained through consultation based on a good evaluation program. Indeed, some companies consider appraisal for counseling purposes a much more important use of evaluation than for rewards and penalties. An excellent system of counseling for executives showing the relations between appraisal, counseling, improvement programs, and information flows is illustrated in Table 12–1.

To be most useful for discussing ratings with employees, evaluations should be made periodically. It is rather common to rate new employees more frequently than old. Thus, in one company, new employees are

TABLE 12–1
Components of an Executive Appraisal System

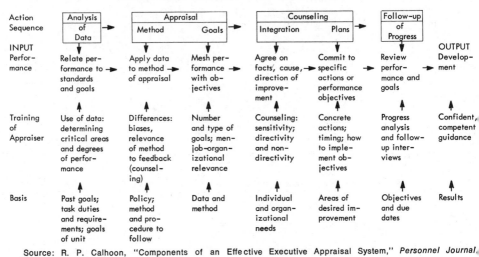

Action Sequence	Analysis of Data	Appraisal		Counseling		Follow-up of Progress	
		Method	Goals	Integration	Plans		
INPUT Performance	Relate performance to standards and goals	Apply data to method of appraisal	Mesh performance with objectives	Agree on facts, cause, direction of improvement	Commit to specific actions or performance objectives	Review performance and goals	OUTPUT Development
Training of Appraiser	Use of data: determining critical areas and degrees of performance	Differences: biases, relevance of method to feedback (counseling)	Number and type of goals; men-job-organizational relevance	Counseling: sensitivity; directivity and non-directivity	Concrete actions; timing; how to implement objectives	Progress analysis and follow-up interviews	Confident, competent guidance
Basis	Past goals; task duties and requirements; goals of unit	Policy; method and procedure to follow	Data and method	Individual and organizational needs	Areas of desired improvement	Objectives and due dates	Results

Source: R. P. Calhoon, "Components of an Effective Executive Appraisal System," *Personnel Journal,* vol. 48, no. 8, p. 618.

rated after one month, three months, six months, and a year. Thereafter, they are rated annually. This practice recognizes that newer employees need more help and also are more likely to be sources of trouble. Overall, good plans of evaluation call for appraisal semiannually or at the least annually.

Designs of Evaluation Forms

Design of forms is an important part of any evaluation plan. Graphical methods are widely used and will be described first. Later in this section attention will be turned to the forced-choice method.

1. Design of Graphical Forms. The use of rating forms can lead to excellent results, provided that practical rules of design are adopted. In the following are listed and described some of the more significant rules:

a. Perhaps the most important step, at least initially, in the design of forms is to determine precisely the objectives of the program. As noted earlier, there are two major uses of evaluation: (1) as the basis for rewards and penalties, and (2) as the basis for counseling. If the first of these objectives is sought, the rating form should include factors that measure employee contributions as much as possible. Figure 12–2 is an example of such selections, in that, except for the last item, all factors relate to output or efficiency in output. If the objective is counseling, factors that cause contributions should be selected, as illustrated by most of the items in Figure 12–1.

b. Having determined the type of factors to be rated, the next step is to determine which factors, and how many, should be selected. This problem is not too difficult when evaluation is restricted to productivity. For example, the factors in Figure 12–2 are very inclusive, covering all aspects of a given individual's work; yet the number of factors to be rated is not unduly large.

Evaluations that delve into personal characteristics present a more difficult problem. To begin with, even a brief review of the following list of personal characteristics reveals differences in specificity and problems of overlapping:

Personality	Honesty	Persistence
Character	Initiative	Imagination
Dependability	Industriousness	Enthusiasm
Attitude	Leadership	Aggressiveness
Adaptability	Judgment	Loyalty
Appearance	Cooperativeness	Creativeness

In selecting the factors to be rated, it has been found that not more than nine to twelve traits should be used. Some investigations have shown that as few as three or four traits are sufficient to give good results. However, until various groups of executives are taught to give up their belief that there is safety in numbers, it is easier to get their cooperation when a higher rather than a lower number of traits is used.

As to the traits to be selected, a better choice can be made if the following rules are watched:

1. Select traits that are specific rather than general; e.g., honesty is more definite than character.
2. Select traits that can be defined in terms understandable in the same way by all raters.
3. Select traits that are common to as many people as possible.
4. Select traits that raters can observe or be taught to observe in the day-to-day performance of employees.

c. Since all factors usually do not have equal weight in all jobs, it is also necessary to determine how much importance should be accorded to each one. This can be accomplished by conference with interested line executives. Some companies provide space for the weights on the form itself, whereas others contend that it is better to omit the weights in order to avoid confusing the raters. In the latter case the weighting is done by the personnel department.

d. In the physical design of rating forms, an important question is that of how to arrange the factors and the spaces for rating. This involves (1) the order of arranging factors and (2) the particulars of rating. There is no general rule that is followed in arranging factors;

some arrange them from specific to general, and others reverse this; some like to list factors easy to rate and then go on to the more difficult; and still others adopt a considered disorder.

In the matter of particulars of rating, there is a diversity of practice, much of which is mere whim. When the graphical plan of rating is to be used, adoption of the following suggestions may be desirable:

1. Do not number all scales in the same direction from high to low or low to high. To do this encourages the tendency of raters to evaluate all factors as they do the first, irrespective of warranted differences.

'   2. Use of scales of varying length, as shown in the following design, also serves to reduce the influence of the rating of earlier or subsequent factors:

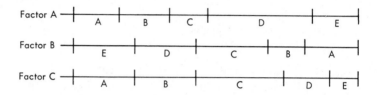

3. Use descriptions to indicate varying degrees of each trait instead of grades and numbers, and omit division points along the scales. As a consequence, the tendency of raters to fit each employee to the scale rather than to concentrate on the employee will be avoided. For example, some raters tend to check the following scale in the center or edge of each grade, depending upon their personal bias:

The following type of scale tends, however, to take the mind of the rater off the scale and encourage concentration on the employee:

e. The description of factors and degrees of factors, already mentioned, deserves special attention. Some of the hypothetical illustrations used in the foregoing would, if adopted, be weak because descriptions are not given. To use such terms as *excellent, above average, average,* and so forth, to describe varying degrees of factors is undesirable because each rater must interpret their meaning. As a result, varying standards are used to rate employees. Much to be preferred is the practice illustrated in Figure 12–3 of providing raters with space under each factor wherein raters can enter comments or significant incidents.

f. And finally, consideration should be given to general rules of form design. That is, size of type, color and weight of paper, size of form, and so forth, should be chosen to conform with such matters as who is to use the form, how long the forms are to be kept, where and how long forms are to be filed, and whether or not information is to be transferred to other records. Unless these matters are also kept in mind, rating forms will be designed, as many have been, that are difficult to handle at various stages of the rating procedure.

g. These recommendations, it is important to note, need not be followed to the letter in every case. Indeed, it is often unwise to insist upon some of these rules when such insistence would lead to objections from executives who must finally approve the program, but who are as yet not sufficiently educated to appreciate the finer details of design. In one case, for example, a personnel director had to violate rules of which he was aware because he knew that to insist upon his views might jeopardize the whole rating program. Wisely, he calculated how far he could go in designing a good system and yet get it approved. He did not confuse top executives with technical details, because he knew that once the program began to show results, he could get the changes that were desirable. Knowing how fast to push the extension of various personnel programs is an absolute requirement if a personnel director expects to be successful, personally as well as professionally.

2. Design of the Forced-Choice Method. The forced-choice method of rating has been developed in an attempt to improve the accuracy of ratings by reducing the biases, intentional or not, of raters. Under the graphical method, for example, a rater may give a particular employee high ratings because of a desire for that person to receive a raise. Under the forced-choice method, the rater, when making choices, cannot tell how the final rating is going to turn out.

This is accomplished by providing the rater with from 30 to 50 sets of statements from which to choose in each set the one that is most and the one that is least descriptive of the person being rated. The following is an example of such a set of statements:

	Most	Least
Unwilling to make long-run decisions	A	A
Willing to make a decision in a new situation	B	B
Tenses in discussions with other supervisors	C	C
Good for technical staff positions	D	D
High potential for limited-task advancement	E	E

FIGURE 12-3

RATING FORM FOR SUPERVISORY CANDIDATE
(For Use In a Rating Interview)

Name of Candidate _Jas. H. Hobsell_   Evaluator _H. Dorner_

Name of Individual Interviewed _W. Schmutz_   Date _6/8/_

Position _Foreman of Assembly Section_

Information sought	Suggested questions for the interviewer

1. PERFORMANCE AS A WORKER

A. TECHNICAL COMPETENCE IN THE PROPOSED SUPERVISORY JOB
—Understand most of the work well?
—Would he be able to answer technical questions?
—Does he often have to get help from supervisor?
—Do others respect him for his technical competence?

Below Average ——————✓—————— Above Average

Seems to understand work fairly well, but lacks experience on all jobs in assembly. Picks things up quickly.

Tell me something about his performance as a worker? (How would you describe him in general?)

How well does he know the different parts of the job? (i.e.; his technical competence)

What parts of the job does he do best? Poorest?

B. WORK HABITS
—Hard worker?
—Turn out good quality work?
—Organize his work well?
—Safety conscious?
—Good housekeeper?
—Thorough?
—Cost conscious? Watch scrap, etc?
—Tend to emphasize one aspect of the job at the expense of others? _No._

Below Average ——————✓—————— Above Average

Eager - hard worker Very good organizer.

Neat, thorough, efficient.

Tell me something about his work habits, such as the kind of work he turns out, how he organizes his work, and the like?

How about the amount of work he turns out? Is he the kind of guy who finds work to do, or does he wait until a new job is assigned?

2. MENTAL AND PHYSICAL QUALIFICATIONS

A. MENTAL ABILITY
—Catch on quickly to new things?
—Does he look ahead to catch things before they happen?
—Use good judgment? Make wise decisions?
—Ever suggest new approaches to problems?
—Could he keep records and write reports if he had to?

Below Average ——————✓—————— Above Average

Catches on quickly. Uses his head - looks ahead.

How well does he catch on to new things? Can he be switched to other jobs easily?

How about his ability to make decisions?

Does he look ahead to catch things before they happen, or is he apt to wait until something has to be done?

B. PHYSICAL CHARACTERISTICS
—In good health?
—Out sick a lot?
—Any defects which would handicap him in a high-pressure job?
—Regular in attendance? (If poor, is it due to sickness?)

Below Average ——————✓—————— Above Average

_O. K._

Good attendance.

How about his health?

Does he have any physical defects which would handicap him in a high-pressure job?

FIGURE 12–3 (continued)

3. PERSONALITY CHARACTERISTICS

A. MATURITY

—Apt to indulge in too much horseplay?

—Show childish reactions (pouting, tattletale, etc.)

—Stand up well under pressure?

—Willing to accept responsibility? (Handle problems or duck them?)

Below Average _____ / _____ ✓ _____ Above Average

Very mature. Good sense of responsibility

How about his personality? Would you describe that in some detail?

Is he always very mature in his actions, or is he sometimes a little childish in some ways?

B. SOCIAL EFFECTIVENESS

Effect on others—

—Others have confidence in him?

—Enjoy working with him?

—Others take their troubles to him?

—Express himself well?

—Too much of a "swell guy"? (others take advantage of him)

Below Average _____ / _____ ✓ _____ Above Average

Others enjoy working with him "One of the best leaders we've had."

What effect does he have on others?

Would he gain the respect and cooperation of others?

Attitude toward others—

—Interest in people?

—Cooperative?

—Fair and objective, or inclined to be prejudiced?

—Tend to blame others for his own mistakes?

—Tend to treat junior members of group as inferiors?

—Inclined to be "cliquish"? (Might have favorites)

—Good reaction to authority? A good follower? Resent criticism? Likely not to obey a rule when it's easier not to?

Very helpful with new men – seems to have a lot of interest in others.

A good follower. Welcomes constructive criticism.

Tell me something about his attitude toward others?

Does he always seem to be thinking of the other person, or does he sometimes tend to be a little self-centered?

How does he react to authority?

C. MOTIVATION

—Is he eager to advance?

—Interested in a career with the Company?

—Understand Company polices and regulations well?

—Can he be counted on in emergencies?

Below Average _____ / _____ ✓ _____ Above Average

Very eager. Has high hopes to get ahead in G. E.

How would you describe his attitude toward his work and the Company?

SUMMARY BY RATER

Assets— *A natural leader.*

All things considered, what do you consider this man's major strong points to be?

Liabilities— *Lacks experience.*

What are his major shortcomings?

Overall recommendation— *Would be an excellent supervisor.*

How would you rate his chances of success as a supervisor?

Recommendations regarding his future in other lines— *Could use a broader experience background – a chance to acquire more technical "know-how."*

If he were not considered to be qualified for a supervisory job, can he advance along other lines?

Courtesy: General Electric Company

Some of these statements sound favorable, and some do not. But from previous research, it will have been found that some of the favorable ones are really meaningful and count for a person if checked; the same is true of the unfavorable. The rater, however, does not know which of the "favorable" ones are really favorable, and which of the "unfavorable" are really unfavorable. So the rater cannot by choice favor friends and purposefully harm those who are not.

The plan, however, has two shortcomings. First, it is practically useless for counseling purposes because it is impossible to explain simply why a person received a rating. Second, its construction requires a great deal of work to arrive at a valid set of statements.

Accuracy of Evaluations

Unless the accuracy of evaluations is checked, they will be unacceptable to employees and useless to the company. Accuracy may be tested by checking the *validity* of evaluations, that is, how well ratings really measure the factors they set out to measure. Thus, if a plan purports to measure (among other things) initiative, it is valid if this trait is really appraised. Second, accuracy must be concerned with *reliability*, or the consistency with which ratings are made. Thus, if a supervisor gives an employee a rating of "very good," let us say, on two successive evaluations of dependability, and the employee deserves this rating, the ratings are said to be reliable. And third, accuracy of raters, one to another, may be checked.

1. Validity of Evaluations. Measuring the validity of evaluations is not easy because criteria are seldom available against which to check ratings. When employees are rated for such a factor as personality, for example, the very fact that they are being rated for it is usually an indication that a better method of estimating it is not available. Yet, by comparing ratings with various aspects of an employee's employment records and performance, adequate checks of validity can be obtained.

Perhaps the simplest overall check of validity is to compare ratings with the performance of employees. For example, when ratings of personal traits compare favorably with ratings of performance, a smooth progression should be obtained when the data for all values are arranged from high to low. The existence of the "halo effect" is also a sign of low validity of ratings. This can be determined by examining ratings to note whether there is a tendency for raters to rate all other factors the same as some one factor about an employee with which they were particularly impressed, favorably or unfavorably.

A check on validity can also be obtained by comparing estimates of two or more raters on the same employees. For example, if two raters, *A* and *B*, rated a given employee as shown in Figure 12–4, the validity of

FIGURE 12–4

Comparison of Profiles

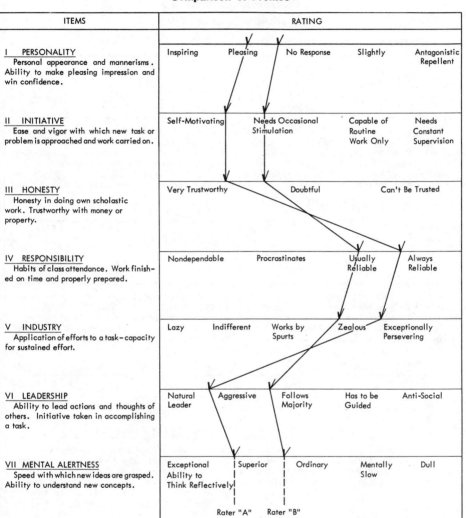

ITEMS	RATING				
I PERSONALITY Personal appearance and mannerisms. Ability to make pleasing impression and win confidence.	Inspiring	Pleasing	No Response	Slightly	Antagonistic Repellent
II INITIATIVE Ease and vigor with which new task or problem is approached and work carried on.	Self-Motivating	Needs Occasional Stimulation		Capable of Routine Work Only	Needs Constant Supervision
III HONESTY Honesty in doing own scholastic work. Trustworthy with money or property.	Very Trustworthy		Doubtful		Can't Be Trusted
IV RESPONSIBILITY Habits of class attendance. Work finished on time and properly prepared.	Nondependable	Procrastinates		Usually Reliable	Always Reliable
V INDUSTRY Application of efforts to a task–capacity for sustained effort.	Lazy	Indifferent	Works by Spurts	Zealous	Exceptionally Persevering
VI LEADERSHIP Ability to lead actions and thoughts of others. Initiative taken in accomplishing a task.	Natural Leader	Aggressive	Follows Majority	Has to be Guided	Anti-Social
VII MENTAL ALERTNESS Speed with which new ideas are grasped. Ability to understand new concepts.	Exceptional Ability to Think Reflectively	Superior	Ordinary	Mentally Slow	Dull

Rater "A"   Rater "B"

one or the other, or both, is in error. The lines connecting the scores for each factor by each rater are called "profiles" and are commonly used because they aid the eye in interpreting the ratings. Such differences in estimates are common because most raters tend to be somewhat easy or harsh. Hence the tendency of each rater must be discovered and either corrected by instruction or allowed for if given raters are too set in their ways.

FIGURE 12–5

Excerpt from a Critical-Incident Rating Form

PERFORMANCE RECORD

WORK HABITS AND ATTITUDES

13. Response to Departmental Needs

4	3	2	1		1	2	3	4
5								5
6								6

a. Tried to get others to slow down, refuse tasks; b. Criticized equipment, facilities, methods unnecessarily; c. Was unwilling to perform work beyond his assignment or responsibility; d. Refused to pass along his idea for an improvement.

A. Tried to get co-workers to accept new rate, job, etc.; B. Increased his efficiency despite co-workers' resentment; C. Accepted extra work in spite of inconvenience; D. Accepted more difficult jobs; E. Suggested improved production procedures.

14. Getting Along with Others

4	3	2	1		1	2	3	4
5								5
6								6

a. Became upset or angry over work; b. Quarreled with fellow employees; c. Criticized, annoyed co-workers; d. Bossed co-worker; e. Interfered with equipment of another; f. Refused help to co-worker.

A. Remained calm under stress; B. Kept temper under provocation; C. Helped co-worker at inconvenience to self; D. Avoided friction by tact, consideration; E. Assisted fellow employee needing help.

15. Initiative

4	3	2	1		1	2	3	4
5								5
6								6

a. Failed to plan work when necessary; b. Failed to obtain tools until need arose; c. Failed to point out defective parts or operation; d. Failed to take action in an emergency.

A. Planned efficient ways of doing work; B. Stocked materials and tools ahead of time; C. Prepared work area, machine in advance; D. Volunteered for more responsible tasks; E. Voluntarily did work in addition to that expected; F. Pointed out defects on the line.

16. Responsibility

4	3	2	1		1	2	3	4
5								5
6								6

a. Passed up chance for more training; b. Passed up chance to learn more about the job; c. Gave misleading, incorrect instructions; d. Poorly directed work in foreman's absence.

A. Got additional information on his job, department; B. Took additional outside training; C. Got information on improving work; D. Planned a schedule for others; E. Trained, instructed other employees; F. Got cooperation between employees.

Source: John C. Flanagan, "Principles and Procedures in Evaluating Performance," *Personnel*, vol. 28, no. 5, p. 383.

The critical-incident technique is an interesting plan for increasing the validity of ratings. It provides for the collection and classification of reports of behavior which represent significant examples of success and failure. The supervisor is first given instruction on traits to be observed and samples of behavior descriptive of successful and unsuccessful application of the traits. Then the supervisor must note when such incidents actually take place. An excerpt from a form for recording the incidents is shown in Figure 12–5. The theory of the plan is that the rating really consists of observed experiences rather than opinions about behavior; like a production report, it shows what happened and not an opinion about happenings.

2. Reliability of Evaluations. The reliability of evaluations is ordinarily checked by comparing the ratings of given raters from period to period. If an employee has improved in certain aspects or remained the same, the ratings should have increased in value or remained the same, as the case may be. Hence, checks should be made also with other measures which indicate the relative changes in employees from period to period.

Reliability may be checked by comparing ratings with records of an employee's performance. Some companies also compare the estimates of a number of raters for the same ratees as a check on their reliability. There is some question whether this is a test of validity or reliability, or both. In any event, its use is advisable for the good it will do in calling attention to variances in raters.

3. Accuracy of Raters. It is also desirable to determine (a) which raters are more lenient than others and (b) which have a tendency toward the halo effect. Leniency of raters can be determined simply by averaging the ratings of each and then getting an average of the averages. Any rater whose average is significantly off the average should be checked for leniency or undue strictness, as the case may be. Another check on leniency can be obtained if two or more raters rate the same employees. Significant deviations can then be readily checked.

In the case of the halo effect, as noted earlier, ratings are influenced by a particularly impressive characteristic of an employee. For example, a given supervisor may be impressed by the neatness of a particular employee. Unconsciously or consciously, the supervisor proceeds to overrate the worker on matters of dependability, initiative, cooperation, etc. Sometimes this tendency can be discovered by a simple examination of ratings. At other times, interviews will be necessary to ascertain the degree to which given supervisors are susceptible to such errors.

Rules of Evaluating

Forms of rating are only tools that must be used properly if desired ends are to be attained. Skill and understanding must be applied in rating employees. Hence, it is now appropriate to suggest a number of rules which, if followed, will increase the contributions of evaluations.

First of all, it is important to select raters carefully. In some companies, two raters, usually the immediate supervisor and the supervisor's superior, evaluate each employee. The purpose of the double evaluation is to derive a check on the ratings and to induce higher executives to keep in closer touch with lower levels of the organization. This practice is, however, debatable. To be sure, the purpose of the double check is admirable, but it is unwise to ask an executive to make estimates about employees with whom association is infrequent or when such association would result in neglect of regular duties. Ordinarily, it is better practice to place the burden of rating on the person best able to assume it—the immediate supervisor.

Second, the rater should be thoroughly instructed in the purposes and values of the program. Hence, it is desirable to hold conferences in which the reasons for the program, the part supervisors are to play, and the advantages to all concerned are carefully explained. Such conferences also can increase the supervisor's prestige and feeling of worthwhileness, and importance to the success of the program.

Third, all factors, degrees of factors, and terms should be meticulously explained to raters. Both verbal and printed explanations are worth using. In this way, there is greater assurance that all raters will interpret all terms in the same way and hence produce ratings that are based on the same standards.

Fourth, it is imperative to recognize the sensitivity factor in rating. Any plan which purports to evaluate employees runs into the feelings of people about what may happen to them. They become concerned about the fairness of the rater. They may even question the right to "measure" any human being. Hence the plan should give assurance that no arbitrary decisions will be reached. Indeed, it might be well to forgo such words as *measure* and *evaluate*. In their place, it would be well to substitute such phrases as "how we are getting along" or "what is happening to performance."

Fifth, along similar lines, rating should be viewed in its psychological and sociological as well as technical framework. This merely is a recognition that any rating affects the attitudes of individuals as individuals and as members of groups. Persons rated can easily react unfavorably even to a fair rating if they feel the system of rating exposes them to a reduction of status in the eyes of coworkers.

Sixth, several suggestions can be made that will improve the accuracy of ratings. Raters should be impressed with the need for observing workers in terms of the factors in which they are to be rated. In this way the task of rating will not be a chore or a matter of guesswork. Raters should also be advised to guard against allowing recent events or isolated cases to influence unduly their decisions. In this connection, the practice of recollecting examples of individual performance and traits is desirable. Then, too, raters should be advised to allow enough time and find a relatively quiet office for the rating job. Interruptions tend to reduce the accuracy of ratings. And finally, it has been found advisable to rate all employees one factor at a time because the consistency of rating is thereby increased.

QUESTIONS

1. What objectives may be sought by employee rating plans?
2. For purposes of rewarding or penalizing employees, what aspects of employees should be evaluated, if possible?
3. For purposes of counseling, what aspects of employees should be appraised?
4. What bases of comparison may be used in comparing employees in an evaluation plan?
5. What are the pros and cons of consulting with employees about their ratings?
6. What rules should be followed in selecting the factors to be included in an employee rating form?
7. Why is it undesirable to use merely the names or grade levels of factors on an employee rating plan?
8. How does the forced-choice plan of rating employees tend to reduce bias of raters?
9. How can the validity and reliability of employee ratings be determined?
10. What rules would it be desirable to follow in evaluating employees?

CASE 12–1.   A SELECTION CHOICE

Two qualified and able workers are being considered for promotion. The job in question is that of department head in a governmental agency responsible for the administration of the procurement and supply of coal.

The two candidates are Mr. Blow, who is currently the chief of a major unit in the coal department, and Mr. Doe, who is a technical consultant to the department chief. Their background and qualifications are as follows:

1. Mr. Blow has been employed by the government for 12 years and had been interested in getting promoted to a higher grade. He has purchased a new home and has a wife and five children to support. He is 40 years of age and expects to work until retirement age.

Mr. Blow belongs to a minority religious group. He worked his way through college and went on to earn a master's degree in business administration. He started his career in the present department as a clerk and has worked his way up to his present position.

After several years' experience in this department, he became an expert in the supply of coal for the government and was of valuable help in establishing procedures and policies in this area. He spent long hours in his office without extra pay in order to accomplish his work.

His superiors regard him as a very capable man. Oftentimes, he is consulted by other agencies on coal problems and is helpful in policy decisions that affect the government. His coworkers respect his ability, admire his efficiency, and enjoy working for him. His department chief has told him on occasion that he would be considered for promotion at the first available opportunity.

Mr. Blow has one shortcoming: He uses flowery language and talks excessively over minor details. He has been cautioned about this, to no avail. In fact, he has been relieved of the duty of attending important conferences because the conferees complained that time was wasted by his pointless talk over details. Since his technical knowledge is respected, his opinions are sought, but they must be submitted in memorandum form.

2. Mr. Doe is approximately at the same grade level as Mr. Blow, but he is a consultant rather than a supervisory executive. He is about 45 years of age and has no children. He enjoys his work and would like to stay on in government service in order to earn retirement benefits.

Mr. Doe is a graduate mining engineer and has had about 20 years' experience with private coal firms. He has held administrative jobs in industry, but his jobs with the government have been primarily technical.

As a technical consultant, he also attends many conferences and is noted for giving clear, concise, and dependable reports. He is well liked and respected by higher officials, and his immediate superior has rated him as a key worker in the organization.

If Mr. Blow is turned down for the job, he may think that he was discriminated against because of his religion, that he is not being rewarded for the many hours he put in without pay, and that his long and loyal service is not appreciated.

If Mr. Doe is turned down he will remain with the agency another year and then return to private industry. It will be difficult to replace him, but he has promised to stay long enough so that a replacement could perhaps be found and trained.

Questions

1. In terms of the available information, which man do you prefer?
2. Is there any other information that would be helpful to you in reaching a correct decision?

CASE 12–2. THE SALES DEPARTMENT STORE

The Sales Department Store is located in a medium-sized city in an agricultural area and does a business of about $2 million annually. It is owned and managed by A. B. Comer, who is elderly, resistant to change, and opinionated in most matters. His son, James Comer, manages one of the large departments, does some of the top administrative work, and also handles the personnel duties. A daughter-in-law, D. E. Jones, runs the accounting office, supervises maintenance, and handles some of the top executive functions. These are the top executives of the company, under whom are the department managers and buyers.

One function that Mr. A. B. Comer and Mr. James Comer will not delegate is that related to personnel. They receive requests for new employees, but they do all of the hiring. However, they give almost unlimited authority to department managers in buying and selling. Their success has been through other people's rather than their own personal merchandising skill. The difference in their ages and background sometimes gives rise to clashes in matters pertaining to employees. This was illustrated in the case of Mrs. Jane Doe, who was hired for the cosmetics department, which is one of the seven departments managed by Mr. John Swift.

A few months later, and after Mrs. Doe had been transferred to the book department, young Comer came to Swift about Mrs. Doe.

JAMES: Mr. Comer is really mad about that Mrs. Doe now. He says fire her today, give her a week's pay in advance, and get her out of the store. He said she's been absent two more times; and he has received a complaint from a customer about her; and every time he sees her, she is sitting around reading a book. This afternoon at 2:30 he saw her sitting in the kitchen drinking coffee and reading a book, and it was 45 minutes before she came out.

SWIFT: Well, he might have bothered to find out why, before jumping to conclusions. One of the women is sick and didn't show up today, but phoned in. That made us shorthanded, with two others away on vacation. Jane volunteered to work in two departments so the women could get away for lunch, then she was going without her own. About 2:30, I insisted that she take time off at least to get a sandwich and rest awhile. It would be unfair to fire her for being considerate of other people—and if he does, I quit, too, right now!

JAMES: Oh, that's different. He wouldn't be sore if he knew that. But what about this reading all the time?

SWIFT: I've asked her to read every chance she gets. That's the only way she can know these new books as they come out. She reads all the book reviews, and keeps the bulletin board posted with them for the benefit of the customers. Have you noticed the board she put up over there? The customers like that. When she isn't busy, she reads the fly leaves of different books. Then, at noon she reads and at night takes books home with her. I check them out to her, and she keeps them in perfect condition, brings them back, and we sell them at no loss. She has a remarkable memory for books and can really talk to customers about them. It used to be that nine out of ten people were just browsing around; now, nine out of ten are buying. Have you noticed those book sales?

JAMES: Yes, but Mary is selling a lot more than she used to. As much as Jane, according to the sales slips.

SWIFT: Mary isn't selling anything. She couldn't sell anything if her life depended on it—you know that. She is a sweet girl that most of the people like, and she just waits on them to get them what they ask for. But that works out swell with Jane. Mary handles the miscellaneous trade on stationery and stuff and writes up the sales tickets on Jane's sales while Jane is waiting on another book customer. That's why Mary has more sales slips now; she writes them out while Jane sells. [*No commission on sales had resulted in such working arrangements between the women.*]

JAMES: Of course, it looks bad if she is reading on the job. But it's fine that she is finding out so much about the merchandise.

SWIFT: She isn't sitting down reading a book out in the department. She stands at a book rack, arranges the books, checks stock, and reads fly leaves, and is Johnny-on-the-spot when a customer approaches. That is exactly what she should be doing. Does Mr. Comer prefer Mary's just standing around doing nothing when a customer isn't there?

JAMES: Can't you keep Mary busy?

SWIFT: By giving her specific tasks, but I can't watch her every minute. She hasn't an ounce of initiative.

JAMES: Would you like to replace her?

SWIFT: Not necessarily. She works out well with Jane. But I'd much rather lose her than Jane.

JAMES: I have suggested to Mr. Comer that we let Mary go or transfer her to the office because she can't sell. She is the complete opposite of the sales type. But Mr. Comer insists on keeping her there. It seems you and I disagree with the boss on people, doesn't it?

SWIFT: Well, a couple of them, anyway. We seem to agree on all the others though. What was the complaint about Jane?

JAMES: An older woman, an acquaintance of Mr. Comer's said she didn't think that woman was the right kind to have working here, especially with a sweet person like Mary. Thought it would contaminate Mary and give the store a bad name having such people for clerks.

SWIFT: Oh, I know who you mean now and what the complaint was about. It was the only real boner Jane has pulled on the sales floor; but oddly enough, it helped business, and I got the best laugh out of it that I've had all year. See that book rack built around that post? Jane was standing on this side of it, that old prude on the left side, and two fellows from the university on the right side of it. All were talking to her. The woman had wondered when Jane had had a chance to read so much, since she knew so many of the books, and Jane told her she read every night when she went to bed. The college fellows asked if she had any more books like *Forever Amber*. Jane pulled three books from the rack and started telling about them. The woman interposed in an insulting tone: "Young lady, do you read such trash as that? I'm surprised that you don't read something to improve your mind!" Jane was half indignant, and said: "Lady, after I work here all day, then go home and cook supper, wash dishes, clean house, and take care of the kids, and finally get to bed, I go to bed to be entertained, not educated!" The boys started roaring; then, it dawned on Jane how it sounded, and she put her hand up to her mouth and started laughing, too. The old lady left in sort of a huff. Mary and I had overheard the thing, and we were both laughing, too. The boys bought all three of the books, have come back twice since then and bought stuff, and brought friends with them both times. That bunch bought almost $100 worth of stuff, including a good suitcase from the luggage department, and they are definitely Jane's customers. Of course, we haven't seen the old lady since.

JAMES: How about her absences lately?

SWIFT: She hasn't been absent. She worked on her scheduled day off last week so Mary could get away for a church function. So this week, Mary worked for her, and that's why she was gone an extra day. And she needed the rest; she's been working at two jobs and is looking rather tired.

JAMES: Where else is she working?

SWIFT: At night, as a waitress. She took on the extra job for a few weeks to make money to pay off the loan she took on the house. Now, she has decided to stay there permanently and quit here because she heard via the grapevine from the office that Mr. Comer wants to get rid of her. She told me just before you came down. She said she would stay here, though, to help me out until I could get someone to replace her. I thanked her for that. I would like her to stay here permanently, but I didn't press the point because she is earning over three times as much there as she is here, counting tips.

JAMES: Well, it's best, in a way. It will get Mr. Comer off our neck.

SWIFT: And lose a lot of business. I'll bet you ten to one you can't find anyone, at her salary, who will sell half as much merchandise in that department as she has. And she would have stayed in spite of the salary difference because she likes to work so well here, except for Mr. Comer. But this case has taught me something. There is no future in working for a place where prejudice overrides facts and business considerations, so I'm leaving. I'll stay till the first of next month. That will give you a chance to find a replacement, and me a chance to make an inventory and get everything shipshape.

JAMES: Do you feel that strongly about the clerk?

SWIFT: Not personally, but as a matter of principle I do. That could happen to any of the individuals here if it happened to her, and it could happen to me. Under such conditions, there is no future in this place.

JAMES: I don't want you to leave, and I know Mr. Comer won't. You have done a grand job with these departments. Think it over, and talk to him before you do anything definite.

Mr. Swift did not leave then but did leave two months later, in good grace, when he accepted a much better job in a salary range the store could not meet. The store lost the top salesclerk in the seven departments and the manager who had the largest volume of business for the seven departments in the history of the store. The elder Mr. Comer was quite pleased to get rid of the woman who was "no good," and young Mr. Comer was relieved of a critical point of friction.

Questions

1. Criticize the handling of this case.
2. Was there any other logical outcome?

part III
The Development Phase of Personnel Management

People do not come complete into an organization. They must learn to adjust to a new environment, increase and sharpen the skills they have, become understanding participants in organizational endeavors, and meet the challenges of changing conditions.

Such improvements may be left to chance or planning. No doubt, many companies rely upon the former alternative. But modern personnel management relies upon formal programs of development for all kinds and all levels of employees. The development of the man at the machine or the man in the executive chair are the concern of personnel management through training, education, and communication. Such developmental programs with their various types, practices and principles are the subjects matter of this Part.

CHAPTER 13

TRAINING OPERATIVE EMPLOYEES

Training and Education

This chapter and the next three are devoted to a study of training and education in business. The term *training* is used here to indicate any process by which the aptitudes, skills, and abilities of employees to perform specific jobs are increased. This task may be contrasted with that of increasing the knowledge, understanding, or attitude of employees so that they are better adjusted to their working environment. The term *education* is used here to denote the latter task.

To clarify these terms, the example of a trainee on a drill press may be considered. Teaching a worker how to operate the drill press is training, whereas giving a course in economics is education. The two may go hand in hand, as in the case of a supervisor who, while showing an operator how to seal a package, also talks about the sales policies of the company and their importance to each factory employee.

Although education in attitudes is often undertaken at the same time as training, and wisely so, it is better for discussional purposes to take up the two phases of learning separately. Hence, in this chapter, operative training will be discussed, and training of executives will be taken up in the next chapter. Following that, educational programs will be taken up in the next chapter. Following that, educational programs will be taken up under the chapter heading "Education."

In the present chapter, training of operative employees is taken up under the following major headings:

1. Justification and scope of training.
2. Courses and programs of training.

3. Factors in a training program.
4. Evaluation of training programs.

JUSTIFICATION AND SCOPE

One of the first questions that must be answered regarding training is whether or not the cost is justified. The simplest argument in favor of a formal program is that a company pays for training whether it has a program or not. Some executives conclude that they do not have any training costs because they have no training program. But are all their employees hired with skills and aptitudes equal to the jobs to be done? Do their employees learn nothing while they are working? Whose machines, materials, and facilities are employees using while their skills improve? Answers would show that the employees learn on the job by themselves, but the company unwittingly foots the bill.

Viewed positively, the values of training are not far to seek. First, training serves to improve employee skill, which in turn increases the quantity and quality of output. Second, the relative amount of equipment and material required to produce a unit of output is decreased. Third, executive effort will tend to shift from the disagreeable need of correcting mistakes to the more pleasant tasks of planning work and of encouraging expert employees. And last, the various increases in productivity should find reflection in increased returns to both employer and employees.

Although all employees should undergo training, all need not be trained to the same degree, and seldom can all be trained at the same time. Company facilities for training are rarely sufficient to undertake such a broad program. Hence the guiding principle should be that of attacking training problems where the needs are greatest. After urgent needs are taken care of, those with lower priority should be served.

As yet, standards as to the amounts of training that should be provided on various types of jobs are practically nonexistent. Even in the field of apprentice training, practice differs considerably. In some trades the apprentice period is two years; and in others, it is as high as seven. Length of training among other job areas is equally variable. Each company must work out time standards of training for itself, changing them as its experience warrants. Standards should be set for such matters as:

1. Total hours of training time.
2. Calendar spacing of the total hours.
3. Parts of the day assigned to training.
4. Scheduling of retraining sessions.

COURSES OF TRAINING

Many approaches to training are being used in industry. To describe and examine them all is beyond the scope of this chapter. However, the more common methods of training operative employees are taken up now. The types of training are not mutually exclusive but invariably overlap and employ many of the same techniques. A few of the more common types are examined more fully in this section.

On-the-Job Training

Undoubtedly, training is most commonly done on the job. It requires no special school, the student is being trained at a point where no changeover will be required, and this output adds to the total of the department. These are favorable points for a training plan that is simple, too.

On-the-job training can be improved if some simple rules are followed. First, what the learner is to be taught, and how, should be determined and preferably set down on paper, at least in major outline. Second, the instructor should be carefully selected and trained. It is well for the supervisor to do the training if time will permit, because it will be a favorable opportunity to get acquainted, with the new worker and to make an impression, personally and for the company. When time does not permit the supervisor to do this work, the next best practice is to have a departmental trainer. When this is not practical, a seasoned and understanding worker should be appointed to teach the new worker. But it is well to pay such part-time instructors a bonus for each learner trained, so that they will not hurry this responsibility in order to return to their own duties on which incentive payments may otherwise be lost. And third, a definite feedback schedule should be provided, so that the results of the training and the progress of the learner can be established.

Vestibule Training

In "vestibule" training, employees are taken through a short course under working conditions that approximate actual sales, shop, or office conditions. It gets its name from the resemblance of the school to a house. Such a course usually takes from a few days to a few weeks at the most and is used where only a few skills are to be acquired. Thus, training may be given to newly hired comptometer operators. As a result, they will be able to do the work required of them when they step into the departments for which they were hired.

Vestibule training has the advantage of training numbers of people in a short period of time without disturbing the flow of normal routines. Moreover, the employees can be adjusted to actual conditions under guided direction and gradually speeded up as they gain confidence. In addition, misfits or poor practices can be eliminated before actual production conditions are encountered.

Vestibule training, however, requires the duplication of sales, shop, or office facilities in a school area. Consequently, it must be limited to types of instruction in which the machinery used is not too expensive to install in a school or which can be used, on and off, as employment demands, without excessive overhead cost. It is also limited to those jobs in which there is high turnover or a continually increasing demand for workers.

Apprenticeship Training

Apprenticeship is followed in trades, crafts, and technical fields in which proficiency can be acquired only after a relatively long period of time in direct association with the work and under the direct supervision of experts. A partial list of areas in which such training is practiced includes the following:

Barbers	Die sinkers	Jewelers	Plumbers
Boilermakers	Drafters	Lens grinders	Printers
Carpenters	Electricians	Millwrights	Shipfitters
Coppersmiths	Engravers	Molders	Stonemasons
Coremakers	Furriers	Painters	Toolmakers

The federal government and the unions have had an impact upon apprenticeship training. The federal government has interested itself in apprentices because of wage rates, training subsidies, and standardized practices. If an employer desires to pay apprentices less than amounts prescribed by wages and hours laws, apprenticeship agreements must be covered in writing and submitted to administrators of these acts in order to obtain a certificate of exemption. Apprentice courses are subject to federal regulation when learners are subsidized by the government. And the federal government, through its Bureau of Apprenticeship and Training, has also cooperated with state apprenticeship councils to standardize apprenticeship practices regarding amounts of training, wages, and measures of progress.

Unions, too, are concerned with apprenticeship programs. First, they are interested in establishing apprentice quotas in order to prevent undue displacement of fully trained workers by learners. Second, they have used such programs to restrict entry into a trade or industry. And third, they have bargained over wage rates and conditions of employment of apprentices.

Internship Training

Internship training refers to a joint program of training in which schools and businesses cooperate. Selected students carry on regular school studies for periods ranging from 3 to 12 months and then work in some factory or office for a designated period of time, alternating in this fashion until the course is completed. The training is usually conducted in connection with highly skilled or professional types of training. Trade and high schools often cooperate with industry in this way to train various vocational workers. And it has been employed by industry and colleges for training for management, accounting, and engineering positions.

By such training, it is hoped to gain a good balance between theory and practice. In addition, students may gain a better appreciation of their school studies by having a practical background against which to visualize classroom principles. Moreover, the students who have a definite vocation or profession in mind are likely to be better motivated because they can see the practical side of their objectives being achieved. From the company's side, the gain is in a better balanced employee and one who has already been exposed to its practices.

Internship has its disadvantages. It is such a slow process as to try the patience of the student as well as the instructor or supervisor. It takes so long that one or both of the parties involved may become discouraged. It suffers when business depressions call for layoffs; and under it, present employees feel that the interns are being favored at their expense.

Outside Courses

A number of agencies and groups have cooperated with industry in the solution of its training problems. Vocational, correspondence, trade, and evening schools have been a constant source of supply of semiskilled, skilled, and technical workers. Such training must be sufficiently broad to qualify graduates for any one of a number of employers.

The federal government has assisted industry in its training work. Vocational training is given support by providing federal funds to match contributions by the states to participating companies. Federal funding is also provided vocational training of the handicapped and veterans. The Manpower Development and Training Act of 1962 has been helpful to those who need retraining and upgrading because their old jobs have been lost in the march of technological progress. And a wide range of programs to help the underprivileged has been funded in recent years.

Programmed Learning

Until recently, learning has normally been associated with a human teacher. Coming into play is the use of mechanical devices to aid the learner. Through audiovisual mechanisms, instruction has been carried on in such fields as company organizations, product knowledge, sales information, office forms, and technical language. These are more or less routine areas, although some effort is being directed toward more creative-type subjects.

With the use of such a mechanism—or programmed instruction as it is better called—material to be learned is fed into a machine. Each bit of information is imprinted on an individual frame, an example of which is shown in Figure 13–1. The machine projects an item, after which the student is asked on a succeeding frame to respond to a question or problem pertaining to the preceding informational frame. The student's response is fed into the machine by selecting from a choice of button switches, or by making a check mark. If the response is correct, the

FIGURE 13–1

Excerpts from Programmed Instructional Materials

1. The 7070 is a data processing system. To prepare a payroll, to maintain an inventory, or to perform other accounting applications, a customer can use the 7070 data_____ _____

   processing system

2. All data processing systems require some type of input unit or units. In order to put information into the 7070_____ _____ _____, an_____unit is required.

   data processing system   input

3. In addition to one or more input units all data processing systems require some sort of processing unit or units to operate on the input data. The 7070 has several_____units to process input data.

   processing

4. Data are put into the 7070 by means of an_____unit. The information (data) is then operated upon by several_____

   input   processing units

5. All data processing systems must also have output units to write out information in a usable form. A mechanical printer is an example of an_____unit.

   output

Source: J. L. Hughes and W. J. McNamara, "The Potential of Programmed Instruction," *Personnel,* vol. 38, no. 6, p. 61.

machine turns up a new frame with additional information, to which the student again responds. If the response is wrong, the machine repeats the original information in the same or a new form. Until a satisfactory response is obtained from the student, no new or more complex informational bits are given.

Such mechanical programming is expensive to construct but has impressive advantages. The instruction is individualized, and a person can go as fast as personal capabilities permit. The material is presented in small segments; this operates on the principle that small-dose learning is best and that small errors can be more quickly unlearned than large ones. Such programming must be constructed with extreme care so that a logical and rigorous lesson plan is provided. And since a student is immediately informed whether the answer is right or wrong, successes reinforce the learning process, while failures lead to immediate corrections.

Retraining and Upgrading

Curiously enough, either a shortage of labor or an excessive supply may necessitate retraining. The case of shortages is well exemplified by war conditions. A need for such training was created because most companies had to change from civilian pursuits to war work and yet increase their output at the same time. Hence, employees who had skills for making automobiles, let us say, had to be retrained to make tanks. And many who were performing semiskilled tasks had to be given additional training so that they might be upgraded to skilled jobs. Their jobs, in turn, were filled by upgraded unskilled workers, and these were replaced by learners, many of whom might be women with no industrial experience whatsoever.

Carefully planned training programs have also been found useful in alleviating ghetto unemployment and helping at the same time to solve industry's need for skilled workers. One company which previously took two years to train relatively proficient machinists reduced the time to six months. This was accomplished through a redesigned program of classroom instruction, machine instruction, and regular production-line experience. And it worked out with disadvantaged people who previously would have been a doubtful source of personnel supply.

The case of excess labor bringing about retraining is illustrated by the recent increase in unemployment brought on by automation. This has become very serious in some areas. As a consequence, the federal government enacted the Manpower Development and Training Act of 1962. This authorized the government to spend millions of dollars to provide free retraining for those with obsolete or inadequate skills.

In some industries, retraining and placement projects have been worked out in conjunction with state employment services and unions.

Through committees encharged with supervising funds allocated to handle problems caused by automation, assistance has been provided to members of the bargaining unit who would be displaced by advancing technology.

This type of training is conducted outside of the business enterprise. As such, it represents a departure which may well be a new trend in training. The government makes studies to determine what skills are needed in various areas. Then, it provides facilities and instruction to the unemployed who do not have these skills. In this manner the unemployed are brought back into the labor market and thereby taken off relief and the unemployment compensation rolls.

FACTORS IN A TRAINING PROGRAM

The operation of a successful program requires that due consideration be given to a number of factors. These include (1) the planning of the program, (2) the organization of a training program, (3) the selection of trainees and instructors, (4) the evaluation of training, and (5) adherence to rules and principles of learning.

Planning the Program

Along with good organization, careful planning is a most important prerequisite of training. When such aspects as where, who, how, what, and when are preplanned in a training program, the result will be fewer mistakes and better trainees when the program gets under way. An excellent example of this is seen in the case of a company which carefully redesigned its training program for office workers. The new method included technical instruction and training of attitudes toward work and other workers. As a result, employees attained efficiency levels in three months which ordinarily took a year, and by the end of a year their productivity had doubled.

Another aspect of planning is that of building training programs on a good foundation of (1) job and employee specifications and (2) measurements of what employees actually know. This follows from the proposition that a training program should be based on the following formula: What should be known *less* what one knows *equals* what must be learned. Thus, job and employee specifications serve to disclose the kind and degree of skills, abilities, and aptitudes required on various jobs; whereas checking of employees through records of past experience and education, interviewing, testing, and surveys of difficulties encountered on the job reveals their current status. The differences shown by these two broad investigations should provide an answer to the question of how much training must be allowed for in the program of a company.

Organizational Aspects

A training program has a much better chance of being effective if it is well organized. To begin with, one person or unit in the organization should be made responsible for training. In a small company, this means that a line executive will have to be given this responsibility. In larger

FIGURE 13–2

Training Aircraft Workers

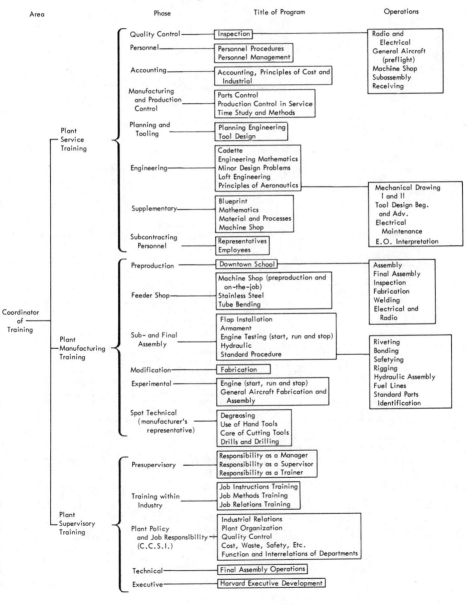

organizations the personnel manager or a training director should be assigned the task of planning, organizing, and evaluating the program. Such division of responsibility should be made with the clear recognition that the line supervisors, supervisors, and other executives assisted by the designated teaching officers possess ultimate authority over and responsibility for training within their respective units. As an example of this, Figure 13–2 shows the various types of training for which a training coordinator in one company was made responsible for planning and

FIGURE 13–3

Training Organization Chart

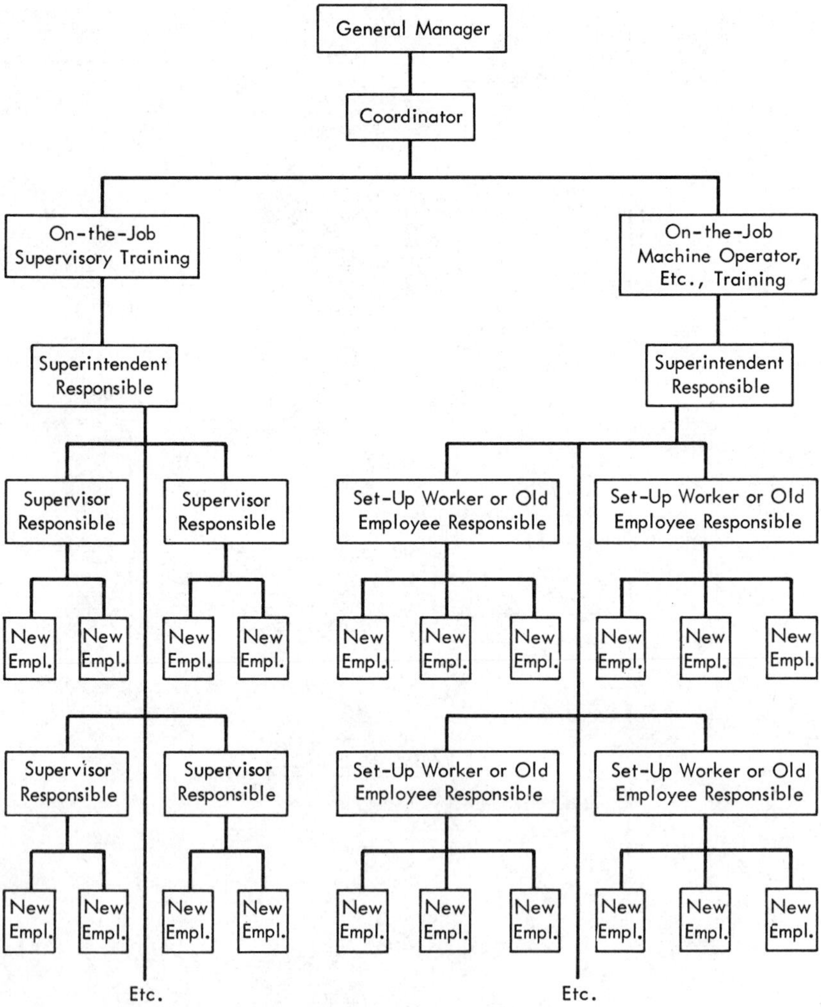

coordination. Figure 13–3 shows how the execution of some of the training work was actually assigned to the shop departments.

Second, unless the interest and prestige of the administrative levels support a training program, it will be accepted with reluctance by the lower levels. Top management is best convinced by facts that disclose the results that can be expected from training. And it has been found desirable to give top management a condensed version of the training so that executives can personally visualize its practicality.

And third, it is well to consider the role of the union in the organization for training. This may include such matters as courses of training, responsibility for selecting or restricting candidates, and evaluation of training work. These matters may be handled through collective bargaining, through joint committees, or informally. In any event, it is probable that with the passing years, union interest in training is likely to grow because of its effect on job placements and wage rates.

Selection of Trainees and Instructors

Another basic factor in training is to select trainable employees. Inasmuch as training costs money, expenditures are warranted only for those from whom the greatest returns will be received. Thus, higher production results are obtained sooner at a lower training cost. Employees may also be preselected for various types of training by having detailed knowledge of their past experience and training. An example of a form which has been used to obtain this information is illustrated in Figure 13–4. In this connection, testing programs are highly worthwhile. As noted in an earlier chapter, employees selected by tests learn faster and better than nontested employees.

The selection and training of instructors also is significant. Here is an excellent opportunity for supervisors. The supervisor who becomes skilled in training methods can demonstrate to employees interest in their welfare. By working with them to help them better themselves, the supervisor will gain their loyalty and their confidence. If lead men or gang bosses are used as trainers, they also deserve careful preparation, if training time and effort are not to be wasted. In the case of regular full-time instructors, special care should be exercised to see that such individuals not only know the rudiments of instruction but also have a sincere interest in the workers and their development.

Evaluation of Training Program

Although it is contended here that training programs are well worth their cost, it is nevertheless argued that the activities of training should

FIGURE 13–4

Experience Record

EXPERIENCE RECORD

NAME: _____ CLOCK NO. _____

ADDRESS: _____ S.S. NO. _____

For the purpose of determining the qualifications and experience of the employees as to their mechanical experience for defense work, the questions below are submitted:

1. Grade completed in school _____

2. Have you completed a school course in:
   (1) Arithmetic _____   (4) Trigonometry _____
   (2) Algebra _____   (5) Shop (Mach.) _____
   (3) Geometry _____

3. Have you served an apprenticeship as:
   (1) Machinist _____ (2) Toolmaker _____ (3) Diemaker _____   (4) Any other _____

4. Can you read blueprints? _____

5. Can you read micrometers? _____

6. Can you read a Vernier? _____

7. Have you had experience operating the following machine tools?

	Prod.	Tool-Room	Specify Type		Prod.	Tool-Room	Specify Type
(1) Lathe	___	___	___	(10) Diamond Boring Mach.	___	___	___
(2) Multiple Turn-				(11) Auto. Screw Mach.	___	___	___
ing Machine				(12) Hand Screw Mach.	___	___	___
(Bullard, etc.)	___	___	___	(13) Chucking Machine			
(3) Milling Machine	___	___	___	(New Britain,			
(4) Drill Press	___	___	___	Cleveland, etc.)	___	___	___
(5) Drill Press (Multi)	___	___	___	(14) Gear Cutter	___	___	___
(6) Grinder External	___	___	___	(15) Broaching Mach.	___	___	___
(7) Grinder Internal	___	___	___	(16) Semi–Automatic			
(8) Planer	___	___	___	Lathe	___	___	___
(9) Shaper	___	___	___	(17) Any other	___	___	___

                                                                      School   Practical

8. Have you had any training in mechanical drawing or design? _____   _____

9. Have you had experience as:
   (1) Mach. shop   (7) Cutter grinder _____   (14) Instructor–
     foreman _____   (8) Tool hardener _____   Machine Shop _____
   (2) Mach. shop   (9) Machine repairman _____   (15) Indicate experience, if
     inspector _____   (10) Welder _____   any, on manufacture of
   (3) Toolmaker _____   (11) Boring mill   ordnance parts; if so,
   (4) Diemaker _____   (toolroom) _____   what parts _____
   (5) Machinist _____   (12) Layout (bench)   (16) Any other (use reverse
   (6) Tool and gage   (Surface Plate) _____   side if necessary) _____
     grinder _____   (13) Patternmaker _____   _____

10. Please indicate any other mechancial qualfications (use reverse side if necessary) _____

_____

11. Indicate class of work you prefer _____

12. Indicate class of work best qualified for _____

    Your answers will be supplemented by further practical examination and demonstration

Source: *Factory Management and Maintenance*, vol. 101, no. 10, p. 117.

be evaluated. This will not only result in getting more for the training dollar but also make it possible to improve training techniques and practices. In the final analysis, the savings and improvements resulting from training must be set off against the cost of training to determine the extent of positive advantage. Such comparisons must be made on a month-to-month, company-to-company, or interdepartmental basis, to establish worthwhile conclusions.

The types of evidence which may be gathered to show savings and improvements include the following:

1. Production factors:
   a. Increase in output.
   b. Decrease in scrap.
   c. Decrease in unit times and unit cost of production.
   d. Reduction in space or machine requirements.

2. Labor factors:
   a. Decrease in labor turnover.
   b. Decrease in absenteeism.
   c. Decrease in number and severity of accidents.
   d. Betterment of employee morale.
   e. Decrease in grievances and disciplinary action.
   f. Reduction in time to earn piece rates.
   g. Decrease in number of discharges or quits.

When such information is gathered, the value of training will seldom be taken for granted or questioned. Yet, it is not an onerous task to collect these data. In gathering them, care should be used to bring out the results of training by comparing the records of trainees with those of employees who were not trained. How this may be done is illustrated in Figure 13–5. There is a striking contrast between the efficiency of trainees and those who learned on the job. Such data establish strongly the desirability of planned training.

Another way of evaluating training programs is that illustrated in Figure 13–6. Here is shown the progress made by two trainees, one who is "too good" for the job and one who is "just right." Certainly, when it is possible to ascertain the future prospects of employees so early in their employment tenure, the tool which helps is deserving of favorable support.

A few words on evaluation also are in order from a legal and professional point of view. Some training programs may have to be measured in terms of legal requirements. For example, a company that desires to qualify war veterans under an approved learner or apprentice course

FIGURE 13–5

The relation between efficiency and weeks of training or experience for trainees and beginners in the operation of disc cutoff machines

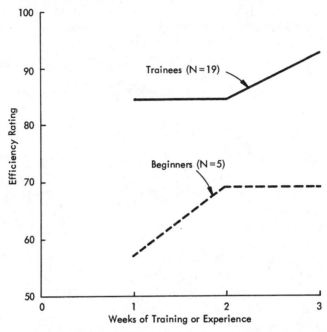

Source: L. G. Lindahl, "Training Operations by Activity Analysis," *Personnel,* vol. 24, no. 5, p. 304.

must meet minimum standards on such matters as quantity and quality of instruction. In cases in which a company seeks exemptions under the Wages and Hours and Walsh-Healey acts, this information must be available. Even when not mandatory, establishing such standards is desirable in order to keep the planning of courses on a definite schedule and to stipulate times for evaluating training results.

If the quantity of training is relatively unstandardized, its quality is even less so. To be sure, where federal or state agencies supervise vocational, learner, apprentice, and rehabilitation training, some review of the quality of courses and instructors is made, but this is as yet largely personal and variable. There is little doubt, however, that the quality of training has improved. Such groups as the American Society of Training and Development and local associations of training directors have had considerable impact upon raising standards of industrial and business training.

FIGURE 13–6

Learning Curves

Grace Was Too Good

Too good, that is, for this particular job. From the start, her progress (*heavy line*) was far better than standard. She'd worked before on repetitive jobs, and was glad to be transferred to the machine shop.

Betty? Just Right

It paid to train her. Her learning curve (*heavy line*) practically coincides with the standard curve. She reached full production on the 21st day, and consistently met standard without difficulty.

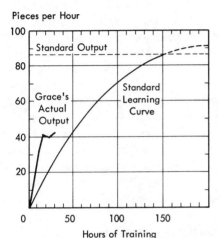

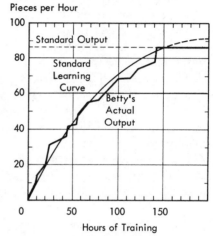

Source: A. R. Knowles and L. F. Bell, "Training Curves," *Factory Management and Maintenance,* vol. 108, no. 6, p. 115.

Rules and Principles of Learning

It is desirable here to note some theories and rules that underlie an effective training program. Although how people learn has long been a concern of psychologists and educators, positive conclusions are still debatable. There is some agreement that much operative learning includes muscular and mental adaptations, attitude and emotional changes, and motivational and environmental influences.

In learning how to operate a drill press, for example, a person should

1. develop new habits of using and coordinating various elements of body, senses, and mind,
2. concentrate attention on and accept the various constraints of this operation, and
3. adapt to the norms of coworkers and to the organizational and motivational factors.

How and to what extent such changes actually take place is, however, not clearly understood. What, for example, happens within the human body and mind when one learns such an operation? If we knew, we could perhaps go directly into the body to effect desired changes. Since we don't know, reliance is placed upon such indirect factors of change as practice, repetition, supervision, encouragement, compensation, and punishment. Our plans of training are based upon practical theories of learning rather than scientifically proved concepts.

There are various suggestions that are useful as rules and principles of learning. To begin with, in planning a program, it is wise to determine how frequently instruction should be given, and to ascertain the effect of recency, types of materials, and audio-visual devices upon the learning process. The conditions and environment of instruction are also items to be considered.

More specifically, industrial training is more effective when shop instruction is correlated with classroom instruction. This follows not only because the learner can see personal improvement in actual production, but also because of the principle that the more specific and concrete the material of instruction, the better the learning. All of this suggests, too, that it is imperative to select trainers who can stimulate the learners to exert themselves. An otherwise admirable plan of training will almost inevitably fail to achieve desired results if this principle of instruction is violated.

Also of interest is the fact that in teaching, it is sometimes best to start describing the middle steps of an operation rather than the first or last, as is usually done. Students who are pushed at the most rapid rate of which they are capable do better than when a more leisurely pace is maintained. It is also well to alternate lectures, demonstrations, and actual shop practice at carefully worked-out time intervals to get the best results. And to cite one more principle of this nature, the instructor should stand beside students when demonstrating, so that students will not have to reverse the images they receive, as is true when the instructor stands facing them.

Another category of rules pertains to the media and mechanics of instruction. These are so numerous that only a few suggestions can be mentioned here:

1. Use graphical, illustrative, and sample materials freely and frequently. Such matters as charts, drawings, and models increase the effectiveness of teaching and learning.
2. Use good classroom facilities, and select the best possible shop areas for instruction purposes.
3. Determine the best time for classroom work. Lectures ordinarily should not be longer than 50 to 60 minutes; discussion periods can be longer, provided that intermissions of about 10 minutes are provided after 45 minutes.

4. Examinations or tests should be scheduled at appropriate intervals in order to check the student and instill a sense of progress.
5. Groups in training together should seldom be larger than 30 persons if discussion is to be encouraged and if instructors are not to be overworked.
6. Questions should emphasize how and why rather than yes or no.
7. The use of pictures, whether shown by movies, slides, strip films, or other methods, cannot be overstressed. It has been discovered that thereby:

    a. Interest of students may be increased up to 40 percent.

    b. Their range of immediate understanding may be increased up to 25 percent.

    c. Their time for completing a course may be decreased up to 25 percent.

    d. Their retention of information may be increased up to 35 percent.

QUESTIONS

1. How might you go about justifying the cost of a formal training program in a business concern?
2. To be most effective, how should on-the-job training programs be conducted?
3. Why do such groups as unions and governmental agencies concern themselves with apprenticeship training in industry?
4. What are the merits and demerits of the internship plan of training in industry?
5. What are the advantages of teaching machines?
6. To whom should organizational responsibility for training be assigned?
7. How do job employee specifications fit into planning a training program?
8. What are the advantages of having supervisors do their own training? The disadvantages?
9. How would you go about evaluating the effectiveness of a training program?
10. What rules and principles of learning would it be desirable to follow in the operation of a training program?

CASE 13–1. TRAINING THE UNDERPRIVILEGED

The Scad Machine Company had until the present followed the practice of selecting machine trainees from candidates who possessed some skill in reading simple machine-shop blueprints, in handling eighth grade arithmetic, and in reading and understanding simple technical language. It then took these candidates and gave them instruction and practice in operating such basic machines as a drill press, a lathe, a milling machine, and a grinding machine. After four to six weeks of such elementary training, the trainees were assigned to regular production units where their skills increased through actual work assignments.

But the regular sources of labor supply had dried up to a point that only candidates were presenting themselves who did not possess the basic skills which the company had taken for granted. It now was faced with the task of training people to prepare them to become machine trainees. After some study of the situation, it found that with the level of people who were presenting themselves, the company would have to spend a minimum of three months just to get people ready for the machine-shop training. The cost of this seemed to be an undue burden.

Question

1. What is the outlook for this company?

CASE 13–2. TRAINING COST/BENEFIT ANALYSIS

The personnel director of a potato chip company has been having difficulty selling top management on the desirability of formal training programs for employees. He concluded that arguments and talk about the benefits of training were not convincing anyone at the top. He decided to seek some "hard" data because management seemed to be very sensitive to such information when plans of any type were suggested.

He sought out an operation which would serve to sell his ideas. He finally selected a simple packaging operation. The operation occured after the potato chips were carried on a conveyor to the packaging machine. Here they are blown off the conveyor into the weighing machine, from which they are dropped into packages. The packages are then automatically sealed and then placed into the shipping cartons.

Not infrequently during a production run, the packaging machine goes out of sequence. Bags of chips pass out of the machine either unsealed or half-sealed. If corrective action is not taken immediately, the machine will continue to produce defectives. Actual corrective action takes about a minute. This includes shutting down the machine, resetting it, and then restarting. The operator of packaging does not perform the corrective action but must call for a maintenance person who does the correcting.

The personnel director has found that on the average about $4 of chips are spoiled a week; labor and machine time down a week loses $4, and maintenance cost are $2 a week. The director figures that it would cost $600 to train the three people who alternately work on this operation.

Question

1. Do the facts seem to justify the training, assuming a 50-week year?
2. Are there any other matters to be considered in making the decision about training?

EXECUTIVE DEVELOPMENT 14

Significance of Executive Development

One of the most encouraging trends in personnel management is the increasing role being given to executive development, at all levels from supervisory management to top management. Few companies once either considered formal training necessary or gave it any thought whatsoever. It was felt that those appointed as supervisors and those who moved up the managerial ladder either possessed leadership aptitudes or could readily acquire needed skills and know-how by experience.

The practice has been common to select for supervisory positions those who have exhibited the most proficiency in technical work. Thus the best salesperson is made the supervisor of the department when a vacancy occurs. Yet the skills which led to that selection are usually of partial value in managing salespeople. There is a significant difference between a being-managed position and a managing position. But the new manager has been expected to learn managing skills independently.

Nor do those who move up the managerial ladder have a happier experience when they must educate themselves. It is one thing to supervise operative employees and another to supervise executives. The task of planning, organizing, directing, and controlling minor areas differs in important degrees, if not in kind, from that assumed by major executives. Yet the acquisition of needed skills, knowledge, and attitudes in higher levels has often been left to individual effort and the laws of chance.

But an encouraging change has been accelerating. More and more companies are giving increased attention to executive development at all levels, from supervisory through middle management levels to the top.

To survey such developmental efforts, the materials in this chapter are divided into the following parts:

1. Planning executive development.
2. Types of programs at various executive levels.
3. Content of developmental materials.
4. Follow-up and evaluation of developmental results.

PLANNING EXECUTIVE DEVELOPMENT

Executive development is the program by which executive capacities to achieve desired objectives are increased. The implications of this definition may be noted by commenting briefly about each of its terms. The word *program* implies that development must be concerned with a number of interrelated subjects, factors, and needs. "Executive capacities" implies consideration for various personal abilities, potential as well as current jobholders, and all managerial levels. "Desired objectives" implies consideration for the goals of the company, of the executives, and of those being managed. And the term *increased* implies that a change must occur in the executive and, subsequently in subordinates in that department.

This overall view of the concept of executive development provides the basis for discussing the planning of a developmental program. In this section, attention is directed to the fundamental questions of the executive capacities that need to be developed, who should be included in the program, and upon what conditions development is contingent.

Executive Capacities

Students of management are generally agreed that an executive's effectiveness depends in large measure upon knowledge, skills, attitudes, and behavioral patterns. How much of each and in what proportion for various executives is debatable; but even here, there is much agreement on specific aspects of each.

Knowledge refers to what an executive must know about the subjects dealt with and the functions performed, as well as knowledge in the technical area managed. Such areas as production, sales, finance, accounting, engineering, and research are examples. Executives must have knowledge in managerial areas—i.e., in planning, organizing, directing, and controlling the work of others. They must have knowledge of people; such areas as psychology and motivation come to mind. And they must have knowledge of the environments in which they work; these include such areas as social, cultural, political, and ethical.

Knowledge must be applied, which calls for skills. Broadly speaking, they must have skill in solving problems; in making decisions; in dealing with things, ideas, and people; and in making personal adjustments to conditions and people. More specifically, the foregoing require such skills as communicating (listening as well as talking), reading, writing, creating, being sensitive to others, concentrating on tasks, and utilizing various tools (such as logic, statistics, mathematics, and psychological principles).

Attitudes are an influential factor affecting leadership. How does one perceive one's job, superiors, subordinates, and company? How does one perceive oneself personally, in relation to others, and in relation to future hopes and ambitions? How does one view challenge, change, and responsibilities? Almost everyone has some answers to these vital questions, but how well they are evaluated is another matter.

And finally, an executive's behavioral pattern is a part of leadership ability. Overt actions of dress, speech, and way of acting in various situations are seen by and affect others. Cooperation with others, the bases for decisions about people, the manner in which authority is used, and the way the executive allows (or does not allow) empathy to develop are examples of behavior discerned quickly by associates who adjust accordingly.

Candidates for Development

Obviously, all executives must possess the foregoing capacities. Equally obvious is the fact that a developmental program must be based upon some policy of who needs training most and which capacities require attention. Some needs are greater than others. High-priority needs should be taken care of first. Later, others will be included. Thus, development is recognized as an ongoing responsibility, yet one with properly evaluated timeliness. Priorities must be established by (1) a guiding principle and (2) needs of organizational levels, particular vacancies, and specific individuals.

1. Guiding Principles.   The foundation for a developmental program is laid on the simple proposition that needed capacities *less* available capacities *equals* capacities to be developed. For each executive position a specification of needed knowledge, skills, attitudes, and behavioral patterns would have to be established. For each person who holds or aspires to an executive position, a statement of personal level of knowledge, skills, attitudes, and behavioral patterns would be derived. Then the difference between what capacities a person should have and does have constitutes developmental needs. A form used in this connection is illustrated in Figure 14–1. And a more complete diagram showing the relation between organizational needs, job performance, appraisals, rewards, and development is well illustrated in Figure 14–2.

If this formula were applied to every position and person, the developmental program, if fully implemented, would in practically every company call for unavailable amounts of time, money, and skills. Hence, how

FIGURE 14–1

Estimating Development Needs

Capacities	Needed	Available	To Be Developed
Knowledge			
Skills			
Attitudes			
Behavioral Patterns			

much can be built upon the foundation laid in the preceding section calls for the exercise of judgment. Where shall the resources which are available be applied? In any company the answer would have to be made after some evaluation of particular needs. All that can be done here is to comment generally on organizational and personal needs.

2. Needs of Organizational Levels. *Executive development* has been applied here to all managerial levels. To some, the term is used only in connection with top-level administrators. Lower levels are encompassed by such terms as *middle management training* or *supervisory training.* Each of these will be considered here.

a. Administrative Levels. In the past, a developmental program for top-level executives would have been placed at the bottom of a priority list, were it placed there at all. The president of a company would have been the butt of the silent scorn of subordinates and open ridicule of friends for any part taken in an executive development program. Indeed, a president would not have admitted to needed development after having worked up through the school of hard knocks.

But now the positive value of participation in developmental programs is openly recognized (and even viewed as a status symbol). A profound influence has been the growing recognition that a top executive is essentially a manager. Effectiveness depends upon how well the executive can manage various experts, not alone upon personal expertise in technical matters. And growth and dynamic changes in companies make concentration on coordination of team effort even more imperative. Executives have recognized, therefore, that to keep abreast of their profession—management—they must take advantage of developmental programs.

Executive development has also appealed to top executives because of

FIGURE 14-2 A Managerial Performance, Appraisal, and Development System

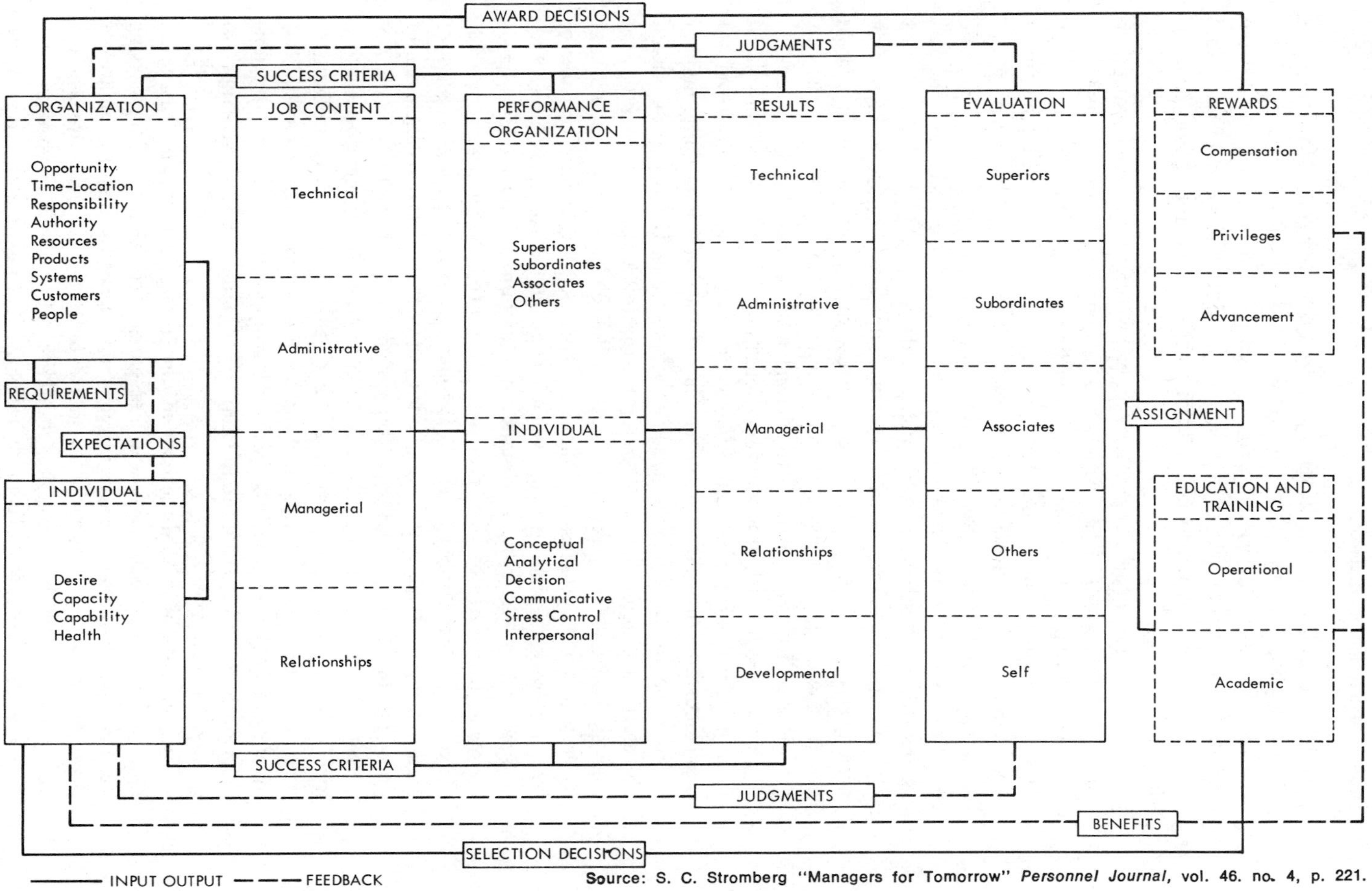

Source: S. C. Stromberg "Managers for Tomorrow" Personnel Journal, vol. 46, no. 4, p. 221.

the broader roles and implications they see in their jobs. How they run their companies is important. But they also see the need to explore such matters as the social, ethical, and political roles of their decisions. They are interested in long-range planning in this dynamic world of ours. And they are concerned with their relations with human forces and community affairs.

b. Lower Executive Levels. Levels below the top management group have developmental needs which are fundamentally more alike than different. The middle manager, like the first-line supervisor, has to pay close attention to the completion of various specific projects; but must also think of them in terms of overall company objectives and plans. Awareness of the need for interdivisional cooperation is necessary. So emphasis of executive development for middle managers has in part tended to direct attention to company-wide factors.

Development efforts for the supervisor are concerned with increasing managerial effectiveness. This is so because the supervisor has to make a drastic change when moving into a managerial role, must learn how to get results through others, not to do the work personally.

In the case of both groups, promotional objectives must be considered in a developmental program. Some supervisors must be prepared for movement into the middle management group, and some middle managers must be prepared for top management positions. Usually, promotional objectives are achieved by stressing on-the-job performance skills and then evaluating closely progress made on the job. The assumption is that those who make progress in managing current assignments because of training are most likely to succeed when promoted to higher jobs.

3. Needs of Particular Individuals or Positions. Development needs may also be ascertained by interpreting the needs of particular individuals or of expected job vacancies. Instead of making overall studies of organizational needs, many companies make their decisions in terms of pressures of current shortages. Expansion of business or loss of key personnel makes it obvious that there are not enough executives or that available executives need training. There then is a hurried program to prepare those at lower levels for promotion or to expand the capabilities of current jobholders to meet expanding opportunities. Such developmental planning is justifiable in smaller companies or in those caught in unexpected changes.

But more sophisticated methods of developing programs may be used. As noted in Chapter 6. "Job and Personnel Requirements," forecasting business and personnel changes can provide a basis for better estimates of training needs. It is possible in many cases to calculate for coming periods of time, within small degrees of error, how much business is to be done and, therefore, executive requirements. It is possible also to estimate turnover of personnel at various levels and, as a consequence, how many executives will have to be replaced. Schedules of personnel needs thus arrived at are an effective means of determining who has to be developed and to what degree.

Conditions of Executive Development

The foregoing discussion has stressed a number of factors that enter into the composition of an executive development program. In describing who has to be trained, how much, on what aspects, and with what resources, vital dimensions of such programs have been covered. But it would be negligent to overlook the environmental factors involved in and group interactions affected by development programs.

Turning first to environmental factors, it must be noted that executive development takes place in a complex and dynamic atmosphere. The physical, economic, and human environment places great demands upon managers. They must be prepared to handle changing as well as current conditions in these areas. How executives perform is affected by such environmental factors. Hence training must help develop contingency flexibility.

The learning process is, as already noted, largely concerned with the economic success of an enterprise. It is restricted by the dollars available to carry on programs and justified by the dollar outputs it can eventually bring forth. But it also affects and is affected by the feelings of people as individuals and as members of groups. Hence, executive development is conditioned by psychological and sociological overtones. It must give due consideration to how people feel about programs, their perceptions of the rewards and obligations which flow from participation in them, and the changes which may take place in their status and roles.

In short, what goes into and comes out of a development program is affected by individual and group feelings, customs, and standards. Placing a seasoned executive into a classroom is different from enrolling a student in a college course. In the former case the marks of the teacher-student relationship must be removed, or resistance to the learning process will be informally significant, if not openly evidenced. The values of the development program, moreover, must be made as directly and immediately apparent as possible to executives. Otherwise, they will conclude that it is below their dignity as well as a waste of their valuable time. They are not students but practitioners. They want the value of the program to be as apparent to others as to themselves.

This brings us to the point of interactions of people involved in executive development. A participant in a program must have assurance that as a result of said participation, there will be favorable relations with superiors, peers, and subordinates. Some programs have suffered because the lessons learned in a program are not supported by the practices or opinions of one's superiors. This is most frustrating after one returns to the job. Or if one's peers believe that favoritism or special treatment is accorded a participant, a less than satisfactory relationship will result in cross-horizontal contacts and cooperation. And if one's subordinates perceive the program as a means of getting more out of them without compensating returns, the participant finds that development experiences bring forth undesirable resistance.

If, then, an executive development program is to achieve desired changes, it must be adapted to the various conditions and people involved in it. To change successfully an executive's knowledge, skill, attitudes, and behavior, it is necessary to know how various people will be affected by and relate to the changes. Action will bring reaction. And the reactions will be along personal lines of attitudes, feelings, perceptions, and reasoning as well as technical lines.

TYPES OF DEVELOPMENT PROGRAMS

Having reviewed the implications and general planning of executive development, it is now appropriate to comment on some of the more common types of such programs and their coverage.

On-the-Job Development

Most executive development is accomplished on the job. Trainees learn the job under actual fire. They can size up subordinates, and in turn be appraised by them, without artificial support or backing. They can demonstrate independently latent leadership aptitudes. Some have argued that the best executives will naturally rise to their opportunities without formal training. And it is also claimed that this path up the executive ladder does not build up false hopes in understudies or destroy the initiative of those not specifically being groomed for promotion.

Undirected on-the-job training, however, has serious disadvantages. One no longer expects such experts as chemists, accountants, or designers to learn on their own. Inadequate programs for managers are equally unjustifiable. Moreover, informal on-the-job training is costly and time-consuming relative to its effectiveness. And finally, such training is wasteful, in that the lessons learned by one generation are not transmitted efficiently to succeeding generations.

It is admitted, of course, that the actual working situation—whether executive, professional, or operative—will always be an important learning situation. But sole reliance on it is defensible only in small companies, or when emergency or expanding conditions preclude other expedients. In most instances, however, it should be buttressed by more formal programs, some of which are now discussed.

Understudy Plans

Executive development by means of understudies also has its proponents. Under this plan, each executive is assigned an understudy who, in addition to regular duties, acquires some familiarity with the responsibilities of the department superior. The understudy is thus expected to be prepared to take over the superior's work when the latter is away; and presumably will be prepared to move into the superior's position when the vacancy occurs.

This plan has a number of advantages. Training-wise, learning takes place in the atmosphere and position in which the executive will be expected to perform. And from the executive's point of view, an excellent opportunity is opened to prepare for advancement.

The understudy system suffers, however, from some disadvantages. First, aspirants for promotion other than the selected understudy may feel that their chances are so remote that it is useless to exert themselves. Second, understudies who have to wait a long time for vacancies may become discouraged, particularly when they see vacancies fortuitously open quickly for understudies in other organizational lines. And third, some superiors, jealous of their positions, refrain from opening their store of knowledge to potential replacements.

Short-Term Courses

A popular type of executive development is that of the short, intensive school program. Executives are brought together for periods of a few days up to a month for training on well-defined topics. These short courses, or workshops, as they are also known, are conducted by companies, by trade and professional associations, and by universities. They are usually restricted to qualified executives and professional staff members. Their purpose is to provide refresher courses as well as instruction in new developments. Specific topics covered in such schools include work in counseling, testing, job evaluation, use of computers in decision making and systems building, and various aspects of collective bargaining. In some cases the subjects covered are very general in nature, such as basic economics, political forces, literature, and social factors.

In addition to the value of the course materials, the opportunity for discussion by small groups of executives with common interests and problems is an advantage of this form of training. A possible shortcoming, which can be minimized by scheduling the courses during seasonal lulls, is that they take executives away from their desks for a relatively extended period of time.

Since such short courses often rely upon guided discussions by small groups of conferees, it is desirable to comment briefly on the features of this phase of these programs. To be most effective, conferences call for the following:

1. A competent conference leader or instructor.
2. A preplanned outline of what the group is to cover and how it is to be conducted.
3. A well-equipped conference room.
4. A limit to the number of conferees, preferably not over 25.
5. An interesting beginning, spirited and pointed discussions, and a good summarization.

Position Rotation Plan

Another plan of training which has had some acceptance in industry, perhaps influenced by assignment shifts in military organizations, is that of rotating key and promising executives and subordinates. The assumptions of such plans are threefold: (1) that by job rotation, executives will tend to think in terms of managerial principles rather than the technical aspects of particular functional fields; (2) that rotating will permit good executives to determine the functional fields in which they would prefer to manage; and (3) that by gaining a broad view of interdivisional problems, the top positions in the company can be filled by better qualified appointees. Against these values must be cited the disadvantages of the disturbances caused in inaugurating the plan and in the periodic changes of leadership in various departments and divisions.

Other Supervisory Programs

A number of programs are directed toward first-line management training, a few of which are noted here. In one case, a program for group leaders has been devised in which trainees are given a three-month course under the guidance of trained instructors and under shop conditions. The trainees are given assignments that are intended to provide working knowledge along technical lines in the application of leadership qualities to improve production, in the relations of various line and staff departments, and in principles of supervision.

In another program, emphasis is laid upon the development of better relations between supervisors and the upper levels of management. This is accomplished by bringing small groups of supervisors into a series of full-day meetings, lectures, and conferences with top management. By means of a carefully planned schedule and a topical outline, various aspects of company and supervisory problems are explained to and discussed with the supervisors. In this way the policies of the company can be instilled, and the association of top and supervisory officials leads to more friendly relations.

Another supervisory program is based upon guided reading of published literature. Books, bulletins, and magazine articles dealing with good foremanship are distributed to the supervisors. At intervals, conferences are held to discuss particular views, and tests are given to determine how much has been read and how well.

Decision-Making Training

Of great interest are attempts to train executives in decision making. Of course, executives have always made decisions. But the processes of decision making have been, and still often are, considered to be beyond the realm of structured training. Some attempts along this line have been made under the general heading of problem solving. This has amounted largely to presenting to executives such well-known stages as stating the problem, making hypotheses, gathering data, testing alternatives, selecting and applying a given alternative, and following up the results.

More recently, decision-making training has taken more rigorous and sophisticated approaches. Logical thinking, mathematical models, electronic computers, and creativity analysis have been explored with a view to reaching a better understanding of how decisions can be improved. Thus, it is not enough, for example, to use case problems as a teaching aid in this area. Instead, it is more important to examine such matters as how one goes about thinking from the known to new insights into the unknown; how to relate various dimensions of a problem; how to utilize various mathematical and computer aids in thinking; and how to establish criteria for optimizing results when interacting objectives must be sought. Practically, such training has been conducted by simulating various kinds of decision-making situations (games, for example) and then conducting intensive reviews on how and why various strategies were selected.

Business Games

An interesting development in executive training is that of business games. This amounts to the design of a simulated situation in which decisions must be made as various events occur. The decisions are made by groups of players. The groups compete with each other in the sense that the one whose decisions bring about the optimum results is the winner. Playing this game is intended, of course, to provide a learning experience, not merely to see who wins.

The value of this type of training may be seen in how the game is constructed and played. A situation is established in which decisions must be made in—and which interact on—all divisions of the company. Such things as the current financial condition, the market situation, production facilities, and available personnel and funds are postulated. Then, at specified periods the players make decisions on how they would spend their money on such items as sales promotion, research and development, personnel services, production facilities, etc. These decisions are recorded on forms provided for the purpose and collected by umpires, who calculate the impact of the decisions on the company. The results are returned to the players, who then make new decisions. These, in turn, are collected and evaluated for impact, and returns are made to the players. This continues for the length of the session—which may be for a period of three or four hours, or longer. The umpires presumably have preestablished criteria for determining the impact of various decisions on the business.

The learning process is enhanced by conducting a critique session. To begin with, the umpires review the game strategies and results of the various teams. Each team reviews its own decisions and reasons therefore in relation to the results obtained. The team benefits also by evaluating what it might do differently were it to replay the game. And a general discussion by all concerned is helpful in summarizing what various members have learned from the process.

Role Playing

A method that has in recent years received much favorable attention is that of "role playing," which was first introduced as the psychodrama or sociodrama. Under this method a group of supervisors meets in conference, and two are selected to act out some situation which is commonly encountered or is causing trouble. For example, the situation might be that of an employee who is seeking a transfer. Then, one of the supervisors is assigned the role of the employee, and the second becomes the supervisor. A few pertinent facts are decided upon, and then the two, without rehearsal, act out how the supervisor and employee would react.

As the two act, the members of the conference observe, make mental notes, and evaluate the performance. After the drama is completed, others may be selected to act out the same situation, or a general discussion of the acting thus far may be reviewed. Often, a recording is made, so that the actors can review their own performances.

The desirable features of this method are centered in the fact that the learners learn by doing. They can observe, sometimes for the first time, their own actions in a critical way, particularly when sound recordings are used. There is a subsidiary value in improving the supervisor's ability to speak effectively and secure acceptance of ideas. But the method does take a lot of time which many find too costly to make available.

Sensitivity Training

Another area to which executive training has been directed in recent years is that of sensitivity to those with whom one must deal. This is an outgrowth of the realization that executives get work done through others and with others. No matter how much an executive knows about the technical phases of the work, achieving the highest possible degree of success necessitates awareness of personal feelings, attitudes, and needs, and those of superiors, subordinates, and associates.

Such awareness may be increased by training. For a long time, executive training has recognized this only within a narrow spectrum. Thus, training has often been directed with a view to improving speaking skills. But other skills are now receiving attention. Does one know how, for example, to listen? To what degree is one aware of the feelings of various classes of people? How does the nature of a particular project or company goal affect the attitudes and desires of various people? How should arguments, orders, discussions, counseling, etc., be communicated? Training along such lines is a rightful recognition that in interacting with others, it is important to work out how to interact as well as the "what" of the interaction. Such training is often conducted through personal interactions although packaged audio- and visual-aided courses are also available.

CONTENT OF DEVELOPMENT PROGRAMS

The foregoing has covered the most important types of executive development programs, and has also noted various techniques and tools used in connection therewith. It is now pertinent to note the subject matter which is covered in such courses.

Perhaps the obvious and simplest approach to the matter of content is to take up tasks the executive is most likely to encounter. Of interest is the fact that most executive development programs, from this angle, take up various subjects connected with handling people—the so-called "human relations" problem. Such subjects as the following are discussed:

1. Present-day labor-management philosophy and policies.
2. Working with others through organizational channels.

3. Communicating up and down organizational channels.
4. Employment policies and practices.
5. Training and education policies and practices.
6. Discipline, grievances, and rules and regulations.
7. Employee services and recreation.
8. Transfers, promotion, merit, and seniority policies.
9. The union contract—its meaning and implications.
10. Community agencies and institutions.

Another basic approach to course content has reference to the basic characteristics a leader should possess. Among the characteristics to which attention has been devoted are the following:

1. Ability to think.
2. Ability to organize.
3. Ability to handle people.
4. Ability to plan.
5. Ability to lead.
6. Ability to get and interpret facts.
7. Loyalty.
8. Decisiveness.
9. Teaching ability.
10. Ability to solve problems.
11. Courage.
12. Self-motivation.
13. Desire for achievement and prestige.
14. Social balance and understanding.
15. Sense of responsibility.
16. Emotional balance and poise.
17. Ability to influence people, individually and in groups.
18. Attitudes toward subordinates and associates.
19. Attitude toward community associations.
20. Attitude toward economic and political systems.

This list is by no means complete, but it does illustrate the wide range of subjects that have been considered basic leadership traits.

Since there is so much variation in content, the best practice for any company in establishing its own program is to give consideration to outside practices, but to build its program in terms of its own needs. This can be done by taking the following steps:

1. Determine as precisely as possible the major objectives or tasks the company faces.
2. Inventory present executive capacities.
3. Compute the shortages of executive capacities as compared to major needs.

4. Establish the content of training required by individual executives to bring them up to desired standards.

FOLLOW-UP AND EVALUATION

Follow-up and evaluation of executive development programs are particularly difficult because it is almost impossible to determine which results of executive efforts are attributable to training and which to other causes. Nevertheless, it is desirable to make an attempt in this direction because a partial answer is better than none. Examples are available of measurements which have been made of training results. In one case, a study of 600 plants gave the results shown in Table 14–1. In another

TABLE 14–1

Training Results

Kind of Result	Percentage of Plants Reporting Results			
	Under 25%	25–49%	50–74%	75% and Over
Production increased	63	16	1	20
Training time reduced	52	25	7	16
Work hours saved	89	9	1	1
Scrap loss reduced	89	5	5	1

instance, learning sessions on "management by objectives," which cost a company $6,000 have resulted in savings of $11,500 with further potential savings estimated at over $400,000.

An interesting summary of the results that should flow from a good program is contained in the following listing (certainly it is a broad-gauge test of this subject, as well it should be):

1. Increased executive management skills
2. Development in each executive of a broad background and appreciation of the company's overall operations and objectives
3. Greater delegation of authority because executives down the line are better qualified and better able to assume increased responsibilities
4. Creation of a reserve of qualified personnel to replace present incumbents and to staff new positions
5. Improved selection for promotion
6. Minimum delay in staffing new positions and minimum disruption of operations during replacements of incumbents
7. Provision for the best combination of youth, vigor, and exexperience in top management and increased span of productive life in high-level positions
8. Improved executive morale

9. Attraction to the company of ambitious people who wish to move ahead as rapidly as their abilities permit

10. Increased effectiveness and reduced costs, resulting in greater assurance of continued profitability[1]

Evaluation of Trainees

Another approach to evaluation is that of determining how well executive trainees have learned. They may be tested and rated after their courses of training. Thus, in some of the plans mentioned in the foregoing, supervisors, and higher executives as well, are rated as to their promise for further training. In addition, regular examinations are scheduled to ascertain how well various phases of technical and descriptive materials have been absorbed. Such tests should be given with care in order to avoid the development of a feeling on the part of trainees that a "school" is being operated; most executives like to feel that the "little red schoolhouse" is a part of their past.

More informal plans of follow-up include conferences and discussions by superiors with those who have taken training work. In this way the supervisors can obtain some measure of the value of the training received, and the trainees will prepare themselves more carefully, knowing that such talks are to take place. An added value of such informal talks is that they bring various levels of leadership together more frequently, giving each the opportunity to get better acquainted with the other.

An inversion of follow-up which has desirable points is that in which trainees are asked to express themselves on the quality or results of training. In one company, for example, executives are asked to comment upon the quality and usefulness of each conference they attend. This acts as a double-edged weapon: (1) The conference leader and training school are alert to build and conduct better sessions, and (2) the conferees must be more attentive in order to be able to express pertinent interpretations and criticisms. In another company, executives who take various forms of training are required to fill out weekly reports indicating progress in various aspects of their work. All that is required is a simple check (without quantitative estimates) opposite any of the following items: reduction of indirect labor, indirect cost, daywork operations, materials, or supplies; and increase or improvement in processes, quality, personnel relations, or suggestions. Here again, knowledge that the training is expected to produce results will keep the trainees alert to see how training material can be applied in various phases of their work.

---

[1] E. W. Reilley and B. J. Muller-Thym, "Executive Development," *Personnel,* vol. 24, no. 6, p. 412.

QUESTIONS

1. What capacities of various levels of managers do developmental programs seek to upgrade?
2. On what principle should an executive development program be built?
3. What developmental needs should be served in the case of first-line supervisory levels?
4. How many environmental and personal conditions affect the operation of an executive development program?
5. What is your opinion of the understudy plan of executive development?
6. How does the "business-game" type of executive training tie in with decision-making training?
7. Where is the role-playing plan most desirable in executive training?
8. Why, or why not, should a company use sensitivity training for executives?
9. Into what classes would you group subject matter to be included in executive development training programs?
10. How may trainees in an executive development program be evaluated?

CASE 14–1. A CHANGE IN LEADERSHIP STYLE

Mr. T. Hatter is the chief executive officer of a company which he once owned but which is now a subsidiary of a large conglomerate. The parent company requires all its executives to attend various executive development programs. Mr. Hatter recently returned from a three-week program in which he had been exposed to new trends in leadership and motivational practices.

Mr. Hatter has been an old-line traditionalist in his methods of dealing with subordinate executives and employees. He has comprehended that the parent company sent him to the development sessions because it would like to have him adopt more participative, permissive, and positive methods of leadership and motivation. Yet he likes his, as he puts it, tried-and-true methods of management and feels he should continue them but clothe them in the appearances of modernity to please the senior company.

His approach to combining the new and the old can be illustrated by what he did in handling the introduction of a new warehousing system. A few weeks before telling his operating executives about the new plan, he made it a point to commend them about various minor suggestions they had made. This was done to give them a feeling of recognition which he had been told in the training sessions was a necessary element in motivating others. Then at the meeting at which he planned to introduce the new warehousing system, he invited participation in the decision-making process, again because this had been stressed in the training sessions. He opened the meeting by asking his subordinates what ideas they had about warehousing (very few came forward because the agenda of the meeting had been unclear). Then he outlined his plan and asked for comments and suggestions (but again very little came forth).

Questions

1. Did or did not Mr. Hatter utilize participation in his motivational approach?
2. What must be true about the use of recognition and participation if they are to be successfully utilized as motivational tools?

CASE 14–2. EXECUTIVE DEVELOPMENT

The Personal Bakery Company has grown rapidly in the past dozen years. Opportunities for employee development, growth, and improvement have been numerous. As a case in point, John Brane has moved through a series of jobs from route man to that of Operating Manager. Under him are six assistant managers, under them about five route supervisors each, and under them the various route people.

John has grown in technical skill and operating managerial skill up to the present. Without any formal training he has, through experience, developed into a capable person and an administrator who is highly respected by all of his people. In the last stage of company expansion, however, it took more than the usual time for him to grow up to the more complicated organizational relationships.

Now the company through normal growth and a couple of contemplated acquisitions expects to triple its business in the next couple of years. The owners are doubtful that John is capable of handling an expanded assignment because it will involve more corporate planning, financial controls, and technical staff relationships which were not present in the operating end in which he has been so successful. There are two courses, as they see it, that are open to them; (1) let him remain as an operating manager or (2) set up a development program for him.

Question

1. Were they to choose the second alternative, set up a developmental program for John Brane.

CHAPTER

EDUCATION 15

___

Importance and Scope of Education

Education (*know why*)—as well as training (*know how*) is essential to effective performance by well-adjusted people. Education must be concerned with the understanding, perceptions, and attitudes of people at all organizational levels. Operative employees, for example, tend to work more effectively when they feel that management's objectives are significant and fair, when they understand what management is doing, and when they agree that management's practices are justifiable. And executives, in turn, can lead more effectively when they understand the motives, expectations, and thinking of employees. Through such mutual understanding comes appreciation for each other's interests and problems, adjustments in their thinking and actions, and fair compromises in their plans and interactions.

This chapter is concerned, therefore, with educational processes. Attention here is directed to the following:

1. Upward education; how executives learn more about the lower levels of an organization.
2. Downward education; how executives seek to increase the understanding of lower levels.
3. Communication practices which are basic to both directions of educational efforts.

UPWARD EDUCATION

Management cannot do an effective job of educating employees unless it is knowledgeable about the thinking and attitudes of employees. To be on firm ground, answers must be sought to two questions: what must be learned about employees and how is this learning to be accomplished?

Subject Matter

There are three broad areas of learning about employees to which management's education should be directed: the employee as an individual, the attitudes of employees toward company practices; and the attitudes of employees toward forces and factors outside the company but which impinge on company interests.

The Employee as an Individual. Basically, the thinking skills of employees will significantly affect a company's educational efforts. If the ability of employees to understand reasonable explanations is low, management, try as it may, will not be able to get across its messages. That is why a company should, among other personnel practices, seek people who not only are technically capable of doing required jobs but also can understand how our business and economic system works.

And management must be a student of the human dimensions of people. As noted earlier, people are more than a factor of production. Employees also have psychological, sociological, and ethical properties which affect performance. It is enough here, therefore, to say that these must also be included in the learning of management. Indeed, it may be argued that ignorance about these matters can negate however much management may know about people as machines.

Company Practices. It may also be argued that an executive who does not know how much understanding employees have about company practices is uneducated. A brief survey of pertinent practices is enough to point up their importance. What, for example, do employees know or feel about the following?

a. Objectives—to what extent the goals of stockholders, customers, and labor are to be served.

b. Policies—the basic guides established in a company relating to such questions as wage levels, seniority versus merit, promotional channels, working conditions, and union-management relations.

c. Procedures—steps to be taken in handling such matters as grievances, disciplinary action, employee services, and counseling.

d. Communications—the extent to which and the channels through which information is to flow back and forth between organizational levels.

And employees not only think about what management does in these areas but also think about how management does what it does. Thus executives may think themselves fair in establishing promotional policies and in selecting a particular person for promotion under the policies.

But to non-successful candidates, both the policies and the particular selection may appear to be examples of favoritism. It is not enough to think its practices are fair; it must seek to learn if employees think they are fair.

The behavioral patterns of management also merit managerial scrutiny. Some executives, for example, are autocratic in their attitude toward subordinates. Others instill a feeling that they are better than their subordinates—that the latter are second-class citizens. Others are suspicious of the motives and actions of employees and indicate a lack of confidence in them. Others avoid, if not despise, the company of their workers. And still others are contemptuous of the intelligence of employees. Of course, such relationships should not exist, but if management is not aware of how employees are reacting to these behavioral patterns, the education of the executives is being neglected.

Outside Factors and Forces. At one time management largely ignored how an employee reacted to or was affected by outside factors. But no more. Increasingly, management is becoming concerned about employee attitudes toward such matters as ecology, politics, energy crises, politics, community agencies, general education, traffic conditions, ghettos, and social relationships. How employees feel about these matters do affect internal company relationships. Hence they are relevant subjects of executive education.

Management must also learn about the associations which tend to affect the thinking and attitudes of its employees. For example, what ideas does an employee get from family background and associations? How does the community affect views? If a member of a union, what may its impact be upon worker's thinking? And how do political affiliations affect attitudes? These are all touchy subjects but nonetheless not to be overlooked in the educational program of an executive.

Learning Methods

A number of methods are available by means of which management may learn about its employees. The major ones are observation, interviews, questionnaires, and record keeping.

Observation. Observation can be one of management's best learning methods. Perhaps its very simplicity lulls some executives into ineptitude. They look but they do not see. Or they are so overloaded with technical details, important tasks, or a wide span of control that they have no time to look. Or they may foolishly pride themselves on an ability to size up individuals by the merest glance. Or they may fear to look lest they find some difficult-to-handle personal problem. Suffering from such failings, an executive will get little use from observation and may indeed get misinformation.

To use observation profitably, an executive must practice it and then apply it consciously and systematically. Much may be learned by watching the behavior of employees, listening to their talk, and noting their actions. People constantly tell us how they feel. They tell us by a shrug of the shoulder, a change of facial expression, a shuffling of feet, a change of tonal expression, a change of work habits, or an avoidance of our company. An observing executive will make note of these.

Interviewing.   Interviewing is another useful learning method. It provides for a face-to-face, personal, and verbal exchange of information, ideas, and points of view. But it is not something that will be satisfactory if done in a casual, unplanned, or careless manner.

To be effective, interviewing must adhere to a number of basic rules. These were reviewed in an earlier chapter, hence only another idea or two are in order here. It is particularly important to make employees feel free about coming in for interviews or they must be sought out at times that will serve to give a good sampling of their thinking and attitudes.

Thus an executive may plan to talk informally to a given number of employees every week or month, or use some anniversary, such as a hiring date, to contact subordinates. If staff members such as personnel department representatives or counselors participate in interviewing, they may schedule interviews in particular departments or among certain types of workers. In this way, trends in given areas may be ascertained and compared with those in other areas or past periods.

Questionnaires.   The questionnaire is a useful method of learning about employees. They are asked to express their opinions on a printed form to specific or open-end questions. In the first type an employee may be asked such questions as the following: Do you get a satisfactory answer from your supervisor when you ask about wages? Then a specific list of answers is provided from which a choice can be made as follows: Always; usually; sometimes; seldom; never. This type of questionnaire makes it easy for the employee to answer and for management to collate and compare answers. But it does restrict the employee, or it may require supply of answers to questions about which no thought has been given.

An open-end question has no terminal limitations. Of this type is the following question: What do you dislike most about your work? Here, employees are restricted neither in what they may say nor in how much they says. It is difficult, however, for management to collate and compare the answers. And many employees do not like to take the time to write out full answers or cannot express themselves satisfactorily.

Record Keeping.   Good records can tell much about employee thinking, attitudes, and reactions. Output and quality records are useful and should be kept by individuals and departments. Absenteeism and tardiness should be recorded on personnel records and summarized on departmental reports. Records should be similarly kept on such matters as morale changes, grievances, disciplinary actions, suggestions, and merit ratings. All are pertinent to executive education about employees.

DOWNWARD EDUCATION

The process of downward education consists of two major phases: what is to be taught and how the subject matter is to be taught.

Subject Matter

The subject matter of downward education takes place in the areas of top management, middle management, and supervision.

Top Management Groups. One of the most significant movements has been that concerned with top-level executive development. Of particular interest here are the employee-related subjects which might well be included in top-level executive programs. A variety of topics suggest themselves. Until top management seeks definite answers to questions such as the following, it can scarcely expect lower levels of management to know how to communicate intelligently.

a. What are the social responsibilities of management?
b. To what extent is business liable for the various risks which endanger employees?
c. What is an optimum balance between reasonable profits and fair wages?
d. Can workers be loyal to both the company and the union?
e. What are realistic policies toward political activities on the part of the company?
f. How do the roles of management and workers interact?
g. To what extent, and how, should employees participate in managerial decisions of importance to them?

These are significant questions. The trend of top executives to take counsel on these matters represents a wholesome advance in labor-management relations.

Middle Management Groups. Subject matter of middle management education usually includes the following major areas:

a. To learn precisely the educational plans and policies of top management.
b. To coordinate horizontally the educational responsibilities of various line and staff units.
c. To transmit specific educational plans to lower supervisory levels, and ultimately to employees at the operative levels.

Since the middle groups stand between the top and the bottom, they occupy a strategic position affecting relations between employees and management. They must therefore be adequately prepared to transmit accurately, and to control constructively, the plans, policies, and ideas of the top levels.

Supervisory Levels. Without doubt, day in and day out, the supervisor is in closer contact with operative employees than any other management or unit. In the formal organization structure, it is the supervisors and superintendents who are management to employees. And even informally, employees tend to feel that the supervisors determine how well they will or will not be treated as individuals.

It is through the supervisors, therefore, that most information will be channeled downward, as well as upward, relative to employees. Therefore, it is manifest that this group must be educated, first, in the various subjects important to the employee, and, second, in how such subject matter should be transmitted to employees.

Learning Methods

The materials in the foregoing two chapters have, in a sense, described the various methods by which all levels of an organization, both managerial and operative, may be taught. Hence, further discussion of this topic would be redundant. It may be well to note, however, that education is concerned with what people think and why. These are subjects in which continuous educational inputs are required. Conditions change, people change, knowledge expands, and needs and perceptions change. There should be no expectation that we will ever arrive at a stage that further education will be unnecessary.

ROLE OF COMMUNICATION

The best of educational methods or intentions will be of little avail if they are not communicated. Hence, in this section attention is directed to, first, some basic concepts of communication, and second, some rules of good communication practices.

Basic Concepts of Communication

Essential to good communication is an understandable model of the ingredients and relationships of a communication system. Thus, in all cases of communication, there will be found to be a communicator, the person communicated to, the message, the communication channel or device, and the purpose of the communication. These can be simply displayed as shown in Figure 15–1. Were this all there was to communi-

FIGURE 15–1

A Simple Communication System

cation, interaction between people would not be unduly complicated nor difficult to understand.

A number of difficulties and complexities interpose themselves. First, the communicator must select words or signals to express the ideas of the message. These are filtered through or affected by the person's logical system, background, experiences, roles, status, feelings, and behavioral patterns. Second, the signals are filtered through, interpreted, or decoded by the recipient's intellectual system, feelings, loyalties, sentiments, attitudes, position, background, experiences, and value system. Third, any communication channel is interfered with by—noises from—messages from other sources which detract and distract from the clarity of the intended messages. Cases in point are others talking, competing messages, and technical inadequacies of the channel or device. And fourth, the result which the communicator had in mind may be in conflict with the goals or needs of the recipient. The communication system thus has to be expanded as shown in Figure 15–2.

To illustrate, an executive seeks to convince a subordinate of the need to increase productivity. To the executive, the relation of productivity to profits, security, and high wages seems to be blatantly obvious. But in talking to the subordinate in these terms, the subordinate thinks (noises distracting attention) how previous increases in output brought no raises, how he or she was called a scab for working hard (filtering system), and so the subordinate is set against cooperating (cross-purposes).

This example also serves to illustrate the importance of having a

FIGURE 15–2

Complexities of a Communication System

Communicator	Filter System		Message		Filter System	Results
his ideas go through his	words and behavior come out and become	affected by noise	comes out as words and behavior perceived by recipient and go through his		comes out as impact on	

FIGURE 15–3

Feedback in the Communication System

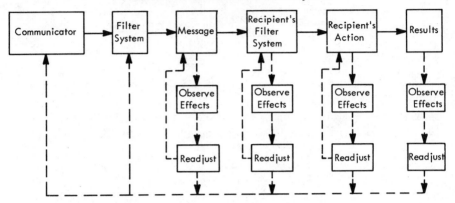

feedback arrangement in the communication system as shown in Figure 15–3. The communicator must observe or measure in some way the effect a communication is having, or has had, on the recipient. Then the message can be recast as it is being carried on or future messages can be redesigned to be more effective. This may involve rechecking the communicator's own filtering system, becoming attuned to the filtering system of the recipient, clearing the noises from the communication channel, and reexamining personally desired results or the goals of the recipient.

Rules of Communication

Some suggestions and some warnings are now in order if the communication model is to be used effectively. These are discussed here under the following headings:

1. The factor of change—resistance to change.
2. The educational process—difficulties of teaching.
3. The individual—obstacles in reaching people.
4. Semantics—the mystery of words.
5. Classes—obstacles of stereotypes.
6. Degrees—questions of how much.

1. The Factor of Change. The need for communication perhaps arises basically out of the dynamics of change. In the first place, if business operations did not change, there would be little need for communications. But they do change. So employees must be convinced to make and accept the changes. They must be convinced for a number of reasons. In the first place, there is the normal human resistance to getting out of a habitual way of doing things. Communications can be helpful in reducing the psychological frictions of this type.

Much more significant, in the second place, is the resistance arising from feelings of insecurity. Almost any change arouses questions of its possible negative impact upon job security, wage levels, social and organizational status, and personal prestige. To counter such feelings calls for considerable communication.

Usually, the practice in such cases has been to explain the nature of proposed change as already decided upon by management. This does not do too much in allaying fears. So explanations of why changes are needed and why they are desirable are communicated. This is of some help if specific attention is directed to advantages accruing to employees. Better still are communications which raise the need of change, without specifying a course of action, but instead inviting suggestions as to what should be done. This approach involves employees in managerial decision making, which few companies have been willing to adopt. If managerial resistance to this change in decision making can be reduced, undoubtedly much progress can be made in reducing employee resistances to change.

2. Educational Process.   Communication is thus for management a task of changing the thinking of employees—an educational process. Yet, frequently, management does not realize it is an educator. During a person's working life, something will be learned—if not from management, then from others. And what is learned elsewhere may not be to management's liking. Hence, it must be concluded that the role of educator must be accepted as a significant part of the job of every executive from the highest to the lowest supervisor.

As educators, management must be skilled in transmitting information and knowledge to subordinates. Each executive must therefore know the subject matter to be taught. This is not enough. A teacher must also be a preacher and a coach—a preacher because convincing employees about the profit system, let us say, is more than a statement of cold logic. All of us learn best when the teacher is enthusiastic, transmits a feeling of conviction, and employs various devices to bring human interest into lessons.

As educators, executives must apply the best techniques of coaching. They must always keep in mind that the employees are to play the game, not they alone. So they must teach workers how to act in the situations in which they will find themselves. This involves insight into the problems to be met and insight into the reactions that people will have in meeting them. Yet, many an executive fails to get across ideas effectively because of lack of cultivation of such insight. It is too easy to forget, once we have learned how to perform some act, how much difficulty we ourselves had in learning. Unless the coach keeps this in mind, the students develop obstructions to learning which make the executive's task even more difficult.

Finally, education has its problems because it is a thinking process. In all human activities, thinking ranks highest in difficulty. It is hard to concentrate for more than short periods of time. And sequential, logical analysis demands intense concentration. To get employees (or executives) to apply themselves, various educational devices must be used. Simple doses, constantly repeated at properly spaced intervals, through the best of conveyers (such as pictures and diagrams), must be used. Much could be learned in this regard from the comic books and movies of Walt Disney. He educated extremely well in a most interesting and painless manner.

3. The Individual. This last point about the thinking process leads naturally to a consideration of the difficulties of reaching individuals

FIGURE 15–4

A Difficulty in Communicating

COMMUNICATOR

Urge
Purpose
Knowledge

RECIPIENT

Capable of Understanding
Willing to Listen

Courtesy: General Electric Company

simply because of their human makeup. We assume that we shall not receive a busy signal when we call up, that they will not be preoccupied with personal problems and interests. We assume employees want to know what our managerial problems are. And we assume that the people have the technical equipment and education to receive the message which is sent. These assumptions are rarely warranted. And so communications based upon them are often bound to be ineffective, as suggested in Figure 15–4.

4. Semantics. One of the most perplexing problems of communications arises in relation to symbols used to transmit messages. A given word, for example, may not mean the same thing to all who hear it. But more important, the image a word creates in the mind, and the action the image initiates, may be far different than that visualized by the transmitter. Nonverbal sounds, too, such as a factory whistle, may connote one thing to the employer and another to the employee. Or a picture of a new machine the company proposes to install may not convey the idea of job security, as the company intends, but rather the idea of technological unemployment and job insecurity. And finally, the actions and trappings of executives may raise in the minds of employees ideas and actions far different than those in the minds or expectations of executives.

This area of the effect of symbols upon the minds and actions of people is entitled "semantics." It is concerned with a study of the meaning of symbols used in communication. Obviously, such study is appropriate to all areas of human endeavor. Only very recently, however, has it received the attention it deserves in the field of business.

The moral of all this to management is twofold: first, it should choose its words (and other symbols, too) carefully in preparing communications; and second, it should examine its own reactions and understanding of the words. This involves a good deal of study. A good place to begin is with past communications. What words were used? Were they simple or complex? Could they have been misconstrued? Then, some studies of employee reactions are called for. How do employees react to such words as *job, profits, boss, work, pay, order, service,* and *business?*

5. Classes. Another difficulty in communications that must be overcome is the obstacle created by the class attitude taken by various groups. Thus, in many instances, workers feel that as a class, they are opposed to the class of executives. It is their duty, then, to refrain from accepting the views expressed by management. This is uniquely illustrated by an employee who gets a promotion to a supervisory position. While at the lower level various coworkers come to her because she is their natural informal leader. They believe whatever she has to say and take whatever action she suggests. After she becomes boss, the visits stop, and such messages as she initiates are scorned or questioned. Yet, both before and after, this worker holds—or so she thinks—the same feelings toward her coworkers. But now she is in another class, and takes on the characteristics, viewpoints, and motives of that class.

Such typing of classes occurs in the executive levels, too. Staff people tend to categorize line executives as biased, relatively ignorant, and noncooperative individuals. The line people return the compliment by classifying staff people as impractical visionaries, who are constantly scheming to take control of their departments. And upper level executives generally are suspicious of lower level supervisors, feeling that the latter are not company-minded, take the side of labor, and generally lack needed managerial qualities. The lower levels have their own picture of the upper levels, viewing them as a group which is simply profit- and cost-minded, with little or no regard for the daily problems of getting work done and for the human factor in the shop.

On top of these organizational stereotypes, there may be overlappings of political, racial, religious, color, and job groupings. It is unwise to group all employees as being under the political influence of Democrats, Republicans, or labor unions. To address communications in terms of one grouping alone will certainly antagonize the others. And similarly, it is unwise to assume that all employees hold the same views on race, color, and creed—even those of the same race, color, and creed.

The design of communications to minimize class distinctions must begin, therefore, with a revision of acts which tend to raise class barriers. Management, for example, must live so that employees will not consider executives as natural enemies. Similarly, staff people should not act as if they alone are repositories of all that is good; line people should have confidence in their own abilities and not reflect characteristic manifestations of an inferiority complex in relation to staff people; upper management should put more managerial responsibilities upon lower supervisors; and the lower levels should take a broader company view and seek to earn the confidence of upper executives.

Thus, good communications really begin with action. The way we live speaks louder than words. But if our actions are good, the words we speak—if carefully chosen—will effectively convey our messages to various selected recipients.

6. Degrees and Quality of Communications.   But how much communication is necessary? Theoretically speaking, enough for an executive to make managerial planning, organizing, directing, and controlling of teamwork effective.

But there is also an ethical aspect to communication. For example, does management have the right to try to change or clarify basic economic, social, or political ideas? To illustrate, a program may be undertaken to convince employees that private enterprise is better than any form of government ownership, that the profit system is superior to national planning, that union membership will bring no lasting benefits, and that management leadership is fairer and more democratic than union leadership or political administration of business. To some, such communications may be termed "indoctrination" or outright propaganda. Such views are based not upon the type of education, but upon its fairness, accuracy, and validity. And those who voice them may themselves indoctrinate or propagandize, but see nothing wrong in that because they believe the content of their programs and messages is right and just.

Hence the right to indoctrinate or propagandize is not the basic issue. Since capitalists (*management* is too often used incorrectly as a synonym for this term) have so much at stake in a business enterprise, they should have the right to protect their investment by all legal and ethical means. But to go beyond the borders of fairness in such efforts by employing high-pressure tactics and partial truths is unjustifiable. The question, however, of what is fair, ethical, and accurate is one that is difficult to answer in many cases. Nevertheless, this should not be reason to remove the rights of management (or for that matter, of unions, political groups, or other agencies) to indoctrinate—communicate.

To sum up, whether the communication is intended to provide information or change the attitudes of employees (even to the extent of indoctrination or propagandizement), the efforts of management are justified. But the premise of fairness, honesty, and ethical standards is assumed and must be maintained. Without this, counterforce will be built up that will result in loss of faith, confidence, and loyalty.

QUESTIONS

1. To what three areas about employees should management's education be directed?
2. What are the methods which managers may use to learn about their employees?
3. What are the advantages of learning about employees through direct observation of employees?
4. What are the advantages and disadvantages of questionnaires as a method of learning the attitudes of employees?
5. What subjects are particularly useful for middle-group managers to learn about?
6. What are the major elements in the process of communication?
7. How does feedback contribute to better communications?
8. What has the factor of change to do with communications?
9. What solutions would you suggest to the problem of semantics in communications?
10. On what grounds would management propaganda to employees be justified? On what grounds would it be justifiably criticized?

CASE 15–1. THE OPEN-DOOR POLICY

Whenever employees of the Proco Company do not get the action or answers they want from their immediate supervisors or from the personnel department, they may take the matter up to higher management or directly to the chief executive. That is what Mr. A. W. Topper, the president, wants them to do. He has found that because they know his door is always open to them, workers ask to see him only when it seems absolutely necessary. And he has not been swamped by employees bearing suggestions, requests, or gripes.

The open-door policy is augmented by morale surveys that are conducted every few years. In these, individual responses are kept confidential. They are sealed by the employees and go to an outside firm of consultants for analysis and review. The company gets detailed reports of the survey results, but no names. The employees have developed faith in the surveys because over the years the items brought to the attention of management have in the main been acted upon.

A newly appointed supervisor has felt somewhat upset by this system of communications. He has found that a number of employees have gone around him to higher management to voice opinions and complaints. In a meeting with his superior, he has argued that company policy should require employees to come to the supervisor either before going to higher levels or before expressing their views on questionnaires. Otherwise, he argues, action cannot be taken at the lowest possible level, and that higher levels must be bothered by details that have to be handled by the lower levels in the final analysis.

Questions

1. What is your opinion of the supervisor's opinion?
2. What is the basis for the company's success in human relations, assuming that it has been successful?

CASE 15–2. INTERPRETING COMMUNICATIONS

Maury, a route manager, had a run-in with Stan, one of his truck salespeople. In the discussion, Maury told Stan that he disapproved of Stan's practices of loading his truck with merchandise not in accord with company practices, humming and singing on the route, carelessness in reporting inventories day, and rendezvousing with other salespeople at lunch breaks.

Afterwards, Stan's views of the conversation could be summarized in his words as follows: "I knew how to load my truck long before he showed up around here. I knew him when he was one of us but he sure has changed. He has lost his friendly ways and just wants to polish the brass. He doesn't know how to manage us. Besides, he's just jealous that I could become a professional singer and am not dependent on him. Well, I'm working on acting lessons. Sure, the other workers like to meet with me. I've been a natural friend of human and beast around here for years. Well, I know how to take care of that spying snake-in-the-grass if he gumshoes around here. I've talked this over with the boys and they agree that any more of this kid stuff and we're talking to the business agent."

And Maury's views could be summarized as follows: "I had to lay into Stan. I told him nicely a couple of times about the loading and the records. I know a thing or two about record-cheating, and I'll pounce on him. He thinks he's a swinging singer and it's gone to his head. The others just egg him on for a joke but he's trying to set them off against me. He's got to be more careful about public relations with that bellowing of his. If he doesn't straighten out, he's on the way out."

Question

1. What has gone on here?

part IV
The Maintenance Phase of Personnel Management

This Part of the text takes up some ways of personnel management by which a relatively effective and satisfied working force is sustained. And without doubt of primary importance in this connection is compensation. What are theories of compensation? How are compensation rates for particular jobs determined? What specific plans are available from which to choose? What indirect plans of compensation are commonly used? And to what governmental regulations must compensation plans conform? These are important questions, the answers to which the maintenance of employee cooperation is largely dependent.

As noted above, this Part takes up some maintenance plans. To attempt to cover all would require a set of encyclopedias. But this Part would be remiss were it to overlook (1) the many service and participation programs which help support a better working force, (2) the health and safety of people at work, and (3) some of the particular problems of various disadvantaged groups, special employee classes, and particular technological conditions. The maintenance aspects of these are of concern here.

REMUNERATION POLICIES 16

Significance of Remuneration

Scarcely any subject is as important to all levels of employees as is financial remuneration. Certainly, many grievances have their source in the feeling that compensation is unfair. Also employees sometimes express their discontent with various management practices by complaining about compensation. Moreover, all employees are continually reminded of compensation by the race between expenditures and the next payday—a matter of purchasing power. And how employees feel about compensation is significantly affected by what their neighbors think about their spending power—in a sense, a status symbol.

The Problems of Remuneration

Such sensitivity is not, however, the critical factor in remuneration. The trouble lies in the lack of a measuring device which can establish to the satisfaction of all concerned what an employee is worth in financial terms. To be sure, many measuring approaches are being used. But all are subject to some question by both the businessman and the recipient. Yet, payments of wages and salaries must be made in the present; neither management nor employee can await the day when a perfect measuring device is invented.

This is not necessarily a pessimistic outlook. Reasonably good remuneration plans and policies can be established. They must be based, however, upon careful consideration of a number of factors. Insofar as management's role in remuneration is concerned, close attention should be directed to the following:

1. General remuneration theories and issues (the subject matter of this chapter).

2. Determination of rates for specific jobs and positions (the subject matter of Chapter 17).
3. Provisions for variations within given job and position rates (the subject matter of Chapter 18).
4. Remuneration allowances in various benefit arrangements (the subject matter of Chapter 19).
5. Considerations of factors related to financial remuneration (the subject matter of Chapter 20).

Scope of Present Discussion

The amount an employee receives on payday is significantly influenced by the company's program of wage and salary administration. And this program, in turn, will have been vitally influenced by the answers the company derived to the following basic questions:

1. What is the economic basis of remuneration?
2. What are non-economic aspects of remuneration?
3. What are practical means of calculating compensation?
4. What are the influences of unions and collective bargaining?
5. What is the impact of governmental influences?
6. What safeguards may be employed in wage programming?

Economic Explanations

In a world in which various groups have recourse so often to the use of force in gaining desired goals, economic principles often seem to be of minor importance. But sooner or later, the millstones of economics grind out their truths to the disadvantage of those who do not obey its precepts. Hence, a brief review of economic wage principles is now in order.

1. Wages as a Price. Without forgetting the human aspects involved, it is nevertheless necessary at the outset to recognize that the term *wage* is a particular kind of price, that is, the price of labor. As such, it is subject to much the same type of analysis as any other price. Assuming, for the moment, the absence of frictions, political regulations, and pressure groups (either managerial or labor), wages are set at the point where the demand curve for labor crosses the supply curve of labor.[1] Hence, to act rationally in setting wage policies, an understanding of the theory of demand and supply curves is very useful. At least the manager who understands such forces will not overlook some very important factors when building a compensation program.

---

[1] This oversimplified statement has the merit of making it possible to discuss, in a limited space, a topic that otherwise would have to be left untouched here.

2. Demand Curve. The demand for labor (to begin with this factor) has two major aspects. First, each company has a demand for labor, that is, the quantities of labor that it is willing to hire at varying prices. Ordinarily, these quantities are increased only if the price of labor is decreased, as indicated in Figure 16–1. This trend is explainable by the general principle of diminishing productivity as increasing numbers of employees are added to a work group. Second, for every company, there usually is a community or industry demand curve, depending upon the number and type of competitors for labor in the area in which a company is operating.

FIGURE 16–1

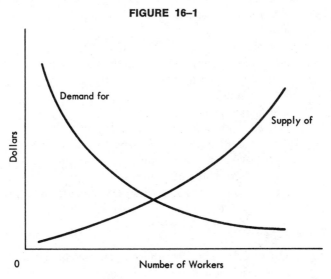

3. Supply Curve. The supply curve, on the other hand, has an upward trend, as indicated in Figure 16–1. This is a recognition of the fact that ordinarily it takes increasing quantities of dollars to lure larger numbers of workers into the employment market. Here again, there are company and area supply curves. Most companies have a supply of labor that is loyal to them irrespective of general wages or competition. And then, there is a general supply curve representing quantities that can be drawn upon or lost by a particular company, depending upon the wages it is willing to pay. Supply curves are difficult to draw, although here, too, approximations can be derived by counting the population by age groups and by getting estimates of types of skills available in the community.

4. Forces Affecting Demand and Supply. To estimate demand and supply curves at any particular time, it is essential to ascertain as accurately as possible the factors that influence such curves. In outline, the following are factors commonly of importance:

A. Demand factors
   1. Short-run changes in:
      a. Company production schedules
      b. Competitors' production schedules
      c. Seasonal production
      d. Consumer demands
   2. Long-run changes in:
      a. Fundamental processes of production
      b. Demands of competitors for labor
      c. Fundamental productivity of labor
      d. Growth or decline of industry
      e. Profitability of the industry
B. Supply factors
   1. Short-run changes in:
      a. Mobility of labor in or out of the community
      b. Seasonal changes in working habits
      c. Union demands
   2. Long-run changes in:
      a. Cyclical depressions or periods of prosperity
      b. Influx of new industries or departure of old
      c. Family size and other population characteristics
      d. Costs and standard of living
      e. Trends in union strength and governmental regulation

Noneconomic Aspects

But wages and salaries are also affected by psychological, sociological, and ethical factors. These determine in significant measure how hard a person will work for the compensation received or what pressures a person will exert to increase compensation.

Looking first at the psychological dimension, people perceive the level of their wages as a measure of themselves. They may as a consequence feel insecure, have an inferiority complex, seem inadequate, indulge in self pity—or feel the reverse of all these. They may or may not take pride in the amount of their paychecks and what it can buy in worldly goods. So their internal reactions are in part due to their perceptions of their price, in wages and salaries. Management must, therefore, not overlook this aspect in establishing its compensation program.

But what about the social aspects of compensation? Why, for example, does a $5 an hour machinist get upset when he learns that a co-worker is receiving five cents an hour more? Why does a $100,000 a year executive seek an increase of $5,000 knowing that taxes will get most of the increase? Answers to such questions lie in the realm of interpersonal status, prestige, and values. Compensation differentials serve to depict social hierarchies. We perceive ourselves in relations to others in terms of how much each of us earns. Management must seek, therefore, to weigh the social impact of its compensation programs.

Running through all compensation decisions are basic questions of equity. Is my salary fair and just in terms of: the job I am on; my contributions to the company; my job compared to other jobs; myself and other employees; my years of education, experience, and, service; myself and those of other races, creeds, colors, and sex; and my family responsibilities? All of these enter into attitudes about fairness and equity. And to all of such matters relating to ethical perceptions, management must include inputs into its compensation programs.

Our knowledge is not great on how to quantify these non-economic aspects of compensation. For example, governmental agencies, unions, and community agencies have on occasion forced business to set wage rates at levels above those which might have otherwise been justified on purely economic grounds. Or when a segment of society achieves a productive capacity beyond a mere subsistence level, various participants seek a share in such affluence. And governmental regulations and bargaining agreements have sought to upgrade the dignity of workers, reduce gross inequities, or minimize class distrust. And most, if not all, are based upon evaluations other than the measurements of supply and demand.

Calculating Compensation Levels

Granted that economic and non-economic factors are significant, including all of them in a precise wage formula is simply impractical. Yet employees must be paid here and now. No one wants to wait for the compilation of demand and supply data. And no one seems capable of weighing the non-economic elements. Hence, it is not unnatural to seek a formula which returns quicker answers and which still has over-all reasonableness.

1. Employee Contributions. A logical approach seemingly is to remunerate employees for the contributions they make to salable goods and services. Thus the company sells the goods and then shares the monies so received with—among other groups—labor. But employees invariably receive wages and salaries before (often months before) goods are sold and sometimes when the finished goods cannot be sold at all. It is obvious, then, that remuneration must be calculated and paid before labor's contribution to sales can thereby be measured. Moreover, it is a difficult—if, indeed, not impossible—task to determine what contribution a specific employee, let us say a typist, makes to a product such as an electronic computer.

If contributions cannot be measured directly, are there factors which

influence contributions, and can they be measured? No involved cogita-
tion is needed to conclude that as far as employees are concerned, their
contributions to a company's success are dependent upon the following:

a. Time spent at work.
b. Energy and skill expended—physical, mental, emotional, and social.
c. Willingness to cooperate.

These can be measured with varying degrees of accuracy. Time, of
course, is readily ascertainable. Energy and skill call for judgmental
evaluations. And willingness to cooperate is undoubtedly the most difficult to measure. Yet, anyone who has worked with or watched people
work soon realizes that willingness to expend energy is an important
factor for which people are paid wages.

The proof of this is immediately seen in cases of method changes. Let
us assume that energy and skill can be expressed in units and that
management improves job methods with the following results:

	Old Method	New Method
Output per hour	100	200
Energy and skill expended by labor	30	20

If the principle of cause and effect were invoked to support its claim,
management presumably should be given credit for the increase in production. Indeed, to follow the argument to its logical end, wages should
be decreased, because labor is spending less energy in working and is
taking no more time.

But in all likelihood, wages will have to be raised! And this despite
the claim that management might make that it caused the increased
output by devising the improved method. Labor would note that output
has now been doubled. It would conclude that it should share in the increase and simply refuse to cooperate if a share were not forthcoming.

Labor expresses its unwillingness to work by a slow down on the job
or in extreme cases by a strike. In the latter case, unwillingness to work
is complete. As a consequence, supply of labor is at zero. It must be concluded, therefore, that the degree of unwillingness (or willingness) to
work affects supply which, as discussed above, is a basic economic factor
of price (wage) determination. To sum up, people must be compensated
for their willingness to work as well as for their time, skill, and energy.

2. Monetary Conversions. While it is possible to measure the foregoing factors, the measurements are not expressed in monetary terms. How
does one convert eight hours of work, 50 units of energy, and 60 units of
cooperation into dollars and cents? One way is to see what others in the
same community or in the same line of business are paying for such em-

ployee contributions. Another is to establish a job evaluation plan by which varying degrees of such factors are given monetary values. Both of these approaches are discussed more fully in a later chapter. For the present, it is sufficient to note that conversions into monetary terms are invariably based upon opinions. Yet, such opinions, when expertly made, can provide reasonably accurate answers to the wage determination problem.

Influence of Unions and Collective Bargaining

Increasingly, the right to make wage determinations is being shared by management with unions. It is therefore desirable to examine some of the concepts which have been given a significant place in remuneration determinations because of union activity. Of particular interest are the concepts of administered wages, productivity increases, ability to pay, cost of living, "equality of workers," power of strikes and bargaining strategies.

1. Administered Wages. There are some who ascribe little practical weight to economic forces as wage determinants. Instead, they contend that representatives of labor and management in the collective bargaining process set wages, i.e., administer wages. Presumably, these parties have the power (and exercise it) to determine rates irrespective of supply and demand factors. There is evidence that wage rates and fringe benefits have been increased when supply-demand conditions would have indicated a reverse action. So it sometimes appears that those in positions of power, rather than economic forces, are the real determiners of wage levels.

To the extent that monopolistic conditions exist, such determinations have current and practical significance. But even the parties to administered wages cannot completely ignore economic forces. The union, for example, must determine how many jobs it is willing to sacrifice if wage demands are set at an unduly high level. And managerial representatives are not unaware of the fact that some sales will be lost if high labor costs result in high sales prices. Sooner or later, adjustments to supply and demand of labor must be made when wage rates are administered, so long as labor leaders and business administrators cannot also control the buyers of their products.

2. Productivity Increases. An interesting development in wage determination has been the productivity increase, as espoused by a number of unions and as used by the federal government as a guide line to noninflationary wage increases. This is based on the fact that overall productivity in this country has tended to increase on the average about three percent a year. So the unions in some industries have gained the concession that employees should share in the annual average increase—and this though there may actually be no increase in some years or in the industry in question.

When management makes such a concession, it is economically justified only when labor makes a contribution to the productivity increase. To accept the conclusion that labor in a given company should be given an annual productivity adjustment based on national averages is scarcely logical. To do so would result in overcompensation in some cases and undercompensation in others. Much more defensible would be a productivity reward based on what occurred in a given company and what labor specifically contributed to the given productivity increase.

3. Ability to Pay. Wage increases based on a company's ability to pay is subject to argument. Unions contend that increases should be given by those that can afford them. Companies that are high earners contend that ability to pay has little if anything to do with current wage levels. The debate can be endless between the two because both are partly right as well as partly wrong.

Simple analysis is enough to show that the contentions of the parties are dependent upon the influence of time on wages. In the short run, the economic influence on wages of ability to pay is practically nil. All employers, irrespective of their profits or losses, must pay no less than their competitors and need pay no more if they wish to attract and keep workers. For example, if those who are operating unprofitably cut wages because of losses, they would soon find that their employees were leaving them, provided that other jobs were available.

In the long run, ability to pay is influential. During times of rising prosperity, individual producers who wish to take advantage of such trends have to bid for labor to help carry on the profitable operations. And the limit to their bidding—which, of course, they hope is not approached too closely—is their increased ability to pay. Conversely, when a general depression hits, wages and/or employment must be cut because needed funds become scarcer.

4. Cost of Living. The relation of cost of living to wages is another basic question in establishing remuneration policies. Its significance has increased because many companies have agreed to tie wage increases to (and decreases, too, in some instances) changes in cost of living as reflected in cost-of-living indexes such as that compiled by the Bureau of Labor Statistics. For example, adjustments in wages are made monthly or quarterly as the index changes. How much of a wage adjustment will be made depends upon the agreement between labor and management as to the percentage of wage change that is to be made for each percentage change in the cost-of-living index.

Such practices seem to have a logical appeal. Yet, analysis will show that cost of living has an indirect, not a direct, bearing upon wages. The reasonableness of cost-of-living clauses, or "escalator clauses," as they are sometimes called, lies in the fact that wages and cost of living tend to go up and down at the same time. For example, in the rising phase of a business cycle, all prices tend to rise. Thus the items labor buys go up in price. And wages of labor do, too. In the case of labor, its requests for increases are then met, for the very simple reason that the supply of labor is relatively less than the demand for labor. The supply-demand relationship also favors price increases in the goods that labor buys in its standard of living.

This analysis would hold true on the down side of a business swing. Then, of course, cost of living and wages would tend to move lower.

So, any way one looks at it, cost of living and wages seem to be related directly, particularly to those whose wages buy their cost of living. The relation is not, however, casual; each goes up or down because of general market and competitive conditions. It is like a cloud and a sailboat moving in the same direction. No one would say the cloud is pushing the sailboat. Rather, the wind would be recognized as the causal factor in the case of cloud and boat. Similarly, with wages and cost of living, the common wind is the force of supply and demand.

Since cost of living and wages tend to move together, it may be practical to use the former as a measure of the latter. But this should be done with a clear understanding that the cost-of-living indexes are an expedient, not the real measure of wages.

But even when used as expedients, the practice of tying wages to cost-of-living indexes eventually runs into one or more difficulties. In the first place, the tie between wages and living costs is usually made during periods of rising prices when employers are not reluctant to grant wage increases. But during deflationary periods, employees are irritated by the periodic (even though small) readjustments of wages that are made as living costs go down. Second, arguments eventually are raised as to how cost-of-living indexes should be computed. In one case, opinions differed as much as 100 percent in regard to how much costs had risen. Finally, a vicious circle would be induced if all employers followed this practice. Thus a price rise would call for a wage increase, which would increase costs, which would lead to an increase in prices, and so on, bringing about an inflationary spiral detrimental to all.

5. Equality-of-Workers Theory. Occasionally the principle is encountered that all workers are economically equal on given types of jobs. An application of this principle is that of paying all workers in a given class of work the same rate, irrespective of individual merit. Its application is desirable for the union because it eliminates the troublesome controversies between workers of varying ability as to the rates they should receive. The union can then concentrate its attention upon other matters than that of reconciling intraunion differences. Such supposed equality is the basis of seniority rules for granting wage increases which otherwise have little validity.

6. Power of Strikes. The strike is a potent weapon of union policies. Through it unions control supply of labor as a basic element of wage determination. By withholding the supply, the number of people legally —and so practically—available to work is temporarily reduced to zero. Hence, the strike, or the threat of one, is invariably capable of forcing management to accept to some degree the wage demands of unions.

7. Union Strategies. It is also imperative for management to be aware of the strategies unions may be pursuing in relation to wage matters. When a union in a given case asks for a large increase in wages, what does it really want? In asking for more money than it expects to get, its strategy may be either to get something else (earlier retirement privileges under the pension plan, for example), or to divert management's attention from various parts of the bargaining package. Of course, management may counter with proposals that tend to offset the strategy of the union; but to do this, it must judge carefully the extent to which the union is using wages as a bargaining device.

Wages are used by unions to control their internal affairs as well as to affect their relations with employers. For example, wage rates have been bargained for that will retard the flow of learners into a trade. In addition, levels of wages between different grades of work are often closely watched so that members do not quarrel among themselves over relative wages. In some instances, wage adjustments have been sought to offset the introduction of laborsaving equipment. And most unions nowadays estimate closely the possible effect upon employment of the levels of wage increases they seek.

Governmental Regulations

If the unions have had an impact upon remuneration practices, so too has the government. The federal government has been particularly influential through such enactments as the Fair Labor Standards Act (FLSA), the Walsh-Healey Act, the Bacon-Davis Act, and Equal Pay Act. Since state regulations, in cases where they have been enacted, tend to follow federal laws, only the latter are described here.

The Fair Labor Standards Act

The FLSA, also known as the Wages and Hours Law, was enacted in 1938 and subsequently amended for the dual purpose of helping to spread employment and to outlaw unsatisfactory wage rates. The latter purpose is accomplished by establishing a minimum pay level of $2.10 an hour, increased to $2.30 after December 31, 1975. The former purpose is achieved by penalizing employers who work their employees beyond 40 hours a week by requiring them to pay 50 percent more for the excess hours. This is where the term *time and one half for overtime* is derived, the actual overtime being paid for at the rate of one and one-half times the regular base rate.

1. Coverage of the Act. The FLSA covers all businesses and employees (with stated exceptions) who engage in interstate commerce or produce goods that enter interstate commerce. But some exceptions are allowed for companies whose gross earnings are less than $250,000, and for some companies in certain seasonal industries. Some exceptions are also allowed, first, for employees such as apprentices, learners, handicapped workers, messengers, and salespeople, and, second, for executives, administrators, and professional workers. But even in these cases of personal exemptions, stated wage and salary minimums must be maintained.

2. Records. Although the FLSA does not require that specific forms of records be kept, rulings of the administrator indicate that certain types of information should be recorded. First, for each employee, such personal data should be kept as name, address, date of birth if under 19, and occupation. Second, time records should be kept regarding the standard workweek, hours worked each day and each week, and absences. Third, payroll records should cover dates of payment, pay periods, daily and weekly earnings, basis on which payment is made, bonuses earned, and any deductions from wages paid. And fourth, if the company hires employees who work at home, detailed records should be kept on the foregoing, as well as the amount of work distributed to and collected from each such worker.

3. Penalties. Employers who violate this Act may be punished in a variety of ways. By injunction, an employer may be forbidden to ship goods interstate, to pay less than minimum wages, or to keep inadequate records. By criminal prosecution, an employer who is convicted of having willfully violated the Act can be fined up to $10,000 or imprisoned for a term of not more than six months, or both. And an employee who has not been paid properly under the law may sue to recover the wages due, plus an equal sum as liquidated damages, plus attorney fees and litigation costs. It is not necessary that the employer's failure to pay be willful.

The Walsh-Healey Public Contracts Act

The Walsh-Healey Act pertains to the parts of an employer's business related to federal contracts of $10,000 or more. The Walsh-Healey Act has rules on overtime and minimum wages as does the FLSA but differs from it in two important respects. First, the overtime provisions are set on a daily (8-hour) as well as a weekly (40-hour) basis. Second, the minimum wages are based upon prevailing community rates, as determined by the Secretary of Labor after public hearings.

1. Exemptions. There are a number of important exemptions under this Act. There are business exemptions, such as the following:

a. Various transportation and communication facilities.
b. Construction contracts.
c. Personal service contracts.
d. Perishable commodities.
e. Stock on hand.

And there are groups of exempt employees, such as the following:

a. Employees not engaged in work directly connected with the manufacturing, fabrication, assembling, handling, or shipment of articles, supplies, and equipment.
b. Office, custodial, and maintenance employees.
c. Executive, administrative, and professional employees.

2. Required Records. The records required by this Act are much the same as by the FLSA. The Walsh-Healey regulations require the same personal data as the Wages and Hours Law, plus these two additional items:

a. The sex of each employee.
b. The number of each contract each employee works on, and the dates when the work is performed.

Except for the overtime column, payroll records and computations under both the Wages and Hours and the Walsh-Healey acts may be identical. The reason for the exception is that the Wages and Hours Law requires overtime pay only for hours worked over 40 per week, whereas the Walsh-Healey Act requires overtime pay for hours worked over 8 per day or 40 per week, whichever is greater.

Firms covered by the Walsh-Healey Act also must keep a record of the "injury frequency rate" in their establishments on a quarterly basis. The injury frequency rate is calculated by multiplying the total number of "disabling injuries" which occur during each three-month period by one million and dividing that sum by the total number of work hours actually worked within the same quarterly period.

3. Penalties for Violations. The penalties for violations of this Act may be very severe. They are as follows:

a. Money damages for child or prison labor.
b. Wage restitutions.

c. Cancellation of contract.

d. Blacklisting.

Perhaps the most effective method of enforcement of the Walsh-Healey Act is that which provides for the assessment of money damages against the contractor.

A contractor who violates the minimum-wage or overtime stipulations has to pay the wages due, equal to the amount of any unlawful deductions, rebates, refunds, or underpayments.

Failure to comply with the stipulations of the Walsh-Healey Act, which are a part of the contract, constitutes breach of contract by the contractor. As in other instances of breach of contract, the penalty is cancellation of the contract. In addition, a contractor can be made to pay any increased costs if the government gets someone else to complete the contract.

The Comptroller General is required to distribute a blacklist to all government agencies. The persons or firms whose names appear on this list cannot be awarded any government contract for a period of three years following the date upon which the Secretary of Labor determines that a breach occurred, unless the Secretary recommends otherwise. Obviously, to be placed upon this list would be a serious penalty in many cases.

The Bacon-Davis (Public Construction) Act

The Bacon-Davis Act is similar to the Walsh-Healey Act, since it too regulates minimum wages on governmental contracts. It relates to contracts in excess of $2,000 for the construction, alteration, and repair of public works. All mechanics and laborers must be paid at least the prevailing rate as established by the Secretary of Labor.

If contractors pay more than prevailing rates, they do so at their own risk, since such additional costs are not reimbursable. If contractors pay less, they are subject to any of the following penalties:

1. The Secretary of Labor may withhold accrued payments due to the contractor from the federal government.
2. The contracts held by the contractor may be canceled outright by the government.
3. The contractor's name may be placed upon the Comptroller General's ineligibility list for further contracts.

Equal Pay Act

This legislation, enacted in 1963, prohibits wage differentials, based on sex, for workers covered by the Fair Labor Standards Act. It requires that pay for given jobs be the same irrespective of the sex of the employee. It seeks to correct the policy followed for such a long period of time of paying women less than men on the same job.

Safeguards in Wage Programming

This discussion of remuneration can best be closed by making a number of suggestions regarding wage programming. In the first place, it should be perfectly obvious that anyone who is convinced of having a perfect answer to wage problems and can correctly set wages is deluding himself. There is as yet no method of such perfection available. To believe so merely establishes a block in the road that otherwise leads to intelligent compromise.

In part, the explanation for the belief that wages can be set accurately derives from false deductions relative to the use of time-study methods. Such methods are very useful in determining a fair day's work. They may serve to establish, for example, that on a given job a well-selected, trained, and experienced worker should be able to produce, let us say, 800 units a day. But what the wage value of the 800 units is cannot be determined by time-study devices. To be sure, time-study analysts often proceed to set value rates, but they are using other yardsticks or techniques in doing so, not time-study.

The use of time-study methods is not criticized here but rather their misuse. To claim for them results that they cannot yield is a serious error which management should avoid. And certainly unions in many cases have become vigorous opponents of time-study methods because of misuse in setting rates.

Another safeguard is that management's wage policies should be based upon a full account of all factors—economic, legal, union, sociological, and psychological—that have some effect on wages. To do this, it is absolutely essential to determine as precisely as possible how these factors exert their influence. Such factors as cost-of-living indexes, union demands, changes in population structure, competition, and federal regulations all have their place in the wage structure. However, some work directly and others indirectly, some work slowly and others rapidly, and some are positive in wage determinations and others negative. Unless the direction and force of the composite of factors is determined, grievous errors will be committed in establishing wage policies.

For example, a personnel manager must properly evaluate short-run influences and long-run influences to help the company reach correct wage decisions. Moreover, companies which foolishly raise arguments that apply in the short run but not in the long run, or vice versa, merely weaken themselves in the eyes of their employees when the truth is known. And when legal and social forces are against the company, the employer should not be the last to adapt to their moves. This does not mean that employers should not seek to protect their interests by legitimate means, but to do so by obstructionist tactics is folly.

Finally, and perhaps most important of all, wage policies should be viewed as an integral part of the structure of a personnel program. Wages are undoubtedly the keystone to the arch of this structure, but not the structure itself, as some employers seem to believe. Indeed, some have been so preoccupied with wages that unions have taken advantage of this bias to gain unwarranted and ill-advised concessions on working conditions and rules. The ill-advised seniority rules accepted by some companies, which they must follow thereafter to their regret, are a case in point.

When wages are given their proper place in the personnel program, they are neither overemphasized or underemphasized. Wages alone cannot bring about higher production, better morale, and better relations with employees. Nonfinancial incentives, proper handling of grievances, good working conditions, availability of various services, and development of confidence in workers are examples of other matters that can add or detract from the effectiveness of the wage program itself.

QUESTIONS

1. Inasmuch as what wage should be paid cannot be measured precisely, what hope is there of ever minimizing wage disputes?
2. What is the economic explanation of wages?
3. What non-economic factors affect wages and salaries?
4. How does "willingness to work" affect wage determination?
5. What is the major weakness of the "administered wages" theory?
6. If Company A made a profit of $1.5 million this year and Company B lost an equal amount, what effect would these data have upon wage levels in these companies that are located side by side and employ approximately the same classes and grades of employees?
7. What effect does productivity of employees have upon wages in theory and in practice?
8. What strategies may a union adopt in its concerns with wage matters?
9. What were the reasons for the passage of the fair labor standards acts? The Walsh-Healey Act? The Bacon-Davis Act? The Equal Pay Act?
10. What can time-study methods contribute to the determination of wages? What can they not contribute?

CASE 16–1. COST OF LIVING INCREASE DEMANDS

In a confrontation between the industrial relations director and the bargaining agent, an impasse has been reached over the amount of a wage increase. The director was authorized to offer an increase which would have amounted to seven percent (direct wage increased by fringe benefits), but the union representative refused to go back to the membership with less than fifteen percent (this also would include fringe benefit as well as direct wage increases) over the next three years—evenly divided, plus a cost-of-living escalator adjustment.

The bargaining agent explained that the fifteen percent increase would take care of some of the cost-of-living increases and some of the productivity increases that had taken place since the last contract was signed. And the escalator clause was intended to take care of such cost-of-living increases that might occur in the future.

The industrial relations director offered to recommend that the cost of living increase for the past and the escalator clause for the future be accepted by the company if the company would arrange to go to its customers and ask them (1) to repay the company for the employees' costs of living increases incurred in the products the customers had bought and (2) to agree to pay for such new increases that might occur.

The bargaining agent retorted that these were facetious answers to the union's bargaining in good faith and that unless the demands were met, the agent would recommend a strike as a means to gaining the legitimate demands.

Question

1. Why should (or should not) the company agree to the demands for the cost of living increases; for the productivity increases?

CASE 16–2. COMPENSATION DIFFERENTIALS

All employees are interested in both the absolute amount of their salaries and the amount relative to others in the organization. As to the latter dimensions, the spread between the highest paid and the lowest can in some companies be very great. This wide spread may not be as noticeable in some companies because the recipients at either end may seldom see each other. But in some instances, the recipients may work in close proximity, and the lower level employees may be prone therefore to seek some form of redress.

As a case in point, the Broad Stock Brokerage Company is particularly having trouble on this score in one of its branch offices. On the one hand, the branch manager and the customer's workers are at the upper end of the compensation scale but the secretaries and account clerks are at the lower end. The latter know that they are widely separated compensationwise from the top people. Being in a small organization, the informal communication network informs most everybody of the salary payments, or at least good guesses about them. And being in a small organization, the lower levels don't think that as far as they can see that the work of the higher levels is worth the difference.

Although the lower levels don't seem to do anything directly about this spread, there is a constant stream of grievances on various matters, mistakes, unreliable cooperation, bickering, turnover, rumor-mongering, and slowdowns to evidence their dissatisfaction.

Question

1. What do you suggest be done to reduce the adverse reactions of the lower levels?

JOB EVALUATION AND 17
WAGE CLASSIFICATION

Introduction

As noted earlier, relative—even more than absolute—compensation is of critical importance in affecting employee morale and effort. It is surprising to see the change in a person who, seemingly satisfied with earned remuneration, learns of the higher earnings of a coworker whom the employee considers inferior. To minimize such occurrences, it is imperative to determine, first, what each job is worth, and, second, what each individual on each job is worth. Determining job values comes under the heading of job evaluation and wage classification (which is the subject of this chapter); and determining the value of employees (which has been discussed in Chapter 12) comes under the province of merit evaluation or seniority plans.

Job evaluation is essentially a process of measurement. This is done by using arbitrarily designed yardsticks to evaluate factors considered of importance in jobs. A quantitative sum is thus derived for each job, and then this sum is converted into a dollar value. Thus, each job has a logical relation to other jobs, since all have been measured by the same yardsticks.

Various methods have been designed to make such measurements. In major outline, all follow the same general pattern, which includes the following major steps:

1. Establishing organizational responsibility.
2. Determining jobs to be evaluated.
3. Making the job analysis.
4. Evaluating the jobs.
5. Preparing wage and salary classifications.

Organizational Aspects

Almost without exception, those who have had experience with job evaluation programs have concluded that such programs should have the approval and sponsorship of top executive levels. Particularly in the initial stages, a committee of major executives should guide the development of job evaluation. This is desirable to convince any doubters that top management is convinced of the value of the program. After the program is well under way, periodic conferences should be scheduled with top executives so that they may be kept informed of progress and have the opportunity to offer suggestions and criticisms.

1. Organizational Responsibility. Responsibility for job evaluation is usually assigned to the personnel department, the industrial engineering section, or some interested operating executive. Its placement in the personnel department has much to commend it because a wage and salary program is of vital importance in a total personnel program. There is sense to its assignment to industrial engineering because of its professional interest in working conditions. The "interested executive" assignment is usually made in smaller companies without specialized service units.

2. Staffing the Unit. Wherever in the organization the job evaluation program is assigned, provision must be made for staffing it with competent help. In some companies, trained and experienced help is hired from the outside. By this method, competent help is secured at once, but it may take some time for the outsider to become acquainted with the policies and characteristics of the company and its employees. In other companies, present members of the staff are given special training. Under this method the staff members are acquainted with the company, its executives, and its employees, but they must acquire skills to carry out the job evaluation program. Both plans have been used successfully, so that the choice in any particular case depends upon which can be installed most economically and effectively. In any event, the staff should be a permanent one because the job evaluation plan will require subsequent adjustments and refinements.

3. Approval of Evaluation Plans. Where authority rests in approving and using job evaluation data should also be specified if all organizational aspects of the program are to be properly considered. Since the personnel department is a staff department, it obviously cannot enforce the program, the development of which has been assigned to it. Hence, approval of the plan must be in the hands of some top-line executive. Even when this is provided for, the personnel department must solve the problem of securing full cooperation of unions and the using departments. More and more, job evaluation has become subject to collective bargaining. Thus, consultation, if not direct cooperation, with unions at all stages of development and use seems desirable. Moreover, building satisfactory relations with supervisors and superintendents is an essential part of the organizational problem. Even though top management approves a job evaluation program, the supervisors can delay or even sabotage its development if they withhold their cooperation or give it grudgingly.

Selection of Jobs to Be Evaluated

Few companies have included all jobs and positions in their evaluation programs. Ordinarily, the programs are limited in most companies to shop jobs or office positions. Or jobs receiving more than a set amount a year in salary—in some cases as low as $8,000 and in others up to $20,000—are excluded. Or a particular level in the organization chart is used: for example, all jobs below the first line of supervision may be included. Executive, professional, and technical jobs are often excluded also at least in the beginning.

Such exclusions should not, however, be made permanent nor have they in some companies. When time and conditions permit, all positions should be brought into the plan. When selling jobs are separated from nonselling, or engineering from technical shop jobs, for example, in order to get an evaluation program done quickly, grievances in the nonstudied jobs will soon appear and be difficult to handle.

Moreover, when companies try to include previously excluded jobs in the program, they find that the new jobs can seldom be fitted into the existing scheme. The alternatives are to have two evaluation programs, which do not quite match, or to start all over and reevaluate the old jobs under an overall program. Either course is unsatisfactory and can be avoided if the evaluation plan is developed with a view to including all jobs ultimately, though at the outset only particular groups of jobs are to be evaluated.

Making the Job Analysis

The basic material of job evaluation is provided by job analysis. Since the nature and scope of job analysis have been described in an earlier chapter, it is necessary here merely to note the information which is secured by job analysis and which is essential to subsequent steps of job evaluation. The following information is usually collected:

1. Job title or titles, including trade nicknames.
2. Number of employees on the job, and their organizational and geographical locations.
3. Names of immediate supervisors.

4. Materials, tools, and equipment used or worked with.
5. From whom work is received and to whom it is delivered.
6. Hours of work and wage levels.
7. Conditions of work.
8. Complete listing of duties, with an estimate of time spent on each group, classified according to daily, weekly, monthly, and occasional.
9. Educational and experience requirements.
10. Skills, aptitudes, and abilities required.
11. Promotional and transfer lines from and to the job.
12. Miscellaneous information and comments.

Job Evaluation Plans

After the foregoing preparations have been made, measurement of jobs in nonfinancial terms may be undertaken. This step, to repeat, is based on the assumption that to develop correct financial relationships between jobs, it is first necessary to set forth quantitative relationships based upon arbitrarily constructed yardsticks. In simple terms, this means that if it is found that job A is worth two units on a predetermined scale and job B is worth four units on the same scale, then, whatever A is worth in dollars, B should be worth about twice as much. How the jobs are quantitatively related to each other depends upon the system employed. The following systems of evaluation are described here:

1. The simple ranking plan.
2. The job classification method.
3. The point system.
4. The factor comparison method.

1. The Simple Ranking Plan. Under the simple ranking plan of evaluation, jobs are arranged in order of increasing value in accordance with the judgment of the arrangers. This is first done on a departmental level by a committee of job analysts and supervisors, and then on interdepartmental levels by a committee which also includes higher line executives. The committee members read the job descriptions or, if descriptions are not available, examine their mental pictures of the jobs and grade the jobs in terms of their individual interpretations of the relative amounts of such elements as the following:

a. Difficulty and volume of work.
b. Responsibilities involved.
c. Supervision given and received.
d. Training and experience requirements.
e. Working conditions.

After all jobs have been ranked, they are grouped into a small number of classes, usually from six to ten. Wage and salary rates are established for each of the classes, either arbitrarily or by job-rating methods to be defined later. All jobs in a given class are then paid within the dollar range established for that class.

This plan is obviously simple, can be done quickly, and does not require a large staff. But it is difficult to explain because the reasons why jobs have been ranked as they are, are locked in the minds of the rankers, whose scales of value vary from one time to another and whose individual concepts of jobs differ. The rankers are ordinarily inexperienced in such work, so that their decisions are uncertain and largely a series of compromises. When it comes to interdepartmental ranking of jobs, their inexperience is even more apparent, because few raters are acquainted with all jobs. Under the circumstances, the job-ranking plan should be used when time or resources to employ a better method are not available or as a check on the accuracy of other methods.

2. The Job Classification Method.   The job classification method is a refinement of the ranking method. Under it, major job classes or grades are first established, and then the various jobs are assigned by rankers to these grades. Figure 17–1 illustrates a gradation of five classes, designated by a title label and increasing in value. The raters read the job

FIGURE 17–1
Description of Job Classification

Third Class Clerk:	Pure routine concentration, speed and accuracy. Works under supervision. May or may not be held responsible for results.
Second Class Clerk:	No supervision of others; especially skilled for the job by having exhaustive knowledge of the details. Person: close application, exceptional accuracy and speed.
First Class Clerk:	Must have characteristics of 2nd class clerk. Assume more responsibility.
Senior Clerk:	Technical, varied work, occasionally independent thinking and action due to difficult work, which requires exceptional clerical ability and extensive knowledge of principles and fundamentals of business of assigned department. Not charged with supervision of others to any extent, work subject to only limited check. Person: dependable, trustworthy, resourceful—able to make decisions.
Interpretive Clerk:	Those handling or capable of doing a major division of the work. Complicated work requiring much independent thinking, able to consider details outside control of supervision or routine.

descriptions and, depending upon their personal interpretations of the relative difficulty of tasks, responsibilities involved, and knowledge and experience required, decide in which of the classes each job should be placed.

This method, too, is relatively simple to operate and to understand, does not take a great deal of time, and does not require technical help. Although it represents an advance in accuracy over the ranking method, it still leaves much to be desired, because personal evaluations by executives unskilled in such work establish the major classes and determine into which class each job shall be placed. In this case, as in job ranking, it is difficult to know how much of a job's rank is influenced by the worker. Although the job and not the employee should be evaluated, the foregoing methods provide practically no safeguards against this form of error. The job classification method should be used when an organization is small, when jobs are not too complex or numerous, or when time and resources to use another method are not available. It will produce better results than the ranking method without great increase in time or cost.

3. The Point System. The point system of job evaluation is the most widely used and, according to its proponents, yields accurate results without undue expense or effort. In simple outline, it values jobs by means of yardsticks, one for each factor that is considered to be common to all jobs. By summing up the readings of the several yardsticks, a quantitative expression is derived for each job. These sums are called points, which must then be converted to dollar values.

In applying a point system, the following steps are taken:

a. Establish and define a list of factors common to all jobs that are being covered.
b. Construct a measuring yardstick for each factor.
c. From the job description, prepare a schedule showing qualitatively to what degree each job possesses the various factors enumerated above.
d. Apply the yardstick to convert the qualitative descriptions to quantitative units.
e. Sum up for each job the reading obtained for the individual factors.
f. Rank the jobs in accordance with the scores obtained in the foregoing steps.
g. Determine the dollar value to be assigned to relative positions in the job ranking.

a. Job Factors. Job factors are characteristics that are common to all jobs to be covered in the program. They can be readily determined by making a survey of representative jobs. Ordinarily, no more than six to nine major factors with appropriate subheadings should be used; otherwise, the ratings will be subject to useless controversy.

TABLE 17–1

Points Assigned to Factors of National Metal Trades Association Plan

Factor	1st Degree	2d Degree	3d Degree	4th Degree	5th Degree
Skill					
1. Education 14	28	42	56	70
2. Experience 22	44	66	88	110
3. Initiative and ingenuity 14	28	42	56	70
Effort					
4. Physical demand 10	20	30	40	50
5. Mental or visual demand 5	10	15	20	25
Responsibility					
6. Equipment or process 5	10	15	20	25
7. Material or product 5	10	15	20	25
8. Safety of others 5	10	15	20	25
9. Work of others 5	10	15	20	25
Job Conditions					
10. Working conditions 10	20	30	40	50
11. Unavoidable hazards 5	10	15	20	25

The major factors found most commonly in job evaluation programs are responsibility, skill, effort, education, required experience, and working conditions. The factors used in a plan for machine operators are shown in Table 17–1 and for office workers in Table 17–2.

TABLE 17–2

Points Assigned to Factors of National Office Managers Association Plan

1. Elemental—250 points
2. Skill—500 points
   a. General or special education 160
   b. Training time on job 40
   c. Memory 40
   d. Analytical 95
   e. Personal contact 35
   f. Dexterity 80
   g. Accuracy 50
3. Responsibility—200 points
   a. For company property 25
   b. For procedure 125
   c. Supervision 50
4. Effort—physical factors—50 points
   a. Place of work 5
   b. Cleanliness of work 5
   c. Position 10
   d. Continuity of work 15
   e. Physical or mental strain 15

Source: National Office Management Association, *Clerical Job Evaluation*, Bulletin no. 1 (New York).

In the case of evaluation plans for managerial positions, the following factors and subfactors have been used in a number of companies:[1]

Know-How:

Requirements of duties	Administration
Knowledge	Original thinking
Planning required	Creative ability
Mental application	Managerial techniques
Understanding required	

Responsibilities:

Initiative	
Accountability	
Effect on profits	
For personnel relations	
For policy making	
For policy interpretation	

Relationships:

Supervision exercised	
Demand for leadership	
Influence	
Influence on policy making	
Influence on methods	

The foregoing plans contain upward of a dozen rating factors. The number of factors needed to rate jobs with a relatively high degree of accuracy can be as few as three to five. But such numbers, although statistically and realistically valid, seem inadequate to the average employee. A full complement of yardsticks must be used to convince them that the plan is complete.

b. Measuring Yardsticks. After the factors to be used are determined, yardsticks must be established by which increasing importance in each of the factors may be measured. This is usually done in two stages. First, the total points that any factor or major subheading of a factor may have are established. Such assignments of points determine the relative value of the several factors. Second, varying degrees of each major factor are then assigned an increasing number of points within the total established for it.

These determinations are arrived at through the pooled opinions of line and staff executives. Cross-checks of various kinds can be employed to compare the accuracy of major divisions and point assignments within divisions. In any event, after the points have been allocated, they, along with verbal descriptions of major classes and grades within classes, should be formally written up, so that all may use and interpret the system similarly.

Although yardsticks are arbitrarily determined and vary in value from company to company, this does not impair their accuracy. As long as the yardsticks in each company are carefully designed and adhered to in measuring jobs, the relative values of all jobs in each company can be established with accuracy.

---

[1] R. E. Sibson, "Plan for Management Salary Administration," *Harvard Business Review,* vol. XXXIV, no. 6, p. 108.

c. Rating Jobs. After the job factors and measuring sticks have been established, the task of evaluating individual jobs can begin. The first step is to translate the job descriptions for each job into a written statement of the various job factors contained in each job. Thus, if the first factor to be measured is education, the amount of education required should be listed on a work sheet for each job. The next step is to apply the education yardstick to the amount of education specified on each job. For example, if a given job calls for four years of high school and the points assigned to that level of education are 92, this amount is written on the work sheet for the job in question.

And so on, in order, each factor of each job is measured until points have been assigned to all. The points for each job are then totaled to get its point rating. Obviously, these steps of rating are largely routine. The big tasks are preparing acceptable job descriptions and yardsticks. When these have been done, the function of applying the yardsticks to each job is relatively easy.

d. Monetary Conversions. The point values assigned to jobs at this juncture are, to repeat, stated in point values which are nonmonetary units. Through such measurements, it has been determined how jobs rate relative to each other. To be of practical use, the relative positions accorded jobs by the point system must be expressed in monetary terms. To accomplish this, two major steps are usually taken. First, a plan is established for determining how nonmonetary units are to be converted into dollar units. And second, a decision is reached as to how jobs of increasing importance are to be grouped into wage classes.

The task of conversion is usually based on a comparison of present company salary rates with those being paid in the community or in the industry for comparable jobs. By making a check with other employers, the data for such a comparison are derived. The comparison need not be made for all jobs; a limited number of selected jobs that are representative of several points on the job list is sufficient. Let us assume, for example, that data on community and company rates, as shown in Table 17–3, are collected for selected jobs.

TABLE 17–3

Selected Jobs	Point Values	Average Company Salary per Week	Average Community Salary per Week
A	400	190	186
B	420	200	202
C	460	220	224
D	500	240	244
E	540	260	270
F	560	270	296
G	600	290	310
H	660	320	350

Study of such figures would indicate that company rates in this case are well in line with community rates. Hence a conversion of point values to dollar values could be undertaken. If company and community rates were not in line, decisions would have to be made as to how rates out of line would be reconciled with community rates.

Careful analysis of these two sets of weekly rates (particularly if charts were prepared) would indicate that company salaries increase in an arithmetic progression, whereas those in the community follow a percentage increase. This provides a clue to two possible bases of conversion—the arithmetic and the percentage bases. In the foregoing case the company salary increase is approximately $10 for each 20-point increase, whereas the community increase is about 5 percent for each 20-point increase. The arithmetic plan results in a straight line when point values are set off against dollar units on a chart. The percentage plan results in a line that curves upward.

The arithmetic plan has simplicity in its favor, but economic principles favor the percentage plan. It has been found, for example, that most companies without a considered wage plan tend to overpay the lower jobs and underpay the higher jobs. Yet the supply of labor available to fill the lower jobs is invariably relatively more plentiful than that to fill the higher jobs. Hence, in developing a salary curve, it is preferable to select the percentage plan of increase. In this way, jobs in the higher point ranges will be accorded a wider dollar range than those in the lower point ranges.

e. Job Class and Rate Ranges. In most job evaluation plans, it is felt to be undesirable to establish a salary curve in which separate dollar values are assigned to each unitary increase in point values. Instead, a number of job classes are established, increasing in point values, with all jobs in each class being paid the same salary base. It might be decided, for example, that all jobs would be grouped and paid as shown in Table 17–4.

As may be noted in Table 17–4, the brackets of one class may overlap somewhat those in the ones below and above it. Indeed, the top rate for the 400-to-439 class, for example, is above that of the lowest rate for the

TABLE 17–4

Point Value Range	Salary Base	Fixed Range ($40)	Percentage Range (20%)
400–439	$200	$180–220	$180–220
440–479	220	200–240	198–242
480–519	240	220–260	216–264
520–559	260	240–280	234–286
560–599	280	260–300	252–308
600–639	300	280–320	270–320
640–679	320	300–340	288–352

440-to-479 class. Such overlapping is a recognition of the fact that each class includes a number of jobs of varying point values. Moreover, it provides an opportunity for employees within a given class to obtain base rate increases if their work and length of service merit them.

The range within each class depends in part upon arbitrary decision and in part upon the number of classes. The ranges in the cases cited above were based upon a fixed rate of $40 and of a 20 percent difference, respectively. The arithmetic base might have been set at more or less than $40, and the percentage might have been set at some figure other than 20 percent. The range in each class is usually set somewhere between 20 percent and 50 percent of the minimum figure; or the percentage is divided by two, and the range for each class is established by adding and subtracting the percentage amount from the average salary rate for each job class. On the other hand, the class range depends upon the number of classes. Thus the more classes there are in a given plan, the narrower is the bracket for each class. An example of a wage chart is shown in Figure 17–2.

FIGURE 17–2

Wage Chart

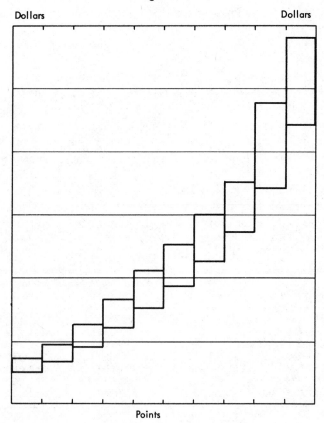

Dollars   Dollars

Points

After the wage brackets are established and jobs are assigned to their respective classes, comparisons will ordinarily show that actual salaries in some cases exceed the maximum for their job class and others fall below the class minimum. These are sometimes called "red circle" rates because they are marked in color to call attention to needed corrections. The usual practice is to raise gradually the underpaid jobs and to allow time to take care of the overpaid employees. The latter will eventually leave the payroll or be promoted to higher job classifications commensurate with the rates they are receiving.

4. The Factor Comparison System. The factor comparison system also has its proponents. It is similar to the point system in that jobs are evaluated by means of standard yardsticks of value. It differs from the latter by using key jobs as the basic yardsticks. Otherwise, the same steps are taken in making preliminary job descriptions and in bringing together the expert opinion of trained specialists and line executives.

The major steps in the program consist of the following:

a. Determination of key jobs.
b. Ranking of key jobs.
c. Valuing of factors into which key jobs are divided.
d. Comparison of all jobs with key job ratings.
e. Establishment of dollar value of all jobs.

The first step in this plan is to determine the key jobs. For this purpose, jobs are selected that cover the range from low- to high-paid jobs. Moreover, the jobs must be ones over which job analysts and executives do not disagree on the amount of pay. The jobs, too, must be definable in accurate and clear terms. Usually, from 10 to 30 jobs are picked at this stage.

Next, the key jobs are ranked. This is first done on an overall basis. Then the jobs are ranked, factor by factor, somewhat similarly to the point system. Here, too, salient factors must be selected, such as mental requirements, skill requirements, etc. An example of how this may be done is shown in Table 17–5. The five key jobs are ranked in the following order for mental requirements: job No. 1 is first, job No. 35 is second, job No. 20 is third, job No. 75 is fourth, and job No. 120 is fifth. On physical requirements, however, the ranking is almost reversed.

After the key jobs are ranked factor by factor, the base pay for each job is allocated to each factor. As may be seen in Table 17–5, the base pay of job No. 35, for example, is divided in the following way:

```
Mental requirements  ..........................$1.84
Skill requirements ...............................  1.92
Physical requirements  ..........................  1.20
Responsibilities  ..................................  1.18
Working conditions ..............................   .60
```

TABLE 17–5

Table of Key Jobs
(rankings and factor values)

Job No.	Total Base Rate	Mental Requirements		Skill Requirements		Physical Requirements		Responsibilities		Working Conditions	
		Ranking	Rate	Ranking	Rate	Ranking	Rate	Ranking	Rate	Ranking	Rate
1	$8.08	1	$2.28	1	$3.00	5	$1.00	2	$1.40	5	$.40
20	7.26	3	1.40	2	2.40	3	1.32	1	1.70	4	.44
35	6.74	2	1.84	3	1.92	4	1.20	3	1.18	2	.60
75	5.82	4	1.36	4	1.64	2	1.60	4	.70	3	.52
120	5.20	5	.84	5	1.08	1	1.72	5	.92	1	.64

Next, all jobs, one at a time, are compared with the table of key job values as just established. This is done by determining for each job the key job to which it is most similar, factor by factor. Assume, for example, that job No. 27 is being checked against Table 18–5. Assume further that it is found to have the following characteristics:

Similar to: For:

Job No. 1 .... Mental requirements
Job No. 20 .... Skill requirements
Job No. 35 .... Physical requirements
Job No. 35 .... Responsibilities
Job No. 20 .... Working conditions

The final step of dollar evaluation can now be taken. The individual jobs are then given the factor values, factor by factor, of the jobs to which they are similar. In the instance just cited, the rate would be $7.50 an hour, which is the sum of the factor values of $2.28 for mental requirements, $2.40 for skill requirements, $1.20 for physical requirements, $1.18 for responsibilities, and $.44 for working conditions.

In carrying out the comparison plan, the various steps included are much more detailed than outlined above. For example, after the key jobs are selected, ranked, and rated, it is usually found desirable to include other jobs, in order to establish a comparison table against which all jobs are to be checked. Thus, to the dozen or two jobs that constitute the master list, there are added up to 50 or 100 supplementary jobs, so that enough detail will be available to fit, without argument, all the other jobs into the table. Moreover, as the rating of jobs progresses, it may be found desirable to make some changes in the master key jobs because some are found, for one reason or another, to be out of line with other jobs. These changes obviously take more time than anticipated at the outset, but they do reduce errors in the plan.

5. Internal and External Consistency. This plan calls for a great deal of work because it is essential to develop consistency not only in the rankings of the key jobs but also in the allocations of the base rates of the key jobs to the various factors. This two-way check, in the eyes of the proponents of the factor comparison system, makes it superior to the point plan. They admit that their system involves more time and effort but insist that the internal consistency of rates is increased by the methods of checking and cross-checking which they employ.

The external consistency of this plan is obtained in the same fashion as in the case of the point rating plan. As noted in connection with the latter, it is necessary to compare company rates with community or industry rates for comparable jobs. Through such a comparison, a smooth progression of rates, from key job to key job, can be obtained. In the case of the comparison method, company rates are related to outside rates before the final selection of key jobs is made, whereas in the point plan the company rates are usually related to outside rates after the point values have been established. To enhance the accuracy, representativeness, and timeliness of outside data, some companies have cooperated in a computer-based system of salary information gathering and retrieval.

Outside comparisons are particularly useful in checking on executive compensation. One such survey has found that subordinate executives receive the following as a percentage of the president's salary in selected companies:[2]

Position	Percentage
Company president	100
Executive vice president	72
Top marketing executive	56
Top financial executive	55
Top production executive	52
Top Industrial relations executive	38

Such information provides a check on relationships within one's own company.

Summary

To conclude this discussion, a number of comments are in order regarding the accuracy of job evaluation plans. In the first place, such plans do not eliminate wage controversies. When questions arise—for example, asking why job X received 87 points and not 89—it is possible to present the analysis by which the decision was made. Attention can be directed to specific factors as proof that thought, not whim, was the basis

---

[2] Kenneth Henry, "The President's Pay Check," *Dun's Review and Modern Industry,* vol. 71, no. 3, p. 40.

of evaluation. But the parties to the disagreement can concern themselves with examining a system rather than unsupported opinions.

In the second place, it must be kept in mind that the factors of a job evaluation plan sometimes do not adequately take account of the marketplace, in spite of what may be done to assure external consistency. Although a particular job may rate only $5.00 an hour according to the evaluation plan, an extreme shortage of help or union bargaining in that category may require the payment of $6.50 an hour. Some companies will insist on fighting for the $5.00 rate to maintain the integrity of the job evaluation plan. Others accept the $6.50 rate, but only as an exception which will not be permitted to affect the relative rates of other jobs. There is no way of proving which course of action is right. Circumstances and managerial discretion are controlling elements in what will or can be done.

In the third place, strict adherence to job factors overlooks the effect of age and seniority of employees in affecting job values. Hence, some companies develop so-called maturity curves which include age and seniority factors for adjusting a given person's place in the job evaluation scheme.

Perhaps this suggests, in the fourth place, that it is well for a company to work with a union, when one is involved, in developing a job evaluation plan. If the union is informed after a plan is adopted, there is a natural objection because it was not consulted on the development. When its cooperation is sought from the start, there may be disagreements, but the final product becomes a "baby" that will be protected as much by the union as by management.

QUESTIONS

1. Who should have the authority to approve job evaluation programs?
2. What jobs should be included in a job evaluation program?
3. In what respects is the job classification method of job evaluation an improvement over the simple ranking plan?
4. What steps are taken when the point system of job evaluation is used?
5. What factors are commonly used as measuring sticks in a point system of job evaluation?
6. How are yardsticks for measuring job factors in a point system developed?
7. What are the relative merits of the arithmetic base and the percentage base in establishing wage classes in job evaluation plans?
8. What policies are most desirable in dealing with wage rates that are found to be above or below the rates set by the respective wage classes?
9. What are the essential features of the factor comparison plan of job evaluation?
10. What must be done to achieve relative "internal consistency" and "external consistency" in job evaluation programs?

CASE 17–1. RED-CIRCLE JOBS

After a company had completed its job evaluation and wage classification program, a number of positions were found to be out of line both above and below the established limits. Two cases of such "red-circled" positions were particularly disturbing.

The first case involved the company's "over-the-highway" truck drivers. These were getting about a dollar an hour more than the evaluation system had set as the upper limit. The drivers were not organized. But if their rates were reduced, the probability of unionization was high, in which event an even higher union rate would have to be met. Yet to let the rate remain, raised the probability of complaints from others who were at lower levels.

The second case involved a senior employee whose rate had for one reason or another been increased over time so that it too was about a dollar an hour above the established rate. To allow the rate to stand, created an inequity; yet to lower it would require the senior employee to pay for the company's mistakes.

Question

1. What should the company do about these cases?

CASE 17–2. AN ANALYSIS OF A WAGE STRUCTURE

With a view to evaluating its wage structure for selected jobs, a company has gathered data both within the company and in the community on wages in the various job classes. The table below contains the data that have been gathered:

Company Wage Class	Points for Class	Company Average Rate of Class	Community Average Rate of Class
1	30	$116	$150
2	40	136	152
3	50	140	180
4	60	152	184
5	70	180	208
6	80	192	222

Question

1. In your opinion, (a) is the wage relation between classes fair? (b) Does the wage curve for the company compare favorably with that of the community? (c) What, if anything, would you propose about changes?

PLANS OF REMUNERATION

CHAPTER 18

Introduction

In addition to determining how much employees are to be paid, it is necessary to select a method for calculating compensation. Two companies may have approximately the same wage and salary schedule, yet each may apply different methods by which compensation is computed. Thus, one company may employ the piecework plan and the other a timesaving bonus plan. Or one company may pay its salespeople on a straight commission plan, and another may use a combination plan of drawing account and commissions. The result in salaries may be approximately the same. Yet, in both of these cases the individual companies may be highly pleased with their selections and would not consider changing to the plan of the other. And each may be justified in concluding that a change would be undesirable.

A compensation method cannot be selected wisely unless the management knows the workings, advantages and disadvantages, and conditions of best usage of available plans. It is the purpose of this chapter to discuss the more common types of wage and salary plans for production employees, clerical and sales employees, and executive groups.

The discussion here is taken up under the following headings:

1. Basic kinds of plans.
2. Tests of a wage plan.
3. Specific wage plans.
4. Remuneration of salespeople.
5. Executive compensation.

Basic Kinds of Plans

There are two major kinds of wage and salary payment plans. In the first category are plans under which remuneration does not vary with

310

output or quality of output. Instead, they are computed in terms of some time unit. Since it once was common to pay workers by the day, time plans of shopworkers are referred to as "daywork," even though the hour is now the standard time unit of calculation. In the case of office and executive employees, the time unit may be the week, the half-month, the month, or rarely the year. Time plans are nonincentive in the sense that earnings during a given time period do not vary with the productivity of an employee during the time period.

The second category is composed of incentive plans, or those in which remuneration depends upon output or some other measure of productivity during a given time period. To earn more, an employee must expend effort to produce more, to sell more, to reduce costs, or to utilize various resources more effectively, as the case may be. There is a direct financial stimulus to incentive plans that is lacking in time-computed remuneration plans.

There is no one plan that is best under all circumstances. A plan (or plans, in some cases) must be selected to do the job that has to be done. Before describing and evaluating in more detail the more common types of compensation plans, it is therefore desirable to outline the tests by which particular plans may be evaluated.

Tests of Wage Plans

The apparent purpose of a wage plan is to remunerate employees for the work they perform. This is only one side of the story because it gives the impression that output is a function of wages alone. Wage plans do more than this; the nature of the plan itself may or may not appeal to workers. Hence, it is important to know what characteristics of wage plans appeal to employees so that they are stimulated to exert greater efforts. The following are desirable qualities in a wage plan:

1. Easily understood.
2. Easily computed.
3. Earnings related to effort.
4. Incentive earnings paid soon after being earned.
5. Relatively stable and unvarying.

1. Understandability of Wage Plans. Obviously, all employees like to know how their wage plan works. If they do not, they are not sure that they are getting what is justly due them. Hence, it is desirable to select a simple wage plan; or if a complicated one is chosen, all employees should be instructed in how it works. For example, a supervisor in one company was asked to explain to a visiting group of supervisors the company's wage plan. After about 15 minutes, everyone was confused.

Obviously, if a supervisor cannot describe the company's incentive plan in 15 minutes, it is scarcely conceivable that subordinates will have a clear understanding of it.

2. Ease of Computation. Somewhat similar to the characteristic of understanding is that of ease of computation. Most employees like to be able (a) to compute daily, from time to time, what they are making; and (b) to check the accuracy of their pay envelopes. If they can do neither without help or without taking too much time, their confidence level in the plan will be low. The effect upon their output will be adverse. Thus a wage payment plan should be sufficiently simple to permit quick calculation, or arithmetic tables should be supplied by reference to which calculations can be quickly made.

3. Effective Motivation. A pay plan should also provide for incentive within the work range of a particular job. To begin with, standards should be set so that they are attainable by competent workers. Obviously, the motivational potential will be low if par is beyond the capacity of employees. But a standard attained without trying is equally poor. Again, if quality of crafting is significant in particular cases, a wage payment plan should not be selected that will stimulate output and affect quality adversely. Or if it is desired to stress output, a wage plan should be selected that pays a high premium at the upper levels and penalizes— or at least does not overcompensate—low production. And finally, if quantity and quality are to be stressed at the same time, a plan should be selected that will not unduly influence the worker to work too fast or to become careless of quality.

4. Relation between Effort and Payday. Incentive wage plans, if adopted, should provide for remuneration to employees as soon as possible after effort is exerted. In this way the reward or penalty is fixed in the minds of the employees in connection with the work they did. Payment at the end of each day would be best from this point of view, were it not for the undue cost of distributing a daily payroll. A weekly period is customary and serves this purpose, provided that the payday is not too distant from the work to which it applies. An interval of three or five days, at most, should be sufficient to calculate and distribute the payroll.

5. Stability of Wage Plans. Finally, a wage plan should be relatively stable and unvarying. Frequent tinkering with wage plans gives the impression that the management is seeking to defraud the employees. Hence, it is imperative thoroughly to consider available plans, so that need for subsequent changes or tinkering is eliminated. But incentive plans particularly, though stable in appearance, may be made variable or given the appearance of variability by rate cutting, changes in time standards, or changes in the value of money. For example, rate cutting has been an evil that has made the piecework plan suspect in some quarters.

Types of Wage Payment Plans

A large number of wage plans have been devised, but relatively few have been used to any significant degree. Various surveys have disclosed that daywork and piecework are used to pay about 90 per cent of all industrial workers. The others are paid under a miscellany of plans, with some variant of the timesaving plan predominating. Hence, only the following plans, which include the more widely used and are representative of various types, are discussed here:

1. Daywork.
2. Measured daywork.
3. Piecework.
4. Timesaving plans.
5. Efficiency bonus plans.
6. Group plans.
7. Overtime calculations.
8. Profit- and revenue-sharing plans.

In the formula of the wage plans the following symbols are used:

W = Wages earned
H = Hours actually worked
S = Standard time
P = Percentage
R = Rate per hour in dollars
U = Rate per unit in dollars
N = Number of units produced

1. Daywork. Daywork is not only the oldest but the most common way of remunerating employees. It refers to all time-payment plans used in paying workers, although the hour is the time unit most commonly employed. Wages are computed under it by multiplying the number of hours worked by the rate per hour, as follows.

$$H \times R = W$$

If an employee worked 40 hours in a given week and at a basic rate of $6 an hour, pay would be calculated as follows:

$$(40 \times \$6) = \$240$$

The daywork plan has been widely adopted for several reasons. It is simplicity itself to compute and to understand. Also, it is unnecessary to set quantity standards as the basis for computing wages. It is also preferred by most unions because the plan does not stimulate speedups or penalize the average or less-than-average worker. And under it, quality is not sacrificed because it does not stimulate workers to concentrate on production alone. On the other side, the major disadvantage of daywork is its lack of motivation, which is very serious if high production is desired. It is also undesirable from the point of view of cost accounting because unit costs are more difficult to compute than under such plans as piecework.

The adoption of daywork is generally advisable under the following conditions:

a. When standards of output cannot be readily or accurately set.
b. When output is mainly made up of odd-lot jobs differing one from another.
c. When quality, material and machine costs, and crafting are more important than quantity.
d. When output can be controlled by management or conveyers and is not subject to individual influence.
e. When employees resist unduly other plans.

2. Measured Daywork. The advantages of daywork may be gained and the disadvantages minimized by the system known as measured daywork. Under this plan, employees are paid under the daywork system, but hourly rates are revised periodically in accordance with measures of their overall qualifications. The following steps are taken under this plan:

a. The base rate for each job class is carefully established by means of job evaluation.
b. A table of values is prepared to show the percentage to be added to the base rate because of varying degrees of personal performance in regard to productivity, quality, dependability, and versatility.
c. Each worker is rated periodically (the period varies in practice from three to six months) on productivity, quality, dependability, and versatility.
d. Each worker is then paid during the next work period at the base rate plus the percentage as determined by individual rating and the table of values.

The advantage of this plan is that wages may be easily computed, yet employees are provided with a motive for improving their performance. Moreover, earnings are not dependent upon one factor, such as output, but are affected by quality of output, dependability, and versatility. In addition, this plan provides supervisors with an opportunity to point out to employees specifically which aspects of their jobs can be improved. Management thereby assumes a job which is often shifted to the workers themselves by other plans.

The disadvantages of this plan are twofold. First, it is not easy to prove exactly why specific percentages are added to the base rate during merit rating of employees. Second, on any given day an employee may let down (lack incentive) and feel no remorse because the effect on the rate for the next period is somewhat remote.

The conditions under which this plan would be most plausible include the following:

a. When overall performance is important in measuring employee worth.
b. When specific output standards cannot be accurately set, yet some incentive for better production is desirable.
c. When gradual and stable improvement in workers is desired rather than variable day-to-day performance.
d. When supervisors are to be impressed with the need for more careful observation of employees and the need for better guidance, training, and improvement.

3. Piecework. The most widely used incentive plan is piecework. As its name denotes, wages are determined by the number of pieces or units of work that are completed. Each piece is given a prescribed value, which is known as the piece rate. Rates are commonly set by time study, although in the past and in some companies in the present, rates have been set by using past experience on similar jobs, or even mere guesswork. The formula for wage computations under this plan is as follows:

$$N \times U = W$$

Thus, if on a particular day an employee produced 1,080 units on a given job, the rate for which was $0.03 a unit, earnings would be:

$$1,080 \times \$0.03 = \$32.40$$

Earnings consequently vary with output. When employees are working on small lots, making more than their hourly rate on some and less on others, it is the usual practice to add the piecework earnings together for a particular period, sometimes for a day but in no case for more than a week, to determine whether total piecework earnings exceed daywork. If they do not, it is customary to pay the hourly rate. Under this practice, piecework is called guaranteed piecework. In most cases, too, output is inspected to determine how many parts have been spoiled, because these are not included in calculating the operator's earnings.

Incentive value, simplicity in calculation, and understandability are the most commanding advantages of this plan. While there may be misunderstandings about the content of a piecework system, the form of it never gives trouble. Piecework is also favorable from a cost accounting point of view because the labor cost of each unit of output is the same, irrespective of output.

The major disadvantage of the plan derives from its misuse. Over the years, some employers, either selfishly or to correct mistakes in setting rates, have cut rates time and time again. To employees at the receiving end of such cuts, it looks like a scheme to get more production at their expense. After this happened a resistance movement would develop along the following lines: (a) workers would loaf while being time-studied, and (b) they would not earn over an amount which would encourage management to cut rates.

Another disadvantage of piecework is that a piece rate must be changed as the dollar changes in value. During a period of rising prices, for example, piece rates have to be revised upward, although the time taken to do jobs still remain the same.

4. Timesaving Plans.   One of the oldest incentive plans is the time-saving plan. Under it, an employee is paid for the time actually spent on a task plus a bonus based upon a percentage of the time saved under the time set for the tasks worked on. Under this plan the following formula is used:

$$(H \times HR) + [(S - H)R]P = W$$

Thus, if a worker whose rate was $5.00 an hour took 8 hours on a job on which the standard allowance was $12\frac{1}{2}$ hours, and the percentage was 75, earnings would be:

$$(8 \times \$5.00) + [(12\frac{1}{2} - 8)\$5.00]75\% = \$56.86$$

The bonus percentage is usually set between 75 and 100.

Timesaving plans have two major advantages. First, since the standard upon which earnings are based is expressed in time units, it is not subject to the random fluctuations of the dollar. If adjustments must be made in earnings, the hourly rate can be changed, leaving the time standard unaffected. Thus the employees are not inclined to lose faith in job standards. Second, since the bonus is based upon time saved, the attitude of employees is conditioned by the positive factor of gaining through saving. This has a better psychological effect than that produced by the pressure of piece rates, for example.

5. Efficiency Bonus Plans.   Another type of incentive is the efficiency bonus plan. Under it, an employee is paid for the time actually spent on assigned tasks plus a bonus based on personal efficiency on those tasks. This plan calls, first of all, for establishing a table of values for increasing degrees of efficiency. Selected values taken from one plant in which bonuses start at 66 percent efficiency are shown in Table 18–1.

For each job a standard time allowance is established, by time study or by reference to records of similar jobs completed in the past. At the end of each week, each worker's efficiency is derived by dividing the time allowed on various jobs by the time taken. To the base wage is then added a percentage for relative efficiency. For example, a worker who took 40 hours to complete jobs on which the allowance was 36 hours,

TABLE 18–1

Efficiency	Percent Added to Basic Earnings
66	1
70	4
75	5
80	8
85	11
90	15
95	20
100	25

and whose hourly rate was $5.00, would be paid $115, computed as follows:

$$(H \times R) + (H \times R) \text{ selected } \% = W$$
$$(40 \times \$5.00) + (40 \times \$5.00)15\% = \$230$$

The major advantage of this plan lies in its emphasis upon efficiency. Comparisons can readily be made from week to week or between employees; thus, personal efficiency tends to rise because of the competitive factor. The plan has two disadvantages: (a) The plan is expressed in efficiency percentages whose establishment is not always understandable, and (b) employees tend to complain about the standards they must surpass in order to earn a bonus.

The plan has the most favorable conditions of use when it is desired to educate workers in the need of efficiency and to bestir them to compete in raising their relative efficiency.

6. Group Plans. The foregoing plans have been discussed on the assumption that each individual is remunerated in terms of individual effort. In addition to such individual or "straight" calculations, plans may be placed upon a group basis. Earnings of individuals are thus computed by prorating the bonus or premium produced by the group. For example, Table 18–2 shows how the individuals in a group would share (prorated on the basis of hours worked and rate per hour) a bonus of $280.20 they had earned as a unit.

In summary, there are numerous plans from which it is possible to

TABLE 18–2

Employee	Hours Worked	Rate per Hour	Basic Wage	Pro Rata Share	Bonus	Total Wage
A	40	$5.40	$216.00	216/799.92	$75.60	$291.60
B	36	6.00	216.00	216/799.92	75.60	291.60
C	38	5.64	214.32	214/799.92	75.00	289.32
D	32	4.80	153.60	153/799.92	54.00	207.60
			799.92			

select one or more that will fit one's requirements. Significant, in any event, is the importance of calculating basic standards fairly and equitably. But perhaps more important of all is the need for determining how much remuneration should be provided to attain varying degrees of employee efficiency. To this aspect of wage plans, there is no generally accepted answer.

Whether or not incentive plans should be used is not debated here for the simple reason that, unless unions or conditions prevent, incentive plans are ordinarily superior to nonincentive plans for the employee as well as the company. It is scarcely conceivable, for example, how some companies could have outproduced some of their competitors had they not used excellent incentive plans. Of course, such a plan is not easy to install in nonstandardized types of work, but even here successful plans have been operated. Maintenance jobs, for example, once thought of as daywork jobs, are often being paid on some incentive plan. The key in all of these instances is careful determination of standards of production and careful establishment of a unit of output.

7. Overtime Calculations. By governmental regulations, union agreements, or voluntary company policies, employees may be paid extra amounts for daily or weekly overtime. Let us assume the following instances:

a. An employee whose hourly rate is $4, works 10 hours on a given day. Then under the Walsh-Healey Act or by union or voluntary agreement, pay for that day would require time-and-a-half compensation after 8 hours (in some union cases after 6 or 7), calculated as follows:

$$(8 \times \$4) + (2 \times \$4)1\frac{1}{2} = \$44, \text{ or}$$
$$(10 \times \$4) + (2 \times \$4)1\frac{1}{2} = \$44$$

b. The given employee works 46 hours in a given week. Then under federal enactments or by union or voluntary agreements, compensation would be at the time-and-a-half rate after 40 hours (at double time in some union agreements or by voluntary company policies), calculated as follows:

$$(40 \times \$4) + (4 \times \$4)\frac{1}{2} = \$184$$

c. When an employee is on some form of incentive wage plan, the hourly rate for overtime purposes is calculated by dividing the incentive pay by the hours worked in the daily or weekly period in which the overtime was worked. For example, an employee had piece work earnings of $210 in a given 42 hour work week. Average hourly earnings would be $5, obtained by dividing $210 by 42. Then the two hours of overtime would be $5 obtained by multiplying 2 by $5 by one half, which would be added to the $210 making total earnings for the week $215.

8. Profit- and Revenue-Sharing Plans. A final group of plans related to compensation is characterized by some form of sharing in profits or revenues. These include (*a*) sharing directly in profits, (*b*) sharing through stock ownership, and (*c*) sharing through royalty payments.

a. Profit-Sharing Plans. Sharing of profits with employees has been used with varying success as a means of incentive compensation. A number of companies have tried this and discarded it because of dissatisfaction with results. Yet, other companies have been more convinced that profit sharing is useful in building productivity and better employee relations. This much can be said, however: A company must have a fairly stable history of profits, or the plan is bound to fail. Employees cannot be stimulated to greater effort or expected to increase their loyalty to a company when there are no profits to divide.

Profit sharing plans as motivators proceed against two fundamentals of wage incentive plans. First, remuneration is spaced too far from the effort of employees. A plan in which profits are shared in February will scarcely possess much stimulating power the preceding July, let us say. Second, the connection between reward and effort is scarcely discernible. Employees may work very conscientiously and get no share in profits because there are none in some years. Or they may see a coworker loaf and get just as much as they do in prosperous years.

As a means of developing team spirit and for educating employees in the risks and interdependencies of business, profit sharing has much to be said for it. Some companies have noted such favorable trends as the following after experience with profit sharing: a sharp decline in labor turnover, a greater loyalty to the company, a better spirit of cooperation with fewer petty grievances, and a generally improved tone of relationships and understanding between employee and employer. And it is difficult for employees to complain about excessive profits when they share in them, too.

Profit-sharing plans will not succeed, however, as a substitute for other personnel practices. Companies that have had the most success with profit sharing are those that stress their other personnel programs. Thus they note that their high wages, savings plans, good supervision, recreational and educational services, and grievance-handling procedures precede and abet the profit-sharing plans. Satisfied with all of these, employees are then stimulated to higher efforts by the prospects of sharing also in profits.

b. Employee Ownership of Stock. From time to time, interest in employee ownership of stock waxes strong as a means of improving employee and employer relations. Not uncommon is the practice to allow employees to purchase stock at prices somewhat below current market levels. The purchases must usually be made on a time basis to encourage the thrift habit. Also, the number of shares for which an employee may subscribe is restricted by seniority or earning power clauses. If an employee leaves the company before the stock is paid for, most plans provide that the employee will receive the amount of the payments plus interest, usually computed above current rates.

Stock plans are preferred by some because employees are made partners of the business in name as well as in fact. It is felt that since employees share in losses as well as profits, they become more conscious of the problems that beset their companies. As a consequence, they become more understanding and effective participants.

Unfortunately, the risks of stock ownership sometimes result in large losses to employees. For example, it is obvious what happened when a stock sold to employees at $30 went up to $150 and then tobogganed to $1.50. Employee morale, in this instance, for a time was not worth the proverbial plugged nickel. As a consequence of such experiences, many have concluded that the risks of stock ownership plans exceed the possible advantages. Moreover, employees can gain little feeling of self-assurance or of contribution when they watch stock prices go up and down for reasons they may not understand.

c. Royalty Provisions. Labor, in its organized endeavors, is seeking to gain a greater share of industry's earnings by royalty demands. These consist of payments, usually to a union organization of employees, based on a levy for each unit of output. The funds thus collected are to be used for a variety of purposes—for example, to aid the unemployed, to supplement payments to those injured on the job, and to support various other welfare activities.

Management cannot be exceedingly happy over such developments because they represent a practice over which it has no control and from which it can seemingly derive no benefit. Perhaps the most significant lesson that management can learn from these demands is that it must anticipate the reasons for which royalty demands are likely to be made, and it must be prepared to rebut them. If labor can prove that royalties are needed to serve welfare needs which management could but does not support, public sympathy will be on the side of labor. And management will have to pay for, but will lose control of, another prerogative.

Remuneration of Salespeople

Remuneration of salespeople may be by straight salary or some form of incentive compensation. Since the salesperson's job is usually more variable than the average factory job, the problem of establishing a stable and satisfactory unit of output is much more difficult; some even conclude that it is impossible. Nevertheless, various incentive plans have been devised that have had varying degrees of success. Although details vary, all plans can be grouped under one or more of the following headings:

1. Straight salary.
2. A commission based upon units sold.
3. A commission based upon factors affecting sales other than units sold.

1. Straight Salary Plans. Straight salary plans include those in which salespeople are paid strictly in accordance with the time they spend on their jobs. The week is the common time unit. This plan finds favor with those who contend (*a*) that the salesperson in the particular case has little or no control over how much he or she sells and (*b*) that the number of factors which are important in affecting sales is so large that it is impossible to give due consideration to all of them in any incentive plan. Some also favor straight salary because they have seen commission plans misused to the point that no one retains confidence in them. Where the foregoing conditions prevail, the use of commission plans is obviously questionable.

2. Unit Commission Plans. Straight salary plans, in and of themselves, contain no incentive value. Hence, when the amount of sales depends largely upon the calls that are made and supervision itself cannot spur sales personnel to take the necessary initiative, commission plans are desirable. Under these plans, salespeople are paid a set commission for each unit sold, a commission that varies as output increases, or a commission that begins only after a set quota has been sold.

The bases for commissions are so numerous that space does not permit full descriptions. However, two opposing theories are worth citing. In some companies the rate of commission decreases as sales increase, and in others the rate increases. In the former case the belief is that salespeople who make too much will lose their zest for work. In the latter case, it is recognized that large volumes are harder to make, yet add greatly to the profit of the company. Hence, it is concluded that increasing commissions are needed to attain the high volumes. Which theory should be followed depends, among other things, upon the nature of the sales problem, the type of salespeople required, and the type of sales executives directing the sales. But in any event, the existence of such opposed theories illustrates the need for care in selecting an appropriate plan.

3. General Commission Plans. Because selling often involves much more than repeated calls to get more business, some incentive plans are based upon other factors as well as volume of sales. For example, bonuses may be computed in terms of such factors as the following:

a. The quantity of various products sold, graded by their profitability to the company.

b. New business obtained.

c. Service calls made.

d. Repeat orders obtained.

e. Sales expenses reduced.

f. Cash business obtained relative to credit accounts.

g. Percentage of bonuses obtained from new or highly competitive areas.

h. Complaints received on old customers' list.

Such plans call for important decisions regarding the weights the various factors will have and how they are to be measured. This is very difficult; yet, if the factors are of importance and the salesperson's attention should be called to them, the work necessary to the development of standards will have to be done.

Executive Compensation Plans

Compensation is of interest to executive but it is also a subject of interest to operative employees. If executive salaries are out of line with employee notions, however arrived at, employees become disgruntled with attendant losses due to industrial unrest. Moreover, large executive salaries are viewed at times as something which is derived at the expense of the shares employees receive. To correct such interpretations, one company illustrates the relation of executive salaries to employee wages by showing that were all salaries of the top executives distributed to employees, the latter would gain the equivalent of a package of cigarettes a week.

Executive compensation is related to the basic question of how much should be paid to obtain their services. It is easy to say that they should be paid what they are worth. Some violent controversies have raged as to whether or not any executive is worth $1 million a year, as some have been paid. One side argues that without the leadership of the executive who received such a salary, the company would not have been so successful as it was, nor could it have employed as many workers at the wages that it did. The other side retorts that the same results could have been attained without such munificent compensation to the executive in question, since a lesser amount and the prestige of the position would have been sufficient compensation. Executive talents are not so scarce, add the opponents, that a few isolated individuals possess a monopoly.

Such disagreements suggest that great care must be used to set compensation for executives, since such decisions affect the attitudes of others in addition to the efficiency of the executives. It is desirable to describe executive compensation methods so that the relative merits of available plans may be noted. This is done here under two headings: (1) major executives and (2) minor executives.

1. Major Executives. Straight salary, bonuses, stock purchase plans, and profit sharing are used to compensate major executives. Straight salary is undoubtedly the most common method. It is often adopted because the task of managing is made up of many variables and imponderables, the direct measurement of which would be a herculean task. Hence, as is true of any job whose units of work cannot be readily defined or measured, the only alternative is the daywork or time interval principle. With top-level executives, the month or the year is commonly used.

However, many companies hold the opinion that the full measure of executive effort cannot be obtained unless some stimulus is applied. In such cases, indirect measures of accomplishment are used to determine how much effort executives have exerted beyond that which is normal for the job and which is compensated for on a salary basis. The most common measures are profits, sales, and expenses. Using these as a base, bonuses are paid in addition to the salary. Thus, one company pays its top executive a percentage of the profits the company earns. Another establishes a quota of profits which must be earned before executives share in profits. And a third establishes a sliding scale of percentages related to sales (a fourth ties this to expenditures) by which the base salary will be increased.

Another plan of compensating executives is that in which stock is offered to them at a nominal figure or at a figure that leaves ample room for speculative profit. The executives are thus given a stake in the business, which can redound to their benefit if their efforts are skillfully applied to its operation. Usually, these plans make handsome rewards possible. For example, an executive who took charge of an ailing business was given the option to buy 100,000 shares at $12 a share. Within a year the stock rose in value to $16, yielding the executive a paper profit of $400,000. Had the stock not risen in price, however, the executive's efforts would have been rewarded only by a small salary. Hence the probability of small earnings as well as of high profits makes such plans highly stimulating. Indeed, the plan is criticized by some on the ground that executives become so conscious of the market price of the stock and the short-run factors that affect prices that they do not pay attention to the fundamentals that make for long-run stable growth of a business.

The theory in these cases is that profits are correlated to executive efforts and thus are an accurate measure of executive contributions.[1] The theory is weak because profits are sometimes made no matter how unwisely executives act and losses are incurred despite the best possible judgment. Prosperity periods and depressions leave in their wake results for which no individual should take credit or be penalized. This condition

---

[1] The favorable incidence of the capital gains tax as opposed to the higher personal income tax is also important.

should be recognized in any plan in which executive compensation is based upon results; otherwise, executives will from time to time be overpaid or underpaid. That the theory is weak is not offered as a reason for not using incentives for executives. It is mentioned so that a plan is not idly adopted, thus inviting the chance of yielding undesirable consequences to all concerned.

All the foregoing methods of compensating executives result in taxable income. Since tax rates take a large part of such increases, there is a trend for companies to pay for a variety of expenses incurred by executives. The range of such payments, or fringe benefits, to executives includes the following:

a. Medical care.
b. Counsel and accountants to assist in legal, tax, and financial problems.
c. Facilities for entertaining customers and for dining.
d. Company recreational areas—golf course, swimming pool, and gymnasium.
e. Membership fees in clubs and business associations.
f. Costs of education and development of executives, scholarships for children of employees, and business magazines and books.

Such benefits may be tax-free to the recipient although the Internal Revenue Service is screening them rather carefully. Were employees to pay for them out of salary, their income would have to be increased a minimum of 30 percent for lower income executives and much higher for executives in the upper tax brackets. Obviously, this is a form of executive compensation that has found adopters.

2. Minor Executives.   Most minor executives are paid on a salary basis, although incentive plans of one form or another are used in a minority of cases. The proponents of the salary plan expound the usual claims for it and make the usual charges against incentive plans, which need not be repeated here. The discussion will be limited to a description of typical plans for incentive compensation of minor executives.

Perhaps the oldest form of compensating superintendents and supervisors on a basis other than straight salary is that of paying them a bonus, depending upon the incentive earnings of their subordinates. For example, in one time saving plan the supervisor shares in part of the time saved by subordinates. Thus the latter receive 75 percent of the time saved, and the supervisor (who presumably helped them indirectly to be more productive) receives the remaining 25 percent. Such practices are commendable because they stress the fundamental responsibility of the supervisor to lead a more effective group of employees.

Another type of incentive plan is based directly upon departmental productivity or cost reductions. Under such plans, it is necessary to take the following steps:

a. Define in quantitative terms the factors to be included in the plan.
b. Establish standards by which to measure varying degrees of success.
c. Establish a sliding scale of bonus percentages for increasing degrees of accomplishing the factors specified in the plan.

For example, in simple outline, the plan of one company is based upon attainment of production schedules. Then the schedule for each job during a particular period is set. Actual completion dates are then compared with scheduled dates, to arrive at a percentage of success. Supervisors receive a bonus, depending upon their effectiveness in meeting schedules. This company stresses meeting of schedules because delivery to customers is a prime factor in its success.

In another plan, reduction in expenditures is the key to supervisory bonuses. A flexible budget is established for each department, depending upon its expected rates of output. If actual expenses of a department are less than budgeted figures, the supervisor receives a bonus varying with the percentage of the saving. In the so-called Scanlon plan, such cost savings are also shared by operative employees. Some unions have strongly supported the Scanlon plan as a fair method of compensation.

Other plans of supervisory bonus payments are more complicated. For example, one company weighs the following factors:

a. Attainment of budgets.
b. Scrap reductions.
c. Direct laborsaving.
d. Efficiency in output.
e. Savings in materials used.
f. Savings in maintenance costs.

Under this plan, standards are established for each of the foregoing factors, their relative importance is determined, and a scale of values for overall achievement is established. The value of all this work, it must be noted, goes beyond the effect upon supervisory efficiency; it has the added value which careful planning brings forth. Although such plans may require a great deal of preliminary thought, the calculations a supervisor must make to compute his earnings can be simplified by preparing statistical tables from which foremen can, at a glance, determine the bonus they have earned.

Records

A significant problem in all wage plans is the effect they have upon record keeping. It has been noted from time to time that some plans aid the work of cost accounting, for example, whereas others are not so simple to handle. The same holds true for payroll computations. Hence, plans should be weighed in terms of the effect they are likely to have upon the work of payroll computations. Of course, the whole problem of payroll calculation has been complicated by the extra records required by the Social Security Act, the Wages and Hours Law, and various deductions, such as "pay-as-you-go" federal income taxes and bond purchase plans. As a consequence, it is desirable to design forms that will make this work as speedy and economical as possible. Illustrative is the growing use of computers and electronic data-processing equipment.

QUESTIONS

1. What is the difference between a wage payment plan and a job evaluation plan?
2. What specific wage plan best meets the characteristics that a good wage plan should possess?
3. Under what conditions is the use of the daywork plan of wage payment desirable?
4. What are the merits of the measured daywork plan of wage payment?
5. What are the advantages of the time saving plans of wage payment?
6. How is the hourly rate calculated for overtime purposes if an employee is on an incentive plan such as piecework?
7. Under what conditions is profit-sharing for operative employees more likely to be successful as an employee motivator?
8. For what factors other than sales may a salesperson be compensated?
9. Why do profit-sharing plans and stock-option plans find favorable use in connection with executive compensation?
10. What incentive compensation plans would you recommend for supervisors?

CASE 18–1.   A COST-SAVING BONUS PLAN

The Fan-Aluminum Company and its employees have become dissatisfied with the profit-sharing plan currently in use because profits are often unrelated to employee efforts. The company believes that an incentive plan based upon cost savings would be fairer because employees can directly influence costs no matter whether or not there are any profits.

After some study of existing plans and theories of cost-saving sharing, the company came up with the following proposal:

1. Employees would receive 30 percent of savings of labor and material costs under budgeted figures for given production quotas.
2. Half of the savings would be paid every two weeks and half would go into the pension and retirement fund.

3. Regular base wages would be maintained at or above competitive community rates.
4. The plan would be monitored by a committee composed of representatives from the company, nonunionized employees, unionized employees, and outside consultants.

From various meetings held to discuss the proposal, it was favorably received by all quarters except for three major questions, as follows:

1. Some company executives thought the 30 percent allocation to employees was too high, arguing that management was usually responsible for all savings. But employee representatives thought it too low arguing that labor really exerts the effort to make the saving.
2. Some argued that cost savings in labor and materials were so intimately related to how much assisting technology was employed that labor essentially was at the mercy of capital expenditures.
3. Some argue that the base from which cost standards were set was an accounting device and not a statement of real costs.

Question

1. How, if at all, can these points be answered?

CASE 18–2. CHOOSING A WAGE INCENTIVE PLAN

In order to provide more financial motivation, a company has decided to place as many of its hourly employees as possible on an incentive plan instead of straight "daywork." It has reduced its choice among the many available plans to do straight piecework and the 100 percent time saving plan. It prepared data for various sample job situations to see how the two plans compared. It set up the jobs so that they could be done on either piecework or the 100 percent plan, set standards so that there was no difference on that score, and then had operators do the work under each plan.

In one case on a given job, during a given week of 40 hours, the following data were collected on the two plans:

a. Under piecework the piece rate was 20 cents per piece and the standard output was 670 pieces.
b. Under the 100% plan with the base hourly rate of $3.00, and the assigned time to do the same job at 46 hours, the time taken was 40 hours.

Question

1. Which plan would you choose, and why?

FRINGE BENEFITS 19

Scope of Discussion

In addition to the compensation employees receive directly, a number of other benefits may accrue to them. A few examples are insurance programs, pension rights, vacations and sick leave with pay, and separation allowances. In a sense, they are delayed forms of compensation, paid in the event of prescribed occurrences or contingencies.

At one time, such benefit allowances were a very small percentage of take-home pay. Hence someone ascribed to them the apt term *fringe benefits*. With the passage of time the percentage has increased substantially, so that the term, although generally used, is not correctly descriptive of the amount or importance of the benefits.

Attention is directed here to this important aspect of compensation under the following headings:

1. Overall coverage and amounts.
2. Insurance plans.
3. Pension plans.
4. Unemployment compensation plans.

Fringe Benefits

In recent years, there has been a trend on the part of unions to make demands which increase the return to employees in ways other than direct wages. Examples are vacations with pay, sick leave with pay, establishment of funds to assist employees injured in accidents, and provision of medical services. These wage supplements provide employees with services or returns they otherwise would have to finance themselves.

The cost of fringe benefits (or "fringes") is by no means insignificant. In a survey conducted by the Chamber of Commerce of the United States, the cost averaged 32.7 percent of the direct labor payroll. This amounts to $1.54 per payroll hour, or $3,230 per employee per year, as seen in Table 19–1. Twenty-five years earlier, the annual bill for fringes, according to a Chamber survey, was $819.

Employers should, therefore, be prepared to expect increasing demands for fringe benefits. One of the tasks of the personnel department should be to anticipate the direction of fringe demands and to prepare recommendations concerning their justification. Management can then react more intelligently to such requests.

TABLE 19–1

Nonwage Payments as Percent of Payroll of 742 Companies, 1973 Items

Employer's share of compulsory old-age insurance, unemployment compensation, and workmen's compensation	7.5%
Employer's share of agreed-upon payments for pensions, insurance programs, separation pay allowances, and miscellaneous payments to employees	10.5
Pay for rest periods, lunch periods, washup time, etc.	3.5
Payments for vacations, holidays, voting time, National Guard duty, time off for personal reasons, etc.	9.2
Bonus, profit sharing, special awards, etc.	2.0
Total	32.7%
Nonwage payments as:	
Percent of payroll	32.7
Cents per hour worked	154.1
Dollars per year per employee	$3,230

Source: Chamber of Commerce of the United States, *Employee Benefits, 1973* (Washington, D.C., 1974), p. 9.

The best preparation is to make studies of various possible demands, so that if they are presented, a reasonable reaction can be established immediately. For example, the demand that employees be paid for sick leave or that their sick-leave allowances be increased cannot be deflected by words alone. Such countercharges that the cost of the program would be excessive or that malingering would be increased excessively must be supported by facts. Carefully prepared studies will carry weight in support of a claim that an increase in sick-leave allowance will tend to increase malingering. Information gathered in advance, analyzed for principles and aptly illustrated, is the substantial basis upon which management can fight fringe demands, anticipate them or agree gracefully that they are warranted, when once presented.

It may be argued, too, that management should attempt to have some fringe plans or parts thereof paid for by the employees themselves. This makes sense because some employees would be better off if they underwrote the plans which best fitted their individual needs. For example, employees do not benefit from a pension plan if they leave a company, yet not to leave restricts their mobility. Or some employees with good health records may feel that they indirectly support but gain little from health insurance programs. It would be better in such cases if the company were to support a basic minimum program, while the employees added at their own expense such additions or plans as they thought best for themselves.

Of greater import, however, is the fact that as costs of current fringe plans rise, and as more plans are added, some companies will find the burden competitively difficult to bear alone. Hence, it is advisable to work toward a division of responsibility. Some plans would be underwritten by the company and others by the employees. The former would include plans generally assumed by business and the latter those which employees wanted in addition to the basic group. Moreover, the company could well help in finding ways by which some plans could be obtained at reduced cost to the employee.

The idea of shared responsibility can also be approached from the angle of productivity. As long as employees are given various benefits, there is little reason to expect anything in return. Yet business must, through increased productivity, earn the funds to cover the expenditures it incurs on behalf of its employees. However, the cooperation of employees in increased productivity should be sought to help defray the cost of employee fringe benefits.

Insurance Programs

Insurance programs have been among the most common types of fringe benefits. These serve to provide financial protection to an employee or his dependents from the risks of death, illness, and accidents.

1. Life Insurance. Life insurance has long been included in the programs of many companies. This is explainable in part by the fact that such financial protection seemed to be an obligation a company should accept for the long service of loyal employees. It was an obligation that had been initiated by companies which paid the funeral expenses of deceased employees. As insurance companies began to offer low-cost group insurance, this method has supplanted the uncertain funeral expense plan. The cost of the insurance has been assumed by the companies. And the forthright acceptance of a contractual insurance obligation provides employees with positive assurance of their company's interest in one of their financial problems.

The range of company-supported insurance plans is so wide that only a few general comments are in order here. Such plans usually cover all employees. They become eligible after a short waiting period after being hired—for example, 90 days. The company's regular physical examination at the time of hiring is usually sufficient evidence of insurability.

The amount of insurance for each employee is related to salary and age. Salary-wise, amounts increase with the level of earnings. Lower levels are insured at minimum amounts, with insurance increasing as the base salary increases. Thus, minimum amounts may be $5,000 or $6,000, whereas the upper limits may be established at the five-figure range. As age increases, most plans provide for a lowering in the insurance. This is based on the assumption that an employee who survives into advancing years does not have the same family obligations as earlier, as well as having had time to save for such incurred obligations.

Most insurance plans are supported entirely by the company. Some have provisions whereby employees may increase their insurance by contributing to the insurance premiums. This opportunity is often offered to executives. And many plans give an employee the right to convert the group plan to an individual policy without further physical examination if his services with the company are terminated; but in such a case the ex-employee pays the premium. Some plans include an employee in the group insurance program after he retires or suffers a permanent disability before retiring.

2. Health and Accident Insurance Programs. Growing in popularity are insurance programs covering financial losses due to illness and accidents. Of course, the employee is protected from losses incurred in connection with company business and operations. These are covered by state industrial compensation laws and are commented upon in Chapter 22. But noncompany-incurred losses to employees or those to their dependents, have long been considered to be matters of their own concern. There is, however, a trend toward company aid and assistance in such areas.

First steps toward company assistance came in the form of making it easier and cheaper to procure protective insurance, but at the expense of the employees themselves. Blue Cross is an example. Employees in such instances pay the premiums but at lower rates because groups of employees participate in the program. The company provides the group for which group rates can be gained. As time passed, some companies have undertaken to share the costs of such insurance, and some now shoulder all the costs themselves. Sharing or full responsibility has in some cases been assumed voluntarily as a gesture of good human relations and in some cases been accepted because of the pressures of collective bargaining.

The risks and benefits included in these programs are varied, but a few comments will serve to provide a general picture. An employee who cannot work because of an accident or illness—noncompany-incurred—is subject to two losses. First, there are medical and hospital bills to be met. The appropriate insurance can pay for these expenses. Hospital costs for a room, medication, nursing services, technical equipment, and operating facilities will be covered up to specified limits. And payments of the doctor's fee is also insurable within given amount and for given services.

Second, there are losses of wages while not working. These, too, may be covered by insurance. The amount received, the duration over which benefits will be paid, and the stated waiting periods vary, depending on the contract which is written.

The dependents of an employee may also be included in some of these insurance coverages. Thus, certain hospital, surgical, and medical expenses of one's family may be covered. And the insurance would apply to expenses due to illness, accidents, or obstetrical and maternity care.

Pension Plans

Pensions have come to be an important type of fringe benefit. The private plans are of course normally a fringe benefit. But even pension plans under the Social Security Act are underwritten in part by the employer and, to that extent, are a fringe benefit to the employee.

1. Private Pension Plans. Private pension plans were once relatively few in number. They were underwritten voluntarily by some companies which took a farsighted view of the need for protecting the employee upon retirement. Or some, in a paternalistic attitude, felt that pensions were good for their employees.

But the gates for private pensions were opened wide in October, 1948, by the U.S. Supreme Court in the Inland Steel decision. Here, it was ruled that pensions were not bargainable only if the union contract expressly excluded pensions from bargainable subjects. As a consequence, union after union—which had previously thought that it was precluded from bargaining about pensions—demanded and won pension benefits for its members.

Since private pension arrangements have increased in importance, it is desirable to survey the following points covering the operation of such plans:

a. Who is eligible for pensions?
b. What is the amount of benefits?
c. How are pensions financed?
d. Who contributes to the financing?
e. What if death occurs before retirement?
f. How is the plan administered?

a. Eligibility. Since pensions are paid to retired employees, the significant question to working employees is: Am I eligible to receive a pension? This depends upon eligibility rules, which usually cover waiting period, length of service, age, work factors, and nature and amount of compensation.

First, most pension plans establish a waiting period before employees become eligible. This may be anywhere from one to five years. The longer period tends to penalize floaters and perhaps reduce turnover. The shorter period tends to give the newer employees a feeling of being part of the total program of his company.

Second, the length of service affects eligibility. This is particularly important as far as the amount of the pension received is concerned, provided that other tests of eligibility are met. Thus a minimum number of years of service must be completed at a before-retirement age if full benefits are to accrue. Lesser service results in smaller payments. It should be noted, however, that some plans provide benefits under the pension program for employees who become disabled before the stated retirement age or seniority requirement.

Third, the question of lower and upper age limits must also be answered. Some companies limit eligibility to those over 25 or 30 years of age, because the clerical cost of administering the plan for such employees offsets any possible advantages the plan might have for the company or the employee. The upper limit, on the other hand, raises important problems. To include older employees raises the cost of the plan, but to exclude them either may arouse employee antagonism or may fail to qualify the plan under the requirements of the Internal Revenue Service.

It is interesting to note that the United Auto Workers union has won an early retirement supplementary pension benefit payment. These are available only for those who retire before age 65. Early retirees who thus make openings for younger workers get more under this agreement until they reach 65 than they get after the statutory retirement age is reached. This union has also expressed the aim for a pension age beginning at 50 years and after 30 years employment.

Fourth, the working situation may also determine eligibility. Employees in certain types of work or locations may be excluded. Or only salaried, clerical, and executive ranks may be included. Or again, nonunion employees may be excluded from a plan negotiated by a union. In any event, exclusions should be logically justifiable; or again, employee enmity may be incurred, or the approval of the Internal Revenue Service may not be forthcoming.

Fifth, the nature and amount of compensation may be determining factors in eligibility. Salespeople on commission, part-time employees or those earning less than some set figure—$8,000 a year—and all hourly rated employees may be excluded. The general trend is, however, away from such compensation exclusions. Certainly, collective bargaining has improved the position of hourly rated employees, who were once rather generally excluded.

The amount of the pension is usually fixed throughout the effective period. But due to inflationary pressures, some companies have moved to the variable annuity which adjusts payments in some relation to changes in the purchasing power of the dollar.

b. Amount of Benefits. Another matter of major concern is the level and amount of benefits. To the employee, this is significant because it determines what will be received—and perhaps contributed, if the plan is contributory. And to the employer, it is significant because it determines in part how costly the plan will be.

Private pension plans have in recent years frequently been tied in with social security payments. In that event, an employee may be entitled to a pension, let us say, of $300 a month. The company makes up the difference between $300 and the amount the pensioner receives from social security payments. Some companies pay a company pension in addition to the social security payments.

c. Financing. Before discussing who contributes to paying for a pension plan, it is desirable to note the various ways in which provision is made for assuring payments. The simplest plan of providing funds is the current expenditure method, in which payments are made out of general cash at the time employees retire. How much must be paid out can be quickly ascertained by listing the pensioners and the amounts due to each. The plan has disadvantages: Cash or assets may not be available when needed, tax advantages may be lost, and the actuarial basis of pensions may not be followed. So, with few exceptions, a plan of advance provision or underwriting of funds is adopted. These are the so-called funded methods and include insured or trusteed plans.

Insured plans are those in which future pension liabilities are assumed by a commercial insurance firm upon payment of premiums to it by the company. Such plans have the usual advantages of having a specialist assume the liability. Under trusteed plans the employer acts, in a sense, as his own insurance company or pays over each year's fund accumulations to a trustee. Such plans are preferred by the larger employers, who feel that they are equipped to do the work the insurance companies do in such matters, thereby saving some of the overhead cost which is loaded into the premium charged by an insurance company.

d. Contributions to Cost of Pensions. Funds may be accumulated by joint payments of employees and employers (the contributory plan) or by payments by the company alone (the noncontributory plan). Which plan should be used has been subject to debate, and it is improbable that universal agreement will ever be reached.

Proponents of the noncontributory plan argue that this is a cost business should assume. Where unions are concerned, they insist on this point and are gaining it increasingly in collective bargaining. Proponents of contributory plans claim that in sharing costs, employees become more interested in the plan and, indirectly, in other affairs and problems of the company.

e. Benefit Payments to Survivors. When death occurs before retirement, benefit payments must take another form. Either a lump sum or an annuity may be paid to survivors or the employee's estate. This must be provided for, or again the plan will not be qualified by the Internal Revenue Service, which requires that a pension plan be for the benefit of employees or their beneficiaries. The employee has the right to select beneficiaries, and his or her wishes must be respected. If the employee has selected no beneficiaries, the plan may provide for an order of priority as follows: the employee's spouse, children, parents, brothers and sisters, and estate. The company cannot be a beneficiary in this listing and still qualify the plan under Internal Revenue Service regulations.

The amount of payment will vary with the particular nature of the plan. This should take into consideration the age of the deceased, length of service, earnings, the employee's contributions, company contributions, interest factors, and rulings of the Internal Revenue Service.

f. Administration. The administration of a pension plan involves a number of phases. First, consideration must be given to legal requirements such as the Welfare and Pension Plan Disclosure Act of 1958. Tax laws and directives must be observed; otherwise, important income tax privileges will be lost. The Taft-Hartley Act requires joint representation of employer and employee with respect to plans in which the union or its appointees are directly involved in fund administration (insured or trusteed plans may sometimes be exempt). And plans must conform to the registration requirements of the Securities and Exchange Act, the insurance and trust provisions of state laws, the wage provisions of the Wages and Hours Act, and various estate and inheritance tax laws.

Perhaps the most important legal requirement is that provided by the Employee Benefit Security Act of 1974. This act insures that benefits of private pension plans will be paid even though a pension fund should go broke, a company fail or merge, or a vested worker (one who has gained pension rights) should be laid off or transfer to another company. The Act is administered by the federal Pension Benefit Guaranty Corp. from which the employer buys insurance to cover pension benefits.

Second, provision must be made for adequate representation by various interested parties. Company executives, union executives, private insurance company executives, and various state and federal agencies may all have a direct or indirect role to play. And the services of such technical specialists as lawyers, accountants, actuaries, tax experts, labor relations experts, corporate and financial experts, investment counselors, and statisticians may also be required.

Third, adequate records must be kept in detail. These will include information on the following:

1. Accession of new employees.
2. Voluntary severance of old employees.
3. Disability severance of old employees.
4. Employees going on retirement rolls.
5. Earnings of employees.
6. Changes in positions or wage rates of employees.
7. Various details of fund investments, changes, and earnings.
8. Premium payments.
9. Pension and supplementary benefit payments.
10. Tax computations.
11. Costs of operating the plan.

And finally, a pension plan should be designed with the assistance of qualified advice on a number of salient points. It should be adequate to meet retirement needs, and it should be fair to employee and employer. It should be actuarially and legally sound. It should be built with due consideration to a firm's place in the industry and the market, and to its future possibilities. Perhaps above all, it should be an integral part of a company's total objectives and programs, not just an adjunct tacked on because of outside pressures or what seems good for employees.

2. Federal Old-Age Assistance. Approved by the President on August 14, 1935, and with several subsequent amendments, the Social Security Act provides, among other benefits, for old-age and survivor benefits.

This aid is financed by means of taxes shared equally by the employee and the employer, or paid entirely by the self-employed. The tax is variable and is collected on earnings up to $13,200 a year. The taxes serve to pay the benefits and the cost of administering the program. The employer collects the taxes and pays over the sum to the Internal Revenue Service. This payment is credited to the account of each employee, to whom has been assigned a social security number.

Retirement benefits are payable to the wage earner and family upon retirement at age 65 for standard benefits, or 62 for lower benefits. Survivor benefits are payable to the insured's family, no matter what the age is at death. Disability benefits accrue to the worker if the insured becomes totally disabled before the age of 65.

The exact amount of benefits cannot be calculated until a claim is filed, being dependent largely on average earnings, period of contributions, and the particular type of claim. By way of illustration, however, Table 19–2 shows payments (rounded to the next lower whole dollar figure) to various classes of beneficiaries.

If a person becomes entitled to benefit payments based on the social security account of more than one person, the amount received will be no more than the larger of the benefits. For example, a woman who is eligible for retirement benefits on her own account as well as that of her

TABLE 19–2

Examples of Monthly Social Security Payments
(effective June 1974)

	Average Yearly Earnings since 1950						
Benefits can be paid to	$4,000	$5,000	$6,000	$7,000	$8,000	$9,000	$10,000
You, the worker							
▶ Retired at 65	228.50	264.90	299.40	335.50	372.20	393.50	412.40
▶ Under 65 and disabled	228.50	264.90	299.40	335.50	372.20	393.50	412.40
▶ Retired at 62	182.80	212.00	239.60	268.40	297.80	314.80	330.00
Your spouse							
▶ At 65	114.30	132.50	149.70	167.80	186.10	196.80	206.20
▶ At 62, with no child	85.80	99.40	112.30	125.90	139.60	147.60	154.70
▶ Under 65 and one child at home	162.00	224.00	249.90	262.40	279.20	295.20	309.40
Your widow(er)							
▶ At 65 (if worker never received reduced retirement benefits)	228.50	264.90	299.40	335.50	372.20	393.50	412.40
▶ At 60 (if sole survivor)	163.40	189.50	214.10	239.90	266.20	281.40	294.90
▶ At 50 and disabled (if sole survivor)	114.30	132.60	149.80	167.80	186.20	196.80	206.30
▶ Widowed mother and one child in her care	342.80	397.40	449.20	503.40	558.40	590.40	618.60
Maximum family payment	390.50	488.90	549.30	597.90	651.40	688.70	721.80

husband would receive no more than the larger of the two accounts. Or her children would receive the benefits of one, but not both, of the parents.

An insured person who becomes totally disabled for work before the age of 65 becomes eligible to receive insurance benefits. The amount will be the same as the old-age benefit would be if the insured were already 65. Dependents, however, do not get any payments while the insured is receiving insurance benefits. But benefits become payable when the insured becomes entitled to old-age insurance, or upon the insured's death.

Unemployment Compensation Plans

Another, and very significant, area of fringe benefits is that relating to compensation when an employee is laid off either temporarily or permanently. Concern here is with plans arrived at by negotiation to provide unemployment benefits, governmental plans of unemployment benefits, and plans of compensation upon an employee's severance from the company payroll.

1. Negotiated Plans. In the early 1950s the unions began to press for a guaranteed annual wage. They achieved partial success in 1955, when agreements were reached in the automobile industry to provide supplemental unemployment benefit (SUB) payments. Subsequently, agreements were similarly reached in other industries. The success is partial in that, with a few exceptions, benefit payments are for 26 rather than 52 weeks, as desired. Moreover, limitations as to employees covered and amounts to be paid have been established.

The supplemental aspects of the plans derives from the fact that they are usually tied in with state unemployment compensation plans. For example, one plan provides for the payment of $25 a week while an employee is receiving state benefits. The payment is increased to almost $50 after state benefits are exhausted. In another company an amount (not to exceed $30) is added to the compensation received from the state, so that a person's weekly benefit would amount to 65 percent of his after-tax, straight-time wage.

The SUB plans also contain specific rules on eligibility for payments. First, some period of seniority is usually required. For example, an employee covered by some of the automobile industry plans must work a year before acquiring benefit credits. Second, the amounts to which an eligible employee is entitled will vary. The credits to an account are granted in accordance with a formula related to time worked. Thus, in one plan an employee is granted a credit unit for each two full weeks of work. In a full year, 26 units would be accumulated, making the worker eligible for 26 weeks of supplementary benefits. It is also common to give shorter service employees a lower credit than longer service employees. This is done so that the former—who would be the first to be laid off—would not exhaust accumulated funds and thus leave the latter unprotected.

Obviously, fund accumulation is significant, particularly during the earlier years of a SUB plan. The usual method has been to have the employer contribute to the fund by a standard amount for each hour of work—e.g., 5 cents per work-hour. Moreover, the benefit payments are normally scaled down until the fund is built up to a satisfactory amount.

2. Governmental Plans. The federal and state governments have also taken steps to stabilize income through a plan of unemployment insurance. The unemployment title of the Social Security Act gives the federal government authority to administer an unemployment insurance plan in cooperation with the states. The Federal Unemployment Tax Act authorizes the collection of a payroll tax for this purpose which amounts to 3.2 percent of the payroll up to $4,200 per employee. But the federal government does not pay benefits. This can only be done through the states. To collect funds for benefits, the states tax the employers. This might seem like double taxation. But in states with federally approved insurance plans, employers may deduct (credit) to the state up to 90 percent of the tax paid to the federal government. All states have passed appropriate laws to take advantage of this credit.

With these funds the states have provided for varying benefits. The benefits vary according to amount, length of time paid, and individual employee records. The maximum payable for a week of unemployment (excluding allowances for dependents, provided by 11 states) ranges from $30 to $60. The maximum weeks of benefits range from 22 to 39. And the qualification of individuals for benefits depends (a) upon how long the individual worked in covered employment before becoming unemployed and (b) upon registration with the state employment office for suitable work, should it become available.

Obviously, this program does not establish wage stabilization. It does provide a buffer while the unemployed are looking for work. Moreover, it indicates the type of program that government may be asked to expand, as some already are demanding, if periods of unemployment should become severe.

3. Severance Benefits. Severance payments refer to the fact that after a certain number of years or after a certain age, or both, an employee acquires a right to a payment, now or in the future, even though leaving the company before the regular retirement age. This right is referred to as a vested right or a vesting of benefits.

The vested right depends upon the method of contributing. It is generally agreed that an employee's contributions are returnable upon severance. Whether or not interest should be paid, and how much, is a matter of company policy. As to the employer's contributions, the Empoyee Benefit Security Act provides for vesting after an employee has worked for a company five years.

QUESTIONS

1. What arguments should management prepare to counter the demands of employees for additional fringe benefits?
2. Since management pays for the fringe benefits, how should it go about seeing that it gets some credit for supporting such benefits?
3. Why have life insurance programs been supported by management, whereas such programs as health and accident insurance have in many cases had to be forced into management's support programs?
4. What lessons does the trend toward private pension plans funded by management have for personnel managers?
5. What effect do you feel the extension of pension plans, both private and governmental, is likely to have upon the hiring of older people?

6. As a personnel manager discussing with employees the question of the amount of pensions, what would you tell them is a reasonable pension?
7. To what must consideration be given in the administration of company pension plans?
8. What is the purpose of SUB plans and who funds them?
9. How is unemployment insurance handled through government programs?
10. What do you think will be the trend of vesting in the operation of pension plans when employees are severed from the payroll?

CASE 19–1. THE FRINGE BENEFIT DILEMMA

When Joseph Grimm started his company in 1935, fringe benefits to his employees were close to the zero level. Currently they are running about 30 percent. He expects them to go higher if what he learns about union demands for the future are true.

He expects that next year the demands are likely to hit 40 percent. If this should transpire then his total labor costs per hour will increase absolutely about $0.65 and relatively about 17 percent. These figures are based on his present hourly rate which now averages $3 but which he expects will go up to $3.25. He wonders how he would cover such an increase.

But he is also bothered by differing views among his employees. The younger ones don't care for increased pensions; they want cash in the paycheck. The older ones are not overly concerned about raises (they're at the upper levels already); they want more in the pension and medical plans. He wonders how he can reconcile the two.

Question

1. What would you suggest?

CASE 19–2. EDUCATIONAL SUBSIDIES

The Scitechno Company has been in the vanguard of manufacturing highly technical machine controls. It has grown to a size of over 5,000 employees. Concern of the executives with technical matters left little or no time for labor relations during its early history. As a consequence, the company, until the 1950s, had no formal personnel program. But in the past several years the company has interested itself, among other things, in education. It inaugurated an educational subsidy for talented young men and women. Under this plan the company employs "co-op" students, offers summer employment to college students, and makes grants to individuals in the form of unrestricted scholarships.

Most of the scholarship recipients were connected with the company in some way or other. They usually slanted their education toward fields in which the company was interested. Such slanting was not, however, stipulated in the grants.

After the scholarship program had been in effect for several years, the company made some casual surveys of those whom it had sent through school. It was found that while the scholarship holders held the company in the highest esteem, few of them sought jobs with the company upon graduation. It was further found that the company itself exerted no effort to recruit any of the graduates, even though it considered some of them to be top managerial material and technically competent. It seemed that the company was underwriting a program for training personnel for other companies, some of whom were competitors.

The president, although a believer in higher education, is wondering whether the scholarship program should be dropped.

Questions

1. What would be your advice to the president?
2. How might the program be retained with more benefit to the company?

RELATED COMPENSATION 20
PROBLEMS

Introduction

Two subjects related to compensation have thus far been ignored but may now be given attention. The first is how time is related to wage and salary administration. The second is concerned with the possibilities of guaranteeing remuneration.

TIME PROBLEMS

Variables

How long should an employee work? This simple question involves numerous problems that are not easy to solve. For example, within this century, the average workweek has decreased from around 70 hours to 40 hours. Some contend that a decrease to 35, or even 30 hours, is justifiable. And the working day has decreased from one of dawn to dusk to an average of eight hours, with some companies on a six-hour day. Then, too, such practices as the five-day week, vacations with pay, rest periods during the working day, and reduced hours for certain labor have not necessarily been standardized beyond change.

As already suggested, the question of the work period resolves itself into a series of questions, depending upon the particular time periods under consideration. The day, the week, and the year are major time periods, and each in turn raises problems. Within the week interval, there are matters of working days, shift changes, and paydays to be considered. And during the year, weeks to be worked, vacation periods, and holidays must be determined.

How these matters should be resolved can easily be stated in principle. The length of working periods should be such that the maximum productivity is derived, at the least cost, with due regard to the health and welfare of the employees. Its application is something else again. Management, unions, employees, governmental agencies, and other groups have disputed and continue to dispute these matters vehemently from time to time. And it may be well to point out at the outset that no final solution is likely because the problems are affected by social and political as well as economic conditions and by the conflicting views various groups bring to bear upon their solution.

Daily Time Problems

At the present time, the eight-hour day is rather general throughout the United States. A number of companies exceed this figure, but only a small percentage work fewer hours. Ordinarily, when a day of less than eight hours is worked, it is usually due to the fact that no time out is taken for lunch—the employees eat while working. A few companies have tried a six-hour day. This practice makes it possible for four shifts to be employed, each shift working six hours without a break for lunch. As the productivity of industry increases, there is no reason why the length of the working day may not be decreased to or below 6 hours, just as in the past it has been decreased from the 14-hour day once worked.

1. Starting and Stopping Time. Although the length of the working day for particular classes of workers is usually the same in particular communities, considerable variation is found in other aspects of daily hours. For example, starting time in some companies is as early as 6:30 A.M. and in others as late as 9:30 A.M. Stopping times differ in like manner. These variations may be explained as follows:

a. Some trades, such as service industries, must start earlier to be ready to meet the needs of other industries.
b. Employee preference; in one company that asked its employees to note their wishes, a starting time of 7:00 A.M. was selected.
c. Staggered starting times are encouraged to permit transportation and restaurant services to handle loads without burdensome peaks.
d. Tradition or growth without plan.

And some companies allow a flexible starting time from 7:00 to 10:00 A.M., so long as the employee then puts in a regular, full working day.

Even within the same company, starting and stopping times may differ for shop and office workers and sometimes between divisions of shop workers. This is done to prevent overloading of various facilities and services or as a form of perquisite of office workers. Of course, maintenance workers usually have to arrive early to get the plant ready for operation.

2. Lunch Periods. Lunch periods constitute another problem of daily working hours. Practice here is varied. As in the preceding instance, office workers often have a longer lunch period than shopworkers. In their case, periods up to 1½ hours are occasionally found, while an hour is the maximum for shop workers.

While employees seem to prefer a shorter lunch period because their overall working day is decreased, there is danger that sufficient time may not be available for getting back to work on time. Employees will then tend to jump the gun in starting their lunch period. A short lunch period may also result in the harmful practice of eating too hurriedly.

3. Rest Periods. Whether or not rest periods should be provided constitutes another problem of daily working hours. Almost without exception, this practice has been found to have favorable effects—fatigue, loitering, visiting, accidents, and spoilage are reduced, and productive efficiency is increased. Breaks of 8 to 12 minutes in the morning and again in the afternoon are found to be effective. Except where the nature of operations prevents, the only obstacle to the universal adoption of this practice is the reluctance of employers to try it. They do not like to break with traditional practice, or they fear that employees will demand a shorter day instead of the rest periods.

4. The Coffee Break. Closely related in nature to the rest periods is the coffee break. Either formally or informally, the practice is growing, particularly among office and technical workers, to allow time to obtain a snack or a drink during working hours. Proponents of the practice contend that the coffee break provides a desirable energy booster as well as a rest period. These advantages are usually worth the time taken provided the interval is not allowed to become overly extended and provided the breaks are not repeated too often.

5. Overall Working Day. And finally, what constitutes the overall working period must be defined for pay purposes. Ordinarily, the stated hours of starting and stopping constitute the limits of the working day. This must be understood by the employees, particularly where time clocks are used and employees must stamp their time cards on the clocks. In such instances the cards will be punched before the starting time and after the stated stopping time by employees who are on time and do not quit early. The time as thus recorded are not used to calculate hours worked but to check an employee's on-time arrival and departure. For example, in the following case the employee would be paid for 8 hours of work and not for 8 hours and 16 minutes:

| | Stated Time | | Time Card Punched | |
	Starting	Stopping	In	Out
Morning	8:00	12:00	7:52	12:01
Afternoon	12:45	4:45	12:40	4:47

Portal-to-Portal Issues

Reaching one's assigned station and departing from it sometimes consumes so much time that compensation must be given either because of union demands or because of legal requirements. For example, the coal miners have won such concessions. And federal rules were incorporated in the Portal-to-Portal Act of 1947, the provisions of which were included in later revisions of the Wages and Hours Law.

Federal legislation spells out what is excluded as well as included in compensable time. Thus the law specifically excludes the time an employee spends going to a workplace, starting a "principal activity," and returning from the workplace. Such activities as going to work, reaching one's station, checking in and out, washing, changing clothes, and getting one's paycheck are not compensable. However, if any one of the foregoing is not for the convenience of the worker but is really an integral part of the job, it is compensable.

More specifically, activities compensable as part of an employee's principal activity include:

1. Waiting to begin or resume work for reasons beyond an employee's control—such as waiting for materials.
2. Getting instructions before going on a shift, or getting materials.
3. Remaining on call on the employer's premises, where the employee is not free to leave the plant (except for scheduled sleeping time).
4. Preparing reports required by the job.
5. Getting medical attention during working hours.
6. Eating meals where the employees must remain at the working post.
7. Rest periods under 20 minutes.
8. Time spent in handling grievances, under an established plan in effect in the company.
9. Attending business conferences or schools in connection with work duties.

Weekly Time Problems

1. Total Hours a Week. The weekly time interval also raises a number of problems. First, there is the question of the total hours to be worked. During normal times the workweek in most companies is about 40 hours. Of course, during peak periods the workweek is extended. On the other hand, the standard workweek of 25 hours has been negotiated by the electrical workers in the New York City area. This illustrates the desire of some unions to get a shorter workweek so as to spread work in the face of the effects of automation upon employment.

The overtime pay provisions of the Wages and Hours Law militate against a workweek of over 40 hours. Obviously, a 50 percent increase in labor costs will not be assumed unless offsetting reductions or customer demands warrant.

In addition to the economic factor, the length of the workweek is also affected by personal feelings and social customs. Physiologically, people could work long hours, as they once did. But psychological feelings and social attitudes favor much shorter periods. People might not get tired physically if hours were somewhat over 40, but they most certainly would react unfavorably.

2. Working Days a Week.   The number of days to be worked is also of importance in the weekly picture. The five-day week is rather common throughout the United States. Even the 5½-day week is disliked by those who once have the opportunity to try the 5-day week. From the employer's point of view, the effectiveness of employees on the half day is not always worth the cost. When the employer can be persuaded, therefore, that no significant loss of business will be incurred, the business will close on Saturday.

There is a movement to a four-day week. Companies which have adopted this plan have concluded that efficiency has increased and that employees like the shortened week. The employees still work 40 hours a week, putting in 10 hours each working day. And as automation comes on further, the four-day week—or even a three-day week—may well be one way of sharing its fruits.

3. Shift Arrangements.   Of course, when the nature of operations or rush of business demands, the workweek may have to be extended and extra shifts of workers employed. The matter of shifts has debatable alternatives. Staying on the same shift means that some employees will have to work nights, a disrupting factor to normal family life. Rotating shifts means that all employees will have to change their life styles periodically.

Yearly Time Problems

In the yearly interval, the major problems revolve about holidays and vacation schedules. Holidays with pay are as common for shop workers as for office workers. Hence, what holidays will be recognized should be specifically stated. Holidays may be important because some companies pay time and one half or even double time to those who have to work on these days. To avoid possible arguments about premium days, therefore, such days should be specified in advance. Since absenteeism after holidays by those who worked on and received double time for holidays is excessive, one company reduced this by providing

FIGURE 20–1

Comparing Vacations Plans

MASS VACATIONS	STAGGERED VACATIONS
ADVANTAGES	
☐ USING THE SLACK SEASON to close the plant for paid vacation period can help avoid the unpleasantness of seasonal layoffs. Especially useful for highly seasonal industries.	☐ CONTINUOUS DELIVERIES to regular customers, and all normal services are possible the year around. Interruption might play into competitors' hands.
☐ CAPACITY OPERATION is easier for 50 weeks of the year. Efficiency isn't cut by vacation absences.	☐ NEW ORDERS CAN BE ACCEPTED at all times and completed on schedule. A maker of cardboard boxes could take a rush order any time, give it priority (or overtime) and complete it even with 20% of his force on vacation.
☐ EXTENSIVE REPAIRS, equipment installation, and inventory taking can be done during the vacation without slowing output or causing lay-offs.	
☐ IT'S EASIER TO SCHEDULE WORK. There's no more need to keep making allowance for employees away on vacation. So every department's output is easier to predict.	☐ RAPID PROCESSING OF PERISHABLE GOODS on hand is assured. Continuous manufacturing would prevent spoilage of goods.
	☐ EMPLOYEES HAVE A WIDER CHOICE of vacation time. Those who want to take their time off during the hunting or fishing season—or in the winter—can be accommodated.
☐ ALL WORKERS ARE TREATED THE SAME. This simplifies the foreman's job of scheduling vacations, and the accounting department's job of issuing vacation pay. It also stops complaints that "Bill got his vacation in July, why must I take mine in May?"	☐ GOOD COMMUNITY RELATIONS are preserved. The load on recreational and travel facilities is spread more evenly.
DISADVANTAGES	
☐ THE EXPENSE OF CLOSING the plant down and of reopening it two weeks later may be high.	☐ PRODUCTION MAY SLOW DOWN because of operation with a reduced labor force.
☐ SOME MAINTENANCE OPERATIONS AND ROUTINE SERVICES must be kept going even while the plant is closed. Don't forget their cost.	☐ BOTTLENECKS MAY BE CREATED by the absence of even a few people—particularly in small plants or in departments with small staffs where the effect of absences is felt more strongly.
☐ YOU MIGHT MISS SOME BUSINESS. And some customers may be inconvenienced.	☐ POORER SUPERVISION and short-range planning may result when an assistant takes over during the key man's vacation.
☐ NEW EMPLOYEES NOT ELIGIBLE for vacations will lose income during the shutdown—unless you can find work for them in the plant.	☐ WORK MAY PILE UP FOR SPECIALISTS, who will then have a heavier than ever load when they return.
☐ SOME EMPLOYEES MAY BE ELIGIBLE for longer vacations than the shutdown period.	☐ RESENTMENT AND FRICTION MAY ARISE among employees if too many want off at the same time. Since it is impossible to satisfy all requests, management is forced to refuse some.
☐ VACATION FACILITIES MAY BE OVERLOADED in the area if too many employees are off at once.	
☐ EMPLOYEES MAY NOT LIKE to have vacation periods fixed for them. It's tougher to tie in with plans of relatives or friends—or with game seasons.	☐ COSTS CAN RUN HIGH for training temporary replacements and for overtime work made necessary by vacation cuts in the work force.

Source: J. B. Bennet, "Vacations—Mass or Staggered," *Factory Management and Maintenance*, Vol. 108, no. 6, p. 128.

that pay would be calculated at straight rather than double rates for holidays in the event of unexcused absences following them.

Vacation periods are also of growing importance, since more and more companies are granting vacations with pay (because of collective bargaining in many instances) to shop as well as office workers. Two problems must be decided here: (1) the length of vacations and (2) the time of taking vacations. Office workers generally get two and in some instances three weeks, and shop workers get one or two and increasingly three weeks, depending upon seniority. Some employees have gained vacation periods up to 5 weeks. In the steel industry a 13-week, time-off option is available to employees with sufficient seniority.

All vacations may be taken at the same time, which has the advantage of avoiding conflicts about selections of calendar periods and the need of replacing key employees. Or they may be staggered, so that business can be conducted as usual with the company's regular staff. Which plan should be used may be determined by checking in a particular case the applicable advantages and disadvantages in the list provided in Figure 20–1.

STABILIZATION PROGRAMS

Employees are interested not only in fair wages but also in uninterrupted wage opportunities. Unfortunately, various seasonal and cyclical disturbances disrupt continued earning power. Many believe that nothing much can be done to secure employees against such risks. Yet a number of programs have been devised to provide some degree of protection against such losses of income.

This is not the place to debate the issue of income stabilization. All that can be done here is to note what has been done by industry and government in this respect. Such programs fall into two major categories:

1. Job stabilization, which seeks to provide continuous work opportunities and thereby assures employees of steady earnings.
2. Wage stabilization, which provides steady wage payments, whether or not employees are actually working.

Job Stabilization

To all concerned, stabilization of jobs would be a real boon. The employer seeks job stability because it leads to production efficiency, which means, in turn, that excess capacity, with its high costs, can be reduced to a minimum. And to employees, the assurance of steady employment is of real significance, dependent as they are on a steady source of income. Unfortunately, cyclical and seasonal fluctuations are formidable obstacles to these hopes. The effect of these fluctuations must be reduced or removed, if possible, if stabilization of jobs is to be attained. Attempts to do this may be classified as follows:

1. By individual companies:
   a. By adoption of sales practices that stabilize production.
   b. By adoption of production practices that stabilize production.
   c. By adoption of personnel practices that stabilize production.
2. By intercompany cooperation in regard to:
   a. Sales practices.
   b. Production practices.
   c. Personnel practices.
3. By governmental regulation and assistance:
   a. Unemployment compensation regulations.
   b. Assistance of employment services.
   c. Assistance of informational service.

Individual Plans

The basic question a company must answer when considering job stabilization is: Is the program worth the cost? Although it has been contended that such is the case, nevertheless any proposals offered by the personnel department should carry schedules of (1) losses due to job fluctuations, (2) costs of programs aimed at reducing fluctuations, and (3) the gains to be derived therefrom. To make such estimates, it is first necessary to examine statistically the seasonal and cyclical fluctuations that have and are likely to beset the company. Only after this has been done can the size of the stabilization job be appreciated and the desirability and flexibility of alternative plans for solving it be considered.

1. Sales Practices. Most stabilization programs start with the sales area, since anything which will stabilize sales will obviously stabilize production, and hence jobs. Much can be done by companies themselves to eliminate practices that tend to destabilize jobs. Unplanned sales programs are cases in point. To correct this, salespeople should be advised regarding products to be pushed, types of sales to be avoided, or what promises may be given on shipping dates to align sales with production and thus stabilize jobs.

And customers should be induced to become more stable buyers. First, in the case of seasonal items, buyers may be encouraged to send in advance orders by allowing special discounts, guaranteeing against price declines, offering exclusive rights of distribution, offering exclusive selection of styles, and permitting purchase on consignment. Second, in the case of items that are being ordered in small lots, buyers may be induced by methods suggested above to place a large order, with deliveries to be made periodically. And third, seasonal buyers may in some cases, as in the soft-drink industry, be converted into year-round buyers.

2. Production Practices. Production practices and policies should also be studied with a view to stabilizing employment. One of the most useful practices in this respect is that of producing to stock during seasons of low sales. This is not a cure-all because it is not universally feasible. When the following conditions prevail, its use should be given favorable consideration:

a. Parts or products can be stored:
   (1) With a minimum of loss to deterioration or evaporation.
   (2) At a minimum cost of handling, storing, and financial investment.
b. Minimum losses will be incurred because of:
   (1) Style changes while goods are stored.
   (2) Declines in price storage.

A number of production practices are helpful in stabilizing employment. For example, available work may be routed and scheduled by production control methods to provide a stable work load. Another practice in this connection is to defer work of certain kinds to slack periods. Maintenance work, construction jobs, and scrap handling are cases in point. Another useful idea is to design products so that various parts are interchangeable, irrespective of exterior style or variations in size. In that way, sales of particular products may fluctuate, yet production can be stabilized by producing to stock, if need be, or by producing to a plan of production control that has, as far as the workers are concerned, removed some of the vagaries of size or style factors.

3. Personnel Practices. Job stabilization may also be favorably affected by planned personnel practices. More accurate analysis of labor requirements, development of versatility of employees, and planned placement of work loads are the major ways in which this may be done.

a. Stabilizing Hiring Practices. Lack of information regarding labor needs and hiring is a major cause of instability. When such poor employment practices are permitted, supervisors in departments in which the work load is increasing will hire extra labor to handle it, not knowing that the load is temporary and that layoffs will soon be in order. Even when it is known that work loads are temporary, some companies proceed to hire willy-nilly, not caring about the disturbing influence to the labor situation. If, then, job stability is a desirable goal, the first and easiest step any company can take in attaining it is to forecast the labor requirements as accurately as possible and, on this basis, to lay down stabilizing rules of hiring. Indiscriminate, inconsistent, and temporary hirings may then be reduced to a minimum.

b. Developing Versatility. The development of versatility in workers also has much to be said for it because varying work loads then can be handled by a smaller number of employees. The theory of this practice is that workers who are kept on the payroll can be shifted, with a minimum loss of effectiveness, from jobs on which output is falling to those on which output is increasing. This makes it unnecessary to hire one worker for the first job, lay him off, and then hire another specialist for the second job, who in turn would have to be laid off when the work load in that area declines.

Versatility may be attained in two major ways—selection and training. By seeking candidates who have all-around abilities, employees selected can be shifted to other jobs as work loads require, thus adding a link to the chain of job security. Training of workers is also a desirable practice in the development of versatility. To be effective, training programs must be started and continued far enough in advance of actual need to allow employees time to gain new and added skills.

c. Leveling Work Loads. A third important way of stabilizing jobs by means of personnel practices is to level work loads. For example, hours of work may be adjusted so that available work is shared by all employees. Ordinarily, this will be practicable on the downward side of the business cycle, so long as reductions in hours of work do not reach the point at which all workers are on starvation wages. When this point is reached (what it is, is a variable depending upon employee opinion and standards of living), employees with seniority lose their desire to share the work with the younger employees and insist that the latter be released. On the upward side, taking care of peak loads by means of overtime, without hiring extra workers who must before long be laid off, depends upon the willingness of employees to give up their leisure and upon their efficiency as the factor of fatigue takes effect. However, within the practicable limits, adjustment of hours is a simple way of stabilizing jobs.

A good system of transfers is also effective in this regard. If work loads of varying amount are scheduled in different departments at different times, transfer programs can be worked out so that employees may be shifted between departments without need for layoffs. This practice can be adopted, however, only if, in addition to the requirements of sales and production tie-ups suggested in the preceding paragraph, employees possess versatility.

Intercompany Cooperation

In a competitive society, no one company can install practices the cost of which will place it in an unfavorable position as compared to other firms. Job security is a goal the attainment of which involves some practices that, if adopted, call for intercompany action to be successful.

Some progress in this direction has been made by a number of groups. Favorable results have been achieved by such groups as local and state chambers of commerce acting in behalf of their areas, trade associations working for the benefit of particular industries, and national business associations such as the National Association of Manufacturers and the more loosely knit Committee of Economic Development, acting for the benefit of all business. Such diverse groups as the American Legion, church bodies, and unions have also interested themselves in ways and means of stabilizing jobs.

A variety of sales, production, and personnel practices have been developed on an intercompany basis. Perhaps the most important contribution in this respect is the collection and dissemination of various types of information. Certainly, information on such subjects as inventory positions, buying potentials and trends in various markets, new developments in materials and machines, trends in employment, and price fluctuations is highly useful in keeping employers from making mistakes that lead to overemployment and the inevitable layoffs. Intercompany cooperation in gathering such information may be obtained through their own bureaus of information or outside bureaus subsidized to carry on this work.

In addition to the contributions to the ability of individual companies to make better decisions which aid in stabilizing production, intercompany cooperation can lead to the elimination of destabilizing practices. For example, fluctuation of output in the automobile industry has been reduced by changing the time of introducing new models from the spring to the fall of the year. And the agreement of various industries to avoid extravagant claims, excessive discounts, and high-pressure salesmanship has tended to reduce unsettling results in the market and thus, in turn, to stabilize employment. More positive action has been taken by industries that have sought on a cooperative basis to educate customers in more stable buying methods.

An intercompany practice which has been successful in stabilizing production is that of interchanging workers as slack periods develop in one company while a peak load must be carried by another. Of course, such interchanges are the responsibility of workers in most markets, but the results of individual search are not always satisfactory to the workers, nor do the companies always get back desirable workers. When companies in a community get together to discuss their work loads, however, employees may be shifted from company to company with a minimum of lost time and effort to the employees. Some interesting problems, such as effect upon seniority, must be worked out; but their solution seems to be a small price to pay compared to the losses that are avoided thereby.

Governmental Influences

Job stabilization has also been influenced by governmental regulation and assistance. Regulatory influences have come chiefly from the Wages and Hours Law and the unemployment compensation laws, while the work of such agencies as the Employment Service and the U.S. Departments of Commerce and Labor has been of an assisting nature.

1. The Wages and Hours Law. As noted earlier, one of the fundamental purposes of the Fair Labor Standards Act (FLSA) is to encourage the sharing of available work by penalizing employers who work their employees more than 40 hours a week. Obviously, an employer who has to increase labor costs by 50 percent for overtime will consider very seriously the advisability of hiring additional workers. If this occurs, the objective of stabilizing employment in the overall sense by reducing unemployment will be attained.

2. The Social Security Act. Another encouragement to stabilized employment stems from the unemployment compensation provisions of the Social Security Act. Under Titles III and IX of this Act, employees of industry, in states that have approved plans, are compensated for periods up to 39 weeks, depending on the legislation of the states in which they reside. The funds for compensation are obtained by taxes computed as a percentage of individual payrolls. Records are kept of the contributions of each company and of compensation paid out against the individual accounts. In most states, adjustments are made in the taxation for particular companies if the withdrawals from the fund, because of a low record of layoffs, are at a minimum. The amount of the adjustments depends upon the system of merit or experience rating particular states have adopted. Obviously, it is to the benefit of companies operating in states in which rating may lead to reduction in taxes to reduce fluctuations in employment whenever possible.

3. Assistance of Federal Agencies. Other federal agencies have lent an assisting hand in reducing job instability. The U.S. Departments of Commerce and Labor have collected a variety of data which are useful to employers in reaching more intelligent decisions regarding business problems, thereby reducing mistakes that lead to layoffs and employment fluctuations. Also, the U.S. Employment Service and the state employment services favorably affect work stabilization, first, by helping companies to select workers who are better suited to their jobs, and, second, by helping employees who lose their jobs to find new ones more quickly.

WAGE STABILIZATION

Scope of Plans

Programs of wage stabilization are based on the proposition that wages and salaries should be continued at a more or less constant rate when it is impossible to stabilize production. A variety of such plans have been developed. The key points of difference pertain to:

1. The employees covered by guarantees.
2. Guarantee periods and amounts.
3. Examples of voluntary plans.
4. Conditions of favorable usage.

Employee Coverage

Most plans are limited to certain classes of workers. Length of service, type of work, and a calculated number of employees are used to establish limits. Length of service is undoubtedly the most popular method for determining the employees who are to participate in wage stabilization plans. It is, of course, easy to calculate and understand and, moreover, has the actual advantage of the test of time—since the company has been able to retain the workers for a length of time, probabilities are in favor of being able to continue their employment. The service requirements of some plans are as low as six months and as high as five years, with a period of one year being favored.

Job classes are also used by some companies because the retention of employees on certain key jobs is highly desirable. Technical, professional, supervisory, and maintenance employees are examples of those to whom guarantees are extended.

And finally, some companies establish the number of employees to whom guarantees can be extended by calculating labor requirements for a future period of time. After this figure is determined, seniority by job classes is then employed to determine which of the employees will be included in the number of employees to whom the guarantee can be extended. This method has the advantage of protecting the company against excessive guarantees, but it has the advantage of making some key employees uncertain about income stability.

Guarantee Periods and Amounts

All plans establish a definite period of time during which guarantees apply or are calculated. In most instances the year is the base period, although some plans limit the time to as low as three months. Obviously, if a plan is to give employees assurance of steady income, it should at least aim toward the annual basis. This provides a sufficiently extended period so that employees are not disturbed by what is going to happen to their income in the near future. Of course, from the company's point of view, guarantees beyond a year's time are full of danger because economic conditions and prices beyond its control and its powers of foresight may lead to impossible financial burdens. However, most companies should be able to forecast within reasonable limits of accuracy the sales they will make during a year's time and hence be able to establish this period as a limit to their guarantees.

Although questions of who is to be covered for how long may be answered with relative ease, how much is to be guaranteed is a much more difficult question. The variations in this regard in actual practice show that differences of opinion are wide. Guarantees differ in terms of liability of payments and amount of payment.

With rare exceptions, most companies limit their guarantees or establish rules for counterbalancing overpayments or underpayments. A common way of doing this is to establish a basic workweek and a basic paycheck for each week. If the actual earnings of employees are less than the basic check, the differences are recorded and must be made up in future weeks when overtime hours raise actual earnings above the basic check. The basic paycheck may be based on a standard workweek of 40 hours (or upon some lesser figure) if actual hours from week to week fluctuate around 40. If the period within which shortages must be made up is definitely stated, let us say a year, as some plans provide, the liability of employers is minimized, yet the wage plan may be termed a guaranteed wage plan.

Many companies limit their ability by agreeing to advance employees, for specified periods of time only, an amount sufficient to make up the difference between the amount earned and the guaranteed weekly paycheck. These advances are continued only for a limited period of time or up to the pay for a given number of hours. Should these limits be reached, the makeups are stopped. And as noted earlier, the advances must be made up by the employee when workweeks exceed the basic week or some percentage of a basic week.

Examples of Voluntary Plans

The specifics of a few examples will serve to illustrate how stabilization has been achieved voluntarily. In one company, permanent factory workers are guaranteed employment for at least 48 weeks of the year. To make the plan feasible, the company had (1) to redesign certain key operations so that year-round instead of seasonal operations could be carried on and (2) to revamp its distribution methods so that retailers purchased on a periodic rather than a random basis. The guarantees are made to employees with two or more years of consecutive service. Employees also are subject to changes in work assignments as loads of various divisions require.

Another company has used a plan of "fifty-two paychecks a year." It, too, worked out very carefully the conditions under which wage guarantees could be made. It has found that the amount that could be paid to employees was about 20 percent of the value of production. Hence, by forecasting sales for any year, it could determine what its payroll would be.

Employees earn bonuses based upon the earnings of the company and upon production in excess of estimated production. Thus, this plan includes a profit-sharing feature.

And to cite one more case, employees in one company are paid a regular weekly amount 52 weeks a year and required to work whatever number of hours (up to but not beyond reasonable limits) are needed to get the work done. Earnings in excess of weekly guarantees are paid at the end of the year. Payments in excess of earnings have been absorbed by the company.

Conditions of Feasible Use

Wage stabilization requires favorable conditions. Such plans are practically limited to a year or less. Even within such time periods, companies with hard-to-predict swings in business—the so-called producer goods industries are a case in point—cannot undertake such plans.

But those in the consumer goods field with more stable volumes may find it easier to adopt such plans. A review of names of companies that have installed them soon indicates the predominance of consumer-type industries. And finally, industries which can economically store parts or finished products are in a better position to stabilize wages than others. Thus, anything a company can do to reduce seasonal fluctuations, to increase the storability of products, and to increase the versatility of employees makes wage stabilization more feasible.

The variations in these conditions explain why some companies can be more liberal in their guarantees than others. Whereas some can guarantee weekly paychecks of fixed amounts without repayment features in the event of overpayments, others must restrict their guarantees to little more than wage advances that must sooner or later be repaid. In any event, the steps taken by any company in this direction serve to reduce one of the most serious threats to labor's security and peace of mind.

How far this movement will go is conjectural. Guaranteed wages have an appeal, however, that is difficult to resist. And it must be granted that most companies never have laid off their employees at any time. At least, guarantees of this amount could be feasible. So it is safe to conclude that negotiations for such guarantees are not likely to abate. How many employees will be covered and the extent of guarantees will depend upon economic conditions, the type of industry, the strength of union bargaining power, the strategy of union drives, and the facts that management can marshall about its industrial situation.

QUESTIONS

1. What is the answer to the question of how long an employee should work in any given time period?
2. What are the arguments for and against the provision of rest periods during the working period?
3. In terms of past trends and current developments, what do you expect the length of the workweek in business is likely to be in the next five years?
4. How does one determine what starting and stopping times are for purposes of computing compensable time?
5. What are the advantages and disadvantages of the fixed- versus the swing-shift plan of handling the multishift problem?
6. What are the advantages and disadvantages of the staggered plan of scheduling employee vacations?
7. What conditions are present in the case of companies which have been relatively successful in stabilizing continuity of jobs.
8. What personnel practices are helpful when undertaking a program of job stabilization?
9. Upon what grounds would you agree or disagree with the argument that guaranteeing wage security is indefensible?
10. Under what conditions is a wage stabilization program likely to be relatively successful?

CASE 20–1.   A SHIFT PROBLEM

The Makem Parts Company had to add a third shift because of increasing business. There are three major divisions in the company. In section A (see diagram), initial manufacture of parts takes place. Here is found the heaviest and dirtiest work. Hourly wages here do not always compensate for these conditions. However, some jobs here are liked better than others. Many good jobs are located in section B (a finishing and paint-spraying unit), but it is also the hottest section. As a consequence, many good jobs go unwanted in the summer but are desired in the winter. Section C is final assembly. Conditions here are generally the best, but the work is controlled by a mechanical conveyor and, as a result, is tiresome and monotonous.

Each section has a supervisor and assistant supervisor for each shift, with a general superintendent over all.

```
┌─────────────┐   ┌─────────────┐   ┌─────────────┐
│  Section A  │   │  Section B  │   │  Section C  │
│             │   │             │   │             │
│    ┌───┐    │   │  ┌─┐ ┌─┐    │   │    ┌─┐      │
│    │ 1 │    │   │  │2│ │2│    │   │    │3│      │
│    └───┘    │   │  └─┘ └─┘    │   │    └─┘      │
└─────────────┘   └─────────────┘   └─────────────┘
```

Note: 1 = Welding and assembling; 2 = Paint spraying and ovens; 3 = Mechanical conveyor.

The company is adding a midnight shift to the day and afternoon shifts. This is being done by hiring more personnel from the outside and training them, by transferring workers between sections, and by promoting employees.

The union contract, which applies to all employees except supervisory and above, states:

All vacancies shall be posted, at least a week before they become available, on the various company bulletin boards. Any employee wishing to bid for a job should do so in the department office for which the vacancy occurs. Employees bidding for jobs will be given preference in the following order:

1. Persons who are in the same section of the same department in which the vacancy occurs will have first choice. However, if two workers from the same section apply, seniority will rule unless the company can prove the senior employee to be incompetent.

2. All other employees in the same department have next preference. Seniority rules here in case more than one worker applies.

3. The rest of the employees have next preference with seniority ruling, of course, in case more than one worker applies.

4. All outside hiring will be in order of application.

Questions

1. What difficulties do you foresee in the light of the union contract?

2. What changes, if any, in the union contract would you try to bring about?

CASE 20–2.   INCOME AND JOB STABILIZATION

The management of the Eyo Company was giving thought and consideration to possible ways and means of stabilizing the wages of its employees. It had hoped to stabilize jobs, which would have automatically stabilized incomes, so it reviewed its past employment variations. On a seasonal basis, it had found that over the past ten years employment in the lowest period of a year was 25 percent below employment in the highest month. On a cyclical basis the data showed that in the poorest year, employment was 30 percent below the year with the highest employment.

Currently employment is running around the 2000 figure for factory employees. Conservative estimates have projected a steady five percent annual growth of the company over the next five years.

Question

1. On the basis of these data, what if anything, do you think this company could do about job stabilization? Income stabilization?

CHAPTER 21

SERVICE AND PARTICIPATION PROGRAMS

Scope of Plans

Over the years, a miscellany of plans which fall outside the borders of affairs strictly related to business has been offered to employees. Some, such as athletic programs, seem well removed from the business of producing and selling goods. Others, such as medical plans, are more closely related, in that they provide services which might otherwise be unavailable. And still others, such as company periodicals, may indirectly affect employee morale, teamwork, and productivity.

How far a company will go in establishing such programs depends upon its basic philosophy, community factors, union relations, and forces pressing for or against particular plans. All that can be done here, therefore, is to comment upon various programs and some guide lines for their operation. This is done under the following headings:

1. Recreational, social, and athletic programs.
2. Participation programs.
3. Services of convenience or personal necessity.
4. Organization of programs.
5. Rules of adoption and operation.

RECREATIONAL, SOCIAL, AND ATHLETIC PROGRAMS

Purposes of Programs

Recreational, social, and athletic programs have a double purpose. They make for a well-rounded life for employees, and they serve thereby to build employees who are better equipped to perform their daily tasks. What specific plans should be provided requires careful consideration of objectives, morale, and environmental factors. For example, answers to such questions as the following should be sought:

1. Are any objectives of the company being missed because facilities for recreation are not available?
2. Does the community provide adequate and usable recreational facilities?
3. Is a union offering such plans or facilities?
4. Is employee morale, and hence willingness to cooperate, weak because of a lack of adequate recreational facilities?
5. If recreational plans are established, will the employees in sufficient numbers take advantage of them?

Recreational and Social Programs

Assuming that favorable answers are derived, a wide range of programs is available from which to make selections. In describing these plans, only a superficial attempt is made to group them in recreational, social, and athletic categories. After all, such plans as bowling leagues have aspects of all of these: they provide physical exercise—the athletic aspect. They provide a change in the tempo of living that brings renewed vigor to employees—the recreational aspect. They encourage gregariousness among employees—the social aspect. Or a company symphony orchestra for example, may be to one individual a recreational opportunity and to another a social event. Hence the groupings here are for purposes of convenience rather than being indicative of exclusive categories.

1. Social Get-Togethers. Occasional events such as company-sponsored dances and picnics are the usual way in which recreational and social programs are initiated. Whereas dances may be operated with relative ease because participation of those who attend the event is assured, such programs as picnics and outings call for a good deal of planning and organizing. Games and contests should be planned for all age groups and for both sexes. The events should be scheduled so that they neither drag nor overlap. Small prizes, too, are a desirable feature for winning contestants. And it is important that the executives attend and participate with unconcealed enjoyment.

Parties organized to suit the season serve to promote interest. Beach parties in the summer, Halloween and Thanksgiving parties in the fall, and Christmas and New Year's parties in the winter are examples of such occasions.

2. Informal Associations. Other recreational activities are provided by informal get-togethers of employees in clubrooms of their own.

During rest periods, lunch hours, or before or after going to work, employees may gather in the club for refreshments or dancing. More elaborate arrangements provide facilities for athletic activities of various kinds.

3. Musical Groups. Music is an area for developing employee participation. The employees of one company have been unusually successful in organizing a symphony orchestra. This activity began with the formation of a group for playing popular music, which evolved after a few years into a symphonic unit. Of interest is the fact that this orchestra has been a success not only for the participants but also for nonparticipating employees who have learned to enjoy classical music. More popular among musical activities are glee clubs, dance bands, and rock and roll musical groups.

4. Drama Clubs. Some companies also have drama clubs. These seem to be very attractive because they provide employees an opportunity to produce and direct stage plays as well as to act in them. Thus a variety of challenges are made available to attract employee participation.

5. Flying Clubs. Flying clubs have been organized by the employees of some companies. This is a relatively expensive activity, but the cost for the individual can be reduced considerably by the formation of clubs. Ordinarily, this activity can be organized only in large companies. The number of potential flyers must be large enough to support a continuing turnover of learners and participants. To the flying activity, whether power or sail planes, some groups have added that of parachute-jumping.

6. Flower and Garden Clubs. Gardening has also proved of some interest. Flower clubs with their discussion sessions and periodic shows have strong adherents.

7. Noon-Hour Programs. The noon hour also provides a recreational opportunity. Horseshoe pitching and softball are indulged in during this time period. Other companies prepare programs encompassing professional talent from the entertainment world, sport figures, and visitors of public renown. The latter types can only be established by large companies. There are inexpensive possibilities of programs, using production and aisle space for noon-time recreation.

8. Special Interests. Groups with special interests may also be served. Chess and checkers clubs, camera clubs, and bridge clubs are examples. These groups, though small, will nevertheless be found to be among the most active that can be established.

9. Physical Facilities. Recreational and social programs require some physical facilities. At times, advantage may be taken of conveniently located community facilities. At other times, it will be found necessary to provide some space on company premises. Arrangements for social events can be provided with relative ease when company restaurants are designed for all types of occasions. Thus the restaurant building of one company is used for dances, parties of all types, educational meetings, and meetings to pass out rewards for seniority and suggestions. In some cases the recreation building is separated from the company building. This has the advantage of removing the employee completely from the working atmosphere. Unusual facilities for various sports and social gatherings are provided by the 180-acre park established by NCR of Dayton for these purposes. Such arrangements are, of course, the exception.

Athletic Programs

1. The Popular Sports. Athletic programs are widely used to engage employees in after-hours activities. Bowling and softball, in season, are particularly popular with many companies. The former has grown widely in employee acceptance because it is a good mixer sport and can be enjoyed by the tyro as well as the expert. Softball teams have grown in popularity, too. Some companies stress intramural teams, whereas others sponsor intercompany leagues. The former provides opportunity for a large number of employees to participate in athletics, while the latter gives employees an opportunity to cheer for their company, thus encouraging institutional pride. Basketball teams require more skilled participants and are usually restricted to intercompany competition, but they do provide much spectator entertainment. These programs sometimes have one serious disadvantage. As one company official noted, the costs of industrial compensation for accidents were higher in the case of recreational programs than for factory operations.

2. The Minor Sports. A variety of other athletic sports is also sponsored. Tennis and golf tournaments or parties are planned by some companies. In a few instances, skeet, trapshooting, and pistol ranges have been provided. Swimming and ice skating facilities are also provided by some companies by renting community facilities at stated times and under qualified supervision. Gymnasiums may also be rented under similar conditions in some cases. In a few instances, companies have built such facilities for the exclusive use of employees.

Horseshoe pitching is also of interest to some employees. This game possesses possibilities in any program because facilities can be provided easily and the playing time of the game is relatively short. Hence, it furnishes an excellent sport for the lunch hour. Continuing interest can be derived by keeping cumulative records and setting up interdepartmental teams. Other sports that have been established in a few instances include ice and field hockey, cricket, squash, badminton, water skiing, and snow skiing. Because of the skill required by most of these sports, they have been less popular.

Enough enthusiasts can usually be found in most companies to organize a fishing club. In addition to organized outings, meetings to discuss fishing and outdoor recreation and to swap "lies" may be planned.

Music in the Plant and Office

Although music in business is a twilight case of a recreational or social program, it is included for discussion here because music does have an aesthetic or emotional appeal that is more related to the recreational or enjoyment capacity of employees than to their physical nature.

For many decades, music, as well as other forms of discussion and entertainment such as the reading of stories, has been employed during working hours in various foreign countries. Until recently, such practices were almost nonexistent in the United States. But in the past several years, there has been a small but growing trend toward the use of music as a means of improving production by relieving monotony and by providing employees with a lift. Conclusive evidence to support the productivity claims for music is not available. Some argue that productivity is not influenced by music. Proponents, such as the Muzak Corporation, report quantity and quality increases as shown in Figures 21–1 and 21–2. And some contend that music may have an impact but that it

FIGURE 21–1
Effect of Music Quantity of Production

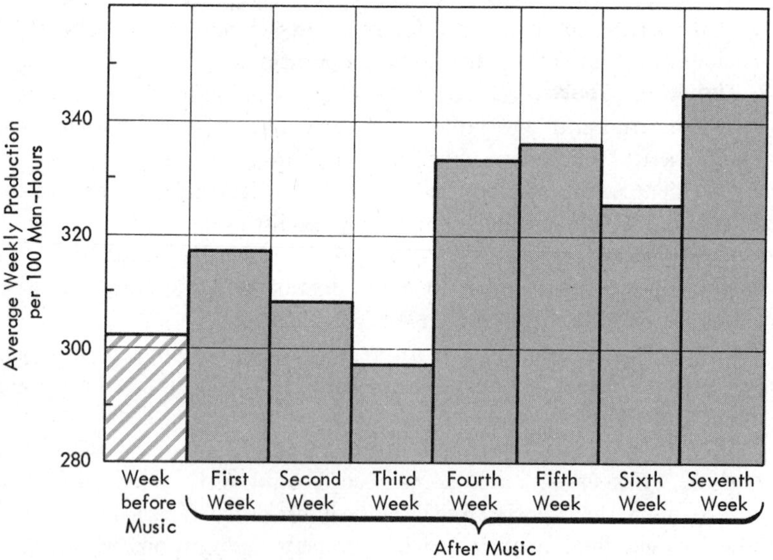

Source: Muzak Corporation.

FIGURE 21-2

Effect of Music upon Quality of Production

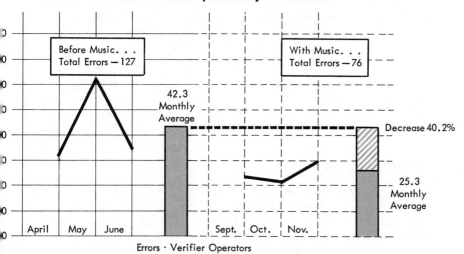

Source: Muzak Corporation.

differs significantly in accordance with a person's makeup, position vertically in the organization, and the nature of job assignments.

The introduction of music in the plant or office calls for good equipment. Modern developments now make possible the distribution of music from central stations to strategically located loudspeakers at reasonably low cost. The musical equipment need not be located in the factory. Such services, in large communities, may be purchased from companies established solely for this purpose.

Another significant factor in the use of music is the building of programs that will not interfere with working rhythms and will appeal to employees. The music suitable for a punch press department may be distracting to a central stenographic department, and vice versa. Usually, some experimentation will be necessary before programs suited to various departments are established. Similarly, experimentation will be necessary to select programs that the majority of employees prefer.

The equipment for sending music may also be employed to broadcast various messages. Although some companies frown upon this practice, others favor it. The latter use the system to make special announcements, to describe lost and found items, to welcome new workers, to send birthday and anniversary greetings, and to broadcast such public events as World Series baseball contests, football games, news reports, and addresses by the President of the United States.

PARTICIPATION PROGRAMS

Although the inclusion is somewhat arbitrary, company periodicals and suggestion systems are discussed here in connection with employee services because both attempt to relate the employee to his working environment. Either might be dispensed with, as some companies have done, on the grounds that periodicals are ineffective and suggestion systems are likely to bring about disputes and controversies between employees and employers. But the supporters of such plans see much good in them as means of improving the ties between the two groups.

Company Periodicals

Company periodicals are publications such as newspapers or magazines issued regularly to employees. Most companies, outside of the small-size group, have such publications. They are discussed here because their content in most cases is devoted to social and personal items of interest to employees. But they also are used for instructional purposes of a general nature and to disseminate information regarding company products, policies, rules, and regulations. However, the latter must be heavily sugarcoated with personal items, or they are not likely to be read.

1. Objectives. The fundamental purpose of company publications of this type is to bring employee and employer closer together. The larger organizations, in particular, have recourse to such devices in order to personalize employee-employer relationships. Employees become better employees, so the theory of company magazines goes, because they have been recognized publicly as a significant part of the organization.

Publication of company rules and of explanations of procedures and plans also can serve indirectly to make employees feel that they are an important part of the organization. In the first place, they are taken into the confidence of the company; and second, their ignorance regarding various aspects of company operations is removed. Hence, when properly handled, which means writing from the employee's viewpoint, company news can be as effective a morale builder as personal items.

2. Layout and Form. To be effective, company periodicals must be made up with care. Much thought and study should be given to such matters as technical form, content, periodicity, method of distribution, and staff for gathering and editing materials. Some companies invest very small amounts in mimeographed sheets, whereas others publish magazines that compare favorably with the finest magazines found on the newsstands. In either event, the important point is to determine carefully what type of magazine will serve the conditions and needs most appropriately.

Several points are well worth noting in regard to the technical composition of periodicals. The size of magazines should be such that they are easy and convenient to handle. Type should be selected that is easy to read, and headings should both attract and guide the reader. And perhaps above all, the style of writing should be somewhat on the breezy side, interesting and appealing to the average employee.

3. Content. In regard to the content, it is generally agreed that personal items, social events, and recreational and athletic news should make up the greatest part of a magazine. Some contend that nothing else should go into a publication intended for employees. Perhaps it would be better to argue that nothing should be included unless it is written or translated for employees. After all, the opening of a new office building, for example, may be company business, but it is also of real interest to employees. So, too, is news about products, processes, and organization changes.

News of personal interest, however, should lead all the rest. New additions to the staff, transfers and promotions, marriages and births, unusual happenings to employees, hobbies and activities, awards and recognitions, leaves of absence, and serious illnesses are examples of items that should be reported. A liberal sprinkling of pictures, particularly of children, is also desirable. After this, social events of personal interest, both within the company and within the community, such as dances, parties, and gatherings, should receive attention. Then, too, the various sports activities of employees, such as standings of teams, personal performances, and game schedules, should be highlighted.

Although some people may state that they do not care whether or not they get their names in the paper, there are few indeed who actually do not like such mention, insignificant though the occasion for it may be. The old rule of the small-town newspaper that each subscriber's name should be mentioned at least twice a year in the paper also holds true of the company periodical.

4. Periodicity and Distribution. How often magazines should be issued and how they are to be distributed must also be considered carefully. In most cases, magazines are published once a month. Periods of greater or less time are selected infrequently. A month provides a convenient interval as well as one that whets the employees' interest and does not overwork the publication staff.

The question of frequency is comparatively easy to answer, but the question of distribution is difficult. There is wide difference of opinion as to methods. Some companies prefer to mail the magazines to the homes of employees. In this way, there is greater assurance that the families will read the magazines. Some pass out the magazines as the employees punch the clock, and others distribute them through the departmental supervisors. The last two methods are used primarily because of their convenience and secondarily because each employee is given a copy on the company premises, providing another direct contact between employee and employer.

The real problem is, of course, to have the magazine read; otherwise, it may as well not be issued. This can be accomplished by including various features such as puzzles, rewards for those who notice special items scattered through the magazine, and contests for such suggestions as names of new sections of the magazine or comic characters that are used to depict safety lessons and other instructions that may be run in the magazine from time to time. Emphasis on personal items serves to promote reader interest.

5. News Gathering and Editing. Finally, arrangements must be made for gathering and editing the content of magazines. A popular method is to hire a full-time magazine editor and to rely upon selected employees from various departments to gather and report the news. This arrangement has the advantage of expert direction and of employee participation, but it suffers from the possibility that the employee reporters will not do a thorough job of news gathering. This may be circumvented by frequent staff meetings in which the departmental reporters are made to feel the importance of their jobs and, at the same time, are instructed in what news to gather and how to do it. In some companies a full-time staff to do all of the work is hired, members being selected from present employees or from sources outside the company. In this way the technical competence of gathering and preparing news items is assured. Whether or not a sense of employee participation is lost depends upon how closely reporters get in touch with employees and how well they ferret out and report their activities.

Suggestion Systems

General education and communication may also be improved by means of a good suggestion system. Although some companies have had unfavorable experience with suggestion plans, favorable results are more common.[1] To be effective, however, suggestion plans should be designed with care in regard to the following aspects:

1. Objectives of suggestion plans.
2. Procedures for collection and evaluation.
3. Policies of compensation.

It is invariably necessary to precede the inauguration of a suggestion system with a campaign of publicity designed to acquaint employees

---

[1] The proponents of suggestion systems have been numerous enough and enthusiastic enough to form a group known as the National Association of Suggestion Systems.

with the values of the system and how it is to operate. Specific notes should be made regarding the gains to the employees. In this connection, it is important to stress that laborsaving suggestions will not result in layoffs.

Then, it is important to publicize the procedures of the system, as illustrated, for example, in Figure 21–3. In particular, employees should be informed as to how suggestions should be made, where they should be deposited, and how they are to be judged. Every effort should be made to indicate how the employee who makes a suggestion is to be protected in any rewards or recognition which may arise from the suggestion. In this connection, some companies have found it desirable to establish judging committees made up of employees as well as executives and technical assistants.

Rewards for acceptable suggestions are a matter of argument. Some companies frown upon any rewards except expressions of congratulation. Others conclude that some form of financial compensation is indispensable. In the latter event, practice varies. Some companies establish maxi-

FIGURE 21–3

Suggestion-Processing Flow Chart

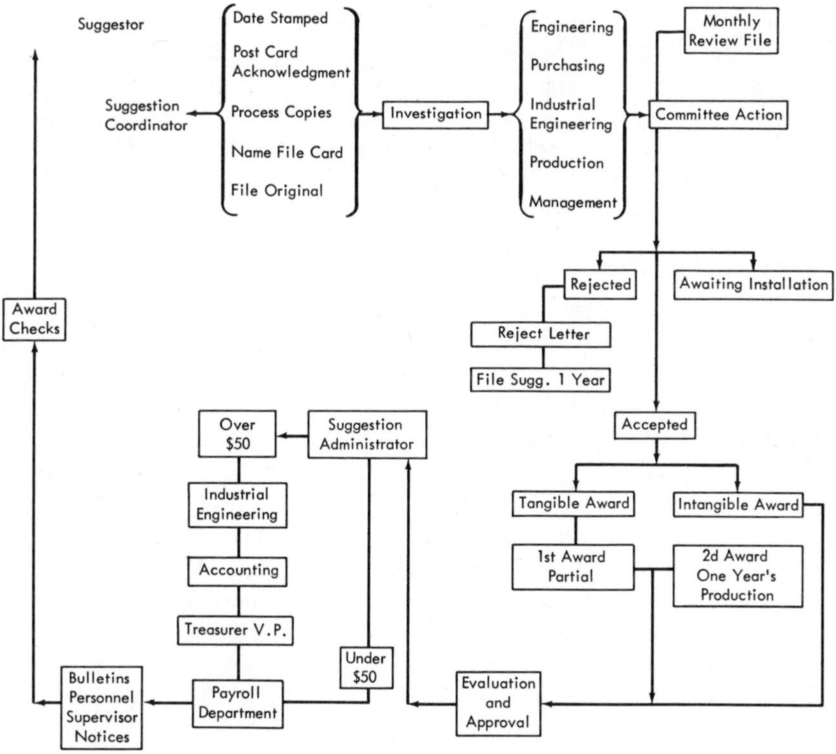

mum rewards of $100 to $200, whereas others use formulas by which employees may be paid up to 25 percent of the first year's savings derived from the suggestion. In the latter case, bonuses have been paid in thousands of dollars in some instances.

Although suggestion plans are largely concerned with ways and means by which production, sales, and office procedures may be improved, they are sometimes used to obtain the views of employees regarding management methods and policies. The latter objective, while desirable, is perhaps better handled in connection with grievance machinery. By making this separation, the suggestion plan can be used to keep the sight of employees upon positive improvements of mutual advantage to employer and employee. Complaints, disputes, and dissatisfactions should be channeled through appropriate executives or an effective and accepted grievance machinery.

CONVENIENCE SERVICES

"Convenience services" refers to the facilities or assistance that are ordinarily available in the community and arranged for by employees themselves, but for one reason or another are provided for employees by the company. Among such services are restaurants, company stores, company nursing and medical assistance, and counselors of various types. Unless made available in convenient form—so it is contended by those that offer these plans—employees will not take advantage of plans that are significant to their health, well-being, or state of mind. When such services are properly installed, the morale and effectiveness of employees can be raised sufficiently to pay for their cost.

Restaurant Facilities

Perhaps no employee service plan has received as much attention in recent years as that of restaurants. Some companies have been forced to provide such facilities because they locate their plants away from central community services. Others have concluded that such facilities have a favorable impact upon productivity. In either event, the actual operation of the facilities is conducted by the company or leased to an outside caterer.

The biggest advances in eating services have been made in physical facilities and planning of diets. Considerable thought has gone into the design and location of restaurants and eating facilities. The technique of layout planning is being adapted to the design of company cafeterias. In addition to fixed restaurant sites, more and more companies are adopting mobile and automatic food-dispensing units. These units are used by some companies to serve employees who are located at inconvenient distances from the regular restaurants of the company. Other companies use these devices to reach workers during working hours and provide them with soft drinks, milk, candy, and sandwiches.

Careful study has been made of the dietary needs of workers. Industrial dietitians and nutritional experts have become permanent members of the personnel staff of many companies. The dietitians must plan meals that not only are well balanced but also will be selected by the employees. To induce good selections, a popular method is to offer the planned meals as "specials" at a relatively low price. One company has gone so far as to serve free meals to employees, so that they have no problem of "selling" the balanced diet. Another method is to feature items, such as salads, that are deemed good for the diet. One company took all soft drinks out of the restaurant so that milk would not have that competition. Another company has used the idea of contests among employees to attract attention to balanced menus. Employees have responded not only by offering menu suggestions but also by buying more of the balanced menus than they did when the company alone decided what the menus were to be.

A final word on nutrition has reference to the practice of some companies of supplying employees with vitamin pills as a supplement to possible dietary deficiencies. Of course, the practice of providing salt tablets to those who work under very hot conditions has for a long time been known to be desirable in replacing body salts lost by perspiration.

Company Stores

Company stores in some localities have had some adoptions. In communities where retail stores are inadequate, company stores perform a needed service. The offerings to employees can be wide, covering food, clothing, sports equipment, automobile supplies, and household furnishings. Many of these items may be available on the store premises. Others may be offered through discount arrangements with dealers, only samples being shown at the store.

In some instances, company stores have acquired a poor reputation. They have been used as a means of making excessive profits. They have also been used to keep employees in debt, thereby assuring the company of little, if any, labor turnover. These instances, although infrequent, occurred often enough in the past that unions at times raise the issue in collective bargaining negotiations. Moreover, the wages and hours administrator has laid down rules governing how employees shall be paid so that they will not fall victims to unscrupulous company-stores practices. Company stores have also been opposed by community retailers, who feel that such profits logically should go to them. And some states have outlawed them.

The charge that company stores are exacting excessive profits can be avoided by turning over their operation to employees. In one company the store is run by the employees for the purpose of financing various employee activities. The profits are used to support various recreational, social, and athletic activities. As a consequence, these programs are run and supported by the employees themselves. The company lends a minimum of support by providing store space at a minimum charge.

Credit Unions

Facilitative services include a variety of plans, only a few of which can be mentioned here. An interesting example is the credit union, which has had a phenomenal growth in the United States. The credit union is essentially a small-loan institution operated by employees for their own benefit. Its purpose is to have a source from which short-term loans may be obtained for personal needs at rates far below those that are charged by commercial institutions. Since some employees are hard pressed for funds occasionally, the credit union offers a worthwhile service to them. And to the employees who invest in the credit union, it offers a combination savings and interest-earning plan, and also a life insurance program based upon the savings and age of the member.

The losses in credit unions are remarkably low, having averaged less than 20 cents per $100 loaned. In the first place, the officers of credit unions review applications for loans from a restricted group with whom they are well acquainted, since they are all fellow employees. Hence, losses are reduced at the source by careful screening of applications. In the second place, most plans have established an upper limit above which loans will not be made to any given individual. In this way, risks are spread over a large number of borrowers. In the third place, credit unions are subject to state and federal regulations, depending upon how the unions are established. Since 1907, when the first state law was enacted, 44 states have enacted legislation governing the operation of credit unions; and in 1934, provision was made for federal incorporation.

Home Purchasing

Assistance to employees in purchasing homes is also a popular plan of employee service. Such assistance is usually provided by a building and loan financial plan. This combines a savings plan, for employees who want to invest their savings, with the loan feature, for those who wish to build or buy homes. The borrower then repays to the loan association a fixed amount each month or payday. In other cases the company itself provides the financial assistance and deducts a fixed amount, covering principal and interest, each payday. Both plans make it possible for employees who so desire to procure long-term loans at reasonable rates with a minimum of red tape. Indeed, some companies make the loans at extremely low rates as an encouragement to homeownership, believing that such acquisitions make for stable employees.

Medical Services

In recent years, there has been a tendency for more and more companies to provide employees with medical service. Such service usually has started with visiting-nurse service for sick employees. It has gradually been extended so that varied medical service is available not only to employees but also to their families. Thus, hospital and surgical facilities are available in some companies for all types of illness and operations. Also, the services of dentists and optometrists are offered in some cases.

Consultative Services

Included among the facilities offered by some companies are consultative services of various kinds. For example, some companies have opened their legal departments to the personal problems of employees. In most instances, this is restricted simply to giving initial advice as to what to do if threatened with legal suits, for example, or what rights one has in various difficulties that may present themselves. In other instances, help is given in instituting a suit, in selecting legal counsel if protracted court action is necessary, and in suggesting the nature of action to be taken. Of course, except in minor cases or actions, the legal departments are not offered to carry on court actions or extended cases. However, limited service is highly desirable because most employees are uncertain of what to do or what not to do when faced with legal difficulties. Hence the availability of this service will be of help to them, at minimum cost to the company.

Other companies have made arrangements whereby employees may discuss various problems with vocational guidance experts, psychologists, psychiatrists, and family relations experts. Such services, too, can do much to find and eliminate sources of trouble that disrupt an employee's ease of mind and, therefore, capacity to produce efficiently and effectively.

Retirement Consultation

An interesting type of service is that related to easing the transition of employees into retirement. Three phases of retirement may be noted: preretirement, actual retirement, and postretirement.

In the preretirement phase, it has been found desirable to discuss with employees and executives their approaching retirement. Problems they are likely to encounter in readjusting, possible plans they may make, and financial changes that will be forced upon them are examined. Each is counseled to consider the new way of life he and his family will soon be facing. And help may be given to plan for new hobbies, to investigate possible activities, and to prepare for changes gradually.

In the actual retirement stage, it has been found desirable to establish a formal program of leavetaking. Such affairs as banquets, with their gifts and speeches, at which are gathered associates and executives, show the appreciation of fellow workers and the company. Making the rounds of one's associates, particularly when accompanied by a high executive, adds to the prestige of an individual and one's pride in the significance attached to this tradition by the company. And a careful explanation of the formal plans and services to which the pensioner is now entitled should also be made at this time.

In the postretirement stage, various activities may be undertaken which serve not only to tie in the pensioner with the company but also to build good will throughout the organization. Literature such as house organs, letters, and periodicals should be sent to pensioners. Participation in social and recreational clubs should be encouraged. Use of company facilities, advisory services, and medical aids should be extended. And the right to visit the plant or office may well be granted. Indeed, in this latter respect, some companies have found it very useful to continue key employees or executives as consultants on a part-time, extra-fee basis. A few have provided special areas where pensioners may continue to work part time or which they may use for their private hobbies.

ORGANIZATION FOR SERVICE PLANS

In most companies the various services plans are operated under the jurisdiction of the personnel department. Within this department a section is established to inaugurate and direct the service plans. This section is often called the employee service department, but it is also known by such names as the welfare department, the recreation and athletic department, the insurance department, and the benefits department.

In performing its duties, this unit may rely upon the assistance of others. Thus, in the establishment of pension plans, for example, the service department would call upon the legal, financial, and statistical departments for advice on technical aspects of pensions. And in the operation of the recreational plan, for example, it would rely in most companies upon the help and cooperation of formal committees or organizations of employees.

Example of Service Organization

To illustrate how the company organization ties in with employee organization, it is well to describe the plans in use by a few companies. Of interest, to begin with, is the plan used by a company employing 10,000 workers in a large city location.

In this case a recreation club, operated by the employees, serves as a nucleus for all social and athletic events within the company. All employees may join, the dues being 25 cents a month. The management of the club is in the hands of officers who are elected by the members. Activities include baseball, bowling, golf, skeet shooting, model auto racing, roller skating, dances, and other social affairs. Annual Halloween and New Year's parties are sponsored. The annual Christmas party is an outstanding event, being given for the children of employees.

The officers are advised and assisted by an activities director, who is on the staff of the personnel division. The director also plans and operates special entertainment and activities for the company. Noonhour entertainment is an example of such activities. The activities director also has charge of the distribution of tickets for special events held outside the company, such as operas, sports events, and circus performances. Thus, much of the work done here is by the company, but the employees are made to feel that they are running the show.

Organizational Plan under Decentralized Operations

In another case an employees' club has been established at each of the several plants operated by the company. The general plan of organization is the same at all of these, but the program and activities of each plant are determined by the people located in them. Each of the clubs is made up of departmental groups averaging from about 50 to 100 members, thus providing a well-knit working unit. The supervisor of the department is a member, but without the privilege of voting or holding office.

In each department, employees elect their own president, vice president, secretary-treasurer, social director, athletics director, and welfare director. It is noteworthy that the greatest interest is in the social activities—dances, parties, picnics, and the functions of hobby and special interest groups. The athletics committee plans activities the employees desire most—archery, table tennis, basketball, softball, golf, swimming, or whatever. Bowling, by the way, has proved the most popular sports activity. Among the activities the welfare committee carries on are building a fund to buy flowers for hospital patients, distributing Christmas baskets, and organizing first-aid or home-nursing classes.

The departmental presidents are then organized into the executive council, and the departmental chairpeople into councils for the plant.

Thus the social directors form the social council, and so on. Each council elects its own officers and meets once a month.

Dues vary from 10 to 50 cents a month, as the members of each department determine. The funds go into the department treasury. In addition, a central club fund, administered by the club's executive council, is built up from vending-machine profits, admission to central club dances, cafeteria profits, and other plantwide social or athletic events, as well as company contributions. Most club affairs are therefore self-supporting. Any employee, however, whether or not a member of the club, may attend any of the central parties or dances.

At most of the plants the employee club has a clubhouse or rooms—one has an auditorium, a kitchen, a game room, a reading room, and one or two meeting rooms. The company provides and owns this property and buys all permanent facilities. The funds of the club are used only for current expenditures.

These clubs, like those in most companies, are not incorporated. Hence, to insure officers against the unlimited liability which may accrue from such organizations, the company has arranged to protect the officers from damage suits by means of a rider on the company's public liability insurance policy.

Company Experts

Another case of organization is illustrated by an employees' club in which the company supplies expert advice and guidance. A member of the staff of the industrial relations department, who is known as the activities director, helps organize and counsels the employee organizations which are a part of the employees' activities association. This is a nonprofit association, organized and supported by the employees. Membership begins automatically for every employee at the time of employment. No dues are paid, the organization's activities being financed by the profits from vending machines.

A board of directors governs the association. It is composed of one representative from each club or activity represented in the association; the activities director, who is an ex officio member; and one other appointed by the president of the company. The latter appointee is an accountant who keeps the books and serves as treasurer of the association.

Whenever at least 50 employees participate in an activity, a petition may be made to the board of directors for representation in the association. Among the activities represented are a band, baseball, basketball, bowling, boxing, a camera club, chess and checkers, fishing, riding, golf, a gun club, horseshoes, a mixed chorus, and tennis. The company provides and maintains an athletic field with night lighting, where baseball and softball games are played. It also provides a darkroom for the camera club and facilities for the gun club and the casting club. It also pays the salaries of the activities director and secretary, and allows for time spent by the other company representatives on work of the employees' association. Beyond these expenditures, the employees carry the financial burden. The management feels that employee interest in recreational and social activities has a direct relationship to the extent to which employees plan, manage, and support their own activities.

The activities director also counsels the women's club, to which all women employees belong automatically and which raises money through social activities for charitable purposes; the employees' relief association, a mutual benefit association; and the employees' credit union.

RULES OF OPERATION

If such plans are to yield the fullest returns, several suggestions are in order regarding the plans and their operations. Worthy of careful consideration are the following points:

1. Primacy of Wages, Hours, and Working Conditions. In the first place, service plans will do little good if a company's wages, hours, and working conditions are not considered satisfactory by the employees. These are the foundation, without which all else is futile. Employee service plans cannot support a weak or unfair structure of wages, hours, and working conditions. Hence the first principle in establishing service plans is to review the basic values of employee relationships. Until questionable features are removed, the installation of service plans should be delayed.

2. The Factor of Need. In the second place, employee service plans should not be installed unless there is a real need for them. They should not be viewed from the moralistic angle of being good for the employees. Rather, the question must be: do the employees want the services? To establish playgrounds, athletic fields, and recreational facilities, for example, just because some executive feels that these will turn employees away from the corner saloon to the good life will almost inevitably lead to failure. Of course, a company should not install features that would lead to moral deterioration, but neither can it succeed in making employees tread the straight and narrow path.

3. Employee Support. In the third place, a service plan should not be sponsored unless the employees are willing to support it with their time, effort, and (sometimes) money. To give employees facilities is dangerous to long-run success for the simple reason that those things that are easily obtained are seldom appreciated. But when employees help to build facilities, such as softball diamonds or vegetable gardens; to manage activities, such as dances or parties; or to finance activities through monthly dues, for example, their attitude changes from that of an outsider to one of personal ownership. Hence, it is invariably wise to provide for employee participation—whether by contributions of time, effort, or money should be determined by the particular circumstances.

4. Stimulating Employee Interest. In the fourth place, the company need not wait for employees to need particular service plans or to display willingness to participate in them. Steps can be taken to suggest, directly or indirectly, the desirability of various plans. One company, for example, has contended that all its plans have been established at the request of its employees. However, it has not been averse to dropping hints where they will do the most good. In one case the company was "surprised" by the request of employees for financial aid in building low-cost housing; but its surprise was only superficial, because company executives had hinted months before to a few key employees that low-cost housing would be a desirable thing for many employees. The idea was subsequently presented at a meeting of the employees' club and soon snowballed into a company-aided program. Such steps must of course be taken with caution, lest any sign of company interference undermine the employees' feeling of possession.

5. Overall Coverage. In the fifth place, service plans should be developed so that all employees have some service or facility in which they have an interest. Not all employees want to participate in or watch softball games, bowling, or fishing, for example. However, if opportunities are provided in a variety of fields, most employees will find some service plan that will interest them. Unless breadth of offerings is sought, the result will be that only a few employees will participate. The service plans in that case are useful only to a restricted part of the payroll. For example, varsity athletic projects have that shortcoming. These should be strengthened by encouraging employees to be spectators at contests or by providing intramural sports that will permit mass participation.

6. "Soft-Pedaling" Expenditures. In the sixth place, it is desirable to operate plans with a minimum of financial fanfare. Otherwise, there is real danger that employees will tend to wonder whether or not the plans are being financed at the expense of lower wages. If employees begin to ask such questions, it is usually certain that trouble is bound to follow. Although costs of such programs are invariably low, they may seem high to employees who note elaborate recreational and sports equipment. Moreover, expenditures for these affairs tend to become a subject of collective bargaining, with consequent loss of control over them by management. Hence, it is well to build facilities conservatively, to indoctrinate employees regarding their low cost, and to encourage employee participation in their management and financing. Under these conditions the facilities will be accepted rather than suspected.

7. Relating Company and Personal Objectives. And finally, service plans should be organized and operated so that employees become a more integral part of the company because of them. In other words, the bowling league should not only result in recreation and exercise but should also build company esprit de corps. Any activity or event should be designed so there is a linkage with company objectives. This is not easy; but unless it is accomplished to some degree, the employee service plans will represent an unconnected appendage that serves no useful organizational purpose. And wholesome and enjoyable though some activities may be, if they are not related to company objectives, they have no reason for taking up company time, resources, or energy.

It is worth repeating in this respect that unions are increasingly interesting themselves in social and athletic programs. They are conducting parties and dances, organizing athletic teams, and operating recreational activities. Whether or not this trend will continue to an extent which will ultimately see unions assuming a predominant role is as yet uncertain. But if it does, management will have lost an opportunity of substantial proportions to build employee relatedness and loyalty.

QUESTIONS

1. What are the major purposes of recreational, social, and athletic programs supported by business?
2. What policies should a company pursue regarding alcoholic beverages at parties of employees administered in a company program?
3. To what extent, if any, should supervisors and executives participate in company-sponsored athletic programs such as bowling and softball?
4. How, and how often, should company periodicals be issued?
5. What should be the place of employee grievances in a company suggestion plan?
6. Why is a preretirement phase important in designing a retirement program for employees?
7. Is socialized medicine and paternalism at the base of medical, dental, and hospital programs underwritten by a company?
8. What are the merits of turning over to employees all recreational and social affairs but making available the services of a trained company counselor?
9. What is the relation between wage administration and employee service programs?
10. How should a company go about determining how many service programs to provide or sponsor for employees?

CASE 21-1. THE BOWLING TEAM

About three years ago, the general manager of a metropolitan delivery company thought it would be a good idea to form a bowling team. The manager reasoned that the drivers were usually out on their separate runs and that a bowling team would help to bring them together as well as develop more company loyalty. Some drivers had on occasion voiced a desire for a company activity of this type. So a bowling setup was organized. In addition to forming company groups, the company put up the money for shirts, entry fees, and half the cost of bowling in a regular league.

Bowling grew into a success in a very short time. Others besides the drivers wanted to get into the act. And soon groups were formed on a company, inter-departmental basis. The company provided only minimum financial help in these offshoots.

But about a year ago, the number of bowlers began to shrink. Soon the informal groups dwindled to zero. The league team continued, but its membership was restricted to a select few.

After noting the decline in interest, the general manager decided to do some casual and private checking. The manager found, for one, that a small clique of five employees constituted the league bowling team. They associated with each other almost exclusively. Their contact with other employees was minimal and they discouraged anyone who wanted to get into the league team. This togetherness was beginning to cause friction around the company. The older employees just kept away from the "bowlers," and those who tried to get into the clique were soon told they were not wanted.

On becoming acquainted with these developments in the athletic program, the general manager is wondering whether to continue supporting it or to disassociate the company from all its phases entirely.

Question

1. What would you do if the decision is negative, and what if positive?

CASE 21-2. A SUGGESTION PLAN

Art Arthur was pleased to accept a position of management trainee with the Nonsuch Retail Company because of the opportunities for advancement. In the period of three months he had been given a number of tasks in three of its chain outlets. Being of an observing turn, he had noticed that lack of information about job openings was a common complaint of many people in the organization.

Even though he was a relative newcomer, Art decided to write a report suggesting a plan for informing employees about, first, job openings, second, requirements of job openings, and third, steps to be taken to become candidates for openings. He submitted it to his training supervisor who praised the plan and who then sent it on to the regional vice president of store operations.

That was the last Art heard of the plan until a routine notice came out in the company news periodical to the effect that a number of improvements were to be made in plans for filling job vacancies. Art looked in vain for any mention of his name or for any other communication about what he thought was his plan.

Question

1. How well is the suggestion plan of this company working?

PHYSICAL SECURITY 22

Introduction

Of significance to both employer and employee is the sense of physical security which surrounds the employee. Working conditions, health, and safety are particularly important in this connection and therefore constitute the major areas of study in this chapter. To these subjects, various fields such as medicine, engineering, psychology, and management have devoted considerable attention. Space here, however, permits only a review of various pertinent practices and principles contributed by these fields to better working conditions, improved health, and increased safety. Before taking up specific aspects of these subjects, it is worth noting (1) the objectives of improved physical security and (2) legal aspects of compensation for employee accidents and health.

Objectives

Numerous objectives may be attained by proper attention to working conditions, health, and safety. From the viewpoint of the individual, the value of these efforts can hardly be overestimated. For example, looked at, first of all, from the side of losses, how can anyone estimate the value of lives lost in industrial accidents? Or how can the loss to the individuals maimed in such accidents be estimated? Of course, insurance benefits may provide some financial relief to these individuals or their beneficiaries, but the personal sufferings and losses are inestimable.

And viewed positively, healthy and safe workers gain personal satisfactions which alone make the effort to improve health, safety, and working conditions worthwhile. A more cooperative spirit, better quality work, better use of materials and equipment, and better discipline are reflected in such workers. Their relationships with their coworkers and superiors are more agreeable. And of course, what happens to the individual—either negatively or positively—is of interest also to the worker's family, relatives, friends, and the community.

To the company the objectives are many and significant. As an example, a quarter of a million working days, and the production thereof, are lost annually by fatal and disabling industrial accidents, according to estimates of the Bureau of Labor Statistics. And there are the corollary losses of idle machinery, working capital, and space; of extra efforts to rearrange schedules and working crews; and of delayed shipments. In the face of these facts, it is apparent why industry places a high priority on meeting the challenge of safer and healthier working conditions.

1. Statutory Enactments. Despite these obvious advantages, industry did not concern itself with the physical well-being of workers until the passage of industrial compensation laws by the various states beginning around the beginning of the Twentieth Century. Industry paid little attention to these matters because their burden and financial costs fell largely upon the worker, family, or the community under earlier common law rulings. But after statutory legislation was enacted, compensatory obligations for accidents and illnesses arising from occupational hazards fell upon industry.

The fundamental advantage of state workmen's compensation laws is that, irrespective of what or who causes an accident, except in instances of outrageous disregard of safety rules, the employee is compensated for financial losses incurred. Compensation is paid in a variety of ways. In the case of death, lump sums or weekly allotments may be paid to dependents. In the event of total or partial disability, the individual may be paid a lump sum and also provided with periodic subsistence payments. And in the event of accidents or illnesses which result in temporary losses of earning power, weekly allotments of varying amounts are provided.

2. Financial Arrangements under Statutory Law. The funds for such compensation are obtained by charges against the employer. This is done through payments of premiums to private insurance systems, to state-operated systems, or through self-accumulated funds. Administrative machinery is provided by which the amount of liability can readily be determined, though in all cases recourse may be had to the judicial branch in the event of disagreement with administrative rulings.

The charges against employers will tend to vary with the number and severity of compensable accidents and illness. Hence, it is to the interest of management to reduce them to the lowest possible number. Such efforts cost money, to be sure, but accident-reduction programs are nevertheless followed because industry has found that they are financially less costly than compensation for accidents.

3. Merit Rating. Further incentive to reduce accidents and hazards is provided by the practice of adjusting insurance premiums in accordance with merit ratings of health and safety practices and results. The most common way of doing this is to adjust an employer's insurance rate in accordance with the company's accident record. This is known as experience merit rating. Another plan—that of schedule merit rating—adjusts rates according to the degree of risk which is present on an employer's premises. Obviously, a factory or office which maintains and safeguards its equipment is likely to have fewer accidents than one in which the reverse is true.

WORKING CONDITIONS

General Considerations

In most companies, attention to safety emphasizes good working conditions. Concern is directed, therefore, to technical tools of production. Machines and equipment used directly in production are designed with a view to the comfort and effective employment of the skills of the operator. For example, levers by which operators make adjustments to the machines are placed with a view to the anatomical features of the human body and not to mechanical demands alone.

The actual design and maintenance of working conditions is largely the work of the engineering and plant maintenance departments. But there are personnel aspects to such work. Personnel has a stake in such matters because of their effect upon the loyalty and attitude of employees. This department should therefore have an advisory relation to the departments that may plan for and maintain physical conditions. In the second place, unions often make an issue of physical conditions. Hence the personnel department should be attentive to such matters, so that disputes or frictions do not arise. And third, the personnel department should keep abreast of new developments in order to be able to advise management on steps that might be taken so that desirable improvements will not be overlooked.

Phases of Working Conditions

This is not to imply that the personnel department must have technicians on its staff. Rather, it should be acquainted with technical working conditions merely to the extent that any shortcomings may be detected, corrections requested, and improvements suggested. In the following, attention is therefore directed to some specific phases of working conditions.

1. Material Handling. Material handling is the source of the greatest number of injuries in industry. Hence the flow of materials in all of its phases should be carefully planned. First, handling of materials and parts at machines and benches should be studied, to the end that physical handling is reduced to a minimum and adequate protective devices are provided. Second, the flow of work between machines and departments

A Safety and Process Chart

From PROCESS 5

Welding Trunion to Bucket — Roller Conveyor

HAZARDS: Eye Injuries, Burns, Fumes
PRECAUTIONS: Shields, Protective Clothing (gloves, goggles, etc.), Ventilation

From Stores (welding rod, etc.)

From PROCESS 8

PROCESS 9 — HAND METHOD: Machining Boil — Skid Material Box, Drill, Ream, Etc. — Fork Lift Truck
HAZARDS: Hand Injuries
PRECAUTIONS: Brushes for Oiling and Cleaning Operations

From PROCESS 7

PROCESS 11 — HAND METHOD: Press Locking Fixture — Skid Material Box, Hand Skid Truck
HAZARDS: Hand Injuries
PRECAUTIONS: Guard Machine, Point of Operator, Automatic Feed to Press Operator

From Stores (hardware, paint, etc.)

PROCESS 12 — HAND METHOD: Assembly Boil on Trunions, Locking Fixtures, Etc. — Overhead Traveling Carrier with Swivel Hooks
HAZARDS: Injuries from Handling Tools, Electric Shock from Portable Power Tools, Dropping Material
PRECAUTIONS: Ground Electrical Tools, Safety Shoes

PROCESS 13 — HAND METHOD: Painting, Drying, Inspection — Overhead Traveling Carrier through Drying Ovens
HAZARDS: Vapor and Spray Inhalation, Eye Injuries, Dermatitis
PRECAUTIONS: Ventilated Booth, Respirators, Goggles, Hood, Hand Protectors

---

PROCESS 14 — HAND METHOD: Shipping Finished Product — Fork Lift Truck from Dryer to Storage to R.R. Car
HAZARDS: Dropping Material
PRECAUTIONS: Use Special Carrier Adapted to Fork Lift Truck

To R.R.

PROCESS 15 — HAND METHOD: Storage Finished Product — Same as Process 14
HAZARDS: Same as Process 14
PRECAUTIONS: Same as Process 14

To R.R.

Source: George Koller, "The Challenge of Post-War Safety," *Personnel*, vol. 22, no. 6, p. 65.

should be facilitated by proper equipment, and should be provided with well-designed and well-marked storage spaces and aisles and roadways. An interesting example of how a study of hazards can be tied in with the design of flow of work is illustrated in Figure 22–1.

2. Machine Guarding. Protection of the worker by the strategic placement of mechanical guards (as shown in Figure 22–2) and electronic controls is another essential of good working conditions. Various devices can be provided to protect workers (a) from the many parts of all equipment that transmit power and (b) from the hazards at the point of work (see Figure 22–3). The dangers arising from the mechanical devices that surround the worker as well as the hazards arising from adjusting, inserting, and manipulating materials and tools should be considered here.

3. Factors of the Work Place. The comfort and efficiency of workers is also affected importantly by the physical factors at the work place. For example, the influence of chairs is not small. In one company, chairs in the factory have been designed that are adjustable to differing sizes of individuals. The chair seats can be moved up and down, the backs both up and down and in and out, and the footrests up and down. Moreover, the chairs have foam-rubber seats and backs. In another company the installation of chairs that can be easily moved on operations that require considerable stretching and movement has increased production 25 percent and decreased fatigue noticeably.

Other aspects of the work place that deserve mention are the safety devices and clothing that should be worn. Consideration should be given to personal comfort and tastes in these matters or cooperation in their adoption and use will be difficult to secure.

4. Disaster Controls. Hazard and disaster controls are also essentials of good working conditions. A well-designed system for detecting, inhibiting, and fighting fires is absolutely essential. In cases where explosions are possible, a program of control should include periodic inspections, isolation from other operations, and devices for reducing igniting factors.

5. Radiation. The nuclear age has brought to industry a new challenge to safety. The consequences of radioactivity are so severe that extreme measures must be adopted to protect employees from exposure. This involves such practices as appropriate buildings, warning devices, protective clothing, handling devices, and safety education. As the trend of nuclear energy accelerates, the needs in this area will become increasingly imperative.

6. Internal Environmental Conditions. Environmental factors are important in good working conditions. Attention needs to be devoted to light, temperature, and atmospheric conditions. Provision should be made for good illumination, comfortable temperatures, and control of dusts, fumes, and gases. And employees should be provided with protective devices, clothing, goggles, and shields in case of unusual conditions (see Figure 22–4).

FIGURE 22-2

Guarding Punch Presses by Automatic Push-Away or Pull-Away Guards

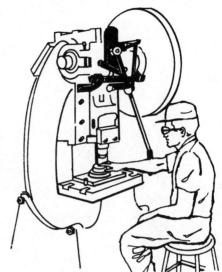

Push-away guard. Sweep guard pushes operator's hand away from the danger zone before ram descends. Double sweep arms are preferable and barrier guards on the sides of the die are desirable to prevent the operator reaching around it.

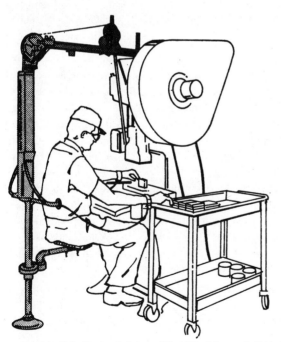

Pull-away guard. Operator's hands are pulled away from danger zone before ram descends.

Source: U.S. Dept. of Labor, "The Principles and Techniques of Machine Guarding," August, 1973, p. 48.

FIGURE 22–3

Protection for Heavy Equipment

Courtesy: The Anaconda Company

Noise control is also of significance in promoting employee comfort and efficiency. In factories, it is possible to segregate noisy equipment, to dampen vibration, and to redesign particularly noisy equipment. In offices, much can be done to soundproof walls, ceilings, machines, and equipment. In very unusual situations, employees may be provided with ear coverings. In one case, the ear protectors were designed to receive radio musical programs.

Since excessive noise can also lead to hearing injuries, which may be compensable under industrial compensation laws, noise measurement surveys are suggested if there is any question about noisy conditions. The threshold of painful noise begins around 110 decibels, the unit used to measure sound. An idea of sound and noise intensities may be gained from the following list of sound conditions:

Type of Sound	Decibels
Rustle of leaves	20
Average office	30
Stenographic room	60
Average conversation	60
Average machine shop	70
Newspaper pressroom	90
Subway train	110
Boiler factory	110

FIGURE 22–4

The Value of Safety Glasses

Courtesy: The Anaconda Company

7. Color. Proper use of color may also have a constructive influence on safety and efficiency. Improvements are noticeable after equipment is painted to conform with safety recommendations instead of a uniform gray. Suggested colors are as follows: yellow or orange for dangerous materials or parts of equipment; green, white, gray, or black for safe materials or machinery parts; blue for protective materials; and red for fire protection materials and equipment.

8. Personal Needs. Good working conditions also call for adequate provision of conveniences of a personal nature. Good drinking water, properly cooled and made available through well-located dispensers, should be supplied. Adequate toilet facilities that are well located, lighted, and ventilated, and carefully cleaned and disinfected, should be provided. Facilities such as shower rooms are also indispensable when working conditions may lead to skin diseases or contamination.

9. External Conditions. The outside of the factory should also be given attention in the matter of employee comfort and attitudes. First, the general appearance and landscaping cast an impression upon employees for good or for bad. Second, strategic arrangement and pleasing appearance of approaches, streets, sidewalks, gates, and entrances can be a part of good working conditions. And third, arrangements for parking of automobiles and areas for waiting for transportation—private or public—can put employees into the right (or wrong) attitude toward their working day.

Although not directly an internal employee matter, growing too is industry's responsibility for external pollution. Air pollution, contamination of water resources, and waste disposal are by voluntary as well as mandatory means receiving attention. Directly the community is thereby affected, and indirectly the employee who then has a more favorable attitude toward employers accepting their community responsibilities.

HEALTH

Pertinent Factors

The health of employees may be influenced by a number of factors. Off-plant living conditions and habits, medical services, environmental conditions, and past personal history are of vital significance. These phases are seldom considered within the domain of management influence and so are not treated here.

Health is also significantly influenced by working conditions and safety practices. This is discussed in other sections of this chapter, so no detailed mention of these phases need to be made here. Of interest here are two commonly encountered health programs: (1) medical examinations and (2) various health services. Discussed in this section, too, is the matter of organizing medical services.

Medical Examinations

Most companies give due recognition to provision for and performance of adequate medical examinations. This may be seen by reviewing (1) coverage of examinations, (2) facilities for examinations, and (3) medical and health records.

1. Coverage of Examinations. A useful survey of the subject may be made by noting who may be examined, when, and how.

A list of those who may be examined would include the following:

a. Applicants for employment or reemployment.
b. Employees who return from extended leaves of absence.
c. Employees who are returning from sick leave.
d. Employees who have been absent, excused or not excused, for a specified number of days, usually 6 to 12 days.
e. Employees engaged in occupations with exposure to disease or illness.
f. Employees whose work might endanger the life or health of customers or fellow workers.
g. All employees, periodically or as new developments in medicine warrant.

The periodicity and frequency of examinations may also vary. A list of the variations follows:

a. An examination of employees only when they enter the employment of the company.
b. Nonperiodic examinations for those returning from sick leave, etc.
c. Periodic examinations: (1) Voluntarily assumed by the company for all employees or those engaged in hazardous or health-affecting occupations; (2) Required by law for those engaged in occupations affecting the health or security of customers or patrons.

A list of types of examinations which may be given follows:

a. Medical examinations of general physical condition.
b. Examinations of communicable disease—e.g., venereal or tuberculosis
c. Visual and dental examinations.
d. Psychiatric examinations.
e. Visits to the homes of employees.

Of course, few companies include all of the foregoing in their examination programs for the reasons that (1) opinions differ as to how far a company should delve into a person's physical and mental makeup, and (2) facilities and staff are not always available or are beyond the resources of some companies, particularly the smaller plants, and (3) opposition from medical and dental associations.

There is a strong tendency, however, toward expansion of such programs. To cite but one example, there is a growing interest in the benefits of psychoanalysis and psychiatry. Various companies have moved slowly and with satisfactory results in this direction. The aim here is not so much to eliminate the obviously unbalanced but rather to help employees and executives who have minor troubles to minimize blocks and obstacles to more effective and satisfying living. This approach has also been useful in dealing with problem drinkers, of whom it is estimated there are about three percent among the employee and executive ranks.

2. Facilities for Examinations. Most companies provide excellent facilities for physical examinations relative to their size and needs. Usually, facilities are provided adjacent to the personnel department office, since most examinations are given in connection with various personnel procedures—e.g., new employees, transfers, employees returning from sick leave, or those absent without permission who are returning to their jobs. This location is also desirable because it gives applicants an opportunity to get a favorable impression of the company. Moreover, it is sufficiently removed from busy traffic to make its location favorable for medical work.

Next to the medical and professional staff, equipment is invariably the most important part of the medical department. What it should contain depends upon the examinations to be given, the hazards that exist in the company, the policy of the company, and the number of workers to be served. Usually, facilities are provided for minor injury cases, chest X-ray pictures, venereal disease tests, and urinalysis, as well as cursory eye, ear, nose, and dental examinations. Some of the larger companies also have completely equipped operating rooms and hospital units. A few have eye and dental dispensaries.

3. Medical and Health Records. All medical, health, and accident procedures should be properly implemented with adequate records and reports. Since vital decisions are based on them, it is doubly essential to gather and report information so that those who use them will be able to interpret them properly. The records which may be kept are so varied that no more can be done here than to list the major categories:

a. Medical examinations.
b. Dispensary cases handled.
c. Reports of accident occurrence.
d. Investigations and surveys of working conditions.
e. Trends of accidents, occupational illness, and first-aid cases.

Health Services

In addition to examining candidates and employees, health services may be expanded to include (1) surveys of plant conditions and (2) off-plant medical care.

1. Plant Surveys. Plant surveys are essential in order to maintain healthful working conditions. They serve to reveal sources of occupational disease, unsafe working conditions, and conditions conducive to the development of fatigue. The surveys should be made periodically or upon special occasions. They should be conducted by skilled technicians operating out of the medical department of the personnel division, since this will insure freedom from interference by or condonation of undesirable conditions by line executives. In addition, the skills of properly trained technicians and professional talent will be brought into play in this important work.

In order to appreciate the types of surveys and checks, some of the more common types will be noted. An important phase of such surveys is that of checking operations that tend toward occupational disease or illness. Examples are making dust counts in core rooms and checking the percentage of carbon monoxide in the air of certain baking rooms.

As important, but less obvious to the observer, are factors leading to the development of excessive fatigue. Surveys of noise, vibration, and material movements may be related to output, scrap, absenteeism, illness, and accidents. Such studies may serve to determine if these factors are present to an undesirable degree.

2. Extension of Health Services. In some companies the health and medical services, originally provided only to serve the internal needs of the company, are now being extended to the families of employees. Such extensions are not to be confused with health and medical service insurance, described in an earlier chapter, which provide for financial assistance to those who require such services from their own doctors. Medical facilities have been made available to employees and their families usually in cases where community facilities are inadequate or where company officials take the view that employees must be given such opportunities or they will not seek medical services, even when financially able, until too late.

The expansion of health services usually takes place by providing visiting-nurse service to employees away from work because of illness. After this, provisions are made for giving free physical examinations to all who desire them. Also, the services of company doctors or hospital facilities are made available in the case of emergency operations due to causes outside the employment contract. From these extensions, it is a simple step to provide free examinations and at-cost, or even free, service in connection with the prevention or cure of visual, aural, and dental problems, as well as general physical ailments.

Some health services are of an educational nature. For example, first-aid courses have been sponsored by many companies. Their effects have external as well as internal value, for the records are replete with cases in which lives have been saved and serious pain and losses prevented by those who had completed Red Cross first-aid courses. Home-nursing courses are another example of training along these lines sponsored by some companies. Company sponsorship has also extended to allied subjects, such as nutrition. Instruction material in this field includes the theory of good nutrition as well as practical applications, such as suggested menus.

Organization for Medical Services

In most large companies, the medical department is made a part of the personnel division. Its work is closely related to the personnel functions of hiring as well as safety. Some companies believe, however, that the relation between physician and employee is so private that the physicians should report to no one but the chief executive of the company.

However, it is essential for the personnel director to have the utmost confidence in and respect for the opinions of the medical unit. For this condition to prevail, the medical staff should be selected and trained so that it understands the relationships involved in industrial medicine. It is necessary to define, therefore, the relations of the medical staff to the following groups:

1. To employees, with whom they should deal strictly in terms of matters arising out of the employment and industrial situations. If it is the policy of the company to offer services and aid beyond this, the doctor, the employee, and executives should be informed of the exact nature and extent of available services.
2. To community physicians and local health agencies, whose availability to workers should be respected and whose cooperation in attacking health problems should be sought, since outside factors are often as significant to physical well-being of workers as plant conditions. Local and state health departments, such agencies as the Red Cross, and medical doctors are as much in the fight for good health as company staff members.
3. To management, through whom the medical staff must frequently work to gain the cooperation necessary to "sell" health and accident programs, and whose proficiency can be increased in reducing hazards to health and safety.

Organization of medical services varies in smaller companies. Some rely solely upon community physicians and hospitals. Some may have a nurse on duty. Some have a doctor on duty part time. And some have worked out intercompany cooperation. One such plan provides for the establishment of a central clinic for three companies having a total of 800 employees. At the central clinic a doctor spends three hours a day, and a nurse five. The nurse spends an hour a day at each of the three plants. In another plan operated by eight companies having a total of 4,000 employees, a full-time nurse is employed in each plant, while a full-time doctor visits each plant each day.

SAFETY

Importance and Scope

In no other phase of physical security has management exerted greater effort than that of accident prevention. In part this is due, as noted earlier, to the passage of state industrial compensation laws which make the employer financially responsible for accident losses to his employees. It is cheaper, therefore, to pay for safety programs than for accident losses. And in part this is due to the strict safety rules established in the administration of the federal Occupational Safety and Health Act (OSHA) of 1970. Failure to meet and abide by these rules can bring very heavy penalties.

Although great progress has been made, there is room for improvement in accident prevention. For example, data on accident frequency rates and accident severity rates shown in Figure 22–5 (on page 396) are not commendable in some industries. Although the frequency rate was as low as 4.45 in the steel industry, it was 35.44 and 27.51 in the coal-mining and meat-packing industries, respectively, in 1974. Mining also shows up poorly in the accident severity column.

These trends, though improving, are evidence why safety activities are strongly supported by industry. To appreciate better the nature of such activities, the following phases are here studied:

1. Measures of accidents.
2. Human aspects.
3. Organizational aspects.

Measures of Accidents

As already noted in the foregoing sections, accidents and safety may be measured in indirect and direct terms. Indirect measures include such information as the effect upon various aspects of production as a result of accidents and illness. For example, data on losses to production, lowered quality of output, and increases in costs of absenteeism and turnover are commonly collected and reported.

The more direct measures are the frequency and severity rates of accidents. The frequency rate is determined by multiplying the number of lost-time accidents during any selected period by one million and dividing the result by the total number of work-hours worked during the same period. The severity rate is computed by multiplying the number of days lost because of accidents during any selected period by one million and dividing the result by the total number of work-hours worked during the same period. The charting of such rates is shown in Figure 22–6. Although it is contended by some that these formulas are arbitrarily established

FIGURE 22–5

Injury Rates, Reported to National Safety Council

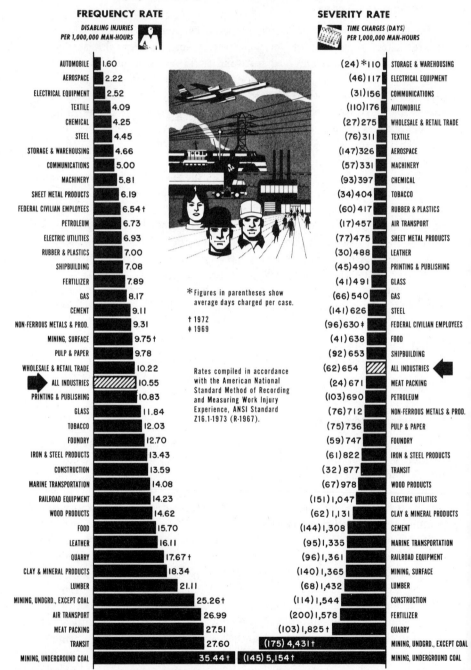

FREQUENCY RATE

DISABLING INJURIES
PER 1,000,000 MAN-HOURS

AUTOMOBILE	1.60
AEROSPACE	2.22
ELECTRICAL EQUIPMENT	2.52
TEXTILE	4.09
CHEMICAL	4.25
STEEL	4.45
STORAGE & WAREHOUSING	4.66
COMMUNICATIONS	5.00
MACHINERY	5.81
SHEET METAL PRODUCTS	6.19
FEDERAL CIVILIAN EMPLOYEES	6.54†
PETROLEUM	6.73
ELECTRIC UTILITIES	6.93
RUBBER & PLASTICS	7.00
SHIPBUILDING	7.08
FERTILIZER	7.89
GAS	8.17
CEMENT	9.11
NON-FERROUS METALS & PROD.	9.31
MINING, SURFACE	9.75†
PULP & PAPER	9.78
WHOLESALE & RETAIL TRADE	10.22
ALL INDUSTRIES	10.55
PRINTING & PUBLISHING	10.83
GLASS	11.84
TOBACCO	12.03
FOUNDRY	12.70
IRON & STEEL PRODUCTS	13.43
CONSTRUCTION	13.59
MARINE TRANSPORTATION	14.08
RAILROAD EQUIPMENT	14.23
WOOD PRODUCTS	14.62
FOOD	15.70
LEATHER	16.11
QUARRY	17.67†
CLAY & MINERAL PRODUCTS	18.34
LUMBER	21.11
MINING, UNDGRD., EXCEPT COAL	25.26†
AIR TRANSPORT	26.99
MEAT PACKING	27.51
TRANSIT	27.60
MINING, UNDERGROUND COAL	35.44†

SEVERITY RATE

TIME CHARGES (DAYS)
PER 1,000,000 MAN-HOURS

(24) *110	STORAGE & WAREHOUSING
(46) 117	ELECTRICAL EQUIPMENT
(31) 156	COMMUNICATIONS
(110) 176	AUTOMOBILE
(27) 275	WHOLESALE & RETAIL TRADE
(76) 311	TEXTILE
(147) 326	AEROSPACE
(57) 331	MACHINERY
(93) 397	CHEMICAL
(34) 404	TOBACCO
(60) 417	RUBBER & PLASTICS
(17) 457	AIR TRANSPORT
(77) 475	SHEET METAL PRODUCTS
(30) 488	LEATHER
(45) 490	PRINTING & PUBLISHING
(41) 491	GLASS
(66) 540	GAS
(141) 626	STEEL
(96) 630‡	FEDERAL CIVILIAN EMPLOYEES
(41) 638	FOOD
(92) 653	SHIPBUILDING
(62) 654	ALL INDUSTRIES
(24) 671	MEAT PACKING
(103) 690	PETROLEUM
(76) 712	NON-FERROUS METALS & PROD.
(75) 736	PULP & PAPER
(59) 747	FOUNDRY
(61) 822	IRON & STEEL PRODUCTS
(32) 877	TRANSIT
(67) 978	WOOD PRODUCTS
(151) 1,047	ELECTRIC UTILITIES
(62) 1,131	CLAY & MINERAL PRODUCTS
(144) 1,308	CEMENT
(95) 1,335	MARINE TRANSPORTATION
(96) 1,361	RAILROAD EQUIPMENT
(140) 1,365	MINING, SURFACE
(68) 1,432	LUMBER
(114) 1,544	CONSTRUCTION
(200) 1,578	FERTILIZER
(103) 1,825†	QUARRY
(175) 4,431†	MINING, UNDGRD., EXCEPT COAL
(145) 5,154†	MINING, UNDERGROUND COAL

*Figures in parentheses show
average days charged per case.

† 1972
‡ 1969

Rates compiled in accordance
with the American National
Standard Method of Recording
and Measuring Work Injury
Experience, ANSI Standard
Z16.1-1973 (R-1967).

Source: National Safety Council, *Accident Facts—1974 Edition* (Chicago, 1974), p. 26.

FIGURE 22–6
A Chart of Accident Rates

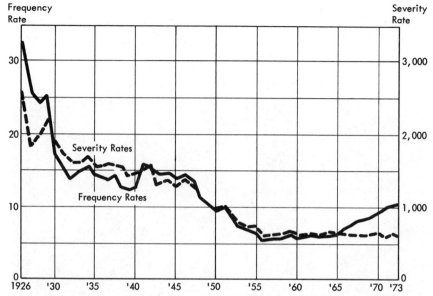

Source: National Safety Council, *Accident Facts—1974 Edition* (Chicago, 1974), p. 28.

and that they do not reflect the real pains and losses of accidents, nevertheless they have the advantages of almost universal acceptance and of comparability.

Human Aspects of Safety

Much has been done to make work mechanically safe. As noted earlier, this phase of safety is largely the province of engineering and maintenance. Hence, attention here is directed instead to the following personnel subjects which can contribute to safety:

1. Accident-prone employees.
2. Selection of employees.
3. Training.
4. Discipline.
5. Supervision.

1. Accident-Prone Employees. It is often found that a few employees in every plant have the most accidents. The term *accident-prone* has consequently been applied to an employee who, in spite of all efforts at safety education, continues to have more accidents than coworkers. What should be done about such employees depends upon the underlying factors. Perhaps discharge is the only cure in some cases, and training may help in others; whereas psychiatric analysis may be necessary in still other cases. In any event, such employees should receive special attention and perhaps care.

2. Selection. An ideal approach to reduction of accidents is by elimination of accident-prone candidates in the selection process. It is possible

FIGURE 22–7
Protective Equipment in Welding

Courtesy: The Anaconda Company

to do some good through interviews and examination of work histories. Evidence can be gathered regarding the accidents candidates have caused or have been involved in during previous employment. Moreover, a forecast of safety proneness can be estimated by the use of psychological tests relating to such factors as physical capabilities and emotional stability. In one company in which interviews, tests, and medical examinations were used along these lines, it was estimated that preventable accidents were reduced by more than one half. To the savings of accident reduction can also be added those of reduced training costs, absenteeism, and sick pay.

3. Training. High on the list of a good safety program is the function of training. This has a number of possibilities. Perhaps the best time to start safety training is when a new worker is being inducted. Through the use of carefully designed lectures, visual aids, demonstrations, and conferences, a lasting impact can be made upon employees when they are in a very receptive frame of mind.

Second, courses completely concerned with safety have been effective. Employees are lectured on or participate in conferences concerned with major causes and examples of accidents, ways and means of prevention, proper use of safety devices and clothing, the services of the medical and accident departments, and what the individual can do to build safety in work.

In the third place, employees may be taught how to use such practices as job analysis in reducing accidents. With this technique the worker learns how to observe the job with a view of determining what aspects of methods, machines, tools, or the operator have dangerous characteristics. Then the worker suggests means by which the danger can be removed or minimized. Figure 22–8 illustrates a change suggested under this program.

In the fourth place, it is often desirable to publicize accident records and safety programs. A rather common plan is to use large displays to illustrate the safety records of various departments or divisions of a company, or to draw attention to unsafe working practices and desirable safety precautions. Some companies have utilized the principle of competition through contests in which the best or worst departments are rewarded or penalized with unfavorable publicity.

4. Discipline. Another tool used in safety work is that of disciplinary action. Penalties are assessed in instances in which employees carelessly break safety rules. Layoff, loss of privileges, demotion, or outright discharge are examples of penalties.

It is good practice to state in advance what penalties will accompany various types of safety violations. For example, employees who participate in horseplay with air-pressure hoses shall be subject to immediate dismissal. Or those who fail to wear safety goggles, let us say, shall be

FIGURE 22–8

A Safety Suggestion

Job Safety Analysis
CHANGE IN PROTECTION

Department: Furnace   Date: August 2
Job: Crane Operator
Operation: Checking crane prior to operation.
Possibility: Someone working on crane or runways.

Present Protection:
1. Danger sign on main
   electrical switch.

Proposed Protection:
1. In addition to the danger
   sign, a padlock should be
   used to inactivate the
   switch. If several crafts
   from the repair crews are
   working on the crane, each
   craft must place its own
   lock on the switch.

Prepared by:_____   Checked by:_____

Source: W. S. Walker and C. J. Potter, "Worker Participation in Safety through Job Analysis." *Personnel*, vol. 31, no. 2, p. 147.

laid off for a specified number of days. And those who come to work under the influence of alcohol or who use drugs during working hours shall be sent home immediately, or in some cases discharged.

5. The Role of the Supervisor. Perhaps even more culpable than the individual who is involved in an accident are the supervisor and superiors. When management is lax in safety matters, its attitude is reflected all down the line. Indeed, workers who, through their own carelessness, have had accidents are often loudest in their criticism of supervisors for having failed to make them toe the mark on safety practices. All the work of engineers and of safety trainers is of little consequence if supervision is weak in these matters.

Obviously, the answer to this aspect of accidents is safety-conscious supervision. First, candidates for supervisory positions who show a lack of appreciation for or a poor record of accident prevention should be given special attention in safety conferences before being assigned higher positions. Second, all supervisors should be given specially designed safety courses. Third, supervisors should be encouraged to show by example, by precept, and, indeed, with occasional dramatics, their intense belief in and demand for adherence to safety rules and practices. And last, supervisors who have excellent records for safety should be rewarded appropriately and openly to prove to them that their efforts are appreciated and so that the recognition receives the benefit of public acclamation.

Safety Organization

Finally, good safety work depends upon proper organization. This means that every company should have someone or some department to whom sufficient authority is given to carry out an effective program, as illustrated in Figure 22–9. In most companies a safety unit in the personnel division is the answer. But intercompany cooperation and education calls for efforts by industrywide organization. As a consequence, various industries have established safety committees in their trade associations to investigate unsafe conditions, to suggest methods of improvement, and to develop educational materials.

Perhaps most influential among the outside agencies is the National Safety Council, organized in 1911 as a nonprofit, nonpolitical, cooperative

FIGURE 22–9

Types of Safety Organization

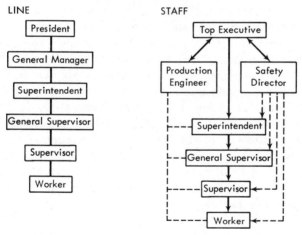

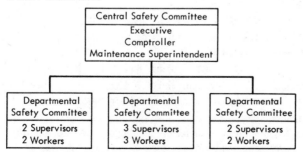

Source: Adapted from "Safety Organization," Bulletin 285, Bureau of Labor Standards, U.S. Department of Labor, p. 4.

organization. Its purpose is to reduce the number and severity of all kinds of accidents. It covers the fields of industrial safety and health, traffic and transportation, other public safety, school and child safety, and home, farm, and general safety.

The Council serves as a national and international clearinghouse to gather and distribute information about causes of accidents and ways to prevent them. Through its headquarters and regional offices and its state and local units, it carries on a continuous and unified program of accident prevention.

The Council receives safety information from its members and through the constant research of its own staff of statistical, educational, and engineering technicians. These facts and figures are tabulated and broken down to show where, when, how, and why people are injured. The information shows whether various safety measures are getting results and what needs to be done.

In regard to the particular field of industrial health and safety, the Council investigates and compares ways of making equipment and working conditions safer. It helps the plant management, the supervisor, and workers to locate hazards and guard against them, as well as to recognize and prevent occupational diseases. It outlines programs for stimulating and maintaining safety interest both on and off the job.

Safety information is disseminated in various ways. The Council prepares and distributes a wide variety of publications, pamphlets, booklets, posters, and other employer and employee educational materials. It also has worked out and supplies material on a complete accident prevention plan applicable to any industry or organization. In addition, the Council works with newspapers, radio and television stations, magazines, and motion pictures in presenting safety information.

Other outside agencies interested in safety work include such groups as the American Society of Safety Engineers, the International Association of Industrial Accident Boards and Commissioners, and individual industry and trade associations.

QUESTIONS

1. What are the objectives of safety and health programs in industry?
2. Why has statutory legislation been necessary to bring about reductions in industrial accidents?
3. How does industrial merit rating serve to reduce accidents?
4. What right does a company have to intrude on the privacy of people by prescribing a physical examination as a condition of employment?
5. Do such health services as hospital and dental services to members of an employee's immediate family go beyond the reasonable obligations of a company to its employees?

6. What safeguards should be adopted to protect the professional role of doctors in a company organization?

7. How valid and realistic are "frequency rate" and "severity rate" as measures of industrial accidents?

8. What role can training play in a safety program?

9. How would you rate the supervisor and the engineer as to their relative importance in safety work?

10. How may a company go about protecting itself from the so-called accident-prone employee?

CASE 22–1.   SAFETY

The Motor Manufacturing Company makes auto parts, which are sold to various automotive companies in and around Detroit. The company employs approximately 500 workers. It was unionized in 1940 by the UAW.

The company uses punch press and drop hammer operations in the manufacture of some of its products. There are about 50 employees in this department who operate approximately 20 machines in two shifts. Operation of these machines is extremely hazardous unless all safety rules are strictly observed. It is the responsibility of the supervisor to enforce these rules, aided in the enforcement by group leaders.

The accident rate in the operation of these machines has been very high. A check of the safety rules shows that the following procedure is to be used in the operation of the machines: The operator picks up the unformed part with the left hand, grips it with tweezers in the right hand, and places it in the machine. The machine is set in motion with the foot. After the machine completes its cycle, the operator removes the part with the tweezers and, at the same time, grasps an unformed part with the left hand. The cycle of operations is then repeated.

The operators are on incentive work and tend to disregard safety in an effort to boost their earnings. Consequently, they have developed the habit of grasping the unformed part with the left hand and placing it in the machine while they remove the formed part with the right hand.

In an effort to reduce the number of accidents, the safety engineer had the machines equipped with a sweep-motion mechanical guard. The guard brushed the operator's hand aside when the machine was set in motion.

This brought a complaint from the operators that the guard was removing their hands far enough to clear the descending die but that their hands were being hit with the guard. The complaints continued, and it was eventually agreed to discontinue the use of the guard, provided that the workers used the tweezers.

However, the rule of using the tweezers was disobeyed, and the accidents continued.

The safety engineer investigated other safety devices in an effort to reduce accidents. The investigation disclosed a device which was being used for similar machines in other plants, which automatically pulled the worker's hand away from the machine when it was set into operation.

At a safety committee meeting of the department the safety engineer explained the device and went into detail as to how it functioned. The supervisor of the department opposed the device on the ground that having seen it in operation at other plants, the supervisors there had found that employees cooperated reluctantly after such devices had been installed.

The committee, because of the supervisor's objections, voted against the use of the safety device.

Later, in a further investigation of the same device, the safety engineer conferred with a representative of the firm that manufactured the device. It was decided to experiment by installing the device on a machine. The supervisor agreed to permit the installation on a machine that was used for odd jobs. The device was installed without any notice to the workers or to the union.

Several workers tried the device, which proved to work satisfactorily, but reserved their opinions on it. Others refused even to try the machine.

At this point, the union steward saw the device and requested that it be removed at once, objecting to it for two main reasons: (1) that the device was not actually foolproof and (2) that the device would restrict the worker's actions and lower worker efficiency.

All efforts by the safety engineer to disprove these beliefs were rejected by the steward. The machine remained in the shop for several days and finally, upon the insistence of the steward, was removed.

In the light of the facts given, the problem still remains of how to cut down an excessively high accident rate. The problem is accentuated by the fact that the attempts to install various devices have been rejected by the employees, the union, or the supervisor.

Questions

1. Who is responsible for safety?
2. Why has management failed to take positive action?
3. Why do employees seem to have insufficient regard for their own safety? What is the moral?
4. What should management do in this case?

CASE 22–2   SAFETY PRACTICES

This case is concerned with safety practices for line repair workers of a utility company. When working on line poles, safety belts are to be worn. All the workers are thoroughly instructed on these practices and rules before they are sent out into the field.

The workers have tended to become careless when they are out on jobs without supervision. It is not practical to have a supervisor on every job or with every person working alone. So some of the repair workers tend to unhook the safety belts claiming that the belts become uncomfortable after a while or that they have no trouble keeping their balance on the poles.

It is the supervisor's job to visit the job sites periodically to check on work and to give technical assistance if needed. One day, while driving up to one of the jobs, the supervisor noticed a repair worker who has been with the company for two years quickly fastening the safety belt. The supervisor had orally disciplined this same person twice in the past month for the same disobedience.

While approaching the worker, the supervisor is gathering thoughts as to what to say or do. The supervisor is disturbed about the negative disciplinary action taken because it obviously has done little good. Does this mean that tougher measures should be taken? Or is some reversal into a more positive posture the better supervisory practice?

Question

1. What advice would you give the supervisor? Keep in mind the supervisor is walking toward the employee.

CHAPTER 23

AREAS OF SPECIAL PERSONNEL INTEREST

Scope

In this chapter a group of subjects of special personnel interest is considered. The subjects are discussed here because their inclusion elsewhere would have been somewhat forced; yet, to exclude them would be to overlook some significant areas. The subjects include the following:

1. Minority and disadvantaged groups.
2. Handicapped workers.
3. Older employees.
4. Women employees.
5. Technological innovations.
6. International Personnel Programs.

Minority and Disadvantaged Groups

Until the 1940s, the prevailing philosophy in American business was that employers, first, had the right to hire (or not hire) whomever they liked, and, second, had no direct obligation towards those who could not be hired. They could refuse to hire otherwise qualified people if they did not like their race, color, creed, age, or sex. They could, if they so chose, discriminate on grounds other than job qualifications. And, on the other hand, they could refuse to concern themselves with the plight of those who could not qualify for jobs because they had not had an opportunity for adequate training, education, and experience. They could, in short, claim that the disadvantaged members of ghettos, for example, were not their problem.

But changes have occurred relative to the responsibilities of business in these matters. Some changes have resulted from legislation and some because of voluntary business actions. A full discussion of these critical matters calls for more space than is available here. All that can be done here is to describe the nature of discriminatory practices, the legislation pertinent to these matters, and the efforts to attack the problems of disadvantaged groups.

1. Nature of Discrimination. Discriminatory employment practices may be defined as those practices which result in decisions regarding the employability of people on the basis of race, color, creed, age, or sex instead of skill, ability, and capacity. In the United States, blacks constitute the largest ethnic minority group. In lesser degree, and varying with localities, such other groups as Jews, Catholics, Seventh-Day Adventists, Jehovah's Witnesses, Mexican-Americans, Puerto Ricans, Indians, and immigrants from various European countries are included with this category. The charge of discrimination is usually shown by comparing the percentage of employment of a particular group with the percentage of that group in the total population. Thus, in a given community in which black workers made up about 10 percent of the working population, a majority of the companies had less than this percentage of black workers, or none at all. And of those that had black workers, none had relatively equal percentages of blacks and whites in all kinds of jobs. The blacks held the poorer and less desirable jobs, were seldom given anything above a minor supervisory position, and were the last to be hired and the first to be laid off. Discrimination has also been noted in respect to wages, seniority rights, and union membership.

Ordinarily, such evidence as the following is cited as proof of discrimination on the part of an employer:

a. The policy of hiring members of a minority group as laborers or in custodial work only, regardless of their particular skills.

b. The recruitment of a substantial number of skilled workers from a technical school with Jews and blacks, but hiring a proportionately small number of Jews and no blacks.

c. Discharge of employees who refuse to salute the American flag or to stand during the playing of the national anthem.

d. A preference for employees of a particular race to be entrusted with hiring.

e. A refusal to hire a black craftsman unless the worker obtains a permit from a labor organization which bars that worker from membership on a parity with white craftsmen.

f. Hiring under a quota system.

2. Governmental Intervention. Finding that many employers were not voluntarily practicing nondiscrimination, the federal and state governments have concerned themselves with discriminatory practices. The federal government, during World War II, by executive order forbade discrimination in public and private employment, and also ordered the administration of government-sponsored training programs to be free of discrimination. In other executive orders, it was required that contracting agencies of the government insert a clause in all defense contracts prohibiting contractors from discriminating against minorities in employment.

But the most important legislative action came in 1964 with the passage of the Civil Rights Act. This Act includes Title VII, the Equal Employment Opportunities Law, which went into effect in 1965. It prohibits employers in interstate commerce from discriminating against applicants or employees because of race, color, religion, national origin, or sex.

This title makes the following practices of an employer unlawful:

a. To fail or refuse to hire or to discharge a person, or otherwise discriminate with respect to that person's compensation, terms, conditions, or privileges of employment because of race, color, religion, national origin, or sex.

b. To limit, segregate, or classify employees in any way that would deprive a person of employment opportunities or otherwise adversely affect an employee's status because of race, color, religion, sex, or national origin.

c. To discriminate against a person because of race, color, religion, national origin, or sex in admission to or employment in any apprenticeship, training, or retraining program.

d. To print or publish an employment notice or advertisement that indicates any preference, limitation, specification, or discrimination based on race, color, religion, sex, or national origin.

e. To discriminate against a job applicant or employee because that person has opposed any unlawful practice under the Act, has made a charge of discrimination, or has testified, assisted, or participated in an investigation, proceeding, or hearing.

It is important to note that the Act makes an exception where religion, sex, or national origin are occupational qualifications reasonably necessary to the normal conduct of an employer's business.

The enforcement of the Act is entrusted to an Equal Employment Opportunity Commission. It works with state and local antidiscrimination agencies, as well as on its own initiative, to act on complaints submitted by job applicants, employees, and employers. If a complaint is not settled by conciliation, it is then taken to a federal court for appropriate consideration and action. The Attorney General of the United States may be invited to intervene in cases of general public importance.

Of the 37 states that have passed such legislation, New York's Law against Discrimination is of typical interest. Its purpose is to guarantee every applicant for employment and every employee the right of equal treatment without regard to race, creed, color, or national origin. In administering the law, the State Commission against Discrimination has promulgated the rules that it shall be unlawful:

a. For an employer to:
  (1) Discriminate in hiring, upgrading, or discharging employees because of race, creed, color, or national origin
  (2) Ask questions before hiring which directly or indirectly would disclose race, creed, color, or national origin
  (3) Print or circulate matter which directly or indirectly indicates discrimination because of race, creed, color, or origin
  (4) Discriminate against anyone who files a complaint or testifies in connection with the Law against Discrimination
b. For a union to:
  (1) Discriminate against members or applicants for membership because of race, creed, color, or national origin
  (2) Discriminate against employers on the same grounds
c. For an employment agency to:
  (1) Discriminate in registering or referring applicants
  (2) Ask questions before hiring which directly or indirectly would disclose race, creed, color, or origin
  (3) Disclose such information to employers
  (4) Print or circulate matter which directly or indirectly expresses discrimination because of race, color, creed, or origin
  (5) Discriminate against anyone who files a complaint or testifies in connection with the Law against Discrimination
d. For employees to:
  (1) Offer resistance to the hiring of anyone on grounds of race, creed, color, or national origin
e. For anyone to:
  (1) Compel, help, or incite or to attempt acts which would lead to discrimination on account of race, creed, color, or national origin

As examples of what may or may not be lawful, Figure 23–1 illustrated the care which must be used in making specific inquiries of applicants in a state where a fair employment practices law has been enacted.

3. Disadvantaged Groups. The 1960s focused particular attention on the plight of those who could not get jobs because of inadequate education and training. The seriousness of the problem is illustrated by the plight of the teenager. The unemployment rate among nonwhite teenagers is close to three times that among white teenagers. These and older disadvantaged came mainly from the ghettos. For one reason or another, they dropped out of school at an early age. They then lacked qualifications for entry into the labor market at levels which technology

FIGURE 23–1

A Guide for Questioning Applicants

Inquiries before Hiring	Lawful	Unlawful
1. Name	a. Maiden name b. Name used if previously employed under different name	Inquiry into previous name where it has been changed by court order, or otherwise
2. Address	Inquiry into place and length of current and previous addresses	Specific inquiry into foreign addresses which would indicate national origin
3. Age	a. Request proof of age in form of work permit issued by school authorities b. Require proof of age by birth certificate after being hired	Require birth certificate or baptismal record
4. Birthplace or national origin .		a. Any inquiry into place of birth b. Any inquiry into place of birth of parents, grandparents or spouse c. Any other inquiry into national origin
5. Race or color .		Any inquiry which would indicate race or color
6. Photographs ..	May be required after hiring for identification purposes	Request photograph
7. Religion·Creed		a. Any inquiry to indicate or identify religious denomination or customs b. May not be told this is a Protestant (Catholic or Jewish) organization c. Request pastor's recommendation or reference
8. Citizenship ...	a. Whether a U.S. citizen. b. If not, whether intends to become one c. If U.S. residence is legal. d. If spouse is citizen e. Require proof of citizenship after being hired	a. If native-born or naturalized b. Date citizenship received c. Proof of citizenship d. Whether parents or spouse are native-born or naturalized
9. Education	a. Inquiry into what academic, professional, or	a. Any inquiry asking specifically the nationality,

FIGURE 23–1 (*continued*)

Inquiries Before Hiring	Lawful	Unlawful
	vocational schools attended	racial, or religious affiliation of a school
	b. Inquiry into language skills, such as reading and writing of foreign languages	b. Inquiry as to what is mother tongue or how foreign language ability was acquired
10. Relatives	a. Inquiry into name, relationship, and address of person to be notified in case of accident	Any inquiry about a relative which is unlawful to ask an applicant
11. Organization ..	a. Inquiry into organization memberships, excluding any organization, the name or character of which indicates the race, creed, color, religion, or national origin of its members b. What offices are held, if any	Inquiry into all clubs and organizations where membership is held
12. Military service	a. Inquiry into service in U.S. Armed Forces. b. Rank attained c. Which branch of service. d. Require military discharge papers after being hired	a. Inquiry into military service in armed service of any other country b. Request military discharge papers
13. Work schedule	Inquire into willingness to work required work-schedule	Any inquiry into willingness to work any particular religious holiday

Note: I. Federal defense contracts: Employers having federal defense contracts are exempt only to the extent that otherwise prohibited inquiries are required by federal law for security purposes.

II. Any inquiry is forbidden which, although not specifically listed among the above, is designed to elicit information as to national origin, race, color, creed, religion, or ancestry in violation of the law.

is demanding. Unless training were provided, there would be a serious loss to the individuals themselves, to industry's labor supply, and to society which has to shoulder the support of this nonworking segment.

Tackling this problem have been a variety of governmental and private-sector efforts. The federal government has sought to help in the training and hiring of the underprivileged through related clauses under the Civil Rights Act, the Area Redevelopment Act, the Public Works Acceleration Act, the Federal Defense Education Act, the Economic

Opportunities Act, and the Manpower Development and Training Act. It also helps through such programs as the Job Corps, the Neighborhood Youth Corps, Volunteers in Service to American program, Concentrated Employment Programs, Community Action Programs, and the various work and education programs of the Department of Health, Education, and Welfare. The Department of Labor is extending its National Computerized Job Bank program to help the underprivileged to learn of job opportunities nationwide.

The private-sector area has helped in the foregoing efforts and also on its own. The National Alliance of Businessmen began in 1968 to help the hard-core unemployed get appropriate training directly in industry and business. Voluntary efforts, such as the "New York Plan," promoted by a joint labor and management committee in the construction industry, provides for classroom and on-the-job training for minority members. This is a development along the lines of the "Philadelphia Plan" promoted by the Department of Labor for the purpose of having a set percentage of minority members on federal construction projects. All such efforts have proved that training of the disadvantaged develops satisfactory employees besides the good it does for them and society.

Handicapped Workers

The handicapped worker also represents a problem that industry in general must face if charity is not to be the answer. Whether crippled, defaced, partially or totally blind, deaf, mute, or otherwise handicapped, this group contains a source of employees which many companies have found useful, and many more could. The case for handicapped people has been well presented in the suggestions of the U.S. Employment Service to its employer service representatives regarding, first, techniques in selling the employer on use of the handicapped, and second, answers to possible objections to hiring the handicapped.

In regard to selling techniques, it has been found desirable at the outset neither to use the word *handicapped* nor to mention specific handicaps by name. Rather a person's good points should be stressed. Moreover, in talking about a disability, it is better to state a specific shortcoming, such as "lame" rather than a broad term, such as "arm disabled." The person's good points should be related to the physical demands of the job to show that a specific disability has no relation to job needs. Also, by referring only suitable handicapped people for particular jobs, the potential employer will have confidence in the applicants referred. Moreover, it may be possible to suggest previous employers who were satisfied with the particular applicant.

In the matter of meeting objections to hiring the handicapped, a number of favorable answers are available. It has been found, for example, that contrary to the opinion of some, all the handicapped do not have higher accident rates on the job nor do they incur higher compensation insurance rates. Similarly, as to sick benefit and group insurance rates, evidence shows that well-selected handicapped people are absent less often than the nonhandicapped. To the claim that handicapped workers cannot be shifted around on jobs or need special attention, that depends entirely on circumstances because in individuals who are well selected and placed, this disadvantage is entirely minimal. Some claim too that other employees do not like to see handicapped people around but this is more fiction than fact with normal people. And some claim that handicapped people cannot pass the normal physical examinations of companies but this only means that the examinations very likely are not pertinent to the demands of specific jobs.

The above arguments in favor of hiring the handicapped can be summed up on the grounds that the disabled can be as efficient as nondisabled people. This is based on the assumption that they are hired for jobs for which their available capacities can meet the physical demands of the job. It has been found, for example, that blind people have been particularly effective on jobs which call for finger dexterity. In brief, the handicapped person is often a self-sufficient, effective producer, not a charity case.

The Older Employee

Older employees have often been considered a poorer investment by business than younger workers. They have been subject to earlier layoffs in some cases during depression times or subject to lower probability of being hired. Yet various experiences support the contention that the older worker is no more a problem than other groups of workers. Indeed, the record of the older worker seems to be better than that of younger groups. Whereas older employees cannot perform the heavy work that younger employees can, this is offset by the following:

1. Greater versatility, with an ability to handle a variety of jobs.
2. Greater dependability, with a better record of absenteeism.
3. Fewer accidents.
4. More stable on the job.
5. Fewer grievances and fewer occasions for disciplinary action.

Thus, older workers make up in steady work and crafting what they may lack in ability to spurt for short periods or to handle heavy jobs. Inasmuch as our population pattern shows a change toward a higher percentage of older people, the place of the older worker in industry must be given more favorable attention. It is estimated that in the seventies, two out of every five employees will be in the 45-or-older age group.

Moreover, the Age Discrimination in Employment Act (ADEA) of 1967, which went into effect in 1968, states that age legally must not be a bar to employment.

Employment of older workers should invariably be handled with thought, as should all employment matters. To begin with, a long-range program of hiring will serve to build a well-balanced force, so that a predominance of age groups of any bracket will not result. In the second place, a variety of procedures may be established for the older workers. Among these are the following:

1. Review of occupations best suited to accommodate employees of advanced years.
2. Review of occupations that lend themselves with some modification to the accommodation of employees of advanced years.
3. Training to increase and prolong the productivity of older workers within a given occupation.
4. Training for other occupations more suited to those of advanced years.
5. Adoption of a pension plan as a bridge between active employment and retirement.
6. Arranging the pay of the employee in keeping with personal productiveness and charging the balance to the pension account.

Women Employees

Women as employees deserve the attention of personnel management because of their increasing numbers, misconceptions about their adaptability in business, and legal regulations. First, as to their numerical importance, the trend has been steadily upward. At one time in the United States, women were not hired in industry or business. Now the number of women working is estimated to be around 35 million. By 1980 the number is expected to increase to 40 million. Thus, more than a third of the working force is made up of women. Obviously, the personnel aspects of such an important class deserve careful attention.

1. Economic Aspects. The trend in the economic treatment of women in business is toward equality with men, both voluntarily and by legal compulsion. More and more companies are adopting the policy of equal pay for equal work, whether they have to or not. Some companies follow only the letter of this policy by claiming that women, even on the same jobs as men, do not do equal work because they must have help in lifting parts, adjusting machines, and meeting emergencies. But on the whole, the adoption of this rule usually leads to its being followed in the full spirit, sooner or later. Moreover, with the passage in 1963 by the federal government of the Equal Pay Act, women doing the same kind of work as men must be paid the same rates.

2. Legal Aspects.[1] Legislation relating to employment of women is sometimes equalizing in effect and sometimes restrictive, as compared to that of men. Discrimination against women on the basis of sex is prohibited by the Equal Pay Act of 1963, the Civil Rights Act of 1964, and the Nondiscrimination in Employment Act of 1970. But it must be noted, as cited below, that some states have passed legislation which restricts the work or conditions under which work can be performed by women. Not every state has legislation in each of the categories, and the standards vary widely, but among the subjects regulated are the following:

1. Minimum Wages. Either by statute or by state wage boards, the base below which rates cannot fall is established for occupations or industries.
2. Equal Pay. Such regulations prohibit discrimination in pay because of sex, the principle being that the pay rate should be based on the job, and not on the sex of the worker.
3. Hours of Work. This category has reference to such aspects as maximum daily and weekly hours, days of rest, meal times, rest periods, and night work.
4. Industrial Homework. Restrictions or prohibitions are placed on work done in the home in order to safeguard minimum-wage rate regulations.
5. Miscellaneous. Here reference is to employment standards and plant facilities such as seats, weight lifting, lunchrooms, rest rooms, and toilet rooms.

But it must be noted that various movements relating to equality of treatment of women may result in removal of favorable protections. Some states have passed equalizing laws, a federal constitutional amendment is in the process of possible passage, and various groups of women are exerting pressure. Women may gain much by such equalization, but may also lose a number of protections.

Technological Innovations

Of unique interest to personnel management is the increased tempo of technological innovations in production, offices, and distribution. Machines are replacing workers and calling for changed skills of needed labor. Attention is directed here (1) to a brief description of new technology and (2) to a summary of the impact upon personnel management and labor.

In the past decade the trend toward mechanized processes has been

---

[1] It may be noted that similar types of regulations are also usually found in some states and municipalities covering the employment of minors, whether male or female.

accelerated. In particular, more and more operations are being automated. Processing of parts, material handling, assembly work, and inspection operations are being highly mechanized and made technologically self-regulating. Such machine control of machines has been made possible by "cybernetics." This is a coined term referred to electronic equipment by which mechanical processes can be automatically and continuously controlled, checked, and corrected. Carried over to the office, such equipment in the form of data-processing components makes it possible to process mechanically all types of quantitative and verbalized information. Even in such marketing areas as retailing, warehousing, and associated office work, automation and computers have made substantial inroads.

The impact upon work is startling. The machines can do routine work faster, more accurately, without tiring, and at less cost than can the human workers. As an example, office work that previously took weeks and even months can be completed in hours. But the machines do displace some workers and do call for new skills.

The matter of unemployment, to look at this first, is indeed challenging. To be sure, in the long run, the history of technological improvements shows that more jobs are created and society's standard of living is increased. But in the short run—and people must live in the "here and now"—technological unemployment causes severe losses to some. To meet this problem, a number of plans are being pursued, as follows:

1. Some companies agree not to lay off employees displaced by machines. These companies (a) rely upon natural quits, deaths, etc., to take care of the excess needs; (b) retrain employees for other jobs; and (c) expect expansion of business to utilize displaced personnel.
2. Some companies have more or less liberal severance pay plans whereby anyone displaced is given, in some cases, up to five years' pay.
3. The manpower retraining program of the federal government has compensation and training provisions for those who lose their jobs because of technological change.
4. Unions have bargained for financial and training benefits for displaced personnel, as well as for shortened hours, as a means of spreading available work over as many people as possible.

On the positive side, technological change will place more burdens upon personnel management. To begin with, the skills of the work force in any given company will be much higher. Drudgery and monotony will be minimized, and jobs will be more interesting. Personnel will be of a higher caliber, more alert, better trained, and more highly educated. Consequently, the job of human relations will have to be on a higher plane.

Briefly, the following shows the variety of subjects which will have to be reexamined or reemphasized:

1. Automation and cybernetics involve complicated equipment and processes. The need is great for highly skilled technical and maintenance personnel. Selection and placement techniques must be perfected to assist in securing capable employees who can operate such plants proficiently.
2. Redesign of plants will call for completely new job and employee specifications. Job analysis and job studies will be prime necessities if selection, placement, and training are to be conducted successfully.
3. The importance of training will increase. More people will require longer periods of training. Engineers and other technical personnel will need supplementary training, maintenance workers will require additional skills and better technical background, and operative employees will have to convert to maintenance and control skills.
4. Automation will not eliminate the need of good relations with organized labor. Indeed, its cooperation will be needed in order to gain acceptance of layoffs and job changes and transfers.
5. The problem of compensation will have to be reviewed again all the way from basic theory to specific wage plans. The basis of incentives is likely to change from that of individual effort to group sharing plans. Undoubtedly, too, supervisors will be included in the incentive plans.
6. It may be necessary to change from a line-and-staff type of organization to a functionalized scheme. The specialists who are required in such an operation must have a more direct control of operations.
7. Employee attitude changes must be expected. Better employee communications, idea sharing, and education are indicated. This will all place a bigger burden not only on the personnel department in designing better plans but also on the executives who must carry them out.
8. Automation should tend to reduce safety hazards, because machines will do the work, and because such devices as television can be used to view dangerous operations.
9. Better housekeeping will also be required in the automatic factory and office.

International Personnel Programs

In recent years the trend toward penetration of foreign markets by overseas subsidiaries and branches has raised the need for various personnel decisions. Because of the wide variations in types of international operations and in the conditions in the many foreign countries, space here permits only a highlighting of personnel problem areas and their possible solutions. The major areas to which consideration must be given are, as follows:

a. Accommodation to local customs and laws.
b. Staffing with American and local personnel.
c. Policies for American and local personnel.
d. Services and maintenance policies for American staff and families.

   a. Local Laws and Customs. Undoubtedly one of the primary principles of international operations is that of making realistic accommodations to the laws and customs of the countries in which a company is to operate. The need of conforming to laws is obvious. Corporate organization, financing, commercial transactions, and labor laws must be strictly followed. This phase is generally recognized, accepted, and obeyed.

   But customs present another matter. It is not easy to learn and adapt oneself to the shadings of customs and mores of correct behavior. Americans normally like to follow the quick, businesslike formulae of our country. But abroad this seldom works out. What to do if a lunch hour is two hours long, if employees are sensitive to class distinctions, if religious and national holidays seem to intrude frequently, if traditions come before business, and if social niceties must always precede any business talks. The answer is learn the customs and always abide by them, and particularly without any expressions of disdain for them.

   b. Staffing Policies. The staffing of overseas operations must also be carefully weighed. The usual practice has been to use American personnel in key positions, managerial and technical. Then the lower supervisory and operative employees have come from the locals. There has been some trend away from this to all local help but with periodic visitations of American staff. This change is coming about for three reasons. First, Americans do not like normally to be located on foreign shores permanently. Second, locals do not cooperate as effectively when they think that upper levels of management and technical positions are closed to them permanently. Third, various countries are insisting by agreements and by laws for local representation on the higher organization levels.

   c. Personnel Policies. Where Americans and locals are working together, the problem of equality of treatment arises. This happens for the simple reason that Americans require higher compensation and perquisites, first, to get them to work abroad, and, second, because of disparities between standards and costs of living. Local employees usually do not mind this when a company first comes into a country and provides jobs. But later, the disparities tend to cause unrest. Yet, however a company might feel about reducing the disparities and inequities, to do so would be unrealistically disruptive to local customs and conditions. The usual solution, eventually, is to supplant the American staff with locals. Thus almost all, if not all, Americans with their disturbing advantages are removed.

d. Service and Maintenance Policies. And finally, international personnel policies must provide guidelines for the maintenance of American staff and, very often, their families. Such matters must be considered as finding appropriate housing, taking care of medical and educational needs, arranging for vacations and leaves in the States, and assisting in social and cultural associations. These are things which do not make themselves available simply because the resident Americans may be receiving superior remuneration. Money alone cannot balance out the disadvantages and difficulties of living in a foreign country. Not, by all means, that there is anything basically wrong with the foreign climate. Indeed, most have many glamorous and attractive features. But help is needed to overcome the difficulties in order to take advantage of the attractions.

If a company does not help to bridge the difficulties, serious disadvantages occur. Too often, Americans living abroad gather into American compounds or communities, failing thereby to melt into the affairs and happenings of the foreign land. The executives will not get the flavor and attitudes needed to effectively carry on their business affairs. Or failure to seriously study the language of the country in which they operate places the American businessman at a major disadvantage. In sum, the need to maintain the American staff abroad has two aspects. First, the worker and worker's family must be made comfortable and at ease. But, second, this must not be done so that the employee is removed from the life of the foreign country which is so necessary to make contributions effective.

QUESTIONS

1. Upon what grounds is discrimination illegal? Legal?
2. What evidence, when available, tends to be proof of discrimination?
3. What steps should be taken to ease the introduction of minority groups into the working situation?
4. What arguments are there to substantiate the claim that handicapped people can and do make effective contributions to the working situation?
5. In what respects have older employees proved themselves the equal to or the superior of younger employees?
6. How do women compare with men as employees?
7. What are the principal subjects which have been covered by legislation regarding women employees?
8. What are some of the technical innovations having an effect upon personnel policies and practices?

9. As a business converts its processes to automation, what personnel problems does it have to solve?

10. What types of personnel problems are faced by a company which undertakes overseas operations?

CASE 23–1. THE BLACK EMPLOYEE

Bill Blake, the supervisor in a repair shop for electronic equipment, had flubbed in handling and relating to the first black employee who had come under his jurisdiction. Not having any training in such relationships he had to learn by experience. And his experience thus far seemed to point to the need for more sensitivity to the feelings of others.

Thus, when his second black employee—Tom Sanders—came his way, he decided to have a talk with him and frankly ask for his opinions. To do this he decided to tell Tom about the problems he had encountered with Lewis, the earlier employee.

In summary, some of the things that Bill Blake said were as follows. Three months ago, Lewis was introduced into my department. His education had been a bit below company standards but the company had decided to shade requirements in favor of underprivileged candidates. He worked hard, learned fast, and seemed like a good candidate for repair work. He was moved around on various tasks so that he could get broad experiences. He even got his picture in the company periodical as an example of how well things were working out for him and the company.

But trouble arose which led to his ultimate discharge. Lewis was a good worker on his own but antagonisms arose in his relations in working with others. When Lewis had to make a joint repair, he handled tools carelessly, he didn't pay careful attention to the instructions of more experienced workers, and he was careless about the safety of others. After being warned about such matters several times, he began to feel he was being discriminated against. And discharge came when his attitude and workmanship caused a serious and painful accident to a coworker.

The supervisor told Tom that he told his story because he admitted he might not have worked well with Lewis, that he wouldn't want the same to happen in their relationships, and that he hoped there would be friendly and open talk between them.

Questions

1. What do you think about this approach?
2. What aspects do you like or dislike?

CASE 23–2. EQUALITY OF WOMEN

The Makem Company had for most of its life been an all-male organization. During World War II, women were hired to a point that they constituted over half the payroll. Without this source of employees, the company would likely have gone out of business.

But even in recent years, women were only on operative and manual jobs. Wage rates were equal on the same jobs for men and women.

Management is worried, however, having read that a number of companies had to pay out large sums of money because of discriminatory practices. Since the company held important government contracts, it was particularly concerned about its current practices in regard to women. To be sure they had hired large numbers of women but only a few were at the straw boss level and not one at higher executive or professional levels.

It has decided, therefore, to start a crash program to improve its image. Hoping to find some women who could be promoted immediately, they reviewed the personnel records of current employees. Nothing was found because the company in the past neither had looked for qualified women nor had it succeeded in attracting any because of its reputation.

Now they are faced with two options; (1) train any current employees who seem to have some potential and (2) attract some good candidates from other companies.

Question

1. What do you think of these options and their practicality?

part V
The Utilization Phase of Personnel Management

Personnel management as a specialized organizational unit or as a part of every executive's job must assume responsibility for the appropriate utilization of people in an organization. In this Part, therefore, attention is directed to some key ideas and tasks of utilization.

At the outset it has been considered important to address attention to the relation of cooperation and conflict to utilization. Management and employees must be aware of the ingredients of cooperation and the useful aspects of conflict if organizational life is to be productive and satisfying. Moving from the theory of these topics, this Part then takes up specific subjects which have a large role in the utilization of people: union-management relations, handling grievances of people, and taking disciplinary action. And finally, utilization—as well as other phases of personnel management—cannot be dealt with effectively unless there is substantial effort to examine one's efforts. So research in and evaluation of personnel practices conclude the materials of this Part.

COOPERATION 24
AND CONFLICT

Scope

Among the unavoidable balancing acts in business (as well as in all of life) is that relating to cooperation and conflict. People with differing interests must work together if their respective interests are to be attained. Yet the very fact of differing interests creates an atmosphere of opposing forces. In organized business life, ways must be sought, therefore, which minimize undesirable tensions which might otherwise inhibit desirable cooperative efforts.

The task of this and following chapters is to take up basic aspects and specific programs relating to cooperation and conflict. In this chapter, attention is directed to fundamental factors underlying cooperation and conflict. Then in succeeding chapters attention is directed to the role of union-management relations, grievance handling, disciplinary action, and research in cooperative-conflict matters.

The success with which specific programs or topics of these matters are handled depend in part on the degree of understanding which management brings to pertinent basic factors. These include—and constitute the major subjects of this chapter—the following:

1. Organizational behavior.
2. Employee morale.
3. Conflict dimensions.

ORGANIZATIONAL BEHAVIOR

To understand how people interact in an organization, one must—among other things—understand the theory of organizations. Hence, the following aspects of organizations are now considered:

1. The nature and characteristics of an organization.
2. The advantages and disadvantages of organizations.
3. Requirements of effective organizational behavior.

Nature and Characteristics of an Organization

An organization may be described in terms of what it is, why organizing is desirable, and conditions of organizational effectiveness.

1. Basic Dimensions. Simply stated, a human organization consists of two or more people in operational, interacting, and purposeful relationships.

Operationally speaking, each person in an organization does something before, after, and simultaneously with someone else. Such arrangements are called operations, procedures, or processes. In addition, operationally, each person is in a superior, subordinate, and peer relationship with other people. Such arrangements consist of authority, responsibility, leadership, and followership relationships. These often are termed organizational structures. More has been said on these operational matters in Chapter 5.

Persons in an organization are also interaffecting. As individuals and as group members they affect each other technically, psychologically, socially, and ethically. Such interactions result in likes, dislikes, perceptions, expectations, attitudes, and value judgments which in turn result in various degrees of cooperation or conflict.

And purposively, an organization is a goal-seeking entity. Various goals are sought for the general society in which it operates and whose members it affects, as well as for the various members of the organization itself. Products and services, profits, wages and salaries, personal needs and wants, and economic survival are examples of organizational purposes. Attendant to all of these are questions of fair and equitable adjustments of possible conflicts among these goals.

But an organization must not be viewed as an isolated unit. It is a suborganization or a subsystem in a larger world, which itself is changing and dynamic. It must adapt itself to the larger economic, social, and political systems in which it operates.

2. Advantages and Disadvantages of Organizations. Organizations are formed because they are often superior to individual action in attaining various goals. This is true in practically every area of human endeavour whether it be religious, social, military, educational, or business. The source of this superiority is found in specialization. Members of an organization take on specialized tasks; they don't try to be "jacks of all trades."

This very desirable aspect of organizations has, however, a number of undesirable features. First, human specialists do not operate nor affect each other harmoniously automatically. Hence, managers (a type of specialist) are needed to attain operational and interacting harmony. They are needed but their cost must be deducted from the benefits of organizing.

Second, participants in an organization must give up some of their time and freedom of action during (and often at other times too) their participation in the organization. If conformance were lacking, specialization and coordination would be reduced. It is assumed that the benefits of organizing offset such disadvantages.

Third, human beings often get bored with the repetitive aspects of their specialized tasks. Unless they are willing to accept reasonable requirements of specialization, the efficiency due to specialization is endangered.

And last, specialized organizations themselves are sometimes changed by taking on a variety of goals. A church may add social activities to its religious ceremonies. A tire company may add on a cinema project. A food company takes on a nuclear operation. The organization thus tends to become non-specialized and in turn to dilute some of its original specialized advantages.

3. Effective Organizational Behavior.   An organization is, therefore, not a thing of unalloyed joy. It has disadvantages as well as advantages: it is dysfunctional as well as functional. To balance these, a number of conditions must be met.

Fundamental to organizational success is an understanding by all participants of its undesirable and desirable features. For example, if specialization is an essential of organizations, its members cannot demand to be non-specialists. If an organization, requires conformance, its members cannot demand freedom. If organizations must divide up their benefits, their members cannot seek individual maximization.

Essentially, an organization requires trade-offs by its members. Members must be willing to make reasonable compromises, to seek balance, and to respect the roles and goals of each other.

An organization will be most effective, therefore, when its members intelligently balance the degree to which they are willing to accept the constraints against the benefits of organizational membership. Taking employee as example of organizational member, one should weigh how much freedom one is willing to give up as a price of gaining the benefits to be derived from conformance to organizational rules. If one values freedom of action while at work, it thereby reduces one's willingness to conform to rules which are needed for effective coordination of specialists. This involves a value judgment as to which personal and organizational goals may be in some opposition but which must be reconciled and balanced.

Interactions of People and Organizations

Undoubtedly, people are the most complex factor in an organization. They possess a wide variety of characteristics, perceptions, needs, attitudes, and behavioral patterns that complicate organizational activities. Yet these must be taken into account by management. The discussion now is concerned with these aspects of people and how they fit into organizations.

1. Attributes of People in an Organization. There is no doubt that an organization needs such human attributes as physical strength and mental skill. These are important contributors to productivity. But people also have other unusual features. They also are psychological, cultural, and ethical creatures. To the degree that these attributes are needed in an organization, people make a very significant contribution to organizational success. But what if some of these are not needed, what then? Two conditions must then be given appropriate treatment.

Excess attributes, first, must somehow be either dampened or accepted as undesirable frictions in the organizational machine. For example, people are emotional and gregarious. If unneeded amounts cannot be suppressed by close supervision or employee self-discipline, then these manifestations on the job have to be accepted despite their undesirable effects.

The excess attributes, second, may be reduced either through screening of candidates or by avoiding managerial acts that stir up trouble. Such actions are certainly taken in connection with material resources; management does not buy a higher quality of steel than is needed, let us say, nor use the steel in such a way that moving parts develop undesirable friction heat. With people, too, more careful selection to fit people into jobs is needed. And once hired, management should avoid practices which arouse destructive frictions.

2. Human Action in an Organization. This leads to another critical and distinctive feature of people. They feel and think, project and reminisce, and exercise some control over their skills as well as over those who seek to control them. Contrariwise, a piece of steel does not try to run the machine in which it is placed, nor worry about the past or the future, nor feel pain when the machine operates on it. But people do all of these things.

It is not enough, therefore, to merely consider how to employ the technical skills of people. Consideration must also be given to how people will react to how they are being used, and how they will react to the user. Moreover, their reactions must be weighed in terms of future as well as current interactions. Thus, I, as an employee may dislike but now accept something my superior has done. But later I may demand, and get, through union action rights that offset past grievances.

The Role of Personnel Management in an Organization

Personnel management deals with these human aspects in an organization. The "management" part of personnel management has a connotation of command which seems to infer a uni-directional flow. It also seems to imply manipulation of others. These interpretations are sometimes well founded. The boss has often acted as a "boss." The manager does direct and expects the subordinate to act as directed. And the manager has found authority for actions in such devices as the rights of private property, the sanctions of cultural patterns, and the traditions of business and political practices.

Such views of the rights of managerial authority do not stand upon unshakeable grounds. To be sure every organization needs leadership. Sooner or later, leadership flows to those who serve all participants in an organization, not alone to just one class.

The right of management in business has often been assigned to the one who risks economic resources. Management has rights on how the resources should be used to reduce financial risks. But is business the only one who takes risks in the organization? Of course not, yet curiously enough, the selected risk of the entrepreneur has often been given preferred rights. Gradually, the risks of others, particularly those of employees, have gained recognition. Thus the employee who works in an organization risks and invests work time. May not that investment be more critical than that of the owner of private property?

This view underlies the contention that management must be as much concerned with rights of employees as well as with entrepreneurs. Thus management must not manipulate people solely in the interests of the financial risk-takers. Rather management must exercise its specialized skills so that both types of risk-takers benefit. It must provide plans and working conditions such that labor can make its most effective contribution to its own success as well as other risk-taking members.

In this interpretation of management, of which personnel management is a specialized segment, any depressing, one-sided connotations of management are reduced. The role of personnel management stands on firmer grounds; leadership for and with due consideration for the benefit of people as well as for the owner.

EMPLOYEE MORALE

Without doubt, organizational cooperation and conflict are significantly affected by employee morale. Hence, in personnel management it is important to understand the meaning of morale, the theory of morale development, and the factors of morale development.

Meaning of Morale

Definitions of morale are many. A review of them would show that morale is defined in terms of what it is, where it resides, whom it affects, and what it affects. Thus, to use this classification, morale is composed of the following:

1. What it is—an attitude of mind, an esprit de corps, a state of well-being (or unwell-being), and an emotional state.
2. Where it resides—in the minds, attitudes, and emotions of individuals as members of a group.
3. Whom it affects—immediately, employees and executives in their interactions; ultimately, the customer and the community.
4. What it affects—immediately, willingness to work and cooperate in the best interests of the enterprise; ultimately, output, quality of output, and costs of operations.

Simply stated, then, morale is a state of mind and spirit, affecting willingness to work, which in turn affects organizational and individual objectives. Morale may range from very high to very low. It is not an absolute but is subject to change, depending upon management's plans and practices.

This simple definition emphasizes willingness to work. This is important. A person contented with one's lot may do only enough to get by. Another person works hard because of dissatisfaction and wants to achieve betterment. Good morale would scarcely be a condition of the former person; it could well be of the latter. Dissatisfaction of a group need not be a sign of poor morale when it is associated with a desire to improve through cooperation with organizational goals. Dissatisfaction with management could, however, well be a sign of poor morale.

The foregoing implies that morale is a group manifestation. A particular person may have a favorable attitude toward her own work and supervisor. But the group with whom she works may take a very unfavorable stand against certain company practices and the group reaction may well offset the effect of the employee's personal opinions.

One more point about this definition: It infers a relation to organizational success. But it also makes reference to individual satisfaction. When morale is low, employees evidently have been driven to this sad state by some poor practice of management or by a mistaken interpretation of a good practice. To develop good morale, management need not conclude that a battle with labor is inevitable. On the contrary, employees are as interested in good morale as is management—perhaps more so, because they suffer not only from the results of but also from the state of poor morale.

Theory of Morale Development

Morale is, in essence, conditioned by a group's understanding of the relation between personal interests and company interests. Employees who conclude that their interests are being served fairly when they contribute to the organization's interests develop a favorable attitude of mind. Conversely, their attitude is poor when they perceive an unfair treatment of their interests.

Essentially, then, morale develops out of a mutual satisfaction of interests. In the case of employees, they understand that to gain their goals, they must help the company achieve its goals. And employees must also believe that the share they get is fair in relation to what they and others contribute. If the interests of all parties to a group endeavor are, in their respective minds, fairly served, their morale will be high. Morale development takes place, therefore, through the process of successfully integrating interests.

Immediately, good morale has some very important results for management and for employees. Management finds that subordinates are willing to follow their requests and commands with enthusiasm and respect. Indeed, work is done without the need of commands or supervision. This is a very pleasant condition for the executive who will find that employees will work hard in the face of difficulties. When overtime or holiday work is called for, the response will be quick and understanding. And most of all, employees openly show the attitude of respect for and confidence in their leaders which is so satisfying to the leaders themselves.

Good morale has immediate effects upon employees, too. They work with satisfaction and pleasure. The hours of work go by in an atmosphere of relaxed effort. Nothing seems to drag, the days are not empty and boring, and a feeling of insignificance is absent. It is, in short, good to be at work and in association with one's coworkers and one's superiors. Work—as much as it can be—is a pleasure and not a misery.

These immediate effects cause some desirable ultimate effects. To management, there is higher output of better products at lower costs. And in turn, there will be more consistent, higher profits. To employees, there are higher wages, more secure employment, and a higher standard of living. And to society in general, there are more goods and services obtained more effectively from the limited supply of resources.

These effects do not all flow from morale itself. Morale should not be looked upon as the only source of success. Even the best employee cannot make bricks without straw. But the best employee can do much, much better given the same materials than can the worker whose morale is low.

Factors of Morale Development

It is now pertinent to note the factors which have an effect upon employee morale. As a broad statement, anything can influence the attitude of employees; the factors are limitless. But practically speaking, morale is related to the following:

1. Employee factors.
2. Management practices.
3. Extracompany forces and factors.

1. Employee Factors. The quality of morale is definitely influenced by the type of employees. As already noted, understanding has a significant effect upon morale. And understanding is dependent, in part, upon the ability of people to understand. If, then, the ability of employees to understand reasonable explanations is low, management, try as it may, will not be able to get across its messages. Thus, in its hiring policies, a company should seek not only people who are capable of doing their jobs but also those who can grasp the logical relationships and rewards involved in group effort.

The status and roles of employees have a bearing upon the possibilities of morale development. Employees may be members of a union. In that case, they will invariably take on attitudes and reactions because of their membership. This does not mean that such attitudes will necessarily be negative. But it does mean that management will have to deal with a group which is not so easy to convince of the views it considers correct. Even when not organized, labor may take on particular attitudes because of such things as the labor-management history in a given community or the manner in which labor looks upon itself in the factory.

2. Management Practices. The most important group of factors affecting morale are those falling within the province of management. Few employees, indeed, would be unaware of or disinterested in how management dealt with such matters of pertinence to them as goals, policies, procedures, and communications. These were noted and discussed in Chapter 15, hence it is sufficient to note here that managerial decisions on any of these subjects can have serious impact upon the morale of employees. Any one of these areas has more than enough powder to blow up the relations between labor and management. Conversely, they can be the source of great good, as illustrated in Figure 24–1, which summarizes the opinions in one company toward two levels of management.

The behavior of executives is particularly significant as a morale factor. Some executives are autocratic in their attitude toward subordinates. Others imply a feeling that they are better than their subordinates —that the latter are second-class citizens. Others are suspicious of the

FIGURE 24–1

Report of Employee Opinions of Management

YOUR SUPERVISOR

Please tell us how you rate your *immediate supervisor* on:

Explaining and teaching the work:
44.8 He's a good teacher.
35.7 He gets by.
9.0 He can't teach.
10.5 He doesn't try to teach or explain.

Treating people fairly:
36.1 He's always fair.
38.9 He's fair most of the time.
15.7 He's fair about half the time.
7.2 He's not often fair.
2.1 He's never fair.

Letting you know the news:
50.5 He keeps me posted.
49.5 We don't get much news from him.

Giving a hand when there's trouble:
52.1 He's good about helping you out.
29.2 He does about what he's supposed to do.
18.7 Don't expect much help from him.

Giving Orders:
73.9 He tells you to do a thing in a way that makes you feel like doing it.
26.1 The way he tells you to do things makes you mad.

Upgrading:
62.4 He usually picks the best people to move along.
12.3 He makes poor selections.
25.3 I think he plays favorites.

Letting you know how you're doing:
48.5 He lets me know in a nice way how I'm doing.
11.1 He lets me know in a poor way how I'm doing.
40.4 He doesn't let me know in any way.

Being a good leader:
36.5 He's a good leader.
42.4 He's an average leader.
21.1 He's not a leader.

★ ★ ★

We are happy that, generally, TP supervisors are given a pretty fair rating. There is room for improvement in the areas of letting people know how they are doing, and in passing along instructions.

BOY, WHAT AN ASSIGNMENT!

GOOD GUY!

LET ME BUZZ YOUR EAR!

C'MON GANG—FOLLOW ME!

YOUR DEPARTMENT FOREMAN

Will you please answer the same questions about your *department foreman*, the man to whom your supervisor reports:

Explaining and teaching the work:
35.1 He's a good teacher.
24.2 He gets by.
5.3 He can't teach.
12.2 He doesn't try to teach or explain.
23.2 His job doesn't call for him to teach or explain.

Treating people fairly:
33.2 He's always fair.
35.4 He's fair most of the time.
17.6 He's fair about half the time.
10.1 He's not often fair.
3.7 He's never fair.

Letting you know the news:
36.7 He keeps me posted.
63.3 We don't get much news from him.

Giving a hand when there's trouble:
40.0 He's good about helping you out.
23.5 He does about what he's supposed to do.
22.4 Don't expect much help from him.
14.1 His job doesn't call for him to help.

Giving Orders:
72.4 He tells you to do a thing in a way that makes you feel like doing it.
27.6 The way he tells you to do things makes you mad.

Upgrading:
57.5 He usually picks the best people to move along.
14.9 He makes poor selections.
27.6 I think he plays favorites.

Letting you know how you're doing:
39.2 He lets me know in a nice way how I'm doing.
9.1 He lets me know in a poor way how I'm doing.
51.7 He doesn't let me know in any way.

Being a good leader:
37.7 He's a good leader.
40.6 He's an average leader.
21.7 He's not a leader.

★ ★ ★

You gave both foremen and supervisors a good rating on their fairness. That foremen as a group did not rate quite as high as supervisors may be explained by their less frequent contacts with employees due to the nature of their duties. We wish that both foremen and supervisors would give you more news.

Courtesy: Thompson Products, Inc., Cleveland, Ohio

motives and actions of employees and openly indicate their lack of confidence. Others avoid, if not despise, the company of their workers. And still others are contemptuous of the intelligence of employees. Such attitudes are quickly noted. Obviously, it is natural for employees to return a negative attitude of mind. To reverse these behaviorisms serves to enhance the morale of employees.

3. *Extracompany Forces and Factors.* Morale may also be affected by forces and factors outside the company itself. The union is a significant example, and various community and family relationships are another.

The union is so closely intertwined, and becoming increasingly more so, with company affairs that it may be incorrect to classify it as an extracompany agency. But legally it is, if not in other relationships. Certainly, it is a potent morale factor. How employees feel toward their company is significantly determined by the indoctrination they receive from their unions. And at times—such as during a strike—their attitude seems to be totally swayed by this force.

Other extracompany forces affecting employee morale are numerous. Though it may not be company business, an employee's attitude toward at work is affected by a variety of things, such as:

a.   How well he gets along with spouse, children, and relatives.
b.   The nature of associations with friends and neighbors.
c.   The state of personal health or of family well-being.
d.   Whether or not the worker has picked a winner in politics, in a favorite team, or in the last football pool.
e.   Environmental factors in the community, such as parking and traffic conditions, housing conditions, and ecological conditions.

It might seem a herculean task to cope with such an infinite variety of morale factors. This is not so. Not all are effective at the same time. But to work with any of them, management should be able to determine which ones are effective at particular times. A check list, expanded from those suggested in the foregoing, will be helpful in that connection.

CONFLICT

The foregoing two sections have noted the importance of organizations and of morale to attainment of various goals. Emphasized in these sections is the need of cooperation by the various participants in an organization. And lurking in these sections is the implication that conflict is a common characteristic of organizations.

Conflict is indeed an indisputable fact of all organized life. Is this necessarily cause for pessimism? Or is there room for positive good? To obtain some answers to these questions, it is proposed here to discuss the following:

1.   Nature and impact of conflict.
2.   Handling conflict.

Nature and Impact

A conflict is an expression of disagreement. The subject of disagreement may be as wide as human experience. The intensity of disagreement may be mild or all-consuming. And those involved in the disgreement may be few in number or innumerable.

Such diversities are common in the organized world of business. Unanimity may be lacking on anything such as goals, methods to accomplish goals, roles of the participants in goal attainment, task assignments, power, privileges, and rewards. Even casual acquaintance with the business world soon enlightens one to the range of topics on which disagreements may occur.

The intensity of disagreements also is wide-ranging. Labor and management on many occasions find that their conflicts are mild and inconsequential. And at the other extreme, it seems that disagreements are intense beyond compromise or reconciliation. It sometimes seems that one or the other must forcibly be removed; labor by automation and management by movement of its powers to organized labor.

And those involved in conflict may be few or many. At times, there is a one-to-one situation; one employee with another or one employee with one management representative. At times, the members of a given working group or organizational sub-unit are at odds with management. And at times, the whole class of workers, whether in one company or an industry at large, are in conflict with management.

The impact of such conflicts in general seems undesirable. Employees and management in conflict are in a poor posture to cooperate, to work together. And without doubt much conflict does lead to conditions undesirable for goal attainment.

But curiously enough, conflict can also be the basis of good. Disagreement may inspire improvement. Employee may be dissatisfied with and criticize working conditions, management policies, and compensation practices. But this may bring about improvements in these matters so that the eventual outcomes are better cooperation, more efficiency, and more equitable goal sharing.

Handling Conflicts

Management is thus faced with two classes of conflicts. Which are bad and must be corrected? And which are good and must be nutured?

In regard to the negative or dysfunctional class of conflicts, dealing with them calls for careful definition of each specific situation. Conflicts in general cannot be handled; rather specific conflicts and causes must be ascertained and handled. Briefly, conflicts will tend to be over the following:

1. Disagreements as to the fair share of rewards, privileges, power sharing, status, and roles.
2. Misunderstandings over the meaning and content of policies, com-

munications, responsibility assignments, job and personal relationships and procedural relationships.

In regard to the positive, constructive class of conflicts, specific analysis is again in order. Usually these are concerned with viewpoints on, first, how improvements can be made over present practices, and, second, how undesirable conditions can best be removed. These aspects of conflict invariably are less concerned with personal interests immediately than with organizational improvements. Hence, the personal element with its sensitivity is far less involved than in the case of the negative class of conflicts.

What is to be done in each general class of conflicts or specific instances thereof is not at issue here. Much has been suggested in earlier chapters on positive programs of personnel management. And more will be taken up in the following chapters. But it has been necessary to suggest that conflict is an essential aspect of cooperation. If conflict is to be handled correctly, both its negative and positive aspects must be correctly understood.

In addition, attention must also be called to another important dimension of conflict, that of change. Both the negative and positive classes of conflict are often causes of or caused by change. People change as do their goals, their aspirations, their expectations, their values, etc. Companies change, as do their goals, methods of operations, environments, competition, etc. The world in which we live changes—culturally, socially, politically, economically, educationally, etc.

All these bring on differences of opinion—conflicts, if you please—on what adaptations to such changes should be made. And in addition people themselves are constantly re-evaluating and developing new ideas about their relationships and thereby seeking to get changes more beneficial to themselves. When people succeed in their efforts, they are as much causes of change as affected by change. These interactions may be simply diagramed as follows:

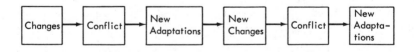

This view of the reciprocal and continuous cycle of cooperation, conflict, and change recognizes an inevitable characteristic of organized life. The lesson to personnel management is obvious and simple. Properly analyzed and handled, much good can be achieved, useful purposes can be served, and negative aspects reduced. Properly managed, they cannot make heaven on earth; but they can make for cooperative interaction with employees. But they must be accepted as normality not abnormality and as an inevitable yet constructive challenge to management.

QUESTIONS

1. What are the advantages and disadvantages of organized activities?
2. If an organization is to be most effective, what must members in it understand about and accept regarding participation in it?
3. Why must management be concerned with the rights of employees as well as with those of owners?
4. What is the role of personnel management in an organization?
5. What should be encompassed in a definition of morale?
6. Essentially, how does employee morale develop, when it does?
7. Into what major classes may the factors affecting morale be grouped?
8. What is the nature and impact of conflict in an organization?
9. How many management attempt to handle conflict in an organization?
10. What impact is change likely to have upon cooperation and conflict in an organization?

CASE 24–1. LIFE STYLES AND PRODUCTIVITY

Mr. Oldmoss, a conservative of the old school, is president of a company specializing in the production of plastic drain pipe. He gives complete control over hiring to his personnel manager, Hal Steven, who is also conservative but respects the personal life style of the employees. But he has cause to wonder about "Shorty" Night.

Shorty is the picture, in his way of thinking, of being "far out." He has past-shoulder-length hair, wears peace patches on his Levis, rides a motorcycle to work, and attends a nearby college where "riots" have not been unknown. Rumors circulating in the plant implied that Shorty had participated in rock throwing, but no one knew for sure. Shorty tended to polarize his coworkers. The older ones disliked his presence and the younger ones enjoyed having him around.

Despite these characteristics, his immediate supervisor was satisfied with Shorty's work and general attitude. One day Shorty asked his supervisor for permission to read his textbooks whenever he worked on the slowmoving pipe machine. Approval was given so long as his attention was not distracted. A few days later, trouble developed on Shorty's machine. A section of pipe, while being extruded, caught on the tray on which it was supposed to rest before being cut off. The tray was broken in half, and the machine, the most vital on the line, became clogged. The supervisor, along with maintenance people, worked for six hours to restore production. Once the machine was fixed, Mr. Oldmoss called the personnel manager and the supervisor into his office for a conference.

Mr. Oldmoss started the conversation by asking, first, if Shorty was the type of person that was a credit to the company, and, second, if part-time students could give adequate attention to their full-time jobs. The personnel manager stated that life styles were always changing and that many of the old standards neither had particular advantages nor could be justified. The supervisor replied that people had outside activities whether school, family, social, or athletic; he couldn't be expected to interfere in any of them; and all he tried to do was to keep on top of job activities.

Question

1. What would you think of these answers were you president?

CASE 24–2.   JOB IMPROVEMENT

Perhaps the most serious complaint of employees against conveyorized-assembly-line operations is their deadening boredom. The design engineer may claim high efficiency for specialized work assignments. But the employees feel that their very sanity is threatened.

Consider the picture in a section of a line of torque converter assemblies. There are five workers in this unit. The first trims excess flash around four drilled holes, the second inserts a drain plug, the third tightens the drain plug, the fourth stamps an identifying letter on the face of the converter, and the fifth lifts the converter onto a conveyor for movement to the next section.

Each of the operations takes no more than several minutes to learn. The pay is good. Working conditions are very noisy. But there is nothing but repetition all day long.

One of the employees has suggested to management that working conditions could be improved by job rotation or job enlargement. The worker also suggested (anonomously) that monkeys be hired as the work might just suit the level of their mentality.

Question

1. What do you think of these suggestions or do you have any of your own?

UNION-MANAGEMENT 25
RELATIONS

Scope of Discussion

Personnel management seeks to establish effective and satisfactory relations with employees. In general, its programs meet with relative success in most companies. Yet, from time to time, conflicts of lesser or greater degree disturb relations in all companies. "Labor relations" refers to the efforts to maintain satisfactory accommodations and to resolve disagreements between employees and management. Implied in the term are organizational arrangements, practices, and policies employed in such efforts.

A detailed examination of these efforts is undertaken in the two chapters that follow under the headings of "Handling Grievances" and "Disciplinary Action," respectively. Inasmuch as organized unions play a significant role in these matters, attention is first directed in this chapter to them, under the following headings:

1. General background of unionization.
2. The Labor Management Relations Act.
3. Stages of union-management relations.

GENERAL BACKGROUND OF UNIONIZATION

The conditions under which and the stages through which management and unions conduct themselves are placed in better perspective by first viewing a number of pertinent aspects of unions themselves. Of importance are the following:

1. The role of unions.
2. Historical aspects of union growth.

3. Legal status of unions.
4. Types of unions.

The Role of Unions

In simple terms, an employee sells skills, time, and willingness to work. The terms of this sales contract presumably are arranged by equals, subject to a free, competitive market. Such presumptions are unrealistic when the mobility and power of a particular employee are arrayed against the average employer. To be sure, the employee can look elsewhere if dissatisfied with an employer's offer. And the weight of the labor market may be promising to the employee when the demand and supply factors are favorable, as in a prosperity period.

Generally speaking, however, the employer usually has the advantages of the power to withhold employment, of the economic strength to withstand the pressures of a particular individual, and of better knowledge of the labor and sales markets. From a bargaining point of view, therefore, the employer is superior to the employee. And business has at times not been above arranging terms of employment more favorable to itself.

Obviously, the employee cannot be blamed for seeking means of balancing the powers of bargaining. A recourse has been to join forces with coworkers. In short, in union there is strength. As a result, the power of management is balanced—and indeed, is sometimes outweighed —so that it must accede to wishes of employees it might otherwise reject.

In bargaining, then, the role of the unions is to balance the economic power of the employer. In its simplest form, this role is played within the confines of a given company. The employees, through their elected representatives, negotiate the terms of employment with the company officials. The agreement thus reached by "equals" becomes the accepted mode of conduct between the parties for a designated period of time.

Much more complicated roles are assumed by unions (and by management) to achieve their goals. The unions (like management) seek the favor of public opinion, of governmental agencies, and of political parties. Legislation, for example, is sought which would protect and enhance the rights of labor, as will be noted in the next section. Moreover, individual unions combine to gain greater power.

So the union is more than an economic institution. It has political characteristics, seeking to use political power to influence governmental agencies in its immediate interests and sometimes on matters far removed from union-management relations. Indeed, at times, unions have been on the verge of forming a political labor party with a view to gaining their economic ends.

The core role of the union is, however, that of collective bargaining. Employees organize and elect representatives who bargain with management for the benefit of the employees. "Collective bargaining" is more complex than this. It is difficult to define because the extent, degree, and kind of bargaining and of "collective" effort depend upon the time, place, and parties of the bargaining process. The subjects over which labor and management will bargain also affect the definitions, and the methods and organizations used in bargaining powers vary from case to case and from time to time.

But broadly speaking, collective bargaining refers to a process by which employers, on the one hand, and representatives of employees, on the other, attempt to arrive at agreements covering the conditions under which employees will contribute and be compensated for their services.

To those who deplore the use of the word *bargaining* as indicative of a struggle between employer and employee, the relationship would be better stated by calling the process "collective cooperation." The role of the union becomes one of a beneficial and understanding partner.

Historical Aspects of Union Growth

Labor unions have not been a significant factor in labor relations generally until the 1930s. Looking back, labor unions had but little success prior to the Civil War. Small-scale manufacturing was not conducive to and legal hindrances obstructed the expansion of such organizations. After the Civil War, from which time modern industrial growth in the United States may be considered to date, labor organizations began to spurt. Of particular interest then was the Noble Order of the Knights of Labor, which flourished briefly but spectacularly during the 1870s and 1880s. Its programs and ambitions, however, were beyond its resources and the opposition industry could muster. As a consequence, it sputtered into insignificance and then extinction during the late 1880s.

This decade is important, however, because it marked the formation of the American Federation of Labor (AFL) in 1886. This group grew to the point that in the early 1930s, it stood as the country's major labor organization. In 1935 a number of unions affiliated with the AFL became dissatisfied with its organizing and jurisdictional policies, and withdrew from it. The new group chose the name Committee of Industrial Organization, which was subsequently changed to Congress of Industrial Organizations (CIO). In 1955 the two decided to rejoin forces in a single group, the American Federation of Labor—Congress of Industrial Organizations (AFL–CIO). Present estimates of union membership of this group and independent unions run up to 20 million. This constitutes about a quarter of the nonagricultural employees. Union membership is relatively concentrated in the industrial areas of business. The office, sales, technical, and professional areas are not well represented, except in isolated cases.

Legal Changes and Status

The answer to why unions grow must be sought in large part in terms of legal strength. Thus, until the thirties, labor unions could gain little momentum because of the legal bulwarks erected against them. In the first place, business by and large had little to do with unions as long as their right to organize and bargain collectively was a matter of mutual consent and not compulsion. Second, legal injunctions could easily be obtained by business to halt a variety of union activities such as strikes, boycotts, picketing, and efforts to increase membership. And third, business could insist upon making employees, as a condition of employment, agree not to join unions (the yellow-dog contract).

Changes in the federal segment favoring unionization, however, started to come after the impact of the depression of the early thirties. The first important change came in 1932 with the passage of the Norris–La Guardia Act, which placed severe restrictions upon the use of court injunctions intended to curb or limit union activities, and which outlawed the yellow-dog contracts; i.e., agreements in which employees agreed not to join a union as a condition of employment. Then, in 1933, the National Industrial Recovery Act gave employees the right to organize and bargain collectively.

Although the Act was short-lived, being declared unconstitutional on May 27, 1935, Congress passed the National Labor Relations Act, which was signed by the President on June 27, 1935. This Act not only gave employees the right to organize but made it mandatory for employers to bargain collectively with representatives of employees. The legal basis for collective bargaining was thus finally laid in the United States. Subsequent federal legislation added protective measures in unionized relationships to both employees and employers. The Labor Management Relations (Taft-Hartley) Act in 1947 and the Labor-Management Reporting and Disclosure (Landrum-Griffin) Act in 1959 are specific cases in point.

Types of Unions

It is now appropriate to note the different organizational forms used to carry on collective bargaining. Of particular interest are differences between representation plans and unions, between craft and industrial unions, and between miscellaneous groups, independent unions, and affiliated unions.

1. Representation Plans. The employee representation plan was once viewed as a promising contributor to better labor relations. Under this plan, employee committees were formed at the behest of management to submit the views and complaints of employees to management.

The National Labor Relations Act, as amended by the Labor Management Relations Act, made it unlawful, however, for a company to interfere with or assist in the organization of employees intended for purposes of collective bargaining. Employee representation plans become illegal because their formation had been assisted by management. They had to be either disbanded or reorganized independently by the employees. And they had to be operated independently of the employer. When so organized and operated, the status of a legal union would be attained.

2. Craft and Industrial Unions. The union is, therefore, the major vehicle by which employees bargain collectively with management. Although the one shades into the other in varying degrees in particular unions, the major types are the craft and the industrial.

The craft union is one in which membership is restricted to employees of a particular trade or craft. The employees may or may not be employed by the same company. For example, carpenters in a given community, irrespective of who employs them, may belong to the same union. Or all the carpenters of a given company may form a craft union and restrict membership to carpenters of the given company. The craft unions are older, more settled, and presumably more attentive to the particular problems and needs of given classes of workers.

The American Federation of Labor was essentially an association of craft unions. Each "local" or union of craftsmen was represented through a sequence of city, state, regional, and national craftsmen organizations, which, in turn, were affiliated with the AFL. The latter group acted as the agency that set national policies for the craft unions and served to protect the labor movement from influences beyond the control of local units. It was subject, however, to the regulation of the local units through the system of state and national representatives, elected by the locals to serve on the boards of the large organizational units.

Different in structure from the craft union is the so-called industrial union, which includes all types of workers in its ranks. Thus, all occupations would be eligible for membership in the same industrial union. Because of this policy of inclusion, it is sometimes referred to as the "vertical" type as opposed to the "horizontal" type of stratification employed by the craft union.

The CIO was the chief exponent of the industrial union. It came into existence largely because of dissatisfaction with the alleged failure of the AFL to pursue vigorously the organization of workers who had no particular skills to qualify them as craftsmen. The industrial unions contended that the AFL catered only to the "elite" of labor, disregarded the millions of workers who belonged to no craft, and had grown stagnant and conservative, if not outright reactionary.

These arguments have not been enough either to keep craft and industrial unions pure in form or to keep the two from combining. There are craft groups which include more than one craft and industrial unions that consist predominantly of one occupation. Moreover, the AFL and the CIO found it desirable to combine forces into the AFL–CIO. Presumably, the labor movement could be better served by bringing all types of workers under one roof. At the local level, craft and industrial distinctions may be retained; but unified direction is provided at the top policy-making level.

3. Miscellaneous Types.   In addition to the AFL–CIO, a number of other unions are of interest. The railroad industry has long been a stronghold of the union movement. It is organized largely on a craft basis, with its various brotherhoods of trainmen, engineers, and other classes of railroad workers. The United Mine Workers (UMW), once led by the militant John L. Lewis, are also deserving of separate mention. They returned to the fold of the AFL after playing a leading role in the formation of the CIO, but are now acting independently. This union, made up of a miscellany of industrial workers as well as of miners, has been in the van of many drives to gain new and added emoluments for labor. And its leadership has displayed cunning in timing drives and choosing strategy so that success attended its efforts much more than failure. Of interest, too, are the strong Teamsters Union and United Auto Workers which have separated from the AFL–CIO because of disagreements on ethical standards of union conduct.

4. Affiliation versus Independence.   Finally, there is a group of unions that act independently and are not associated with any national group. For this reason, they are called independent unions. Ordinarily, they are formed by employees of a given company, exclusively from which members may be selected, for the purpose of dealing solely with the company in question. Sometimes, they take members from a group of companies in a given locality. When an independent union is formed to bargain with a particular company, it may also be called a company union. This connotation must be distinguished from company-dominated independent unions, which are outlawed by the Labor Management Relations Act.

THE LABOR MANAGEMENT RELATIONS ACT

Scope of Act

As already noted, the Labor Management Relations Act (LMRA, or Taft-Hartley Act), which amended the National Labor Relations Act (NLRA) of 1935, is the federal legislation currently significant in organized relations and collective bargaining. It is based upon the power of Congress to regulate interstate commerce and applies, therefore, only to businesses which enter into or affect interstate commerce. In particular, Congress seeks through this law to reduce interferences to the free flow of such commerce caused by labor-management disputes. To this end, labor is given rights of organizing and collective bargaining. If management transgresses these rights, it is guilty, by definition of the Act, of unfair labor practices and is therefore subject to punitive measures. Management is provided with certain protections against certain practices of labor organizations stated to be unfair.

The machinery of the Act has one purpose—to facilitate the process of collective bargaining. In other words, it does not prevent or settle disputes. It serves to bring labor and management together so that they may resolve their difficulties and arrive at agreements as to how they shall work together. It requires all parties to bargain and confer in good faith.

If management is to conduct its labor relations affairs correctly, it must be aware of the proscriptions of this Act in regard to the rights of various parties, coverage, and modes of operation.

Rights of Parties

The LMRA, or the Taft-Hartley Act, as it is sometimes called, establishes rights not only for employees but also for employers and for unions. Interferences with any of these rights may be construed as an unfair labor practice, with relief therefrom, or penalties, as noted in a later section.

Unfair labor practices of employers, as defined by the NLRA and the LMRA, include the following:

1. Interference, restraint, or coercion of employees in the exercise of their right freely to organize.
2. Domination and interference with the formation or administration of a labor organization.
3. Encouragement or discouragement of membership in a labor organization by discrimination in regard to hire or tenure.
4. Discrimination because of filing charges or giving testimony under the Act.
5. Refusal to bargain collectively with properly chosen representatives of the employees.

The LMRA added protections for employees from certain union actions or relationships. The Act outlawed the *closed shop,* in which all workers eligible to belong to a union must be members in good standing and new workers must become, or be, union members at time of hiring. The *union shop,* in which all employees must join a union after hiring, is permissible only if the union can gain such a concession through the process of collective bargaining. Moreover, the Act leaves it to the option of the states, of which about 19 have so acted, to restrict the closed and union shops, under the so-called *right-to-work* laws. The Act also permits deduction of dues from an employee's paycheck and payment of the deductions by the employer to the union only if this is authorized in writing by the employee (the so-called *checkoff*). Employees need not pay excessive initiation fees. But nonpayment of initiation fees and dues is the only reason why a union can ask for a member's dismissal. And the Act permits an employee to take grievances through the union up to management, or do it alone if that is the choice, but any settlements reached individually must not undermine the union contract.

Employers have been given rights under the LMRA regarding protection from practices which might be unfair to them, as follows:

1. They may express themselves freely about labor matters so long as no threat or coercion to employees is implied.
2. They may discharge, without obligation to rehire, employees who engage in illegal strikes, such as those intended to force employers to refuse to handle the products of another producer (the secondary boycott).
3. They may ask the National Labor Relations Board (NLRB) for a vote to be taken to determine whether or not a union claiming to be recognized as the bargaining agent has a majority of employees signed up.
4. They must bargain in good faith, but can now insist that the union also do so.
5. They can sue unions in the federal courts as entities, whose agents by their acts can be held liable.
6. They can set in force a 60-day "cooling-off" period before a strike can be legally called, when a contract is due to terminate or be modified.
7. They are freed from "featherbedding," or rules requiring that pay be given for work not done.
8. They may refuse to bargain with unions representing supervisors.

The Taft-Hartley Act has undoubtedly imposed certain responsibilities upon unions, as to both management and workers. On the other hand, practically all the rights unions gained under the National Labor Relations Act (Wagner Act) are still retained. Employees retained all rights to organize and bargain collectively through representatives of their own choosing. Moreover, the union has the right, under proper conditions, to:

1. Ask the NLRB for recognition elections.
2. Ask the employer to bargain in good faith.
3. Represent all employees who are eligible to vote.

4. Maintain its status for one year without fear of jurisdictional disputes.
5. Represent all employees who ask its assistance in processing grievances.
6. File charges with the NLRB against unfair labor practices.
7. Appeal to various government boards or the courts.
8. Call strikes.

Coverage of the Act

Not all companies and employees are subject to the provisions of the Act. There are three major tests of coverage relating to businesses, employers, and employees.

1. Business Coverage. As already noted, "interstate commerce" is the governing test for businesses that are included under the provisions of the Act. The Act does not specify which businesses are subject to it but includes all those "affecting" interstate commerce. The Supreme Court, in cases arising under the LMRA, and the National Labor Relations Board, in viewing its responsibilities, have interpreted "interstate" so broadly that practically all businesses are included. For example, the Act has been construed to cover such a wide range as transportation, communications, manufacturing, mining, public utilities, banks, brokers, and insurance businesses. Retailing has been included when there is some integration with interstate commerce, but purely local retail sales have thus far been construed as exempt.

2. Definition of Employer. The definition of "employer" is equally broad. It pertains not only to the general areas of management normally understood to be the employer group, but also to any person acting as an agent of an employer, directly or indirectly. Hence the rules of agency apply, and an employer is liable for the acts of representing agents.

In addition, no employer may move a plant to a new locality and then transfer it to a new and purportedly independent corporation without remaining the employer. The employer is still responsible for the unfair labor practice of the "independent" corporation.

3. Definition of Employee. The benefits of the Act are limited to all who normally would be considered employees. Of import is the status of strikers. Those who strike against an unfair labor practice of an employer are employees protected by the law against discrimination or replacement. Also, those who participate in an economic strike (in which a 60-day notice of intent to strike has been given and during which time the status quo has been maintained) are employees. But those who participate in illegal strikes—e.g., boycotts, sympathetic strikes, jurisdictional strikes, and those to gain "featherbedding" rules—lose the benefits of the Act or may be enjoined by the courts to desist from such practices.

Several exceptions and exclusions are worthy of mention. Intermittent workers are excluded only if they actually are casual employees. Seasonal and part-time workers are not generally construed to be employees. Excluded also are agricultural labor, domestics in the service of a family or a person working at home, and persons employed by a parent or spouse. Of particular interest is the exclusion of supervisors, the attempted unionization of whom under the NLRA was opposed by many employers.

Operations under the Act

The operations of the LMRA are handled through the National Labor Relations Board and a general counsel. The Board consists of five members appointed by the President with the consent of the United States Senate. It acts as a judicial body—a labor court. The administrative functions of the Act are assigned to the general counsel. This individual, appointed like the Board members, is responsible for investigating charges of unfair labor practices, issuing complaints, and prosecuting unfair labor practices. But it is the Board which decides whether or not the law has been violated. In a word, the judicial duties are assigned to the Board and the administrative functions to the general counsel.

The Board cannot compel violators to obey its orders. To gain compliance, it must petition a circuit court of appeals in the area wherein an unfair labor practice is alleged to occur or wherein the person proceeded against resides or transacts business. The jurisdiction of the court is exclusive, and its judgment and decree are final except upon review by the Supreme Court of the United States.

RELATIONS WITH THE UNION

The basic objective of union-management relations is to establish an agreement regarding the conditions under which employees will render their services to the employer. These relations, as already noted, are governed in part by legislative rules. They are also subject to a variety of economic, administrative, and personal forces which the parties can bring to bear. When one of these parties is a union, the following are the stages through which management's relations with it tend to be conducted:

1. Preparing to negotiate agreements.
2. Negotiating with unions.
3. Subject matter of agreements.
4. Living with the contract.

Preparing for Negotiation

In many ways, preparing to negotiate a contract is the most crucial stage of union-management relations. What can be accomplished at the bargaining table depends largely upon what management brings to it. Blustering and obstructionist tactics are poor substitutes for solid facts and logical analyses about wages, hours, and working conditions. Good

FIGURE 25–1

Sample Page from a Clause Comparison Chart

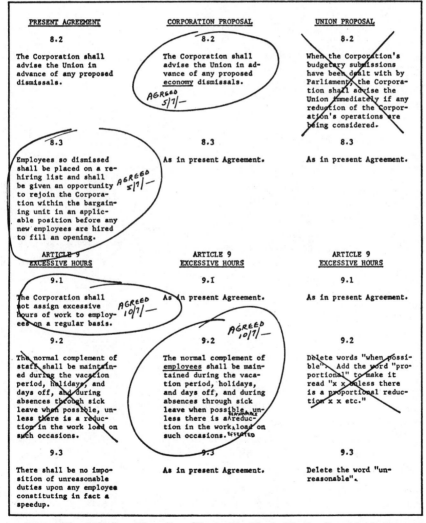

Source: Clive B. McKee, "Know Your Climate—The Key to Effective Bargaining," *Personnel,* vol. 34, no. 4, pp. 58–59.

FIGURE 25–1 (*continued*)

8.2

30/6/— Impossible. Management right to determine size of work force.

8.2

30/6/— Union claims examination should be permitted prior to any economy dismissals.

5/7/— WITHDRAWN.

9.2

7/7/— What is proportional? No better than reasonable & has implications. Proposed "EFFECTED"

8/7/— Agreed as in Corp. proposals with amendments as voted.

9.2

7/7/— Union claims workloads should be reduced mathematically.

8/7/— Union agrees to "effected" & "reasonable" together.

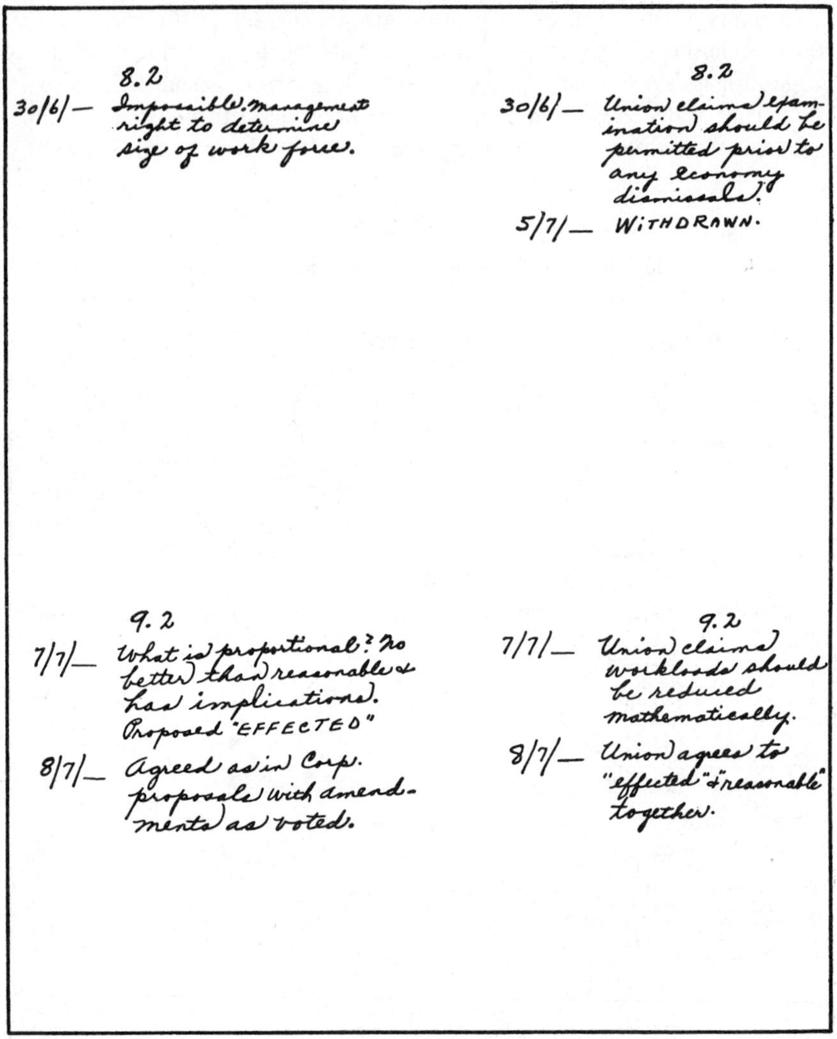

preparation calls for a considered program of information to be gathered, subjects to be studied, and assignment of responsibilities.

The foundation for negotiation is laid by fact gathering. To begin with, information should be collected, day by day, on how relations are progressing under the current contract. Such instances as grievances, disciplinary action, and disputes should be recorded under the sections or clauses to which they apply. Information should also be gathered on contract clauses of other companies in one's own community and industry. Estimates should also be made of the possible impact of economic and political trends. And finally, additional sources of information or access to experts should be provided for in the event negotiations take unexpected turns.

Preparation should include attention to appropriate subject matter. Obviously, the current contract is a good place to begin. The present clauses should therefore be carefully reviewed, as illustrated in Figure 25–1. Then, current business literature, trade periodicals, and union publications should be closely scrutinized to ascertain what new subjects are likely to come up. The unions invariably give clues to the topics they may bring up. The guaranteed annual wage, for example, which led to supplementary unemployment benefits, was noised about for a few years before it was brought to the forefront of negotiations. A close study of business conditions also can throw light on the types of demands which are likely to be made or which the company may want to make.

And finally, careful assignments of responsibility should be made for gathering information, analyzing information and suggested proposals, and deciding upon the company's position. Supervisors and superintendents, for example, are excellent sources of information on how the current contract is operating. They should be asked to submit regular as well as special reports on these matters. Staff members in the legal, personnel, commercial and economic research, and statistical departments should be assigned specific topics regarding which they are expected to collect pertinent information. Such materials should be funneled to one department or person who will be responsible for classifying, summarizing, and interpreting the findings. The personnel or industrial relations department would be the logical choice for this assignment. Of course, the ultimate authority for strategy to be pursued must rest with top management. If such departments do not exist, some line executive will have to assume this task.

Negotiating

For a number of years after the Wagner Act was passed, many top executives attempted to carry on the work of bargaining with unions. Although they recognized the need for experts in such fields as engineering, purchasing, sales, and production, they felt capable of handling personnel functions themselves. The results were to be expected. The unions, with full-time specialists on their staffs, gained many concessions unnoticed by the top executives, who seemed to think that wages alone were of importance in union negotiations. The advantages gained by unions in regard to such matters as grievance machinery, seniority rules, and discharge rules are evidences of the ineptness displayed by some top executives.

Again, personnel departments in some companies were little more than employment clerks and record keepers, so that they were in no position to advise management in negotiations. Indeed, the personnel manager seemed to be the last one to consult in such instances. Although lawyers were often called in, the company personnel department was invariably ignored. Only in recent years has there been a growing tendency to develop a strong labor relations division in the personnel department and to make it responsible for handling contract negotiations.

Although union-management relations are generally handled by each company on an individualized basis, there are instances in which bargaining and dispute settlements have been handled on an industrywide or area basis.[1] Cases in point are the steel and coal industries. For example, the UMW has carried on bargaining with the coal operators through their southern, northern, and anthracite producer groups. Agreements must be approved, however, by the individual companies and local unions with whom contracts are signed. Another interesting approach is found in the Mountain States Employers Council. This group, composed largely of employers in Wyoming, New Mexico, and Colorado, provides such services as information on wages, personnel policies, and labor relations; a staff to assist in negotiations; management workshops and conferences; and bulletins and surveys. Some of the larger airlines have also experimented with group talks, in an attempt to conduct mediation before troubles get far out of line and to negotiate on an informal basis.

Also of significance are attempts in various cities to bring all interested parties together with a view to better labor-management relations. In such instances a committee is formed representing various community, civic, and business interests. It discusses current industrial problems, formulates policies, and helps settle disputes through available mediation, conciliation, and arbitration services. Variations of this program have been undertaken in a number of cities, including Boston, San Francisco, St. Louis, Buffalo, Minneapolis, Newark, Pittsburgh, Tacoma, and South Bend.

Subject Matter of Agreements

The range of subjects covered in union contracts does not differ significantly. These usually include:

1. Management prerogatives.
2. Union recognition.
3. Hours of work.
4. Wages.

---

[1] In some cases, a number of unions sit in while another union is bargaining so as to be in a better position to coordinate their bargaining when their turn comes up. This is termed "coordinated bargaining."

5. Vacations and holidays.
6. Seniority.
7. Working conditions.
8. Layoffs and rehirings.
9. Arbitration and mediation.
10. Renewal clauses.

The details and treatment of these subjects differ so much that it is impractical even to begin to cite examples here. Most of these subjects are discussed in preceding or succeeding chapters. In a sense, the union contract merely formalizes what should be good personnel practice on all these subjects. However, some comment is needed on management prerogatives, union recognition, renewal clauses, and inter-company cooperation.

1. Management Prerogatives. A clause of management prerogatives pertains to the rights, responsibilities, and areas of action which it retains, free from questioning or joint action by the union. It may be stated in general terms such as the following:

Except as otherwise in this agreement expressly provided, nothing in this agreement contained shall be deemed to limit the company in any way in the exercise of the regular and customary functions of management, including the making in connection therewith of such rules relating to operations as it shall deem advisable.

Or it may be more explicit, as in the following:

Nothing in this agreement shall limit the company in the exercise of its function of management, under which it shall have, among others, the right to hire new employees and to direct the working force; to discipline, suspend, or discharge for cause; transfer or lay off employees because of lack of work; to require employees to observe company rules and regulations, not inconsistent with the provisions of this agreement; to decide the number and location of its plants, products to be manufactured, and the methods and schedules of production, including the means and processes of manufacturing, provided that the company will not use these prerogatives for the purpose of discrimination. It is agreed that these enumerations of management prerogatives shall not be deemed to exclude other prerogatives not enumerated.

The former is preferred by some because it is general and all-inclusive. However, those who favor the latter statement argue that generalized clauses leave their meaning open to questioning by the union. But the latter is weak in the sense that what is not specifically reserved by management is presumably open to bargaining or union action. Some students also feel that all prerogative clauses are useless because labor will not countenance them if it feels its rights are injured. Moreover, labor is moving in on so many areas that were once construed to be out of bounds that there are few, if any, subjects that have not come within the scope of bargaining in some company or another.[2]

2. Recognition of Union Clause.   Whereas clauses of management's prerogatives are not written into all contracts, clauses covering union recognition and prerogatives are invariably included. The recognition clause is necessary to indicate specifically the bargaining agency and the unit covered. Although not universal practice, the rights of unions and permissible activities are also included. Examples of clauses in this category are the following:

a.   The company recognizes the union as the sole representative of its hourly and piece rate employees, including employees in the retail store, but excluding executive supervisory employees, guards, office employees, and technical advisers, for the purpose of collective bargaining in respect to rates of pay, wages, hours of work, and other conditions of employment.

b.   The company recognizes the union as the sole collective bargaining agency of the workers in those departments in which the union has a majority of the workers.

c.   Union activities may be conducted by employees on the company property on the free time of such employees, but, except as provided herein under the subject of "grievances," the union shall not engage in any union business, discussions, or activities during working hours, and shall not solicit memberships, collect dues, or conduct organizing activities on the company property on the company time. The company will not permit any antiunion activities or discussions during working hours.

3. Renewal Clauses.   The term of the contract and arrangements for renewals are also included in union contracts. Two examples of such clauses are shown in the following:

a.   This agreement shall remain in force for one year from the date hereof and shall automatically renew itself from year to year, unless written notice of desire to terminate or to modify any portion or any of the terms hereof is given by either party to the other at least 30 days prior to the expiration of any such annual period.

  If notice of desire to terminate or to amend shall have been given, negotiations for a new or amended agreement shall begin not later than 20 days prior to the expiration of the current yearly period and shall continue until an agreement has been reached. During such negotiations, this agreement shall remain in full force and effect, provided, however, that if negotiations continue beyond the termination of the annual period, either party may then terminate this agreement at any time upon 30 days' written notice to the other party.

b.   This agreement becomes effective as of May 1, 19—, and shall remain in ef-

---

[2] Worth watching in this connection is the movement toward "codetermination" in Germany, where labor representatives by law are given a place on the board of directors. The exclusive rights of management are in such an event significantly diluted.

fect until May 1, 19—, and each year thereafter unless written notice of cancellation or changes desired is given 60 days prior to any yearly expiration date by any of the other parties of this agreement. If changes or amendments are desired, such written notice shall contain a complete list of the changes and amendments proposed. In that case, conferences shall be arranged to begin during the 15 days immediately following the 60 days' notice date.

Living with the Contract

An agreement, once reached, is not self-effectuating. It must, in the first place, be communicated to all affected levels. This means more than the printing of the union contract. Meetings with supervisors, for example, are desirable to point out the significant features of the new contract. This not only makes the supervisors feel that they are important factors in labor relations but also prepares them to face employees with a greater feeling of assurance.

It would also be desirable to hold extended training sessions based on the contract. Clause by clause, the various management levels could be shown the nature of the clauses, why they were adopted, what they really mean, and how they must be interpreted. Answers can be supplied to many questions which will be raised on the floor by the employees. And courses of action to be taken and executives to be consulted in the event of doubt can be suggested to help resolve difficulties that are apt to be encountered.

All of this prepares executives, in the second place, to handle labor relations matters day by day, as they pertain to or involve the union contract. The supervisors, in particular, will not only know their responsibilities and rights, but will also be more effective in communicating their arguments and the company's position. They will not make mistakes due to ignorance which the union might interpret as a prejudiced desire to undercut the union and to shortchange the employees in what is coming to them.

And in the third place, living with the contract involves knowing what to do about disagreements that arise but cannot be settled at the point of issue. Grievance channels, arbitration procedures, and provisions for mediation should be known, understood, and correctly practiced. These are merely mentioned here because they are discussed more fully in the next chapter.

In discussing these matters of union-management relations, no attempt has been made to pass judgment on the labor union movement. To some executives, it is an anathema. It is viewed not only as an interference with management prerogatives but sometimes as a parasitic if not corrupt blight upon civilization. An appraisal of such views is out of place here. And no matter what one's views are, business often must deal with unions. Consequently, it has been intended here to outline the basic considerations of which management must be aware in labor relations matters.

It may be noted, however, that both management and labor are made up of human beings—not one side solely of angels and the other solely of devils. Each can suffer from the ills of unethical, ignorant, and prejudiced motives. And as one studies union-management relations, it is equally clear that sound labor relations are essentially found in good personnel practices and human relations, whether in a unionized or a nonunionized setup.

QUESTIONS

1. What is the justification for unions?
2. What is the difference between craft and industrial unions?
3. In what ways do independent unions differ from those affiliated with national organizations?
4. For what purpose did the Congress of the United States pass the National Labor Relations Act?
5. What acts of management could be construed to constitute unfair labor practices under the Labor Management Relations Act?
6. Since employers in some instances have been prevented from going out of business because they used this as a threat against unionizing, is not this a threat to freedom of private property usage?
7. Under the Labor Management Relations Act, what is the status of an employee who is out on strike?
8. In what ways can first-line supervisors contribute to collective bargaining by their company?
9. How should a company go about preparing for negotiating a contract with a union?
10. What steps should management take to make day-to-day living with a union contract more effective?

CASE 25–1. AN ALLEGED LAYOFF INEQUITY

The Tool Help Manufacturing Company has two unions, one of which represents the shop and the other the office. There also are nonunionized employees consisting of management and management staff people, the personnel department being an example of the latter.

During a decline in business, it was found necessary to lay off a number of people. In both the shop and office, separations were based on seniority according to the union agreements. Enough of the newer service employees were separated from the payroll until the available work matched the number of people for whom work could be provided.

Dissatisfaction arose when it was learned that some office workers in the personnel department were retained though their length of service was shorter than laid off workers in the general offices. As a case in point: Mary Withe—with three years service—a general office clerk doing payroll and personnel record work was to be laid off whereas Luanne Jones—with one year of service—doing similar work but located in the personnel department was to be retained. Mary could not understand this apparent breach of fairness, particularly because both she and Luanne were doing almost exactly the same kind of work, at the same rate of pay, and with the same fringe benefits.

Question

1. What, if any, is the justification for this apparent inequity?

CASE 25–2. A LETTER TO EMPLOYEES

To counter some of the claims a union had been making during a strike, the director of industrial relations of the struck company decided to send the following letter to the striking employees:

To ALL OUR EMPLOYEES:

You have now been out a week on your union's strike. We have heard it said that we "forced" you out on strike. Nothing is more ridiculous. We would be pleased to have you return. Some already have. We deny we forced you out.

We have heard it said that you must struggle against the company to secure justice. May we point out that our wage offer would place our rates at or above every company in this neighborhood. We deny that you must struggle with us to get a fair offer.

We have heard it said that your union has received congratulations for taking a militant stand against a repressive company. We question that militancy is a part of good collective bargaining. And we deny that we have ever been or intend to be repressive.

We have heard it said that a strike is necessary to get an honorable settlement. We have been honorable in our dealings with the employees from the day the factory opened, and with the union from the day it came into the lives of our employees. We deny that a strike creates honor.

To repeat, you have lost a week's wages already. Besides, it would take a year to make up the week's wage loss from the increase per hour which the company is ready to grant. Why add to your losses? We deny that these losses by strike are needed.

Question

1. What is your judgment of countering the union through this medium of a letter and through such arguments?

HANDLING GRIEVANCES 26

Employee Dissatisfactions

A common impression of labor-management relations is that they are generally unsatisfactory. This is questionable when it is seen that employee dissatisfaction as measured by time lost through strikes averages less than one quarter of 1 percent of total hours worked. But what about dissatisfied employees who are at work but who are not working at their full capacity. Though unmeasured, the general opinion is that such unrest causes significant losses of productivity.

Hence, it behooves management to exert effort to reduce employee dissatisfactions. Whether management proceeds on an individual basis or operates in conjunction with unions, it is argued here that the basic steps and principles of handling grievances—the particular subject of dissatisfactions discussed in this chapter—are much the same. Thus, grievance handling is taken up here first without reference to union relations. Then, note is made of some specific grievance procedures of interest when unions are involved. In either case, grievance handling is assumed to be as much a responsibility of line executives as of specialized staff personnel departments.

Specifically, the subject of grievances is discussed here under the following broad headings:

1. Basic considerations of grievance handling.
2. Steps in handling grievances.
3. Principles of handling grievances.
4. Machinery for handling grievances.

BASIC CONSIDERATIONS

Before getting into specifics of grievance handling, it is desirable at the outset to define the concept of grievances, to note some of its im-

plications, and to comment on organizational responsibilities for grievance handling.

Meaning of Grievances

Although definitions are sometimes considered sophomoric, in few
cases are definitions more useful than in the matter of grievances. This
is so because making a mistake about what is or is not a grievance can
only lead to added trouble in relations with employees.

Broadly speaking, a grievance is any dissatisfaction that adversely
affects organizational relations and productivity. But it is simply impractical to adopt such a broad definition. No company has the resources, skill, or time to handle all grievances.

To be workable, a definition must be more restrictive. Noncompany
sources usually have to be excluded because they are out of the control
of a company. Highly emotionalized grievances may well have to be
excluded because of the lack of skill to handle them. And unexpressed
dissatisfactions have to be excluded because of their nebulous character.
So it is common to define a grievance as a complaint expressed in writing
(or orally) on a company-related matter.

Implications of the Definition

Even this definition needs some explanation. In the first place, it is
presumed that there are, or will be, adverse effects upon productivity.
Some types of dissatisfaction are sources of good. Some of our greatest
advances have been made by dissatisfied people. The removal of such
motivators could scarcely be justified. But the irritants that reduce
productivity are another matter.

In the second place, the definition does not separate the subject matter
of the grievance from the undesirable attitude of the aggrieved. Let us
assume that an employee is disgruntled because of failure to receive a
raise. Will giving a raise remove the dissatisfaction; or must something
be done, in addition, about the wounded feelings? Obviously, the two
aspects need consideration; the term *grievance* must imply both subject
matter and personal attitudes.

In the third place, the definition must be accepted to mean that
anything—activity, policy, executive, or practice—in the company may
be the source of grievances. As a consequence, there is the implication
that a company is willing to consider whatever or whoever is causing
grievances.

In the fourth place, does the reference to expressed grievances imply
the exclusion of unexpressed grievances? Requiring an expressed statement may serve to formalize the grievance processes. But it would not be
wise to assume that no discontent exists unless it is stated in writing. On

the contrary, implied grievances are very dangerous because it is not known when they may erupt. Moreover, the damage dissatisfied workers do to productivity goes on unimpaired. Hence, such efforts as close supervisory observation and attitude surveys should be employed to ascertain if there are smoldering areas of unrest.

And finally, the definition does not imply any judgment about the injustice, unfairness, rationality, or emotionality of the grievance. It implies, therefore, respect for the opinion of the aggrieved. Grievances based on misconceptions, lack of thinking, or emotionalism may be very hard to handle. But they may become harder to handle if the aggrieved is accused of stupidity. Better by far to give a case every appearance of its being fully worthy of serious consideration.

Channels for Handling Grievances

Channels for handling grievances are needful organizational matters, and should be carefully developed and information about them fully disseminated. The labor relations department, various levels of executives, and the employees should know what relationships exist among them and how the various groups should work together. As noted earlier, grievances may be handled by the company and the employees themselves, or through unions. This phase of the subject is discussed more fully later in this chapter in relation to the machinery for handling grievances.

STEPS IN HANDLING GRIEVANCES

Grievance handling requires that certain steps be taken and that basic guidelines be adopted. Both are done in conjunction in actual cases. But for purposes of discussion, it is better to take them up separately. Steps are discussed in this section and principles in the next section.

Grievances must be handled in some systematic manner, the machinery of which is described in the last section of this chapter. No matter what the machinery, however, grievance handling calls for a number of common steps based on good ground rules. For convenience of discussion, steps are taken up in this section and rules in the next, although steps and rules are interdependent.

In handling grievances, the following steps should be taken:

1. Define, describe, or express the nature of the grievance as clearly and as fully as possible.
2. Gather all the facts that serve to explain when, how, where, to whom, and why the grievance occurred.
3. Establish tentative solutions or answers to the grievance.

4. Gather additional information to check the validity of the tentative solutions, and thus ascertain the best possible solution.
5. Apply the solution.
6. Follow up the case to see that it has been handled satisfactorily and the trouble eliminated.

Describing Grievances

It is patent that good grievance handling should start with a clear and full statement of an employee's complaint. This calls for being sure existing dissatisfactions are expressed correctly. This section is concerned with (1) reliability of expressed complaints and (2) discovery of unexpressed grievances.

1. Determining the Correct Grievance. Many grievances, after being "settled," turn up again to plague management. The trouble in such instances invariably is that the wrong grievance has been handled. This could have been avoided if care had been taken at the outset to describe as accurately as possible the issue at the heart of the employee's complaint. As it is, superficial aspects of grievances are adjusted, while the fundamental cause of trouble remains untouched.

The chances of getting at the right grievances are increased if care is used in the initial contact with the employee. Encouraging a person to talk is one means of getting closer to the truth. And the practice of asking the aggrieved to put the case in writing is also desirable. A good example of a form for this purpose and one that would be useful for recording the entire history of a case is shown in Figure 26–1. This form could also be used in disciplinary cases.

2. Unexpressed Grievances. There are cases, however, when individual grievances go unexpressed and unexposed for long periods of time. If these were discovered earlier, the intensity of feeling which is ultimately generated would be largely minimized.

Various methods are useful in this connection. Statistical studies of turnover, complaints, transfers, earnings, and sources of suggestions and lack thereof can provide clues to actual or probable grievances. And skill in observation of the behaviorisms, attitudes, and habits of one's subordinates is particularly helpful in detecting signs of changes due to unexpected grievances.

Gathering Facts

Having defined grievances as accurately as possible, the next step is to gather all relevant facts about the issue. It is important to know when the alleged grievance was first experienced, whether or not it has been repeated, how and where it took place, and the circumstances under

FIGURE 26-1

INCIDENT REPORT

REPORTED BY _____

Name _____

Position _____

TO _____

Location _____

Name _____   Title _____

Name _____   Title _____

DETERMINE OBJECTIVE — What I am trying to accomplish —

1. GET THE FACTS
(Be sure you have the whole story)

2. WEIGH AND DECIDE
(Don't jump at conclusions)
(Possible actions)

3. ACTION I HAVE TAKEN

RECOMMENDED ACTION FOR MY SUPERVISOR
(Don't Pass the Buck)

4. CHECK RESULTS

Date _____   Condition Found _____

Date _____   Condition Found _____

HOW TO HANDLE A PROBLEM
DETERMINE OBJECTIVES

1.—GET THE FACTS.
Review the record.
Find out what rules and plant customs apply.
Talk with individuals concerned.
Get opinions and feelings.
Be sure you have the whole story.

2.—WEIGH AND DECIDE.
Fit the facts together.
Consider their bearing on each other.
What possible actions are there?
Check practices and policies.
Consider objective and effect on individual, group, and production.
Don't jump at conclusions.

3.—TAKE ACTION.
Are you going to handle this yourself?
Do you need help in handling?
Should you refer this to your supervisor?
Watch the timing of your action.
Don't pass the buck.

4.—CHECK RESULTS.
How soon will you follow up?
How often will you need to check?
Watch for changes in output, attitudes, and relationships.
Did your action help production?

DID YOUR ACTION HELP TO SOLVE YOUR PROBLEM?

If you were the employee involved, would you be satisfied with the action taken?

CHECK RESULTS _____ DID YOUR ACTION SOLVE YOUR PROBLEM? _____ HAS THIS INCIDENT BEEN HANDLED TO THE SATISFACTION

OF THE EMPLOYEE? _____ FOREMAN? _____ SUPERINTENDENT? _____ MANAGEMENT? _____ HOW OFTEN HAS THIS CASE BEEN FOLLOWED UP

BY YOU? _____ DAYS, WEEKS? _____ HAVE YOU SEEN ANY CHANGES IN OUTPUT, ATTITUDE, RELATIONSHIPS?

BETTER OR WORSE? _____

APPROVED: _____

Could this problem be avoided through the use of the foundations?

which it transpired. This does not imply that grievances should be handled like law cases. It does mean that if the confidence of employees is to be gained and held, they must be thoroughly convinced that management is completely sincere in seeing that justice is done. Such fact gathering or sifting requires a knack in interviewing and listening to employees, the principles of which were discussed in an earlier chapter.

1. Nature of Facts. Besides serving to convince the employee of the employer's sincerity, the step of gathering data is indispensable to a fair decision.

But what are facts, and what are opinions? Practically speaking, any claim which can be substantiated to the satisfaction of a reasonable person may be tagged as a fact; otherwise, it is an opinion.

It is well to note here that both labor and management tend to perceive or evaluate facts according to their particular roles in the business and social world. Management should be aware of these predispositions. If it is, it will deal more carefully with grievances and consequently gain the confidence of employees which is so necessary in gaining acceptance of opinions that cannot be proved.

2. Importance of Records. Since fact gathering is not an easy task, after a grievance arises it is perhaps wise to develop a set of records and keep them up to date. For example, such records as merit rating, job progression, attendance records, educational records, and suggestions are invaluable. They serve to show in advance, for example, who should get a promotion, and to warn others why their chances of advancing are not good.

Establishing Tentative Solutions

After getting a clear picture of the grievance, the next step in the procedure calls for the establishment of tentative solutions or answers.

But how are tentative solutions determined? In the first place, management has its own experience to fall back upon. Very likely, it will have had similar cases in the past, and these should provide it with the perspective required to figure out solutions applicable to the present case. In addition, it should have observed how other companies have handled similar grievances. In the third place, alternative answers may be collected from technical and trade publications. And if all the foregoing fail, the best possible guesses will have to be made. The important point is that a thorough search, commensurate with the importance of the case, should be made for alternative solutions.

Checking Tentative Solutions

Unfortunately, the executive cannot check tentative solutions as the scientist can in the laboratory. There are two possible courses of action.

First, the executive can rely on trial and error, or can check by applying a decision. This is a risky course; but often, it must be done because of the lack of time for further analysis. The second choice is to evaluate alternatives on the basis of personal experience or the experiences of others. This presupposes that there exists information on past successes and failures with similar cases. And as an executive gains experience, and as a company compiles grievance records, there is good reason to believe that this method can be very useful in checking out tentative solutions.

Applying Solutions

Having reached a decision, it seems common sense that it should be applied. Yet, it is not uncommon to find executives who shrink from making an unfavorable, although warranted, decision. Indeed, some avoid making decisions favorable to employees for fear of spoiling them or because it would signify that they themselves were wrong in the first place. Yet, subordinates dislike supervisors who refuse to take a definite stand, one way or the other.

The decision, having finally been reached, should then be passed along in clear, unequivocal terms. After all, a grievance cannot be handled just by listening to an employee's complaint; something must be done about it. The ultimate decision is the tool of action.

Follow-Up of the Grievance

It is unsafe to conclude that a grievance has been well handled until a check is made to determine whether the employee's attitude has been favorably changed. To assure themselves along these lines, executives concerned need a timetable and a method of follow-up, or feedback.

As far as a timetable is concerned, many executives rely upon their memories to check on how grievances have been handled. This is simple, but if there is any danger of forgetting, a written record should be made. Records require paper work, but they do minimize serious losses.

As for feedback methods, several are available. Perhaps the most common is casual observation—just see how the employee is taking the decision, whether favorably or unfavorably. Next in order is to ask whether or not the employee is satisfied with the decision. Somewhat similar in nature, but more subtle, is the practice of a general discussion with the employee with a view to indirectly deducing attitudes. A fourth method is to ask others about a given employee's reactions. This latter is dangerous because it smacks of spying. However, when used in the hands of an expert, it is desirable because it takes place away from the particular person involved.

PRINCIPLES OF HANDLING GRIEVANCES

The foregoing steps will be little more than a superficial routine unless they are based upon well-considered principles. Such principles are not absolute insurance of success in dealing with grievances because laws of human behavior are nonexistent. However, principles do work most of the time; hence, it is desirable to search them out and then rely on them as guides.

In the field of handling grievances, a number of principles have been distilled from the experiences of many companies. Grouping of these for purposes of discussion is at best a makeshift. Thus the classification here merely lumps available suggestions under the general headings of interviewing, attitudes toward employees, attitudes toward supervision, and long-run rules.

Principles of Interviewing

In handling grievances, a considerable amount of time must be spent talking to employees, gathering data from them, and passing on various types of information. Such talks, to be most effective, should follow definite patterns and adhere to some well-tested rules. These have been discussed in an earlier chapter, so it is unnecessary to repeat the materials here.

Management's Attitude toward Employees

During the interview and afterward, and in other connections, the wise executive seeks to develop an attitude toward employees that will result in gaining their confidence. In the first place, avoid giving the impression that subordinates are ignorant. No matter how ignorant one may be (and we all are, more or less, about different subjects), reacts favorably to those who deride one's intelligence. Besides, sooner or later, the executive will underestimate the intelligence of some employee, to the executive's own chagrin.

To develop confidence, in the second place, it is also wise to take the stand that employees are fair in presenting their grievances. This does not mean that care should not be exercised to guard against unwarranted or prejudiced demands. It does mean, however, that management should give the impression that the viewpoints of employees are considered to be fair unless proved otherwise.

And finally, in handling grievances, management should display a sincere interest in the problems of employees and a constructive willingness to be of help. Take, for example, the supervisor: supervisors are the representatives of management to employees, but are also representatives of employees to management. If they do not accept the latter responsibility with a full spirit of helpfulness, the confidence and loyalty of employees will be difficult to attain.

Management's Responsibilities

In handling grievances, all executives must have confidence in themselves, be fully aware of their responsibilities, and be willing to carry these burdens. Such a positive attitude must be apparent to employees in order to gain their respect and cooperation.

An executive who lacks self-confidence soon finds that employees are aware of this and tend to beware. Employees do not like to place their grievances in insecure or incompetent hands. They will tend to go around or over the head of such an executive. In either case the prestige and the effectiveness of the executive suffer.

Likewise, executives should recognize the serious responsibilities undertaken. They have obligated themselves in many ways for the success, happiness, and well-being of a number of human beings. Within their capacities and opportunities, they must seek to carry out those responsibilities. In dealing with grievances, they must give the impression of serious consideration. There must be no light-minded attitude or flippant remarks about the grievances of employees—they are no joking matter.

Long-Run Principles

In handling grievances, it is important that consideration be given not only to effects in the present but also to long-run and sometimes far-distant implications. As a consequence, grievances should be handled in terms of their total effect upon the organization and not solely their immediate or individual effect.

1. Long-Run Effects.   As an example, take the case of an employee who complains that he or she rather than someone else should have received a particular promotion. How this case is handled and what decision is reached will certainly have an effect upon the individual in question. But others, too, will watch the case; they will note the decision and reach conclusions. And conclusions are guides to behavior. Hence each case should be handled so that all parties, whether directly involved or indirectly interested, are convinced of the fundamental integrity of management.

2. Dangers of Losing Confidence.   Another truth to be remembered in the process of handling grievances is that it takes a long time to gain the confidence of employees but that, once gained, it can be lost overnight by a foolish decision or inept handling of a single case. In other words, eternal vigilance is the price of good labor relations. Every grievance must be considered important, no matter how irrelevant or insignificant it is. If an executive is tired, in a bad temper, or otherwise feeling out of sorts, it would be much smarter to ask for a postponement of a grievance hearing; but it should be done courteously, apologetically, and with an apparent attitude of regret. It is harder to overcome the results of hotheaded blundering, for example, than those caused by delays.

3. Human Nature. In the long run, too, it is well to remember that human nature will not change much, if at all. People will become neither much better nor much worse. In handling grievances, people should be taken for what they are—including their strengths and their weaknesses. For example, fairness has been desired for ages past and will be for ages to come; hence, a basic question will always be: "what is fair?" It will be standards of fairness that are likely to change much more than the desire for fairness.

4. Effects of the Past. This leads to the thought that a manager should weigh decisions not only in terms of their future impact but should also give consideration to what has happened in the past. Often, when an employee complains, the source of the complaint may actually be found in the past, not present, conditions. But to make the complaint sound credible, the worker may blame some present condition. For example, an employee who complained about wages in a given case was really angry because of open criticism by a supervisor six months previously. In short, grievances of today often have their roots in the acts of yesterday and their branches in the effects of tomorrow. The roots are sometimes difficult to locate, and how the branches will grow is difficult to forecast. But hard though the task may be, it must be tackled as best one can; otherwise, grievance handling becomes grievance fighting.

MACHINERY FOR HANDLING GRIEVANCES

Appropriate machinery must be established to take the steps and to apply the principles discussed in the preceding sections. Responsibility must be assigned to given organization units and executives. And the systematic flow of grievances through various stages and units must be encouraged through appropriate procedural designs. Hence, grievance handling requires attention to organizational responsibility and procedures.

Organizational Responsibility

Organizationally, grievance handling is divided between and shared by first-line supervision, staff and middle management executives, top management, and labor union representatives (when involved).

1. First-Line Supervision. First-line supervision should be accorded the first opportunity to handle grievances. It should be empowered to pass upon grievances within policies, rules, and jurisdictional limits established by the company. And it is good practice to require employees to present their grievances to their immediate superior, even though the final disposition must await higher authority. Otherwise, supervisors are in danger of losing any importance in the organization and the respect of their subordinates.

2. Staff and Middle Management Executives. All grievances cannot be handled at the lowest levels because some involve issues or policies beyond their authority or capacity. Hence, responsibility is placed upon divisional, group, and area managers to handle grievance cases with broader implications. And these may be aided by a staff labor relations unit in three ways: The staff may supply line executives with advice or information on grievance handling; it may help executives in the processing of cases; or it may be given authority actually to settle certain classes of cases.

3. Top Management Levels. Top management has three large areas of responsibility in grievance handling. First, it must assume jurisdiction of cases which are companywide in nature or significant as precedent makers. While the help of lower levels or staff units may be sought in such cases, they are of a nature the responsibility for which should not be evaded or delegated. Second, top management must establish the broad policies and rules upon which grievance handling in the company will be based. And third, it must check on how grievance handling is being carried out by lower organizational levels; it has a control function.

4. Outside Agencies. The use of an "ombudsman," or an independent, outside party, is suggested in Figure 26–2, as the final step in resolving grievances in nonunion companies.

5. Labor Union Representatives. And finally, in many companies, labor union representatives interact in the various organizational segments of the company. Shop and office stewards work at supervisory levels; higher level stewards and union agents work with upper management levels; and officials of union locals, business agents of unions, and representatives of national union offices work at key points of grievance cases wherever they develop.

Superimposed upon or paralleling the formal company organization structure is that of the union structure. The role the union plays often encompasses informal relations. Union representatives work out with their company counterparts decisions that bend contractual agreements or are based on timesaving shortcuts. But space here permits only touching upon formal relationships. These can be seen more clearly in the discussion of procedural aspects of grievance handling.

FIGURE 26–2

**Ombudsman and Grievance
Handling in a Nonunionized Plant**

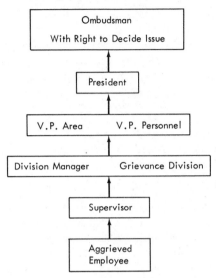

An important question in grievance procedures is how union represent-atives should be compensated. In some instances time spent in the procedures are paid for by the union and in other instances by the company.

Grievance-Handling Procedures

Grievance handling usually involves a number of people, dealing with problems that often go through a number of stages, and sometimes extends over days to months of time. A well-designed procedure is needed if these variables are to be effectively coordinated. It must prescribe how various aspects of grievances are to be handled, by whom, in what order, and in what time periods. This section is concerned, therefore, with a discussion of such procedures and of arbitration, which is often an important part of such procedures.

1. Design of Procedures. Grievance-handling procedures are desir-able whether a company is or is not unionized. In nonunionized firms, a representative procedure is that of a company which has established a clear line for an aggrieved employee to follow first to the immediate supervisor; then to the personnel department supervisor; then to a joint meeting of the vice president of personnel, the personnel manager, and the plant manager; and then, if need be, to the president of the company. An interesting example of the procedure in a unionized situation is detailed in the following statement:

All disputes and grievances arising under the terms of this agreement shall be adjusted in the following manner:

The union grievance committee shall consist of five members, each of whom shall be responsible for grievances in a zone of the plant. The entire plant, for purposes of this Article, will be separated into five zones.

First Step. A grievance will be taken up by the employee and the shop steward or committeeman with the supervisor of the department.

Second Step. If a satisfactory adjustment is not reached, the shop steward will refer the grievance to the member of the grievance committee responsible for that zone. This member of the grievance committee, with or without the shop steward, will take the matter up with the department superintendent.

Third Step. If a satisfactory adjustment is not reached, the member of the grievance committee herein referred to will refer the grievance to the business agent of the union, who will present these grievances to the company each day at 10.00 A.M. The company at that time will return to the business agent of the union in written form any grievances which have been investigated.

The grievance committee of the union will meet with the labor relations manager or assistant or someone of higher authority in the industrial relations department of the company each Tuesday and Friday to discuss grievances which the union feels require clarification and/or additional investigation.

Fourth Step. If a satisfactory adjustment is not reached, grievances may be referred in writing to arbitration.

Time limits on these procedures are as follows:

First Step. One day or 24 hours.
Second Step. One day or 24 hours.
Third Step. Five days, or sooner if answers are available.
Fourth Step. One week for submission.

Any dispute or grievance arising under the terms of this agreement which cannot be settled between the parties involved may be submitted by either party on written notice to the other party to an arbitration committee for their determination.

The arbitration committee shall consist of three representatives of the company and three of the union, the seventh and impartial arbiter to be selected by the six members designated.

If no agreement can be reached as to the seventh and impartial arbiter within three days after the first meeting of the six members of the committee, then they shall jointly petition the American Arbitration Association to make the appointment within five days after notification has been received.

The decision of the seventh and impartial member of the committee shall be final and binding upon both parties to this agreement. Every effort shall be made by the impartial arbiter to render a decision to both parties within 10 days after the conclusion of the hearing.

The parties shall equally bear the expense of the impartial arbiter.

2. Arbitration. Ideally, the grievances of employees should be resolved by management and employees themselves. In practice, the two often cannot reach mutually satisfactory agreements. The alternatives then are a power struggle or arbitration. Obviously, the former is still often chosen. But the discussion here is with the latter, which is also often selected.

In arbitration, the services of an outside third party are sought to settle a grievance (or for that matter, other types of disputes, such as interpretation of contract clauses). The assumption is that an impartial, competent outsider can render a fair verdict not attainable from the parties themselves because of their prejudiced viewpoints or highly emotionalized stands. Moreover, by forgoing the costs of a power struggle, arbitration is not only a faster and less costly method of settling grievances, but is also one that reduces the chances of an escalation of the disagreement. Care must be used, however, in selecting a good arbitrator and in establishing rules governing this role in the grievance-handling procedure.

Arbitrators in a given case may be selected by the parties themselves or, upon their agreement, by some outside group. Thus, labor and management may themselves select an arbitrator. Or they may turn to the American Arbitration Association (a privately organized, nonprofit national organization founded in 1926) to recommend someone from its roster of accredited arbitrators. During disputes, the Federal Mediation and Conciliation Service may be called upon to exercise its good offices in bringing the parties together or to recommend an arbitrator. And an example at the state level is provided by the New York State Board of Mediation, which can offer mediation services or lend assistance in arbitration.

It is imperative to agree on the role and jurisdiction of the arbitrator. The agreement should be included as a clause in the union contract. It should specify how the arbitrator is to be selected and the term of his service. It should clearly state which grievances or aspects of grievances are arbitrable and which are not. It should prescribe how cases may go to arbitration. It should list the rules of procedure for hearing cases in arbitration. It should state whether the decision of the arbitrator is final or is reviewable in the courts. And it should specify how the arbitrator is to be paid, and by whom.

This section on arbitration may be summarized by reference to Table 26–1. This table lists various operational aspects of arbitration. And it is also of interest because it makes note of other devices for settling disputes. To those who contend that management gives up its rights of final decision to outsiders, no matter how experienced and impartial, when arbitrators are used, conciliation and mediation, for example, may be preferable. These are processes by which outside parties, usually

TABLE 26–1 Comparison of Procedures to Settle Industrial Disputes*

	How and by Whom Initiated	Procedure	Administrator	Who Selects Arbitrator, Mediator, Board, etc.	Decision	Appeals	Conclusion
Voluntary arbitration	By mutual agreement, or on demand of one party pursuant to prior agreement	Under rules chosen by the parties	The parties themselves or AAA, or any other agency set up or chosen by parties	The parties, by mutual agreement	Award, based on evidence presented by parties at hearings and which parties agree in advance to accept	To court for enforcement or judgment, if good faith fails, or for correction of errors or misconduct	Execution of award in all but rare instances
Compulsory arbitration	By government agency or decree	As provided by government agency, or improvised by arbitrator	Whatever government agency orders the arbitration, or the arbitrator himself	Usually appointed by government agency	Enforceable award	To the courts	Acceptance of award, or strike or lock-out, or seizure
Conciliation	By invitation of parties, or in initiation by outside person or agency, or by conciliator, or government agency	Improvised—no set procedure	None	Named by government agency or outside person; parties may or may not agree to accept his services	None; result is compromise, agreement, or rejection	To public opinion	Compromise, agreement to arbitrate, or strike or lock-out, or seizure
Mediation	By agreement of parties, or in initiation by outside efforts, or by government order or government agency	Improvised	The mediator, or the agency chosen to mediate	Named by mediation agency or chosen by parties	Compromise, or recommendation which parties are at liberty to reject	To public opinion	Compromise, agreement to arbitrate, or strike or lock-out, or seizure
Fact-finding	By government agency or decree, or by agreement of the parties	As set by government agency, or the board	The board	Government agency	Recommendation	To public opinion	Acceptance or recommendation, compromise, or strike or lockout, or seizure
Litigation	By summons of one party to other to appear in court	Rules of the court	The court	The court	Decision of the court	To a higher court	Enforcement of eventual court decision

* Prepared by the American Arbitration Association.

governmental agencies, attempt to bring the conflicting parties together, to clarify issues, and to examine the various contentions. But they exert no powers of decision. As a consequence, this form of intervention appeals to some students of labor-management relations.

QUESTIONS

1. On what grounds may it be argued that some employee dissatisfactions are desirable but that some are undesirable?
2. What is the difference between subject matter of and attitudes in employee grievances?
3. Why is it desirable to make the supervisor the first stage in handling grievances?
4. What are the basic steps in handling grievances?
5. How may attitude surveys provide information about specific grievances or possible sources of grievances?
6. What methods are useful in deriving feedback on the handling of employee grievances?
7. What attitudes, if held by management, are helpful in grievance handling?
8. What is the role of unions in grievance handling?
9. Distinguish between arbitration, mediation, and conciliation.
10. What role may the American Arbitration Association play in grievance handling in a company?

CASE 26–1. COMPULSORY OVERTIME

The work load of the Job Shop Company is rather variable. As a consequence, daily and weekly working hours are not constant. Although the standard working day is eight hours, overtime is not uncommon so that extra hours may run from one to three. Similarly, the standard work week is five days but Saturday overtime is also common. Of course, such overtime is paid at the rate of time-and-one-half.

The employees like the overtime rate. They do not like to be asked to work overtime on short notice. For example, some employees may be told in the afternoon of a given day that extra hours must be worked. Or, on Friday they may be told to report the next day on Saturday. Family or personal reasons are not permitted as excuses. The argument of the company is that the demands of the customers must be met or business (and jobs) will be lost to competitors.

This arrangement has in recent months been meeting with opposition from employees. And now a unionization movement is gaining momentum. Organizers are inciting action by pointing out that among the demands that would be taken up under collective bargaining would be that for the right of voluntary overtime.

Question

1. In its arguments on the issue of overtime, what can it do to reconcile personal needs of employees and the facts of economic competition whether or not a union is involved?

CASE 26-2. THE TRAINEE

Jill Smate was thinking about her experiences in the business world six months after graduation. She has been employed as a trainee in the trust department of a branch bank operation, a job in which she had been led to believe that great opportunities lay ahead. After an initial orientation period of three weeks she had been assigned to the portfolio management section as an assistant to the officer in charge.

In this capacity, her experiences had three questionable features. First, as an assistant to an officer, it was her job to perform what she found to be tasks of a dull, repetitive nature. As an example of this were standard form letters in which she merely filled in pre-established figures. Any significant matters were always decided by the officer.

Second, was the matter of personal evaluation. A person was not expected to confer with an immediate superior on ratings. Instead she might talk to the chief branch manager who had received the ratings from the personnel department which in turn had received the evaluation report from the immediate supervisor. This second-hand method lacked a personal touch.

And third, was the matter of salary. Even if a person had an excellent rating, she could expect to receive only a few dollars more than a person with an average rating. Besides, new trainees entering the bank were paid about as much as those who had entered one to three years earlier and who had excellent ratings in all that time.

Questions

1. Is there any justification for these practices of the bank?
2. Is Jill too good for her job and its prospects?

CHAPTER 27

DISCIPLINARY ACTION

INTRODUCTION

Management's job is made unpleasant at times because employees have grievances against the company or the company has complaints against employees. In the foregoing chapter, therefore, attention was directed to management's tasks in handling grievances of employees. The present chapter is concerned with disciplinary action, or what management must do when the employee is, or is alleged to be, at fault.

Since disciplinary action implies penalties which have undesirable implications, management must be fully aware of when, how, against whom, and why disciplinary action should be taken. Only then will this action, however unpleasant, be likely to gain its purposes with a minimum loss of employee goodwill. Even when an employee fully deserves punishment, it is invariably accepted with some amount of ill feeling.

It is well to point out that penalties as the basis of disciplinary action have some challengers. Both in industry, and in civil cases, punishment has not always proved to be an effective deterrent to repetition of deviant behavior. Hence, some argue that penalties should be replaced by constructive plans which show the wrong-doer why the transgressions were wrong and why good behavior is better for the worker and the company (or society, in the latter case). And some evidence has been adduced to support this view. Desirable though it may eventually be, such a constructive attitude toward discipline on a general basis is not likely to supplant punishment in the near future.

In the discussion that follows, it has been found desirable, first, to examine the meaning of discipline and disciplinary action. Second, the steps to be taken in disciplinary action are noted. Third, some principles to be followed in taking the steps are suggested.

In the case of disciplinary action, as with grievance handling, management may act jointly with unions. Later in the chapter, therefore, mention is made of this phase of disciplinary action.

Disciplinary action is most cases is taken by line executives. The personnel department may be responsible for advising the line on desirable practices or for taking final action on such serious penalties as discharge. Hence, in this chapter the discussion of methods and principles is pertinent to both line and staff executives.

Definition of Terms

A common complaint about employees is that they do not always do what they are told. Why do they fail to follow orders? There are several possible explanations. The employees may be ignorant; they may misunderstand orders and instructions; they may be careless; they may have little sense of responsibility; or they may purposely and with malice disobey orders or waste property. These explanations indicate that employees approach their work with a variety of attitudes toward their coworkers, management, and the company.

Their attitudes may be summed up in the concept of discipline. Discipline is said to be good when employees willingly follow the rules of their superiors and their company. Discipline is said to be bad when employees either follow rules unwillingly or actually disobey regulations. Poor discipline customarily suggests the need for corrective action.

When the attitude is unfavorable due to faults in the worker, however, the action to be taken is known as disciplinary action. It involves warnings, suggestions, and other penalties by the company to the worker. The correction, as noted earlier, implies some degree of force and penalty.

In handling disciplinary cases, there are two major aspects that must be watched: (1) the steps to be taken and (2) the principles to follow in each step. The two must be considered together in actual practice; but for purposes of discussion, it is simpler to take up each separately. Attention is now directed to the first of these aspects.

Procedures of Disciplinary Action

Although it is not always possible or practical to follow a set routine in taking disciplinary action, nevertheless, there are certain steps or stages to which attention must be directed at one time or another. These steps include the following:

1. Accurate statement of the disciplinary problem.
2. Collection of full information on the case.
3. Selection of tentative penalties to be applied.
4. Choice of the alternative penalties.

5. Application of the penalty.
6. Follow-up of the case.

Statement of Problem

Perhaps no more important step can be taken in the whole process of disciplinary action than to ascertain the problem that calls for discipline. This may be done by seeking answers to the following questions:

1. Is this case one calling for disciplinary action?
2. Exactly what is the nature of the violation?
3. Under what conditions did it occur?
4. What individual or individuals are involved?
5. When or how often have the violations occurred?

1. Determining the Nature of the Violation. The first of the foregoing questions can seldom be answered first. Nevertheless, it is stated first because that question should be a caution to all of the proceedings. For example, to mistakenly classify a grievance as one calling for disciplinary action is bound to have unfortunate repercussions. Indeed, as far as possible executives must assure themselves that a violation has occurred and that the violation is entirely or in part the fault of one or more subordinates.

2. Stating the Violation. With this in mind, the next step is to state precisely the nature of the alleged violation. The specific rule, regulation, policy, request, or order that was broken and the degree to which it was broken must be determined. There should be no generalities or vaporizing here; or certainly the less, the better. For example, the following statement, "My request that the materials on his workbench be moved immediately was not obeyed until the next day," is much better than "He didn't follow my orders." There is a specificity about the former that gives a quantitative as well as a qualitative measurement of the violation, which the latter lacks.

3. Determining the Circumstances. Of course, a violation may be excusable or not, depending upon the circumstances. In the example just cited, it might have been that the order was given shortly before quitting time. The worker might well have felt that he was not expected to work overtime but could finish the next day. Thus the worker might be excused for violating the order because the conditions, in the mind of the worker, justified quitting on time. After all, most employees leave their work places without reporting before leaving—in most instances, this is customary practice. In short, do employees have a clear idea of what is expected of them?

4. Individuals Involved. It is also significant to know exactly what individual or individuals were involved in a violation. For example, if one individual has broken a safety rule, that person alone should be punished; but if someone else has been involved in the case, the second party too should be included in the penalty. Thus a given employee may have been cut, let us say, while sharpening a tool against company rules, which state that only a toolmaker shall perform this operation. Yet the toolmaker might have refused to do the job for one reason or another when requested to do so by the other employee. Of course, the injured employee had no right to proceed with the sharpening, but the toolmaker should also be included for possible discipline. Such multiple aspects of discipline must not be overlooked.

5. Number of Repetitions. And finally, it is desirable to state as precisely as possible when or how often the alleged violations occurred. Here again, the seriousness of a violation is dependent upon the number of violations. For example, a person who has been absent without excuse several times in a given month deserves a more serious reprimand than one who has been absent but once. Or again, if a violation occurs during a particularly busy or rush period, it should be weighed more heavily than one that takes place during a lull.

Gathering Facts

Gathering facts is essentially supplementary to the preceding step as well as others to follow. Nevertheless, as in the case of handling grievances, pertinent data are essential. How these may be collected was discussed rather fully in the preceding chapter; hence, it is suggested that a review of that material be made.

It is worthwhile here merely to highlight some of the significant aspects of fact gathering. First, as noted in the preceding chapter, fact gathering is often a process of fact sifting. If opinions are mistaken for facts, it is easy to reach wrong conclusions. Second, a thorough examination of every case is suggested. An executive who has worked with a group over a period of time should know it well enough to expedite the search for facts. Third, the facts of the case should be so well culled that an executive should be willing to produce them should they be called for. And fourth, management should be respectful of others when gathering information to avoid losing the confidence of employees.

Establishing Tentative Penalties

But, as noted earlier, at this juncture the question of punishment or nonpunishment should be weighed. If nonpunishment, then a plan of constructive, positive self-discipline should be undertaken. But if punishment is to be used, one should be aware of types of penalties and of the usefulness of standard penalties.

Types of Penalties. Disciplinary action may take a variety of forms. Perhaps the most common type is the simple reprimand. This is sufficient in most instances to change the attitude of an employee who has broken some regulation. After all, most of us do not like to be criticized, no matter how gently, and will seek to avoid incurring such disciplinary action. Indeed, with some individuals, it is enough merely to point out their mistakes; they can be relied upon to reprimand themselves.

Another form of discipline is the mild penalty, but nevertheless a penalty. The penalties may be financial or nonfinancial. For example, tardiness may subject the employee to a small loss of wage. Or an excessive number of tardinesses or absences may remove the possibility of a merit increase. Nonfinancial penalties may involve loss of preference for a transfer, various privileges, and assignment to favored jobs or tasks.

FIGURE 27–1

Disciplinary Penalties

19. Posting or removal of any matter on bulletin boards or company property at any time unless specifically authorized by Industrial Relations Department.	1 day off	3 days off	Discharge		
20. Theft or removal from the premises without proper authorization of any company property or property of the government or of any employee.	Discharge				
21. Gambling or engaging in a lottery on company premises.	Discharge				
22. Misusing, destroying, or damaging any company property or property of any employee.	Discharge				
23. Deliberately restricting output.	Discharge				
24. Making of false, vicious, or malicious statements concerning any employee, the company, or its product.	Warning	3 days off	1 week off	Discharge	
25. Provoking, or instigating a fight, or fighting during working hours or on company premises.	1 week off or discharge	Discharge			
26. Drinking any alcoholic beverage on premises or on company time.	1 week off	Discharge			
27. Reporting for work obviously under the influence of alcohol or drugs.	1 day off	3 days off	1 week off	Discharge	
28. Engaging in sabotage or espionage.	Discharge				
29. Violating a safety rule or safety practice.	Warning	1 day off	3 days off	1 week off	Discharge
30. Immoral conduct or indecency.	Discharge				
31. Interfering or refusing to cooperate with Plant Protection officers in the performance of their duties.	Discharge				
32. Sleeping on job during working hours.	Discharge				
33. Entering restricted areas without specific permission.	Warning	3 days off	Discharge		
34. Refusal to show badge at the request of any member of supervisison or Plant Protection.	Discharge				
35. Leaving plant during work shift without permission.	1 day off	1 week off	Discharge		
36. Insubordination.	1 week off or discharge	Discharge			
37. Failure to observe parking and traffic regulations on premises.	Warning	1 day off	3 days off	1 week off	Discharge
38. Mistakes due to lack of knowledge.	Warning	1 day off	Demotion		
39. Leaving work area without permission before final whistle blows indicating end of shift.	Warning	3 days off	1 week off	Discharge	
40. Failure to report for overtime work without good reason after being scheduled to work according to overtime policy.	Warning	1 day off	3 days off	1 week off	Discharge

Source: "Simplifies Discipline Procedure," *Factory Management and Maintenance*, vol. 108, no. 10, p. 458.

And finally, there are the more drastic penalties. These include demotion, temporary layoffs, and outright discharges. As noted earlier, such disciplinary actions are so serious that they require authorization by the personnel department as well as the immediate executive. This does not weaken the hand of the executive because an executive who has carefully considered such a decision will seldom be overruled. Moreover, the best interests of the company may be better served sometimes by transferring a worker to another department rather than by outright discharge. Removing the worker from the present department protects the accusing supervisor, and transfer to another department saves the investment in the employee. If discharge is warranted, joint line-staff action is desirable; the line recommends discharge and the staff (or a higher line executive) gives final approval.

Choosing the Penalty

After a case calling for disciplinary action has been thoroughly examined and alternative penalties weighed, the particular penalty to be applied should be chosen. In principle, the penalty to be chosen is that which will serve to prevent a recurrence of disobedience. A lesser one will not serve to prevent; a greater one may lead to a grievance.

The choice usually is made upon the basis of one's experience and on a comparison of the case at hand with previous similar cases. Also, it is wise to consult with others, particularly when a case evidently falls outside the jurisdiction of a given executive. But even on matters that come completely within one's scope, consultation with one's own superior, some other supervisor, or the personnel department serves to derive the benefit of their advice and also gives one an opportunity to recheck himself.

In the case of a penalty, it should be remembered that it will serve somewhat as a precedent. Employees are quick to compare current decisions with what has gone before as well as what to expect in the future.

Applying Penalties

The next step, the application of the penalty, involves a positive and assured attitude on the part of management. If executives are to convey the idea that they are confident of the fairness of their decisions, their very attitude and conduct should be in accord with the decision.

In other words, if the disciplinary action is a simple reprimand, an executive should calmly and quickly dispose of the matter. When drastic action is called for, a forthright, serious, and determined attitude is highly desirable. Then the case is not overdone, nor is the severity of the case minimized. In this regard, it is best to minimize one's personal feelings or desire to dramatize. Reprimands and penalties are always unpleasant to hand out; hence the quicker and more impersonally the matters are handled, the fewer the undesirable effects.

Nor should this step be delayed. Penalties are most effective when punishment is closely associated in the mind of the wrongdoer with the act that brought it on. If a penalty is delayed unduly, the employee may have concluded the case is closed and therefore that the company is fault-finding.

Follow-Up of Disciplinary Action

The ultimate purpose of disciplinary action is, of course, to assure good productivity by developing good discipline. Its aim is to reduce repetition of disobedience. It cannot repair the damage done. Hence, disciplinary action must be evaluated in terms of its effectiveness after it has been applied. That means more careful supervision of those who were disciplined. But in its most constructive form, follow-up involves steps to motivate employees to want to cooperate fully for their own good as well as that of the company.

PRINCIPLES OF DISCIPLINARY ACTION

Although it is essential to know what steps should be taken in handling disciplinary cases, it is of equal importance to know the whys and wherefores of the steps being taken. Much remains to be learned about the underlying principles of disciplinary action. Yet, much useful experience is available in most companies. This may be seen by commenting on the desirability of disciplinary action, rules of dealing with employees, implications of disciplinary action, and union-management relations in disciplinary action.

Desirability of Disciplinary Action

At the moment disciplinary action is being taken, an employee may dislike being criticized, reprimanded, or discharged; but it may be beneficial over a period of time. However, it should be good for the company both now and in the future.

1. Responsibility of Line Executives. Executives must be sold on the need of discipline from the company's viewpoint. After all, to be profitable, the company must be efficient. To be efficient, it must, among other things, have employees who do not excessively disregard rules, disobey orders, or work carelessly. Hence, to protect its own interests and those of the customers it serves, disciplinary action is essential to the company. Obviously, an employee who kills time is not helping the company; yet that person was hired to do a fair day's work, presumably at a fair day's pay.

2. *Responsibility of Personnel Department.* Executives should be convinced that disciplinary action is a tool that must be used for the company's benefit, even though it would be temporarily more pleasant if such action were not taken. Hence the personnel department can do much good by training executives not to shrink from taking disciplinary action when it is justified. That is one of their responsibilities as executives. It is one of their unpleasant duties and one for the assumption of which they are compensated.

3. *Confidence in Company Policies.* What if executives believe that certain rules of the company are unfair? Several angles must be discussed regarding such a situation. In the first place, they should nevertheless continue to enforce the rules as though they had confidence in them. Executives who in any way lead employees to believe that they have no confidence in the company will soon find that the subordinates do not trust them. In the second place, they should make certain that they know precisely why a rule was established. Often, we do not like what we do not understand, even though the lack of understanding may lie in our own failure to take steps to find out the meaning and reason for rules. If, after the second step, an executive is convinced that a rule is wrong, an attempt should be made to clear up the matter by presenting another side, to the superiors with a view to suggesting a change. And finally, if a change is not made and the executive remains convinced of the inequity of the rule, the choice is to either accept the rule notwithstanding or seek another position.

This does not mean that every time one disagrees with one's superiors, the executive should resign. After all, no matter where or with whom one works, there will always be points upon which agreement is not unanimous. Hence, some disagreement does not mean disloyalty. But after going through the steps outlined in the foregoing, an executive who disagrees with some company rules nevertheless should follow them implicitly or give up the position.

Asking an executive to do this is no more than the executive asks of subordinates. Reasonable executives know that they may be wrong at times but that they must continue to do their job as best they can. And in this vein, they must attempt to explain rules and regulations to all subordinates. If these views are not seen clearly after reasonable effort, the executive must refer the case elsewhere or personally take steps to close the case. Similarly, in dealing with superiors about company policy, an executive cannot expect to see through the implications of all rules.

4. *Developing Confidence in Employees.* These remarks about the attitude of executives toward company rules and policies have been somewhat extended because bad discipline is bound to result when executives do not have or fail to display confidence in company rules. Moreover, employees themselves lack confidence in rules and in executives who display an attitude of disregard for rules. For example, the supervisor who says to an employee, "Well, that rule was figured out by some brass hat who doesn't know what's going on down here," is inviting rule violations.

Confidence of employees in rules and management is based on respectful executives and reasonable rules. Employees like to have a clear and unmuddied idea of what is expected of them. And to a set of reasonably written rules must be added a set of executives who explain and enforce them without confusing contradictions.

Attitude toward Employees

To confidence in company policies on disciplinary matters must be added confidence in the innate goodness of the worker. It is essential to believe that employees can be trusted even though they occasionally break rules. After all, even the best workers make mistakes of omission and commission. To be sure, it is hard to trust employees when, at times, a wave of rule breaking takes place. Unless a fundamental faith is held in the trustworthiness of labor, management will have little else to look forward to than a future of watching for and disciplining rule-breakers.

1. Importance of Attitudes. All of us influence people not only by what we do but also by the innumerable mannerisms that are inadvertent expressions of our feelings. In other words, our attitudes toward others show through our actions and behaviorisms. Hence, when an executive assumes that employees are untrustworthy, that attitude will be discovered by the employees, and they will return in kind.

The point is that even though some penalizing is inevitable, all employees should not be considered as inveterate rule-breakers. On the contrary, an underlying current of confidence in the fundamental integrity of employees must run through all disciplinary action.

2. The Value of Disciplinary Action. Executives must be convinced that disciplinary action is needful and effective. In particular, they must feel that any penalties assigned in given cases were not only merited but were also beneficial to employees. If, in the future, wrongdoings are reduced, the resulting harmonious atmosphere can be in part ascribed to earlier instances of negative motivation. Such a happier state can be achieved because most people prefer to conform. The effectiveness of disciplinary action in attaining this goal can be increased by adding to penalties constructive suggestions on how transgressions can be avoided.

3. The Use of Fear. Good does not derive from correcting the damage done—that is a loss, more or less. It must come from a changed attitude toward the company's rules and regulations. It is too bad that some employees are willing to obey rules only for fear of penalties. But if it is to their benefit to have jobs, and if fear keeps them on the straight and narrow, the use of reasonable penalties is of benefit to the employees themselves. It must be remembered that to some degree, fear rules the lives of all of us. The wise person can get along with a minimum of fear yet recognize that it acts as a spur in personal activities.

This brief comment upon fear, upon which penalties essentially rest, is not intended as justification for irresponsible employment of it. The role of fear should be restricted; nevertheless, when its use is called for, executives should be trained to employ it intelligently.

4. Individual Differences. Moreover, executives should be impressed with the fact that some people are very sensitive, whereas others are not at all. As a consequence, it is essential to adopt disciplinary practices that fit the case. That is why such rules as "reprimand in private" are often cited. Not that some people should not be penalized publicly. Rather, there is greater danger in using an occasional public reprimand than when private penalties are always assigned. Indeed, with some employees a good all-out airing in public works best, but one cannot always be certain that such a reprimand is best for the person in question. Hence, in dealing out penalties, it is wise to be conservative and gradually to step up the penalty, if need be.

Implications of Disciplinary Action

Disciplinary action can be successful only if an executive takes into account the implications of such action upon self, upon others, and upon future relationships.

1. Disciplinary Action as a Tool. An executive must consider disciplinary action as a tool, not as a weapon of supervision; should see penalties and reprimands in the same light as brakes on a car. They slow down employees when needed, they act as a preventive, but they cannot cure an accident. Hence, when a penalty is applied, it should be in the manner of a needed tool and not as a threatening, emotional, or sadistic gesture.

2. Cooperation with Others. Moreover, an executive's attitude toward disciplinary action should be respectful of disciplinary efforts of other executives. Any indication of laughing at, ridiculing, or undermining the work of others will encourage repercussions from other executives and result in a loss of prestige in the eyes of one's own subordinates. To destroy confidence in one's own efforts, one need only go about destroying confidence in those who are doing similar work.

3. After Effects. In taking disciplinary action, it is also imperative to remember that disciplinary action has its after effects. A given penalty in a given case is considered as a precedent for similar cases in the future.

As an example, if some infraction previously has been punished lightly, such as reprimanding a person found smoking in a prohibited area, to later discharge someone else under similar circumstances is asking for trouble. It is far better to announce that thereafter the rule is going to be enforced strictly. Although the legal right to discharge in such cases without warning seems to exist, some companies have found to their sorrow that an unannounced change in policy toward the enforcement of company rules has been considered an unfair labor practice by the National Labor Relations Board.

Union-Management Relations

Most companies take the stand that disciplinary action is a prerogative of management. They contend that management must have the unrestricted right to discipline employees, or else it will be impossible to produce the right quality of goods economically and effectively. In essence, the argument is that in accepting the responsibilities that go with operating a business, there must be a counterbalancing weight of authority. This attitude is held so strongly by some companies that they will neither relinquish any aspects of discipline to joint action with unions nor include any phase of it as a subject for collective bargaining.

Such a stand runs the risk of converting some disciplinary decisions into grievances. Employees who consider themselves treated harshly are in essence aggrieved. They may, particularly in unionized cases, raise in point of "just cause." Does the company have good reason to penalize as it did? When such questions reach arbitrators, they invariably check the evidence and grounds on which a given penalty has supposedly been justified by the company.

There are companies which accept the offices of the unions in various aspects of disciplinary action. Some have agreed that the union may challenge cases in which it feels that punishment has been excessive, partial, or misdirected. In other cases, unions are given the right to participate in hearings in which the type of disciplinary action to be taken is being considered. And in still other cases the union itself may take disciplinary steps, such as layoffs or a reduction of status on a priority list. While direct participation in disciplinary action is not common, it does indicate how far some companies have gone in accepting union action in this area.

As time goes on, it is probable that unions will play a larger role in disciplinary matters. In the final analysis, such participation must be based on good principles and procedures. It is as much to the advantage of the union to be fair to employees as it is to management. Hence, if good principles must prevail eventually, it would seem to be the wise thing for management to adopt such plans and practices before they are forced upon it by outsiders. When outsiders force changes, they take credit for them; yet, it is management which must make them work.

QUESTIONS

1. What is the essential difference between the terms discipline and disciplinary action?
2. Why is the accurate determination and statement of the nature of an alleged violation so important in disciplinary action cases?
3. How does the examination of circumstances surrounding an alleged violation fit into the process of taking disciplinary action?
4. What is the purpose of having levels of increasing penalties which may be imposed?
5. Why is it desirable to have standard penalties for various types of violations?
6. Why is it desirable to divide up the work of taking disciplinary action between line executives and the personnel department? Between various levels of executives?
7. What is the role of follow-up in the process of taking disciplinary action?
8. What does one's attitude toward the basic goodness or badness of people have to do with disciplinary action?
9. What is the justification, if any, for employing fear as a tool of disciplinary action?
10. If you were a manager, would you prefer to have the sole prerogative for taking disciplinary action or to share this task with a union?

CASE 27–1. COOPERATION WITH ORDERS

You are the director of office services of the Soho Advertising Agency. In this department is a steno pool of 20 employees whose work consists of taking dictation, transcribing, and typing. You have just hired Mamie Marion, formerly an officer in the WAVES, to supervise this pool.

Because of the scarcity of qualified office help and because the previous pool supervisor had been lax, the employees in the pool have been coming in at various times in the morning—any time from 8:35 to 9:15. The starting time is 8:30.

Mamie Marion decided to take action on this tardiness and called the workers together a few days after she had come to work. Her opening remarks were, "As your new supervisor I hope we get along together. I think I know my job as a supervisor having been in charge of a group of women in the WAVES in which I was an officer. I feel sure you know your responsibilities in the pool. I am disappointed in your arrival times at work in the morning. Please be at your desks by 8:30."

Nothing further was mentioned on this point. But the next day, the arrival times showed no improvement over the past.

Question

1. You as director of office services have observed the performance of the employees and the new supervisor; what actions would you take?

CASE 27–2. LOITERING ON THE JOB

John, a college student, was working for an electric utility company during the summer vacation. This was his third summer assignment. He had an excellent work record and liked the variety of jobs he worked on.

The company is unionized, wages and benefits are equal to or above community levels, and opportunities for improvement are relatively good.

The crew with which John worked was one of a number supervised by a working, nonunion supervisor. The supervisor is responsible for job assignments among the various crews and for checking the various jobs from time to time during the day.

John was impressed by the fact that his crew, as well as the others as far as he could observe, avoided working whenever possible. Although John liked a break now and then, the regular crew members criticized him whenever they thought he was working too hard. Yet he disliked standing around with nothing to do. To him loafing made the day last longer and the jobs boring when he did work. Yet the regular crew members would leave the garage early, return late, stretch work on the job, and often go through the motions of working without accomplishing much.

John thinks that were he in charge such conditions would not prevail particularly because he believes that not only is there room for better motivation but also the field operations of the jobs have all of the elements of job enlargement about which he has been reading.

Question

1. What would you (John) like to try were you in a position to do something?

PERSONNEL RESEARCH AND 28
EVALUATION

Introduction

At the outset of this text, it was noted that personnel management has to do with planning, organizing, directing, and controlling various tasks of procuring, developing, maintaining, and utilizing an effective work force. And the foregoing chapters have been concerned with practices related to these functions. By these means, it is hoped to increase goal attainment, increase cooperation, reduce conflict, and to adapt to change.

Such aims would be difficult to attain, however, were management to forego research and evaluation of its various activities. Indeed, every chapter in this text deserves expanded sections on these subjects were space no object. But much duplication can be avoided and useful purposes served by summarizing some comments in this chapter. The first section of this chapter is devoted, therefore, to research, and the second to evaluation.

PERSONNEL RESEARCH

Nature and Scope

Personnel research, defined simply, is the task of searching for and analyzing facts to the end that personnel problems may be solved or that guide lines governing their solutions may be deduced. Its scope is all-inclusive. There are no subjects in personnel about which so much is known that no further research is justified. On the contrary, our tested knowledge of basic relationships is so meager that it is a wonder that we get along as well as we do in working with people.

Obviously, it is impossible here to survey the fields of needed research or what has been done. All that can be done here is (1) to comment briefly on some basic considerations in research and (2) to illustrate with an example or two the task and value of careful data gathering.

Basic Considerations

A number of comments are in order regarding how and why research should be carried on.

1. Uses of Research. The objective of research is the truth. This simple statement should be sufficient to support the claim that research is for the use of everyone concerned with a personnel problem. Labor, management, the general public, governmental agencies, and the consumer are its beneficiaries. Each gains, or none does. Unless this attitude is accepted by the researcher, the results will be rejected on the grounds that "figures may not lie, but liars may figure."

Nowhere is this more obvious than in the case of collective bargaining. Disagreements over the question of what is a fair wage are seldom answered by research; rather force—the strike or lockout—is the path to the "truth." How much better off would everyone be if the money, skill, and time spent on fighting were directed to seeking factual answers to the wage problem. It is imperative, therefore, that in undertaking research, investigations should be conducted with a view to finding the correct answer—not the answer some particular group wants.

The need for research is seen in disagreements about the roles and contributions of women in business. Certainly women have generally been held in low esteem except for positions of low organizational rank. Is this factually justified? The few researches we are getting incline toward the negative. Take as an example, the question of how a female leader who has a high need for dominance would handle team interaction of male subordinates as compared to a low need female leader. It has been found in one case that the high need leader was better than the low need leader.[1] Such oncoming research—as well as laws—suggest that one would be well to disabuse oneself of unproved opinions that women are less effective or qualified than men in various organizational positions.

More specifically, uses of research would be related to the following aspects of personnel management, human relations, and labor-management relations:

a. To measure and evaluate present conditions.

b. To predict future conditions, events, and behavioral patterns.

---

[1] Kathryn M. Bartol, "Male Versus Female Leaders: The Effect of Leader Need for Dominance on Followers Satisfaction," *Academy of Management Journal,* vol. 17, no. 2, June 1974, pp. 225–233.

c. To evaluate effects and results of current policies, programs, and activities.

d. To provide an objective basis for revising current policies, programs, and activities.

e. To appraise proposed policies, programs, and activities.

2. Responsibility for Research. The foregoing suggests, in turn, that research is not the sole responsibility or within the sole jurisdiction of any particular group, interest, or department. To be sure, for present purposes, it might be argued that a research section should be established in the personnel department of most companies. This is a fine practice because it serves to focus attention on research, to help establish a research program, and to provide for experts and facilities of research.

But others, too, can and should be brought into the fold. Line supervisors and executives at all levels can help with research projects as well as carry on their own projects. Where unions are in the picture, their help and cooperation should be sought. Nor should such outside organizations as educational institutions, private research groups, endowed foundations, and governmental agencies be overlooked.[2]

3. Facilities of Research. The suggestion is in order that extensive facilities, desirable though they may be, are not indispensable to carry on much useful research. The records of every company contain a wealth of information. All that is needed is the effort to examine them. For example, a simple survey, such as the question of why employees have left the company, will serve to improve personnel practices. In one company that made such a survey, it was found that a majority of quits occurred in two departments. Following up this trail with an attitude survey, poor supervision was discovered to be the cause. After this was cleared up by retaining the supervisors, the quits in these departments fell to a normal figure. Such research can be carried on without excessive cost or effort.

Some research techniques involve high skills and considerable outlays for equipment. Some tabulating equipment falls into this category. Or linear programming, a mathematical and graphical method, is useful (but complicated) in arriving at decisions involving situations where several choices, with variations of degree in each choice, are available. And cybernetics, which employs sophisticated techniques of information feedback and control, involves skills of a high order. But in complicated and important problems, decision making is dependent on such techniques.

4. Importance of Pure Research. One of the lessons that industry in

---

[2] Invaluable is the work of such organizations as the Academy of Management, the American Management Association, the National Industrial Conference Board, the Bureau of Labor Statistics, the Bureau of Foreign and Domestic Commerce, the Administrative Management Association, and the Society for the Advancement of Management.

general as yet must learn about personnel research is that pure research in this area is as useful as it is in physics and chemistry. It is not uncommon to read reports issued by various companies announcing the projected opening of new and complete facilities for research and testing in the physical sciences. But provision of facilities for research in personnel problems is rarely made. Yet, human problems of industry, it is generally agreed, are far more complex and numerous than physical problems. Unfortunately, research in human problems seems to many to be frosting on a cake, whereas technical research leads to direct results in the competitive battle for markets. Failure to learn how to handle labor problems, however, may eat up most of the profits technical research may be providing. A number of universities have in the past decade dedicated themselves to pure research in the personnel area, but substantial progress cannot be expected until industry joins ranks in examining human problems.

5. Relation of Research and Collective Bargaining.   Another lesson that industry must learn is that it must undertake research if it is to bargain successfully with unions. The latter, in some instances, are so far advanced in their researches on wages, economic trends, bargaining processes, and labor relations that the efforts of management to refute labor's arguments are often pathetic. No other road will lead to stable labor relations but that which is paved with facts, information, and statistics. Until industry travels that road, it can look forward to nothing but emotional bombast, name calling, and pressure politics.

6. Priority Lists.   Earlier, it was noted that establishing a priority of research projects is perhaps of greater practical significance than determining subjects of research. The tests of priority should be importance of problems and timeliness.

A useful way of developing such a list is to sample executive judgment. For example, a list such as that illustrated in Figure 28–1 could be sent to various executives. They could be asked to number, from the sample list, the first 10 projects—or any other number—they considered most significant. The results would be most helpful in determining where money, talents, and time should be allocated.

7. Attitude of Mind.   Research is conditioned, too, by attitude toward accepted principles and practices. Executives who do not question the way things have always been done are likely to make mistakes in working with their associates and subordinates. For example, it would be easy to reach incorrect conclusions about one's employees if one failed to gather information on their attitudes toward their jobs as was done in Table 28–1. Or another commonly held but questionable opinion is that high morale and high production always go together. Rather, a number of studies have shown that low morale may at times be the source of high production, and high morale of low production. Occasions are not rare that high morale has caused employees to relax and low to stimulate

FIGURE 28–1

Suggested Research Projects

Please check the areas which you consider worthy of research efforts.

Area

— a. Discovery of new principles of human relations
— b. Application of known principles of human relations
— c. Human characteristics and attributes
— d. Measurement of human characteristics and attributes
— e. Forecasting future of company with reference to its human relations position

— f. Personnel policies
— g. Labor market
— h. Job analysis and evaluation
— i. Recruitment, selection, and placement
— j. Individual testing

— k. Operator training
— l. Supervisor training
— m. Administrator training
— n. Performance rating
— o. Employee services

— p. Personnel records and reports
— q. Promotions, demotions, transfers, layoffs, and separations
— r. Health
— s. Safety
— t. Communications

— u. Employee attitude
— v. Adjustments and social relationships
— w. Wages and salaries
— x. Hours of work, rests
— y. Working conditions

— z. Production standards
— a'. Labor turnover
— b'. Absenteeism
— c'. Measures of effectiveness of personnel program
— d'. Legislation affecting human relations

— e'. Relationship with union
— f'. Collective bargaining
— g'. Clauses for union contracts
— h'. Grievance procedures
— i'. Mediation and arbitration

— j'. Other (*Please specify.*)

_____

_____

TABLE 28–1

Percentage of Workers Rating Job Facets as "Very Important" to Them

Job Facet	All Workers (N = 1500)*	White-Collar Workers (N = 730)*	Blue-Collar Workerst (N = 685)*
RESOURCES			
I receive enough help and equipment to get the job done	68.4	64.5	71.9
I have enough information to get the job done	68.1	67.4	68.5
My responsibilities are clearly defined	61.2	57.6	64.6
My supervisor is competent in supervising	61.1	59.7	63.0
FINANCIAL REWARDS			
The pay is good	64.2	57.4	72.5
The job security is good	62.5	54.2	71.5
My fringe benefits are good	50.6	39.7	62.4
CHALLENGE			
The work is interesting	73.0	78.5	68.2
I have enough authority to do my job	65.6	66.8	63.5
I have an opportunity to develop my special abilities	63.3	69.4	57.2
I can see the results of my work	61.7	60.0	63.8
I am given a chance to do the things I do best	54.3	54.0	55.0
I am given a lot of freedom to decide how I do my work	52.9	56.4	49.8
The problems I am asked to solve are hard enough	30.4	31.2	29.3
RELATIONS WITH COWORKERS			
My coworkers are friendly and helpful	63.4	60.9	67.0
I am given a lot of chances to make friends	44.0	39.3	48.6
COMFORT			
I have enough time to get the job done	54.4	47.7	60.3
The hours are good	50.8	41.0	61.6
Travel to and from work is convenient	46.2	42.4	49.7
Physical surroundings are pleasant	40.2	32.3	47.8
I am free from conflicting demands that other people make of me	33.1	25.8	40.0
I can forget about my personal problems	30.8	26.5	35.3
I am not asked to do excessive amounts of work	23.0	15.7	29.5

* Base Ns vary slightly from row to row due to nonresponse to individual questions.
† Farmworkers have been excluded.
Source: "Job Satisfaction: Is There a Trend?" Manpower Research Monograph No. 30. U.S. Department of Labor (Washington, D.C., 1974), p. 16.

people to improve. Only research can serve to determine under what conditions each type of morale is best.

8. Specialists and Their Techniques.   And finally, a word more is in order on the importance of looking to various fields and their tools for help. Research emphasizes a search for facts. It is therefore quantitative in nature. The most useful tools in this connection are mathematics and statistics. Hence, in the gathering, analysis, and interpretation of data, reliance upon and understanding of statistical methods are indispensable. This does not mean that involved and intricate formulas and calculations are the test of good research. It does mean that relative to the nature of each particular research project, the quantitative tools should be adequate.

And the range of specialists from whom help may be sought is broad indeed. The assistance of psychologists has, of course, long been sought and generally respected. And the statistician, too, has contributed much. Recently, the services of others have proved most useful. For example, the psychiatrist has been called into help solve individual problems of an emotional and mental character that were disturbing company efficiency and individual happiness. And increasingly, the sociologists and anthropologists have carried on significant research and investigations concerning group relations, customs, and status in industry.

The moral is obvious; the field of research requires the services of numerous types of researchers and several kinds of tools. To seek answers through the methodology and principles of a single specialty is to build upon a weak foundation. Rather, research calls for a cosmopolitan attitude and interdisciplinary cooperation. The specialists who try to build a fence around all aspects of research do themselves and industry a serious disfavor.

EXAMPLES OF RESEARCH

To provide some substance to the foregoing discussion of personnel research, it is desirable (1) to show how research can contribute to a better understanding of a particular problem and (2) to note some recent contributors to personnel research.

Absenteeism[3]

The usefulness of research in reaching wise decisions and logical conclusions can be shown in connection with the problem of absenteeism. This discussion is taken up under the headings of importance, measurement, causes, factors, and control of absenteeism.

---

[3] Tardiness is a problem similar to that of absenteeism. Its treatment might well follow the general pattern accorded absenteeism.

1. Importance. During periods when production is at a peak and labor is scarce, the absence of some workers from their appointed stations can be disruptive to production and morale. To illustrate, in a certain company, there were, in one department, eight absentees on one day after payday, and four others were sent home on the same day because of hazardous hangovers, making a total of 12 workers (or 25 percent in this instance) absent from their work. In the chart in Figure 28–2, for example, absenteeism in the worst departments is about five times as high as in the best departments, and this unbalances production in all departments.

2. Measurements of Absenteeism. To combat absenteeism, it is necessary to determine its extent and causes. To do this, a definition of absenteeism should be established and records kept by departments for various causes of absenteeism by such divisions as seniority, sex, days of the week, and classes of jobs. Although there is no standard definition of absenteeism, the following definition of the Bureau of Labor Statistics is widely used:

"Absenteeism" is the failure of workers to report on the job when they are scheduled to work. It is a broad term which is applied to time lost because sickness or accident prevents a worker from being on the job, as well as unauthorized time away from the job for other reasons. Workers who quit without notice are also counted as absentees until they are officially removed from the payroll.

In order to have a common and comparable basis for measuring absenteeism in various plants, the Bureau of Labor Statistics suggest the following formula:

$$\frac{\text{Rate of}}{\text{absenteeism}} = \frac{\text{Work-days lost during a period} \times 100}{\substack{\text{Average number} \\ \text{of workers} \times \text{Number of} \\ \text{work days}}}$$

3. Causes and Distribution of Absenteeism. The specific causes of absenteeism are numerous and devious. To attribute absenteeism in a given case to illness, for example, may result in overlooking the fact that incorrect job placement may have led first to boredom, then to fatigue, and then to physical illness. Hence, in listing the following causes, no attempt is made to determine priority or immediacy of cause and effect. This can only be done by study of individual cases.

Among the reasons for absenteeism, the following list contains those cited frequently:

a. Ordinarily, illness is high on the list of absenteeism causes, running as high as 50 percent of the absenteeism in some cases.

FIGURE 28-2

Chart of Absenteeism

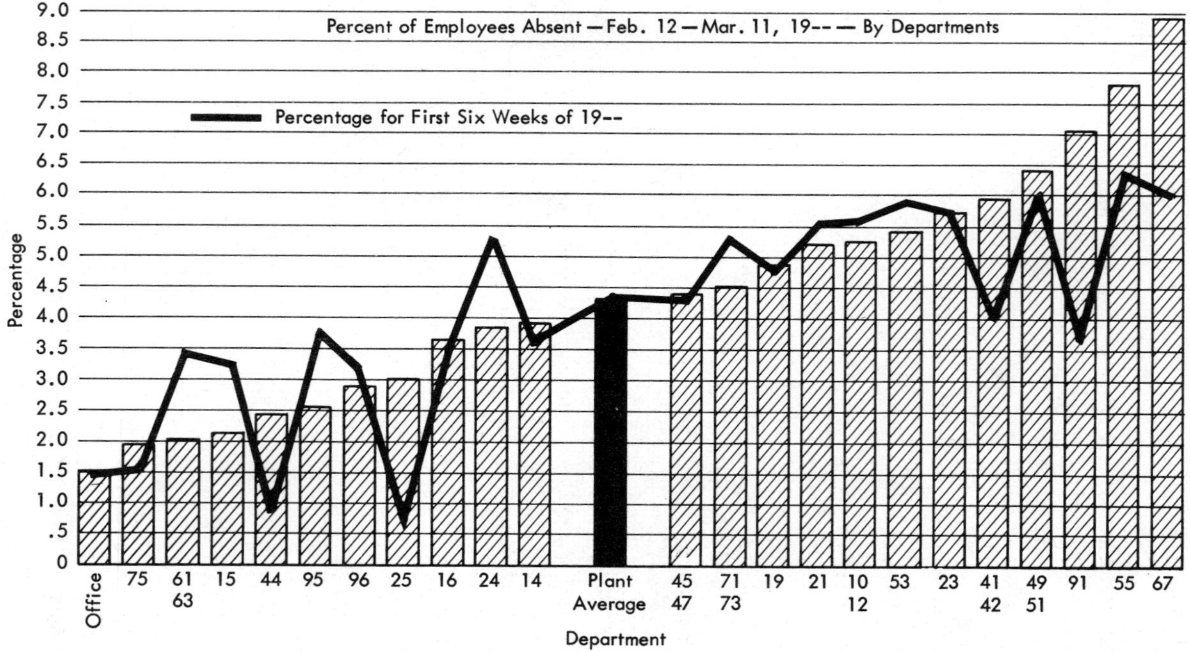

b. Industrial accidents and occupational disease bring on much absenteeism. In one year the equivalent of the production of a million employees for one year was lost due to industrial accidents.

c. Poor production and material control can result in absenteeism. Unless the flow of work between departments is balanced and maintained, workers may stay away from their jobs because they lose interest in their work and lose the feeling of the importance of being dependable.

d. Hours of work can contribute to absenteeism. Scheduled increases in overtime hours are sometimes almost entirely offset by hours of absenteeism. In one plant, employees working seven days a week, 9½ hours a day, lost twice as much time as employees working six days a week.

e. Lack of interest or of a feeling of responsibility and worthwhileness are fundamental causes of absenteeism. It has been found, for example, that campaigns intended to show employees the significance of their efforts have cut absenteeism as much as 50 percent.

f. After-payday sickness and hangovers contribute to absenteeism, particularly when combined with poor working conditions, lack of interest in work, and high wages.

g. A miscellaneous group of causes would include such factors as bad weather, lack of transportation, search for another job, personal business, oversleeping, and friends visiting from out of town (see Figure 28–3).

h. Attitude of mind—caused by environmental factors, sociological factors, or opinions of neighbors—may condition some to develop a feeling of irresponsibility about coming to work.

4. Location of Absentees. Study of absenteeism shows that its incidence is related to whom, when, and where. Some have argued that there are absence-prone workers who account for a major proportion of absences. Although data are not conclusive, there is reason to believe that absences differ in terms of sex, age groups, ethnic groups, and job classes.

Absenteeism is also related to the time factor. Thus, first and last days of the week and the day after payday are usually the worst. Monthly trends are also discernible. November and December, with their year-end holidays, are usually the months with the poorest records, in some cases running two or three times as many absences as the average of the other months.

Departments or geographical areas also vary in these absence rates. Departments or locations distant from the homes of workers will usually have higher rates than others. There is occasional but not indisputable evidence that departments that call for heavy exertion or have monoto-

FIGURE 28–3

Percent of Time Lost for Personal Reasons

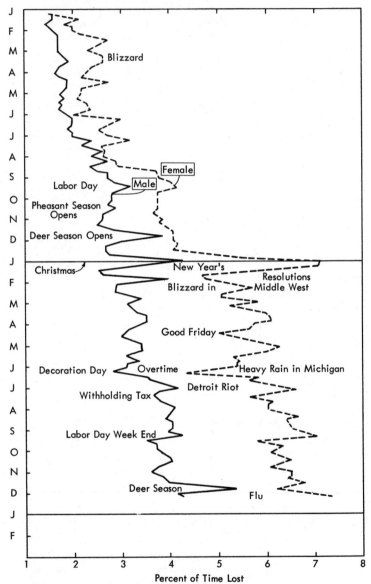

Source: General Motors Corp., *An Analysis of the Paid Sick-Leave Plan* (Detroit).

nous operation and obnoxious conditions tend to have higher rates of absences. What the rates are in any company must be determined by statistical analysis.

5. Control of Absenteeism. The control of absenteeism depends upon its causes. When these are uncovered by study and analysis, steps can be taken to eliminate them. Some of the cases are relatively simple to isolate and attack, but all are difficult to eliminate. For example, if it is discovered that illness of employees in a few departments is the major source of absenteeism, there is a real problem of how to combat the illness. Some companies have found vitamin tablets of use in such cases; others have insisted upon health examinations; and others have installed job rotation plans with success. In other words, there is no one sure cure for absence causes, once discovered.

All that can be done here is to list a variety of plans that have been used in this connection. The following are examples of control efforts:

a. Experiment with hours of work per day and per week to find the number at which absenteeism is reduced to reasonable limits.

b. Select employees with greater care to eliminate at the beginning the irresponsible, the illness-prone, and the unreliable.

c. Induct new employees in such a way that their critical attitude is reduced as quickly as possible and, with it, absenteeism from this source.

d. Plan the flow of production and materials so that workers do not on occasion find themselves without work.

e. Discipline chronic offenders by means of reprimands, layoffs, discharges, and loss of promotions and other privileges.

f. Provide rewards and bonuses for good attendance records.

g. Strengthen the hands of supervisors so that they know how to handle absenteeism.

h. Ridicule chronic offenders by publicizing names.

i. Interview all absent workers upon their return to determine causes and to impress upon them the seriousness of their absence.

j. Work with unions or labor-management committees so that the force of labor is applied against absenteeism.

In conclusion, it is interesting to compare rates of absenteeism among supervisors with those of operative employees. In the former group, among whom the feeling of responsibility ordinarily runs high, absenteeism will usually be near the zero mark, as compared to the usual 3 to 6 percent general average of absenteeism among the latter. Hence the moral is obvious: Develop in employees a sense of individual importance and worthwhileness, and their absenteeism will go down drastically. On the contrary, whatever causes employees to feel insignificant or useless will tend to increase the absentee rates.

Contributors to Personnel Research

As noted earlier, many disciplines have contributed to personnel research. All cannot be given space here. The debt of personnel management to psychology, psychiatry, medicine, statistics, and economics, for example, is large and well recognized. But such areas as sociology, group dynamics, and operations research are newer and deserve more than passing comment.

1. Sociological Research. The famous Hawthorne experiments are an example of research which illustrates the unpredictable sources of valuable information that may be uncovered. During experiments conducted at the Hawthorne Works of the Western Electric Company to ascertain the effect of working conditions upon output, it was found that social and organizational relationships between employees are a most potent force in influencing employee output and morale. The status an employee enjoys because of the job held has much to do with productivity, perhaps more than had ever been previously realized. Also, the roles which operators, supervisors, staff specialists, and union representatives assume have an impact upon interpersonal relations and group dynamics. Indeed, good human relations is often dependent on how groups feel about company policies and practices. All of these represent a sociological influence on the work of personnel management.

2. Group Dynamics. Of great interest recently has been the matter of how individuals work together and interact in small groups. This interest has been generated out of the recognition that people are associated in small groups either through geographical proximity or through project requirements. Since such is often the case, management should direct attention to how such groups can best work together. This implies concern with technical cooperation but, even more so, with what kinds of people should be associated together, how communications should be directed to them, how they should be motivated, and the consideration that should be given to leader-follower relationships. As yet, research here is in its early stages but has given evidence of becoming a rewarding form of investigation.

3. Operations Research. One of the greatest needs of personnel management is to derive quantitative support for the many decisions which must be made. In part, help comes from statistical and factual analysis. Another contributor may be operations research.

Operations research attempts to weigh the alternative courses of action that might be taken in a given situation and supply by mathematical analysis an answer to the most appropriate course of action. It often involves a team of experts to establish the factors in a problem, a model for describing a team of experts to establish the factors in a problem, a model for describing how the factors interact, and a mathematical formula to evaluate the forces at work in the model.

While operations research in business has been utilized largely in connection with production problems, it has possibilities for use in the personnel area. For example, it has been used to analyze such problems as the optimum limits of executive compensation, when to work overtime, how to assign work to minimize labor costs, how best to word contracts, how much work should be done in how much time, the best incentive system for salespeople, and how to speed interplant communications. But it is obvious that it requires a great deal of time, expert staff, and money, factors which most companies as yet have been unwilling to assign to research in sufficient quantities.

EVALUATION

Nature and Scope

Closely akin to research is personnel evaluation. It has to do with (1) measurement of the effectiveness of personnel programs and activities and (2) determination of what should or should not be done in the future as a result of such measurements. Its effectiveness, as with research, is dependent upon information. And like research, its scope is as broad as the field of personnel management. The significant problem here, too, is what phases of personnel activities should be given priority. Available resources are seldom sufficient to permit an evaluation of all functions to an equal degree.

In this discussion of evaluation, it is impractical to examine various methods of evaluation. All that can be done is (1) to comment upon some basic considerations and (2) to summarize the subjects and methods of evaluation.

Basic Considerations

Evaluation of personnel programs and policies may be backward- or forward-looking. The former tends toward fault-finding and scapegoats. So people begin to have alibis ready, to shirk responsibilities, to pass the buck, and to mistrust each other. Under such conditions, the evaluation has become worse than useless.

Forward-looking evaluation still has the determination of faults, mistakes, and errors in mind. But the purpose is not to assess penalties—although that may be done on occasions. The purpose is to find out what went wrong so that the mistake will not be repeated. In such an atmosphere the wrongdoer is as much interested in unearthing causes of failure as anyone else. With improvement being emphasized, pride in making progress is enlisted. The philosophy is positive, not negative.

Another consideration in evaluations is that of how often they should be made. A common plan is the annual evaluation or audit. At the end of the calendar or fiscal year a report with statistical surveys covering such information as activities performed, results achieved, costs and expenditures, and comparison of objectives and accomplishments is presented.

Monthly summaries are also commonly used. For example, the report

TABLE 28–2

Selected Items of Personnel Report

	Current Month	Previous Month	Cumulative This Year
Employees, wages, and hours			
No. of salaried employees			
No. of hourly employees			
Total man-hours			
Average weekly salaries			
Average hourly rate			
Employment			
Applicants			
New hirings			
Separations			
Turnover rate			
Labor relations			
Grievances pending, first of month ..			
Grievances filed			
Grievances settled			
Grievances pending, end of month ...			
Work stoppages, work-hours lost			
Safety and Accidents			
Frequency rate			
Severity rate			
Hospital visits			
Suggestions			
Received			
Adopted			
Declined			
Dollar awards			
Training			
Employee class hours			
Supervisory class hours			

in Table 28–2 provides must useful information on personnel activities. As a consequence, appropriate and timely action can be taken. Moreover, responsible executives are more likely to keep abreast of their personnel duties, so that undesirable exceptions will not have occurred to make such reports necessary.

In addition to periodic audits, there is the practice of conducting special studies as needed. For example, attitude surveys on particular topics may be conducted as occasion demands. Or special reports may be prepared on such matters as grievance cases, workings of seniority rules, or effect of overtime practices, for use in forthcoming bargaining sessions. Or new legislation may necessitate a review of a company's practices to see what changes, if any, need to be made.

Another basic consideration is that of who should conduct evaluations and audits. Some companies hire outside consultants for these purposes, whereas others perform these tasks themselves. The former course has the advantage of being conducted by impartial specialists. They have no axes to grind and can evaluate a particular set of practices against a broad background of experience. They can present their findings without respect to fear or favor of any individuals. The outsiders are not always in the plant a sufficient length of time to get a complete and balanced picture of what is going on. And after they have presented their report, there may be no one to integrate their suggestions into future practices. However, the good in most cases outweighs the shortcomings, so that outside help is often used in conjunction with other plans, though seldom alone.

Most companies conduct their own audits. The examinations are most frequently assigned to the functional heads of the personnel division, although occasionally an audit and research unit is formed. The latter practice is limited to the larger companies. Under the former practice the employment manager reports on the achievement of hiring goals, the training manager on training accomplishments, and the labor relations manager on progress in collective bargaining. This seems to make the executives their own judge, but there are offsetting "juries." The conclusions of the various reports will be inconsistent and require reconciliation and explanation. Superior executives will find that reports do not agree with their own interpretations of past events. And employees, through attitude surveys or expressed conflict, may enter counterevidence to the story told by reports.

But the personnel division need not be the sole appraiser of personnel practices. It is well to adopt the policy followed by some companies of having each line executive incorporate as part of his annual or monthly report a section on personnel accomplishments and shortcomings. This has the advantage of underlining the sound premise that every executive is a personnel manager. It has the further advantage of interpreting personnel policies and practices at their most vital point, and not solely from the viewpoint of a staff bystander.

In short, evaluation can embrace the services of several groups and levels. The warning that must be called out here is: if many are made responsible, no one may tie all the loose ends together. Hence, whatever plan is followed, some one individual or organizational unit—senior vice president or personnel manager or personnel evaluation division—should have the tasks of (1) bringing together all audit reports, (2) arranging meetings for their discussion, and (3) following up action taken on recommendations of such meetings.

Subjects and Methods of Evaluation

As in the case of research, there is no subject that is being performed so well that evaluation is unnecessary. Rather, all phases of personnel practice should be audited. In this way, it can be determined more accurately whether or not a company is getting the most out of the practices it is pursuing. Audits are also desirable to ascertain whether all practices that might be of advantage to a company are being pursued. Each of these is now received.

1. Appraising Current Practices. The field of evaluation is so broad that all that can be done here is to outline the areas and methods of evaluation. Merely by way of illustration, it is well to outline the field of coverage to be certain that nothing is overlooked, as follows:

a.   Personnel functions to be evaluated:
    (1)   Conforming to governmental civil rights regulations
    (2)   Job analysis
    (3)   Recruitment
    (4)   Selection
    (5)   Training
    (6)   Rating
    (7)   Transfers and promotions
    (8)   Morale development
    (9)   Health and safety
    (10)   Employment stabilization
    (11)   Wage and salary administration
    (12)   Collective bargaining

b.   Records and statistics to be used:
    (1)   Time standards
    (2)   Cost records
    (3)   Test scores
    (4)   Training scores
    (5)   Interview records
    (6)   Work stoppages
    (7)   Numbers of medical reports
    (8)   Accident reports
    (9)   Grievance reports
    (10)   Turnover rate
    (11)   Unit labor costs
    (12)   Payroll data

c. Methods of analysis:
- (1)   Comparisons between various time periods
- (2)   Comparisons between departments and with other companies
- (3)   Trend lines, frequency distributions, and statistical correlations
- (4)   Ratio analysis—e.g., labor costs per unit of output
- (5)   Classification of data by kinds of employees, products, departments, etc.
- (6)   Graphical or pictorial displays

It is well also to determine what the personnel division itself is doing. A useful approach here is that of keeping records of how personnel are spending their time. Such a breakdown as illustrated in Table 28–3 is

TABLE 28–3

Percentage of Total Work Time Spent with Various Categories of Persons

Category of Person	Five Clerical Workers		Four Personnel Dept. Mgrs.		Total Staff in Department	
	No. of Observations	Percentage of Total Work Time	No. of Observations	Percentage of Total Work Time	No. of Observations	Percentage of Total Work Time
Superior (own department)	29	02%	54	06%	83	04%
Subordinate (own department)	0	00	97	10	97	05
Manager (other department)	7	01	184	19	191	09
Nonmanager (other department)	48	04	111	12	159	08
Person outside company	32	03	126	13	158	07
Associate	36	30	0	00	36	02
Combination of above ...	10	01	84	09	94	04
None	922	81	237	25	1,159	55
Personal activities ...	43	04	61	06	104	05
Insufficient data	16	01	4	00	20	01
Total	1,143	100%	958	100%	2,101	100%

Source: Stephen J. Carroll, Jr. "Measuring the Work of a Personnel Department," *Personnel,* vol. 37, no. 4, p. 55.

helpful particularly if comparisons are made over time to check on trends of work allocation.

An excellent example of evaluation is found in the Employee Relations Index (ERI) used by the General Electric Company. It is an attempt to measure the extent to which groups of employees accept, and perform in accordance with, the objectives and policies of the company. It is based on the following eight indicators, which were selected after detailed study of numerous aspects of employee behavior:

a. Periods of absence.
b. Initial dispensary visits for occupational reasons.
c. Separations from payroll.
d. Grievances.
e. Work stoppages.
f. Number of suggestions.
g. Disciplinary suspension.
h. Participation in insurance plans.

The indicators are combined by means of the following multiple regression formulae to yield the ERI:

$$ERI = B_1K_1X_1 + B_2K_2X_2 + B_3K_3X_3$$
$$+ B_4K_4X_4 + B_5K_5X_5 + B_6K_6X_6$$
$$+ B_7K_7X_7 + B_8K_8X_8 + C$$

where the Bs refer to the weights for each element, the Ks refer to constants depending on the level of the element in the plant, the Xs refer to the respective indicators, and C is an overall constant for the plant or group in question.

Figure 28–4 shows how data are collected to compute the ERI, and Figure 28–5 shows a quarterly summary form. The ERI is intended to help managers evaluate policies and practices, trace trends in employee relations, find trouble spots, perform their human relations duties more effectively, and control personnel costs.

2. Adequacy of Program. In the matter of determining whether or not a company is pursuing all practices which are of advantage to it, two major alternatives are available. First, outside consultants may be called in to review a company's program. This is highly desirable, because it is difficult for any company to examine itself. An outsider, however, who knows the practices of others, and particularly the breadth of programs found elsewhere, can do a good job of sizing up inadequacies, weak points, and gaps.

If a company desires to do this job itself, check lists such as the selected illustration shown in Figure 28–6 may be used. In this system of check lists, emphasis is placed upon the use of questions that may be answered either yes or no. On the surface, this may appear to be an

FIGURE 28–4

ERI Data-Collection Form

Fabrication: Jones, Foreman
Work Group

Second Shift
Shift

12-31
Summary for ERI Period Ending

Element	10/13	10/10	10/17	10/24	10/31	11/7	11/14	11/21	11/25	12/5	12/12	12/19	12/26	Sum for 13 Weeks	Add Sum for Previous 13 Weeks	Score
Number of Employees	57	55	54	54	54	53	52	52	52	52	52	52	46	685		
Absentees	4	8	7	5	7	7	6	12	8	4	3	2	3	76		.11
Disciplinary Suspensions	0	0	0	0	0	0	0	0	0	0	0	0	0	0		0
Work Stoppages	0	0	0	0	0	0	0	0	0	0	0	0	0	0		0
Separations from Plant	0	0	1	1	0	1	1	0	0	0	0	2	4	10		.015
Separations from Work Group	0	4	1	1	3	2	1	0	0	0	0	2	8	22		X
Number "Bumped"	0	2	1	1	4	2	0	0	0	0	0	2	3	15		
Initial Occupational Dispensary Visits	5	1	3	2	3	1	3	2	1	2	3	1	3	30		.04
Grievances	0	0	0	0	0	0	0	0	0	0	0	0	0	0		.001
Suggestions	0	0	0	0	0	0	0	0	0	0	0	0	0	0		0
Group Insurance																96
Overtime	16	0	0	0	0	0	0	0	0	0	0	0	0	16		.02
Average Rate of Pay																2.45
Average Years Continuous Service																10.2
Average Number Dependents																1.8
% Male Employees																100
Average Age																38.3
% Union Dues Check-Off																89.2

Source: Willard V. Merrihue, *General Electric Employee Relations Index*, Personnel Series, no. 168 (New York: American Management Association), p. 47.

oversimplification. However, it must be remembered that problems cannot be solved or plans laid for their solution until they are uncovered. Hence the use of such audit forms is desirable, in that they serve to reveal areas of personal practices in which improvements may be desirable. Once ascertained in this manner, the next step—and a very significant one, of course—is that of determining what is to be done about the practices in question.

Another interesting aspect of such check lists is that they focus attention upon the wide range of personnel policies and practices that various companies have found it desirable to include in their programs. The mere fact that these plans are cited in the check lists is sufficient to cause some employers to wonder whether or not they, too, should take a broader view in their personnel practices.

It is well to guard against unnecessary dissatisfaction with one's per-

FIGURE 28-5

ERI Quarterly Summary Form

Work Group	No. Emp.	ERI	Absentees*	Disciplin. Suspens.**	Work Stoppages*	Plant Separations**	In. Occup.* Disp. Visits	Grievances**	Suggestions**	Insurance %	Overtime	Average Rate of Pay	Continuous Service	No. of Dependents	% Male	Average Age	Union Dues Check-Off	Shift
Test	43	107	11	0	0	13	3	0	2	93	51	$1.86	5.0	1.1	95.5	30	71.5	2 & 3
Insp. & Q.C.	21	96	6	0	0	4	2	4	73	100	115	2.19	18.2	1.5	100.0	45	66.7	1 & 2
Maint.	28	90	7	0	19	11	4	6	0	100	66	1.96	14.4	1.8	80.0	50	76.1	All
Maint.	28	101	8	0	27	11	3	1	3	100	126	2.04	8.3	2.3	96.0	46	100.0	1 & 2
Loading	17	105	17	0	0	9	3	2	0	100	182	1.74	9.5	2.7	100.0	45	81.4	1 & 2
Panel & Packing	30	117	5	0	0	3	5	0	3	100	177	1.85	17.0	1.8	93.5	47	63.3	1 & 2
Supply	30	111	10	0	0	10	5	0	0	100	91	1.74	11.1	1.8	93.5	42	63.3	1 & 2
Mach. Shop	35	82	24	0	0	24	6	4	0	100	22	2.40	13.1	1.9	100.0	40	100.0	Day
Mach. Shop	27	101	12	0	41	3	3	0	6	100	300	2.19	13.4	1.7	100.0	38	96.5	1
Mach. Shop	31	55	25	1	25	35	7	2	5	96	13	2.02	5.3	1.8	100.0	37	87.6	2
Fabrication	47	94	9	0	0	15	3	0	3	100	17	2.45	14.9	2.0	100.0	42	90.8	1
Fabrication	53	102	11	0	0	15	4	1	0	96	2	2.45	10.2	1.8	100.0	38	89.2	2
Fabrication	29	90	18	0	24	3	7	3	5	100	7	2.81	15.0	2.5	100.0	38	96.6	1
Assem.-Wire	48	112	12	0	0	8	3	0	2	98	72	2.42	11.3	1.9	91.5	36	89.4	1
Assem.-Wire	66	100	11	1	0	5	4	0	2	98	63	2.17	12.0	1.4	100.0	39	92.4	1
Assem.-Wire	51	115	6	0	0	3	5	0	9	100	3	2.18	13.2	2.1	100.0	40	99.7	1
Assem.-Wire & Paint	65	78	9	1	0	33	4	1	6	95	39	2.04	6.8	1.6	100.0	33	79.0	2
Supv. & Panel	44	100	9	0	31	12	3	1	0	100	13	2.22	12.3	1.7	97.1	35	100.0	1
Stockroom	38	102	10	0	0	20	4	0	2	95	76	1.67	6.1	1.3	100.0	34	89.5	1 & 2
Fab.	36	94	19	0	1	19	5	1	0	94	275	2.45	11.8	1.9	100.0	37	88.7	1
Fab.	18	92	15	0	20	21	5	0	0	95	58	1.96	5.4	1.4	100.0	32	94.5	2
Assembly	49	111	10	0	0	2	2	0	46	100	130	2.31	12.7	2.3	100.0	37	91.9	1
Assembly	10	115	8	0	0	0	4	0	23	100	145	2.36	9.0	2.3	100.0	36	91.0	2
Herkolite	18	104	13	0	0	12	5	0	8	95	112	2.44	16.3	1.7	100.0	45	89.5	1
Herkolite	8	97	19	0	0	20	1	0	0	88	24	1.85	6.9	2.2	100.0	36	100.0	2
Mean			13.0	.1	6.7	11.8	3.6	1.3	8.8	98.2	126.5	2.17	10.9	1.45	96.7	38.8	87.7	
Standard Deviation			8.0	.3	11.3	9.0	1.6	1.7	17.4	2.9	141.8	.3	3.7	.6	3.8	4.6	10.2	

*Expressed as per 100 employees per week.
** Expressed as per 10 000 employees per week.

Source: Willard V. Merrihue, *General Electric Employee Relations Index*, Personnel Series, no. 168 (New York: American Management Association), p. 48.

sonnel program because of the use of such check lists. As one reviews personal practices against a list which is a composite of numerous plans, it is easy to conclude that one's present program is inadequate. While it is well to have plans for future expansion, it is perhaps more undesirable to undertake an overly ambitious program which is likely to fail because of hurried installation than it is to proceed with a limited personnel program that is gradually expanded.

In any event, check lists do perform a function of indicating a type of practice that is useful in auditing personnel practices. It is simple, yet comprehensive. As a consequence, such a plan of auditing is more likely to catch the attention of busy top executives than extended descriptive reports.

FIGURE 28–6

Excerpt from a Check List on Morale Building

	Yes	No

I. Does the company—
   A. Explain to all employees the rules and policies of the company?
     (Necessary to prevent misunderstanding of rules and possible later
     disciplinary action. May increase employee participation in in-
     surance, safety, health and other programs.)
   B. Explain the labor policy of the company?
     (To avoid misunderstandings and maintain better relations.)
   C. Show employees the importance of being at work every day as
     scheduled?
     (May prevent employee becoming an absentee.)
   D. Promote the feeling of employee's personal participation in
     work?
     (Every worker is an important cog in the production wheel.)
   E. Show all employees the use to which their products are put?
     (Employees are interested in final use to which products are put.)
   F. Appeal directly to workers by means of posters, bulletins and
     speakers of importance of their work?
     (These programs usually help in utilization of personnel.)
   G. Have a merit rating plan?
     (Employee is given an incentive to make a good record.)

II. Does company have an organization for the sympathetic discussion of
employee problems in order to help solve them?
(Employee counsellors properly trained can analyze employee problems and propose programs to improve morale.)

III. Are the following investigated as possible employee problems?
   A. Housing?
   B. Child-care?
   C. Transportation problem?
     1. Share-the-ride?
     2. Mechanical service to employee's car?
   D. A legal problem?
   E. A medical or dental problem?
   F. An eating facility problem?
   G. Fatigue due to too long working periods?
   H. Misunderstanding due to material shortages?
     (Lowered morale of employees is often caused by a problem on
     which employee needs advice.)

IV. Does the company have program of providing recreation to
employees such as —
   A. Morning and afternoon recess periods?
   B. Definite schedule of vacations?
   C. Interdepartmental baseball?
   D. Interdepartmental football?
   E. Interdepartmental basketball?
   F. Bowling team?
   G. Family picnics?

SUMMARY

Perhaps it can be said in summary that research and evaluation reflect the philosophy of personnel management adopted by a company. In the last analysis, the particular attitude taken toward how problems of labor-management relations are to be solved will determine more than anything else the quality of a company's labor relations. This is so, but not because one's solutions are bound to be accurate—such an ideal state can scarcely ever be expected. It is so because others soon become impressed with the attitude management takes.

If the attitude is that of searching for the truth—let the chips fall where they may—the confidence and respect of employees will be increased. If the attitude is self-seeking, people will tend to return a similar attitude. These developments may be very slow in coming, but come they will. Perhaps that is why management so often despairs. It does what it considers good but sees no immediate results. It does not realize that in personnel management, time—much time—must elapse before we can reap what we have sown. But reap we shall; so, if a harvest is expected, the seeds must be planted early and cultivated with patience.

QUESTIONS

1. What have research and evaluation to do with which management functions of personnel management?
2. Who in an organization should help carry on personnel research?
3. What can conclusively be said about the relation between employee morale and productivity?
4. What are the major causes of absenteeism?
5. A company reported that over half its male employees were absent on the first day of hunting one year. What would be your suggestion for handling the situation in the future?
6. In what aspects of personnel management would sociological research be particularly applicable?
7. To what problems are the techniques of group dynamics particularly applicable?
8. By what methods may personnel programs be evaluated?
9. What do you think of the suggestion that any proposed personnel plan be accompanied by how it should eventually be controlled and evaluated?
10. What are the uses of such evaluation devices as the ERI Index?

CASE 28–1.   SUPERVISORY-SUBORDINATE PERCEPTIONS

A given company has been concerned about the quality of leadership of its first-line supervisors. Among other matters, the personnel director was asked to examine the attitudes that supervisors and employees held in regard to each other. One approach the personnel director took was to survey how supervisors perceived their jobs in relation to subordinates and how subordinates in turn perceived the job the supervisor was doing in relation to them.

To take the examination out of the realm of qualitative conceptions, the personnel director developed a set of scales to measure perceptions. Reproduced below are two of the scales administered to the subordinates and two to the supervisors:

Subordinate Scale #1—Taken all in all, do you have enough knowledge about your leader's evaluation of your work to know where you stand in the leader's opinion?

| Know very well where I stand | Know fairly clearly | Don't know too clearly | Don't know at all clearly |

Subordinate Scale #2—How would you rate your supervisor on knowledge about the attitudes and feelings of the people in the department?

| Perfect | Excellent | Good | Poor |

Supervisor Scale #1—To what degree do you think your subordinates accept the evaluations you communicate to them about their work?

| Very high | Above average | Below average | Quite low |

Supervisor Scale #2—To what degree do you think that logic, as opposed to feelings, influences opinions of employees about departmental matters?

| Very much | Often | Moderately | Very little |

After tabulating the ratings, the personnel director obtained the following results:

On Subordinate Scale #1:
  5 rated between "Know very well where I stand" and "Know fairly clearly."
 11 rated as "Know fairly clearly."
 16 rated between "Know fairly clearly" and "Don't know too clearly."
 42 rated as "Don't know too clearly."
 22 rated between "Don't know too clearly" and "Don't know at all clearly."
  4 rated as "Don't know at all clearly."

On Subordinate Scale #2:
  2 rated between "Perfect" and "Excellent."
  8 rated as "Excellent."
 12 rated between "Excellent" and "Good."
 18 rated as "Good."
 55 rated between "Good" and "Poor."
  5 rated as "Poor."

On Supervisor Scale #1:
  3 rated between "Very high" and "Above average."
  2 rated as "Above average."

On Supervisor Scale #2:
  1 rated between "Very much" and "Often."
  2 rated as "Often."
  2 rated between "Often" and "Moderately."

Question

1. What conclusions would you draw from this sample of the study (recognizing, of course, that this is a very small sample)?

CASE 28–2.   LABOR ALLOCATIONS

The Outdoor Tent Company makes two standard products: tents and sleeping bags. Its machine installations are relatively simple. Hence, labor is the biggest element of cost of manufacturing operations, with more labor being utilized in the production of sleeping bags than in tents. This (apart from respective selling prices) explains why the contribution to marginal income by each unit of output is $6 for tents and $4 for sleeping bags.

The company is desirous of allocating labor to that product mix which would yield the greatest contribution to total marginal income. The technical limitations on output are as follows:

	Tents per Month	Sleeping Bags per Month
Cutting operation	300	600
Sewing operation	400	500
Finishing operation	600	500

Question

1. Assuming that the company can sell any amount within its technical limitations, what would be the best allocation of labor to possible product mixes?

EXAMPLE OF A JOB ANALYSIS SCHEDULE

FIGURE A–1

Job Analysis Schedule

1. Job Title *POLISHER*	2. Schedule No.
3. Number Employed *30 (25-60)*	4. Establishment No.
6. Title of Verified Job *0*	5. Date *November 17, 192*
8. Alternate Titles *JEWELRY POLISHER*	Number of Pages *6*
(see VIII)	7. Industry *Jewelry*
10. Dictionary Title *BUFFER I*	9. Branch *Costume*
11. Code *6-77.020*	12. Department *Polishing*
13. Analysis Prepared by *J. O. B. Analyzer*	14. Field Office *Watucca*

15. JOB SUMMARY

Holds pieces of costume jewelry and manipulates them against the surface of laminated muslin, flannel, and wire polishing wheels which are power-rotated, to produce polished surfaces of various types on them before they are plated and painted.

MINIMUM QUALIFICATIONS FOR EMPLOYMENT

16. Sex   _0_   Age   _0_

17. Necessary Physical Requirements (including height and weight): *Strong, dextrous hands to hold small objects while they are polished.*

18. Education: *S   R   W*   English: Other: *0*

19. Experience: *6 months in the same job, served within the past five years.* *(See VIII).*

20. RELATION TO OTHER JOBS

May be promoted from WASH BOY; JIGGER (See VIII).
May be promoted to FOREMAN (Polishing Room).

21. Supervision Received: General   Medium *X*   Close   By (Title)
    Supervisor *(Polishing Room)*

22. Supervision Given: None   *X*   No. Supervised   Titles

23. Seasonality: Industry   Peak: *August to December.*   Trough: *May to July*
    Job: *Same as Industry*

Supplementary sheets should include the following items: I. WORK PERFORMED; II. EQUIPMENT; III. MATERIAL; IV. SURROUNDINGS; V. HAZARDS; VI. SPECIAL INFORMATION; VII. DEFINITION OF TERMS; VIII. COMMENTS.

Supplementary Sheet

Schedule Number _____

Date   11/17/7_ _____

Sheet 2 of 6 Sheets _____

Job Title *POLISHER*		
	Per Cent of Time	Degree of Skill

I. *WORK PERFORMED*

Note: The polishing work done here falls into six groups: (1) *oiling* (2) *gloss* (3) *cut and gloss* (4) *mat* (5) *satin* (6) *clean wheel*. By using different *polishing* wheels and *polishing compounds* varied results are obtained. Each POLISHER is expected to and at times does perform all of the six polishing operations but the POLISHING Supervisor confines them as much as possible to one of the groups. The work in each case is essentially the same and is covered by the following description.

1. Prepares for polishing: Mounts a polishing wheel on the horizontal arbor of a *Polishing Lathe* and locks it in position with a washer and a nut; dresses the wheel to make its sections even and somewhat softer by starting the Lathe and holding a small hand *rake* and then an *emery stone* against the rapidly revolving wheel; holds a stick of compound against the wheel to make it more abrasive and smooths this off by holding a pad (usually a used wheel) against it to remove excess; repeats the dressing operation whenever the wheel wears unevenly; applies compound frequently.

    Strong hands are required to dress the wheel and knowledge, gained through experience, is required to recognize when the wheel is satisfactorily dressed.

                                    10   2

2. Polishes metal jewelry: Receives trays of jewelry from the POLISHING Supervisor with oral instructions regarding the surfaces to be polished; holds a piece of jewelry against the rotating polishing wheel by hand, with pliers, or with the aid of a *hook*; develops a polishing routine for the job and follows it for each piece, skillfully turning and shifting the piece to produce an evenly polished surface; makes a rapid visual inspection and, finding the finish satisfactory, lays the piece in the tray, using layers of paper to prevent scratching the pieces; carries the tray of completed work to the PAY ROLL CLERK.

                                    85   3

FIGURE A–1 *(continued)*

Supplementary Sheet

Schedule Number _____

Date   11/17/7_

Sheet 3 of 6 Sheets

Job Title   POLISHER

	Per Cent of Time	Degree of Skill
I. *WORK PERFORMED* (Continued)		
Strong and dextrous fingers, hands and arms and well-coordinated use of hands are required to hold the pieces of jewelry against the wheel; good vision is necessary to recognize spots requiring further polishing.		
3. Makes simple *forms* from wood and nails to facilitate holding particular pieces of jewelry while polishing, using hammer, saw, and knife.	5	1

II. *EQUIPMENT*

Pliers; hammer; saw; and knife are supplied by worker.

Polishing wheels: Usually laminated muslin wheels having the circles of muslin sewed together near the center but with the outer edges loose. A hole through the center of the wheel is provided for mounting it on the arbor of a Polishing Lathe. Muslin is used for oiling and cut and gloss operations. Other wheels are (1) felt, for a coarser finish called mat (2) wire wheel for a coarser finish called satin (3) special bristle brushes usually used for oiling operations.

Polishing compounds of varying abrasiveness: Abrasive compounds which (in the order of their abrasiveness) are known as lea, tripoli, white diamond, and crocus are available in the form of sticks about 6 to 10 inches long and 2 inches in diameter. Lea is used to produce mat finishes. Tripoli is used for oiling (a cutting operation in which much oil is used.) White diamond is used for light cutting and is advantageous because it is less oily than tripoli and the articles need not be cleaned after polishing. Crocus, which is a very fine abrasive, is used for polishing to a high gloss.

Polishing Lathe: (Polishing Lathe, Bench Model, ¾ H.P., 3600 R.P.M., manufactured by the Diamond Machine Company, Providence, Rhode Island). A variable speed electric motor having an arbor extending from one side

FIGURE A–1 (*continued*)

Supplementary Sheet

Schedule Number _____

Date _____ 11/17/7_ _____

Sheet 4 of 6 Sheets

Job Title   *POLISHER*

II. *EQUIPMENT* (Continued)

on which interchangeable polishing wheels can be mounted. Different speeds are required for different polishing operations; 1700 R.P.M. being desirable for coarser finishes like mat and satin, and speeds as high as 3600 R.P.M. being used for the gloss finishes.

Rake: A simple tool made by driving many nails through a short length of wood so that their points project; this is used to dress the polishing wheels.

Emery stone: A piece of broken emery wheel used to dress the polishing wheels.

Hook: A steel wire hook with a wooden handle; by hooking this into a piece of jewelry, especially initials, it is possible to hold a piece that would otherwise be pulled out of hand by the polishing wheel.

Forms: Simple wooden jigs made by the worker to facilitate holding of the pieces of jewelry; some are made to hold several pieces at one time.

III. *MATERIAL*

None.

IV. *SURROUNDINGS*

There is a constant, noisy hum from the many Polishing Lathes and the exhaust system in the workroom. Each Polishing Lathe is hooded and is locally exhausted to draw off dust from the wheels. Despite these provisions the surroundings are quite dirty. The worker's hands and clothing are soiled by the compounds used.

V. *HAZARDS*

There is danger of injuring the hands when the article being polished catches in the revolving wheel and is pulled from the worker's hands. Slight burns from the heated articles of jewelry may be incurred.

FIGURE A–1 (*continued*)

Supplementary Sheet

Schedule Number _____

Date   11/17/7_ _____

Sheet 5 of 6 Sheets

Job Title   *POLISHER*

VI. *REGISTRATION AND PLACEMENT AIDS*

Basic Requirements: Some polishing experience is required, in which the worker has learned the "feel of the wheel" sufficiently to be able to control the pressure against the wheel to produce the desired surfaces.

A knowledge of polishing compounds and the polishing operations for which they are appropriate is required.

Must be able to distinguish between shades of color or luster to produce evenly polished surfaces.

Variable Requirements: Determine:

What kinds of metal worker will polish.
(Brass, silver, gold, aluminum and plated articles are polished.)

What kind of articles worker will polish.
(Slightly different skill is required to polish costume jewelry, rings, chains, cases, and bracelets.)

What polishing operations worker will do.
(Some workers specialize on such operations as cut and gloss, oil, mat, satin, or gloss finish; while others are able to do all.)

VII. *DEFINITION OF TERMS*

Oiling: The act of cutting through the surface of metal using an oily compound which must be washed off.

Gloss: A high luster finish produced by polishing with a fine abrasive; also a term applied to the operation of producing such a finish.

Cut and Gloss: The procedure of smoothing metal surfaces with a fairly abrasive compound which requires little oil and the immediate polishing to high luster on another wheel with a fine abrasive. The operations are combined when the cutting can be done with a compound which need not be washed off before glossing.

FIGURE A-1 *(concluded)*

Supplementary Sheet

Schedule Number _____

Date   11/17/7_ _____

Sheet 6 of 6 Sheets _____

Job Title   *POLISHER*

VII. *DEFINITION OF TERMS* (Continued)

    Mat: A dull finish produced by polishing with a coarse abrasive; also the act of producing such a finish.

    Satin: A soft finish produced with a wire brush wheel.

    Clean Wheel: A light polishing operation in which no compound is used on the polishing wheel.

VIII. *COMMENTS*

Job Title and Alternate Title: There is some justification for using the alternate title JEWELRY POLISHER in these items because there are POLISHERS in other industries who while using somewhat different techniques, are capable of being confused with this job.

Relation to Other Jobs: Experienced POLISHERS are usually hired, but occasionally WASH BOYS or JIGGERS may be promoted to the job.

Instructions for Filling Out the Job Analysis Schedule

1. *Headings.* Items 1–14 on the Job Analysis Schedule are included in the term *headings*. This part of the schedule provides for naming and locating the job industrially and for recording of certain identification data which are needed for every job.

2. *Item 1, Job Title.* Here should be entered the name by which the job being analyzed is commonly called in the establishment (plant title). All job titles (Item 1) or alternate titles (Item 8) should be written in capital letters in the singular and in the natural form as used in industry, such as *Bartender,* not *Tender, Bar.* The only exception to this rule is that the words "assistant," "helper," and "apprentice" should not be used to begin a title. A descriptive word should precede these such as *Machinist Apprentice, Pressman Helper.*

3. *General Terms.* Such general terms as *manager, foreman,* and the like should always be editorially qualified by a descriptive phrase if these titles stand alone. For example, *Foreman (Bricklaying)*; but *Bricklayer Foreman* would require no editorial qualifications.

4. *Agreement with Dictionary Form.* Extreme care should be exercised to make all titles other than plant titles in the Job Analysis Schedule and in the *Occupational Dictionary* agree in form; that is, if a title appears in inverted from in the *Occupational Dictionary*, it should be used in inverted form in the Job Analysis Schedule. A few titles are always used in inverted form, to avoid unreasonable alphabetic placement. The words *assistant, helper, apprentice,* and *supervisor* always follow the descriptive portion of the title showing the type of assistant, helper, apprentice, and supervisor.

5. *Item 2, Schedule Number.* This item is used for identification and filing purposes primarily.

6. *Item 3, Number Employed.* Here is entered the number of workers engaged in jobs identical with the job being analyzed in this particular establishment.

7. *Item 4, Establishment Number.* This entry is used for identification and filing purposes.

8. *Item 5, Date.* Enter here the date on which the job analysis is completed.

9. *Item 6, Title of Verified Job.* This entry is left blank until the job under consideration is verified as to content.

10. *Item 8, Alternate Titles.* All names by which the job is known, other than the one entered in Item 1 above, should be entered in the space opposite Item 8. These job names should not include slang terms unless such terms are widely used and recognized in the industry.

11. *Items 10 and 11, Dictionary Title and Code Number.* If the job which is described in this analysis is defined in the *Dictionary of Occupational Titles,* enter the specific dictionary title and code number here.

12. *Item 7, Industry.* Here enter the accepted name of the industry in which the analyzed job is observed.

13. *Item 9, Branch.* A branch represents a larger division of an industry, made according to type of activity carried on, as contrasted with a department, which represents a division made according to phases of a single activity or process.

14. *Item 12, Department.* Enter here the name of the department of the industry in which the analyzed job is found. The analyst is responsible for specifying either the division in which this job exists, or the fact that no division exists.

15. *Item 13, Analysis Prepared by.* Here is entered the name of the person who is responsible for preparing the job analysis.

16. *Item 14, Field Office.* Enter here the name and the code number of the field office which services the area in which the industry is located.

17. *Item 16, Job Summary.* The job summary presents in concise form the essential and distinguishing characteristics of the occupation. Since it is a summary of all the information collected by the job analysis, it is not written until all of the job analysis has been completed. Hence the details for preparing the job summary will be discussed in paragraph 53 of these instructions.

18. *Minimum Qualifications.* The source of information included in Items 16 to 19 is the person responsible for hiring workers for the job under analysis. This person should define the minimum acceptable standards for employment. It should be recognized, however, that employers generally have a tendency to demand higher qualifications when discussing jobs than when they actually hire workers. It is the problem of the

analyst to determine tactfully and accurately the actual minimum requirements and to record these rather than the ideal standards.

19. *Minimum qualifications for employment* always remain the minimum requirements for success on the job, even though an employer may at the moment prefer applicants of higher educational requirements than necessary. The employer may feel that these requirements are necessary to meet the needs of other jobs in the plant when promoting or transferring workers from one job to another. Minimum qualifications for employment at the time of analysis are not necessarily permanent hiring factors, since hiring requirements readily fluctuate with changes in the labor market. If other than actual minimum job requirements are noted, the entry should be qualified with an explanation.

20. *Item 16, Sex.* Enter here the answer to the question, "Does the employer have the legal right to hire men exclusively, women exclusively, or either men or women, for this job?" Enter M for male, F for female, and O if there is no preference.

21. *Item 16, Age.* Enter here the minimum and maximum age which the employer may legally require in hiring people for this job. If no special range is designated, enter a zero (0). Thus if the employer is willing to accept people between the ages of 18 and 25 only, the entry in Item 16 appears as "18–25."

22. *Item 17, Necessary Physical Requirements.* Here are entered any special physical requirements that are necessary to adequate performance of the job. If average, ordinary, not unusual requirements are specified, the entry should be zero (0). The data should include all necessary characteristics, such as: "Small and agile to climb between girders"; "Not under 5'10" tall to reach high shelves"; or, "Strong and husky, weight 160 pounds or over, to carry heavy lumber."

23. *Item 18, Education.* Encircle S, R, or W, or all three, to indicate that the ability to speak, read or write English, respectively, is the minimum literacy requirement for employment. If the minimum education required is more than ability to read and write, it should appear after other; as "8 years elementary school"; "business-school secretarial training"; "college graduation with major in chemistry."

24. *Item 19, Experience.* Here indicate any prior work experience which may be required of the applicant. When questioning, it is important to determine exactly what the employer considers as minimum experience requirements in the light of the normal labor market situation.

25. *Item 20, Relation to Other Jobs.* Item 20 is intended to provide information with reference to the job which qualified workers come to the job under analysis, as well as the jobs to which qualified workers may be promoted. It points out ways in which workers are or can be interchanged between jobs within the establishment, as well as the manner in which interindustry transfers may readily be made.

26. *Item 21, Supervision Received.* Here enter a rating of the degree of supervision received by the worker, by marking an X in the space after the appropriate item: general, close, or medium. It is essential that the analyst indicate the amount of responsibility placed on the worker for quality and quantity of product or performance. The term *general* indicates the usual type of overseeing which most workers receive. *Close,* at the other extreme, denotes a constant overseeing of the worker by the supervisor, with almost no responsibility placed on the worker. *Medium,* between these extremes, indicates that the worker is given specific detailed instructions, particularly at the beginning of a task and, hence, is assigned a certain amount of responsibility.

27. *Item 22, Supervision Given.* If no supervision is given to other workers by the worker under observation, an X should be entered in the space after the word *none.* If the worker whose job is being analyzed has, as part of the duties, the supervision of others, the number of workers supervised should be entered following *no. supervised.* The titles of the jobs supervised should be entered following the word *title.* Where the titles of the job supervised are numerous, an indication of the group supervised is sufficient, but it should be possible to ascertain the title from the statement made, supplemented by a note in Item VIII, Comments, if necessary.

28. *Item 23, Seasonality.* In certain industries, as in canning, the number of workers employed is closely related to the season of the year. In canning, the greatest number of workers are employed during the months of September and October and the smallest number in February. If the job being analyzed, or the industry in which it exists, is affected by seasonal fluctuations, the weeks and months in which the hiring and the laying-off occurs should be recorded. The weeks or months during which employment is above normal are known as the "peak" of employment, and the period during which employment is below normal is known as the "trough."

Filling Out Supplementary Sheets

29. *Certain kinds of information* which are needed to describe a job fully, vary so much in form, extent, and content, that little more than a heading and a general explanation can be given. Of such a nature are the eight items of the supplementary material. These items are:

I.	Work performed	V.	Hazards
II.	Equipment	VI.	Special information
III.	Material	VII.	Definitions of terms
IV.	Surroundings	VIII.	Comments.

30. *Not all* of these eight supplementary items will be of value on every job. On some jobs the detailed treatment of work performed may

be unnecessary, especially if ample descriptive material is contained in the job summary. In jobs in which no hazards exist, or in jobs which involve few or no special terms, these items will not be required.

31. *Work Performed.* The primary purpose of this supplementary item is the description of the duties of the job concisely, precisely, and explicitly so that a reader may be able to visualize the tasks composing the job, preferably in the sequence of steps taken, and may be able to recognize the skills, knowledges, and judgments or responsibilities involved, with a minimum of mental reorganization of the data after reading. The purpose of the information on work performed is to furnish the interviewer with enough detail about the job to accomplish effective interviewing, selection, and placement work.

32. In *Supplementary Item I* should be entered a statement or description of what the worker does in a series of either chronological or logical steps, setting forth what is done, how it is done, and why it is done.

33. *A statement of work* performed will usually consist of a series of numbered statements, each comprising a description of a task or major step in the job. The statements should be brief, and the job title of the worker is implied as the subject of each sentence.

34. *Knowledges and Judgments.* It is not enough to record simply a description of the motions performed by the worker; it is generally of greater importance that the interviewer have a record of the knowledges, training, and experience necessary to perform these motions at the right time, in the right order, and in the right manner. Consequently, it is vitally necessary in every instance that the analyst determine whether execution of the motions depends on any skills, knowledges, exercise of judgments, or other intangible factors, and so make specific statements emphasizing the significance of such factors. This comment applies to each separate task in the job, as well as to the job as a whole.

35. *Rating of Percent of Time.* After each numbered element of the work performed, in the column headed Percent of Time should be indicated the percentage of the worker's time that the element occupies as compared with the job as a whole.

36. *Rating of Degree of Skill.* After each element in the second column headed Degree of Skill, should be indicated a rating of the skill that is required of the worker to perform the element. Expressions of the degree or rate of skill are indicated by the figures 1, 2, and 3; 1 being used to express the lowest amount of skill, and 3 the highest amount. When assigning the ratings to job elements, only the job being analyzed is to be considered. This practice must be followed strictly because it is not possible to compare the skills involved in different jobs, since what might be rated a 3 skill for the element of one job might deserve only the rating of 1 in another job.

37. *The Work Performed* item should include a statement of the duties

that are performed infrequently, as well as in the normal work cycle. Such tasks as the occasional setting up of a machine, occasional repairs, infrequent reports, and the like, should here be included. In each case a notation should be made concerning the frequency of occurrence of the performance.

38. *"May" Tasks and Alternative Tasks.* If a task may be performed by one worker or by another, the description of it should be introduced with the word *may.* All alternative methods of performing a task should be stated: "Either . . . (the one) . . . or . . . (the other) . . . ."

39. *Simultaneous Tasks.* In cases in which a worker may start several tasks at the same time, none of which is completed for several days, each task should be completely described before beginning the description of a second task.

40. *Miscellaneous Cautions.* In preparing the Work Performed item, care should be exercised to avoid the simple listing of the tasks performed by the worker without any explanation of how they are performed. The inclusion of too many duties in one work element should be avoided. Even closely related duties should be broken up into more than one element if the item has become too long and involved.

41. *Equipment.* Under this item enumerate, in the order mentioned under Work Performed, all machines and all special or unusual equipment used by the worker on the job that is being analyzed.

42. Under *Description of a Machine* should appear the following: a statement of the function of the machine; a description of the physical appearance of the machine and its essential parts; and a description of the operation of the machine and its relation to the worker. Only essential features of the mechanical equipment should be included in the description. Structural details, such as gear ratios, types of power drive, and other technical features, need not be included unless some specific job duties are performed in relation to these features.

43. *Tools.* For simpler devices, particularly for hand tools, it will be necessary to include only a definition of the device rather than a complete description. In every case the purpose for which the device is used should be shown.

44. *Relating the Description to the Drawing.* If a drawing has been included in the Schedule, all descriptions of equipment should be related to the drawing by placing the letters appearing on the drawing in parentheses after the names of the component parts of the device to which they refer.

45. *Material.* Under this item should be listed and described the components used by the worker to make a finished product, if such activity is being performed on the job. For example, a baker makes bread from flour. A core maker makes cores from sand, but a cab driver or elevator operator does not use material in this sense.

46. *Surroundings.* Under this item will be described the physical

conditions under which the job is performed. The statement should show the nature of the conditions and the manner in which they affect the worker. The statement of the surroundings may begin with the word *inside* or the word *outside* if this fact is not obvious from the statement to follow. Three situations may arise in analyzing surroundings. These are: First, situations in which the analyst determines that no significant entries need to be made concerning surroundings, such as might be typified by a large group of clerical workers who perform their duties in "normal office surroundings." In preparing schedules for such jobs, a zero (0) should be placed after Item IV, Surrounding. Second, situations in which the surroundings are significant and inherent factors on the job. Third, situations in which the analyst is in doubt whether the significance of the surroundings or their inherent identification with the job adds to the job analysis. When in doubt, the analyst should include the data as reference information, leaving to others who use the information the decision as to its relevance.

47. *Hazards.* If the job is of such a nature that its performance involves possible injury, death, or damage to health, these dangers should be described. Only those hazards that can be connected with the job itself should be included. For example, traffic hazards to which everyone is subjected are not considered occupational hazards for most jobs, but in the case of a traffic patrol-officer, the danger of being struck by a passing vehicle is a very real occupational hazard.

48. *Special Information.* The material in this section should enumerate the factors in the job, the presence or absence of which may have a direct bearing on occupational classification or on placement. A substitute heading for this item might be Registration and Placement Aids. This item should be used to emphasize characteristics in which the job under analysis differs in important respects from other jobs of its kind. It should assist in anticipating variations in the job which may occur in different establishments.

In this item two main headings are kept in mind, Basic Requirements and Variable Requirements.

Basic requirements are the "performance" characteristics—those qualifications which are definitely required by the nature of the job itself. These may be beyond or aside from any qualifications of "evidential" nature which may be demanded by individual employers in keeping with their labor policies. Such factors as "the ability to do art work," or "the possession of engineering training," should be mentioned here. The analyst must be careful in all cases to state the minimum rather than the maximum qualifications for success on the job. Even when no experience is required for the job, some knowledge or ability may be specified as needed for its successful performance. For example, the employer may specify one of the following: "Eighth-grade education or its equivalent, to provide ability to solve problems involving multiplication and division of fractions"; "Sufficient physical strength to stand continuously and lift articles weighing approximately 50 pounds from the floor into the feed hopper at frequent intervals"; or "Worker must possess or obtain a food-handler certificate."

The description of variable requirements should bring out the differences that may be expected between workers, all of whom are employed in the same job, in either the same or different establishments. This information should guide interviewers in obtaining supplementary information that will indicate a worker's fitness for a special position after it has been determined that the worker is qualified to perform the duties of the occupation. Here would be noted such factors as wide variation in procedure followed, equipment used, or the number of workers supervised.

49. *Information for the Applicant.* In Supplementary Item VI, information should be included such as the applicant might request concerning the job. Obviously, all factors listed below will not necessarily apply to any one job, nor does the list include all of the possible items that might apply. Among the more common types of information requested by applicants are: specialized knowledge of machine operation which is required, use of attachments, tolerances or accuracy required, rate of production required by employer, opportunities for training on the job and in the community, length of the learning period, base rate of pay, hours of work shifts, transportation to and from the job, housing and boarding facilities in the neighborhood of the plant, etc.

50. *Definition of Terms.* All unusual or technical terms that are used throughout the analysis should be underlined as they are used. In Item VII, these technical terms should be listed in the order in which they appear in Work Performed. Each term should be defined. The definitions will vary with the terms to be explained. Each definition should include a clear statement or explanation of the word or thing by describing the attributes, properties, or relations which distinguish it from all other words or things. The term may be defined by stating its use.

51. The style to be used in preparing Definitions of Terms is illustrated in the following examples derived from an analysis of the job of polisher in an establishment where costume jewelry is produced.

Gloss: A high-luster finish produced by polishing with fine abrasives; also, a term applied to the operation of producing such a finish.

Satin: A soft finish produced with a wire-brush wheel.

Cut and Gloss: The process of smoothing metal surfaces with a medium fine abrasive compound which requires little oil, and the immediately polishing or high luster on another wheel with a fine abrasive.

52. *Miscellaneous.* This item contains material not elsewhere classified. It should be used for footnoting all other parts of the job analysis.

If the space allotted in the printed form is insufficient at any point, the information to be entered may be continued in Item VIII.

53. *Job Summary.* Refer again to paragraph 17 of these instructions. The job summary presents in concise form the essential and distinguishing characteristics of the occupation. It should be so constructed that it characterizes the job accurately. The job summary must be an abstract of the entire analysis; hence, it is written after the Job Analysis Schedule proper has been completed. It should be so complete that it can be used independently as an adequate presentation of the essential facts about the job. It should be a concise overall definition of the job, and not simply a summary of the work performed. Such items as the following should be taken into account in determining the content of the job summary:

What the worker does.
How it is done.
Why it is done (for what purpose) and worker's in the process.
Under what conditions work is done.
The degree of responsibility.
The kind of establishment in which the work is done (if the industry includes more than one).
Considerations controlling trade judgments or decisions.
The special qualifications which worker must possess.

Undesirable Differentiations	*Desirable Differentiations*
ADJUSTER.—Receives complaints from customers in person or by telephone concerning merchandise and bills; investigates complaints and makes adjustments.	ADJUSTER.—Receives complaints from customers concerning qualities of merchandise, credits to be allowed for defective merchandise, and the like. Investigates complaints, decides what adjustment is to be made, and authorizes replacement of merchandise or the giving of credit.
ADJUSTMENT CLERK.—Notes complaints made by customers; as TRACER checks complaints and informs customer what adjustment will be made.	ADJUSTMENT CLERK.—Receives complaints of customers concerning routine matters such as nondelivery of merchandise and erroneous charges. As TRACER ascertains reason for the complaint, what adjustment will be made, and informs customer.

Another example is cited of an unacceptable job summary and an acceptable revision:

Unacceptable Job Summary	*Acceptable Job Summary*
CORE PASTER.—Mixes paste; removes baked core from rack; cuts	CORE PASTER.—Assembles baked sand core sections to form a core by

vent holes through sections; applies paste, presses sections together; spreads flurry on seams, checks dimensions. brushing the adjoining surfaces with flour paste, to make them adhesive, and fitting the section accurately together, smoothing the surfaces with a plastic mixture and inspecting the dimensions for accuracy.

Two acceptable job summaries are cited in conclusion:

PUNCH PRESS OPERATOR. Sets up and operates a punch press to punch or shape small aircraft pieces from sheet aluminum. Checks dies against blue-prints and fits dies into press, bolting them securely in place. Sets gauges and makes trial run to test position of dies and gauges, making adjustments so that the completed work conforms to specifications recorded on blueprints. Places piece of aluminum stock in position against gauges on the punch press and operates the machine by stepping on a pedal, periodically checking completed pieces to be sure they are according to requirements. Supervises a PUNCH PRESS OPERATOR HELPER.

ROAD PAVER OPERATOR. Operates a one-yard capacity gasoline-powered road paver to mix wet concrete and spread it on a roadbed by manipulating hand levers and foot treadles to lift and dump the ingredients from the skip (loading hopper) into the rotating mixing drum of the machine. Empties the drum contents into a bucket, moves the bucket horizontally along the boom, and distributes the contents of the bucket onto the roadbed as the bucket is being emptied. Moves the road paver on its crawler treads during the paving process.

SELECTED BIBLIOGRAPHY

Magazines and Periodicals

Academy of Management Journal; Administrative Management; Administrative Science Quarterly; Advanced Management; American Journal of Sociology; American Psychologist; American Sociological Review; Factory; Fortune; Harvard Business Review; Human Relations; Industrial and Labor Relations Review; Industrial Relations; International Labor Review; Journal of Applied Behavioral Science; Journal of Applied Psychology; Labor History; Management Review; Management of Personal Quarterly; Management Science; Monthly Labor Review; NTL Institute News and Reports; Office Administration; Personnel; Personnel Administration; Personnel and Guidance Journal; Personnel Journal; Personnel Psychology; Training and Development Journal; Training in Business and Industry.

Loose Leaf Services

The Bureau of National Affairs, Inc., Washington, D.C.; *Commerce Clearing House,* Chicago, Illinois; *Executive Sciences Institute,* Whippany, New Jersey; *Prentice-Hall, Inc.;* Englewood Cliffs, New Jersey; *Research Institute of America,* New York.

Information on current developments, practices, laws, legal interpretations, and administrative rulings may be found in the foregoing services, on various aspects of employment, collective bargaining, compensation, labor relations, personnel policies and practices, pensions, profit sharing, safety and health, training, and wages and hours.

Books

Argyris, Chris. *Integrating the Individual and the Organization.* New York: John Wiley & Sons, Inc., 1964.

Baker, Frank. *Organization Systems.* Homewood, Illinois: Richard D. Irwin, Inc., 1973.

Bakke, E. Wright; Kerr, Clark; and Anrod, Charles W. *Unions, Management, and the Public.* 3d ed. New York: Harcourt, Brace & World, Inc., 1967.

Bartlett, Alton C., and Kayser, Thomas A., eds. *Changing Organizational Behavior.* Englewood Cliffs, New Jersey: Prentice Hall, Inc., 1973.

Bass, Bernard M., and Barrett, Gerald V. *Man, Work, and Organizations.* Boston, Mass.: Allyn and Bacon, Inc., 1973.

Beal, Edwin F.; Wickersham, Edward D.; and Kienast, Philip. *The Practice of Collective Bargaining.* Homewood, Illinois: Richard D. Irwin, Inc., 1972.

Belcher, David W. *Compensation Administration.* 3rd ed. Englewood Cliffs, New Jersey: Prentice-Hall, Inc., 1974.

Berliner, William M., and McLarney, William J. *Management Training.* 6th ed. Homewood, Illinois: Richard D. Irwin, Inc., 1974.

Bloom, Gordon F., and Northrup, Herbert R. *Economics of Labor Relations.* 7th ed. Homewood, Illinois: Richard D. Irwin, Inc., 1973.

Bok, Derek C., and Dunlop, John T. *Labor and the American Community.* New York: Simon and Schuster, 1970.

Burack, Elmer H. *Strategies for Manpower Planning and Programming.* Morristown, New Jersey: General Learning Corporation, 1972.

Campbell, John P.; Dunnette, Marvin D.; Lawler, Edward E. III; and Weick, Karl E. Jr. *Managerial Behavior, Performance, and Effectiveness.* New York: McGraw-Hill, Inc., 1970.

Cohen, Sanford. *Labor in the United States.* 3d ed. Columbus, Ohio: Charles E. Merrill Books, Inc., 1970.

Davey, Harold W. *Contemporary Collective Bargaining.* 3d ed. Englewood Cliffs, New Jersey: Prentice-Hall, Inc., 1972.

Davis, Keith. *Human Behavior at Work.* 4th ed. New York: McGraw-Hill Book Company, 1972.

Drucker, Peter F. *Management: Tasks, Responsibilities, Practices.* New York: Harper and Row, 1974.

Finkle, Robert B., and Jones, William S. *Assessing Corporate Talent.* New York: John Wiley and Sons, Inc., 1970.

French, Wendell L., and Hellriegal, Don. *Personnel Management and Organization Development: Fields in Transition.* Boston, Mass.: Houghton Mifflin Company, 1971.

Ghiselli, Ewin E. *The Validity of Occupational Aptitude Tests.* New York: John Wiley & Sons, Inc., 1966.

Gibson, James L.; Ivancevich, John M.; and Donnelly, James H. Jr. *Organizations: Structure, Processes and Behavior.* Dallas, Texas: Business Publications, Inc., 1973.

Golembiewski, Robert T., and Cohen, Michael, eds. *People in Public Service.* Itasca, Illinois: F. E. Peacock, 1970.

Greenman, Russell L., and Schmertz, Eric J. *Personnel Administration and the Law.* Rockville, Maryland: Bureau of National Affairs, Inc., 1972.

Haner, F. T. *Multinational Management.* Columbus, Ohio: Charles E. Merrill Publishing Company, 1973.

Herzberg, Frederick. *Work and the Nature of Man.* Cleveland: The World Publishing Company, 1966.

Kahn, Robert L., and Cannell, Charles F. *The Dynamics of Interviewing.* 11th ed. New York: John Wiley & Sons, Inc., 1967.

Katz, Daniel, and Kahn, Robert L. *The Social Psychology of Organizations.* New York: John Wiley & Sons, Inc., 1966.

Koontz, Harold. *Appraising Managers as Managers.* New York: McGraw-Hill Book Company, 1971.

Leavitt, Harold J., and Pondy, Louis R. *Readings in Managerial Psychology.* 2d ed. Chicago: University of Chicago Press, 1973.

Levitan, Sar A.; Mangum, Garth L.; and Marshall, Ray. *Human Resources and Labor Markets.* New York: Harper and Row, 1972.

McGregor, Douglas. *The Human Side of Enterprise.* New York: McGraw-Hill Book Company, 1960.

Margules, Newton, and Raia, Anthony P. *Organizational Development.* New York: McGraw-Hill Book Company, 1972.

Maslow, A. H. *Motivation and Personality.* New York: Harper & Brothers, 1954.

Mayo, Elton. *The Social Problems of an Industrial Civilization.* Boston: Harvard University, 1945.

Mills, E. P. *Listening: Key to Communication.* New York: Mason and Lipscomb Publishers, Inc., 1974.

Milton, Charles R. *Ethics and Expediency in Personnel Management.* Columbia, South Carolina: University of South Carolina Press, 1970.

Myers, M. Scott. *Every Employee a Manager.* New York: McGraw-Hill Book Company, 1970.

Nash, Allan N., and Miner, John B., eds. *Personnel and Labor Relations: An Evolutionary Approach.* Riverside, New Jersey: Macmillan Publishing Company, Inc., 1973.

Roethlisberger, F. J. *Management and Morale.* Cambridge: Harvard University Press, 1946.

Sanford, Aubrey C. *Human Relations: Theory and Practice.* Columbus, Ohio: Charles E. Merrill Publishing Company, 1973.

Scheer, Wilbert E. *Personnel Director's Handbook.* Chicago: The Dartnell Corp., 1969.

Schein, Edgar H. *Organizational Psychology.* 2d ed. Englewood Cliffs, New Jersey: Prentice-Hall, Inc., 1970.

Sedwick, Robert C. *Interaction: Interpersonal Relationships in Organizations.* Englewood Cliffs, New Jersey: Prentice-Hall, Inc., 1974.

Siegel, Lawrence, and Lane, Irving M. *Psychology in Industrial Organizations.* 3d ed. Homewood, Illinois: Richard D. Irwin, Inc., 1974.

Stahl, O. Glenn. *Public Personnel Administration,* 6th ed. New York: Harper and Row, 1971.

Tosi, Henry L.; House, Robert J.; and Dunnette, Marvin D., eds. *Managerial*

Motivation and Compensation. East Lansing, Michigan: Michigan State University, 1972.

Vroom, V. H. *Work and Motivation.* New York: John Wiley & Sons, Inc., 1964.

Weber, Max. *The Theory of Social and Economic Organizations.* New York: Oxford University Press, 1967.

Zollitsch, Herbert G., and Langsner, Adolph. *Wage and Salary Administration.* Cincinnati: South-Western Publishing Company, 1970.

index

INDEX

A

Ability to pay, 284
Absenteeism, 494
Academy of Management, 490
Accident insurance plans, 331
Accident-prone employees, 397
Accidents
  frequency, 395
  severity, 395
Administered wages, 283
Advertising for labor, 114
Affiliated unions, 443
Alliance for Labor Action, 25
American Arbitration Association, 471
American Federation of Labor, 441
American Federation of Labor—Congress of Industrial Organizations, 441
American Legion, 352
American Management Association, 490
American Society of Safety Engineers, 402
American Society of Training and Development, 238
Application blank, 128
Apprenticeship training, 228
Aptitude tests, 166
Arbitration, 471
Assessment centers, 185
Athletic programs, 363
Audits, personnel, 502
Authority
  informal, 75
  responsibility and, 77
Authorization of transfers, 189
Automation, 417

B

Bacon-Davis Act, 289
Bargaining agent, 454

Battery of tests, 169

Battery of tests, 169
Behavioral specifications, 101
Blue Cross Plan, 331
Budgets, personnel, 62
Bureau of Labor Statistics, 284
Business games, 253

C

Candidates, executive development, 245
Chamber of Commerce of the United States, 329
Checkoff, 446
Civil Rights Act, 175, 408, 415
Closed shop, 445
Coaching, 269
Co-determination, 24
Coffee break, 344
Collective bargaining, scope of, 448
College recruiting, 117
Commission plans, 321
Committee of Economic Development, 352
Committee on Political Education, 25
Communication
  basic concepts, 266
  feedback, 268
  lines of, 76
  rules, 268
  systems, 267
Community objectives, 54
Company
  periodicals, 366
  stores, 371
  unions, 444
Conciliation, 472
Conflict, 434
Congress of Industrial Organizations, 441
Contracts
  living with, 455

Contracts—*Cont.*
  negotiating, 449
  subject matter, 452
Convenience services, 370
Cooperation, 425
Cost of living, 284
Counseling
  merit evaluation, 203
  role of, 144
Craft unions, 443
Credit unions, 372
Critical incident rating, 215
Critical test scores, 177
Cybernetics, 416

D

Daily time problems, 343
Daywork wages, 313
Decision-making training, 253
Depth interview, 150
Development
  executive, 243
  human factor, 37
  needs, 245
Dictionary of Occupational Titles, 95
Dietitians, 371
Disadvantaged groups, 406, 409
Disaster controls, 386
Disciplinary action
  follow-up, 481
  penalties, 478
  principles, 481
  procedures, 476
  safety and, 399
  terms defined, 476
  union-management relations, 485
Discriminatory practices, 406
Drama clubs, 362

E

Economics, remuneration and, 278
Education, defined, 225, 261
Efficiency Bonus Plan, 316
Emotional specifications, 100
Employee
  audit, 502
  defined, 3
  evaluation, 198
  roles, 23
  sources, 109
  specifications, 98
  training, 225
  types, 3, 98
Employee Benefit Security Act, 335
Employee Relations Index, 506

Employer, defined, 447
Employment agencies
  private, 113
  public, 111
Employment office, 118
Environmental conditions, 79, 382–90
Equal Employment Opportunities Law,
    176, 408
Equal Pay Act, 289, 414–15
Equality-of-workers theory, 285
Escalator clauses, 285
Ethics, 36
Evaluation
  employee, 198
  executive development, 257
  job, 294
  merit, 198
  methods, 206
  personnel, 198
  rules, 215
  sources of labor, 117
  trainee, 258
  training programs, 235, 257
Executive
  appraisal, 205
  behavior, 44
  capacities, 244
  compensation, 322
Executive development
  conditions of, 249
  education, 261
  evaluation, 257
  needs, 246, 248
  planning, 244
  program content, 255
  significance, 243
Exemptions, Wages and Hours Law, 330
Exit interview, 146
External consistency, 307
External source, employee, 111

F

Factor comparison plan, 305
Fair Labor Standards Act, 286, 318, 335,
    353
Featherbedding, 446
Federal Mediation and Conciliation
    Service, 471
Feedback, communication, 268
Flexible work hours, 343
Flower clubs, 362
Flying clubs, 362
Forced choice evaluations, 209
Frequency accident rates, 395
Fringe benefits
  employee, 328
  executive, 324

Functional organizations, 72
Functions
  nature, 55
  responsibility for, 56

G

Garden clubs, 362
General counsel, 448
Ghetto
  labor supply, 115
  training, 231
Governmental relations, 22
Graphical forms of evaluation, 206
Grid structure, 46, 75
Grievances
  channels, 460
  machinery, 467
  meaning, 459
  principles, 465
  steps, 460
Group
  behavior, 43
  dynamics, 500
  interview, 151
  wage plans, 317
Guaranteed annual wage, 354
Guidance, tests and, 163

H

"Halo effect," 212
Handicapped workers, 412
Hawthorne experiments, 500
Health
  insurance plans, 331
  medical examinations, 390
  services, 390
Herzberg, F., 40
Hiring
  function, 89
  halls, 117, 130
  system, 69
Home purchase plans, 372
Hourly wage plans, 313
Human factor
  dimensions, 35
  dynamics, 36
  maturation, 36
  motivation, 37
  personnel management, 34
Human relations, interviewing and, 146

I

Incentive plans, 315
Independent unions, 444
Indoctrination, 140
Induction, 134

Industrial compensation, 383
Industrial relations, 3
Industrial unions, 443
Informal authority, 75
Information programming, 65
Insurance programs, 330
Interest tests, 168
Internal consistency, 307
Internal Revenue Service, 335
Internal source, employees, 110
International Association of Industrial
  Accident Boards and Commissioners,
  402
International personnel programs, 417
Internship training, 228
Interviewer development, 153
Interviewing
  procedures, 153
  purposes, 144
  rules, 155
  technical factors, 151
  types, 147

J

Job
  classification, 91
  definition, 90
  description, 91
  enlargement, 98
  enrichment, 98
  evaluation, 91
  requirements, 95
  terms, 90
Job analysis
  questionnaire, 95
  schedule, 513
Job evaluation
  classification plan, 298
  defined, 294
  organization, 295
  plans, 297
Job families, 91
Job posting, 189, 191
Job relationships, 181
Job specifications
  information, 94
  transfers and, 181
Job stabilization
  Social Security Act and, 353
  Wages and Hours Law and, 353

K–L

Knights of Labor, 441
Labor
  casual sources, 115
  dimensions of, 5
  recommended, 115

Labor Management Relations Act
coverage, 447
rights of parties, 445
scope, 444
Labor-Management Reporting and Disclosure Act, 442
Labor relations, interviewing and, 147
Labor sources, 109
Labor turnover, 104
Landrum-Griffin Act, 442
Language, interviewing and, 151
Learning
curves, 239
executive, 243
methods, 263
principles, 239
Legal aspects, women employees and, 415
Lewis, John L., 444
Life insurance plans, 330
Line and staff structures, 73
Line structures, 71
Lunch periods, 344

M

Maintenance of human relations, 37
Management
attitudes, 24
communication, 272
grid, 75
objectives and, 6
prerogatives, 453
Manpower Development and Training Act, 231, 412
Maslow, A. H., 39
Matrix structures, 75
Maturation, 36
Measured daywork plan, 314
Mechanical aids, interviewing, 152
Mediation, 472
Medical
examinations, 390
service organization, 394
services, 373
Mental specification, 98
Merit, seniority and, 193
Merit evaluation
accuracy, 212
comparison bases, 202
consultation, 203
form design, 206
objectives, 199
programs, 198
rules, 215
theory, 199
Merit rating, accident, 383
Minority groups, 115
Monetary conversions, 282

Morale, 429
group, 431
Motivation, 37
basic aspects, 38
classes, 39
human aspects, 37
rules, 42
steps, 40
Music in the plant, 364
Musical groups, 362

N

National Alliance of Businessmen, 412
National Association of Manufacturers, 352
National Association of Suggestion Systems, 368
National Industrial Recovery Act, 442
National Labor Relations Act, 442, 446
National Labor Relations Board, 448
National Safety Council, 401
Negotiations, contract, 449
Noise, 388
Nondirective interview, 148
Noon-hour programs, 362
Norris-LaGuardia Act, 442

O

Objectives
classes, 51
management by, 47
personal, 52
personnel, 51
personnel management, 6
Occupation, defined, 90
Occupational Safety and Health Act, 395
Older employees, 413
Ombudsman, 469
On-the-job
executive development, 250
operative training, 227
Operations research, 500
Operative training
courses, 226
employee, 225
evaluation, 235
factors, 232
scope, 226
Organization
behavior, 425
job evaluation, 295
operative training, 233
personnel management, 68
safety, 401
service plans, 374
Organization structure
authority, 76
design, 77

Organization structure—*Cont.*
  formal, 71
  responsibility, 57, 77
  tests, 82
Overall working day, 344
Overtime compensation, 318

P

Participation programs, 366
Paternalism, 25
Penalties, disciplinary, 476
Pension Benefit Guaranty Corporation, 335
Pension plans,
  federal, 336
  private, 332
Periodicals, 366
Personal
  audits, 502
  objectives, 52
  observation, 130
Personnel
  evaluation, 501
  functional integration, 83
  objectives, 51
  policies, 58
  problems, 26
  programming, 50
  supply sources, 109
  terms, 4
Personnel executives
  education, 13
  fields of knowledge, 12
  qualifications, 11
Personnel management
  basic guides, 8
  concept, 3
  definition, 5
  educational institutions and, 26
  employee roles, 23
  future prospects, 30
  governmental relations, 22
  historical changes, 17
  human aspects, 34
  management attitudes, 24
  managerial phases, 5
  objectives, 5
  operative phases, 6
  organization, 68
  philosophy, 8
  present status, 26
  principles, 9
  problems, 26
  procurement phase, 37
  responsibility, 7
  social aspects, 20
  systems, 68

Personnel management—*Cont.*
  unions and, 24
  technical phases, 6
Personnel problems
  approaches to, 27
  factual basis, 28
  nature, 27
  obstacles, 29
Personnel programs
  budgets, 62
  international, 417
Personnel requirements, 89, 103
Personnel research
  basic considerations, 489
  managerial, 488
  production estimates, 103
  quantitative, 500
  scope, 488
  technical, 491
Personnel services
  evaluation, 377
  types, 376
Philadelphia Plan, 412
Physical demands record, 98
Physical security, 382
Physical specifications, 98
Piecework plans, 315
Planned interviews, 148
Point systems of evaluation, 299
Policies
  control, 61
  coverage, 59
  personnel, 58
  responsibility, 60
Pollution, 390
Portal-to-portal issue, 345
Position
  defined, 90
  rotation plan, 252
Principles, learning, 239
Private employment agencies, 113
Problem-solving learning, 253
Procedural responsibility, 56
Procedure, selection, 122
Procurement, human relations, 37
Production estimates, 103
Productivity, wages and, 283
Profiles
  merit evaluation, 213
  test, 172
Profit-sharing plans
  executive, 322
  operative employee, 319
Programmed instruction, 229
Programming
  budgets and, 62
  operative training, 229
  personnel, 50

Progression charts, 183–84
Project management, 74
Promotions, 180
Propaganda, communications and, 272
Public employment agencies, 111

Q–R

Questionnaires
  job analysis, 94
  morale, 264
Rate ranges, 303
Recreational programs, 361
Recruitment
  college, 117
  employee, 116
  programs, 116
"Red circle" rates, 305
Reference letters, 129
Reliability
  merit evaluation, 212, 215
  test, 175
Remuneration
  economic aspects, 278
  noneconomic aspects, 280
  problems, 277
  safeguards, 290
  social aspects, 280
  time problems, 342
  union aspects, 283
Remuneration plans
  basic kinds, 310
  executive, 322
  salesmen, 320
  tests, 311
Representation plans, 442
Requisition, employment, 126
Research
  collective bargaining and, 491
  facilities, 490
  personnel, 488
  programming, 65
  pure, 490
  responsibility, 490
  sociological, 500
  specialists, 494
  uses, 489
Responsibility
  authority and, 77
  organizational, 76
  procedural, 70
Rest periods, 344
Restaurant facilities, 370
Retirement consultation, 373
Revenue sharing plans, 319
Right-to-work laws, 446
"Role playing," 254
Royalty plans, 320

S

Safety
  accident measures, 395
  human phases, 397
  mechanical phases, 386
  organization, 401
  scope of, 395
  working conditions, 384
Salespeople, remuneration of, 321
Samples, test, 162
Scanlon Plan, 325
Security, physical, 384
Selection
  employee, 89
  instructor, 235
  promotion, 184
  safety and, 398
  trainee, 235
Selection procedure
  design, 123
  initiation, 125
  organization, 123
  records, 131
  scope, 122
  tests, 125
Semantics, 270
Seniority
  application area, 194
  calculating, 191
  employment privileges, 193
  merit and, 193
Sensitivity training, 255
Service objectives, 51
Service plans
  organization, 374
  rules of, 377
Severance benefits, 339
Shift arrangements, 346
Short-term executive courses, 251
Simple ranking job evaluation, 297
Social
  conditions, 21
  objectives, 54
  parties, 361
  programs, 361
  specifications, 100
Social Security Act, 112, 336, 353
Sociological patterns, 21
Sociometric analysis, 76
Sources, personnel, 109
Specifications
  data gathering, 101
  employee, 90
  job, 90
  responsibility, 101
  writing, 102

Stabilization programs
 job, 348
 wage, 354
State employment agencies, 111
Station, defined, 90
Stock ownership
 employee, 319
 executive, 323
Stress-type interviews, 146
Structure
 design factors, 77
 organization, 71
 tests, 83
 unions and, 81
Suggestion systems, 368
Supervision, safety and, 400
Supplemental unemployment benefits,
 338
Systems
 communication, 267
 informational, 85
 nature, 69
 personnel, 70
 personnel management, 68

T

Taft-Hartley Act, 442, 446
Teamsters Union, 444
Technological
 conditions, 18
 innovations, 415
Technology, personnel management and,
 18
Tests
 accuracy of, 173
 areas of usage, 162
 basic fundamentals, 161
 general aptitude, 170
 measures of, 173
 popularity of, 161
 programs, 171
 records, 171
 remuneration plans, 311
 rules, 175
 staffing programs, 171
 types, 167
Time problems, 342
Time study, remuneration and, 290
Timesaving incentive plans, 316
Training
 courses, 226
 defined, 225
 evaluation, 235
 interviewing, 155
 operative employees, 225
 rules, 239
 safety, 399

Training—*Cont.*
 tests, 164
 underprivileged, 229
Transfers and promotions
 limitations, 191
 operational aspects, 181
 purposes, 180
 records, 186
 reports, 186

U

Underprivileged training, 229
Understudy plans, 251
Unemployment compensation, 337
Union-management relations, 439
Union shop, 445
Unions
 credit, 372
 hall, 130
 historical growth, 24
 labor supply and, 117, 130
 membership, 24
 personnel management and, 23
 recognition clause, 452
 relations with, 448
 remuneration and, 283
 role, 440
 strategies, 286
 types, 442
United Auto Workers, 333
United Mine Workers, 444
U.S. Bureau of Apprenticeship and
 Training, 228
U.S. Department of Commerce, 353
U.S. Department of Labor, 111, 353
U.S. Employment Service, 111, 114, 353
Urban conditions, 20
Utilization, human factor, 37

V

Vacancies
 forecasting, 187
 reporting, 187
Vacation plans, 348
Validity
 merit evaluation, 212
 test, 173
Vestibule training, 227
Vesting, 335
Vocational training, 229

W

Wage plans, 310
Wage stabilization
 feasibility, 356
 voluntary plans, 355

Wages and Hours Law; *see* Fair Labor
    Standards Act
Walsh-Healey Public Contracts Act, 287
Weekly time problems, 345
Welfare and Pension Plan Disclosure
    Act, 335
Women employees, 414

Working conditions
    phases, 384
    safety, 384

Y

Yearly time problems, 346
Yellow-dog contracts, 442

*This book has been set in 10 and 9 point
Modern #21, leaded 2 points. Part numbers and
titles are 24 point (small) Helvetica Medium
and 24 point (small) Helvetica. Chapter numbers are 10 point Helvetica and 48 point Caslon
and chapter titles are 18 point Helvetica Medium. The size of the type page is 27 x 45½
picas.*